Foundations of
Business Systems
Second Edition

Foundations of
Business Systems
Second Edition

Andersen Consulting Arthur Andersen & Co ., S.C.
Per O. Flaatten
Donald J. McCubbrey
P. Declan O'Riordan
Keith Burgess

The Dryden Press
A Harcourt Brace Jovanovich College Publisher
Fort Worth Philadelphia San Diego New York Orlando Austin San Antonio
Toronto Montreal London Sydney Tokyo

Acquisitions Editor: DeVilla Williams
Project Editor: Jan Huskisson
Art and Design Manager: Alan Wendt
Production Manager: Barb Bahnsen
Director of Editing, Design, and Production: Jane Perkins

Text and Cover Designer: Becky Lemna
Copy Editor: Kathy Pruno
Indexer: Leoni McVey
Compositor: HBJ Graphic Services
Text Type: 10/12 Garamond Light

Library of Congress Cataloging-in-Publication Data

Foundations of business systems/Andersen Consulting, Arthur Andersen
  & Co., Per O. Flaatten . . . [et al.].—2nd ed.
    p. cm.
Includes bibliographical references and index.
ISBN 0-03-076481-5
1. Management information systems.   I. Flaatten, Per O.
II. Arthur Andersen Consulting.
T58.6.F68   1991
658.4'038—-dc20   91-24811

Printed in the United States of America
123-040-987654321
Copyright © 1992, 1989 by The Dryden Press.

Address orders:
The Dryden Press
Orlando, FL 32887

Address editorial correspondence:
The Dryden Press
301 Commerce Street, Suite 3700
Fort Worth, TX 76102

The Dryden Press
Harcourt Brace Jovanovich

Cover source: Copyright © Herb Comess

To our wives and families

The Dryden Press Series in Information Systems

Arthur Andersen & Co.,
Boynton and Shank
**Foundations of
Business Systems:
Projects and Cases**

Arthur Andersen & Co.,
Flaatten, McCubbrey,
O'Riordan, and Burgess
**Foundations of
Business Systems,**
Second Edition

Andersen
**Structured Programming
Using Turbo Pascal:
A Brief Introduction**

Bradley
**Introduction to Data Base
Management in Business**
Second Edition

Brown and McKeown
**Structured Programming
with Microsoft BASIC**

Burstein and Martin
Computer Information Systems

Carney
**Advanced Structured
BASIC for the IBM PC**

Coburn
Beginning Structured COBOL

Coburn
Advanced Structured COBOL

Dean and Effinger
**Common-Sense BASIC:
Structured Programming
with Microsoft QuickBASIC**

Electronic Learning
Facilitators, Inc.
The DOS Book

Electronic Learning
Facilitators, Inc.
The Lotus 1-2-3 Book

Electronic Learning
Facilitators, Inc.
Working with WordPerfect 5.0

Electronic Learning
Facilitators, Inc.
Working with WordPerfect 5.1

Ellis and Lodi
**Structured Programming
Using True BASIC**

Federico
WordPerfect 5.1 Primer

Feiler
**Database Management
with FoxPro**

Goldstein Software, Inc.
**Joe Spreadsheet,
Macintosh Version**

Goldstein Software, Inc.
Joe Spreadsheet, Statistical

Harrington
**Making Database
Management Work**

Harrington
**Microsoft Works:
A Window to Computing**

Harrington
**Relational Database Manage-
ment for Microcomputers:
Design and Implementation**

Laudon and Laudon
**Business Information Systems:
A Problem-Solving Approach**

Laudon, Laudon, and Weill
The Integrated Solution

Lawlor
Computer Information Systems
Second Edition

Lawlor
**Introducing BASIC:
A Structured Approach**

Liebowitz
**The Dynamics of Decision
Support Systems and
Expert Systems**

McKeown
Living with Computers
Third Edition

McKeown
Working with Computers

McKeown
**Working with Computers
with Software Tutorials**

Martin and Burstein
**Computer Systems
Fundamentals**

Martin and Parker
Mastering Today's Software
*(DOS, WordPerfect 5.0/5.1,
Lotus 1-2-3, dBASE III PLUS, BASIC)*

Martin and Parker
Mastering Today's Software
*(DOS, WordPerfect 5.0/5.1,
Lotus 1-2-3, dBASE IV, BASIC)*

Martin and Parker
Mastering Today's Software
*(DOS, WordPerfect 5.0/5.1,
Lotus 1-2-3, dBASE III PLUS)*

Martin and Parker
Mastering Today's Software
*(DOS, WordPerfect 5.0/5.1,
Lotus 1-2-3, dBASE IV)*

Mason
**Using IBM Microcomputers
in Business: Decision Making
with Lotus 1-2-3 and
dBASE III PLUS**

Parker
A Beginner's Guide to BASIC

Parker
**Computers and Their
Applications**
Second Edition

Parker
**Computers and Their
Applications with
Productivity Software Tools**
Second Edition

Parker
**Microcomputers:
Concepts and Applications**

Parker
Productivity Software Guide
Third Edition

Parker
**Understanding Computers
and Information Processing:
Today and Tomorrow**
Fourth Edition

Price
Microcomputer Applications

Price
**Microcomputer Applications
Workbook**

Robertson and Robertson
**Microcomputer Applications
and Programming: A Complete
Computer Course with DOS,
WordPerfect 5.1, Lotus 1-2-3,
dBASE III PLUS, and BASIC**

Robertson and Robertson
**Microcomputer Applications
and Programming: A Complete
Computer Course with DOS,
WordPerfect 5.1, Lotus 1-2-3,
dBASE IV, and BASIC**

Robertson and Robertson
**Using Microcomputer
Applications**
*(A Series of Computer
Lab Manuals)*

Roche
**Telecommunications and
Business Strategy**

Swafford and Haff
dBASE III PLUS

FOREWORD

Since the 1960s, virtually every industry worldwide has become increasingly competitive. Around 1980, Michael Porter and others developed new approaches and methods of strategic planning that shifted the focus from internal concerns to issues of competition. Later, these approaches and methods were extended to consider the use of information and information technology to gain an advantage.

Porter's approaches have gained wide use. We have witnessed not only a change in the amount of systems development activity but also a change in the nature of the systems being developed for business. Strategic planners increasingly realize that using information technology simply to improve clerical efficiency is not enough. Rather, information technology must support deep changes in the business process itself.

In the past, most data processing applications were limited to a single organizational unit or department. Today's systems offer cross organizational lines and even reach to other enterprises—customers and suppliers. Second, these systems are the heart of the business; they often transform such basic processes as order fulfillment and plant scheduling, and they have significant performance, security, and control requirements. Third, these new systems must increasingly be responsive to change because they tend to be part of the enterprise's competitive posture and will therefore be duplicated by competitors. Last, these systems are developed by very large project teams of sophisticated, seasoned information systems professionals.

This book is intended to assist in the education of college-level students who are interested in studying how business information systems are planned, built, and implemented. Andersen Consulting has been developing systems since the mid-1950s, when we assisted in the first business application of computers, a payroll system for General Electric on a UNIVAC machine. Since then, we have developed thousands of business systems for clients in every industry, in virtually every country, on all sorts of hardware and software platforms, and to perform every business function imaginable. Andersen Consulting, which at the time of printing numbers some 25,000 people, is considered to be the leading provider of these services in the world.

We have witnessed through the years the metamorphosis of the information systems developer from eccentric scientist to egocentric artist to organizational neophyte to professional contributor to the strategic health of the enterprise he or she serves.

Our interest in writing this book is to demonstrate our corporate commitment to improving the education of future information systems professionals by sharing our experience and the resulting methods with students who are interested in this rewarding domain. Few fields of endeavor are as important, as challenging, and as open to opportunity.

Carl G. Longnecker, Jr.
Partner in Charge—Advanced Development
Andersen Consulting

Preface

Systems analysis and design are the fundamental skills required by information systems professionals who are to develop, implement, and maintain computer-based business systems. Systems analysis is deciding what a system is to do; systems design is deciding how it is to do its work.

For some years—the late 1970s and early 1980s—systems analysis and design were de-emphasized in favor of end-user computing using fourth-generation languages and application software package installation. Since then, however, the increased use of information technology as a strategic weapon in the competitive arsenal of large corporations has redirected the focus on the custom development of applications by information systems professionals. This textbook recognizes that trend: it applies current theory about systems development to today's competitive environment, emphasizing teamwork, change management, and usability and giving a wealth of practical examples and advice. The book also attempts to update some of the techniques traditionally taught in systems analysis and design so that they more closely resemble current tools and techniques in information systems departments, particularly in the domain of computer-aided software engineering (CASE).

ABOUT THE TEXTBOOK

Foundations of Business Systems is about the initial phases of the systems development life cycle, systems analysis, and design. It focuses on day-to-day transaction processing and management information systems in businesses and similar organizations. It meets the guidelines for the first course in systems analysis and design set by the Data Processing Management Association (DPMA) and those set by the Association for Computing Machinery (ACM).

The book is divided into seven sections:

- Section I, "Information Systems in the Business," is an introduction to the environment in which today's systems are being built: the competitive motivation for building or extending systems, the changes in business process brought about by information technology, and the organization of the information systems (IS) department.

- Section II, "Systems Planning," describes how systems development projects originate: one at a time through feasibility studies or in a coordinated whole through an enterprisewide systems plan.

- Section III, "Requirements Analysis," covers the first part of the analysis and design curriculum. The emphasis is on how to understand and document the functions of the system—either by interviewing users individually or by a group interviewing technique such as Joint Application Design (JAD)—how to determine and document functional requirements, and how to analyze quality requirements.

- Sections IV to VI cover the design part of the curriculum. Section IV, "User Interface Design," emphasizes the current focus on users, whether they are dedicated clerks or end users such as financial analysts, marketing professionals, and engineers. Both alphanumeric and graphical user interfaces are covered.

- Section V, "Data Design," covers recent developments in data modeling, which is increasingly recognized as one of the most important tools of the system designer. The coverage stops short of data base design, concentrating on the functional aspects of the data structures manipulated by typical transaction processing and management information systems.

- Section VI, "Process Design," concentrates on proven elements of technical architectures for on-line and batch processing: single-exchange and multi-exchange conversations, recovery and restart, and batch updating and reporting. Also covered are controls and performance. The final chapter in this section, "Installation Planning, Economic Analysis, and Management Approval," describes the synthesis of the results of the three design activities: user interface, data, and processes.

- Section VII, "Implementation," rounds out the description of the systems development life cycle by covering the remaining activities: programming, testing, installation, and maintenance.

The core of the book is constituted by Sections III to VI, which are designed to give the student majoring in information systems knowledge of and skills in analysis and design. The remaining sections give useful background information. It is not expected that the student will single-handedly be able to apply Michael Porter's approach to the use of information technology for competitive advantage, manage technology insertion, reorganize an information systems department, or even complete a systems planning project: all these activities require a team approach, led by seasoned professionals. Nor is the book designed to cover programming, testing, and maintenance in depth: the student is assumed to have knowledge in at least one commercial programming language and to have written, tested, debugged, and possibly modified at least one program.

It is hoped that the book, including the initial and final sections, can also be helpful to students majoring in subjects other than information processing. And although the book is primarily directed to undergraduates, there is sufficient substance to justify its use in selected graduate courses.

FLEXIBLE ORGANIZATION

Each section of the book is essentially autonomous and can be taught in any sequence. The book follows the generic systems development life cycle chronologically; however, it is possible to teach implementation before design, design before analysis, and analysis before strategic systems planning, conforming to the conventional wisdom that the objectives and deliverables of an activity are best understood by those who have had a chance to use those deliverables as input to a subsequent activity.

There is one exception to the book's flexibility: the techniques at the end of each section are best taught in the sequence in which they appear in the text.

The boxed vignette appearing at the beginning of each section may be used to introduce a topic and thus make it more lively, or it may be used at the end of teaching the section to illustrate applications of the concepts taught. In addition, the techniques may be taught before, during, or after the detailed chapters in the section.

PEDAGOGICAL HIGHLIGHTS

A boxed vignette opens each section. The vignettes illustrate modern systems design practice in actual companies. Each chapter begins with learning objectives and chapter overviews to prepare the student for the topic and closes with review and discussion questions to reinforce the material presented. In addition, several features support the text discussion. Real-world perspectives, highlighted in color in the text, realistically relate the strategy described in the section-opening vignette to the relevant management concerns, placing particular emphasis on competitive advantage and current systems development practice. Boxed features enhance textual material with real-world examples and applications of concepts, plus examinations of special interest topics. Mini-Cases link business issues and chapter contents through real-world cases with questions. Selected readings provide a capsule summary of major works in the subject area.

PACKAGE

Software/Case Tools Casebook

Foundations of Business Systems: Projects and Cases
By Andrew C. Boynton, *The Darden School of the University of Virginia*
Michael E. Shank, *University of North Carolina at Chapel Hill*

An ideal companion to *Foundations of Business Systems*, this realistic case-book utilizes the same seven-section organization as the text. The cases simulate the real-world business environment, covering the entire systems development life cycle. The integration between the ongoing cases and exercises allows your students to work independently or in groups.

The "projects" section of the casebook corresponds to the end-of-section techniques found in the main text. Projects incorporate the use of a special educational version of Andersen Consulting's *Foundation*® software.

Foundation® **Software**

Adopters of *Foundations of Business Systems* will have access to a special educational version of Andersen Consulting's *Foundation*®, a CASE tool that covers the entire systems development life cycle. The software includes techniques from the text such as Data Flow Diagrams, Hierarchical Diagramming, and Entity-Relationship Diagrams.

Ancillaries

A complete instructional support package is offered with *Foundations of Business Systems:*

- Instructor's Manual
- Test Bank
- Computerized Test Bank
- Transparency Acetates

ACKNOWLEDGMENTS

The writing of *Foundations of Business Systems* has been a team effort, and the authors wish to thank all of those who have contributed to it. Particular thanks are due to Bob Evanson, Senior Vice-President of Harcourt Brace Jovanovich, Inc., for the idea for this book and to the leadership of Andersen Consulting's Technology Services, past and present, for their enthusiastic reception and continuing support for the idea. Thanks are also due to the following for contributing, reviewing, and critiquing substantial contents of various portions of the book: Gip Bonar, Bill Bramer, Glover Ferguson, Carl Longnecker, Jill Smith, Peter Wenzlick, Will Zachman. Special thanks go to the members of the Editorial Review Board, who reviewed the entire manuscript and whose suggestions have immeasurably improved the text.

The development of *Foundations of Business Systems* would not have been possible without the input and responsiveness of those in the academic field: Gary R. Armstrong, Shippensburg University; Paul T. Cooke, Dalhousie University; Jeffrey P. Corcoran, Nichols College; Eric L. Denna, Brigham Young University; William Eddins, York College; David VanOver, The University of Georgia; James Woolever, Cerritos College; Margaret S.

Wu, The University of Iowa; and Bayard E. Wynne, Indiana University; and those of the marketplace: Robert Ashenhurt, University of Chicago; Don Amoroso, University of Colorado, Colorado Springs; Roger Hayen, Central Michigan University; Khaleeb Hussain, New Mexico State University; William Konn, University of Wisconsin, Eau Claire; Khris McAlister, University of Alabama, Birmingham; William Moates, Indiana State University; Tarun Sen, Virginia Polytechnic & State University; Robert Trent, University of Virginia; and Ira Weiss, University of Houston, University Park are to be thanked for their participation in our focus groups. Marketing research also played a critical role in the production of this text. The following are to be thanked for their time, information, and ideas:

Joyce Abler
Central Michigan University

Joseph Adamski
Grand Valley State College

Robert Ader
Middle Tennessee State University

Gary Baram
Temple University

William Beidler
University of Southern Mississippi

Virginia Bender
William Rainey Harper Community College

Charles Bilbrey
James Madison University

David A. Bird
University of Missouri—St. Louis

Stephen Bird
New Mexico State University

James Blaisdoll
Humboldt State University

Mark Blank
San Francisco State University

Roy Boggs
University of South Florida

Michael Brendler
Louisiana State University—Shreveport

Elias Callahan
Mississippi State University

Jan Carey
Texas A & M University

Carol Chrisman
Illinois State University

Frank David
Bloomsburg University

Sasa Dekleva
DePaul University

E.Reed Doke
Southwest Missouri State

Peter Duchessi
State University of New York at Albany

John Durham
Fort Harris State

Henry Etlinger
Rochester Institute of Technology

Robert Fleck
Columbus College

Jack Fuller
West Virginia University

Jack Gilman
Florida International University

Carol Grimm
Palm Beach Community College

Ted Grossman
Babson College

Patricia Guinan
Boston University

Dennis Guster
St. Louis Meramec Community College

Maurice Halloday
Suffolk University

Fred Harold
Florida Atlantic University

Brian Honess
University of South Carolina

Jeretha Horn
Oklahoma State University

Wallace Jewell
Edinboro State University

Ernest Kallman
Bentley College

Dale Kewitz
Marshall University

Chuck Litecky
University of Missouri

Rebecca Litner
St. Joseph's University

Thomas MacBeth
University of Lowell

Roy Martin
Southwest Texas State University

Thomas Mason
Florida A & M University

M. Khris McAlister
University of Alabama—Birmingham

Roger McGrath
University of South Florida

William McHenry
Georgetown University

Bruce McLaren
Indiana State University

Rich Montague
Western Connecticut State University

Lewis Myers
Texas A & M University

Lowell Needham
Pittsburgh State University

Ronald Norman
San Diego State University

Shailendra Palvia
Babson College

Gehrhard Plenert
California State University, Chico

David Russell
Western New England College

Bruce Saulrigs
Quinnipiac College

Carol Saunders
Texas Christian University

Valerie Schmeider
Western Connecticut State University

Tarun Sen
Virginia Polytechnic & State University

Jerri Frances Sitek
Southern Illinois University—Edwardsville

Craig Slinkman
University of Texas—Arlington

Ralph Stair
Florida State University

Fred Stiner
University of Delaware

Stephen Strane
Western Illinois University

Joel Stutz
University of Miami

Madjid Tavana
LaSalle University

James Teng
University of Pittsburgh

Robert Trent
University of Virginia

Michael Varano
Villanova University

Lawig Weathe
University of Texas—Austin

John Willhardt
Alabama State University

Mustafa Yilmiz
Northeastern University

Ron Zigli
Memphis State University

Great improvements were also brought to the book by Mark Fitzgerald, Bonnie Carter, and Craig Skates.

Heartfelt thanks are due to the people at Harcourt Brace Jovanovich, Inc., at The Dryden Press, and at Andersen Consulting who helped with design, production, and marketing: David Bassin, Mike Brown, Manuel Castro, Ben Elderd, Leng Eng, Butch Gemin, David Hall, MaryEllen McKee, John Sulzycki, Alan Wendt, and Shari Wenker. Jan Huskisson kept tireless track of where each part of the book stood and what remained due: without her, chapters, vignettes, techniques, and figures would be a hopeless jumble today, rather than a whole book. For the second edition, we wish to thank John Saaty, Mike Sijacic, and Cassandra Cole. We also thank all our friends and colleagues at Andersen Consulting and at the University of Denver College of Business Administration for their contributions and support, in the small and in the large.

Last but not least, we wish to thank DeVilla Williams, our beloved editor and Chief Whip. This book is as much hers as it is ours.

ABOUT THE AUTHORS

Per O. Flaatten is Associate Partner of Methodology Research and Communications at Andersen Consulting in Chicago. He has more than twenty years of experience developing information systems in the United States and Europe and has taught several courses in Systems Development and Methodology. Mr. Flaatten is at present responsible for formulating and communicating Andersen Consulting's methodology strategy.

Donald J. McCubbrey is Chair of the Management Information Systems Department at the University of Denver. Before joining the University of Denver faculty in 1984, he served as a partner in Andersen Consulting, Arthur Andersen & Co., where he was responsible for a large number of Information Systems planning, design, and installation engagements throughout the United States, Canada, Europe, and Latin America.

P. Declan O'Riordan, who is now located in the Washington, D.C., office of Andersen Consulting, has twenty-six years of experience in information systems design and installation at both IBM and Andersen Consulting. He is currently a member of the firm's Technology Advisory Committee and has previously served as a Director of Information Technology Research for the firm. He has also served as the firm's representative on the Sponsor's Advisory Board of the Center for Information System Research at the Sloan School of Management, Massachusetts Institute of Technology.

Keith Burgess is Country Managing Partner of Andersen Consulting in the United Kingdom. He is currently chairman of the Technical Advisory Committee, which is responsible for overseeing the technical direction of the firm's practice.

Contents in Brief

Section I   INFORMATION SYSTEMS IN THE BUSINESS   1

   Chapter 1   Information Technology and Competitive Advantage   13

   Chapter 2   Business Process Change   33

   Chapter 3   Systems Projects and the Systems Life Cycle   59

   Technique   Hierarchical Diagramming   83

Section II   SYSTEMS PLANNING   99

   Chapter 4   Feasibility Studies   105

   Chapter 5   Establishing the Systems Plan   125

   Chapter 6   IS Infrastructure Planning   163

   Technique   Matrix Affinity Analysis   183

Section III   REQUIREMENTS ANALYSIS   191

   Chapter 7   Interviewing and JAD   197

   Chapter 8   Functional Requirements   225

   Chapter 9   Quality Requirements   249

   Technique   Data Flow Diagrams   267

Section IV   USER INTERFACE DESIGN   279

   Chapter 10   Designing Dialogs and Document Flows   287

   Chapter 11   Designing Forms, Screens, and Reports   329

   Chapter 12   Graphical User Interfaces   349

   Technique   Tools for Prototyping   367

Section V   DATA DESIGN 371
  Chapter 13   Entity-Relationship Modeling 379
  Chapter 14   Data Element Design   421
  Chapter 15   Specification of Integrity Constraints   445
  Technique   Entity-Relationship Diagrams   459

Section VI   PROCESS DESIGN   471
  Chapter 16   Program Design   479
  Chapter 17   Controls and Security   527
  Chapter 18   Designing for Performance   553
  Chapter 19   Installation Planning, Economic Analysis,
                 and Management Approval   581
  Technique   Program Structure Charting 603

Section VII   IMPLEMENTATION   611
  Chapter 20   Programming and Testing   617
  Chapter 21   Installing the System   653
  Chapter 22   Maintenance   671
  Technique   Implementation Data Dictionary   687

  Appendix 1   Value Chain Analysis   699
  Appendix 2   State Transition Diagrams   713
  Appendix 3   Computer Graphics   717

Contents

Section I   **INFORMATION SYSTEMS IN THE BUSINESS**   1

        The Hospitals of Kalamazoo   *2*

Chapter 1   **Information Technology and Competitive Advantage**   13

        A Brief Historical Perspective   *14*
        Box 1–1 Top Management's Understanding of Information Technology   *16*
        Information Technology's Role Today   *16*
        A Framework for Strategic Business Planning   *17*
           Five Forces Model   *17*
           Three Generic Strategies   *20*
           The Value Chain   *21*
        Box 1–2 Systems That Have Changed an Industry Structure   *22*
        Box 1–3 Companies That Have Improved Existing Products or Services   *23*
        The Strategic Grid   *24*
        Box 1–4 Companies That Have Created New Products or Services   *25*
        First-Mover Disadvantages   *26*
        Applicability to the Not-For-Profit Sector   *27*

Chapter 2   **Business Process Change**   33

        Systems Are Composed of People, Technology, and Business Processes   *33*
        Changing Systems Changes People   *35*
        Box 2–1 The Need for Change   *36*
        The New Industrial Engineering   *37*
           Historical Nature of Clerical Work   *37*
           Initial Automation Strategies   *38*
           Widening the Scope of Integration   *38*
        Box 2–2 Business Process Change at Ford Motor Company   *39*
           Empowering the Knowledge Worker   *40*
        Reengineering the Business Process   *40*
           Overall Approach   *40*
           Principles of Reengineering   *40*
           Interorganizational Systems and Process Integration   *47*
        The Nature of Change   *48*
        Resistance to Change   *48*
           Diagnosing and Dealing with Resistance to Change   *49*
        Implementing the Organizational Change   *51*

Chapter 3   **Systems Projects and the Systems Life Cycle**   59

The Place of the IS Department in the Organization   *60*
Merging the Islands of Technology   *60*
The Supportive Role of the IS Department   *63*
Organization of the IS Department   *65*
Form of Organization   *65*
Centralization versus Decentralization   *68*
More Recent Trends   *70*
Project Management and the Systems Development Life Cycle   *72*
Project Organization   *72*
Project Planning   *74*
Project Execution   *75*
Project Control   *75*
The Design Process in the Systems Development Life Cycle   *76*
System Design as Problem Solving   *77*
System Design as Modeling   *77*
System Design from Models   *78*
System Design as Transformation   *78*

Technique   **Hierarchical Diagramming**   83

Section II   **SYSTEMS PLANNING**   99

Social Security Administration Revamps Software, Data Structures   *100*

Chapter 4   **Feasibility Studies**   105

Objectives and Organization of a Feasibility Study   *105*
Examples of the Use of Feasibility Studies   *106*
Types of Feasibility   *109*
Technical Feasibility   *109*
Operational Feasibility   *109*
Economic Feasibility   *110*
Schedule Feasibility   *110*
Motivational Feasibility   *110*
Approaches to Determining Project Feasibility   *110*
Solving Operational Problems   *111*
Replacing Existing Technology   *112*
Mechanizing a Manual System   *113*
Creating a New Activity   *114*
Cost/Benefit Analysis   *116*

Chapter 5   **Establishing the Systems Plan**   125

Benefits of Systems Planning   *125*
Shared Data   *126*

Shared Strategy   *126*
Cost Reduction   *126*
Four Approaches to Systems Planning   *127*
Application Portfolio Planning   *127*
Enterprise Modeling   *128*
Technology Infrastructure Planning   *128*
Linking Business and Technology Strategies   *129*
Understanding the Strategic Business Plan   *129*
Identifying Criteria for Evaluating Application Development Projects   *131*
Understanding the Operation of the Business   *131*
Identify Products (or Services) and Supporting Resources   *136*
Identify Strategic Planning and Management Control Processes   *136*
Identify Operational Processes   *138*
Group/Split the Processes   *138*
Box 5–1 Types of Systems   *140*
Write a Description of Each Process   *143*
Relate the Business Process to the Organization   *143*
Analyzing Data Requirements   *144*
Identify Business Entities   *144*
Determine Data Usage by Process   *144*
Identify Data Classes   *145*
Develop a Process/Data Matrix   *145*
Some Practical Considerations   *149*
Identifying Systems Projects   *149*
Evaluating Systems Projects   *153*
Box 5–2 Sources of Systems   *154*
Organizing the Systems Planning Effort   *155*

Chapter 6   **IS Infrastructure Planning**   163

Problems Solved by Proper Infrastructure Planning   *163*
Lack of Development Resources   *164*
Equipment and Software Disparity   *165*
Information Technology for the Developers   *166*
Planning for the Development Environment   *166*
Planning for the Production Environment   *169*
Capacity   *170*
Data Communications   *171*
Planning for Personnel Requirements   *172*
Box 6–1 Distributed Data Processing   *174*
Handling Organizational Issues   *176*

Technique   **Matrix Affinity Analysis**   183

Section III   **REQUIREMENTS ANALYSIS**   191

Lone Wolf Timber & Mining Company   *192*

Chapter 7   **Interviewing and JAD**   197

Reviewing the Current System   *197*
  Understanding the Business Problem   *198*
  Understanding the Operating Environment   *199*
  Considering All Requirements   *199*
  Anchoring the New System in the Old   *199*
  Enhancing User Relationships   *200*
  Box 7–1 Permanence versus Change   *201*
Interviewing   *201*
  Preparing for the Interview   *202*
  Planning and Scheduling the Interview   *202*
  Opening and Closing the Interview   *204*
  Conducting the Interview   *205*
  Following Up for Clarification   *210*
When to Use Joint Application Design (JAD)   *210*
Six Types of Participants   *211*
Preparing for the Workshop   *213*
Conducting the Session   *216*
Documenting the Results   *217*
Alternative Methods   *217*
Costs and Benefits of JAD   *218*
Other Information-Gathering Techniques   *218*
  Questionnaires   *218*
  Observation   *218*
  Sampling   *219*

Chapter 8   **Functional Requirements**   225

Functional Requirements Defined   *225*
Strategies for Analyzing Functional Requirements   *226*
  Structured Systems Analysis   *227*
  Essential Systems Analysis   *229*
  Business Area Analysis   *231*
  Box 8–1 Top-Down versus Bottom-Up Analysis   *232*
  Object-Oriented Analysis   *233*
Strategies for Documenting Functional Requirements   *235*
  Behavior   *236*
  Data Structure   *237*
  Data Flow   *237*
Deducing Processing and Information Requirements: Lessons from Practice   *240*
Achieving Business Integration   *243*

Chapter 9   **Quality Requirements**   249

Functional versus Quality Requirements   *249*
Definition of Quality   *250*
  Historical Background   *250*

Quality as Absence of Defects   *252*
Quality as Meeting User Expectations   *254*
Quality Attributes of Systems   *255*
Benefits   *256*
Budget and Schedule   *256*
Performance   *257*
Reliability   *257*
Usability   *258*
Flexibility   *258*
Quality Characteristics as Design Drivers   *259*
Relationship to Development Process   *260*
Evaluation Methods   *260*
Measurement of Quality   *261*
Selecting Metrics   *261*
Setting Goals   *262*
Measuring Results   *262*
Total Quality Management in the Design Process   *263*

Technique   **Data Flow Diagrams**   263

Section IV   **USER INTERFACE DESIGN**   279
Videotex: A Success Story   *280*

Chapter 10   **Designing Dialogs and Document Flows**   287
On-Line versus Batch   *287*
Box 10–1 Good Design   *288*
Data Flows from an External Entity   *289*
Data Flows to an External Entity   *290*
Data Flows That Do Not Involve an External Entity   *295*
Box 10–2 Ad Hoc Inquiry and Data Storage   *296*
Data Flow That Cycles through Several Activities   *297*
Design of Document Flows   *297*
Dialog Design   *299*
Box 10–3 Logical Units of Work   *300*
Determining the Logical Unit of Work   *301*
Box 10–4 Ease of Use   *303*
Choosing the Type of Dialog   *304*
Choosing the Technology, Dialog, and Help Styles   *314*
Box 10–5 User Dialog and Natural Language   *316*
Elements of Good Dialog Design   *318*
Clarity   *318*
Consistency   *318*
Performance   *319*
Respect for the User   *320*
Documenting the Conversation Flow   *320*

Chapter 11   **Designing Forms, Screens, and Reports**   329

Significance of Form, Screen, and Report Design   *329*
  Decreasing Emphasis on Reports and Forms   *330*
  Increasing Emphasis on Screen Design   *331*
The Choice of the Medium   *331*
General Principles of Form, Report, and Screen Design   *333*
  Ease of Use   *333*
  Fulfilling the Purpose   *334*
  Benefits and Costs   *334*
Design of Input Forms   *334*
Report Design   *335*
Screen Design   *342*
  Operator Guidance   *342*
  Highlighting, Aesthetics, and Ergonomics   *343*
  Paging and Scrolling   *344*

Chapter 12   **Graphical User Interfaces**   349

Interface Requirements for Knowledge Workers   *349*
  Self-Learning Systems   *350*
  Box 12–1 Ticket Stub Auditing at Northwest Airlines   *351*
  The Direct Manipulation Metaphor   *353*
  Image Processing   *356*
Guidelines for Design   *358*
  Windows   *359*
  Alerts and Warnings   *361*
  Pull-Down Menus   *363*
  Dialog Boxes   *363*

Technique   **Tools for Prototyping**   367

Section V   **DATA DESIGN**   371

Data Modeling at Bailis, Kronberg, Kendall & Son   *372*

Chapter 13   **Entity-Relationship Modeling**   379

Benefits of Entity-Relationship Modeling   *379*
Box 13–1 Information Modeling   *380*
Entities, Attributes, and Relationships   *382*
Top-Down Analysis   *384*
  Creating the Initial Project Data Model   *385*
  Analyzing Relationships   *388*
  Selecting Attributes   *397*
  Assigning Attributes to Entities   *398*
Box 13–2 Integrating Data, Text, Voice, and Graphics   *403*
Bottom-Up Analysis   *404*

Starting Points   *404*
Business Function Data Models and User Views   *405*
Project Data Model   *406*
Normalization   *406*
Box 13–3 Definition of the Five Normal Forms   *408*
Analysis of Probable Changes   *410*

Chapter 14   **Data Element Design**   421

Naming Data Elements: Homonyms, Synonyms, and Qualifiers   *421*
Data Type Analysis   *423*
Definition of Data Types   *424*
Examples of Data Types: Date   *425*
Defining Operations on Data Types   *426*
Documentation Requirements for Data Types   *428*
Key Analysis   *429*
Purpose of Key Analysis   *429*
Choosing the Identifying Key   *431*
Implementing Relationships with Keys   *435*
Documentation Requirements for Implementing Relationships   *437*
Codes and Tables   *437*
Documentation Requirements for Codes   *441*

Chapter 15   **Specification of Integrity Constraints**   445

Data Base Integrity   *445*
Reasons for Errors in the Data Base   *445*
Types of Errors   *446*
The Referential Integrity Problem   *447*
Implementing Relationships   *448*
Checking for Referential Integrity   *448*
Other Integrity Constraints   *450*
Illegal Transactions versus Transactions That Cause an Illegal State   *453*
Documentation Requirements for Integrity Constraints   *454*

Technique   **Entity-Relationship Diagrams**   459

Section VI   **PROCESS DESIGN**   471

The New York State Retirement System   *472*

Chapter 16   **Program Design**   479

On-Line versus Batch Program Design   *479*
On-Line Program Design   *481*
Session Sign-On   *481*
Box 16–1 Strategies for Program Design   *482*
Conversation Design   *485*

Box 16–2 Distributed Processing   *492*
   Backup, Recovery, and Restart in On-Line Systems   *497*
Batch Processing   *502*
   Standard Batch Architecture   *502*
   Validation   *502*
   Update   *503*
Box 16–3 Process-Driven Design   *504*
Box 16–4 Data-Driven Design   *506*
Box 16–5 Object-Oriented Design   *510*
   Reporting   *511*
Interfaces to Other Systems   *514*
Cut-Off Processing   *518*
Box 16–6 Impact of Fourth-Generation Tools and Prototyping   *519*
Box 16–7 Cooperative Processing   *520*
Recent Trends in Batch Processing   *521*

Chapter 17   **Controls and Security**   **527**

Management Control over Information Systems   *528*
Sources of Errors   *529*
   Human Errors   *529*
   Technical Failures   *529*
   Natural Forces   *530*
General Systems Controls   *531*
Box 17–1 Turning a Computer into a Better Vault   *532*
Application Controls   *533*
   Specification of Application Controls   *534*
   Application Control Objectives   *535*
Examples of Transaction Processing Control Techniques   *539*
   Controls over Transaction Origination   *540*
   Controls over Data Entry   *540*
   Controls over Processing   *543*
   Controls over Reporting   *546*
   Data Base Controls   *547*
   Systems Interface Controls   *547*
Privacy Issues and the Rights of the Individual   *547*

Chapter 18   **Designing for Performance**   **553**

Definition of Performance   *553*
Usual Measures of Performance   *554*
   Response Time   *554*
   Throughput   *557*
   Availability   *557*
How to Design for Performance   *560*
   Response Time Problems   *561*
   Throughput Problems   *562*
   Availability Problems   *563*
Estimating Resource Requirements   *564*

Transmission Time   *565*
Processor Time   *568*
Disk Access Time   *569*
Calculation of the Response Time   *572*
Total On-Line Resource Consumption   *573*
Other Resources   *573*
Resource Consumption in Batch Processing   *573*

Chapter 19   **Installation Planning, Economic Analysis, and Management Approval**   581

Completing the Design   *582*
Planning the Installation   *583*
  The Test Plan   *583*
  The User Training Plan   *584*
  The Conversion Plan   *584*
  The Detailed Installation Plan   *586*
Cost/Benefit Analysis   *588*
  Components of the Cost/Benefit Analysis   *588*
Overall Economic Summary   *591*
Presenting the Analysis to Management   *596*
  The Management Report   *596*
  The Management Review Meeting   *596*
Freezing the Specifications   *597*

Technique   **Program Structure Charting**   603

Section VII   **IMPLEMENTATION**   611

IBM's Multiples Marketing Program   *612*

Chapter 20   **Programming and Testing**   617

Organizing and Managing the Programming Effort   *618*
Planning the Programming Effort   *619*
The Programming Specification   *620*
  Level of Detail   *620*
  Content   *621*
Structured Walk-throughs   *622*
  Participants   *622*
  Preparation of the Walk-through   *623*
  Conduct of the Meeting   *623*
  Follow-Up   *625*
The Role of the Programming Supervisor   *625*
The Importance of Testing   *628*
Box 20–1 Why Is Testing Necessary?   *629*
Unit Testing   *630*
  Objectives and Responsibility   *630*

Planning the Tests   *630*
Preparing Test Data   *633*
Executing the Test   *637*
Evaluating the Results   *638*
Integration, System, and Acceptance Testing   *641*
Definitions   *641*
Planning the Tests   *642*
Preparing Test Data   *642*
Executing the Tests   *643*
Evaluating the Results   *643*
Other Debugging Techniques   *644*
Box 20–2 Alternative Testing Techniques   *645*

Chapter 21   **Installing the System**   653

Preparing Users for Change   653
User Procedure Development and User Training   655
On-Line versus Paper-based Documentation   655
Types of Manuals   655
Contents of Procedure Manuals   657
User Training Planning   659
Training Development and Conduct   660
Operations Procedures Development   662
File Conversion   663
Cutover and Follow-Up   667

Chapter 22   **Maintenance**   671

The Maintenance Problem   *671*
Types of Maintenance   *673*
Versions, Releases, and Fixes   *675*
Box 22–1 Configuration Control   *676*
Processing Change Requests   *677*
Organization of the Maintenance Team   *679*
Performing the Work   *681*
Relationship with Systems Planning   *683*

Technique   **Implementation Data Dictionary**   687

Appendix 1   **Value Chain Analysis**   699

Appendix 2   **State Transition Diagrams**   713

Appendix 3   **Computer Graphics**   717

Index   *727*

Information Systems in the Business

The purpose of Section I is not to teach the practice of systems analysis and design, but to show how successful organizations view today's information technology and information systems professionals in relation to the rest of the enterprise—executive management and information systems users.

Chapter 1 describes how information technology is increasingly used by creative organizations to achieve competitive advantage. For the past few years, the use of information technology has been shifting from transaction recording and management reporting systems, which process information about business activities after the fact, to transaction processing and management information systems, which use information technology to actually help carry out the business activity. This shift has taken place against the backdrop of an increasingly competitive economic environment. One approach to the use of information technology—that of Michael Porter of Harvard—has been effective in achieving success in this environment, as described in Chapter 1.

As information systems have become both more pervasive and more strategic, they are used by more and more people as an integral part of their work. Chapter 2 describes how business processes can be deeply changed by information technology. It then points out some of the factors causing resistance to change and suggests how proper systems development practices can help overcome this resistance.

Chapter 3 examines the place of the information systems (IS) department in the organization and the way the department is organized internally. Because of the increasing importance of information systems in most companies, it is only to be expected that the organizational environment in which the information systems professionals work would change. This change is emphasized by the greater complexity of the technology and the greater demands that users place on systems. The chapter then describes how the systems development life cycle affects project management and the system design process.

The Hospitals of Kalamazoo

♦

Kalamazoo, Michigan, is a city of 125,000 people located in the southwestern part of the state, about midway between Detroit and Chicago. It is the site of Western Michigan University and the home office of such companies as Upjohn. It is known as a pleasant place in which to live and raise a family.

The health care market in Kalamazoo is dominated by two major acute-care hospitals, both close in size. In early 1985, the competition between Borgess Medical Center and Bronson Methodist Hospital intensified. Because of increased outpatient treatment and early patient discharges, both hospitals found that a greater percentage of their beds were unoccupied at any point in time. An empty bed in a hospital is like an empty seat in an airplane or at a concert. It is capacity underutilized and revenue lost. The question both hospitals were asking themselves was "How can we get an increasing share of a decreasing market?" Because patients would travel only so far for hospital care, the market for both hospitals was limited to the city of Kalamazoo and the surrounding areas. Clearly, if one hospital were to find a way to increase its inpatient population, it could only do so by taking patients away from the other.

One hospital, Borgess Medical Center, developed an information system that enabled it to increase its inpatient population at the expense of its crosstown rival, Bronson Methodist Hospital. The project to achieve a competitive advantage began when planners realized that the customers of hospitals were physicians, not patients. In a market such as Kalamazoo, physicians tended to be on the medical staffs of both major hospitals, which meant they were permitted to admit their patients to either one. Hospitals that find themselves in such a position generally try to make themselves the more attractive alternative to physicians by offering the latest in medical technology, building medical office buildings nearby, and generally offering amenities such as attractively furnished lounges and preferred park-

ing. All other things being equal, the physicians would tend to suggest the hospital he or she preferred when it came time to discuss hospitalization with the patient.

The planners at Borgess also realized that a physician's time was valuable. If a way could be found to both make Borgess a more attractive facility and save the physicians' time, physicians would be more likely to admit their patients to Borgess instead of its rival.

The solution they developed involved the creative use of information technology. They offered to place personal computers in the physicians' offices at no cost. Software was provided to perform routine office management functions such as patient billing and accounts receivable, appointment scheduling, and patient records. More important, the personal computers were able to connect with the hospital's computer over telecommunications lines.

The telecommunications capability made it much easier for the physicians to communicate with the hospital for such purposes as scheduling admissions and operating rooms, and also for scheduling patients for laboratory and radiology examinations administered to outpatients. Previously, making such arrangements was often a frustrating and time-consuming process for physicians and their office support personnel. When results of laboratory tests or radiology exams were needed, they could be obtained in the physicians' offices through computer-to-computer links, avoiding the same frustrations.

In addition, Borgess offered physicians who signed up for the program membership in a physicians' referral service operated by the hospital. Advertising programs for the service were developed for television and newspapers, giving people a telephone number to call when they needed a physician but did not know whom to call. Most physicians welcomed this service, particularly those just starting their practices, because the same pressures that made hospitals compete also exerted themselves on the physicians. Moreover, the number of physicians was on the increase. This meant that physicians were competing for patient volumes as well.

Physicians soon discovered the many advantages to the new service provided by Borgess Medical Center:

- They began seeing more patients as a result of the referral service.

- They saved time, as did their office staffs, by making appointments and receiving results through computer-to-computer communications rather than by using the telephone. In addition, there was much less aggravation associated with the new system.

- Their cash flow increased because of an increased patient volume and the more effective billing and accounts receivable operations provided by the software.

Consequently, the physicians sent more of their patients to Borgess and Borgess filled more of its beds.

The success of the system was described in *Modern Healthcare* as follows:

"Frank Tiedemann, vice president for marketing at Borgess, said the network is largely responsible for 'our most profitable year in history.' In the year ended June 30, Borgess had more than $14 million in net income, double projections and up about 40% from the previous year. Net operating revenues were up 18% to $130 million.

"The financial success was attributable largely to a 3% increase in admissions during the first nine months the network was operating, Mr. Tiedemann said. In the year since the network began, admissions have risen about 5% at a time when most of the state's hospitals are experiencing declines in admissions, he said."[1]

Thus, Borgess Medical Center achieved its goal of increasing its share of a decreasing market through the innovative use of information technology, at the expense of its chief competitor, Bronson Methodist Hospital

SYSTEMS DEVELOPMENT LIFE CYCLE

The first section is an overview of the traditional systems development life cycle and shows how the various parts fit together. Each subsequent section of the book deals with one phase of the systems development life cycle.

The systems development life cycle is an approach to developing systems in an organized and disciplined manner. In its most general form, the approach consists of four components:

- Define the objectives of the system to be developed.

- Define indicators of success that will measure whether the objectives have been met.

- Generate alternative strategies.

- Select and implement a strategy.

Although this approach appears simple and almost self-evident, many systems efforts flounder, especially through failing to address the first two steps. If the objectives are not clear or not universally accepted, the systems developers will be in the position of Alice in Wonderland: "Cheshire-Puss," she began, "Would you tell me, please, where I ought to go from here?" "That depends a great deal on where you want to get to," said the Cat.

As an IS professional, if you have not established measurable indicators of success, you may know where you are going, but you will never know whether you are there yet. You may meet your own expectations and those of some others; you will have exceeded those of some users and fallen short of those of others. You will be criticized for doing too much and not doing enough. The system will fail because disappointed users will not make the necessary effort to make the system work.

The Phases of the Systems Development Life Cycle

All systems development life cycle variations in use today divide the life of a system into phases, from the initial idea to its full implementation, followed by enhancements and possibly replacement by a new system based on a fresh idea. Not only is the cycle of defining objectives, defining indicators of success, generating alternatives, and developing an operational plan applicable to a system as a whole, but also to each successive development phase.

The Waterfall Life Cycle

The basic life cycle is called the waterfall life cycle. It is adapted to both custom development and implementation of packaged application software. However, the waterfall life cycle has some problems. More recently developed life cycles—iterative development and prototyping—have addressed some of these problems.

The waterfall life cycle arose from the problems caused by starting to program a solution as soon as the problem to be solved was stated. This might work well for isolated, small programs, but it fell short for larger team efforts. Then, many more activities were required. The waterfall life cycle forced users and developers to accept these activities, which did not appear as immediately productive as the coding effort. Also, each type of activity is executed differently; each must be planned and staffed on its own.

In this approach, each successive phase can be started only after the previous phase has been completed and a formal decision has been made by management whether the results obtained so far justify continuing the project. The name *waterfall life cycle* stems from the way the life cycle was depicted in a seminal presentation by W. W. Royce (see Figure I–1).[2]

There are a great number of versions of the waterfall life cycle on the market. They generally differ in how many phases are recognized, typically from two to ten. The number of phases need not always be the same. For example, some phases could be combined if a systems project is small and time is short. The generic life cycle used in this book has five phases: systems planning, requirements analysis, design (divided into user interface design, data design, and process design subphases), implementation, and maintenance (see Figure I–2).

Figure I–1 Waterfall Systems Development Life Cycle

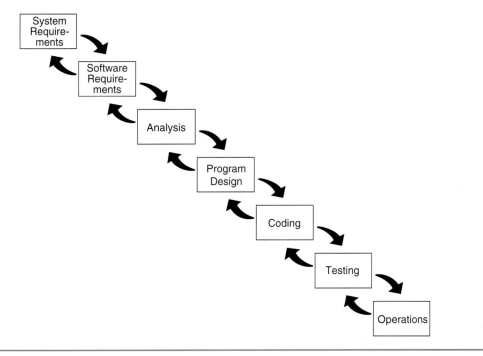

Source: W.W. Royce. "Managing the Development of Large Software Systems." *Proceedings of IEEE WESCON,* 1970.

Figure I–2 Generic Systems Development Life Cycle Used in This Book

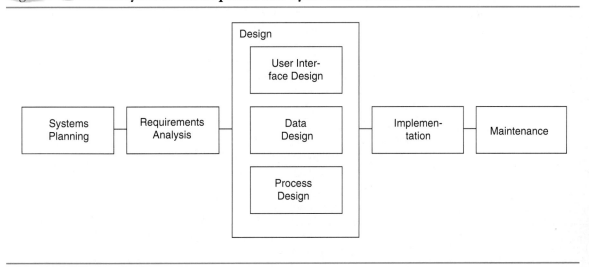

Figure I–3 **Phases, Objectives, and Deliverables**

Phase/Subphase	Objective	Deliverable
Systems Planning	Identify projects and resources over next 3–5 years	Systems Plan
Requirements Analysis	Determine the scope of a system and success factors	Requirements Specification
User Interface Design	Design the external behavior of the system	Dialog and Document Flow Design
Data Design	Design the logical structure of the bases and files	Entity, Relationship, and Attribute
Process Design	Design the internal behavior of the system	Program/Module Descriptions
Implementation	Program and test the system; prepare users; convert	Operational System
Maintenance	Correct and enhance the system	Operational System

As shown in Figure I–3, each phase has an overall objective and an end product (often called deliverable), which serves as the measure of success: when the deliverable is ready and approved by all interested parties, the phase is finished. In addition, each phase has generally accepted methods and techniques for selecting and implementing the alternatives. This process is what this book is all about.

Figure I–4 shows typical relative costs of each phase of the waterfall life cycle for custom systems development and packaged software installation. These costs assume that the system is to be installed in one location only. Multilocation systems require an additional phase, often called rollout, which can easily surpass the cost of all the other phases combined. Imagine, for instance, a new mail sorting and delivery system to be installed in every post office in an entire country.

Problems with the Waterfall Life Cycle. The waterfall life cycle has fallen into disrepute over the last few years. The main problem is the length of time that it can take to go through the life cycle. In particular, once a design is approved, it may typically be 18 months before the system is actually implemented. By that time, requirements have changed and users have forgotten why a design decision was adopted. On the other hand, if new requirements are incorporated into the design throughout the implementation phase, programmers and analysts must work towards a moving target, and the implementation effort becomes difficult or impossible to manage.

The top-down approach inherent in the waterfall model assumes that one can move from one phase to the next with little or no need to return to a previous phase to adjust the design. As Royce pointed out as early as 1970, such a process only happens if the program or system being delivered is not

Figure I–4   **Relative Development Cost by Phase**

Phase/Subphase	Custom Systems Percentage Range of Effort	Packaged Software Percentage Range of Effort
Requirements Analysis	2–5%	10–20%
User Interface Design	5–10	0–5
Data Design	5–10	0–2
Process Design	5–15	0–5
Design	15–40	10–30
Program Specification	10–20	20–30
Program Coding and Unit Test	15–50	10–30
User Procedures and Training	5–25	5–20
Conversion	5–30	15–40
System Test	5–25	5–25
Total	100%	100%

very original. If it contains innovations, then it is likely that the testing phase will reveal performance problems, inconsistencies in interface assumptions, and other errors that could not be predicted during the design and analysis phases.

The waterfall life cycle assumes a different skill set and therefore a different team for each phase. Passing the torch from one phase to the next is done by transmitting to the next team complete documentation of all the decisions made in the previous phase—throwing it over the wall, as it were. This lack of continuity inevitably causes misunderstandings and wrong assumptions. Another problem is that users are typically not associated with the design and coding. Absent from the project for several months, they are unlikely to have maintained their enthusiasm and sense of ownership. The IS department often gets the reputation of working on its own, concentrating only on technical issues, and being out of touch with the real world of the users.

Contributing to this perception of IS departments is that, until recently, the cost of the technology was so high that IS departments concentrated on maximizing the use of the equipment and neglected human factors. Users, typically clerical workers, were trained to conform to the demands of the system instead of the system being designed to conform to the needs of the users. This attitude is rapidly giving way to the opposite. Today, good designers recognize that humans are inherently conservative and do not particularly want to change. Modern methods therefore encourage designing systems in such a way that users will respond positively to the changes that the systems require.

This attention to the user has resulted in a major and a minor change in methodology. The minor change is the added emphasis on user interface design. This added emphasis is apparent in so-called heart-of-the-business systems, where the computer technology is used to help carry out an organization's main tasks, rather than to record data about those tasks after the fact. The change is reinforced by the emergence of personal computers and computer literacy. Users who are accustomed to good interfaces such as those of spreadsheets, graphics, and mice do not readily accept black-and-white terminals with high response times and cryptic or missing instructions.

The major shift in methodology is towards a much more participative style of systems development. Two modern approaches illustrate this shift: iterative development and prototyping.

Iterative Development

With the iterative approach, the development team can avoid long projects and make sure something of value is delivered to the users of an application every few weeks. For example, as soon as a report is found to be required, it can be designed, programmed, tested, and implemented, perhaps in less than two weeks. The development team then goes on to diagnose the next requirement (see Figure I–5).

The iterative development approach has both merits and problems. The merits of the approach are obvious—increased user involvement and returns on investment. Users remain involved because very little time goes by between being promised something and seeing it actually delivered. Returns on investment are increased because the average time to implement a given function is roughly divided in half for the same total cost. Therefore, the breakeven point of the application, the moment when accumulated benefits or savings overtake accumulated costs, can easily come several months or a year earlier than with the waterfall style.

To people who are used to the waterfall methodology, the problems with this approach seem equally obvious. One problem is the difficulty in evaluating the total economics of an entire system before implementation starts. This objection is often met by the argument that each step must pay for itself, thus ensuring that the entire system will achieve at least the sum of the savings of each individual deliverable.

In practice, some systems functions that are a prerequisite for others may not pay for themselves, may take long to implement, and may consequently make the iterative approach impossible. Although invoicing cannot be implemented before a customer data base is established, the customer data base may not pay for itself, especially if the full-fledged, integrated, total customer data base is implemented. It only pays in terms of the applications—order entry, invoicing, marketing, and so on—that it makes possible. If only the small part of the data base actually required for invoicing were implemented in an initial step, and then the other applications were added as they were implemented, an unstable data structure with difficult maintenance problems would result. This problem is getting easier to solve with relational data bases, but it is by no means negligible.

As a consequence, iterative development is much more difficult to apply to transaction processing systems than to management information systems

Figure I–5   **Impact of Iterative Development on the Life Cycle**

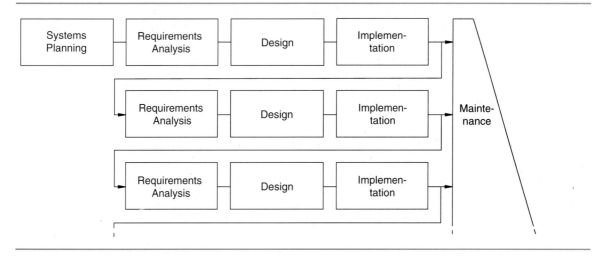

and decision support systems. Transaction processing systems tend to be integrated and operate as a whole. Management information and decision support systems are much easier to subdivide into smaller units and tend to use already existing data bases.

For transaction processing systems, iterative development requires an initial phase of fairly detailed systems planning. The plan lays out the overall data structure and the technical architecture of the system as well as a general sequence of implementation. Then, both infrastructure systems (e.g., data base management, utilities, report distribution, security) and business applications can be implemented in small chunks. The systems plan must also be constantly maintained, and changes must be communicated to the systems developers so that they can continue to aim for the right target, even though it keeps moving.

For the initial planning effort to be successful, there must not be too many surprises along the road. Iterative development is best suited to those efforts where there is relatively little innovation—functional as well as technical—which might cause the initial design to be scrapped midway through the long-term effort.

In summary, iterative development is difficult and requires experienced planners and excellent project leaders, but its rewards can be immense.

Prototyping

In addition to iterative development, another style of participative development has emerged—prototyping. Prototyping is creating a working design rather than a design on paper. In Royce's words, when the solution is innovative, "develop it twice." Barry Boehm has carried the logic even further.

Figure I–6 **The Spiral Model of the Systems Development Life Cycle**

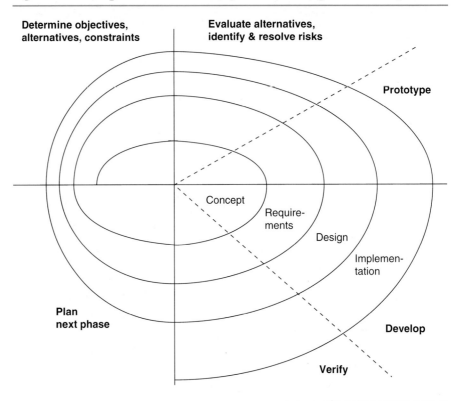

Source: Adapted from B.W. Boehm, "A Spiral Model of Software Development and Enhancement." *IEEE Computer,* 21, No. 5 (May 1988): 61.

He advocates that all projects that have some risk associated with them be developed according to a spiral model (see Figure I–6).[3]

Royce's life cycle is an image of the design process: the work in each phase is of a different nature. Boehm's spiral deemphasizes the differences between the nature of the work in the successive phases and concentrates on a project management view: limiting the risks of systems development by investigating early on those areas where the least is known about the system. Many life-cycle methodologies (including Royce's own suggestion for perfecting the waterfall model) recognize this by distinguishing between preliminary and detailed design. Preliminary design includes just enough work to be reasonably certain that the remaining work can be estimated and controlled. Boehm's work suggests that prototyping is one of the most effective ways to investigate risk-laden or innovative designs.

Part of the difficulty is that users often have little experience with modern systems. When faced with a design on paper—screen layouts, English language descriptions of procedures, flowcharts, and data flow diagrams—the

Figure I–7 **Impact of Prototyping on the Life Cycle**

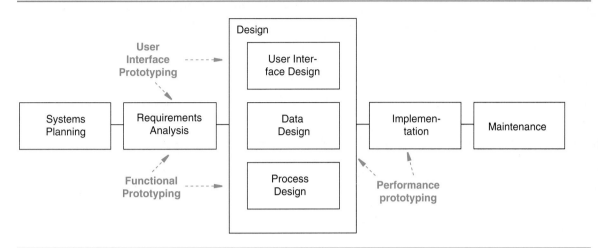

users may sign off on the design without realizing its impact. They may then object to the implementation later on, saying that what they had approved was different or that they had understood the design differently. Sometimes, the users approve something they would have objected to had they read the specification more carefully. Often, however, there is a genuine difference of interpretation that can only be resolved when the actual system is seen.

Instead of a design on paper, prototyping creates a demonstration model of the part of the design that is innovative. The prototype is analogous to the clay model of automobile stylists, the scale model that airplane engineers use for wind-tunnel tests, and the cardboard replicas that architects use.

Prototyping is found in three distinct areas: user interface design, performance design, and functional requirements determination. In practice, it is most often used to demonstrate the flow of human-computer interactions. In particular, it can demonstrate the layout of a screen on an actual display and the succession of operator actions—menu choices, data entry, function keys—together with typical system responses.

The second most frequent use of prototyping is to simulate the performance of a system under conditions that are close to real volumes. A prototype data base can be developed, and a program can then simulate a large number of simultaneous users. This process is usually applied to the evaluation of a technical design or the suitability of a piece of hardware. It generally only involves the technical part of the team, not the users.

Finally, prototyping is proving useful when users have difficulty formulating requirements. The main symptom of this difficulty is when someone says, "I don't know what I want, but I will know it when I see it." Another typical indication is when a user states a processing rule and then never seems to run out of exceptions to the rule. When this problem occurs, artificial intelligence techniques and tools can often be used to develop a working prototype that gives satisfactory results. The requirements analysis process can then pull the prototype apart to ascertain which rules actually made the result come out right. Prototyping is explored in more detail in Section IV.

Notes

1. Anderson, Howard J. "Physician Computer Network Moves into New Markets after Michigan Test." *Modern Healthcare* (November 21, 1986): 50.

2. Royce, W. W. "Managing the Development of Large Software Systems." *Proceedings of IEEE WESCON,* 1970.

3. Boehm, B.W. "A Spiral Model of Software Development and Enhancement." *IEEE Computer,* 21, No. 5 (May 1988): 61.

Information Technology and Competitive Advantage

After a brief historical perspective, Chapter 1 describes the impact of today's rapidly changing and highly competitive environment on the use of information technology. The framework for strategic business planning in this environment is built on Professor Michael Porter's approach: the five forces model, the three generic strategies, and the value chain analysis. Described next are two areas in which work has been done to complete this framework. The first is the strategic grid. This grid enables planners to analyze how important information technology is to a specific organization. The second area is that it may not always be advantageous to pioneer, even when the objective is to achieve an advantage over the competition. Finally, the notion of competitive advantage, which applies mainly to profit-oriented businesses, is extended to not-for-profit organizations.

Learning Objectives

- Describe how management attitudes towards information technology are changing from the view that the technology is useful for recording routine business transactions to the view that information is a valuable corporate resource.

- Recognize how information technology supports the management and use of the information resource.

- Understand how strategic planning is used to anticipate and instigate change.

- Become aware of how Michael Porter's model can be used as a framework for thinking about ways to use information technology to achieve a competitive advantage.

- Understand how the model developed by Cash, McFarlan, and McKenney—the strategic grid—can be used to evaluate the strategic significance of an organization's existing and projected information technology applications.

- Recognize that an organization should consider possible repercussions before introducing a system designed to yield a competitive advantage.

- Realize that applications to achieve a competitive advantage are applicable to the not-for-profit sector as well.

A BRIEF HISTORICAL PERSPECTIVE

Business managers today are much more concerned about the effects of competition than they were even a few short years ago. They must react to competitive threats not only from local sources but also from regional, national, and international sources. Deregulation in such industries as airlines and banking in the United States has also increased competitive pressure. For organizations to survive, much less grow and prosper, in such a competitive environment, managers must employ all of the resources at their command as efficiently and effectively as possible. They, the managers, are responsible for their organizations being better than the competition.

One potentially powerful resource available to managers is information technology. More and more stories tell how information technology has successfully given some companies an advantage over their competitors. Also, companies that are forced to react to a competitor's innovative use of information technology are at a disadvantage.

Computers have been available for business use since 1954, when a Univac 1 was installed at General Electric's Appliance Park facility in Louisville, Kentucky. If computers have been around this long, why is it that the use of information technology for competitive advantage is a relatively recent phenomenon?

Several factors help explain why:

- Early applications focused on the mechanization of existing procedures.
- A gap between technicians and users emerged in many organizations.
- The environment has only recently become more changing, more competitive.

At Appliance Park, the first computer was used to prepare the plant's payroll. In the early years of computer systems, the **application focus** of most companies that used computers was to mechanize existing manual or punched-card transaction processing systems such as payroll, billing and accounts receivable, and general ledger. Most often the data processing group reported to the accounting function. This tended to keep them focused on the development of accounting and related applications in all but the most enlightened of environments.

In addition, because the technology was changing so rapidly, data processing professionals were hard pressed to keep up. As a result, more and more data processing specialists emerged. They were experts in such areas as computer operating systems, data base, telecommunications, and higher-level languages. In many companies, the specialization caused a **technician-user gap;** information systems specialists spoke a language all their own, unintelligible to all but other specialists. They placed a higher value on competence in information technology than on company or industry expertise and tended to change employers frequently to work with the latest technology. Thus, a gap developed between the IS professionals and the users they were supposed to support. In extreme situations, users' needs for information systems remained unmet while the information systems department specialists struggled with backlogs of many years of work or pursued technical adventures of their own.

Many companies are now discovering the contribution that information technology can make to overall corporate effectiveness by developing innovative systems themselves, by reading about systems developed by others, or by experiencing the sting of a system developed by one of their competitors. The **change in the nature of applications**, from routine back-office systems such as payroll and billing to systems such as the airline reservation systems that increase competitiveness, makes a profound contribution to an organization's strategic goals. Information has been added to the traditional physical, human, and financial resources available to organizations. In the words of one prominent practitioner: "The relative performance of companies in the future will increasingly depend on how effectively they use information."

The competitive use of information technology will affect national economies as well, for nations compete with each other in today's global economy. Michael Blumenthal, former chairman of UNISYS Corporation, stated it this way: "Increasingly, then, a country's comparative advantage lies in its ability to utilize effectively the new information technology, in the speed of its absorption into the productive process, and in the relative efficiency with which it is applied. Less and less it is the other factor endowments, the availability of raw materials or the cost of labor, that determines which country has the advantage and which has the lowest cost."[1]

An ancient Chinese proverb states that change is the only constant. Not only is this truth as valid as ever, but the pace of **change in the business environment** is more rapid than before and seems to be constantly increasing. All businesses have to be prepared to operate in an environment of accelerating change. For example, computer-aided design and manufacturing (CAD/CAM) techniques have shortened product development life cycles by several years in some cases. Technological advances have created new products where none existed before. One such new product is the facsimile machine, which transmits copies of documents from one location to another using the dial-up telephone network. Facsimile transmission will no doubt continue to force change in the overnight express delivery industry, and existing players in that industry will have to react willy-nilly.

Although traditional uses of information technology still exist, including reductions of clerical personnel cost and paperwork turnaround times, achieving a competitive edge has become the single most powerful motivation for the creation of new systems. Those organizations that recognize information as a resource to achieve their strategic goals are the ones where new application development is the most vigorous.

Box 1–1

Top Management's Understanding of Information Technology

Top management's understanding of information technology varies. In many organizations, top management views information technology as useful for getting out the payroll or for processing payments, but fails to appreciate the potential it has for doing much more: for leveraging management talent through decision support and expert systems, for information systems tailored for top executives, and for information systems designed to be used as competitive weapons. Part of the explanation for this failure is that information technology is still a young field compared with other areas of business such as manufacturing or marketing. As a result, the techniques for managing information technology effectively are still evolving. Many of today's top managers were not exposed to information technology in their formal training or when they were rising through the ranks except for its use in basic transaction processing systems. Thus, there is little in their backgrounds that prepares them to view information and information technology as a valuable corporate resource.

INFORMATION TECHNOLOGY'S ROLE TODAY

As just noted, increased recognition is being given to information as a valuable corporate resource, one that must be managed as carefully as other corporate resources. A new domain has appeared, **information resource management**, whose purpose is to find ways to ensure that corporations are making the most effective use of this increasingly valuable resource. In some organizations a new executive position, the chief information officer (CIO), has been created to make sure that the information resource receives the appropriate level of executive attention.

At a more fundamental level, management must recognize the **supportive role of information systems**, enabling the organization to operate smoothly and economically. In this role, the information systems function must be properly channeled and directed by senior management in pursuit of overall corporate goals. However, in many organizations top management has not understood the potential of information technology. Many examples exist of a business moving in one direction and its information systems function moving in a direction all its own, almost oblivious that it was supposed to contribute to corporate goals.

For information systems to support overall organizational goals, these goals must be defined and expressed. This process is typically labeled strategic business planning or long-range planning. Strategic business planning is particularly important in a rapidly changing competitive environment. Without it, companies might not be able to survive and prosper.

A FRAMEWORK FOR STRATEGIC BUSINESS PLANNING

Change is inevitable. If an organization does not change on its own, the competitive environment will force it to. Strategic business planning can help companies anticipate change. More important, planning can help companies instigate change rather than be its victims. Instead of letting unexpected change threaten its stability, an organization can capitalize on the opportunities that change presents. To anticipate or, even better, to plan for change, a company can use the traditional strategic planning model, which involves three steps:

- Defining the mission of the organization.

- Identifying strategic goals and objectives in support of the mission.

- Developing strategies to achieve these goals and objectives.

These three steps constitute the strategic planning process itself. Further steps are required to put the strategy into action: development of tactical measures and monitoring results.

One of the challenges of strategic planning is to develop alternative views, or scenarios, of what the future business environment will be like and then to plan corporate strategies appropriate for each scenario. Without the aid of information technology, only a small number of alternative scenarios can be evaluated. For some time, computer-based corporate models and other forecasting techniques have been available to assist organizations in strategic planning and in monitoring progress towards the plan's goals and objectives.

Professor Michael Porter has created a conceptual model for strategic planning that planners can use as a framework for thinking about ways to use information systems to achieve competitive advantage. This model uses information technology not just for planning the strategy, but also for implementing the strategy that is being planned. The three key concepts in Michael Porter's approach are the five forces model, the three generic strategies, and the value chain.

Five Forces Model

Porter defines five competitive forces that collectively determine an industry's overall attractiveness. The opportunities for growth and investment return will vary by industry. Hence, planners first evaluate the areas of attractiveness before committing resources to any particular strategy.

As illustrated in Figure 1–1, the five forces are:

- Threat of New Entrants
    An industry is deemed less attractive if it is relatively easy for new competitors to enter, more attractive if existing competitors can raise barriers against potential new entrants.

- Threat of Substitute Products or Services

Figure 1–1 **The Five Forces Model**

An industry's attractiveness is diminished if substitute products or services are easy for its customers to obtain.

- Bargaining Power of Buyers

    An industry becomes less attractive when the bargaining power of its buyers increases, more attractive when the bargaining power of its buyers decreases.

- Bargaining Power of Suppliers

    As with buyers, the attractiveness of an industry decreases as the bargaining power of its suppliers increases, and vice versa.

- Rivalry among Existing Competitors

    A slow-growth industry with many vigorous competitors and high exit barriers, for example, is inherently less attractive than a high-growth industry with a few relatively courteous competitors.

Let us examine each of the five forces and their interaction in greater detail.

Threat of New Entrants. Members of a particular industry will find it advantageous to erect entry barriers against potential new entrants, thus keeping the number of competitors to a minimum. Traditional barriers to entry have been such factors as economies of scale, large capital requirements, high switching costs, and proprietary technology. For example, an entry barrier exists if large volumes or heavy investments are necessary for new entrants to be cost-efficient producers, because their fixed costs will be very high. It is not until they have reached a sufficient volume of production that the total revenue will be sufficient to cover both variable and fixed costs, thus achieving the required economies of scale. Companies such as Sears that have attempted to enter the credit card market have had to face formidable entry barriers based on economies of scale. Another example of a barrier is the switching costs associated with changing from one supplier to another. For example, if a large organization were to switch from using Lotus 1–2–3 to another spreadsheet package with different layouts and key usage, it would incur large costs in retraining its personnel to use the new spreadsheet. Some of Lotus's competitors have attempted to make Lotus look-alike spreadsheets. No doubt Lotus Development Corporation was aware that the barriers to entry were being lowered when it sued a competitor for having created a look-alike.

Threat of Substitute Products or Services. The availability of substitute products or services may make an industry less attractive. For example, someone wishing to open a restaurant would do well to consider potential competition not only from other restaurants in the market area but also from establishments that offer consumers alternative ways to spend an evening out, such as theaters, athletic clubs, and cultural and sporting events.

Bargaining Power of Buyers. Buyers are likely to have an advantage when negotiating for prices and terms with their suppliers if the product they are purchasing is a highly standardized one. Then they can fairly easily switch to other sources. They also have the advantage if their purchases constitute a major portion of a supplier's business. For example, in the automobile industry, automotive manufacturers ask much from their parts suppliers. A GM, Ford, or Chrysler is often so important to parts suppliers that the suppliers are willing to do whatever is asked of them. The manufacturers typically ask for such things as just-in-time inventory systems (transferring some of the costs of carrying inventory to the supplier) and electronic data interchange systems in formats compatible with the manufacturers' internal systems. The seller is dependent on the buyer, and because moving from one supplier to another is inexpensive, the buyer has the advantage.

Bargaining Power of Suppliers. When there are relatively few suppliers and few substitute products, and when the threat of forward integration (the supplier entering the business of the customer) exists, the supplier has an advantage. When OPEC was at the height of its power and influence during the energy crisis of the mid-1970s, the advantage in the oil industry tilted heavily towards the suppliers and against buyers. Even though the power of OPEC subsequently waned, primarily because of increased supplies and a greater reliance on substitute products, a few OPEC members such as Kuwait and Saudi Arabia seized the opportunity to pursue a strategy of forward integration by entering the petroleum refining and retail distribution businesses.

Rivalry among Existing Competitors. Intensely competitive industries have many competitors, relatively slow growth, high fixed costs, significant

Figure 1–2 **The Strategic Options**

Overall Cost Leader	Overall Differentiation
Cost Focus	Cost Differentiation

Scope

Strategy

exit costs, a lack of buyer switching costs, and diverse competitors. For example, acute-care hospitals in large metropolitan areas are in an intensely competitive industry. In most cases, the nature of the health care industry changed when the government imposed greater cost controls and third-party insurers insisted on lower costs. The challenge to hospitals has become to find ways to get an increasing share of a decreasing market for inpatients.

Interaction of the Five Forces. The way in which the five forces interact determines the overall attractiveness of an industry. The strategic plan of an organization takes into account both the basic attractiveness of its industry and its individual performance. The attractiveness of companies that compete in several industries depends on the performance of its component strategic business units, or SBUs, in their respective industries. The overall performance of the corporation will be the sum of the performances of the SBUs it controls.

Three Generic Strategies

According to Porter, there are three generic strategies an organization can use to create a sustainable competitive advantage for itself: it can alter the structure of the industry; it can improve its position; or it can create a new product.

Altering the Industry Structure. Recall that an industry's basic attractiveness results from the interaction of the five forces in Porter's model. An organization can attempt to improve its position by altering the industry structure in its favor by creating entry barriers or by creating stronger linkages between an organization and its suppliers or customers. The creative use of information technology can make the structural alteration possible.

Figure 1–3 **The Value Chain**

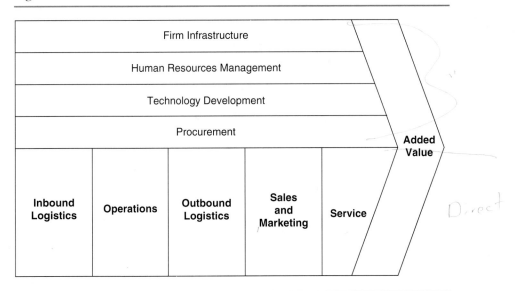

Improving a Position in Existing Lines of Business. A company that sets out to enhance its existing position without changing the industry structure can strive either to become the low-cost producer or to produce a differentiated product. Within both of these strategies a company can choose to focus on broad or narrow market segments. As illustrated in Figure 1–2, the choices are to become an overall cost leader, an overall provider of differentiated products or services, or a more narrowly focused cost leader or differentiator.

Creating New Products. The third strategy is to move to another product or a new market altogether. Information technology can be used to develop and offer entirely new products. Quite often, this can be done simply by delivering and using information that is already available in the organization.

The Value Chain

Porter's framework includes an analytical tool called the value chain, an aid in highlighting the role of information technology in achieving a sustainable competitive advantage (see Figure 1–3). The value chain, a diagram of the functional activities performed by a strategic business unit, highlights the contribution of both direct and supportive activities to the delivery of a product or service to the buyers. A generic value chain, as shown in Figure 1–3, consists of the direct functions of inbound logistics, operations, out-

Box
1–2

Systems That Have Changed an Industry Structure

Cash Management Accounts in the Securities Industry

Merrill-Lynch introduced its innovative Cash Management Account (CMA) a few years ago. The CMA automatically placed customers' cash balances resulting from securities sales into money market interest accounts and also gave the customers limited check-writing privileges. All activity during a given month was shown on an easy-to-read statement that also summarized the customers' holdings placed with the firm. The CMA met such success that it soon became a prerequisite for any firm who wished to compete for the individual investor's business. It was not too long before Merrill-Lynch's competitors had similar products of their own, but Merrill-Lynch gained market share during the intervening period. A product such as the Cash Management Account would have been impossible without information technology. It also raised an entry barrier to any other firm that wished to enter the industry. Any new entrant would have to create its own version of the information technology-based Cash Management Account.

Automatic Teller Machines

Automatic teller machines (ATMs) are an example of a substitute product created with the help of information technology. Many routine banking transactions can be handled directly by the ATMs with no need for human interaction. Moreover, the ATMs are available 24 hours per day. Their acceptance by consumers has been so dramatic that in 1988 there were over 40,000 ATMs installed in the United States. Two competing nationwide (soon to be worldwide) networks permit a customer of a bank located in Lincoln, Nebraska, to obtain cash from an ATM in Orlando, Florida. Banks that were slow to install ATMs ran the risk of losing their customers as a result. Banks that failed to anticipate the wide acceptance of ATMs and that built traditional branches may be burdened today with unwanted

real estate. A secondary effect of the use of ATMs has been to make bank tellers' jobs more challenging as, increasingly, machines handle the more routine transactions.

American Hospital Supply's ASAP System

American Hospital Supply's ASAP system is one of the most oft-cited examples of a use of information technology for competitive advantage. The system evolved over many years, but its main purpose always was to tie hospitals, the company's primary customers, more closely to American Hospital Supply by making ordering faster and more convenient. ASAP permitted hospital purchasing agents to place orders using computer-to-computer communication. It also transmitted confirmations back and suggested substitute products if a desired item was not in stock. Hospital purchasing agents could also inquire to determine the status of open orders and back orders and have certain materials management functions performed for them as well. The system changed the traditional buyer-supplier relationships by making satisfied customers more reluctant to order from competitors. The system tended to decrease the buyers' power and increase the power of the supplier.

American Hospital Supply merged with Baxter Healthcare Corporation in 1985. In 1987, a new version of the system was introduced to counter competitors who had introduced systems that were ASAP look-alikes. Entitled "ASAP Express," it listed products of any vendor who sold items to hospitals and wished to have them included in the system, whereas ASAP listed only those items carried by American Hospital Supply. According to Michael Hudson, president of Baxter's Hospital Systems Division, "ASAP Express opens a new era of electronic entry in which suppliers must compete in other areas such as product line breadth, distribution capabilities, and value added services. This is where Baxter truly excels."[2]

Companies That Have Improved Existing Products or Services

To reduce costs, *Deere & Company* created a computerized parts data base system for the 300,000 parts it uses in production. Having information on existing parts available in an easily accessible form enables the company to determine quickly if needed parts are available, thus avoiding unnecessary duplication in design and production. In two recent years, the company estimated that the system saved it over $9 million.

Aetna Life & Casualty developed a system called AECLAIMS, which automatically maintains insurance contracts and processes claims and insurance premiums. The system has significantly reduced the time and clerical effort required to process claims.

An example of the use of information technology in marketing and sales is the computerized bridal gift registry developed by the *Dayton-Hudson Department Stores*. Previously, a prospective bride would register in a single store, making it difficult to keep track of gifts purchased at other stores. The new system maintains a chainwide data base that records all

purchases in a computer record. Store sales of wedding gifts increased 20 percent annually in the first two years after the system was installed. Dayton-Hudson is presently applying the same concept to baby gifts, calling it "The Stork Club." The company plans to use information about what newlyweds and new parents have been given through the registry to improve their marketing to these prospective customers.

In the highly competitive credit card industry, *American Express* used information technology to create a differentiated product, the Year-End Summary of Charges, first offered to GoldCard members. The computer-prepared report showed each charge the cardholder made during the year in many categories such as airline tickets, lodging, restaurants, car rentals, and merchandise. The report provided the detail of each charge and also summarized the charges in each category by month for the entire year. Many cardholders found the documentation useful for tax purposes.

bound logistics, sales and marketing, and service. Support functions consist of procurement, technology development, human resource management, and firm infrastructure. Added value represents the difference between the product cost determined as the sum of the value chain functions and the price the buyer is willing to pay. Detailed coverage of the way systems analysts use the value chain concept and related analytical tools is presented in Appendix 1.

In analyzing the value chain for a strategic business unit, it is important to remember that the value chain is, indeed, a chain, with linkages between its various functions. For example, increasing the quality (and cost) of raw materials may reduce manufacturing (i.e., operations) costs and reduce the overall cost of the SBU's product. If the market price remains constant, returns to the SBU will increase. Similarly, costly technological development

Figure 1–4 **The Strategic Grid**

Categories of Strategic Relevance and Impact

		Low	High
Strategic Impact of Existing Systems	**High**	Factory	Strategic
	Low	Support	Turnaround
		Low	**High**

Strategic Impact of Applications Development Portfolio

may create a differentiated product for which the market may be willing to pay a premium. The systems analyst's challenge is to search for ways to use information technology to decrease costs or increase product differentiation, thereby increasing the added value segment of the value chain.

The five forces model, the three generic strategies, and the value chain are analytical tools that can help an organization create and sustain a competitive advantage for itself. Firms that fail to do this will have to settle for average returns at best. Superior performers will generate the profit margins necessary to sustain themselves. Some will also generate the additional capital required to flourish in their existing industry or to expand into other, more attractive ones.

THE STRATEGIC GRID

In most businesses, information technology does not contribute nearly as much to create a competitive advantage as it could. The examples cited in this chapter are clearly occurring in companies that are on the leading edge. Others have not nearly tapped the potential of the information technology resource. This potential will vary from company to company, depending on individual industry or company circumstances. A useful framework for the analysis of a company's potential is the strategic grid developed by Cash, McFarlan, and McKenney, which describes four different environments (see Figure 1–4).

An organization belongs in one of the four quadrants as a function of the strategic significance of its existing applications and applications development plan, or portfolio.

A company is in the **strategic quadrant** if both its existing and planned applications are of strategic importance. An example might be a bank that

Box
1–4

Companies That Have Created New Products or Services

Dow Jones News/Retrieval offers subscribers access to many data bases through a dial-up connection from a personal computer located at a business office, a home, or even the subscriber's resort condominium. In addition to company and industry news from such sources as back issues of *The Wall Street Journal* and *Barron's*, the service offers current stock quotes and general services such as news, sports, and weather and on-line shopping, travel, and mail.

Often, a new product is spawned through the creative use of information a company already has available. TRW, the largest credit rating service in the United States, maintains credit histories on millions of people. The credit histories are maintained on a large computer system that is updated by businesses to reflect experiences they have had with consumers and accessed by businesses to obtain a credit report on individuals to whom they are considering granting credit.

TRW developed a differentiated product called TRW CREDENTIALS, which it is marketing to consumers. For a fee of $35 per year, individuals who sign up for the service can review their own credit report, receive notification when a third party receives a copy of their credit report, add supplemental information to their credit history, apply for credit or financing through an electronic network, and finally, register their credit cards in case of loss or theft.

One of TRW's choices was whether to focus on a market segment or on a broad market. It could have made other choices: bundling more services with the product, charging a higher price, or directing its marketing towards high-income individuals. (TRW should certainly know who they are!) TRW apparently decided that its best returns would come from a product-pricing strategy aimed at the broader market.

depends on the smooth functioning of existing applications for doing business and that is currently working on a new loan approval system that will use expert systems technology to give it an edge over the competition by approving more loans more quickly at reduced risks.

A company is in the **factory quadrant** if its existing applications are of strategic significance, but it does not have any applications of strategic importance in its development plans. An example might be an airline that depends on its on-line reservation system to do business but has only non-strategic systems currently under development.

A company in the **support quadrant** has no systems of strategic importance in its applications development portfolio and its existing systems are noncritical data processing applications. The company would not be severely damaged even if the application suffered deterioration or breakdown of service. An example might be a high-fashion retailer that has mechanized customer billing and accounts receivable but has no significant systems development projects under way. The difference between good and bad years depends on the expertise of the store's buyers in anticipating which merchandise will appeal to customers, not on the quality of the information technology used.

A company in the **turnaround quadrant** has existing applications similar to a company in the support quadrant and development plans similar to a company in the strategic quadrant. An example might be a retailer developing a computer system to track sales of high-fashion items on a daily basis. With this system, managers can determine optimal times either to order more merchandise (if an item is moving faster than expected) or to mark down the prices (on items that are moving too slowly). Waiting too long to reorder may cause lost sales from unavailable merchandise. Waiting too long to reduce prices may result in large inventories of unsold items that must be sold at even lower prices or possibly held until the next season.

Information technology should be managed differently in companies in each of the four quadrants. Companies in the strategic quadrant should manage computer operations as efficiently as companies in the factory quadrant, should have the applications development resources to create innovative systems using leading-edge technologies, and should have the support and attention of top management. Similar comments apply to the operations of firms in the factory quadrant and to the applications development function for firms in the turnaround quadrant. For firms in the support quadrant, corporate priorities are likely to lie in areas other than information technology.

Although information technology will vary from company to company in its actual or potential strategic significance, its potential should not be dismissed too easily lest a company be taken by surprise by a competitor who suddenly introduces a system giving a competitive advantage, as is typically the case.

FIRST-MOVER DISADVANTAGES

Michael Vitale, in an article entitled "The Growing Risks of Information Systems Success,"[3] introduced a note of caution when he suggested that companies would be well advised to consider certain undesirable repercussions if they are the first to introduce a system designed to give them a sustainable competitive advantage. Certain events could keep a competitive advantage, if achieved at all, from being sustainable. Vitale identified the following events as the kind that could cause undesirable results:

- Systems that change the basis of competition to a company's disadvantage.

    A company could introduce an information technology-based product to permit its customers to enter orders on-line. It might find that the competition reacts by lowering prices and that the lower prices are more appealing to the market than the added value of the system.

- Systems that lower entry barriers.

    A health and casualty insurance company that markets its policies primarily to smaller businesses discovered that the bookkeepers of potential customers were reluctant to process another payroll deduction. The company considered offering a computerized payroll service as a way of getting over this obstacle but decided that this new service would open up the sale of insurance policies by the much more entrenched companies that already offer computerized payroll preparation services.

- Systems that bring on litigation or regulation.

  The airline reservation systems developed by American and United were so effective that they eventually brought on charges of unfair competition. Eleven competing airlines that purchased services from the two airlines claimed that the prices they had to pay and the treatment they received put them at a competitive disadvantage. The competitors sued and asked that the reservation systems be spun off into separate subsidiaries.

- Systems that increase the power of buyers or suppliers.

  An order entry system that permits buyers to examine a company's inventory files prior to placing an order may place too much power in the hands of the buyer. The knowledge of item availability may give the buyer a bargaining advantage: a buyer who sees that an item is in short supply may choose to negotiate for a price break in exchange for a longer delivery time.

In another article, entitled "A Hard Look at Strategic Systems," Robert F. Morison and Kirtland C. Mead note that obtaining a sustainable competitive advantage from strategic systems is sometimes easier said than done.[4] In particular, they point out that in most cases "an information system does not provide lasting competitive advantage. What it can provide is the base and environment for ongoing innovation that creates a moving target for would-be imitators. Advantage can be sustained by continual enhancement and development." The continuing evolution of the ASAP system discussed in Box 1-2 is but one example of this.

As in any planning process, possible outcomes must be analyzed before initiating a change to be sure that the change does not bring about undesirable side effects.

APPLICABILITY TO THE NOT-FOR-PROFIT SECTOR

Up to this point, the discussion of the use of information technology for competitive advantage has applied to a profit-seeking environment. The approaches can apply in the not-for-profit and public sectors as well. In the story of the two competing hospitals in Kalamazoo, the hospitals were not competing to make a profit but rather to reduce the deleterious effect of high fixed costs when volumes were dwindling. In the not-for-profit sector, the measures of success tend to be whether the application of information technology leads to greater efficiency or effectiveness in an organization rather than whether an organization achieves a sustainable competitive advantage. The following examples illustrate the successful use of information technology in this sector:

- Law enforcement officials in many countries have access to data bases containing records of drivers and vehicles. If a driver is stopped for a traffic violation, a police officer can determine if there are outstanding arrest warrants for the driver or if the car is stolen or has recently been used in a crime. By using the driver's license number and the vehicle's license plate number, a police officer can use a terminal in the police vehicle that is connected by shortwave radio to the computer where the records are stored.

- Several universities have devised systems that permit students to register for classes by using a touch-tone telephone, thereby avoiding the long lines, stress, and inconvenience associated with traditional registration processes.

Thus, the innovative use of information technology is not confined to profit-oriented businesses. Although not-for-profit organizations are not subject to the same competitive forces as business firms, they have to compete for scarce resources such as qualified personnel and financial grants. Therefore, the use of information technology for competitive advantage is just as relevant as in the business sector.

Summary

Increased competition and the pace of technological change have combined to give organizations unprecedented opportunities to achieve a competitive advantage through the creative application of information technology. Although information technology has long been used to support the strategic planning process, Michael Porter's recently developed analytical framework composed of the five forces, the three generic strategies, and the value chain have proved particularly useful in helping organizations identify applications that can have a significant strategic impact.

The strategic grid designed by Cash, McFarlan, and McKenney can also help organizations analyze their needs. The four quadrants of the grid indicate the different levels of significance that information technology may have for different kinds of organizations.

In addition, the work of Michael Vitale points out certain disadvantages that may be associated with being the first organization to introduce an application intended to have strategic impact.

Finally, examples of creative uses of information technology in the public and not-for-profit sectors point out that the concepts in this chapter can be applied in those areas as well as in the profit-making sector.

Selected Readings

Porter, Michael E. *Competitive Strategy.* New York: Free Press, 1981.

Porter, Michael E. *Competitive Advantage: Creating and Sustaining Superior Performance.* New York: Free Press, 1985.
Michael Porter's books have had enormous influence on management thinking in the 1980s. They are indispensable reading for systems analysts who want to understand how the information systems department can support executive management's objectives.

Cash, James I., McFarlan, F. Warren, and McKenney, James L. *Corporate Information Systems Management—The Issues Facing Senior Executives,* 2d ed. Homewood, Illinois: Irwin, 1988.
This book extends the theories created by Michael Porter and others. It is representative of the lines of thought that have led to the emergence of the chief information officer as a member of the executive leadership of organizations.

Wiseman, Charles. *Strategic Information Systems.* Homewood, Illinois: Irwin, 1988.
A thorough review of the subject including implementation techniques. In addition, this text is rich with examples culled from the author's extensive collection of successful and unsuccessful examples of strategic information systems.

Review Questions

Traditionally, the management of many organizations has thought that information technology was useful for transaction processing systems such as payroll or billing, but not much else. This attitude is now changing.

1. Explain the emerging management attitude towards information technology.

2. Describe how the rapidly changing business environment has stimulated the change in attitude.

3. What are the responsibilities of the information resource management function?

4. Explain why aiming to achieve a sustainable competitive advantage has become a major preoccupation in most organizations.

5. What role does technology play in the management of an organization's information resource?

6. What are the five competitive forces that collectively define an industry's overall attractiveness? Describe the forces that make an industry more or less attractive.

7. Summarize the three strategies that managers can use to find ways for information systems to give their organization a sustainable competitive advantage.

8. Why should management consider the first-mover disadvantages described by Michael Vitale before introducing an information system that may give their organization a competitive advantage?

9. Differentiate between the measures of success used for information technology applications in the for-profit and not-for-profit sectors.

Discussion Questions

1. Electronic data interchange (EDI) is a technology whereby purchase orders, invoices, and other order-related documents are exchanged electronically between purchaser and supplier. How might a supplier use EDI to improve its business position?

2. Not all organizations are ready to use information technology to achieve a competitive advantage. Select an industry of interest to you. Explain how Cash, McFarlan, and McKenney's strategic grid may aid a company within that industry to examine its readiness to use information technology for competitive advantage.

Mini-Cases

Bauersfeld's Supermarket. The following excerpt is from an article in *The Wall Street Journal*:

Electronic Price Labels Tested in Supermarkets
Prices of more than 500 items will change today at Bauersfeld's supermarket in Topeka, Kansas, but the clerks won't have to peel outdated labels off the shelves.

Instead, they will change the prices electronically, plugging a hand-held computer into programmable labels clipped to the store's shelves. The computer sends a signal to a microchip in the molded plastic label, which then displays the new price in half-inch-high liquid crystal numbers.

Such devices are part of the grocery industry's continuing effort to reduce overhead with technology. Already more than half of the nation's supermarkets have electronic scanners at check-outs to ring up prices of bar-coded packages. Programmable shelf labeling promises to trim labor costs further and allow quicker price changes than are now possible.

Last week, a big scanner company acquired North American distribution rights for one of two electronic labels on the market. Datachecker Systems, Inc., a unit of National Semiconductor Corp., signed a five-year agreement to sell labels made by Telepanel, Inc., a Canadian concern.

Its rival is Graphic Technology, Inc., of Olathe, Kansas, which makes the labels being tested in Bauersfeld's store. While Graphic Technology's labels must be touched by hand-held computer, Telepanel's labels needn't be. They contain FM transceivers and can be programmed in virtually no time by a store computer sending out a different radio signal to each of the potentially thousands of shelf labels.[5]

Questions for Discussion

1. In what ways could the technology be used to give supermarket operators a competitive advantage?

2. What are some potential first-mover disadvantages?

3. In what other industries could the technology be applied?

High Country Resort, Inc. Brad Stocki, president of High Country Resort, Inc., just returned from a seminar in New York where, among other things, he heard a presentation on ways companies are using information technology to create a competitive advantage. Brad's personal background was in ski resort operations before assuming his present post. The only real exposure he has had to information systems is the basic transaction processing systems such as payroll, hotel reservations, and billing that had been in place at High Country the last several years. The notion that companies could use information technology to gain a competitive advantage was a new one to Brad.

Shortly after his return, he convened a meeting of the Executive Committee, composed of the vice-presidents of the various functional areas. Based on what he had just learned, he said he was concerned that one of the competitor resorts might be working on an application of information technology in their business that would have a negative impact on High Country. Therefore, he wanted assurance from you, as his director of MIS, that High Country was doing everything it should be doing to use information technology for competitive advantage.

Question for Discussion

1. How would you approach this assignment?

Notes

1. Blumenthal, Michael. "Change and Technology." *Foreign Affairs* Special issue: America and the World 1987/1988 (March 1988): 529–550.

2. Konsynski, B., and Vitale, M. "Baxter Healthcare Corporation." *Case No. 9–188–080.* Harvard Business School, 1988. Rev. 1990.

3. Vitale, Michael R. "The Growing Risks of Information Systems Success." *MIS Quarterly* (December 1986): 327–334.

4. Morison, R. F., and Mead, K. C. "A Hard Look at Strategic Systems." *INDICATIONS*, 6, 1 (January-February 1989). © 1989 by Index Group, Inc.

5. "Electronic Price Labels Tested in Supermarkets," by Richard Gibson *The Wall Street Journal* (March 31, 1988), p. 25. Reprinted by permission of *The Wall Street Journal*, © Dow Jones & Company, Inc. 1988. All Rights Reserved.

2

Business Process Change

Chapter 1 covered how businesses use information technology to give them a competitive edge in a rapidly changing environment. This chapter covers the changes in an organization made necessary by the very introduction of information technology-based solutions. The first part describes the nature and depth of these changes, some of which may revolutionize an organization's underlying business processes. The second part describes the challenges in implementing changes caused by new technology, users' resistance to such change, and some approaches to overcome this resistance.

Learning Objectives

*   Understand that business systems are composed of people, technology, and business processes, designed so that they work in harmony towards a common purpose.

*   Realize that if systems are to change, people must change as well.

*   Appreciate the need for a "new industrial engineering" in response to competitive pressures.

*   Understand the goals of business process reengineering.

*   Identify the five steps of business process reengineering.

*   Appreciate the nature of change.

*   Understand how to diagnose and deal with resistance to change.

*   Identify the four phases of organizational change.

SYSTEMS ARE COMPOSED OF PEOPLE, TECHNOLOGY, AND BUSINESS PROCESSES

A system can be defined as a set of interrelated components that interact with each other, with the whole set interacting with the environment. In business systems, each of the components can be viewed as a system in its own right. As illustrated in Figure 2–1, a business process such as product delivery may consist of subsystems for order entry, manufacturing, shipping, billing, etc. Each subsystem is often composed of a combination of people and machines working together to achieve a desired result. Business pro-

Figure 2–1 **Product Delivery Process**

Organizational Unit	Work Task
Sales	Order entry
Credit	Credit check
Production Control	Order scheduling
Manufacturing	Order production
Shipping	Shipment
Accounts Receivable	Billing
	Collection

cesses have two characteristics: they have "customers," the person or group who is the recipient of the defined business outcome of the process; and they cross organizational boundaries.

In subsystems based on information technology, the "machine" is made up of several layers of software and hardware: business application, common architecture, systems software and hardware, for example, as shown in Figure 2–2. Each layer interacts with its environment, i.e., the next layer up. Each environment views the next layer down as a system that responds to certain events in accordance with certain rules, although the details of how a response arises is often hidden. For example, a data entry clerk knows very little about the structure of programs being executed, but can still accomplish a data entry operation.

The organization itself, together with its business processes, is seen as a system by its environment: customers, suppliers, competitors, regulators, and consumers.

In years past, most business computing was done on large mainframe computers. Humans had to perform their complementary tasks in a way that made the most efficient use of the computer because it was a very expensive asset. Technological advances have reduced the cost of computing power in a remarkable way, and further cost reductions will no doubt occur in the coming years. In the meantime, labor costs have continued to rise. As a result, IS professionals are now designing computer systems that are easier for humans to use even though they may consume more computer resources.

Organizations have always had three challenges in the use of information technology. The first was simply understanding the machines themselves and how they worked. This challenge is largely behind us now, but it occupied the majority of the time of IS professionals in the past. The second challenge, that of understanding how to design systems so that human beings and computers work well together, is currently receiving a great deal of attention. The third challenge is to find ways to make our systems (composed of humans and machines) more effective than the systems of our competitors.

Figure 2–2 **System Layers**

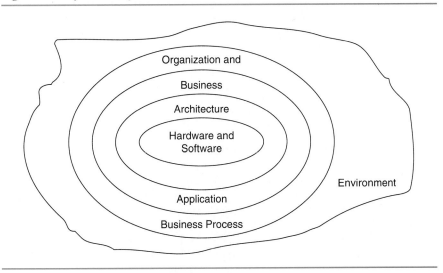

CHANGING SYSTEMS CHANGES PEOPLE

We have seen in Chapter 1 that creatively designed information systems have often given organizations a competitive advantage. Information systems alone, however, do not yield an advantage to an organization. Instead, information systems leverage the human resources of an organization to make them more effective in carrying out their responsibilities. In some cases we find that a department (inventory control, for example) can manage a large amount of information more effectively with a computerized system. In other cases we find that the quality and timeliness of executive decisions are improved if they are supported by a computer-based executive information system. Expert systems used to support, rather than replace, human knowledge are good examples of how human talent can be leveraged with the support of well-designed and accepted information systems.

Information systems are installed in an organizational setting composed of people with their own sets of values and goals and with their own understanding of the organization with its set of values and goals. It is not enough to develop an information system that supports an organization's objectives. The people who will use the information system must also understand the organization's objectives and the way the new system will help them play their parts in achieving these objectives. Information systems are tools. Just as with other tools, people must want to use them and often must be trained to use them in the most effective manner. IS professionals must be aware that the most brilliantly conceived system is of little value to the organization if it is not accepted and used by the people for whom it was designed.

The Need for Change

Top management in any organization is only too familiar with the challenge of introducing change. The pressure of competition together with advances in technology has made doing "business as usual" a thing of the past. As one top executive in a fast-changing industry said, "Nothing's easy anymore."

Examples can be found in many industries, but here are two:

Automobile manufacturers in the United States used to take five years to bring out a new model car, from the time a development project was approved until the time new models were on the dealers' floors. International competition, particularly from the Japanese, has forced U.S. manufacturers to shorten the product development cycle from five to three years in order to stay competitive. Information technology has helped by using computers to support human efforts in every step of the cycle, from computer-aided design through automated inventory control, factory robotics, and marketing. Even after-sale service is improved with information technology: microchip processors in the automobile yield diagnostic readouts to assist the service mechanics.

Airlines have been among the most creative users of information technology to force change in their industry. Those entering the airline business today must offer not only a computerized reservation system, but also:

- A frequent-flier awards program.
- An advanced seat selection service.
- An advanced special menu selection service.
- A locator system for lost baggage.

All of these computer-based systems are used in U.S. airlines today; none were in existence a few years ago. An airline operating without such systems would be at a clear disadvantage compared with its competitors.

Changing the direction of a large corporation has been likened to turning an aircraft carrier around: it is not as easy as turning a smaller vessel. Likewise, smaller corporations have had the advantage of being able to adapt more quickly to changes in their industries while larger organizations have struggled to catch up. We have come to expect more innovation from smaller, more nimble companies.

Competition has changed this, however, and large companies have discovered that they must adapt to change more quickly because their competitors have managed to do so. Some of the techniques used have been based on "intrapreneurship," a technique designed to foster within a corporate giant the entrepreneurial spirit so typical of smaller companies. The IBM PC was developed by a team of IBM "intrapreneurs," who were left to organize their own work autonomously in an organization known for its high degree of central control. The normal product planning and investment cycles were bypassed and management reporting was reduced to a minimum. As a result, the IBM PC was created in approximately 11 months and was introduced on the market in a very timely fashion. This timing contributed for a large part to its success.

The normal resistance so often experienced when managers attempt to implement change can no longer be condoned in the competitive environment of today. Information technology holds great promise as a powerful change agent if properly and creatively applied. To be effective, IS professionals must realize that the bottom line is to get human beings to change. If that does not happen, the systems they attempt to implement will not meet their objectives of improving the way the business is conducted.

THE NEW INDUSTRIAL ENGINEERING

In a recent issue of the *Sloan Management Review*, Thomas H. Davenport and James E. Short described a new way to combine the techniques of information technology with those of industrial engineering to transform an organization more profoundly than simply mechanizing existing work.[1] In another article that appeared about the same time in the *Harvard Business Review*, Michael Hammer told managers "it is time to stop paving the cow paths. Instead of embedding outdated processes in silicon and software we should obliterate them and start over. We should 'reengineer' our businesses: use the power of modern information technology to redesign our business processes radically in order to achieve dramatic improvements in their performance."[2] Both articles describe the new techniques businesses are beginning to employ to radically change their business processes in their search for competitive advantage. Termed *business process change* by some and *business process reengineering* by others, the new techniques hold great promise of transforming our corporations in preparation for the global competitive arena they will face in the 1990s. Information technology and IS professionals have key roles to play in bringing these changes about.

Historical Nature of Clerical Work

Since the early 1900s, industrial engineering has focused on work simplification, inspired by the ideas of Frederick Taylor. Clerical work has been organized along assembly-line principles, with batches of documents passed from one department, section, or work position to the next. Each clerk involved in a process performed just a small part of it. Controls such as batch totals and segregation of duties ensured the reliability that might have been lost due to excessive fragmentation of the work.

Our organizations reflected this philosophy. Employees who performed similar functions were grouped into departments such as accounts payable, purchasing, or sales. Managers were installed to administer each department. Groups of departments were formed, led by vice-presidents, and placed into an organizational hierarchy led by a president or chief executive officer. The organization chart of a typical manufacturing company looked something like the one in Figure 2–3, with vice-presidents of each functional area (marketing, manufacturing, finance, etc.) reporting to a president.

This method of organizing, although promoting the goals of efficiency and control, all too often subtly encouraged functional areas and departments to place their individual goals ahead of organizational goals. Thus, accounting often had a reputation as ones who "after the battle was over, came in and counted the wounded," rather than as resources on the same side as other functional areas. Manufacturing was sometimes perceived as working at cross-purposes to sales when they held back a new product until they were satisfied with their ability to produce it efficiently and with high quality.

Figure 2–3 **High-Level Organization Chart—Manufacturing Company**

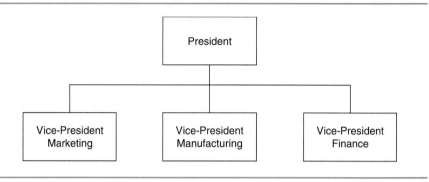

Initial Automation Strategies

The first round of automation, in the 1950s and 1960s, did not reduce the fragmentation. Rather, the work was moved to large mainframe computers without much change. Repetitive, simple operations were carried out on batches of "documents" to create output files, which were then transmitted from one processing unit (in the form of computer programs) to the next. The leftover manual work was simplified even further, to the point where the main role of clerical personnel was data entry. Information systems tended to be developed for single departments or functional areas. Thus, accounting had its set of applications, sales its set, and manufacturing its set, etc. Little information was shared between the applications of the various functional areas even though the computer records of each often contained similar information, such as customer data.

The 1970s and 1980s brought some integration. Data bases rather than files provided for data sharing among work units, and on-line transaction processing software moved some decision-making authority back to the clerks. But the essence of the work was unchanged; so were the organization of the enterprise and its management and control techniques.

Widening the Scope of Integration

One objective of business process reengineering is to increase the scope of integration of business processes. Frequently, this implies the creation of applications that cross the traditional functional boundaries of departments, divisions, or even firms. Experiences with attempts at data integration have led to the conclusion that integrating the data used by various business processes is not enough; the processes themselves must be appropriately integrated to achieve meaningful gains. An example of this can be seen at Ford Motor Company, where the reengineering of the purchasing/receiving/accounts payable process has eliminated the need for vendor invoices. Ford now pays its suppliers based on electronic receiving reports and the accounts payable department has shrunk by 75 percent (see Box 2–2).

Business Process Change at Ford Motor Company

Mr. Michael Treacy, an information technology consultant, tells an instructive tale about Ford's efforts to reduce the number of paper shufflers. What seemed at first to be a mundane efficiency campaign became a challenge to Ford's long-established ways of doing business. Ford employed about 500 people to order components, receive the parts, and pay suppliers. Mazda, a Japanese carmaker with which Ford has formed an alliance cemented by a 25 percent shareholding, did the same job with less than 100. An elaborate automated system cut Ford's order shufflers only to about 400. So Ford's folk took a harder look at Mazda. Mazda, Ford discovered, had fewer computers than Ford. Its secret was that it did not wait for invoices from its suppliers. When goods arrive at the loading dock, a warehouseman waves a bar-code reader over each box. That single action enters the parts into inventory, updates production schedules (if necessary), and sends electronic payment to the supplier.

This seemed like a bit of magic to some of Ford's managers. They had viewed invoices as a capitalist essential, like double-entry book-keeping. Once shown the trick, the possibilities for boosting efficiency by eliminating the complications of matching parts and invoices seem obvious. But tapping these efficiencies requires changes in the way people work: close relations with suppliers, a warehouse that can talk directly to the finance department, and workers who happily adapt to new ways of doing things. Ford is working on all those, and it hopes within a few years to institute payment on receipt worldwide.

Source: "The Ubiquitous Machine" Survey: Information Technology. *The Economist* (June 16, 1990).

Integrated systems developed during the 1980s generally achieved one-time benefits; they did not provide increasing value to the organization because they could not evolve over time. There were two reasons for this lack of flexibility. First, the systems often assumed a particular form of business process. Typically, it was that of a business process embedded in a hierarchical, functionally oriented organization such as the ones described earlier in this chapter. Work necessary to completely perform a business process such as processing a customer order was divided into many tasks and spread across departmental boundaries.

Second, the very content of the business process, the critical rules for processing transactions, was hard-coded into computer programs. Thus, a pattern of *freezing* the business process emerged. While the initial implementation of an automated application reaped the benefits of increased efficiency, it did so at a cost: the new computer application became a hindrance to further change because it could not be easily modified to respond to changes in the business environment.

Empowering the Knowledge Worker

Business process reengineering does not constitute an additional step in the direction of "clerical Taylorism." Rather, it requires that the people who carry out the reengineered process increase their understanding of the entire process, not just some fragmented part of it. Mutual Benefit Life, for example, created a new job position called the "case manager" to permit one person to perform all necessary processing of new applications for insurance. Case managers were supported by new computer systems that gave them all the information necessary to process an application at their workstations. Expert systems were also provided to assist in certain decisions that needed to be made. The new process replaced one in which an application required 19 people in 5 separate departments performing up to 30 individual processing steps. The casework approach is discussed more completely in Chapter 10.

In her book *In the Age of the Smart Machine: The Future of Work and Power*, Shoshana Zuboff argues that traditional industrial engineering approaches can make it harder for employees to understand their work. When work is broken down into small tasks, employees do not have the chance to see the big picture. Using information technology to reengineer tasks along the lines of the Mutual Benefit example results in knowledge workers becoming empowered. Their skills, in combination with the resources provided by well-designed computer systems, give them the ability to take responsibility for a much larger portion of a business process.

REENGINEERING THE BUSINESS PROCESS

Reengineering differs from conventional approaches in that it seeks radical change. The challenges facing our organizations demand it; simply automating the old ways of doing things will not be enough.

Overall Approach

Successful reengineering projects often begin with a strategic goal expressed by top management, such as drastic cost reduction, significant reduction in product development/delivery times, or maximum utilization of an organization's human capital through worker empowerment. A project task force formed to accomplish business process reengineering needs representatives from all functional areas likely to be affected by the resultant changes. IS professionals and industrial engineering specialists are usually included as members of the task force. A key point is to have the task force led by a senior executive to ensure that solutions embrace a broad business perspective rather than ones that protect the interests of individual departments or functional areas.

Principles of Reengineering

Davenport and Short identified five steps in business process redesign (or reengineering), as shown in Figure 2–4. Each is discussed in more detail below.

Figure 2–4 **Five Steps in Process Redesign**

Develop Business Vision and Process Objectives
Identify Processes to be Redesigned
Understand and Measure Existing Processes
Identify IT Levers
Design and Build a Prototype of the Process

Source: Thomas H. Davenport and James E. Short. "The New Industrial Engineering: Information Technology and Business Process Redesign." *Sloan Management Review* (Summer 1990).

Develop Business Vision and Process Objectives. Attempts at reengineering business processes in prior years frequently were mere attempts to rationalize or streamline an existing process. Although this approach could yield greater efficiencies, it all too often fell short of what could be achieved with more radical change. Successful reengineering efforts are more ensured if they start from a broad strategic vision from senior management. Examples of such starting points include:

- Reducing the cost of performing a business process .
- Reducing the time taken to perform a business process.
- Building quality into a business process.
- Building knowledge worker empowerment into a business process.

Multiple objectives can be set and achieved in reengineering a particular business process. One important tactic to ensure dramatic change is to set goals that will "stretch" the organization and thereby encourage creative solutions. Another tactic to remember is to place no limitation on the redesign options, or as few as possible. Process simplification, the traditional approach to improving work processes that focuses on efficiency and control, rarely leads to radical improvements because too much reliance is placed on the way the process is executed now. It is essentially evolutionary. In contrast, process reengineering focuses on effectiveness: innovation, speed, service, and quality. It is more likely to offer revolutionary changes.

Identify Processes to Be Redesigned. While most, if not all, of an organization's processes could benefit from reengineering with information technology, the most critical processes must be selected first. If the most critical processes are not immediately obvious, convening a meeting of senior managers to select them is often the most efficient way to develop a list of high-priority candidates. For example, senior administrators at a university might quickly agree that both student registration and the procurement process should appear at the top of the list of candidates for reengineering.

Within each process, its beginning and end points should be identified, together with the organizational units involved in all work tasks needed to complete the process. The principal "owner" of each process should also be identified. For example, as illustrated in Figure 2–5, the student registration process at a university might involve academic departments, the registrar's office, the financial aid office, the finance office, and the information systems department. Each organizational unit would perform a particular task related to the registration process. The owner of the process, that is, the manager identified as the one most responsible for seeing that student registration is efficient and effective, might be the registrar.

Understand and Measure Existing Processes. The second step, that of understanding and measuring the existing process, is important for two reasons. First, any problems with the current process should be surfaced so they can be understood and not replicated in the redesigned process. Second, a baseline of current process performance is established against which performance of the reengineered process can be measured. Designers must keep an open mind during this step, so that they are not unduly influenced by the way the current tasks are organized. They should adopt a questioning attitude and be continually alert for unnecessary or wasteful steps in the process. For example, in redesigning the accounts payable process at Ford, consider how easy it would have been to quickly accept the time-honored practice of paying vendor invoices when they had been matched with the purchase order and receiving report. Designers must continually ask themselves *why* a particular task is necessary and whether there might not be a shorter way to reach the goal of a particular business process.

Identify Information Technology Levers. Identification of information technology levers, or ways that information technology can be used to enhance the way a business process is performed, requires knowledge of both the business process and of the information technology that could enhance the process. Davenport and Short identified nine ways that information technology could have a favorable impact on a business process, as shown in Figure 2–6 and summarized below.

- Transactional

    The transformation of unstructured processes into routinized transactions. For example, changing the method by which students register for classes from one like the process depicted in Figure 2–5 to one that permits students to register for classes using a touch-tone telephone.

- Geographical

    Information technology can make geographically separate work units operate as if they were physically adjacent because of information technology's ability to transmit large amounts of information over great distances.

Figure 2–5 **Student Registration Process**

Department	Work Task
Academic Departments	Develop course schedule
	Admit students to closed classes
Registrar	Assign rooms
	Assign schedule
	Accept registrations
	Close classes
Financial Aid	Approve requests
	Submit approbation to Finance Office
Finance Office	Accept payments
	Hold unpaid registrations
	Accounts receivable follow-up
Information Systems	Registration
	Financial aid billing and collection

- Automational
    Information technology has the ability to supplement or replace human labor in a process. Automatic teller machines (ATMs) are but one of many examples that could be cited.

- Analytical
    Information technology-based analytical techniques such as spreadsheets or more complex models (e.g., simulations) can be utilized.

- Informational
    Information technology can be used to introduce information drawn from many different sources into a process. For example, corporate intelligence groups routinely extract and summarize data from many different on-line data bases of business media for daily distribution to key members of management.

- Sequential
    Oftentimes business processes are organized in a way that requires work tasks to be performed in a certain sequence. Information technology has been used to either reorder the tasks or, more commonly, to permit certain tasks to be performed simultaneously to reduce the elapsed time required to complete a process. *to speed-up processes*

- Knowledge Management
    Information technology can be used to make specialized knowledge, previously accessible to only a few individuals, accessible to all persons involved in a process. For example, Digital Equipment Corporation makes an expert system available to its field sales force that assists them in putting together the configuration specifications for complex systems. *E-mail Network*

Figure 2–6 **IT Capabilities and Their Organizational Impacts**

Capability	Organizational Impact/Benefit
Transactional	IT can transform unstructured processes into routinized transactions
Geographical	IT can transform information with rapidity and ease across large distances, making processes independent of geography
Automational	IT can reduce or replace human labor in a process
Analytical	IT can bring complex analytical methods to bear on a process
Informational	IT can bring vast amounts of detailed information into a process
Sequential	IT can enable changes in the sequence of tasks in a process, often allowing multiple tasks to be worked on simultaneously
Knowledge Management	IT allows the capture and dissemination of knowledge and expertise to improve the process
Tracking	IT allows the detailed tracking of task status, inputs, and outputs
Disintermediation	IT can be used to connect two parties within a process that would otherwise communicate through an intermediary (internal or external)

Source: Thomas H. Davenport and James E. Short. "The New Industrial Engineering: Information Technology and Business Process Redesign." *Sloan Management Review* (Summer 1990):17.

- Tracking

     Information technology can be used to track the status of processes and report on them either periodically or on demand. The Package Locator System developed by Federal Express tracks the current location of all Fed-Ex packages. Bar-coded package identification is scanned by hand-held readers as packages move from trucks to airplanes and back to trucks. The scanned information is transmitted to computers that keep track of the location of each package as it progresses towards its final destination.

- Disintermediation

     eliminate the middleman

     Information technology can be used to directly connect two parties performing tasks in a process that previously had been connected by an intermediary. Those of us who have used the Prodigy interactive personal service to order a CD from Sam Goody rather than having to write or go through a telephone order clerk have experienced disintermediation.

Design and Build a Prototype of the Process.   Various criteria are employed by companies to evaluate a redesigned business process. The foremost criterion, of course, is that the newly designed process continue to meet its business objectives, as well as the objectives identified by the senior management sponsor of the redesign effort. Additional design techniques used include:

- Designing for simplicity

  Much of the complexity built into existing processes came about as the result of designers simply automating the underlying manual work tasks. In addition to keeping the process fragmented, controls were required to ensure that information was passed from department to department correctly. Reengineering permits business processes to be simplified by attempting to have one person, working in harmony with a supporting computer system, perform all of the tasks in a business process wherever possible. Controls can be designed as an integral part of the process, rather than as separate work tasks performed by specialized departments. The casework approach described earlier in this chapter is an example of this technique.

- Eliminating buffers and intermediaries

  Dividing the work tasks necessary to complete a business process among several departments or functional areas often requires the installation of workstations, which accumulate groups of transactions (buffers) in order to balance the work loads between departments or intermediaries. If the work tasks are concentrated at one point, the time and cost of buffers and intermediaries can be saved. A variation of this principle is to encourage users of a business process to perform that process themselves. For example, some organizations permit individual departments to purchase items from external vendors directly, rather than routing purchase requisitions through an internal purchasing department. Ordering departments have much of the purchasing "expertise" that was previously resident in the minds of humans in the purchasing department made available to them on readily accessible computer data bases.

- Entering information once

  Many existing systems required information to be captured at multiple points in the process. Individual departments had their own forms or systems for data collection. By capturing information only once, at the beginning of a business process, the burden of entering redundant data with its accompanying opportunity for error can be eliminated.

Business process reengineering is usually more radical (a change in kind rather than degree) than traditional systems development, and the risks therefore tend to be higher. Stakeholders, especially, middle management and workers may feel threatened and resist the change, passively or actively. Because business process change touches the core of the business, the stakes are also much higher. A risk is more likely to materialize, and if it does, the penalty could be much higher.

Figure 2–7 **Ford's Accounts Payable Process Was Slow and Cumbersome Until . . .**

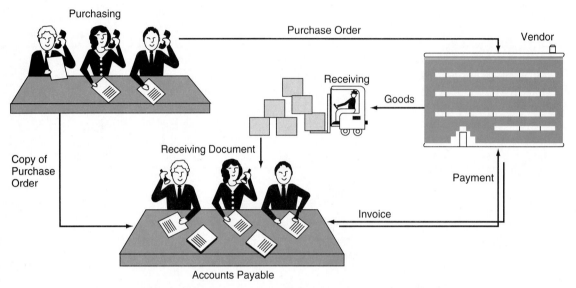

Purchasing

Purchase Order

Vendor

Receiving

Goods

Copy of Purchase Order

Receiving Document

Payment

Invoice

Accounts Payable

More than 500 accounts payable clerks matched purchase orders, receiving documents, and invoices and then issued payment. Mismatches were common.

To reduce the risk, prototyping and experimentation are commonly recommended. This is certainly wise, but organizational change may not always be possible to prototype or implement incrementally (as in the proposed time-phased implementation of changing the side of the road vehicles drive on: cars today and trucks next week). In any case, it becomes important to innovate in stages, so that management can lead the organization through a series of feasible changes. Simultaneous innovation in multiple areas (e.g., business process, organization, technology, and application architecture) can be extremely difficult to control.

Finally, it is worth reemphasizing the importance of setting ambitious goals for a reengineering project. Setting high targets for cost reduction, time compression, quality improvement, or knowledge worker empowerment will increase the likelihood of achieving major benefits. For example, after having their sights raised by observing what Mazda was able to

Figure 2–8 **Ford Reengineered the Process—Now It's Fast and Efficient**

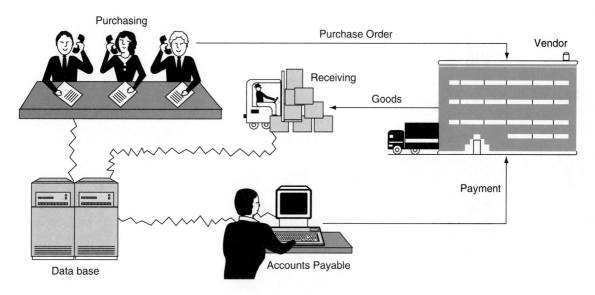

The new process cuts head count in accounts payable by 75%,
eliminates invoices, and improves accuracy. Matching is computerized.

achieve, Ford reduced their head count by 75 percent rather than the 20
percent reduction they had initially hoped to achieve. The old and new
business processes for the accounts payable function at Ford are illustrated
in Figures 2–7 and 2–8.

Interorganizational Systems and Process Integration

An additional degree of business process integration is possible when two
separate firms realize that their respective outbound and inbound logistics
cycles have more in common than either do with their own firm's operations
cycle. For example, Procter & Gamble and Wal-Mart have an agreement
about labeling, shipping, billing, and paying for Pampers wherein Wal-Mart
sends cash register tapes to Procter & Gamble. Procter & Gamble then automatically replenishes Wal-Mart's store inventories, based on sales, with
boxes of Pampers already labeled with each store's specific selling price.

This type of system, called an interorganizational system (IOS) goes considerably beyond conventional electronic data interchange (EDI) systems, which tend to reinforce the idea of batch transmission and traditional break points in the process. The trend towards open systems architectures, as discussed in Chapter 6, should reduce some of the technical hurdles in the adoption and use of IOS. IOS will become more widespread as a result.

THE NATURE OF CHANGE

People are generally reluctant to leave the comfort of the status quo for the unknowns associated with a new way of doing things. This resistance to change, while quite normal, must be managed in the interest of permitting the organization to transform itself by instituting business process change. To know how to manage change, an IS professional must understand the nature of the change process itself.

The most widely accepted model of social change is that of Kurt Lewin, who postulated a model with three stages: unfreezing, moving, and refreezing, as illustrated in Figure 2–9.[3] Groups of people (for example, members of a department in a business organization) are accustomed to performing their daily assignments in a certain way. They have been trained to do so and have become comfortable with their abilities to carry out their assigned duties. To introduce a new way of carrying out their tasks, it is first necessary to prepare them to accept a change. This is the "unfreezing" step. Attempting to impose a change on people unprepared for the change is almost always a mistake. Once the group members have been prepared, the change can be introduced, but it should be followed by a "refreezing" step in which their understanding of the new methods is solidified.

RESISTANCE TO CHANGE

IS professionals must understand that they serve as catalysts for change, or change agents, and that a key requirement to be effective in this role is gaining the acceptance and trust of the users. IS professionals should understand the nature of change and should expect a natural resistance to change on the parts of affected individuals and groups. This resistance does not mean that users are ignorant, uncooperative, obstructionist, or even wrong. Resistance comes from human beings who have honest disagreements or concerns that must be diagnosed and dealt with. The biggest mistake an IS professional can make is to try to brush disagreements under the rug. They do not disappear. They remain and grow, eventually emerging as much larger problems, possibly impinging on the IS professional's own career.

Figure 2–9 **Lewin's Three Stages of Organizational Change**

Stage	Description
Unfreezing	Increasing the receptivity of the organization to a possible change
Moving	Choosing a course of action and following it
Refreezing	Reinforcing the "equilibrium" of the organization at a new level after the change has occurred

Source: G. Davis and M. Olson. *Management Information Systems*. New York: McGraw-Hill, 1985.

Diagnosing and Dealing with Resistance to Change

The first step in overcoming resistance to change is to understand the reasons for it. Peter G. W. Keen identified four specific reasons in an article in *Computerworld*:

- Resistance to computer personnel.

- A feeling that the project is not good, that the cost/benefit assumptions are invalid.

- A lack of felt need: things are satisfactory as they are and this innovation simply disturbs the situation.

- A fear of social uncertainty, which is sometimes mistaken for a fear of computers.[4]

We will add a fifth reason, not so apparent at the time Keen wrote his article, but which is now significant:

- An unwillingness to bend to the requirements of poorly designed systems.

Depending on the situation, some or all of these reasons for resistance to change may apply, and the reason for resistance usually affects the choice of remedy to deal with it.

Resistance to computer personnel can be diagnosed by observing the interactions between users and IS personnel. A good working relationship between the two groups is characterized by feelings of mutual trust and understanding. A poor working relationship is often marked by recriminations for past failures and statements implying that one side does not understand the other's problems. The following techniques have proven useful in overcoming resistance to computer personnel:

- A good working relationship between the higher levels of management to whom the IS department and the affected user department report. Higher levels of management can be role models for cooperative action among subordinates.

- Joint project teams of information systems and user personnel to undertake systems projects. As will be discussed, bringing users and information systems professionals together to work towards a common goal can be very helpful in overcoming gaps in understanding.

- Support and understanding of the user's perspective by IS personnel. It is the IS professional's responsibility to adopt the user's viewpoint, not vice versa.

- Training for the users in computer concepts and the role that information technology can play in modern organizations. This training removes much of the mystique of the technology and helps close the gap between user and technician. Often, hands-on experience can also convert a user from skepticism to acceptance.

Users often resist a systems proposal because they **feel that the project is not good** or that the cost/benefit analysis is inaccurate. In such cases, they have usually been insufficiently involved in determining the feasibility, the scope, or the requirements of the system. Users must be significantly involved in developing the systems proposal as a part of a project team, and they must accept the assumptions and the conclusions of the cost/benefit analysis. As we will discuss in Chapter 19, one of the steps in the systems development process is to put together a project proposal for management approval before proceeding with a project. A cost/benefit analysis is usually a part of the proposal. It is much more convincing to have a representative of the user department describe the system concept and the benefits to be derived from its installation. This technique lets management know that the users understand what the system will do for them and will attest to a set of expected benefits offsetting the cost of installing the system.

We often hear the phrase "If it ain't broke, don't fix it." This is essentially what users are saying when they resist a proposed change because of the **lack of a felt need**. They see no reason to change because they are comfortable with the status quo. Viewing a situation this way has been called the "problem of no problem." Rather than saying "if it ain't broke, don't fix it," users should be saying "fix it before it breaks." This insight is particularly important in today's environment when organizations can expect their competition to be constantly seeking to improve current ways of doing things. In addition to using the techniques mentioned in the previous paragraph, we can best deal with resistance due to lack of a felt need by demonstrating that a proposed systems change will aid the users in meeting goals and objectives in accordance with the organization's strategic plan.

Resistance to change often arises because users **fear social uncertainty** about how the change will affect existing relationships between members of a given department, the roles assigned to members of the affected department, and the power and influence they currently possess. For example, Peter F. Drucker says that a company's organization structure is affected when it begins to concentrate its information technology resources on producing information rather than merely crunching numbers:

> Almost immediately, it becomes clear that both the number of management levels and the number of managers can be sharply cut. The reason is straightforward: it turns out that whole layers of management neither make decisions nor lead. Instead, their main, if not their only, function is to serve as "relays"—human boosters for the faint, unfocused signals that pass for communication in the traditional pre-information organization.[5]

Middle managers are all too conscious of the corporate penchant for becoming "lean and mean" by eliminating white-collar workers. A week rarely goes by without at least one story of a large corporation streamlining operations out of competitive necessity by eliminating staff positions. User resistance is understandable in this type of environment.

It is critical to address this problem because changes can scarcely be implemented without the support of middle management, even if the changes do not affect them directly.

When a user is unsure of the way a proposed change will affect him or her personally, the change is often resisted. However, the concern may be expressed as a fear of computers rather than as the underlying, more personal, concern. The systems professional acting as the change agent must be able to listen to objections and isolate the real reasons for resistance.

Finally, another reason for resistance to change is that users have seen too many **systems with poor human factors**. Before the so-called microcomputer revolution, systems were generally designed to optimize use of technology rather than human resources. Job descriptions and clerical procedures were designed to fit the system requirements rather than the system being designed to fit the human requirements. With the advent of reasonably priced personal computers and widely available, well-designed software, users have come to expect more. The nature of the applications themselves have changed, partly because of the availability of workstation technology and partly because of competitive pressures. Computer-based applications are now much more integrated into the operation of the business, rather than being simple back-office transaction recording systems.

In summary, IS professionals can expect to encounter resistance to change. They can overcome the resistance only by understanding its nature and developing a plan for dealing with it.

IMPLEMENTING THE ORGANIZATIONAL CHANGE

IS professionals can easily underestimate the human component of a new information system. System failures have often been the result when IS professionals did not devote enough resources to preparing employees for changes

Figure 2–10 **Phases of Organizational Change**

brought about by a new information system and training them in its use. In a recent interview published in *CIO Magazine*, Professor Rosabeth Moss Kanter, author of the influential book *The Changemasters*, commented on the importance of companies investing in change: "Everybody underestimates the cost of change and the time change takes, so they underinvest. That's the biggest mistake companies make." Kanter went on to say that the one point she wishes she had given more emphasis to in her earlier writings was "the staying power of the bureaucracy and the inertia of the big corporation. Implementation, acting on new ideas is a longer, harder process than I [originally thought it was]."[6] The process can be better managed if information systems professionals take the time to develop a thoughtful, four-phase program for organizational change, as illustrated in Figure 2–10 and discussed below.

Diagnostic Assessment. First, a diagnostic assessment is performed to determine the organization's readiness to absorb the changes necessitated by a new information system. This is the time to clarify the imperatives to change as well as to uncover any resistance that might be present. IS professionals performing this review will usually assess the change climate by interviewing affected members of the organization or by using survey or other data-gathering and analysis techniques. Different parts of the organization may exhibit different degrees of receptivity to a proposed change, so all significant levels should be assessed. For example, top management is generally much more supportive of a proposed business process change than the layers of middle management more directly affected.

After completing the diagnosis, a description of the changed organization, or *vision*, is developed. Next, a communication strategy is created that will help everyone in the organization to articulate the vision. The current organization is compared to the vision to identify changes that will be required if the organization is to attain it.

Organization Redesign. Once changes have been identified, a strategy for introducing them is developed. Significant business process changes may well require changing the existing organization structure. If so, such changes are identified and designed.

A decision whether or not to start with a pilot program should be made early in this phase. While often desirable, it is not always necessary to begin with a pilot program Such factors as the size, scope, and nature of the change will have a bearing on the decision.

Next, the leadership skills required to manage in the new environment are determined. If they are to be significantly different in the future, the means of obtaining them will need to be identified. A similar effort must be undertaken in determining the skills required of the work force and developing a means of achieving them, such as a training program. The end result of this phase is a formal, management-approved change strategy, including a high-level design of the new organization structure.

Organization Transformation.   The implementation phase of the change project is next. Critical jobs, business processes, organization structure, and the target culture are implemented. New leadership, if required, is selected and installed. Training programs for the work force are conducted.

Coincident with the implementation, a system of tracking and measuring performance of the new system should be installed. This will permit reporting to management on the effectiveness of the change in comparison to the baseline performance of the old system.

Continuous Improvement.   One thing we have learned from the way Japanese firms employ quality control techniques is the importance of instituting a program of continuous process improvement. Continuous improvement ensures that changes made are sustained over time. It also enhances the organization's ability to adapt its business processes to future changes in the business environment.

A well-designed continuous improvement process consists of an infrastructure for evaluating and maintaining changed business processes as well as the basis for identifying new areas of change.

Summary

Most business systems are composed of people and machines that work together toward a common business objective. In the past, humans had to adapt their behavior to what was best for the computer because of the high cost of the computer relative to labor costs. Advances in technology have reversed this relationship. Today, we are now less concerned about the consumption of computing resources and more concerned about making the systems easier to use.

When information systems change, people must change as well. The challenge for top managers is to be sure that the combination of people and machines in their organization performs better than the people and machines of the competition.

Influenced by the work of Frederick Taylor, managers have organized clerical tasks on a fragmented basis since the early 1900s. Organization charts reflect the same philosophy, with their hierarchies and specialized departments. Early information systems tended to follow the organization and resulted in the installation of systems that were narrow and inflexible. In response to competitive pressures, organizations are reengineering their business processes, utilizing information technology to obtain major improvements in their operations.

In addition to searching for radical change, business process reengineering often empowers the knowledge worker by making it possible for one person, supported by information technology, to perform all or most of a business process.

Davenport and Short identified five steps in business process reengineering: Develop a business vision and process objectives; identify the business processes to be redesigned; understand and measure the existing processes; identify the information technology levers that can be used in redesigning the process (nine examples of levers were discussed); and design and build a prototype of the process. Design techniques can include designing for simplicity, eliminating buffers or intermediaries, and entering information only once.

Setting ambitious goals for a reengineering project makes it more likely that dramatic results will be achieved. Much of the benefit of business process reengineering occurs because the reengineered process cuts across the organization and integrates work tasks that were previously fragmented. An additional degree of integration can occur between organizations when business processes of two organizations,—customer and supplier, for example—are integrated.

A new information system will not be successful unless it is accepted by the people for whom it is designed. Human beings have a natural resistance to change, which has been well studied in its organizational setting. Resistance to change must be diagnosed and overcome if the introduction of new technology is to work. For these reasons, information systems professionals must understand the nature of the change process and ways to overcome resistance.

Lewin's three-stage model of change illustrates the need to prepare the organization and to solidify changes once they are made. A plan for overcoming resistance should be developed once the nature of resistance has been diagnosed. Peter Keen cited four reasons for resistance to computer-based innovations. This analysis is a useful framework for diagnosing reasons for resistance to change.

A careful plan for implementing change should be developed containing four phases: diagnostic assessment, organization redesign, organization transformation, and continuous improvement. All too many organizations fail to adequately plan for organizational change; spending time in this area will increase the likelihood of success.

Selected Readings

Davenport, Thomas H., and Short, James E. "The New Industrial Engineering: Information Technology and Business Process Redesign." *Sloan Management Review* (Summer 1990).

This article discusses the natural partnership between information technology and industrial engineering, which, to this point, has been largely unexploited. The authors give a step-by-step approach to business process reengineering and cite examples of companies that have successfully used information technology to redesign boundary-crossing, customer-driven business processes.

Gildersleeve, Thomas R. *Successful Data Processing System Analysis*, 2d ed. Englewood Cliffs, New Jersey: Prentice-Hall, Inc., 1985.
Gildersleeve is the proponent of "fix it before it breaks."

Hammer, Michael. "Reengineering Work: Don't Automate, Obliterate." *Harvard Business Review* (July-August 1990): 104–112.
A persuasive treatise on the benefits of employing information technology in reengineering business processes, including examples.

Kanter, Rosabeth Moss. *The Changemasters: Innovation and Entrepreneurship in the American Corporation.* New York: Simon & Schuster, 1983.

Konsynski, Benn R., and McFarlan, F. Warren. "Information Partnerships—Shared Data, Shared Scale." *Harvard Business Review* (September-October 1990): 114–120.
This article describes how IOSs have enabled companies to gain the benefits of business combinations without the disadvantages of formal associations. Several examples of successful IOS are described.

Mumford, Enid, and Weir, Mary. *Computer Systems in Work Design: The ETHICS Method.* New York: Halsted, 1979.
This work describes the socio-technical approach to systems development and the implementation of change. This method is particularly appropriate in environments where change will affect multiple categories of users (for instance, sales personnel, accounting clerks, and data entry operators) or where substantial changes are anticipated (goals and objectives as well as environment and procedures).

Review Questions

1. What is the role of information technology in the ever-increasing pace of change in the business environment?

2. What are some of the reasons IS professionals have tended to concentrate their efforts on the technological component of information systems?

3. What are the two characteristics of a business process?

4. Describe the concept of "knowledge worker empowerment."

5. Define "business process reengineering." How does it differ from approaches that have been used in the past?

6. What are the five steps in a business process reengineering effort?

7. List four top management visions for the organization that could serve as goals of business processing reengineering.

8. List nine "information technology levers" that could be used in redesigning a business process.

9. Why is it important to set ambitious goals for a business process reengineering project?

10. Give an example of process integration in an IOS environment other than the one referred to in the chapter.

11. What are five specific reasons for human resistance to computer-based innovations? If these reasons apply to a given situation, there are often clues to determine if people feel resistant as well as countermeasures available to information systems personnel. What are the clues and countermeasures for each reason cited above?

12. What are the four phases to be included in a plan for organizational change?

Discussion Questions

1. Innovations made by airline companies for competitive advantage (or for survival) were discussed in this chapter. Expand the discussion by describing innovations made in other industries.

2. Why does the success of organizational change pivot on human acceptance of the change?

3. Business process reengineering has as one of its goals the introduction of "radical change." What is meant by radical change, and how does business process reengineering go about achieving radical change?

4. What are some of the difficulties IS professionals might encounter when they attempt to reengineer a business process that crosses several internal departments? What are some of the techniques that can be employed to overcome these difficulties?

5. What techniques might information systems personnel employ to overcome resistance to change in a situation where users express discontent with past projects and an unwillingness to work with project team personnel?

6. IS personnel have educational backgrounds and experience that are primarily technical. Explain how this background might hinder them in dealing with user resistance to change.

Mini-Cases

Avion Corporation. Avion, a major credit corporation in the southwestern United States, recently automated its customer service and credit authorization procedures. Benefits included reduced clerical costs and more effective use of management time. Clerks, aided by computer terminals, are now able to handle considerably more customer inquiries and credit authorizations without management assistance than they could with the previous system.

One expensive technological innovation at Avion, however, did not fare as well. The innovation, voice mail, was implemented by information systems professionals at the same time as the customer service and credit authorization system. It seems that whenever anyone telephoned an Avion employee directly and had to leave a message because the employee was unavailable, the caller was forced to leave a voice message. Complaints soared as callers claimed they were never able to speak to a human being. There were other technical problems, and the system was eventually scrapped.

Questions for Discussion

1. What was the probable rationale for the voice mail system?

2. Recall the suggested roles of management, users, and information systems professionals in preparing the organization for change discussed in the chapter. What are some possible reasons the customer service and credit authorization system was successful but the voice mail was not?

Mining Industry Research Council. The Mining Industry Research Council (MIRC) is an agency established by contributions from mining industry companies. Its purpose is to serve as a granting agency and project manager for research carried out by independent investigators on topics of interest to the mining industry. Research funds are received from sponsoring companies and the U.S. federal government. Proposals for projects are submitted to a peer review, and awarded annually. Research progress reports are submitted to MIRC each quarter. Financial progress reports and purchase commitments are submitted monthly.

MIRC is currently managing 250 active projects and 800 individual grants. The process is complicated because an individual research project may have several researchers working on it, or just one. Some projects are inactive at any point in time. MIRC has 14 project managers who are responsible for monitoring the progress of projects and grants. One year ago, an on-line data base system was installed to assist the project managers in monitoring project milestones, coordinating individual contracts, and forward planning. The system is built around a state-of-the-art relational DBMS and took two years to develop.

Tom Hutton, the executive director of MIRC has called you and asked for your help in resolving a problem with the new system.

> The problem is that I think the new system is great, my MIS people think it's great, the manager of the Project Administration Department (Bob Scudder) thinks it's great, three of the project managers think it's great, but the rest of the project managers think it's worthless. Despite all of our efforts in training them, and despite the fact that they've been ordered to use the system, the majority of the project managers prefer to do their jobs the old way. Bob's getting ready to fire a few people, but before we disrupt the organization with an action as drastic as that, I thought I'd see if you had any bright ideas we could use. These folks are highly skilled, and if we fired them it would take months to bring new people up to speed.

Questions for Discussion

1. How can you help Tom develop a plan to deal with his problem?

2. How might the problem have been avoided in the first place?

Notes

1. Davenport, T., and Short, J. "The New Industrial Engineering: Information Technology and Business Process Redesign." *Sloan Management Review* (Summer 1990): 11–27.

2. Hammer, Michael. "Reengineering Work: Don't Automate, Obliterate." *Harvard Business Review* (July–August 1990): 104–112.

3. Lewin, Kurt. "The Coming of the New Organization." *Human Frontiers* 1 (1947).

4. Keen, Peter G. W. "Introducing Change." *Computerworld* (September 29, 1982): 10.

5. Drucker, Peter F. "The Coming of the New Organization." *Harvard Business Review* (January–February 1988): 45–53.

6. Alter, Allan E. "Putting Genius to Work." *CIO Magazine* 3, 1 (August 1990): 34.

3

Systems Projects and the Systems Life Cycle

The charge of the information systems department is to design, install, operate, and maintain information systems that truly meet the needs of users. This chapter covers the principal organizational factors that determine how effectively an IS department discharges its responsibilities.

- The placement of the IS department in an organization's hierarchy.
- The internal organization of the IS department.
- The relationship between project management and the systems development life cycle.
- The relationship between the design process and the systems development life cycle.

Learning Objectives

- Understand the traditional placement of information systems (IS) department in organizations and the trends promoting a change in placement.
- Realize the impact on IS of the merging islands of technology—data processing, telecommunications, and office automation.
- Describe three forms of IS department organization—functional, product line, and matrix.
- Recognize issues affecting the degree of centralization or decentralization of an organization's IS resources (hardware, data, and personnel).
- Describe the principal activities of project management—project organization, planning, execution, and control.
- Understand the metaphors for systems design: problem solving, modeling, and transformation.
- Relate the systems development life cycles described in the section introduction to project management and the system design process.

THE PLACE OF THE IS DEPARTMENT IN THE ORGANIZATION

This chapter explains how to set up and manage projects involving the design and installation of new systems. First, however, two broader topics will be discussed: where the IS department fits in the overall organization and how an IS department is organized internally.

An IS department can have the following responsibilities:

- Designing, installing, operating, and maintaining infrastructure applications (i.e., those that provide data and services to the entire organization).

- In most cases, providing resources and support to end users, functional departments, and other organizational units, so that the information technology needs of smaller groups can be satisfied.

- Increasingly, managing other information technology areas such as telecommunications and office automation.

Which of these responsibilities are actually in the province of the IS department depends on the degree of evolution reached by the organization. In turn, the function to which the IS department reports most often depends on the extent of its responsibilities.

Since the first business-oriented computer was installed at General Electric in 1954, there has been a continuous evolution in the perception of information technology and of its proper place within an organization. As previously mentioned, businesses initially used computers for accounting and related applications, thus reducing costs by substituting computers for clerks. Examples of early computer applications are customer billing, demand deposit accounting, policyholder accounting, payroll, and general accounting. Organizations typically delegated the responsibility for these applications to the chief accounting officer (i.e., the controller or financial vice-president). In many organizations, the responsibility remains there today. A high-level organization chart of such a company is pictured in Figure 3–1.

Two recent trends are changing the way top managers view information technology and where they place the IS function for maximum effectiveness:

- The IS department increasingly encompasses not only data processing but also all information technology functions, including office automation and telecommunications.

- The IS department has the potential to support many parts of the organization at all levels of its hierarchy.

Merging the Islands of Technology

In 1982, James McKenney and F. Warren McFarlan proposed that the three separate "islands of technology" (data processing, telecommunications, and office automation) be placed under integrated control because they were

Figure 3–1 **Organization Chart Showing Traditional Placement of Data Processing**

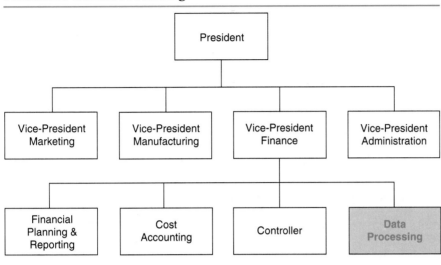

likely to converge in advanced information systems.[1] Under integrated control, the three technologies would be more likely to be managed in a coordinated fashion to the benefit of the organization. For example, a computerized payroll system in the 1960s most probably operated as illustrated in Figure 3–2. Payroll time cards and other transactions needed to produce a paycheck were collected from user areas and sent to the corporate data center. The transactions were converted from paper forms into media readable by the computers of that time, most probably punched cards. These transactions on punched cards were then read by the computer. Through a series of related programs, employees' pay was calculated, employee computer records were updated, and checks were printed along with reports such as the payroll register.

If that same payroll system were to be installed using today's technology, it might appear as in Figure 3–3. Payroll transactions would be entered through computer terminals located in user departments and sent over communications lines directly to the computer in the corporate data center. The payroll transactions would be processed, pay would be calculated, and the employees' records would be updated. Checks would be prepared along with the payroll register and other reports. In this system, employees could request that their checks be deposited directly into their checking accounts. For these employees, deposit data would be sent to their bank over telecommunications lines. Various departments needing access to payroll information could inquire against the computer records. Extracts from the payroll data base could be transmitted to departmental microcomputers where analysis could

Figure 3–2 **Payroll System (ca. 1960)**

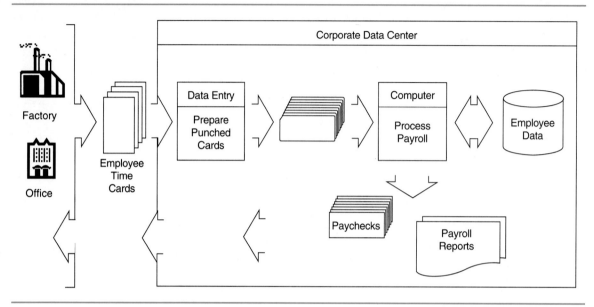

be performed using spreadsheet software. Exhibits such as tables and graphs thus created could be incorporated into reports prepared with office automation software such as a word processor or in-house publishing software.

At the time of payroll systems such as the one in Figure 3–2, there were corporate functions labeled data processing, telecommunications, and office automation. However, these functions were not interconnected as they are in the second example. Data processing took place exclusively at the corporate data center; telecommunications consisted of the public telephone service, internal telephones, and perhaps a telex machine; and office automation consisted of electric typewriters and photocopiers.

In the second example, the design of the payroll system uses today's technology to improve service to the users. Personal computers in user departments perform many office functions such as word processing and spreadsheet applications. Some of these computers are also connected over telecommunications networks to a large computer in the corporate data center. Systems taking advantage of office automation, telecommunications technology, and data processing technology are becoming the norm rather than the exception. Accordingly, in many organizations the responsibility for managing the three areas is given to the IS department.

Systems integration is the name given to a strategy that formally recognizes the convergence of data processing, telecommunications, office automation, and where applicable, process control. The objective is organi-

Figure 3–3 **Payroll System (ca. 1990)**

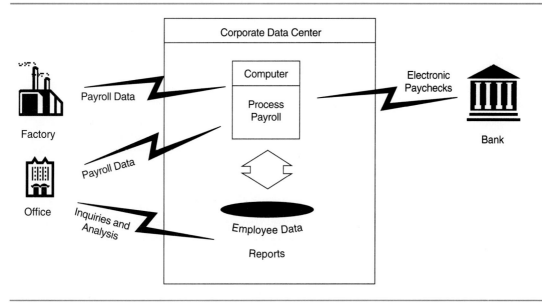

zation-wide integration of systems. Because an organization's many systems were typically installed over a period of years, they use different vendors and serve different users. However, many users need the same information. To satisfy them, information is frequently moved manually from one system to another. Unfortunately, manual interfaces are inefficient and error-prone. As a result, secondary users of the information (in many cases management personnel) receive outdated or inaccurate data. To overcome this problem, organizations are recognizing the convergence of these branches of information systems and beginning to integrate them. A successful integration strategy requires the development of organization-wide standards for information resource management and communications. The strategy also requires IS personnel to recognize that formerly disparate systems must fit together if the organization is to be well served.

The Supportive Role of the IS Department

Information technology applications have expanded to include all functional areas of an organization. A new information system being installed today could be one that improves operations on the factory floor, permitting better utilization of raw materials and factory resources through better production scheduling and control. It could be a marketing information system that permits precise identification of sales prospects. Or it could be a system tailored to meet the specific information requirements of a top executive.

Figure 3–4 **How IS Departments Report**

Level of Reporting of Information Systems

		Low	High
Strategic Impact of Existing Systems	**High**	Under Chief Operating Officer	Chief Information Officer
	Low	Indifferent	Chief Information Officer or Own Vice-President

Strategic Impact of Applications Development Portfolio

The specific location of IS in the organization and the level at which it reports varies from company to company. In some, it reports to the chief financial officer, in keeping with tradition. In others, it reports directly to the chief executive officer (CEO) or to an administrative vice-president.

In searching for guidelines for positioning the IS department, the CEO must recognize the supportive role of IS within the organization: it renders service to other functional areas of the organization. The IS department should be placed so that it can provide its services according to organizational priorities rather than the priorities of the vice-president to whom it happens to report. Thus, in many cases the IS executive should be part of the management team.

In practice, however, many IS directors have risen through the technical ranks and lack the interpersonal and managerial skills expected from a high-level executive. Effective communication and good personal relationships between IS personnel and their counterparts in user departments are as important to the effective delivery of information technology services as more concrete measures of performance. Management should consider this fact when deciding where to place the IS department. Often, the IS director reports to someone who can serve as an ambassador to improve relations with the rest of the organization. This ambassador is often a vice-president with other operational or functional responsibilities and a good working relationship with contemporaries throughout the organization.

Increasingly, organizations are establishing a new executive position called the *chief information officer* (CIO). We referred briefly to this trend in Chapter 1. The CIO is most likely to be found in organizations that recognize the strategic value of information and manage it accordingly. The CIO is most often positioned at the vice-presidential level, on a par with executive

Figure 3–5 **IS Department Organized along Functional Lines**

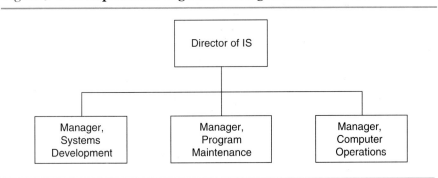

managers of other key functional areas. The charge of the CIO is to see that the available information resources are managed in a manner consistent with their importance to the organization. Usually, the CIO is not a technician, although he or she should understand the technology well enough to manage the IS professionals. In addition, the CIO should possess broad management skills and an understanding of the business so that information technology is appropriately used throughout the organization. The CIO should also have the political and interpersonal skills to serve as the liaison for the IS technicians as previously discussed.

The strategic grid discussed in Chapter 1 provides additional guidelines for determining the level to which the IS department should report. The more important information technology is to an organization, the more attention it should receive from top management and the higher up it should report. Therefore, if an organization places itself in the strategic or turnaround quadrants, the IS department would report to an executive such as a CIO. If an organization is in the factory quadrant, IS would report to an executive who can ensure delivery of high-quality, uninterrupted service. If an organization is in the support quadrant, IS can safely report to a lower level of the organization, since other matters will be of a higher priority to top management (see Figure 3–4).

ORGANIZATION OF THE IS DEPARTMENT

Form of Organization

As pointed out by Davis and Olson, the three major variations in the organization of IS departments are by function, by product line, or as a matrix.

Functional Organization. The IS department is usually organized along functional lines, as illustrated in Figure 3–5. The three primary tasks of the IS department are development of new applications, maintenance and

Figure 3–6 **IS Department Organized along Product Lines**

enhancement of existing applications, and computer operations. In the functional organization, these functions are typically headed by managers who report to the director of information systems. Applications development is responsible for performing the tasks necessary to design and install a new computer system from the project approval through its subsequent conversion and acceptance by the users. At that time, computer operations assumes responsibility for the operation of the system. The program maintenance group performs subsequent changes or enhancements.

New applications are typically developed by project teams composed of users and IS personnel formed specifically to design and install an application. The formation and management of project teams are discussed in a later section of this chapter.

Product Line Organization. An IS department organized along product lines commonly has groups of IS personnel devoted to particular user departments or to types of IS products. For example, Figure 3–6 shows an IS department with groups of personnel dedicated to financial systems, manufacturing systems, and marketing systems. One portion of the personnel in each product group is devoted to building new applications and another portion to maintaining existing systems. Frequently this division can prevent politically difficult resource allocation problems with the user departments. A specific level of IS personnel is dedicated to each product line, and user personnel are deeply involved in deciding which new applications and which existing applications should be worked on. This arrangement is often used by decentralized

Figure 3–7 **Matrix Organization of IS**

organizations. It dedicates resources to functional areas or operating groups which are themselves decentralized. (The next section of this chapter contains a more complete discussion of considerations regarding the centralization and decentralizat'on of IS resources.) The product line approach to organizing IS departments illustrated in Figure 3–6 shows that a single computer center operates existing systems for all product groups, although as an alternative, each product group can have its own computer center as well.

Matrix Organization. In a matrix organization, IS resources are dispersed to various organizational units on a product group basis, a geographical basis, or some other basis. The dispersed IS groups report hierarchically to the operational head of the unit to which they are attached and functionally to an IS director, who is responsible for maintaining technical competence, tools, and infrastructure. An example of an IS function organized on a matrix basis is shown in Figure 3–7. In a manner similar to the product group form of organization, the purpose of the matrix approach is to give users more control over information systems resources. Again, there are many options regarding which functions are retained by the IS director. In the example shown in Figure 3–7, all major functions are dispersed. The IS director retains responsibility for overall coordination and such corporate-level functions as standards setting, long-range systems planning, and IS research and development.

Figure 3–8 **Three Patterns of Overall Technical Architecture**

Centralization versus Decentralization

The Chinese saying "It doesn't matter if a cat is black or white as long as it catches mice" can be applied to issues of centralization versus decentralization of IS resources. It does not matter whether resources are highly centralized or highly decentralized as long as the choice permits the IS resource to serve the entire organization as effectively as possible. In other words, the IS department should fit the company that it serves—its organization, management style, geographical distribution, channels of communications, and culture.

When organizations review their options in deciding the degree of centralization or decentralization of IS resources, they normally take three resources into consideration: hardware, data, and systems development personnel.

Hardware and Data Considerations. Initially, organizations using computers tended towards a centralized approach for computer operations, largely because a central site permitted them to realize economies of scale. (The cost per unit of processing power tended to decrease as the size of the processor increased.) A centralized approach also permitted experts in computer operations, telecommunications, and systems software to be concentrated at a single site. In recent years, advances in technology have permitted organizations more options in the way they distribute their computer processing resources. The economies of scale once so generally accepted no longer apply to computer hardware, and the range of options with telecommunications is increasing. For example, many large organizations have created private telecommunications networks for their own use at significant cost savings. Such trends in technology have allowed organizations considerably more flexibility in placing hardware and data for a given cost.

The development of minicomputers and microcomputers has permitted the placement of powerful computers close to the users. In raw computing power, the personal computers of today rival the mainframes of ten years ago. Telecommunications capabilities and networking techniques permit computers to be tied together in local, regional, or international networks, public and private, enabling users to access and use data stored in computer files thousands of miles away.

Three common patterns of technical architecture are illustrated in Figure 3–8. Company A has chosen a centralized approach built around a large mainframe computer. All applications for the organization are run on this mainframe. Company B has chosen to establish several data centers located near key user concentrations. Each data center serves a specified community of users. Company C has chosen to combine a large mainframe computer with departmental minicomputers located in certain departments. In each case, terminals and desktop personal computers are in place throughout the organization. In most cases, the specific resource configuration derives from the organization's application requirements and the users' requirements for data access. Once these requirements are known, the cost and performance of alternative patterns of hardware and data distribution are analyzed, and a specific alternative is selected. Backup, security, and personnel issues are additional factors to be taken into consideration. Additional information on this subject can be found in the selected readings listed at the end of this chapter.

Systems Development Personnel Considerations. As with hardware and data, most companies initially had a single systems development group, centrally located to serve the needs of the entire organization. Later, some organizations decentralized the group along divisional or geographic lines. Usually, the purpose of decentralization was to place systems development resources more closely under user control or to make them more responsive to user demands for service. Also, when the organization itself operates on a highly decentralized basis, a decentralized IS development function is more consistent with the prevailing corporate culture. Here, too, an organization may choose from a wide spectrum of solutions, ranging from complete centralization to complete decentralization (see Figure 3–9).

Summary of Centralization/Decentralization Issues. Alternative ways of organizing resources range from highly centralized to highly decentralized. All can work well if the alternative chosen is right for a specific organization. Even if an organization chooses a decentralized model, some tasks could be

Figure 3–9 **Three Patterns of Organizing Systems Development Personnel**

handled either by a small central staff or by a coordinating body representing each of the decentralized locations. These tasks include recommending standards for hardware, software, and documentation; recommending systems development methodologies; planning cooperative development projects; overseeing information technology research and development; and coordinating personnel policies and training programs. The final task relates to controlling the corporate data resource. Regardless of the degree of decentralization, procedures should be in place to ensure the integrity of corporate data no matter who is responsible for updating or changing records on computer files. Cash, McFarlan, and McKenney refer to this fundamental responsibility as long-term data hygiene.

More Recent Trends

When computers were first used, one person could often perform all of the functions necessary to bring an application to operating status and then operate the computer as well. In other words, a single individual could (and often did) perform the tasks of systems analysis and design, programming, testing, conversion, and maintenance. Today, with the introduction of more complex computers and operating systems, one person is rarely capable of performing all such tasks in a mainframe computer environment. The tasks of the IS department have continually subdivided into specialized areas. This trend continues. The 1980s saw the emergence of end-user computing specialists; the 1990s are predicted to see the creation of infrastructure specialists and systems architects.

End-User Computing Specialists. The rise in end-user computing has profoundly affected computing within most organizations. End-user computing in business started in the mid-1970s with IBM Canada's creation of the Information Center concept and gathered momentum in 1981 with the introduction of the personal computer and business-oriented software packages such as spreadsheets, word processors, and data base management systems.

In the early days, end-user computing took place on mainframes separated from the transaction processing applications run by the IS department. In general, the IS department procured hardware and software for the Information Center (or Infocenter, for short). The IS department also supplied specialists to help novice users with product and methodology training and troubleshooting. But high costs and a hostile environment prevented the Infocenter from catching on in most environments.

The availability of personal computers and associated friendly, easy-to-learn, easy-to-use software provided the real impetus to end-user computing. At first, the trend had a mixed reception by the IS community. Later, most IS departments came to believe that properly supported end-user computing benefits them and the organization. It benefits IS departments because they need not devote limited resources to smaller systems, when there is typically a multiyear backlog of large project requests that only the IS department can handle.

End-user computing benefits users because they need not go through the centralized IS department priority-setting process and wait in line to get a small project approved; instead, they can build it themselves. On the other hand, users often lack expertise in development and operations. Systems developed by end users often lack adequate documentation, have poor controls, and run on a variety of hardware and software platforms, thus proving hard to integrate.

Many IS departments have now adopted the Information Center approach to supply some professional guidance to end-user computing. For example, some IS departments are providing users with a way to manage the variety of hardware and software products. Others provide users with a quality control function that can help evaluate whether an end-user application is likely to cause data integrity or maintenance problems in the future.

Infrastructure Specialists. In recent years, the number of tools to streamline systems analysis, design, and programming tasks has greatly increased. Prototyping, application generators, and computer-aided software engineering (CASE) tools are the most important of these. Many applications developed with such tools will share common, cross-application functions developed by the IS department in addition to the vendor-provided systems software. In combination with modern development methods, these tools enable IS departments to build systems that are more complex and highly integrated and that are used by more people than before. Just as a manufacturing firm needs tool and die makers, so does a well-equipped IS department require infrastructure specialists.

Systems Architects. Systems that are developed one by one with small teams can be designed collectively; each team member understands the design fully and participates permanently in its evolution. With larger teams, one individual usually emerges as being the leader of the design effort, the one who can answer questions about the latest design modifications or the probable impact of a contemplated change. With very large teams (typically over 25 persons), this role must be formalized. The systems architect's role is to maintain conceptual integrity of the design throughout the development effort.

PROJECT MANAGEMENT AND THE SYSTEMS DEVELOPMENT LIFE CYCLE

In the section introduction, we saw that the systems development life cycle is influenced by two imperatives: project management and the nature of the design process.

Viewed from the project management perspective, the systems development life cycle is divided into phases the structure of which is similar from one phase to another. This similarity can be seen in Barry Boehm's spiral: each turn of the spiral has a set of project management-related activities that repeat at each turn (see Figure I–6). A more traditional view is the management cycle depicted in Figure 3–10: plan, execute, and control. Before the cycle can start, however, the project needs to be organized.

Project Organization

The standard form of organization for systems development today is the project team under a full-time project manager. The project manager reports to a management body that has authority over the project: either a single executive or, more frequently, a steering committee made up of the main stakeholders interested in the project.

Project Team Members. Project team members are selected according to the skill requirements for the particular phase being undertaken. During analysis and user interface design, for instance, IS analysts and users make up the bulk of the team. During the design and the programming phases, technical analysts, programmers, and infrastructure specialists are likely to dominate.

How many roles are identified and how specific they are depends mostly on the size and the complexity of the project. Small projects are informally organized, with each team member potentially capable of playing any of the roles.

Figure 3–10 **The Traditional Management Cycle**

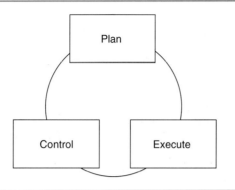

Medium-sized teams have a more rigorous specialization. This special-ization may be along functional or technical lines. For instance, a functional subdivision of a project team might identify some people responsible for the order entry portion of the applications and others for the accounts receivable and general ledger interfaces. A technical subdivision (perhaps later in the same project) might be into on-line, batch, and infrastructure.

Large projects need both functional and technical subdivisions at the same time. In addition, project management is usually not performed by a single individual. There can be separate roles for the following:

- The project leader represents the team to the outside and implements the steering committee's decisions. He or she also defends the project team vis-à-vis the steering committee.

- A project administrator performs all the progress reporting and person-nel administration tasks.

- A contract administrator negotiates and administers contracts with third parties: hardware and software suppliers, consultants, and training firms.

- A systems architect or chief designer is responsible for keeping the over-all design of the system up to date and communicating it to the project team members.

Other project team member roles are dictated by the nature of the work to be performed and the skills required. Users, functional analysts, technical analysts, programmers, data administrators and infrastructure specialists are the most common.

Other Resources. In addition to personnel resources, project organization entails mustering other resources, such as working space (having offices or cubicles close together encourages teamwork), hardware and software for the workstations, and a training program for the team members. The training program typically includes both technical training (for example, in the use of the selected CASE tool) and functional training, to understand the nature of the application and the analysis or design activities that may already have been executed.

Project Planning

While the project team is being organized, the project manager plans the project. First, an analysis of the scope of the project helps select the appropriate form of life cycle. Next, the work to be performed is broken down into a series of tasks or activities. Finally, the effort associated with each task is estimated and the sequence of tasks is laid out in a project schedule.

Selecting the Life-Cycle Approach. The single most important variable when selecting a life-cycle approach for a given project is the degree of innovation that is likely to be required. The more management desires a deep change in business process, the higher the risks associated with the development effort and the more a prototyping style of life cycle is indicated. If, on the other hand, management just wants to mechanize or remechanize current operations, the life cycle to be selected is closer to a waterfall style, possibly modified to include incremental delivery.

The project may be part of a multiple-project effort to implement a major new series of applications. In that case, the later projects in the series are less risky than the earlier ones and can be planned according to a waterfall style life cycle.

The degree to which the sponsor of the project is risk tolerant or risk averse is also an important factor. Some styles of management may be quite comfortable with only a loose idea of probable costs and benefits, whereas others require a much more stringent analysis and therefore a more predictable approach.

Work Breakdown Structure. Next, the project manager creates the work breakdown structure, a hierarchical representation of the parts of the product to be delivered at the end of the project and of the process by which it is delivered. For instance, a large application would be divided into subprojects along functional lines, for example, order entry, order picking, order delivery, and invoicing. More technical distinctions are also made, for example, between the operational system itself, file conversion, and testing activities. Then each subproject is divided into activities, such as requirements analysis, user interface design, data design, and process design. Each activity is in turn broken down, as appropriate, until a level is reached where it becomes possible to control the work effort, each task usually being limited to two weeks or less. For each task one or more deliverables are identified.

Estimating and Scheduling. For each element of the work breakdown structure, the project manager identifies the skill and the time required to perform the task by referring to experience, if possible backed up by historical data. One reason the work is broken down into fairly small pieces is to make it easier to estimate. The more activities that are identified, the more realistic the estimate tends to be.

Finally, the dependencies between the parts of the work breakdown structure are identified. The project manager considers the sequence of activities for a given part of the project, analysis preceding design and conversation design preceding screen design, for example. Dependencies between major parts are also considered. For instance, it may be decided to complete the on-line portion of the project before the batch portion, or order entry may need to precede order delivery. These major dependencies are often dictated by the system test and file conversion approaches.

If necessary, project scheduling software can be used to keep track of these dependencies according to PERT (Project Evaluation and Review Technique) or CPM (Critical Path Method) techniques, two popular methods for scheduling a complex network of interdependent activities.

Project Execution

During project execution, the project manager is responsible for allocating work to the various team members, making sure that the team resources are used where most needed, and ensuring that the workload is balanced.

As intermediate deliverables are completed, they are reviewed for verification (that they are correct and abide by project standards) and validation (that they conform to previous work). Design decisions are traced back to the requirements that influenced them; at major checkpoints, all the requirements identified early are checked against the design to determine whether they are met.

The project manager also supervises the scope of the project to make sure that the project results in what the users expect of it, neither more nor less. In many cases, unexpected difficulties will make it necessary to increase cost, delay delivery, or cut scope: the project manager must manage the steering committee's and users' expectations continuously in these three areas.

Project Control

The project team reports its activities to the project manager all along the project: weekly or twice-monthly time and progress reports are the norm. Each project member reports the time that he or she has spent against each work breakdown structure item and whether the item has been completed.

The project manager consolidates these figures and reports performance of the team against two standards: budget and schedule. A budget discrep-

Figure 3–11 **Creative Nature of Design**

ancy means that the project team members have spent more or less time than estimated on a given deliverable. An accumulation of budget overruns means that the project is costing more than anticipated; it does not necessarily mean that the project will come in late.

Schedule variances can be due to budget variances, but they can also occur because of staffing variances—when the project members spend more or less time than planned away from the project through illness, turnover, or other unplanned absences. If the team is overrunning the budget, it can in some cases stay on schedule by working overtime, compensating with a favorable staffing variance. Of course, if the initial schedule called for planned overtime, this solution becomes less effective.

Generally, favorable budget variances do not get reported: if the estimate is generous, workers have a tendency to use it all up, simply increasing the quality of the deliverable. If the estimate is too small, however, the unfavorable budget variance does get reported. Alternatively, and this is much more dangerous, the team may undercut the quality of the deliverable (by curtailing unit testing, for instance). This is usually an ill-conceived solution: the lack of quality invariably manifests itself at a later stage. Another dangerous factor is that team members may fudge their time reports if they feel that they are being evaluated on their ability to deliver strictly within the estimate. Thus, many a project manager has decreed that the team would work overtime to catch up, only to discover that many of the team members have already been working overtime without reporting it. The project manager must counter the resulting tendency to overrun projects.

THE DESIGN PROCESS IN THE SYSTEMS DEVELOPMENT LIFE CYCLE

The very idea of a systems development life cycle implies that the activity of design can be codified, at least to the extent that a representative work breakdown structure can be created. On the other hand, design is a creative act, as illustrated in Figure 3–11. To reconcile these two views, several metaphors have been proposed for the design activity: system design as

Figure 3–12 **Design as Modeling**

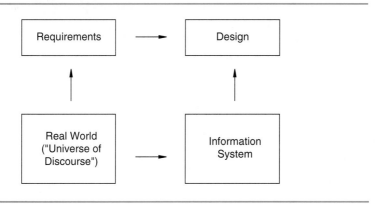

problem solving, as modeling, and as a series of transformations. Although each metaphor represents a viable alternative, it is currently an issue as to how to choose which is the most appropriate technique.[2]

System Design as Problem Solving

System design as problem solving is the most traditional view. Problem solving entails four phases: stating the problem, generating multiple alternative solutions, evaluating the alternatives to find the best one, and implementing it.

The traditional waterfall life cycle is strongly associated with this view. Most authors do not recommend generating multiple solutions to any great degree of details; they all assume that the general shape of the solution is known beforehand and that the only evaluation problem is to decide whether the new system is worth implementing at all. One could say that the new system is compared with the alternative of doing nothing, i.e., letting the current system continue to operate.

The problems that systems building are being likened to are fairly routine; they are not the kind that require great insight—a mental leap, as it were. Rather, they are problems that lend themselves to top-down analysis ("divide and conquer") and straightforward transposition of the elements of the decomposition ("functions") into a set of routine programs.

System Design as Modeling

A more modern view is that of systems design as modeling. This view is strongly held by the data-driven methodology espoused by James Martin.[3] The overall idea is represented in Figure 3–12, which shows that an information system is a model of some part of the real world and that a design is an abstraction (another kind of model, really) of the information system. The design is a model of an abstraction in the real world, just as the system is a model of the world.

This metaphor to explains what goes on in requirements analysis and the earlier stages of design. Analysis consists of abstracting essential features from the real-world system that is being studied, those features that are independent of any physical implementation of the system. Design then is the modeling of this abstraction by applying it to a given technology (for example, mainframe, on-line, buffered terminal, data base, clerk operated). The design decisions that are made are those required to make the best use of this technology or to live within the constraints of its imperfection.

System Design from Models

Since a design is a model, it has potentially several possible implementations. Model-based design exploits this fact by using a common design model across multiple applications in different corporations of the same industry (or different industries for some generic applications such as general ledger or payroll). The basis for model-based design is a conceptual design of a system documented on a CASE tool. This conceptual design can then serve as a shortcut for the requirements analysis phase.

Obviously, the design model must come from some corporation that has experience with many different systems of the same type—systems integrator, software vendor, computer manufacturer. The concept has been piloted in the utilities industry where its success can at least be partially ascribed to the relatively benign competitive atmosphere.

System Design as Transformation

The emerging view of systems development as a series of transformations is akin to the previous view of design as modeling. This view acknowledges that there are several successive models of a system during the development process. The first one is usually an English-language description, informal and by necessity somewhat imprecise; the last one is a very formal one, in source language (COBOL, Data Description Language, Job Control Language) statements that are interpreted by the systems software (compiler, data base management system, operating system) totally mechanically. From one extreme to the other, there are usually several different representations, each with its own syntax and conventions.

When design was manual and paper based, these intermediate representations could still be fairly informal. Any minor error in syntax was automatically corrected by the user of the representation, always a human being. With the advent of CASE tools, however, the representations must become much more formalized and adhere much more strictly to a set of syntactical rules. Moreover, the representations must be chosen with care: each CASE tool normally only supports one. In fact, it is most often the choice of a CASE tool that forces the choice of a representation scheme or a set of representation schemes. For instance, information engineering-oriented CASE tools such as IEW from KnowledgeWare and IEF from Texas Instruments support entity-relationship diagrams according to the James Martin conventions and the particular form of pseudocode known as action diagrams. Other CASE tools such as Excelerator from Index Technologies and FOUNDATION from Andersen Consulting may support data flow diagrams and the Chen convention for entity-relationship diagrams. In either case, when the tool is chosen, the users must abide by the syntax.

The two extreme representations, natural language and source code, are likely to remain with us for a long time. There is at least one, often two intermediate forms of representation, which rely heavily on graphics. Design then becomes a process of transforming each form of representation into the next one—from natural language to graphical form, and from graphical form to source code. The first transformation cannot be fully automated until we can interpret natural language. But why shouldn't we suppress the second transformation and go directly from pictures to code?

The answer is that we can—but only for mundane, relatively uninteresting systems—those for which there is little or no innovation, performance is unimportant because volumes are low and response times are not critical, and the user interface can be glossed over because the system has little impact on the user. These systems are unlikely to have much of an impact on the organization's bottom line either way.

For more complex systems, the performance, reliability, flexibility, and usability characteristics are critical. We do not know how to express these requirements in a language from which we can generate code directly. Moreover, these characteristics cannot be designed as system modules, because they are really a result of the interactions of the system's many parts: they are so-called *emergent* properties. There cannot be a reliability module in the way that there is an invoicing module; nor can there be a flexibility table in the way that there is a customer address table.

Summary

The IS function in most organizations originally consisted of a data processing department reporting to the chief accounting officer. With the advances in office automation, telecommunications technology, and data processing, today's information systems take advantage of all three. Because all three areas are technology based and often require project management skills, the management of office automation, telecommunications, and data processing is increasingly consolidated under the director of IS.

The IS department can now be found reporting to functions other than accounting, as organizations have realized the potential of information technology to serve all areas. In organizations where information technology is valued as a competitive weapon, the IS function is more likely to report to higher levels, even to the CEO. The chief information officer is gaining increasing favor as an executive-level officer responsible for managing an organization's information resources.

The IS department can be organized in many different ways to serve the rest of the organization. The three most common patterns are according to function, product, or a matrix. The IS function can be centralized or decentralized with respect to hardware, data, and personnel resources. The constantly changing environment has seen new groups emerge in some IS departments, an Information Center to support end-user computing, infrastructure specialists to support the use of new development tools, and systems architects, whose role is to ensure the conceptual integrity of large, integrated systems.

The systems development life cycle is considered under two aspects: project management and the design process. Project management consists of project organization, planning, execution, and control activities.

The design process has several interrelated aspects. It can be viewed as problem solving or as modeling. A recent trend is to view it as a series of transformations in representation mode. Each representation is supported by a CASE tool, which requires a greater degree of formalization than was necessary with manual development techniques.

Selected Readings

Davis, Gordon B., and Olson, Margrethe H. *Management Information Systems, Conceptual Foundations, Structure and Development*, 2d ed. New York: McGraw-Hill, 1985.
  This book contains a complete description of the organization of a typical IS department.

Martin, James. *The Information Systems Manifesto.* Englewood Cliffs, NJ: Prentice-Hall, 1984.
  This book is a plea for end-user computing and information centers. It contains the story of how the Santa Fe Railway end users successfully implemented a complex system with a fourth-generation language. The book's weakness is that it does not sufficiently recognize the dangers and shortcomings of end-user computing.

Cleland, D., and King, W., eds. *Project Management Handbook*, 2d ed. New York: Van Nostrand Reinhold, 1988.
  This book contains excellent articles on project management in general. The techniques described are applicable either as is or with minor modifications to systems development projects.

Gilbreath, R. *Winning at Project Management: What Works, What Fails, and Why.* New York: John Wiley & Sons, 1986.
  A well-written perspective on the human side of project management.

Review Questions

1. What is the fundamental mission of the IS department in a typical organization?

2. Why did organizational responsibility for early information systems most often lie with the accounting department?

3. Explain why the management of telecommunications and office automation has been or is being transferred to the IS department in many organizations.

4. Why is it so important that the IS department be placed where it can provide service according to overall organizational priorities?

5. How can the strategic grid be used to help decide the proper organizational placement of the IS department?

6. What are the key considerations for management in deciding whether to centralize or decentralize IS hardware, data, and personnel?

7. What skills will be important for personnel working in end-user computing? As infrastructure specialists? As systems architects?

8. What measures can be taken to ensure management commitment to a systems project?

9. What are the key project management and control considerations described in the chapter?

Discussion Questions

1. Identify and describe two or three IS applications used in organizations today that combine functions of office automation, telecommunications, and data processing.

2. Obtain an organization chart of an IS department of a local company. Compare and contrast the organization chart of the selected firm with the IS organizations described in this chapter—functional, product line, and matrix.

3. Discuss the view that systems design is problem solving. Compare and contrast systems design with other kinds of problems, for example, a math assignment, finding one's way in an unknown city, a problematical relationship with a family member, or the problem of urban planning.

4. Discuss the view that systems design is modeling. Review different meanings of the word *model*. Which ones apply to systems development and which ones do not? One common trait of models is that they never represent the whole reality. Which aspects of reality are left out of an information system, considered as a model of the "real world"? Which are left out of the design, considered as a model for the information system?

Mini-Case

Assume you are an independent consultant specializing in information systems. The vice-president of finance of Midwestern Insurance (to whom the internal information systems department reports) calls and asks you to come to his office. When you arrive, he asks you to help him deal with the following problem.

The vice-president of marketing has proposed to purchase a personal computer for each one of the company's agencies located across the United States and put policyholder information on them so that agents can answer policyholder inquiries better. The vice-president of marketing feels that the present method of having agents telephone the home office is inadequate. Agents tell him that sometimes they cannot get through. When they do, they often have to talk with clerks in the policyholder service department (which also reports to the vice-president of finance) who are ill-trained and rude. Several agents have already purchased personal computers on their own and have placed policyholder data on them. These agents find that because most changes originate in the field, they can keep their own files current, reducing their aggravation levels enormously. Some have purchased IBM PCs, while others have purchased Macintoshes or SUN workstations. Various other manufacturers are also represented.

The director of IS is violently opposed to the proposal. He was just in the final stages of preparing a proposal for a distributed data system that would link personal computers in the agents' offices to the home office computer. He maintains that his approach would be best in the long run even though it will probably require about two years to get it off the ground. In the meantime, he wants all personal computer purchases to be approved by his department because MIS has responsibility for computer hardware purchases. The vice-president of marketing has said he cannot wait two years for action; he wants results now. Furthermore, he maintains that personal computers cost so little that they should be considered office equipment and not come under the purchase supervision of IS.

Question for Discussion

1. The vice-president of finance has asked for your help. What advice can you give him?

Notes

1. McKenney, James, and McFarlan, F. Warren. "The Information Archipelago—Maps and Bridges." *Harvard Business Review* (September 1982): 109–120.

2. Davis, A. M. *Software Requirements Analysis and Specification.* Englewood Cliffs, NJ: Prentice-Hall, 1990.

3. Martin, J. *Information Engineering.* 3 vols. Englewood Cliffs, NJ: Prentice-Hall, 1990.

Technique

Hierarchical Diagramming

INTRODUCTION

One of the most frequently used documentation techniques is the hierarchy chart. It is used whenever there is a need to represent a structure of divisions and subdivisions throughout the systems development life cycle. Chapter 3 alluded to the hierarchical nature of a work breakdown structure. Each of the remaining sections of this book makes use of hierarchical diagramming for some purpose. Indeed, the technique is used even more frequently outside the realm of systems development itself.

All CASE tools have some way of representing hierarchical structures.

DEFINITION

A hierarchy chart depicts relationships between entities or concepts as a tree-like structure, where each entity or concept is related to one and only one higher-level entity. A higher-level entity may have several lower-level entities attached to it. Some entities have no lower-level entities related to them and are considered the leaves of the tree. The highest-level entity is the root, and the intermediate entities are nodes. The number of nodes between a node and the root, including the root itself, represents the level of the node. Thus, the root has a level of zero. The highest level of any node is called the depth of the hierarchy. The number of nodes at a given level characterizes the breadth of the hierarchy, also called fan-out. A node is often called a child and its next higher level node is called a parent. The root is a parent only. Leaves are children only.

EXAMPLES

As Figures 1 through 11 illustrate, relationships expressed by hierarchy charts are quite common.

*   Figure 1. A family tree is a hierarchy with the person whose family tree is being traced placed at the root (the left side of the figure), with that person's mother and father at level 1, the grandparents at level 2, and so on.

*   Figure 2. The line of succession of English kings from 1327 to 1499 shows a hierarchy with Edward III at the root.

Figure 1 **Family Tree**

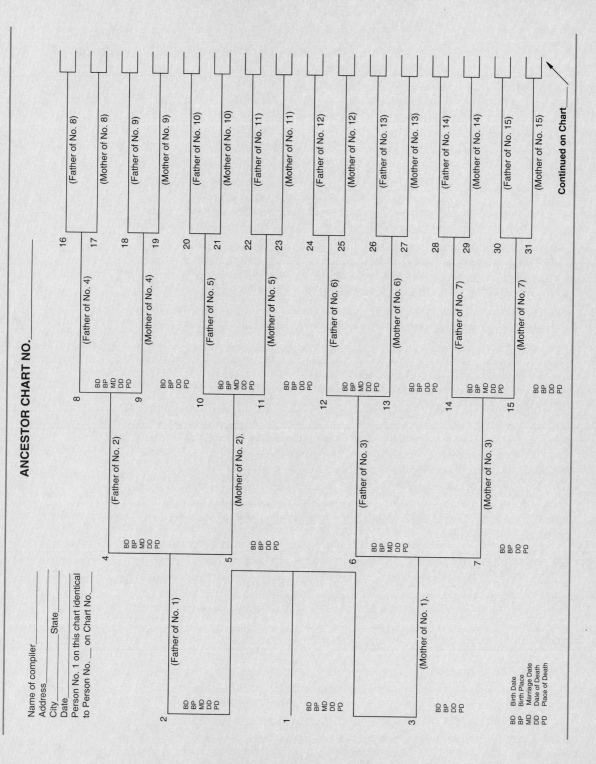

Figure 2 **Line of Succession to the Throne of England**

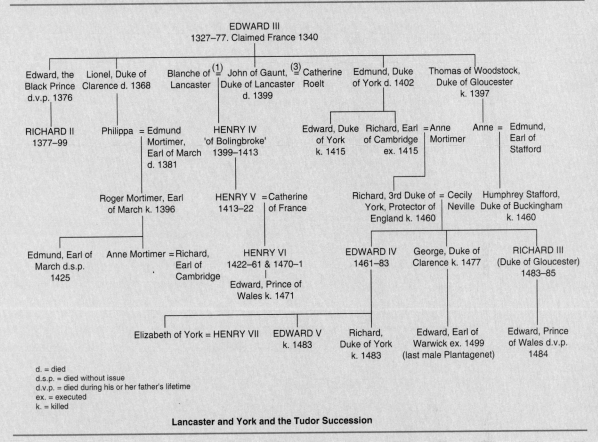

Lancaster and York and the Tudor Succession

- Figure 3. The table of contents of this book is a hierarchy: the entire book (the root) is subdivided into sections, chapters, and paragraphs (the nodes).

- Figure 4. The structure of this book is an abstraction of its table of contents, with the same number of levels, but fewer nodes at each level.

- Figure 5. A program structure chart is a hierarchy of modules with the program name at the root.

- Figure 6. In the hierarchy of the pseudo-code of a structured module, the module is the root and each statement is a node. Indentation of the code indicates the level of the node.

- Figure 7. A COBOL program is a hierarchy in which the first levels are the divisions and the sections. The next levels are paragraphs and the text of the program (except in the data division, where level numbers are used to denote further levels of the hierarchy).

Figure 3 **Partial Table of Contents of This Book**

SECTION I	INFORMATION SYSTEMS IN THE BUSINESS	1
	The Hospitals of Kalamazoo *2*	
Chapter 1	Information Technology and Competitive Advantage	13
	A Brief Historical Perspective *14*	
	Box 1–1 Top Management's Understanding of Information Technology *16*	
	Information Technology's Role Today *16*	
	A Framework for Strategic Business Planning *17*	
	Five Forces Model *17*	
	Three Generic Strategies *20*	
	The Value Chain *21*	
	Box 1–2 Systems That Have Changed an Industry Structure *22*	
	Box 1–3 Companies That Have Improved Existing Products or Services *23*	
	The Strategic Grid *24*	
	Box 1–4 Companies That Have Created New Products or Services *25*	
	First-Mover Disadvantages *26*	
	Applicability to the Not-For-Profit Sector *27*	

- Figure 8. French schoolchildren learn that an essay has a hierarchical structure.

- Figure 9. In the hierarchy of military ranks, the general is at the root and the soldier is the leaf.

- Figure 10. The order of battle is a hierarchy—the breakdown of the armed forces into armies, divisions, battalions, and so on.

- Figure 11. A corporation's organization chart is a hierarchy similar to that of the order of battle.

WHERE USED IN THE LIFE CYCLE

Hierarchical charts are primarily used in two places in systems development. One is the program structure chart, for example, the VTOC (Visual Table of Contents), which is part of IBM's approach to structured program design (Figure 5); the Warnier chart (Figure 12); or the Jackson chart (Figure 13). The other place is in functional decomposition, an alternative to data flow diagramming (Figure 14). Function charts are easier to establish than data flow diagrams, but they are a less powerful mode of representation.

Figure 4 **Structure of This Book**

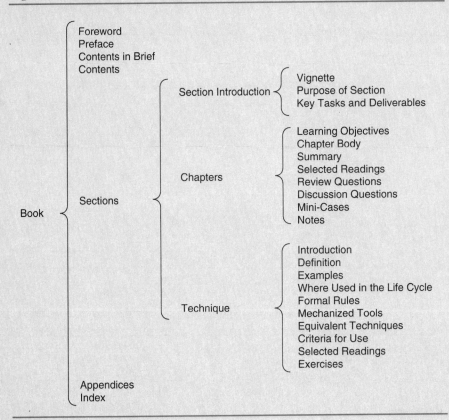

Hierarchical techniques are used whenever a top-down approach is appropriate, although the documentation technique may not reflect the approach directly. For instance, data flow diagrams (DFDs) can be leveled. Each subdivision of an entire domain may be detailed on a different page. Further divisions appear on other pages. These pages have an obvious hierarchical relationship that may be clearer in a numbering scheme or in a table of contents (see Figure 15). (The DFD is further explained at the end of Section III.)

Another illustration of the concept of leveling is a world atlas, which contains a world map, maps of each continent, and detailed maps of countries, regions, and even cities.

FORMAL RULES

Hierarchies can be depicted in any of three ways—top to bottom, left to right, and bottom to top—according to where the root is. Generally, the bottom-to-top representation is chosen only when a tree effect is aimed for; it is seldom used in business charts.

Figure 5 **Program Structure Chart**

Top to bottom is the best representation for deep hierarchies with little fan-out, as in Figure 9. Left to right is best for shallow hierarchies with high fan-out, as in Figure 4. The indented representation used for book outlines and pseudo-code are also suitable for high fan-out (Figures 3 and 6).

The two most important types of hierarchies are the Is-A and Is-Made-Up-Of hierarchies. The relationship between military units in the order of battle is Is-Made-Up-Of. The Is-A relationship is also called a taxonomy, or classification, scheme. Here, the nodes are classes or sets of individuals, and the leaves are subclasses or individuals. The most frequently encountered hierarchy relationship in data processing is Is-Made-Up-Of. (The process of documenting Is-Made-Up-Of is called decomposition; hence the name functional decomposition has been given to the process of documenting the hierarchy of functions or processes during the user requirements phase.) The Is-A hierarchy is frequently encountered in object-oriented analysis.

In a hierarchy chart, only a single type of relationship between nodes should appear. The family tree contains two types of relationships, Has-Mother and Has-Father. These are symmetrical forms of the same, more general relationship. Hierarchies that mix two truly different types of relationships are problematic and should be avoided. For instance, the taxonomy of animals, an Is-A hierarchy, could be mixed with notations that each animal has a head, a body, limbs, and possibly a tail, an Is-Made-Up-Of hierarchy. However, to mix these two independent hierarchies, the Is-A and the Is-Made-Up-Of would be extremely confusing. If mixing is required, it should only occur either at the root or at the leaves, never at intermediate nodes.

Figure 6 **Pseudo-Code**

```
get Card_Stripe_Content
get User_Entered_PIN
if User_Entered_PIN = Card_Stripe_PIN
then
        dountil Trans_Code_Done
            get Trans_Code
            case
                Trans_Code = Withdrawal
                    perform Withdrawal_Process
                Trans_Code = Transfer
                    perform Transfer_Process
                Trans_Code = Deposit
                    perform Deposit_Process
                Trans_Code = Query
                    perform Query_Process
            endcase
        enddo
        put Return_Card
else
        perform Confiscate_Card
        print Error_Message
endif
```

Implied relationships of another nature may be incorporated into the hierarchical diagrams. Both the Warnier and Jackson program structure charts generally incorporate the main three programming structures— sequence, iteration, and alternative. Sequence is implied by the physical disposition of the diagrams; alternatives and iterations must be represented by special conventions (Figures 12 and 13).

A hierarchy chart produced by functional decomposition can be read in different sequences. Consider the example in Figure 14. If it is read from the top of the page down (at the lowest level in the hierarchy), it answers the question "What?" If it is read from left to right, it answers the question "How?" If it is read from right to left, it answers the question "Why?"

Often a numbering scheme for the nodes in a hierarchy helps reflect that hierarchy. There are two main types of numbering schemes. The first is suitable for shallow hierarchies with high fan-out. The root node number is 0, and each of the children of the root is numbered from 1 to n. Then, each entity within node 1 is numbered 1.1 through 1.x. Each additional level adds another level of numbering. For three or four levels, this system is manageable; the most complex number might look like 4.13.2.7. With ten levels, one of the nodes would awkwardly be numbered 1.1.1.1.1.1.1.1.1.2 and another one 1.1.1.1.1.1.1.1.2.1. This powerful numbering scheme actually contains all the information about the hierarchy; in theory, no diagram is

Figure 7 **COBOL Program Structure**

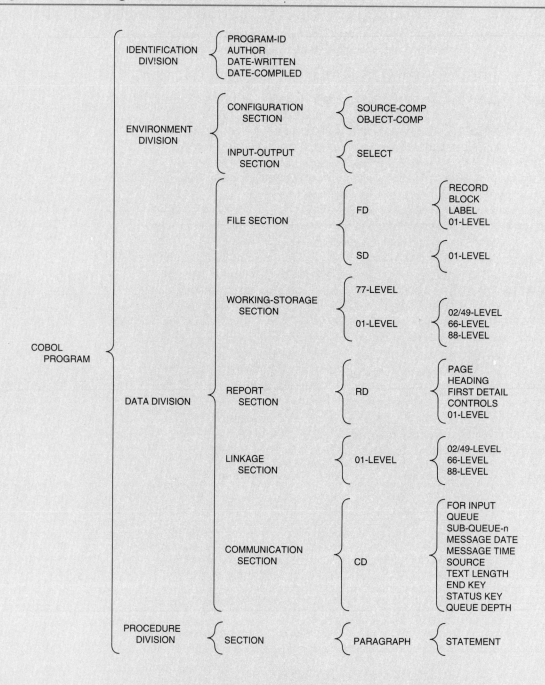

Figure 8 **Structure of an Essay**

required. (A diagram is still useful since a pictorial representation is a superior way of communicating.)

A useful device, often used in business reports, is to alternate numbers and letters, Roman and Arabic numerals, upper and lower case, so that a section of a report might be numbered I.A.1.a.iii. This scheme is useful when each level has a different name, such as section, chapter, paragraph, and the number of levels is fairly homogeneous. It is less useful when the levels are not distinguishable and the depth of the hierarchy varies according to the branch.

The second approach, suitable for deep hierarchies with little fan-out, is to number the levels and then number the nodes across the entire level. The number would then combine the two components. This method is less powerful than the previous one, because it does not show exactly where in a hierarchy the numbered node is located. For a deep hierarchy with high fan-out, combinations of the two approaches can often be devised.

Many authors recommend reducing the fan-out at each node to some number bearing a relationship to the "magical number seven plus or minus two."[1] This system is especially useful during analysis. One of the purposes of leveling structure charts is to present a manageable amount of information at a time. In addition, a criterion for grouping functions under a more general label is that this label be understandable—logical, if you will—to the reader of the chart. Thus, at a given level functions and their relationships can be discussed without worrying about the details of each. Only if there is uncertainty about how functions documented at a lower level affect higher levels is it necessary to explore the depths of the hierarchy.

Reducing fan-out does not have any adverse effects in the analysis stage because the only purpose of the intermediate levels is to organize and communicate ideas. Reducing fan-out merely for the sake of reducing fan-out in a program structure chart is another matter altogether. If the documentation is of modules that will be developed, called, and maintained as independent entities, the rules of good module design take precedence over the rules of presentation. Arbitrarily increasing the number of levels in a program hierarchy increases execution overhead unnecessarily. More seriously, module cohesion and coupling may suffer. The increase can in turn

Figure 9 **United States Army Ranks**

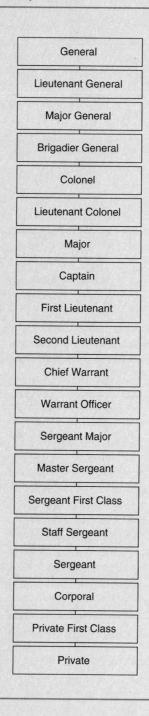

Figure 10 **Order of Battle**

Figure 11 **Organization Chart**

add to maintenance and destroy reusability of components that could otherwise be standardized.

MECHANIZED TOOLS

Most CASE tools support the creation of hierarchical diagrams in appropriate places of the life cycle, especially program structure charts and equivalent forms such as pseudo-code. In addition, hierarchical data base design tools have facilities for preparing charts representing the data base structure. These specialized tools, however, cannot readily be used to create general-purpose hierarchies.

Figure 12 **Warnier Diagram of a Program Structure**

Figure 13 **Jackson Diagram of a Program Structure**

Figure 14 **Function Chart**

Some CASE tools incorporate a general-purpose facility that can be used to prepare any hierarchical documentation from function decomposition to report outlines. An outliner such as ThinkTank or Idea Processor is a useful adjunct if the CASE tool does not have a general-purpose hierarchy diagrammer.

CRITERIA FOR USE

The main criterion for using hierarchical charts is that they depict what is really a hierarchy. To force nonhierarchical structures such as entity-relationship diagrams or data flow diagrams into the mold of a hierarchy is counterproductive.

Also, it is not much use to prepare multiple levels in hierarchical diagrams unless the levels contribute additional information or clarity. If each component of the system is independent of the others and can be reviewed with each user separately, then multiple levels should not be created. For instance, if a new code is being created to designate geographical areas and there is no organizational entity that groups these areas, it is useless to create a regional level.

EXERCISES

1. Create several hierarchical charts using a CASE tool and noting how to insert new levels in an existing tree and how to move entire sections of the diagram from one node to another. Critique the presentation obtained. Is the CASE tool most appropriate for high or low fan-out, high or low depth? If the chart is on several pages, are page connectors clear and easy to follow? Use the following domains as examples of charts that you draw:

Figure 15 **Leveling of Data Flow Diagrams**

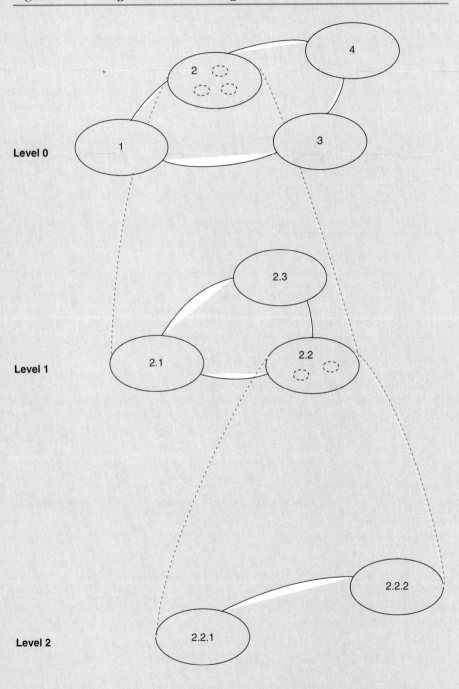

Level 0

Level 1

Level 2

    a. The organization of the university you are attending.
    b. The curriculum that will lead to your bachelor's or master's degree.
    c. The outline of an editorial or in-depth article that you have recently read.
    d. The Dewey classification scheme.

2. Search other textbooks for examples of hierarchies. Critique their presentation and content. Do they mix different types of concepts and relationships?

3. Examine the geopolitical subdivisions of your state—counties, townships, cities, villages, wards, school districts, and so on. Can these divisions be represented in a single hierarchy? If not, discuss whether it would be opportune to restructure the subdivisions.

4. If you play chess, discuss the requirements for a hierarchy representing chess openings with their main variations. What is the theoretical fan-out at ten moves on the part of each opponent? What is the practical fan-out? Can the problem be solved by creating catchall categories? How do you treat openings that transpose into one another?

5. Imagine that you were to create your own family tree going back 930 years (to William the Conqueror or thereabouts). Assume that each successive generation has its children at the average age of 30. How many forebears would you have in the year 1066? Estimate what percentage of the world's population is represented by your ancestors. What does this prove?

Note

1. Miller, G. A. "The Magical Number 7 Plus or Minus Two: Some Limits on Our Capacity for Processing Information." *Psychology Review* (1957): 63, 81–97.

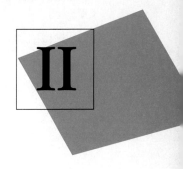

Systems Planning

There are two possible approaches to planning systems projects. The first approach, covered in Chapter 4, Feasibility Studies, is to evaluate each project in isolation, as the need for it is realized. The second approach is to create a global plan. Systems planners consider in a single study all the applications that the organization is likely to require over the next few years. This approach is covered in Chapter 5, Establishing the Systems Plan, and Chapter 6, IS Infrastructure Planning.

Social Security Administration Revamps Software, Data Structures

♦

The Social Security Administration's director of system modernization requirements spoke of some of the daunting problems his agency has faced in bringing its software up to date, as well as the methods used to launch the improvement, during a speech at the recent Federal Office Systems Expo in Washington, D.C.

Richard Gonzalez said at the session on "Strategic Information Systems Planning and Implementation" that after initial analysis of the agency's long-standing software systems, SSA determined none of the software in place at the time was acceptable. Estimates were that 38 percent of the software could be kept with modifications, but that 62 percent needed replacement.

Gonzalez said the review and documentation of existing software asked what pieces of data exist and how they are used and what functions are performed by which software modules. He said the process is a labor-intensive activity.

He also said although strides have been made, full results are "still not there."

Data content and structure analysis has been another important part of the modernization process. "The critical thing in building information systems is having data that everybody understands," Gonzalez said. He said for the purpose of understanding the 1.2 trillion bytes of data in SSA's systems, "we're trying to separate the data from the functions for which it is used." He said different modules of the old software contain nominally duplicative data items that often don't agree, compounding the modernization problem.

Unvalidated Data
The example he gave was birth dates. He said the modular, non-relational system of data in place virtually guarantees that many people's data will include multiple birth dates, with obviously only one being objectively correct. He said this has come about because of different requirements for proving birth date, depending on whether someone is applying for a Social Security number or applying for benefits, for example.

The lack of a central data repository and validation point has conspired with variant data collection policies to corrupt the data base. Gonzalez said, "When I ask for a birth date, the data base administrator is going to say, 'I have three or four. Which one do you want?' "

This problem has led to a data purification project. "We had to somehow look at the existing data and define a logical equivalent for it. We looked at 5,000 elements and were able to reduce that to 600 logical equivalents," Gonzalez said. He said this would expand, but the data analysis requires as few logical equivalents as possible initially. Each logical equivalent could point to up to 10 individual elements. An example would be a client's mailing address. If this is in five old files, it's at least five elements and probably more. The paring down effort would make it one unit, possibly with subcomponents for its identifiable parts.

Gonzalez said this smorgasbord of data is going to be a huge problem.

Gonzalez said the magnitude of the project, encompassing a system tracking 350 million Social Security numbers, past and present, with the attendant payroll tax records and claims, and using 12 million lines of code and 1,500 processing locations to do it, required a proven methodology for planning and mapping requirements. He said the agency chose IBM Corp.'s Business Systems Planning methodology, because it is comprehensive and people in the industry have experience with it.

Gonzalez and SSA also got references. "We asked the Postal Service. They said, 'Yes, it's good.' "

He said the methodology, as its name suggests, relies on defining the business of the agency and the information needed to carry out the business of the agency. The major steps, according to Gonzalez, include analysis of the business and the data used; development of an application architecture, which outlines the applications that will be applied to the functions of the organization's basic business; and the assessment of current systems.

Interdisciplinary Teams
A core tactic in the BSP process is forming an interdisciplinary team of users and systems personnel "as senior as you can get," said Gonzalez. IBM recommends 10 on the team, but SSA went with 25 to ensure all the major players would be included, helping to ensure the success of the plan.

An advantage SSA found was that "we are centralized in terms of our management and software development," Gonzalez said. He said the constant coordination of diverse interests takes a great deal of organizational perseverance. He added, "I am now convinced planning is not so much planning as doing."

The most difficult part of keeping a large-scale planning process on track in a federal agency is the broad consensus required, and understanding that managers must maintain, even though it doesn't yield short-term, immediate payoffs, he said.[1]

PURPOSE OF SECTION

This section describes how systems development projects come into being and how organizations try to ensure that the right project gets done at the right time.

When most systems were developed to automate some existing manual system, systems planning was done system by system. The cost of each system was justified based on its own merit. Its scope was generally reduced to a single department, and the hardware and software architecture was chosen without regard to existing technical environments in other departments. The initial phase of systems development was the feasibility study. It was designed to provide an overview of costs and benefits for a single system. If there was a greater plan, it was usually reduced to a sequence of development projects based on the ranking of the anticipated return on investment of the various projects.

When more integrated systems became possible with the advent of hardware and systems software that could be shared among several applications, large centralized data processing equipment became the rule, dictated by the economies of scale. It was then realized that additional benefits could be drawn from sharing the technical architecture, the systems software platforms (such as access methods, data base management systems, on-line transaction monitors), and above all the data.

In nonintegrated systems, the same data is partly duplicated in many systems. The source of the data, although theoretically the same, is viewed as distinct for each application; therefore, data collection is duplicated. As a result, the integrity of the data—its consistency in all the different places where it appears—is difficult or impossible to ensure.

These problems gave rise to more sophisticated methods of systems planning. Most of the methods in use today emphasize two aspects of over-all planning: planning for the sharing of data across applications and organizational units (Chapter 5), and planning for the sharing of technology, both hardware and software (Chapter 6).

KEY TASKS AND DELIVERABLES

The purpose of systems planning is twofold: to identify and assign priorities to development projects to be undertaken in the next few years and to make sure that the resources to implement the plan are available. Systems planning, therefore, typically includes the following steps.

The first step, which is the responsibility of IS management and executive management, is to ensure that the systems plan will support the strategy of the business. Unless a well-understood business plan already exists, the planning team establishes lines of communication and defines the criteria for deciding on the systems to develop first.

Then, the planners study the business processes, the information needs of management, and the data required to support the processes and fulfill the needs. As a result of this study, high-level functions are grouped into systems according to data usage and the ideal applications of the organization are identified.

The current status of existing applications must be assessed to identify how close they are to this ideal. Also, the costs, benefits, and risks associated with enhancing or redeveloping the applications to make them closer to the ideal are weighed. This analysis forms the basis for the application development plan, which identifies projects, development resources, migration strategies, and the preferred sequence of development. The deliverable from this stage is an application and data plan.

Next, the infrastructure required to develop and operate the applications is analyzed. This includes personnel, development tools (such as CASE, application generators, and data dictionary), and the operating environment (including the data base management system, the transaction processing monitor, communications software, network equipment, and central and departmental hardware). The deliverable from this stage is the infrastructure plan (or the technology plan).

Finally, required compromises are made among the speed of development, the level of ambition of the projects, and the resources that are likely to be available. The resulting deliverable is a time line for project development and for the acquisition of resources: hiring and training personnel, acquiring software, and procuring hardware.

In many corporations, the systems plan is much less formal. In practically every IS department, the IS manager has a fairly explicit strategy. Increasingly, this strategy is in tune with the strategic thinking of top management. However, the strategy is rarely formally documented. One of the main drawbacks of this lack of documentation is that neither users nor top management can know precisely what the IS department will achieve over the next few years.

When there is no formal plan or when an unanticipated application is suddenly needed, the project must be reviewed before starting the development cycle. The review defines the project's scope, the order of magnitude of benefits that can be expected, and the resources that management is willing to commit to achieve these expectations. The steps to perform such a feasibility study, as it is called, are much the same as for the systems plan, but the scope of the study is reduced to a single project.

At this point, the requirements, features, and functions do not determine the cost. It is rather the other way around; only those functions and features that can be implemented within the overall budget of the project will be incorporated into the system, which may therefore fall somewhat short of the description in the feasibility study or the systems plan. At such an early stage, the development cost cannot be predicted accurately based on the functions of the system. Management generally prefers to set a budget constraint and leave some uncertainty about the functions and features of the system, rather than decide on all the functions and be uncertain about the cost.

Note

1. "SSA Revamps Software, Data Structures," *Government Computer News* (April 10, 1987): 65–67.

CHAPTER

Feasibility Studies

Chapter 4 first describes the objectives of a feasibility study and gives examples of situations where feasibility studies are appropriate. It then describes the criteria for deciding whether a project is feasible and explains how to evaluate whether those criteria are met. A detailed section on cost/benefit analysis, the most important criterion of feasibility, concludes the chapter.

Learning Objectives

- Understand how management uses the feasibility study early in the systems development life cycle for a quick evaluation of the potential costs and benefits of a proposed system.

- Become aware that the feasibility study is particularly appropriate for organizations that consider projects one at a time and have not yet adopted an enterprise-wide approach to systems planning.

- Describe four common reasons for initiating a feasibility study and understand the specific approach to be followed for conducting each type of study.

- Identify five types of feasibility that should be addressed in a feasibility study.

- Understand those aspects of a cost/benefit analysis important to management at the feasibility study stage.

OBJECTIVES AND ORGANIZATION OF A FEASIBILITY STUDY

The feasibility study is a quick review of a proposed information systems development project. The study determines whether it makes sense to allocate resources to a project, whether the project is worth doing but should be postponed, or whether the project is worth doing at all. A feasibility study refines a system's concept to the point where the benefits to the organization are more clearly understood. In addition, the study predicts the costs associated with proceeding with the project's development and installation with a degree of accuracy appropriate for this stage of the life cycle, i.e., well enough for management to decide whether continuing is worthwhile, and if so, when.

To understand how a feasibility study is conducted, you should know when it is done, by whom, and with what result.

One common characteristic of the life-cycle methodologies used in the design and installation of information systems is the *phased approach* concept described in Section I. In this approach, the steps necessary to design and install an information system are divided into natural phases, with management approval of the end products of one phase being required before continuing on to the next phase. Gildersleeve calls this approach the *creeping commitment* approach.[1] Management commits resources to a large information systems project little by little, as the project team presents evidence at the conclusion of each phase in the life cycle that the project continues to be viable.

A feasibility study is the first phase of a project to which resources are committed. It occurs at the beginning of the life cycle. Figure 4–1 shows how the feasibility study fits in with the generic life cycle introduced in Section I. It generally substitutes for the systems planning phase; in some cases, when a project was omitted from the systems plan or was studied in insufficient detail, a separate feasibility study may be done in addition to what was done during the preparation of the systems plan.

The feasibility study is best prepared by a project team consisting of users and IS personnel. In practice, however, one group may have the primary responsibility for the study.

The end product of a feasibility study is a report that outlines the concept of a proposed system with sufficient clarity that a distinction can be made between the proposed system and the present system. Costs and benefits of moving to the proposed system are presented in enough detail to permit management to decide whether it is worthwhile to move on to the analysis and design phases. Typically, a management group making the decision is described as an executive steering committee. However, the decision could be, and often is, made by other types of management groups or by individual executives.

When systems planning is performed in an organization, as will be discussed in Chapter 5, steps similar to those performed in a feasibility study are performed for projects identified as part of the planning process. The difference is that in systems planning the team takes an overall view of the organization's requirements. In contrast, those who perform a feasibility study view one project at a time.

EXAMPLES OF THE USE OF FEASIBILITY STUDIES

IS departments usually have more requests for new applications and maintenance of existing systems than they can handle immediately. The list of approved projects waiting for IS resources to become available is called the application development backlog. Some observers estimate the extent of the application development backlog in a typical large IS department at two to four years with an additional "invisible backlog" on top of that.[2] The invisible

Figure 4–1 **The Place of the Feasibility Study in the Generic Systems Development Life Cycle**

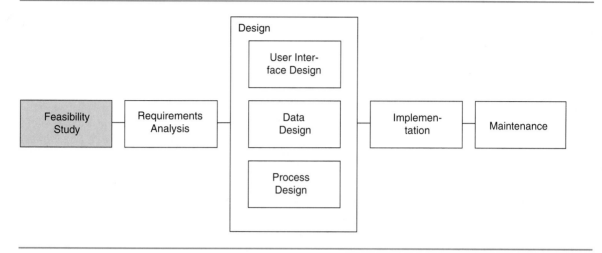

backlog is work that would be requested by users if the visible backlog were not so high. The size of the application development backlog is a major reason for the rise in popularity of end-user computing, CASE technology, code generators, and other tools to shorten the time required to implement systems.

An organization with a large application development backlog and with no formal long-range systems planning approach might use feasibility studies to select and assign priorities to projects in a manner similar to that illustrated in Figure 4–2. The key components in the organization are user departments, the IS department, and an executive steering committee made up of the vice-presidents to whom the heads of each user department report. The executive steering committee meets with the director of information systems once a month to review the list of approved feasibility studies for projects in the backlog, to discuss new feasibility studies that have been received in the current month, and to decide (after considering availability of IS resources) which projects should be initiated in the current month. The executive steering committee, after discussing a new feasibility study, either approves it for placement in the backlog queue in its proper priority sequence or decides that it is currently not worthy of further consideration.

Ideas for new projects (or for major enhancements to existing applications) are almost always initiated by a user department in response to a business problem or opportunity. If a department head thinks that a suggestion from a department member has merit, a feasibility study will be prepared and submitted to the executive steering committee at its next monthly meeting.

One of the shortcomings of a process such as the one illustrated in Figure 4–2 is that the executive steering committee considers only projects

Figure 4–2 **The Feasibility Approach for Selecting and Assigning Priorities to Projects**

User Departments Provide
New Project Feasibility Studies

IS Department

A   B   C   D   E

Executive
Steering
Committee

Agenda

• Review List of Approved Feasibility Studies
• Discuss New Feasibility Studies
• Decide New Projects to Initiate
• Decide Status of New Feasibility Studies

for which feasibility studies have been prepared. If a project is not suggested by a user department, it may never be considered by the executive steering committee. Another issue is that politically powerful members of the executive steering committee may find that they are able to get projects approved for their departments even though other projects may be more beneficial to the organization. (In some cases, the idea for a project comes from a member of the executive steering committee, who then asks someone in one of his or her departments to prepare the necessary feasibility study.) Organizations following this approach often fail to communicate organizational objectives very far down in the organization. Therefore, while members of the executive steering committee may have a good understanding of the objectives, other members of the organization who initiate most of the ideas do not. These members cannot be expected to suggest projects that clearly support organizational objectives.

Even though the preceding process for determining project priorities has shortcomings, it is still often encountered in practice today. In such environments, the preparation of feasibility studies is a generally accepted method for reviewing projects that arise one at a time rather than as the result of an overall systems planning process. Feasibility studies are useful tools for management decision making in such environments.

TYPES OF FEASIBILITY

Five types of feasibility should be evaluated in a feasibility study, according to Davis and Olson:

- Technical
- Operational
- Economic
- Schedule
- Motivational[3]

Most authors only consider the first three, but all five are important.

Technical Feasibility

Technical feasibility addresses the issue of whether the technical aspects of a proposal are practical and achievable. Usually this feasibility is more of an issue if the technology involved in the proposal is generally new or new to the organization. For example, suppose an organization is considering the installation of a computer integrated manufacturing system that depends for part of its data input on quality control readings from automatic sensors. The feasibility study would have to present evidence that the sensor technology was sufficiently accurate and reliable to use as a component of the proposed system. Some of the ways this evidence could be presented include representations (and guarantees, if possible) by the sensor equipment manufacturer, site visits to other installations using the same equipment for similar applications, and pilot tests in the environment where the equipment will be expected to operate.

In addition, technical feasibility is lacking when problems have no known algorithms, or when the algorithm is not efficient enough. Some scheduling problems and many problems currently being researched in artificial intelligence have this characteristic. For example, unconstrained natural language cannot today be used to communicate between a user and a program.

Operational Feasibility

Operational feasibility involves whether the system concept is appropriate for the operating environment for which it is proposed. For example, a feasibility study for a system to support student registration by touch-tone telephone would have to show the university executive steering committee some evidence that the system was operationally feasible. The committee might question not only whether the system would be accepted by the students (almost certainly), but also whether security features could be built into the system to deter mischievous tampering by creative minds. Without such controls, the system would probably fail in actual operation.

Economic Feasibility

Economic feasibility addresses the issue of whether the resources needed to develop and operate the proposed system can be justified by the returns from installing it. A section on costs and benefits is included as an important part of the feasibility study. This inclusion, however, does not imply that all systems should have direct cost savings as a part of their justification. Whether the potential benefits from a system's installation justify its cost is a matter of management judgment. Increasingly, economic feasibility has to be determined by intangible elements such as an increase in the quality of managerial decision making or an increase in customer satisfaction. Placing a value on these intangible elements is difficult. In these cases, decisions to proceed with a system's installation may be based on management's opinion that the system is in the long-term interest of the organization, regardless of immediate payback. Cost/benefit analyses will be covered in more detail later in this chapter.

Schedule Feasibility

The executive steering committee will want assurance that the schedule for developing and installing the proposed system is realistic and reasonable in the light of the business requirements. There are certain times of the year that are natural conversion dates. For example, financial planning and reporting systems are usually scheduled to convert at the beginning of the organization's fiscal year. A feasibility study normally does not identify a specific changeover date because the installation effort cannot be identified precisely until after analysis and design have been completed. The feasibility study should give a realistic estimate of the time required to perform the next phase and should present a range of possible conversion dates with a target date to be established when the necessary analysis and design tasks are completed. The executive steering committee will expect to see the target dates supported.

Motivational Feasibility

Finally, the feasibility study should assure the executive steering committee that the users want the proposed system badly enough that they are willing to participate in a development project and undergo disruption in their daily routines to absorb the changes introduced by the new system. The best evidence of user support is active user participation in preparing the feasibility study.

Motivational feasibility could also be termed political feasibility.

APPROACHES TO DETERMINING PROJECT FEASIBILITY

Projects are commonly instigated for one of four reasons:

- To solve operational problems
- To replace existing technology

Figure 4–3 **Example of Comparison between Current and Proposed System for a Hospital Billing System**

Problems: Accounts receivable balances are too high relative to the level of billing activity. Uncollectible accounts receivable are too high.

Current Operations	**Proposed Operations**
1. Four days between patient discharge and bill preparation.	1. One day between patient discharge and bill preparation.
2. Maximum of 3 percent charge error rate.	2. Maximum of 1 percent charge error rate.
3. No reports generated for management follow-up activity on delinquent accounts.	3. Two reports prepared: Aged analysis of open patient accounts. Adjustments to patient account.

- To mechanize a manual system
- To create a new activity

The preparation of the feasibility study will often vary according to the reason it is undertaken. But all studies have in common the need for a precise definition of the business problem being addressed. Without this definition, management cannot evaluate whether the proposed project adequately addresses the problem. A useful technique is to contrast the current operations with the proposed operations to convey their differences. How this contrast might be portrayed is exemplified in the case of a billing system in Figure 4–3.

Solving Operational Problems

With the passage of time, operational problems often occur in even the best of systems. Such problems are typically associated with costs, volumes, speed, or errors, individually or in combination. For example, many hospitals have problems with their patient billing and accounts receivable systems. The accounts receivable balances are too high and, consequently, an unacceptably large number of receivables must be written off as uncollectible. The problem can usually be traced to several causes: billing systems that take too long to prepare bills once a patient is discharged, charge collection systems that are inaccurate, and accounts receivable systems that do not provide the necessary management reports for an effective follow-up on delinquent accounts. A proposal to solve these problems should specifically identify the problems to be addressed by the proposed changes and should describe in detail how the solutions will eliminate the problems. A proposal to solve the hospitals' problem, for example, might show how the number of days between patient discharge and preparation of the bill could be reduced by three days and how controls could be established to reduce the number of errors in charges by a specified percentage. Also, the proposal

Figure 4–4 **Examples of Operational Problems That May Warrant a Feasibility Study**

Over 25 percent return rate on mail-order catalogs.

Over 30 days wait on back orders.

Excess inventory to store. Inventory shortage on customer requests. Long lines for banking service, student registration, fast-food service, grocery lanes.

High error rate in entering customer orders.

Excessive time between requisition and receipt of raw materials.

might include sample accounts receivable reports containing information needed for follow-up of delinquent accounts. Other examples of operational problems that feasibility studies might address are shown in Figure 4–4.

Replacing Existing Technology

Existing systems have to be replaced from time to time. Systems grow old and have been changed so often that proper maintenance becomes almost impossible. For example, an inventory control system installed in the early 1960s contains the technology available at that time. If it was installed on a large IBM mainframe, the computer was probably a second-generation computer, and the language an assembly-level programming language or perhaps an early version of COBOL. Vendor support for both hardware and software is likely to have been long since withdrawn. The expertise that the IS department once had in this technology has almost certainly disappeared, although both the machine and the programs may continue to function. Machines that were technologically outdated more than 20 years ago may still be operational today. A system's functions may have been well thought out and advanced for its time, with meaningful user involvement in setting the system's requirements. In a situation such as this, the user may be satisfied with the system as it was originally designed, perhaps with minor enhancements made during the intervening years.

A feasibility study to replace the existing technology with current technology must make the change clear to the user. The study must show that the technology will be changed to bring the system up to date so that it can be more easily maintained and perhaps operate more efficiently. The user may be unaware that the technology has changed because the existing system continues to function as it always has. In this situation, the existing system should, in fact, be moved to the current technology even if the user is satisfied. The study should compare the out-of-date system with state-of-the-art systems to make sure that the user understands that technological changes or upgrades have occurred. In addition, a feasibility study to replace existing technology should point out the shortest and simplest way to move to the new technology with the least disruption of user department operations. Examples of systems that might need replacing are shown in Figure 4–5.

Figure 4–5 **Examples of Systems Where Existing Technology May Need Replacement without Change in User Function**

General ledger
Billing
Accounts receivable
Accounts payable
Payroll
Order entry
Inventory control

Mechanizing a Manual System

Feasibility studies that consider the mechanization of a manual system often involve dealing with users who have little experience with information technology. Some users may need to be educated on the technology so that they can contribute to the study. And personnel at all levels may need their fears about the effect of a change put to rest (see some of the techniques discussed in Chapter 2). For this type of feasibility study, acquiring a good understanding of the current system is more important than in the two previous types. Because management will be asked to decide whether to approve the mechanized system or to stay with the present manual system, a comparison of the alternative modes of operation is the basis for the decision. In the two previous types of studies, the existing system is likely to be already understood, because it is already mechanized. Where the present system is a manual system, system characteristics are often not well documented. They must be analyzed by the team performing the feasibility study. At this time, the team needs to gather only those details necessary to compare the present system with alternative proposed systems for management's understanding. Because one of management's options is to decide to stay with the present system, knowledge of the present system is required for an informed decision.

With the status of technology today, most large companies have long since mechanized their routine transaction processing systems such as payroll, order entry, billing, and accounts receivable. As illustrated in Figure 4–5, it is just such systems that are the most likely candidates for replacement with current technologies. As computer processing capability has dropped in price, the technology is now practical for very small companies. Physicians' offices now have mechanized patient records, attorneys have systems for time accounting and client billing, and small retailers or distributors have inventory control systems.

Other manual applications being mechanized for the first time are systems to support high levels of management, often in very personal ways and on a one-on-one basis. Examples of such systems are an expert system that aids physicians in forming diagnoses, a decision support system that helps

Figure 4–6 Examples of Systems for High-Level Users That May Require a Feasibility Study

Debt restructuring
Financial planning
Cash flow management
Pricing strategy analysis
Group decision support
Revenue optimization

an associate dean schedule classes, and an executive information system that is tailored to the specific needs of top management and often contains both internal and external information. Additional examples of systems for high-level users are illustrated in Figure 4–6.

Creating a New Activity

New activities are created when a business is just beginning or when an activity is added to an existing organization. Feasibility studies analyzing a proposed new activity typically require more creativity by the project team than most of the previous examples because no present system exists that can be used as a basis for developing the proposed system. Creative solutions are also important in the other situations; however, creative solutions are even more important when a new activity must be planned, because they can help an organization meet its goals. As a result, the organization is more likely to accept the solution. In addition, a creative solution will take longer to become obsolete. Thus, the organization will get a better return on its investment in the system's development.

There are many examples of creative new systems that have brought organizations a competitive advantage. One example of such a system is the Care Monitoring System developed at Providence Hospital in Southfield, Michigan, over ten years ago.[1] At that time, hospitals were not overly concerned about cost control because they were being reimbursed on what was, in effect, a cost-plus basis. Providence Hospital officials, however, were able to foresee the time when reimbursement policies would be changed to put more pressure on hospitals to control costs. The officials also realized that the people most responsible for cost control were the physicians, not the heads of hospital departments such as nursing, laboratory, and radiology. Physicians admitted patients, ordered tests and procedures, performed operations, ordered medications, and decided on the times for discharging patients. Yet, even though physicians were becoming aware of the rising public concern over increases in health care costs, they were receiving no feedback on the cost consequences of their actions. The Care Monitoring System changed that

Figure 4–7 **Examples of Systems Created to Support New Activities**

Hotel Reservations   Using a system developed by Eloquent Systems Corporation of Manchester, New Hampshire, the Balsams Grand Resort Hotel at Dixville, New Hampshire, has added new functions to its hotel reservation systems. When a guest calls for a reservation, the system will match available rooms with guest preferences. Much of this is done automatically by the system, which has information on up to a million customers stored on optical disk. Other systems capabilities include (1) a faster reservation process, (2) special arrangements for guest activities, (3) automatic generation of confirmation, correspondence, and management reports, (4) reduction of occupancy gaps, and (5) easy modification of rates, hotel policies, and guidelines.

Flight Scheduling   United Airlines and Texas Instruments have developed the Gate Assignment Display System (GADS), a knowledge-based system to handle irregularities in the flight scheduling process. Gate scheduling may become a quagmire when the weather or other operational problems require schedule adjustments affecting hundreds of aircraft using a limited number of gates. GADS facilitates and optimizes United's scheduling process for Chicago O'Hare and Denver Stapleton airports. GADS is also used to aid in scheduling aircraft maintenance, enabling the airline to effectively reduce the aircraft downtime for maintenance, thereby allowing more aircraft to be scheduled for revenue-producing flights.

by gathering cost information and presenting it to physicians in a series of reports that gave them the information they needed to seek out ways to reduce costs without compromising the quality of care delivered to patients. A technique adapted from manufacturing was used to determine costs according to a particular patient diagnosis. Historical information on the costs of treating patients with specific diagnoses proved to be very useful, especially after the federal government changed the method for reimbursing hospitals for Medicare and Medicaid patients. Hospitals without similar systems (the majority by far) had to find a way to generate similar information. Otherwise, they would be handicapped by the lack of it. Additional examples of systems created to support new activities are shown in Figure 4–7.

Project teams conducting feasibility studies for creating a new activity often benefit from visiting other organizations that have recently added a similar activity. In other words, the team learns from the experiences of early users. For example, Providence Hospital found itself entertaining visitors from hospitals around the United States. The visitors had heard of Providence's system and were interested in seeing it firsthand and talking to the physicians, administrators, and IS professionals involved in its development. Project teams can also benefit from industry symposia, consultants, software vendors, equipment manufacturers, and literature searches that can uncover examples of state-of-the-art systems.

COST/BENEFIT ANALYSIS

The purpose of the cost/benefit analysis in a feasibility study is to summarize the relevant costs and benefits of the proposed project in sufficient detail to permit management to decide whether to proceed any further with the project.

In the feasibility study, many of the estimates are probable ranges of costs and benefits. Management should not expect precise estimates at this stage because there is still much that is not yet known about the costs of installing and operating a proposed system. Each additional phase of the development allows a more accurate cost/benefit analysis as more detail is gathered. Estimating has been likened to "trying to guess what the core of an onion will look like as you peel off its outside layers."[5]

The general format of a cost/benefit analysis is illustrated in Figure 4–8. The following information is needed before the analysis can be prepared:

- An estimate of the cost of operating the current system.

- An estimate of the cost of operating the proposed system.

- An estimate of costs for subsequent phases of the development project.

- A description of intangible benefits.

- A basis for estimating how the above costs and benefits will change over the next few years (e.g., assumptions regarding volume increases, inflation).

- An identification of the risks associated with either doing or not doing the project.

Different organizational units should assume primary responsibility for the various components of the cost/benefit analysis under the overall coordination of the project team.

Economic analyses prepared at the completion of the design phase are much more comprehensive than this analysis though the format is essentially the same (see Chapter 19). The following characteristics apply to feasibility study cost/benefit analyses:

- State the cost/benefit analysis conservatively.

    In subsequent stages of the systems development life cycle, experience has shown that costs of installing and operating a new system tend to exceed estimates made in feasibility studies while realized benefits tend to be less than what was estimated. The project team should present ranges of probable costs and benefits; however, if an error is made, it should err on the side of conservatism. An effective technique is to assign the user responsibility for estimating savings and benefits from installation of the new system and be sure this responsibility is noted in the feasibility study document. When users are made aware that they will subsequently be held accountable for achieving savings or benefits, they will tend towards conservative estimates. The IS department should be responsible for estimating the cost of developing the system and of the information technology to be used when the system is in operation.

Figure 4–8 **Typical Cost/Benefit Analysis Worksheet**

```
PERSONNEL                     PROJECT MANAGEMENT TOOL                    CD-20
SKILLS SYSTEM                      SUBURBAN PUMPS                        CBSUM
                                 COST/BENEFIT SUMMARY

PREPARED BY: RON TURNER        DATE: 27NOV88          VERSION: 1         PAGE 1
APPROVED BY: JOE DAVIS         DATE: 05DEC88          STATUS:  F


                                                                  Amount
                                                                  ------

        1. One-time Change Costs
        -----------------------------------------------------------


                      Personnel expense -

                          50 workdays analyst               6,000
                          100 workdays programmer            8,000
                          30 workdays clerical                 960

                      Machine hours cost -
                          20 CPU hours                      12,250
                      Equipment and supplies -
                          Paper and office supplies            100
                          25 reels magnetic tape               625
                                                          ----------
                                      Subtotal              27,935
                                                          ----------
        2. Recurring Costs and Savings
        -----------------------------------------------------------


                      Clerical savings - Annual -
                          25 workdays/month                (9,600)
                          Supplies                           (100)


        3. Intangible Costs and Benefits
        -----------------------------------------------------------


                      Information available earlier (not
                          quantified)                          (0)

                                                          ----------
                                      Subtotal             (9,700)
                                                          ----------
        4. Payback Period
        -----------------------------------------------------------

                  27,935/9,700 = less than 3 years
```

One risk of trying to be conservative in a cost/benefit analysis is that users and IS departments may be so overconservative that nothing gets done. The executive steering committee must make sure this does not occur. Periodic reviews by qualified outsiders, for example, will give the steering committee assurance that internal estimates are in line.

- Make assumptions for financial projections.

Feasibility study cost/benefit analyses require that certain assumptions be made about the behavior of future costs and/or activities. Assumptions can be made about inflation, interest rates, growth projections, volume increases, wage increases, and the like. In most organizations, similar assumptions are made as a routine matter in medium- and long-range financial plans. The project team's best strategy is to use the same assumptions in its cost/benefit analysis as are used in an organization's financial plans. Thus, assumptions in the cost/benefit analysis will be consistent with the other financial projections that members of the executive steering committee review when they carry out their other responsibilities.

- Assess the elements of project risk.

Some proposed projects are inherently more risky than others. Risky projects are likely to exceed their estimated costs of installation and operation; they may take much longer to install than predicted; the technology suggested may not be appropriate or work effectively; users may not accept the system once it has been installed; and business operations may be disrupted. Such a list could go on and on, and unfortunately, many real-life examples could be furnished for each item on the list. Often, IS professionals in particular are aware that a proposed project carries a higher-than-normal degree of risk, but they have not found a way to convey that awareness to the executive steering committee at the feasibility study stage.

F. Warren McFarlan developed a framework for assessing project risk that consists of three components:

1. The familiarity of the company with the technology proposed for the project.

2. The project "structure," i.e., the extent to which user requirements are known at the outset.

3. The size of the project relative to those normally undertaken.[6]

Figure 4–9 illustrates the way these three factors can interrelate to create an overall project risk profile. McFarlan also discusses techniques for managing projects with differing risk profiles. Project risk is an important concept to consider in the feasibility study not only because it can be an important element in evaluating whether to proceed, but also because it puts the executive steering committee on notice that this particular project will require close scrutiny as it goes forward.

Figure 4–9 **Project Implementation Risk**

		High Structure	**Low Structure**
Low Company-Relative Technology	**Large Project**	Low Risk	Low Risk (very susceptible to mismanagement)
	Small Project	Very Low Risk	Very Low Risk (very susceptible to mismanagement)
High Company-Relative Technology	**Large Project**	Medium Risk	Very High Risk
	Small Project	Medium to Low Risk	High Risk

Source: McFarlan, F. Warren. "Portfolio Approach to Information Systems." *Harvard Business Review* (September-October 1981): 142–150.

The concept of project risk also applies to a group of projects. As pointed out by McFarlan, a group of systems development projects can be examined for the collective risk when all the projects are considered at one time.

Different companies will respond differently to risk. For example, companies in the strategic or turnaround quadrants of the strategic grid would be expected to assume a greater degree of risk than companies in the factory or support quadrants. If a company places itself in the strategic quadrant and yet has a low risk profile, the executive steering committee would do well to inquire why. The inquiry may be just the catalyst needed to convince the company that it is time to undertake a systematic approach to systems planning, the subject of the next two chapters.

Summary

A feasibility study, a quick assessment of a proposed system, is performed as one of the first steps in the systems development life cycle, particularly for an organization that does not use a systematic approach to systems planning. The study's purpose is to determine whether a project should be pursued or rejected.

A feasibility study is normally performed by a project team consisting of users and IS professionals. The team's findings are put into a report that is presented to an executive steering committee or its equivalent so that a decision can be made.

Five types of feasibility should be evaluated: technical, operational, economic, schedule, and motivational.

The focus of a feasibility study can vary depending on the reason the study is performed. Feasibility studies are most frequently done for the following four reasons:

- To solve operational problems
- To replace existing technology
- To mechanize a manual system
- To create a new activity

The cost/benefit analysis section of a feasibility study should contain a conservative treatment of costs and benefits, should include assumptions consistent with those typically used for making projections, and should assess project risk.

Selected Readings

Biggs, Charles L., Birks, Evan G., and Atkins, William. *Managing the Systems Development Process*. Englewood Cliffs, NJ: Prentice-Hall, 1980.
Written by practicing information systems consultants, this book is a practical guide to the tasks performed in each phase of the systems development life cycle. Deliverables expected at the end of each phase are described, and many sample forms used in documenting a systems project, including a feasibility study, are illustrated.

Davis, Gordon B., and Olson, Margrethe H. *Management Information Systems: Conceptual Foundations, Structure and Development*, 2d ed. New York: McGraw-Hill, 1985.
This book is one of the most complete and influential textbooks on management information systems. It contains a concise description of feasibility studies. It correctly adds schedule and motivational feasibility to the more commonly listed factors of technical, operational, and economic feasibility.

Gildersleeve, Thomas R. *Successful Data Processing Systems Analysis*, 2d ed. Englewood Cliffs, NJ: Prentice-Hall, 1985.
This book contains a lengthy chapter on cost/benefit analysis from an investment standpoint. For example, it covers such concepts as differential costs, payback, cash flow, and net present value as applied to a feasibility study. It also discusses techniques that systems analysts can use to place a value on intangible benefits.

McFarlan, F. Warren. "Portfolio Approach to Information Systems." *Harvard Business Review* (September-October 1981): 142–150.
This article notes that traditional feasibility studies fail to consider cer-

tain risks that are usually present in computer systems projects. It discusses the consequences of risk as well as the dimensions influencing risk. It suggests that companies develop an aggregate risk profile of their systems development projects.

Review Questions

1. What factors may prompt an organization to use feasibility studies for selecting and assigning priorities to projects?

2. Describe the shortcomings of the executive steering committee approach to IS project selection.

3. Explain the five types of feasibility that should be evaluated in a feasibility study.

4. Provide examples of how the following organizational problems may lead to the initiation of a feasibility study:
   a. Recognized operational problem
   b. Need to replace an existing system
   c. Desire to mechanize a manual system
   d. Strategy to create a new activity

5. Describe the kinds of information needed to prepare a cost/benefit analysis. Who is responsible for providing the information?

6. Why should the cost/benefit analysis be stated conservatively?

7. Explain McFarlan's framework for assessing project risk.

Discussion Questions

1. Do feasibility studies necessarily have to include a cost/benefit analysis in those cases where management is certain it will proceed with a project?

2. Consider the five types of feasibility (technical, operational, economic, schedule, and motivational) in relation to the following proposed projects:
   a. Expert system to make hotel reservations
   b. Replacement order entry system that would require operators to telephone prospective customers and read a tailored sales message directly from a CRT screen
   c. Personal income tax software package that will be available on March 1
   d. Quality control system to be used to reduce the number of defective gaskets on newly manufactured engines

Mini-Cases

St. Clair Shores Community Theater. St. Clair Shores Community Theater depends on private contributions for a substantial portion of its operating funds. Two direct mail campaigns are conducted each year. A data base of contributors is maintained on a large computer located at the offices of a computer service bureau company, Stan Burns Associates. Stan is a resident of St. Clair Shores and an enthusiastic supporter of the Community Theater. His fees for consultation in designing the computer data base, masterminding the direct mail campaigns, and performing all associated computer processing total $70,000 per year. Stan bills the theater for this amount, but then donates $10,000 of it back, making him the largest individual contributor.

The contributor data base was placed on the computer two years ago. Information on contributors was obtained from paper-based records that had been maintained in the theater office for the seven prior years. The paper-based records had been updated by various members of the "Friends of the Theater" who worked in the office as part-time volunteers. There are about 12,000 donor records on the computer at the present time.

Since converting to the computer, the contributor data base has been updated by Stan Burns Associates from information obtained from persons who ordered tickets over the phone or by mail. One of the problems that Susan Bolt, the theater manager, is having is that the theater office staff is not able to obtain all of the information they would like to obtain from ticket purchasers. In addition, donors are often irritated when asked to supply information because they expect box office personnel to recognize their names as supporters of the theater of several years' standing.

Susan has a few other problems with the way the system is working. In the first place, the direct mail efforts are raising only $65,000. Stan says that this is a start-up problem and that any direct mail campaign needs five years to mature. On the other hand, the MIS director for the city has offered to run the theater's system on the city's computer. Susan feels she could probably save some money this way, but she values Stan's consultative services and also worries about the city's ability to perform.

Susan is also concerned about the accuracy of data in the computer system. She is constantly getting complaints about misspelled names and duplicate mailings. She also feels that theater staff does not know enough about major contributors (current, past, and potential) and would like to have specific information readily available on people who contribute more than $500 per year so they can receive special attention. Finally, she would feel a whole lot better if she had a computer of her own, at least for the 400 major contributors, because she really does not think that either Stan Burns or the city are capable of giving her the high-quality information system she needs. She has heard a lot about microcomputers lately and is wondering whether she should consider getting one for the theater office.

Question for Discussion

1. Assume that Susan has asked you to help her find and select the best option for handling the information systems needs of the theater. How would you proceed?

Dunlop State University. Dunlop State University is considering a new system that would computerize all student transcripts. Presently, all transcripts are filed, updated, and copied manually. In the proposed system, current transcripts would be updated at the end of each semester. Corrections, inquiries, and printing would be handled on-line.

Advocates predict a significantly lower error rate for updating and correcting procedures. They also believe goodwill with students and alumni will increase. With proper identification and fee payment, a student or alumnus would be able to have a transcript immediately, as opposed to the five-day delay with the present system.

The university's executive steering committee will meet in one month to consider the feasibility study for the transcript project along with other prospective projects. You are on the project team and are responsible for drafting the feasibility study for the transcript project.

Questions for Discussion

1. How would you classify the reason for initiating this feasibility study? What approach would you use for conducting the study?

2. Consider each type of feasibility for the proposed transcript system.

3. What specific kinds of information would be included in the cost/benefit analysis? Who would supply this information?

Notes

1. Gildersleeve, Thomas R. *Successful Data Processing Systems Analysis*, 2d ed. Englewood Cliffs, NJ: Prentice-Hall, 1985.

2. Martin, James. *An Information Systems Manifesto.* Englewood Cliffs, NJ: Prentice-Hall, 1984.

3. Davis, Gordon B., and Olson, Margrethe H. *Management Information Systems: Conceptual Foundations, Structure and Development*, 2d ed. New York: McGraw-Hill, 1985.

4. Rinaldo, J. A. Jr., McCubbrey, D. J., and Shryock, J. R. "The Care Monitoring, Cost Forecasting and Cost Monitoring System." *Journal of Clinical Computing,* IX, no. 3, 1981.

5. Biggs, Charles L., Birks, Evans G., and Atkins, William. *Managing the Systems Development Process.* Englewood Cliffs, NJ: Prentice-Hall, 1980.

6. McFarlan, F. Warren. "Portfolio Approach to Information Systems." *Harvard Business Review* (September-October 1981): 142–150.

5

Establishing the Systems Plan

After describing the benefits of a formal systems plan and the most frequent approaches to systems planning, this chapter explains the relationship between the strategic business plan of an organization and its systems plan. Then, the development of a systems plan is described: identifying application selection criteria, understanding how the business operates, analyzing data requirements, and identifying and evaluating systems projects. The chapter concludes with some advice on how to organize a systems planning project.

Learning Objectives

- Describe the benefits of preparing a formal systems plan.
- Identify four approaches to systems planning.
- Understand the relationship between a strategic business plan and a systems plan.
- Be aware of the steps required to identify and assign priorities to the applications of an entire organization or a strategic business unit.
- Describe the three dimensions of analysis of systems requirements: information needs, processing requirements, and data structure.
- Recognize how a systems planning effort can be organized to maximize its impact on management and to ensure that its results actually are used.
- Understand the level of documentation typically produced in a systems plan.

BENEFITS OF SYSTEMS PLANNING

A formal systems plan has three benefits. First, a systems plan that covers multiple applications within an organization has technical merit. The plan enables applications to share data, thereby minimizing redundant acquisition and storage, reducing systems development and operations costs, and lowering the costs associated with inconsistent versions of the same data stored in different places. Second, the systems plan serves to promote harmony between the corporate strategy set by top management and the tactical and operational plans of both users and the IS department. Finally, the systems plan helps reduce costs.

Shared Data

Most of the data maintained by a company's information systems are of interest to multiple departments. Experience has shown that data sharing across organizational boundaries does not come naturally. The requirement to share must be explicitly recognized and addressed in the systems development effort. If this requirement is not explicit, each application will tend to be limited to a single department. The data of the application could then be duplicated in other departments' systems; the result will be higher costs.

Shared Strategy

Another merit of a formal systems plan is that it will help middle management understand the organization's objectives, and it will minimize the effect of the interdepartmental rivalries that usually exist. It will show how top management views the contribution to overall goals made by each user department and by the IS department. Thus, the plan can increase users' understanding and acceptance of the sequence assigned to applications development.

The systems plan can also help explain corporate policies on hardware, software, and systems procurement. User management can understand why there must be limits to departmental autonomy in hardware selection and in end-user development.

IS departments have in the past come under heavy fire for being technocratic, unresponsive to the real needs of users, and out of touch with reality. By establishing a systems plan, an IS department can demonstrate that it understands top management's strategies as thoroughly as do the users.

Cost Reduction

Finally, the systems plan is a valuable cost-containment tool because organizations can plan ahead for the resources required, in particular the development resources. An IS department can use a systems plan to avoid hiring people to meet a peak in demand, who will later go idle or underutilized because of a slowdown in development. The next chapter treats resource planning in depth.

Despite all of these benefits, many organizations do not put together a formal systems plan. Some organizations have not yet reached the stage where the plan is necessary; others believe that the strategy is so well understood that there is no need for a formal document. The following types of organizations—those that would fit in the support quadrant of the strategic grid (see Chapter 1)—might not need a systems plan:

- Small organizations, where information can be obtained and communicated informally.

- Organizations where the bulk of mechanization so far has concentrated on automating labor-intensive applications.

- Organizations where end users are only superficially involved in computing.

For other organizations, a coherent strategy is required. Often, a strategy does exist; however, it did not result from a formal study and it has not been documented in a single report. Rather, the strategy resulted from a consensus of a tightly knit management team, of which the IS department head is a part. If enough mutual trust exists among the IS department, top management, and user departments, most of the objectives of systems planning can be met without a formal document. This hinges on mutual trust and on a certain permanence of the management team. The lack of a formal plan is probably reasonable only in a medium-sized company; and even in such a company, not preparing a formal plan has its risks. Many assumptions could go unchallenged, and many important issues could remain hidden. There is also a technical risk: the data architecture might not be the best and could ultimately cause higher maintenance costs than necessary.

Although the absence of a systems plan increases the risks, an organization may successfully implement systems without one. On the other hand, a systems plan is no panacea. In many cases, systems plans have been created only to remain on paper. The value of a systems plan is in its implementation. The systems identified in the plan, and the data and network architecture that it describes, must serve as the focus for all applications development. This is not to say that the plan must be followed slavishly. New requirements may crop up through technological innovation, competitive pressure, or regulatory changes. The systems plan must not be so rigid as to forbid the creation of applications that are not in the plan.

FOUR APPROACHES TO SYSTEMS PLANNING

Systems planning can be approached in a variety of ways depending on the needs of the organization, the state of its current information systems, the sponsor of the planning effort, and the strategic nature of information technology for the business. These approaches can be divided into four groups:

- Application portfolio planning
- Enterprise modeling
- Technology infrastructure planning
- Linking business and technology strategies

Application Portfolio Planning

Application portfolio planning is the most traditional approach to systems planning. It consists of reviewing the current state of the information systems in the organization to locate the greatest needs and opportunities. Each opportunity is analyzed for costs and benefits and the resulting projects are ranked by some priority scheme such as the greatest return on investment or the greatest cost savings. The result is a plan laying out the sequence of projects to be undertaken over the next three to five years and the resources required to implement these projects.

Application portfolio planning was appropriate in the 1960s and 1970s, when many applications were being mechanized for the first time. The scarce resource was qualified systems development personnel; most development projects paid for themselves in less than two years, mainly through personnel cost savings. Each application was typically developed for a single department; little thought was given to the integration of projects across applications.

Enterprise Modeling

Enterprise modeling arose in the late 1970s and early 1980s from the perceived need to integrate data across applications. Enterprise modeling consists of analyzing the current business processes and the data they use to identify shared data structures. A new set of systems is proposed, clustering around groups of shared data. For instance, all customer-oriented systems such as order entry, billing, accounts receivable, and service contract management are grouped around the central customer data base.

The advantage of enterprise modeling over application portfolio planning is that integration between systems increases; it becomes easy to relate data about the same entities from different applications. Another advantage is that data structures are generally considered more stable than business functions; thus, the architecture of the applications identified in the enterprise model should last longer than if no enterprise model is built.

There are two disadvantages to enterprise modeling. First, the planning process usually takes longer than application portfolio planning. This is especially true if the project team is inexperienced; it then tends to fall into the trap of analyzing too deeply, of not knowing when to stop. Second, the logical sequence of projects emerging from an enterprise model is to attack infrastructure projects first. It is difficult to create a series of integrated applications unless there already is the application that creates and feeds the data base which the applications are to share. However, it is usually very difficult to show economic benefits for a data base maintenance application. A systems plan based on enterprise modeling may therefore not show adequate return on investment to sustain top management's interest, especially if the economy took a downturn during the execution of the plan.

Nevertheless, enterprise modeling is today the most popular form of systems planning, and it is the approach that is described in this chapter. The chapter uses IBM's Business Systems Planning (BSP) as its central example. Other popular methodologies are the different varieties of Information Engineering popularized by James Martin and Clive Finkelstein in the 1980s. All these approaches vary more in vocabulary and emphasis than in substance. Many of the activities of enterprise modeling also apply to application portfolio planning.

Technology Infrastructure Planning

Technology infrastructure planning concentrates on the resources required to implement and run applications rather than on the applications themselves, as do application portfolio planning and enterprise modeling.   The resources to be planned for include:

- IS personnel for development, maintenance, and operations
- Computer hardware and systems software
- Development tools—workstations and CASE software
- Telecommunications networks hardware and software

Technology infrastructure planning became critical when incompatible hardware and software platforms started to proliferate in the late 1970s and early 1980s. Regardless of how application development projects were identified, by application portfolio planning, enterprise modeling, or just natural growth of the backlog of requested work, standardization and rationalization was (and still is) required.

Infrastructure planning is the subject of the next chapter.

Linking Business and Technology Strategies

When Michael Porter started publishing his works on competitive advantage, a new motivator for application development was added. In many cases, information technology was the factor that enabled a change in the competitive landscape. Thus, opportunities arose for information technology to fuel new business strategies, rather than simply support the management information system that controlled the execution of a business strategy which was indifferent to technology.

John Henderson and N. Venkatraman have studied the linkage of business and technology strategies and concluded that the enterprise needs to position itself in the information technology marketplace (as a customer rather than as a supplier).[1] This position includes adopting selected marketplace standards (for instance, UNIX or a proprietary *de facto* standard such as IBM's MVS), making strategic alliances with certain vendors, or even retreating from the market altogether by outsourcing the entire IS department as Kodak did recently when entrusting its IS operations to IBM.

UNDERSTANDING THE STRATEGIC BUSINESS PLAN

Regardless of the approach adopted, the first requirement for a systems planning project is to understand the value system, the culture, and the strategies of the organization for which the systems plan is being developed. How easy this understanding is depends very much on how explicitly top management has stated its strategy. In those comparatively rare instances where a strategic business plan has been established, understanding is no problem. In fact, for companies in the strategic or turnaround quadrants as defined by Cash, McFarlan, and McKenney, the existence of a strategic business plan usually implies the existence of a systems plan; the two are almost inseparable.

Most organizations, however, have no formal business strategy. In this case, two solutions are possible: the systems planning effort can be suspended

Figure 5–1 **Schematic Representation of the BSP Methology**

Source: *Business Systems Planning: Information Systems Planning Guide*, IBM Manual No. GE20-0527.

until a strategic business plan has been developed, or the systems planning team can attempt to articulate enough guiding principles within the systems plan itself to ensure that top management and the IS department are in step.

Most systems planning methodologies in use today realistically take this approach, as strategic business planning is not yet in general use. Among the first to realize the importance of tying the systems plan to the business strategy was IBM's Business Systems Planning (BSP) methodology, created in 1970 (see Figure 5–1). The first step in a BSP study is to determine the business objectives and environment. The study team determines these by interviewing top executives to determine the corporation's view on such topics as the following:

- Industry trends
- Business strategies
- Critical success factors
- Current problem areas
- Forecast of where the organization is going over the next few years

A number of business planning tools have emerged in recent years. Some examples were covered in Chapter 1. Others include the use of critical success factors described by John F. Rockart[2] and the six stages of growth in data processing described by Richard L. Nolan.[3] Which of these tools is the best depends on the circumstances. The project team should pick the tool that is most likely to strike some responsive chord in top management, thereby contributing to both management commitment and insight. In fact, it may well be appropriate to combine several of these tools to obtain the best result.

In addition to these tools, which are business rather than system related, many systems planners include the analysis of information needs. Information needs are the needs addressed by the most critical output of the enterprise-wide information system. Each information need can be tied to a critical success factor which it helps satisfy. A matrix of typical information needs in the discrete manufacturing industry is depicted in Figure 5–2.

IDENTIFYING CRITERIA FOR EVALUATING APPLICATION DEVELOPMENT PROJECTS

The next step of the systems planning project is to identify a specific set of measurable criteria by which the merit of proposed application development projects can be judged. It is not enough to enumerate benefit-oriented criteria, as shown in Figure 5–3. It is also necessary to consider the risk factors: uncertainty about how much the project will cost, whether it will actually achieve the benefits, and whether it might turn out to counteract some other project (lack of synergy). The main risk factors are summarized in Figure 5–4.

Most of the criteria will naturally fall out from the study of the strategic business plan. Others may come from well-documented corporate policies, for example, the required return on investment that any project must achieve to be approved. Yet other criteria, such as the willingness of the corporation to take technological risks, are less likely to be explicitly stated on paper and can only be ascertained by someone who understands the corporate culture.

These factors may be tied together in a rating system that defines measures and assigns weights to the factors, so that each project will have a numerical score. In most cases, however, the additional precision gained with this method is not required (and it is somewhat illusory because the measuring systems and the weights are assigned in a fairly arbitrary manner). Projects will naturally tend to fall into three or four categories, as shown in Figure 5–5. Once the criteria have been tentatively identified, they should be presented to all the interested parties to obtain consensus on the criteria and the weights attached to them. The acceptance of these criteria by the entire management team, top executives, and middle management alike is a powerful way to ensure consensus about which projects get the most attention during the implementation of the systems plan. It also provides an excellent tool for updating the systems plan when unanticipated needs arise that require priorities to be reassigned. Obtaining acceptance of the project evaluation criteria, although not specifically described in the BSP methodology, is nevertheless a required step.

UNDERSTANDING THE OPERATION OF THE BUSINESS

Most enterprise modeling methodologies follow BSP in advocating the identification of business processes and decision-making activities executed by middle management. Each process must be defined and analyzed to determine which part of the organization has responsibility for it. A matrix such as the one represented in Figure 5–6 documents the results of this kind of analysis.

An important framework for the analysis is the classical pyramid of strategic, tactical, and operational activities (see Figure 5–7). Transaction processing appears at the operational level. Transaction processing concerns capturing information about the selling or purchasing of products or services. At the tactical level are management information systems (accounting

Figure 5–2 **Sample Information Needs Matrix**

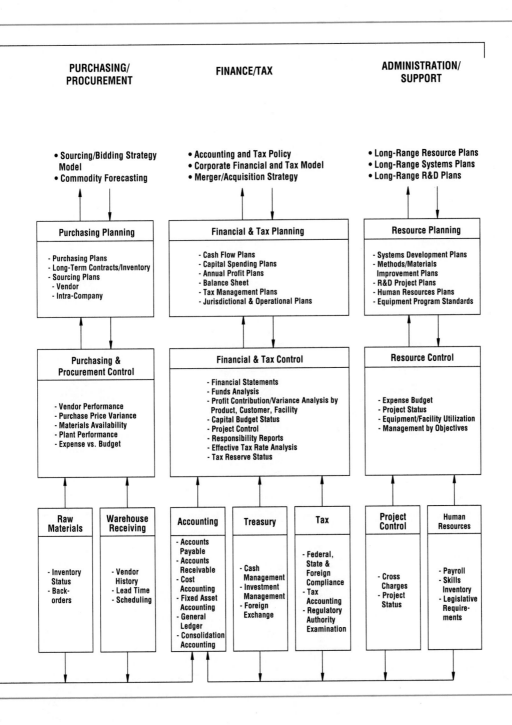

PURCHASING/ PROCUREMENT

- Sourcing/Bidding Strategy Model
- Commodity Forecasting

Purchasing Planning

- Purchasing Plans
- Long-Term Contracts/Inventory
- Sourcing Plans
  - Vendor
  - Intra-Company

Purchasing & Procurement Control

- Vendor Performance
- Purchase Price Variance
- Materials Availability
- Plant Performance
- Expense vs. Budget

Raw Materials

- Inventory Status
- Back-orders

Warehouse Receiving

- Vendor History
- Lead Time
- Scheduling

FINANCE/TAX

- Accounting and Tax Policy
- Corporate Financial and Tax Model
- Merger/Acquisition Strategy

Financial & Tax Planning

- Cash Flow Plans
- Capital Spending Plans
- Annual Profit Plans
- Balance Sheet
- Tax Management Plans
- Jurisdictional & Operational Plans

Financial & Tax Control

- Financial Statements
- Funds Analysis
- Profit Contribution/Variance Analysis by Product, Customer, Facility
- Capital Budget Status
- Project Control
- Responsibility Reports
- Effective Tax Rate Analysis
- Tax Reserve Status

Accounting

- Accounts Payable
- Accounts Receivable
- Cost Accounting
- Fixed Asset Accounting
- General Ledger
- Consolidation Accounting

Treasury

- Cash Management
- Investment Management
- Foreign Exchange

Tax

- Federal, State & Foreign Compliance
- Tax Accounting
- Regulatory Authority Examination

ADMINISTRATION/ SUPPORT

- Long-Range Resource Plans
- Long-Range Systems Plans
- Long-Range R&D Plans

Resource Planning

- Systems Development Plans
- Methods/Materials Improvement Plans
- R&D Project Plans
- Human Resources Plans
- Equipment Program Standards

Resource Control

- Expense Budget
- Project Status
- Equipment/Facility Utilization
- Management by Objectives

Project Control

- Cross Charges
- Project Status

Human Resources

- Payroll
- Skills Inventory
- Legislative Requirements

Figure 5–3 **Benefits-Related Criteria for Evaluating Systems Projects**

```
SYSTEMS                         PLANNING TOOL                    CD-20
PLAN                            SUBURBAN PUMPS                    BCRIT
                           BENEFITS-RELATED CRITERIA


PREPARED BY:  J. WEBER          DATE: 06AUG88      VERSION: 1.1   PAGE 1
APPROVED BY:  JACK CROFT        DATE: 15AUG88      STATUS:  D


I.   Increase Profits/Avoid or Reduce Costs

     A. To satisfy this criterion, a prospective systems development project must
        result in a measurable increase in earnings brought on by:

        1. An increase in product sales
        2. A cost reduction
        3. A favorable change in asset levels

        A prospective project satisfies this criterion to the extent that the source
        of earnings can be identified and the magnitude and timing of the earnings can
        be quantified.

        Where a prospective project's primary benefit criterion is increased profits,
        cost avoidance or reduced costs, it must also meet the normal financial
        justification screens imposed on all other investments (A&FM Policy #19,
        sections IV, V and VI).

II.  Improve Information Available for Decision Making

     A. To satisfy this criterion, a prospective systems development project must
        produce a management support system structured to provide immediately
        accessible information for decision making.

        A prospective project satisfies this criterion to the extent that it provides:

        1. Data collected and arrayed on a comparable basis together with pertinent
           analysis; or
        2. Sophisticated data management, communications, and processing techniques to
           meet an immediate "need to know"; or
        3. Environmental and/or competitive information in a form useful for decision
           making.

III. Support Strategic/Tactical/Operational Objectives

     A. To satisfy this criterion, a prospective systems development project must
        directly support business objectives of a Corporate function or Division
        business organization.
```

Figure 5–4 **Risk-Related Criteria for Evaluating Systems Projects**

```
SYSTEMS                      PLANNING TOOL                       CD-20
PLAN                         SUBURBAN PUMPS                      RCRIT
                          RISK-RELATED CRITERIA


PREPARED BY:  J. WEBER        DATE: 06AUG88        VERSION: 1.1     PAGE 1
APPROVED BY:  JACK CROFT      DATE: 15AUG88        STATUS:  D




A.   Factors

     1. Implementation Risk

        a. Level of internal experience
        b. Degree of design complexity
        c. Degree of technical complexity
        d. Magnitude of effort required for implementation
        e. Time constraints for implementation
        f. Degree of management support

     2. Benefits Risk

        a. Possibility that anticipated benefits will not be achieved
        b. Ease of measurement of benefits actually attained
        c. Quality of estimating assumptions

     3. Synergistic Risk

        a. Interrelationship within the portfolio of proposed systems development
           projects
        b. Interface within the organization of different projects in development


B.   Definition of Process

     1. Systems projects differ in their difficulty of implementation.

     2. This perceived difficulty puts the achievement of benefits at risk.

     3. A measure of this perceived difficulty of implementation may be expressed in
        degrees of risk that can significantly affect achieving benefits.
```

Figure 5–5 **Groups into Which Systems Projects Tend to Fall**

Benefits	Risk	Priority	Comment
Quick	Low	1–2	Need at least one such project
High	High	1	Mainstay of strategic systems plan
Slow	Low	2	Second tier
Low	Low	3	Should be considered for elimination
Medium	High	3	Should be considered for elimination

and responsibility reporting, for example), which use data from operational systems to keep management informed about how well the organization is operating. Also, tactical planning applications such as budgeting and forecasting, which communicate objectives and plans to the operational level, are included at the tactical level. The strategic level typically contains executive support systems. In many cases, these systems rely more on external data sources than on summarized data from the enterprise itself. Top management is usually more interested in analyzing the possible impact of outside events—changes in regulations, in the economic climate, and in specific competitors, suppliers, and customers—than in the daily running of the business, which has been delegated to middle management.

Let us consider how a representative methodology, BSP, advocates understanding and documenting how the business operates. BSP prescribes the following six steps.

Identify Products (or Services) and Supporting Resources

For each basic group of products or resources (in many cases there is only one), the project identifies how the product is planned for, how it is developed and manufactured (or otherwise created), how it is stored, and how it is disposed of (sold or scrapped). This analysis is done for:

- Products
- Services
- Materials
- Money
- Facilities and equipment
- Personnel

Identify Strategic Planning and Management Control Processes

These processes should be easily identifiable from the previous stage, which identified management's strategies and critical success factors. The strategic planning process concerns the corporation as a whole and usually has a horizon of several years. The management control processes can often be deter-

Figure 5–6 **Sample Organization/Function Matrix**

```
SYSTEMS                      PLANNING TOOL                           CD-20
PLAN                         SUBURBAN PUMPS                          ORGFN
                   ORGANIZATION/FUNCTION MATRIX

PREPARED BY: J. WEBER        DATE: 27AUG88        VERSION: 1.1      PAGE 1
APPROVED BY: JACK CROFT      DATE: 05SEP88        STATUS:  D
```

BUSINESS FUNCTION	SENIOR MANAGEMENT						MARKETING			FINANCIAL				MANUFACTURING				SUPPORT		
ORGANIZATION	Managing Director	VP Manufacturing	VP Marketing	VP International	VP Financial	VP I/S	Sales Manager	Advertising Manager	Market Research Mgr	Corporate Planner	Controller	Budgeting Director	Internal Audit Dir	Operations	Materials	Equipment Control	Quality Control	Information Sces	Personnel	Office Support
Strategic Planning	1	1	1	1	1	1														
Financial Planning	2	2	2	2	1	2				1	2	1	3							
Information Systems Planning	2	2	2	2	2	1				3								1		
Research & Development	1																			
Payroll											2								1	
Employee Relations																			1	
Employee Benefits																			1	
Government Relations																			1	
Employee Development																			1	
Recruiting																			1	
Operations	2													1						
Process Engineering														1		3				
Equipment Control																1				
Quality Control																3	1			
Purchasing															1					
Materials Requirements Planning														1	1					
Inventory Control															1					
Distribution							3							1						
Market Intelligence			2	2					1											
Sales			2	2			1													
Advertising			2	2			3	1												
Budgeting					2					3	1									
Financial Reporting					2						1	1								
Accounting					2						1	1								
Information Processing						2				3								1		
Property Management																				1
Security							3							2	1			2		

```
    (1-Major Responsibility    2-Significant Involvement    3-Some Involvement)
```

Figure 5–7 **Pyramid of Strategic, Tactical, and Operational Systems**

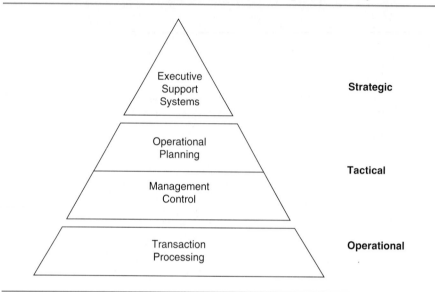

mined by reviewing a corporation's operating plan or budget system; its scope is usually a department or a product group; its horizon is one year or less.

Identify Operational Processes

Identifying operational processes consists of taking each of the products, services, and resources defined in the first step and identifying the business functions required to perform each of the four stages in its life—planning, acquiring, storing, and disposing. An example of the result of this process for a pumping equipment manufacturer is shown in Figure 5–8.

Other methodologies use different techniques. Some advocate tying the processes together by using a data flow diagram (see Section III). This approach generally takes longer than the simple identification of functions. Others use hierarchical representations such as Warnier charts or boxes such as organization charts (see Section I); the result may then be less structured than the BSP matrix. These differences are not material and are not likely to have a bearing on the quality of the systems plan.

Group/Split the Processes

Once the processes have been identified, they are grouped or split so as to be understandable to all concerned, to reduce inconsistencies in levels, or to combine processes that are similar (for instance, purchasing materials might be the same process as purchasing equipment).

Figure 5–8 **Sample Process Identification**

```
SYSTEMS                    PLANNING TOOL                              CD-20
PLAN                       SUBURBAN PUMPS                               PID
                           PROCESS IDENTIFICATION

PREPARED BY: J. WEBER      DATE: 27AUG88      VERSION: 1.1      PAGE 1
APPROVED BY: JACK CROFT    DATE: 05SEP88      STATUS:  D
```

	PRODUCT/SERVICE Pumping Equipment	SUPPORTING RESOURCES Raw Materials			
Requirements	-------Establish Business Direction-------				
	-------Comply with Legal Requirements-------		Determine Control and Financial Requirements	Determine Personnel Requirements	
	Forecast Product Requirements	---Plan Seasonal Production---			
	Analyze Marketplace		Determine Facilities and Equipment Requirements		
	Design Product				
Acquisition	Schedule and Control Production	Purchase Raw Materials	Acquire Facilities and Equipment	Manage Cash Receipts	Hire Personnel
Stewardship	Control Product Inventory	Control Raw Materials Inventory	Maintain Equipment	Determine Product Profitability	Manage Personnel
	Ship Product		Manage Facilities	Manage Accounts	
Disposition	Advertise and Promote Product	Schedule and Control Production	Dispose of Facilities and Equipment	Manage Cash Disbursements	Terminate Personnel
	Market Product				
	Enter and Control Customer Order				

**Box
5–1**

Types of Systems

The types of systems that fall into the framework of the pyramid of operational, tactical, and strategic uses of information can be analyzed somewhat more precisely. The most frequently used categories of systems are:

- Transaction processing systems
- Management information systems
- Decision support systems
- Office automation systems
- Departmental systems
- Expert systems
- Executive information systems

Transaction processing systems are the successors of the initial payroll system at General Electric. In the era of batch, these systems were designed to mechanize the work of clerical personnel such as payroll and invoicing clerks. A side effect was to create a new class of less specialized clerks for data entry (then called keypunch).

The advent of on-line systems has reversed the trend. Now, the users of transaction processing systems are increasingly qualified to make decisions or otherwise contribute to corporate goals as they operate the system. For example, order entry is increasingly done by people who have a marketing function as well, suggesting substitutes, upgrades, and promotional offerings.

The increasing integration of transaction processing systems has also brought about a trend towards so-called subject data bases. These are data bases that centralize all the data about a single entity and are shared across all the departments of an organization.

Management information systems have their roots in budgeting and cost accounting systems.

In the past, these systems produced large amounts of printed output. A typical example would be responsibility reports, made up of a series of detailed reports about budgeted amounts versus actual spending at the lowest levels of the organization's hierarchy, then rolled up into summary reports by section, department, division, and so on. The recipient of these reports would use them to find action items and as a detailed reference.

The trend here is twofold. Actual reports are less and less frequently produced on paper. Instead, they are stored in electronic form so that users can query the data on-line, choosing their own data content, sequence, and level of detail. If on-line query is impractical from a cost-effectiveness standpoint, ad hoc reports can be requested, most often overnight.

In addition, many users receive periodic extracts from the activity files of the management information system and can use these extracts for their own analysis purposes. This is described in detail under decision support systems.

Although the trend is towards integration of data, these management information systems do not necessarily use the subject data bases of the transaction processing system. Subject data bases are generally reserved for operational use. An inquiry against a subject data base is about a subject or a list of subjects satisfying a number of criteria, for example, the list of customers served by the Phoenix branch who have a particular item on order.

Subject data bases, and more generally transaction processing data bases, are not suitable for management information systems for two reasons. First, they are volatile, since they are updated as the business activity is conducted. Second, they reflect the current state of affairs

Continued

Continued

rather than the historical figures. To solve these problems, a periodical (monthly, weekly, or even daily) program reviews activity records and creates management information that is properly cut off, i.e., assigned to a definite period in time. Generally, the information is also summarized to some extent, so that the system does not need to carry full details of every single business event over the period that management may want to analyze—often several years.

This summarization poses a problem because the criteria that appear appropriate for what is retained can vary over the years. As a result, the historical and statistical data that a corporation accumulates can become useless because it does not correspond to the categories of analysis that are of current interest to management.

Decision support systems are in reality an outgrowth of management information systems. These systems are capable of providing varying analyses of the same data without programming effort. It becomes possible to search for correlations between data without rewriting part of the management information system for every new idea to be tested. Often, these systems also have graphics capabilities, making both trend analysis and reporting on the analysis to top executives much easier. Finally, modeling capabilities make it possible to explore many alternative scenarios, answering management's "what-if" questions.

When decision support tools are used on management information data (such as the data supplied by the various cut-off processes in the organization), they support tactical decisions. They can also support strategic decisions. In that case, they will usually be based on different data, as described under executive information systems.

A problem with decision support systems is that they are often PC-based and the mechanism for distributing cut-off data to a large number of PCs is usually lacking today. As a bypass, many decision support users have to rekey data off management reports onto a spreadsheet of their choice. This is obviously inefficient, error-prone, and, one hopes, temporary.

A more serious problem is that conclusions drawn by manipulating data in a decision support system are not always warranted. There are statistical traps that are known to trained statisticians but not necessarily to financial analysts. The use, or misuse, of graphics is another source of erroneous conclusions. Worst are clerical mistakes such as those that can arise when a row on a spreadsheet is set to total some of the rows above, and an additional row is inserted outside the scope of the total. The impeccable presentation that can be obtained on workstation printers and the reputation for hardware reliability can make management rely excessively on corrupted data.

Office automation systems have emerged as a vehicle for processing documents. They are neither transaction processing systems, since they do not recognize business transactions and rules that apply to them, nor management information systems in the usual sense. They may seem to have little to do with our purpose, but they are of interest in two domains.

First, the desktop metaphor of user interfaces was primarily invented as an office automation system. This metaphor, which is incorporated in Apple's Macintosh and on the IBM PS/2 under the name Presentation Manager, has been tremendously influential and will probably be the basis for standard user interface design in all types of systems in the future. (Standard does not mean invariable. Rather, the standard approach is defined as the one taken unless you can justify that some other approach meets your particular requirements better.)

Second, the distinction between transaction processing, done by clerks, and office work, done by secretaries, is beginning to fade. With the help of information technology, professionals can now do some of both. Many transac-

Continued

Continued

tion processing systems today incorporate elements of correspondence management. Examples are claims processing in the insurance industry, mortgage applications in the banking industry, and benefits systems in government and health care.

Departmental systems are often distinguished as a separate category. In truth, departmental systems are often a mix of transaction processing, decision support, and office automation, but with a scope that is reduced to a single department (most often a single location). An example today might be a lab system in a hospital, tracking requests for work and communicating results back. Similar systems might be in the X-ray department, the pharmacy, and the operating room of a large hospital. Each of these departments has requirements for processing and data storage that are distinct from other departments.

This example is intentionally defective. In fact, all the information is about patients, and it is all being produced for the same persons: physicians, nurses, and hospital administrators (billing and accounts receivable, in particular). There is already a growing demand for integration of all these partial systems.

A better example of departmental systems is when a department performs a differentiated support function which is only incidental to the main purpose of the organization, such as facilities management in a large legal firm or the hospital cafeteria. Here, departmental systems may well be justified because the need for integration will remain much lower.

Expert systems are often also mentioned as a separate category. Expert systems are usually rule-based systems that help the not-so-expert perform tasks, often of a diagnostic nature. Thus, the terminology designates both a technology and a goal for the system. The goal is to leverage knowledge that is possessed by a small number of experts, often only one. The technology is artificial intelligence (AI).

The use of AI technology implies that knowledge is not embodied in programs on the one hand and data on the other, but that both the procedural part and the data part are united in a knowledge representation scheme, most often of the Post production rule type. This consists in maintaining a set of facts in memory, for example: "The patient has a temperature of 103 degrees" and "the bacteria isolated are gram-positive." A so-called rule base, a collection of If-Then phrases, is then reviewed. For each rule whose If-part is true, the Then-part is added as an assertion in memory. For example: "If the patient has no fever, then the infection may be bacterial" is not acted on; "If the bacteria is gram-positive, then there is evidence for such and such an illness" is acted on and the evidence of the illness is added as a fact. At the end of this process, if there is enough data and the rule base is correct, a more or less tentative diagnosis is derived.

This type of system has been applied in the medical field, in the maintenance of steam locomotives, in troubleshooting oil drilling bits, in configuring computer hardware, and in analyzing chemical compounds among many others.

Expert systems can have a deep impact on the business environment. We have just seen that information technology can tend to displace unskilled personnel such as data entry operators and typists, transferring work to above-average employees. This has an obvious limit: not everybody can be above average. It therefore becomes important to find applications where expertise—the high competence and reliable judgment that comes from years of experience—can be leveraged, i.e., used by people who are younger or less gifted.

Increasingly, there will be scope for integrating expert systems approaches with mainstream transaction processing and decision support.

Of almost equal importance is that AI technology, in expert systems and elsewhere, is breaking down the dichotomy between pro-
Continued

grams and data, preferring to see both as aspects of knowledge. This is already enriching our repertoire of systems development techniques. Although the results are not yet generally embodied into commercially available tools and generally adopted methodologies, the next decade should see considerable progress. The earliest concrete embodiment of this trend may be object-oriented design and programming, which is described in Section VI.

Executive information systems or executive support systems are the current terms for the top of the pyramid. Executive information systems are distinguished from management information systems because top executives are generally much more interested in information generated outside the organization, about the industry, the competition, and technical innovations. As a result, executive information systems tend to be designed to give executives access to external data bases and to a top-level summary of internal enterprise information.

Executive information systems have been slow to take off, both because the IS department tended not to realize that top management was mainly interested in outside information and because most top executives had keyboard fright. Both of these factors will be overcome with time.

Some interesting experiments with user interfaces have taken place in the efforts to sell information systems to top executives. In one case, a corporation founded by ex-Air Force pilots used a set of dials, reminiscent of a cockpit layout, to display the key indicators of the business. Another scheme which has been successfully used is to display a matrix of green, amber, and red squares, highlighting the areas that need management attention.

Write a Description of Each Process

Each process is then described, usually on one-half page to two pages. A guideline is that each process should be decomposed into three to seven components and a paragraph defining each should be written. These descriptions ensure that everyone has the same understanding of what a given process does and does not include. They are particularly valuable for team members who have not been involved with the analysis of a particular area. The write-up is less useful to users, who usually understand each process under their control on the basis of a process name. They typically do not need a detailed description.

If hierarchical representation techniques are used, the written descriptions may be replaced by adding one or two levels of detail to the hierarchical chart.

Relate the Business Process to the Organization

Each business process is then reviewed to determine which parts of the organization play a role in it. The usual technique is to create a matrix such as the one in Figure 5–6.

ANALYZING DATA REQUIREMENTS

The next stage in the planning process is to group data into what has been called *subject data bases* (because each data base is devoted to a single subject of interest to the corporation, rather than to serving a single group of users). Again, the methodology used by BSP can serve as a model for understanding the process. Typically, four steps are involved: identify business entities, determine data usage by process, identify data classes, and develop a process/data matrix.

Identify Business Entities

The business entities are those persons, things, or concepts that are of lasting interest to the business and about which data needs to be stored. Examples range from customers to warehouses, departments, products, and shipments. There are several strategies for defining these entities:

- By using an iterative approach, through group discussions. (An initial list of, say, 10 to 20 entities is proposed and is then gradually refined until the group feels comfortable.)

- By analyzing present mechanized systems and assuming that one record type in an existing file represents one entity, then factoring similar entities to reduce their number.

- By analyzing existing documents exchanged with the outside world (customers, suppliers, government, etc.) to develop an understanding of the primary entities and the type of data to be stored about them.

- By using checklists available from suppliers or colleagues in professional associations. (Such checklists are usually specific to a given industry.)

The approach selected is not critical. In practical terms, the only risk is to identify too many entities, so that the output becomes unwieldy. In a large organization, it is usually possible to identify several hundred of them; this number is in all probability too large, and related entities should be consolidated to provide a higher level of abstraction.

If too few entities have been proposed, the lack will be discovered in the next step, and it is fairly easy to complete the list.

Determine Data Usage by Process

The next step is to determine which entities are required by each process and which entities the process creates or updates. Not only is the entity identified, but the type of data that is involved is also identified. In general, each process only requires part of the data about an entity. For instance, the data about the employee entity might be divided into several categories such as vital statistics, status, employment history, skills, salary and withholding data, and so on. Each process might use only one or two of these categories.

Identify Data Classes

From the data types for each process, the data classes are defined. A data class is a category of information about an entity with a single source of creation. If a data class is created by several processes rather than just one, then the data class must be decomposed, or the processes must be factored or combined.

Develop a Process/Data Matrix

The result of the above analysis is documented in matrix form (see Figure 5–9). For each process, the data that it uses is marked with an A (for "access only"), and that which it creates or updates with a U (for "update"). The matrix is manipulated until natural groupings fall out. This is fairly easy to do with a spreadsheet, but is much more painful by hand. If the matrix is drawn by someone with good knowledge of the industry and previous BSP experience, this grouping will tend to become apparent after the first attempt (see Figure 5–10).

In addition, data/organization matrices (see Figure 5–11) showing the responsibility and use of data across organizational and geographical boundaries should be established whenever there is considerable sharing of data across organizational boundaries or whenever there may be a case for implementing distributed systems. It is fairly easy to see the need for this additional analysis based on comparing the process/organization matrix developed earlier with the data/process matrix in Figure 5–10.

Both processes and data groupings are relatively standard within an industry. Identifying the categories listed along the rows and columns of the matrix is usually not extremely difficult. Some practitioners recommend establishing a corporate data model before doing the data/process matrix. The model is created by enumerating all the external entities of interest to the organization, such as customers, suppliers, and third parties. Internal entities such as products, parts, and employees that are of interest to the external entities are then added. Then, the relationships between all these entities are charted according to the rules of a data modeling technique—usually entity-relationship modeling, as described in Section V. This modeling technique, related to the approach by products, services, markets, and channels, is most useful for transaction processing systems. In contrast, management planning and reporting are more related to the internal activities and processes than to the data entities (see Figure 5–12). Regardless of when such a corporate data model is undertaken, it is a part of the end product of the systems planning process.

The data/process matrix designed here is the essential component of the systems architecture that BSP establishes. It identifies how data entities are grouped into logically coherent data bases and how groups of processes make up systems and subsystems that maintain and use the data.

Figure 5–9 **Sample Process/Data Matrix—Initial Version**

SYSTEMS
PLAN
PLANNING TOOL
SUBURBAN PUMPS
PROCESS/DATA MATRIX
CD-20
PDMTX

PREPARED BY: J. WEBER   DATE: 27AUG88   VERSION: 1.1   PAGE 1
APPROVED BY: JACK CROFT   DATE: 05SEP88   STATUS: D

A-Access Only
U-Update

DATA ENTITIES

BUSINESS FUNCTIONS	Strategic Plans	Annual Plans	Vendor	Raw Materials	Materials Inventory	Purchase Order	Finished Goods Inventory	Finished Goods Warehouse	Competitor	Market Sector	Product	Product Structure	Manufacturing Process	Work Center	Plant	Department	Employee	Process Type	Equipment Type	Sales Region	Salesperson	Customer	Order Agent	Financial
Strategic Planning	U	A							A	A	A													A
Financial Planning	A	A																						
Research & Development									A	A	A	A	A					A	A					U
Payroll																U	U							
Employee Relations																	U							
Employee Benefits																	U							
Government Relations																	U							
Employee Development																	U							
Recruiting																								
Operations							U				U	U	U	U	U			U	U					U
Process Engineering											U	U	U	U	U			U	U					
Equipment Control													A	A	U			A	A					
Quality Control											A	A	A	A				A	A					
Purchasing			U	U	U	U																		U
Materials Requirements Planning			A	A	U						A	A	A					U	A					
Inventory Control				A			U	U			A													U
Distribution							U	U														U	U	
Market Intelligence									U	U	A									U	U			
Sales										A	A									A	A	A	A	
Advertising						A																		
Budgeting		A																						U
General Financial Administration																								U
Reports																								U
Accounting																								U
Administrative Reporting																								U

Figure 5–10 **Sample Process/Data Matrix—Final Version**

```
SYSTEMS                    PLANNING TOOL                              CD-20
PLAN                       SUBURBAN PUMPS                             PDMTX
                           PROCESS/DATA MATRIX


PREPARED BY: J. WEBER          DATE: 27OCT88          VERSION: 3      PAGE 1
APPROVED BY: JACK CROFT        DATE: 28OCT88          STATUS:  F
```

SUBJECT DATA BASES   EMPLOYEE   MANUFACTURING   MARKETING   MATERIALS   FIN

APPLICATION SYSTEMS	Department	Employee	Benefits	Payroll	Training	Product	Product Structure	Manufacturing Process	Work Center	Plant	Process Type	Equipment Type	Competitor	Sector	Region	Salesperson	Customer	Order	Agent	Finished Goods Inv	Warehouse	Vendor	Raw Materials	Raw Materials Inv	Purchase Order	Financial Info	Strategic Planning	Annual Planning
FINANCIAL																												
Purchasing						A																U	U	U	U			
Accounts Payable																							A	A		U		
Accounts Receivable																				A	A					U		
General Ledger																				A				A		U		
Cost Accounting						U	A	A															U	A		U		
MANUFACTURING																												
Production Scheduling							U	U																				
Plant Process Control								U	U		U	U																
Inventory Control						A														U	U							
ADMINISTRATION																												
Personnel Planning	U	U	A	A																								
Payroll/Personnel	A	U	U	U																								
Training	A	A			U																							
MARKETING																												
Sales Analysis						A							A		U	U	A	A	A									
Profitability Reporting		A				A																						A
Order Entry						A							A	A	U	U	U	U		A	A							
DECISION SUPPORT																												
Strategic Planning													A		A	A										A	U	A
Budegeting																										A	A	U

A-Access Only   U-Update

Figure 5–11 **Sample Organization/Data Matrix**

```
SYSTEMS                    PLANNING TOOL                              CD-20
PLAN                       SUBURBAN PUMPS                             ODMTX
                           ORGANIZATION/DATA MATRIX

PREPARED BY: J. WEBER      DATE: 27AUG88        VERSION: 1.1          PAGE 1
APPROVED BY: JACK CROFT    DATE: 05SEP88        STATUS: D
```

DATA ENTITIES → BUSINESS LOCATIONS ↓	Strategic Plans	Annual Plans	Vendor	Raw Materials Inventory	Materials Purchase Order	Finished Goods Inventory	Finished Goods Warehouse	Competitor	Market Sector	Product	Product Structure	Manufacturing Process	Work Center	Plant	Department	Employee	Process Type	Equipment Type	Sales Region	Salesperson	Customer	Order	Agent	Financial
Headquarters	D	D	S		S	S		D	D	D	D		S	S	S	S	S	S	S	S	S	S	D	D
Plants	D	D	D	D				P	D	P	P	P	D	D	P	P	P	D				P		
Regional Sales Offices								D	D	P									D	D	D	D		
Finished Goods Warehouses						D	D			D	P										P	D	P	

Data Volumes	L	L	M	M	H	H	H	L	H	L	L	M	M	L	L	L	H	L	L	L	M	H	H	M

D–Detailed Data
P–Partial Copy of Detailed Data
S–Summary Only

L–Low
M–Medium
H–High

Some Practical Considerations

Two refinements, not explicitly covered in BSP, tend to cause difficulties later if glossed over now. One is the identification of data ownership. The problem involves who is responsible for defining the meaning of data and authorizing others to use it, on the one hand, and who is responsible for data integrity on the other. Because subject data bases tend to cross organizational boundaries, often the data in one part of the data base is maintained by one group, and the data in another part by another group. In that case, who has responsibility for seeing that the data in the two parts are coherent? For instance, if a human resources department has the responsibility for maintaining personnel records—date of hire, job experience, and so on—and a separate payroll department maintains payroll data—salary, deductions, and so on—who is responsible for ensuring that each employee qualifies for each benefit? What happens if the human resources department changes some characteristic, such as age (because of a previous error), and does not check whether the employee is still eligible for age-related benefits?

A similar difficulty arises when one organizational group is responsible for maintaining data that is used exclusively by another group. One of Murphy's laws pertaining to data is the following: "Data not used by the persons who maintain it becomes erroneous."

The second problem, not generally addressed explicitly by most methodologies, is that transaction processing systems do not view data in the same way as do tactical or strategic systems. The difference is that transaction processing needs the most recently known value of each piece of data; this value changes as transactions are processed. Other types of systems contain data that has been *cut off*, i.e., assigned to a specific period. In addition, the historical data may go back several years. Generally, this difference implies the use of separate data bases because it is technically quite difficult to store both current and cut-off data on the same data bases. Moreover, it implies a cut-off function, or information-delivery function, in each transaction processing system.

IDENTIFYING SYSTEMS PROJECTS

At this stage of the systems planning project, the identification of new systems to be developed can be based on two sources: a natural grouping of processes and data and a list of unsatisfied information needs of top and middle management. Most systems planning methodologies do not prescribe that one source should be used rather than another. The practical consequences of preferring one or the other are described below.

Systems plans have historically relied heavily on the information needs analysis. The information needs approach appeals to top management (it is the one that results naturally if Porter and Rockart are followed) and tends to yield more immediate payback. It also corresponds best to the earlier stages in Nolan's analysis. The systems identified in this way are usually imple-

Figure 5–12 **Sample Corporate Data Model**

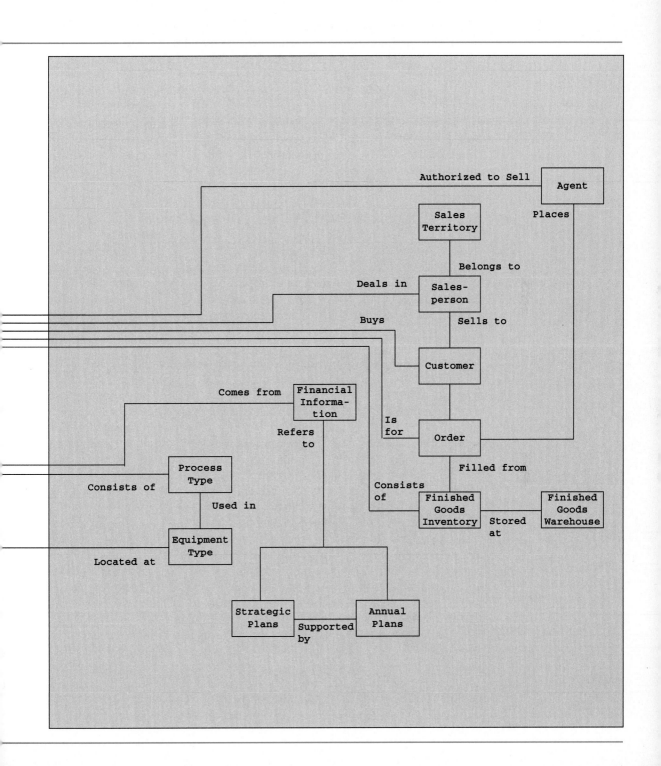

mented by using data from existing transaction processing systems and data bases, thus requiring few infrastructure modifications. These systems are usually either management information systems or data delivery systems for decision support.

The systems plans that rely more on enterprise modeling and subject data bases tend to be more comprehensive. Most of the data bases identified during this process already exist in the form of nonintegrated, partially redundant files serving current transaction processing systems. To implement the subject data base approach usually means replacing, little by little, most or all of the existing transaction processing applications. As a result, these plans are more costly, take longer to implement, and have a higher degree of risk because they present a higher degree of integration. However, the promised benefits are greater than in the previous approach because the systems developed under this approach will have an architecture that lends itself better to maintenance and evolution, while maintaining the proper degree of data integration. So far, few success stories have been associated with this type of systems planning, both because it is more recent (and fewer companies have used it) and because it takes longer to show positive results. Some companies have also fallen into the "analysis-paralysis" trap, in which the planning process bogs down because it has become an end unto itself.

A great danger with the subject data base approach is that too much attention is paid to the target that is aimed for, and not enough to the strategy for reaching the target. Any organization has systems today, and these systems cannot all be instantaneously replaced by the new systems. The plan for migrating towards the ideal architecture represented by the future subject data bases and integrated applications must take into account that, while an application is being developed, its predecessor has to make do. In particular, when the first new application is installed, it has to interface to all the old applications that it does not replace. As more applications are developed and replace older ones, these interfaces will continue to be changed. Finding a workable, low-cost strategy to deal with this problem is one of the main challenges to the systems planner.

Most planning methodologies do not specify which approach to use. Some implicitly favor one over the other, simply by the way the different tasks are executed. The fact that information needs analysis leads to short-term improvements and subject data base analysis leads to long-term integration is not explicitly recognized. (We are indebted to John Zachman, from IBM Corporation, for pointing out this essential difference.)

The obvious recommendation is to combine the best of both approaches—to solve the most glaring operational and informational problems immediately while undertaking a longer-term, deeper renovation of the application structure. In fact, it may be a good idea to start some of the shorter-term projects even before the systems plan is completed, so as to demonstrate conclusively the benefits of the systems plan at a very early stage.

EVALUATING SYSTEMS PROJECTS

The final step in preparing the application part of the systems plan is to evaluate the benefits, risks, and possible sources for each of the systems projects just identified. This evaluation serves as the basis for assigning priorities and developing an initial phased plan with development schedules.

Once the new systems or groups of systems have been identified, the analysis of how well the objectives of these systems are carried out by today's applications will identify which systems, groups of systems, and subsystems are candidates for development projects. The benefits and risks of those that are candidates must then be evaluated, using the criteria agreed upon earlier. If required, a brief study akin to the feasibility study described in the previous chapter is conducted. Once a project's benefits have been evaluated, the amount of resource to be allocated to it is estimated. This estimate is partly based on the systems planners' perception of the probable development and running costs, but also, more realistically, it is based on what the organization is willing to invest to achieve the benefit. The analysis determines the orders of magnitude of the benefits and risks; the analysis is not a rigorous economic analysis using net present value techniques, for example.

As a simplified illustration, suppose an electronic mail system is estimated to save $5 million in postage over the next four years. (This period was evaluated to be the economic life of the required hardware.) The hardware cost is estimated not to exceed $3 million. Thus, $2 million is left as the upper limit on development cost. The question then becomes whether, in the planners' judgment, there is a strong chance of developing the system for, say, $1.5 million. The experience of the systems planners will usually tell them whether the risk of exceeding the benefit is very high or very low. (Gray areas are, by definition, high-risk.)

At this point, the probable source for each system is initially evaluated. In particular, all those systems that qualify for application software packages are identified. Systems for which no application software package is known to exist and those heart-of-the-business systems that are being deployed for a competitive edge are normally excluded.

Systems that are to be entirely developed by the users themselves are also identified at this point. The criteria for end-user development are the following:

- The application should not be on a critical path.
- The application should be limited in scope to the department or division that develops it.
- Data integrity and privacy should not be a major issue.
- The system should preferably use proven technology.

The result of this phase is a document for each identified system, depicting its general principles, its use of subject data bases, and its score against the criteria identified earlier.

Box
5–2

Sources of Systems

In Section I, the discussion of the systems development life cycle assumed tacitly that all systems were developed by the personnel of the organization, working either in the IS department or in user departments. There are other sources of systems. The two main alternatives to the classical approach are packaged application software and turnkey systems.

Packaged application software consists of prewritten programs that perform a function that is similar from one organization to another, in the same industry (for example, materials requirements planning for discrete manufacturing) or across industries (for example, project control, general accounting, and payroll systems).

The advantages of packages are obvious: the cost and time of preparing detailed programming specifications, coding, and testing is replaced by a lump sum. The application software vendor can afford to charge much less per copy of the system because many copies will be sold.

Application software packages cannot be installed overnight. The life cycle activities associated with packages are requirements analysis, application software selection, interfacing to other systems, creation of data bases, and installation (user training and system test). In addition, the package may require customization when the specifications of the software do not meet those of the organization exactly. For instance, a user may prefer a different report sequence than the standard one or request that an additional piece of information be included.

In general, the more options the package has and the more flexible it is, the longer it may take to install, but the better it will ultimately meet the specific requirements of the users.

There are no hard-and-fast guidelines; whether you select a no-frills, no-options product which can be installed quickly (but may force solutions that you may not be completely happy with) or a more sophisticated and difficult to install product is an individual decision for each new application.

When are application packages appropriate? In general, packaged application software is a good solution for nonstrategic systems. Payroll and general accounting are two examples of functions which generally do not provide strategic competitive advantage to an organization. For a retail chain, purchasing is a very important function and may not be appropriately filled by a package. For a firm of architects, purchasing is not critical, and application software is likely to be adequate. The reason behind this analysis is that if one firm can buy application software, then so can all its competitors. It is therefore difficult to differentiate based on application software. Moreover, the installation time of application software is short, so the possible competitive edge gained from installing it is not sustainable over the long run.

End-user computing has been mentioned as a source of departmental systems. It is difficult to have end users develop heart-of-the-business systems because the scale and scope of such systems generally require full-time IS professionals. End users can be expected to develop smaller systems, such as those that are to be used within their own departments and do not have the strong data integrity requirements of major transactions processing applications. End users who develop systems could be compared to do-it-yourself carpenters, who may be expected to build a deck or garage on their own, but not a house.

Continued

Continued

Turnkey systems, or systems specified by the organization and developed exclusively for it by third parties, are generally chosen as a solution to the lack of personnel to develop the system in-house. The requirements specifications and the final integration testing must remain with the organization itself, just as with application software. In fact, custom-developed turnkey systems have a lot in common with application software, but they are more costly and take longer to implement. They are perhaps most appropriate where an application software package would have been a good solution had one existed.

The greatest disadvantage of turnkey development is that the organization may lose touch with the project during the development stage (which may last for many months, sometimes years). The result is the loss of the sense of ownership that comes from continuing user participation.

In-house custom development, the traditional approach, is likely to continue to be the choice for implementing critical systems in large organizations. If the organization does not have a sufficient number of developers or lacks experience in some of the fields, the team can be completed with temporary resources, be they programmers, analysts, or project leaders. In some cases, the leadership of the whole effort may be delegated to a systems integrator who can command all the hardware, software, and personnel resources required. However, it is prudent to insist on substantial participation of the client organization's personnel—top management (on a steering committee), users, and IS department personnel, who will run the system and maintain it.

Even though the proportion of systems coming from in-house development is likely to diminish relative to other sources, end-user computing and application software in particular, its total volume will continue to increase.

When logical constraints are added—no system can use a subject data base until that data base exists—this document forms the basis for assigning priorities to the application development projects according to the policy set out at the beginning of the planning project.

ORGANIZING THE SYSTEMS PLANNING EFFORT

Little has been said so far about how the systems planning project itself is set up, who should participate, how long it is likely to last, and what practical problems have to be resolved.

First, a systems plan always covers multiple systems and multiple organizational units. For most medium-sized businesses, the plan covers the entire business. For very large enterprises, the plan may only cover a single strategic business unit (SBU). The requirement is that the SBU be quite independent, both in its operation and in its management, from the rest of the enterprise.

For a systems plan to be successful, it must first and foremost have the full **support of top management.** For example, IBM's BSP methodology recommends devoting a substantial part of the effort to gaining executive commitment. Perhaps as much as one-third of the elapsed time is spent up front planning and preparing the study. IBM also gives several types of briefings and courses to non-IS executives to prepare them for a BSP study by training them in the uses of information technology, discussing potential uses to solve the executives' day-to-day problems, and developing techniques to evaluate whether an information technology investment is worthwhile. IBM has recently been offering Information Systems Investment Strategy sessions as an addendum to BSP.

IBM recommends that the BSP team be led by an "executive with broad business perspective," who is supported by two to five managers from various functional areas and by one representative from the IS department. The **ideal user representative** on any project is the user who is absolutely indispensable in his or her own department and has no time available. To secure the cooperation of such an individual, it is all the more important to have executive commitment to the systems planning project.

IBM's BSP methodology aims at **a project of six to eight weeks.** Other methodologies tend to take more time, often as much as six months. A great deal of the value of systems planning lies in doing it quickly. If it lasts for longer than a few months, there is a significant risk that top management support will flag, as will user interest.

Three practical problems have to be addressed in planning and executing a systems planning project. The first is related to what has just been said about BSP, which prescribes the participation of about a half dozen high-level users for several weeks. Although this participation is an ideal to strive for, it is practically impossible to achieve. Compromises usually have to be made on the level and degree of involvement of the users. The compromises must then be compensated for by making sure that the best possible resources from the IS department are assigned to the project. Another partial solution is to hire consultants with good knowledge of the industry. It may also be necessary to exceed the eight-week guideline.

The second problem is that it is very difficult for the systems planners to stay at a general enough level of analysis. The criticism that has been leveled at some methodologies is that they encourage the team to go into too much detail. There are not enough firm guidelines on when to stop analyzing and start doing. A good indicator is that the project should under no circumstance exceed six months in duration. The tendency to generate excessive details is tied to the previous problem: it is much easier for high-level people to stay at a high level of abstraction. People with less experience and perspective need a deeper level of detail before they can be satisfied that they have understood all the critical aspects of a problem.

Finally, any successful systems planning project must result almost immediately in the implementation of some of the high-priority opportunities. How to translate the systems plan into a usable project plan for the IS department is one of the themes of the next chapter. Here suffice it to say that if the IS department is not ready to start delivering almost as soon as the systems plan is ready, the planning effort may well turn out to have been wasted.

Summary

Management's first goal in establishing a systems plan is to create systems that serve the organization better through the sharing of data across the entire organization. The second goal is to ensure better communications, understanding, and support among the three principal actors in information technology: top management, the users, and IS professionals. Harmony can be achieved by increasing the users' understanding of corporate goals and information technology policies and by making sure that the IS department takes the business view of the systems it develops rather than the technocrats'.

The first requirement of a systems planning project is therefore to ascertain the corporation's goals and strategies, either by reviewing the strategic business plan, if it exists, or by interviewing top management to develop the guiding principles that can help direct the study.

The knowledge of these goals and strategies enables the systems planning team to identify the commonly accepted criteria by which a proposed project's merits will be evaluated. Both potential paybacks and risks associated with the projects should be incorporated in these criteria.

When criteria are identified, the analysis of the organization's systems needs can proceed. Although this analysis can be undertaken in several ways, BSP is an effective example.

Most formal methodologies group data and functions around a fairly small number of subject data bases. These groups make up the ideal architecture towards which future systems development will attempt to evolve. Depending on how far the present systems are from this architecture and how much the organization is willing to spend on long-term versus short-term improvements, the systems actually identified in the systems plan will vary from situation to situation.

Some of the factors that will make a systems planning project successful are to keep the duration of the project short, to obtain sufficient top management commitment and user involvement, and to identify projects with quick payback that should be undertaken immediately following the conclusion of the systems planning project, or even earlier if possible.

Selected Readings

IBM Corporation, *Business Systems Planning: Information Systems Planning Guide* (Order No. GE20–0527), IBM, White Plains.
This manual is IBM's description of BSP. The current edition can be obtained through local IBM branch offices.

Zachman, John. "Business Systems Planning and Business Information Control Study: A Comparison." *IBM Systems Journal,* Vol. 21, No. 1, 1982.
In this article, John Zachman, IBM's foremost authority on systems plan-

ning, compares BSP and BICS, another methodology researched by IBM in the 1970s. This issue also contains interesting articles on information requirements analysis by Gordon Davis and on cost-benefit analysis by M. Parker. The best way to obtain a copy of the entire issue is from University Microfilms, Inc., Ann Arbor, Michigan.

Martin, James. *Strategic Data-Planning Methodologies.* Englewood Cliffs, NJ: Prentice-Hall, 1982.

This book justifies top management involvement, the subject data base approach, and the analysis of processes to get at the data structure. It refers to BSP and extends the planning process to distributed environments.

Martin, James. *Information Engineering.* 3 vols. Englewood Cliffs, NJ: Prentice-Hall, 1990.

This book covers systems planning as well as the subsequent phases of the life cycle in great detail. It is of special interest to students of data-driven methodologies. It presents a very coherent view of how systems planning arises and is exploited later in the life cycle.

Finkelstein, Clive. *An Introduction to Information Engineering: From Strategic Planning to Information Systems.* Sydney, Australia: Addison-Wesley, 1989.

From one of the creators of Information Engineering (James Martin is the other), this book gives a slightly different view. The treatment of the relationship among strategic, tactical, and operational needs is quite original.

Goodhue, Kirsch, Quillard, J., and Rockart, J. "Managing the Data Resource: A Contingency Approach." *Working Paper 150.* Cambridge, Massachusetts: Center for Information Systems Research, January 1987.

Goodhue, Kirsch, Quillard, J., and Rockart, J. "Strategic Data Planning: Lessons from the Field." *Working Paper 215.* Cambridge, Massachusetts: Center for Information Systems Research, October 1990.

A series of case studies of corporations that have tried enterprise modeling. These two papers have some very good lessons on the dangers of "paralysis from analysis."

Cotterman, W. W., Couger, J. D., Enger, N. L., and Harold, F., eds. *Systems Analysis and Design: A Foundation for the 1980s.* New York: North Holland, 1980.

This collection of papers was presented at a symposium at Georgia State University in 1980. It contains a number of thought-provoking articles that still have a great deal of interest ten years later, although some of the technical discussions are outdated.

Review Questions

1. Enumerate the steps that lead to the establishment of a systems plan. Which steps can be omitted and under what conditions?

2. What are the three main benefits of a formal systems plan? What are the risks inherent in not having one?

3. List some typical criteria that are used to evaluate systems projects in a systems plan. Why are these criteria not identical from one organization to another?

4. What are the two main sources for identifying systems projects? Explain why both sources are necessary for a balanced view.

5. How can a systems planning study team best ensure top management commitment to the study and to the resulting plan?

Discussion Question

1. The text implies that methods based on the analysis of management information needs tend to result in short-term improvements and that methods that use a subject data base approach have a more long-term perspective. Discuss how these approaches are likely to affect the search for the use of information technology to competitive advantage.

Mini-Cases

First Mercantile Bank & Trust. The First Mercantile Bank & Trust is a large bank with $20 billion in assets and 700,000 customers, individuals and corporations alike. Cynthia Kline, vice-president of information systems, tells you that First Mercantile does not have a formally documented systems plan. She explains that it is not really necessary, because:

- She attends meetings with top management regularly, at least once a month if not more frequently. Information technology is a regular topic in these meetings, and she feels she has top management's support in the current direction of the IS department.

- All IS analysts and programmers are currently busy either with maintenance or with one of the two very large development projects currently under way: branch banking and commercial loans.

- Any additional need must be met with minimal assistance from the IS department, a case in point being the mortgage application approval system being developed by the user department with assistance from an artificial intelligence firm and outside consultants, analysts, and programmers.

- Subject data bases are not yet implemented, except for a shared Customer Information File, which uses hierarchical data base technology. However, account and balance information is maintained by separate systems for checking, savings, NOW, commercial loans, mortgages, and consumer loans.

- There is a hardware acquisition plan based on a capacity planning study first done two years ago with the help of the hardware vendor and updated every six months. The plan covers the next three years and takes into account the central mainframe, computing equipment in branches, office automation and departmental computing, and teleprocessing network needs.

The IS department has about 140 programmers, analysts, and project managers. Of these, approximately 105 are full-time on maintenance, and the rest are doing development work.

Questions for Discussion

1. How would you try to convince Ms. Kline to do a formal systems planning study?

2. If you succeeded in convincing her, what overall approach to the study would you recommend to her?

Mercy Medical Center. Mercy Medical Center is a 550-bed community hospital located in a large U.S. city. Mercy has a board of directors comprised of influential members of the community. Bob MacLeod has been president for a year, having held a similar position with a smaller hospital on the other side of town. Since coming to Mercy, he has done well and has good rapport with the board. He has also maintained good relations with the hospital's many stakeholders: doctors, employees, insurers, employers, municipal officials, community groups, and the press.

Bob was upset by something that occurred at the most recent board meeting. It was the first time since coming to Mercy that he felt a member of his staff embarrassed him in front of the board. Bob had invited Ron Allen, the chief information officer, to assist him in presenting the IS budget for next year because it contained a sizable increase for all areas of IS: hardware, software, internal staff, and outside consultants. Since IS was not Bob's area of expertise, he wanted to have Ron at his side to help in answering questions.

The first question came from George Fischer, who interrupted before Ron had a chance to begin commenting on his budget request. "I've had a chance to review this request and find that I can't put it in any sort of context," he said. "At my company, we have information systems people prepare a systems plan subordinate to and supportive of the strategic plan of the company. When we review a budget for the IS department, or any other department for that matter, we verify that it is carrying out the plans we've previously approved. I assume a similar process is in place here at Mercy, and I would like to see a copy of the IS plan before discussing your budget request. Do you have one?"

Ron's response was immediate. "Mr. Fischer, I've wanted to prepare an IS strategic plan ever since I came here six years ago. We always had one at my previous employer, St. Vincent's Hospital, and it made my life a lot easier. The problem is, as you have said, IS planning must have a strategic plan for the hospital as its starting point, and as long as I've been at Mercy, we've never been able to get the other departments to sit still long enough to develop a strategic plan. They had one at St. Vincent's, so I know it can be done. Nevertheless, we have to move ahead in IS. We can't wait until the hospital gets its act together, so I hope the board will see fit to approve my budget request."

Ron's comments set off a discussion that lasted over 20 minutes, during which time Bob became increasingly uncomfortable. Some board members wanted to approve Ron's request and move on. Others saw the merit of what Fischer was saying. Bob was concerned that the board would ask for a strategic plan for the hospital. He knew that would take more time and resources than he could spare right now. "Maybe two years from now," he thought, "but not now. Not when I'm still getting my feet on the ground and dealing with short-term problems that needed to be solved immediately."

Bob breathed a sigh of relief when the chairman suggested the formation of a subcommittee. Its charge would be to suggest a framework for moving forward with the evaluation of IS requests in the absence of an IS plan or to develop an approach to IS planning in the absence of a strategic plan for the hospital. Without saying so out loud, the chairman agreed with what he knew Bob's position to be. "There's no way the hospital was ready to devote resources to strategic planning," he thought. "Not until they'd put out a few more fires."

Question for Discussion

1. You have been appointed a member of the subcommittee. What approaches do you want the subcommittee to evaluate?

Notes

1. Henderson, J., and Venkatraman, N. "Strategic Alignment: A Framework for Strategic IT Planning." *Working Paper* 190. Cambridge, Massachusetts: Center for Information Systems Research, May 1985.

2. Rockart, John F. "Critical Success Factors." *Harvard Business Review* 57, no. 2 (March-April 1979): 81–91.

3. Nolan, Richard L. "Managing the Crises in Data Processing." *Harvard Business Review* 57, no. 2 (March-April 1979): 115–126.

6

IS Infrastructure Planning

IS management can use the systems planning process to plan for the IS department's organization and resources. The process will ensure that the systems plan can actually be implemented and will eliminate some of the pitfalls that result from initiating one project at a time.

The chapter first outlines the advantages of the infrastructure planning process. Next, it describes the process of planning for technology. This process is divided into two parts: planning for the resources used to develop applications and planning for the resources used to run the applications, once they are developed. The chapter concludes with sections on planning the personnel requirements and the organization of the IS department. Throughout the chapter, less emphasis is placed on describing the management planning process itself than on describing practical, real-world choices that need to be made.

Learning Objectives

- Understand the need to plan for the availability of personnel, software, and hardware resources required to implement a systems plan.

- Describe the main considerations in establishing the plan for a development hardware and software environment.

- Recognize the factors that preside over planning for the operating environment.

- Evaluate personnel planning requirements.

- Understand how infrastructure planning considerations can affect the implementation strategy for the systems plan.

PROBLEMS SOLVED BY PROPER INFRASTRUCTURE PLANNING

Many of the problems facing IS departments in the 1990s could have been avoided, or at least minimized, by better infrastructure planning in the 1960s and 1970s. Three of these problems are described more fully here: the lack of availability of development resources due to excessive maintenance, the consequences of disparity in hardware and software, and the information technology needs of the IS department.

Lack of Development Resources

This problem manifests itself in the reputation of IS departments for not being able to take on new projects in a timely manner. The reputation for untimeliness is partly due to the nature of systems projects, which are more difficult and take longer to implement than most users realize. But it is also partly due to poor personnel planning. Maintenance tends to take up more than 50 percent—often up to 80 percent—of the IS department's personnel, leaving few resources available to cope with new development. Planning for maintenance has been inadequate. Improvements in this area would contribute to resolving several problems: unreasonable expectations about development speed, a lack of quality in the systems developed, and an unrealistic view of the benefits of end-user computing.

Good planning probably does not reduce the requirement for maintenance, but it can point out to top management the need for more staff if new development is to take place (with consequently higher budgets), or alternatively the need for lower expectations on the users' part. In other words, user and management expectations for the speed with which new projects can be developed could be better managed with effective planning.

Planning for realistic levels of maintenance could also help management realize the need for higher quality in the initial development of projects. Many IS departments tend to skimp on design, documentation, and reviews under the pressure of both top management and users to produce operational applications quickly and within the initial budget.

This problem is not easy to solve because of today's imperfect techniques for reducing maintenance by increasing the quality of the systems design and implementation techniques and tools. Moreover, IS professionals do not yet have reliable mechanisms for predicting maintenance efforts as a percentage of development effort or as a function of system size.

In the early days of end-user computing, the cost of maintenance of user-developed systems was even less well recognized than that of applications developed by the IS department. In many organizations, this is still the case.

There are two common results of this lack of recognition. First, many end users who develop their own applications because the IS department does not have sufficient resources find the development project to be challenging and rewarding, but they run out of steam when it comes to maintenance. In other words, they commit the same mistakes as early IS departments in failing to plan for high maintenance levels. Some of these user departments ask the IS department to take over the responsibility for the application, thus adding to the maintenance burden of the IS department.

A more frequent cause of added maintenance is that end-user computing usually places demands for data delivery systems on the central IS facility. Analysts and programmers have to be assigned to writing programs to cut off, extract, format, and deliver data to Infocenters, departmental computers, or PCs.

Even though proper planning does not by itself reduce the levels of maintenance in an organization, the systems plan should be the first step towards recognizing the problem and bringing it under control.

Equipment and Software Disparity

Equipment and software disparity occurs when multiple types of hardware and software coexist within an organization. Some of the resources may be incompatible. For instance, an IBM 3270 terminal cannot be attached to a Digital VAX or a Tandem computer. Other resources may be compatible, for instance, multiple programming languages such as COBOL, PL/I, Fortran, Assembler, and C. These languages may all be compatible; they can usually all be intermixed in the same application. Nevertheless, having too many products with the same purpose can cause problems.

The most frequent reason for disparity is that applications have been developed in isolation, and each application development team has chosen the hardware and software that suited the particular application, without regard to other applications. Another reason for disparity is that an IS department may be the result of a merger between firms and has therefore inherited multiple environments.

The two major difficulties associated with disparity are the lack of integration and the fragmentation of expertise. A minor problem is software cost: having five compilers instead of two is bound to be more costly.

The lack of integration caused by disparity is usually found when each application has been developed with its own tools and architecture, without regard to other applications. It will then be difficult to make Application A deliver data to or use data from Application B.

The fragmentation of expertise results because each developer can only be proficient in a small number of products and techniques. When developers or maintainers are moved from one application to another with different tools and techniques, their productivity is greatly reduced for substantial time periods. The alternative is to assign developers to specific applications and avoid moving them. This alternative is frequently unacceptable because it reduces personnel planning flexibility too much.

The proper planning for software and hardware environments can force the systems planners to choose the environment that best suits the organization over the long term. Properly done, the plan also stresses that the technological environment is going to change and that these changes are independent of the requirements of the applications that are identified today. As a result, it can become somewhat easier to design applications that are less intimately coupled with the technical environment and that will therefore cause fewer maintenance and integration problems in the future. As an example, most on-line data base applications today are designed with a specific teleprocessing (TP) monitor and data base management system (DBMS) in mind. If recognition is given to the fact that the choices made today may not be appropriate three, five, or ten years hence, the development team may try to design these applications so that the functional part—what the user sees—is less intimately tied to the technical part—the specific DBMS and TP monitor.

This kind of design is just as difficult to achieve as the proper planning for maintenance, but if the effort is not made, it is certain that progress will not be achieved.

Information Technology for the Developers

Finally, infrastructure planning can also point out the information technology needs of the development teams themselves, long treated as shoemakers' children. Traditionally, IS departments have concentrated on satisfying the customers, i.e., the users, first and their own employees second. Most programmers continued to maintain their source programs on cards long after their users had started converting to on-line transaction processing.

This situation can be alleviated today with the widespread availability of intelligent workstations for developers and reasonably priced CASE tools. An additional condition is necessary. For productivity tools to be effective, their installation must be treated just like any other application. The analysts' and programmers' requirements must be analyzed, the tools selected, the users (IS professionals) trained, and the process of change managed. In too many cases, tool selection is left to individual project leaders. As a result, the tools are adopted only by the members of that project. Other project leaders, partly suffering from the "not-invented-here" syndrome, may select other tools, thus creating a tools proliferation problem.

Frequently, the impact of tools on methodology is neglected. The use of some tools practically forces the use of a methodology. Tool proliferation then also leads to methodology proliferation, which, in turn, causes integration, management, and quality problems. The choice should be made the other way around: select and implement a department-wide methodology first, then pick the tools to support it.

PLANNING FOR THE DEVELOPMENT ENVIRONMENT

The objective of planning for the development environment is to avoid, as much as possible, the disparity problem described above. During the systems planning project, the main activity is to select those components of the development environment that are the most critical and that will contribute the most to high productivity (including the avoidance of disparity). A second important consideration is software costs. The components to be selected typically include the following:

- The data base management system (DBMS).
- The transaction processing monitor.
- Methods and tools such as programming languages, CASE tools, application generators, and fourth-generation languages.

The first critical choice for the technology planners is probably that of a **data base management system (DBMS).** This has an impact on all the other development tools and on the production environment.

In the 1990s, the situation is often that an organization is committed to relational data base technology for its management information systems, end-user computing, departmental systems, and decision support data base. There are numerous merits to relational technology, one of which is flexibility in selecting and presenting information.

The question that often arises is that of transaction processing data bases. Is relational technology efficient enough to accommodate the volumes of transaction processing? Do end users need access to the production data bases as well as the information data bases? Does the organization already have a nonrelational DBMS, and if so, how can existing data bases migrate to relational technology? Can the organization afford to support multiple DBMS products?

Many of these questions, in particular those concerning performance, will be resolved in time, as relational technology grows more efficient and hardware becomes less costly. A strong indicator of the tendency towards relational DBMS as a generally accepted choice is that SQL, the premier relational data manipulation language, has been standardized by the American National Standards Institute. It therefore has the required stability and industry-wide support.

If data need to be shared across geographical boundaries, distributed data base becomes an issue. Distributed DBMS products are barely emerging on the market, and although distributed systems are becoming more widespread, they are still difficult to plan and implement. Distributing information to end users from a central clearinghouse for data is difficult enough to manage. On-demand access to data located in another part of the network, possibly with the intention to update it, requires a great deal of computing and communications power as well as considerable design expertise.

A final question to be addressed concerning DBMS is that of how well the DBMS is supported by the main application software packages that the organization uses or is planning to implement in the future. Is there a requirement for the application software to access existing subject data bases? Will end users be able to get the required data from the application software transparently? Are batch file interfaces needed between the application software and the rest of the organization's systems?

Once the DBMS has been chosen, the next choice is usually the **transaction processing monitor** to be used for operational systems. This is an easier question to resolve, because it has an impact only on the IS department professionals who will be developing transaction systems. Even here, the choices are not as simple as a few years ago: new solutions for high-volume transaction processing are appearing with front-end, fault-tolerant machines with operating systems specifically designed for easy transaction processing. More importantly, these systems facilitate distributed processing and gradual, modular growth. As their name indicates, fault-tolerant machines can continue to operate even in the presence of failing components. (Nonspecialized processors can increasingly do this, but not quite to the full extent of the fault-tolerant alternatives.)

The next question concerns development **methods and tools** such as programming languages, application generators, fourth-generation languages, and CASE. A large number of tools claim to increase programming productivity and enable end users to develop systems. The contingency approach applied to the choice of style and language weighs project size, degree of integration, and processing volumes against the use of high-level tools.

The general guideline is that the larger the project, the less time is spent, in proportion, on programming and the more on other tasks. The need for communicating specifications and design documents between project members grows exponentially with the size of the project team. It becomes necessary to make sure of the coherence of design choices in different parts of the system. Much time is also spent on integration testing, i.e., testing to see that all the parts of the application fit together as planned. As a result, extremely large projects (say 500,000 lines of code and up) do not benefit nearly as much from advanced tools such as fourth-generation languages or application generators. The tendency today is to choose third-generation languages for very large systems, because the toolset that covers activities outside the coding effort tends to be much better established than for more recent languages. Because third-generation languages have been in existence for a long time and are highly standardized, tools working in this environment are easier to leverage.

Choosing a third-generation language as the core development language should not preclude the IS department from using a report writer, a query processor, or a program generator for low-volume, nonintegrated tasks such as ad hoc query.

A psychological factor to take into account is that fourth-generation languages and application generators are usually associated with prototyping and iterative development because of the speed with which code can be written. The temptation can then be to curtail design. This is fine if the prototype developed is truly a prototype with the objective of experimenting with a specific aspect of the application—the user interface, the data base performance, the functional rules—and if the intention is to throw the prototype out in favor of a designed solution. It is more of a problem if the prototype becomes the operational system, as sometimes happens. In iterative development, care should be taken that the design phase that precedes the first of the iterations is solid enough.

It may prove easy to code an insufficiently designed application the first time. The problem comes with maintaining it and trying to integrate it with other applications. The lack of design and the ease with which code is produced and modified can easily produce such a large number of different successive or even parallel versions of the same program that all control is lost.

In a number of instances, the use of a fourth-generation language has been unsuccessful in handling high volumes. The cause is not necessarily that fourth-generation languages are inherently inefficient. Rather, the trade-off between development productivity and flexibility has been made to favor development productivity. As a result, more architectural decisions have already been made and are embedded in the product. These can easily be incompatible with the volume requirements of the application.

An example of this problem occurs in one of the oldest types of produc-tivity tools, report writers. A report writer generally reads a sequential file and produces a printout of selected parts of the file, possibly in a different sequence, with totals and summaries where required. A good report writer can easily save 80 percent of the coding effort that would be required to write the corresponding program in COBOL. The problem is that many report writers can only produce a single output report in each pass of the file. If this report writer is used to produce ten or more daily reports, the file will be read ten or more times in a day. A custom-written program or a more perfected (but less easy-to-use) report writer could read the file once, extracting all the data required as each record is read, do all the required manipulations, and print the reports, thus eliminating nine passes of the file.

The range is wide from application generators and fourth-generation languages to third-generation languages with tools concentrating on docu-mentation, testing, integration, and design. Most large installations will require both categories of products.

An IS department with multiple tools needs guidelines on which tool to use under which circumstances and on the acquisition of new tools when they are required. The degree of end-user computing; the balance of central-ized, integrated versus departmental systems; and the corporate culture should determine how stringently these guidelines are enforced.

Once the development tools and methodology strategy have been deter-mined, a **plan for implementing** them must be devised. This plan includes a schedule for acquiring the tools and provisions for training the users, building up expertise, and gradually extending the use of the tool throughout the IS organization. The effort to implement new methods and tools is no different from any other project aiming to change the way people work. As outlined in Chapter 2, this change must be managed; it cannot be implemented at break-neck speed, and it requires absolute management commitment and support.

PLANNING FOR THE PRODUCTION ENVIRONMENT

This book is mainly about development; planning for a production environ-ment is not its central theme. However, many production issues have an impact on design and implementation, and they therefore affect the mainte-nance, disparity, and technology problems indirectly. Two areas are covered here: planning for capacity and planning the communications network.

Capacity

The main role of planning for production resources is to match hardware and software to processing volumes and characteristics. The planning for capacity is quite different for production systems and for end-user computing.

Production. Most production applications run on centralized mainframes or departmental minicomputers. For transaction processing, there are fairly well-developed capacity planning tools, especially on the more popular mainframes, that can help predict hardware requirements.

Because the trend has been towards on-line processing, batch problems have been largely glossed over. However, in most transaction processing systems, batch processing still plays a large role. With most of the working day devoted to on-line activity, the so-called batch window, the time frame in which the day's batch processing must be done, must be strictly respected. Within this time frame, the day's activities must be cut off, interface files to other systems created, data bases backed up and possibly reorganized, daily reports produced (possibly in time for a postal deadline to be met), and any other ad hoc or periodic processing completed.

All these processes may be easy to complete if nothing goes wrong. If anything does, there must be sufficient time for the night shift personnel to find out what the problem is, get the solution, implement it, and redo the work before the on-line program is started in the morning. Ideally, the batch window should contain provisions for such incidents and the time required to recover from them. In other words, the night work should probably be scheduled to be over around 2 or 3 A.M. Despite appearances, the entire night is not available for batch work. Also, for centralized systems that process transactions from several different time zones, the batch window may have to be further contracted.

Historically, most on-line systems have been designed to be stopped at the end of the day to let the batch system take over. A serious problem occurs if the batch window gets too small. A recent trend has been to design applications that can operate continuously, continuing to process transactions while the day's processing is being cut off and the data bases are unloaded.

The requirement for continuous operations must be diagnosed early so that operating systems, TP monitors, and DBMS can be selected to support this requirement.

End-User Computing. End-user computing is increasingly done on personal computers or intelligent workstations, connected by local area networks that give the PCs access to local data bases and telecommunications networks. The required capacity of shared central resources, local networks, telecommunications facilities, and data base machines is difficult to predict because the architecture and the offerings are newer. If end-user computing is done from terminals on a departmental computer or a central mainframe, the difficulty stems from the fact that some users tend to consume a great deal of resources whereas others are much more modest in their demands. An "average" user cannot be reliably defined when the extremes range so far.

The best approach is probably to use historical data to estimate the needs of various classes of users and to extrapolate growth trends. If the cost of end-user computing thus estimated is substantial, top management should be informed that there is a high risk of the actual need being quite different from the plan after a few years.

Data Communications

In addition to the plan for processors and operating systems, planning for the operating environment requires that consideration be given to the communications network and the related software. In general, the communications software selected is the proprietary software of the main hardware vendor, such as SNA for IBM and DECNet for Digital.

Special considerations apply when multiple systems from different vendors need to communicate. If these systems are all within the organization, it is usually feasible either to standardize on one communications standard that can be accommodated by all the equipment or to provide protocol converters, which can enable two incompatible pieces of equipment to converse through a translator.

The Open Systems Interconnect (OSI) model promulgated by the International Standards Organization (ISO) is designed to permit the hardware and software products of any vendor to be installed on any network. Companies that adopt the OSI model for their internal standard should have greater flexibility in the future in the selection of products to attach to their networks.

The network itself must be designed. Because network design is the work of telecommunications specialists, it will not be covered in detail here. The technology is changing very fast, as are the offerings of the various vendors. Basically, the planning activity consists of anticipating peak and average data transmission volumes between different sites. The planners then decide whether to install leased communications lines (unlike switched telephone lines, these lines are always available and do not require one site to dial up the other in order to connect), to use the switched (or dial-up) public telephone network, or to use a dedicated data network offered by a third party such as Tymnet, Telenet, Autonet, General Electric, or IBM. With increasing frequency, the question concerns not only the network for transmitting data between locations but also intracompany telephone conversations, image (as in facsimile), and electronic mail.

Within each of these options, the many choices of capacity, quality, and reliability of service make decisions extremely complex. In those cases where the organization routinely exchanges large volumes of data with its suppliers, vendors, or competitors, the choices are more limited, because they must be negotiated and agreed upon by several independent organizations. For instance, a bank that wishes to execute international funds transfers to its correspondent banks abroad has little choice but to connect to the S.W.I.F.T. network, based in Brussels, Belgium. This network has its own well-defined transmission disciplines. Most vendors of communications software to the banking industry offer an interface to S.W.I.F.T. Another emerging example of intercompany data transfer is electronic data interchange (EDI), which enables corporate customers and suppliers to transmit ordering, invoicing, and shipping data among themselves. EDI data is usually transmitted over either a third-party network or the switched telephone network.

Distributed data processing offers even more alternatives than telecommunications networks. Box 6–1 (page 174) details some considerations that apply when planning for distributed data processing.

PLANNING FOR PERSONNEL REQUIREMENTS

Given the applications to be developed and the development environment (methodology and tools), overall personnel requirements to implement the systems plan can be estimated. The best way to plan the level and sources of personnel required is a spreadsheet such as the one in Figure 6–1. This spreadsheet shows the required level of staffing by project and by category for each month of the plan. Analyst and programmer are the two main categories; if personnel from user departments is to be assigned full time to the project, user analysts may make up a third category. The lower part of the spreadsheet shows gross and net available personnel, the unfulfilled requirement, and the proposed solution to this requirement.

The technique used is that of resource loading. For large projects, mechanized tools can help. For smaller projects, the steps are as follows:

- Identify the amount of resource required per project (divided into design and installation) and personnel type.

- Summarize the resource required for the period of the plan by adding up all the projects.

- Summarize the available personnel and identify the net personnel requirement (the difference between the gross requirement and the available resource). Remember to subtract the requirement for maintenance from the gross availability figure.

- Prepare a strategy for filling the net requirement: recruiting and temporary personnel.

- Add the recruited personnel to existing available personnel and distribute it over the duration of the plan on a spreadsheet.

- Start loading the highest-priority projects by spreading the available personnel evenly over these projects, from the start of the plan. Adjust this loading by adding temporary personnel, if that strategy is to be used, wherever needed.

Figure 6–1 **Personnel Requirements Plans**

SYSTEMS PLAN — PLANNING TOOL — SUBURBAN PUMPS — DEVELOPMENT PERSONNEL REQUIREMENTS — CD-20 / DPREQ

PREPARED BY: J. WEBER   DATE: 28AUG88   VERSION: 1.1   PAGE 1
APPROVED BY: JACK CROFT   DATE: 06SEP88   STATUS: D

APPLICATION

	1989 Q4 PM	Q4 AP	1990 Q1 PM	Q1 AP	Q2 PM	Q2 AP	Q3 PM	Q3 AP	Q4 PM	Q4 AP	1991 Q1 PM	Q1 AP	Q2 PM	Q2 AP	Q3 PM	Q3 AP	Q4 PM	Q4 AP	1992 Q1 PM	Q1 AP	Q2 PM	Q2 AP	Q3 PM	Q3 AP
Document Existing Systems	1	3																						
Automate Delivery Tickets	1		1	2	1	2																		
Develop Procedures for Training			1	1	1	2																		
Develop Purchased Products	1	1	1	2	1	5	1	5	1	5														
Rewrite and Enhance Batch	1	1	1	1	1	2	1	3	1	3	1	3												
Major Systems Enhancements																								
Order Status Change					1	1																		
Commit/Decommit Fabrication					1	1	1	1																
Inventory Improvements							1	1	1															
Production Scheduling									1	1														
Pricing Support											1	1	1	1										
Install New General Ledger																1	1	3	1	3	1	4	1	4
Other																								
Alpha Cargo			1	1	1																			
Plant and Fleet Maintenance			1	1	1																			
Payroll Data Collection			1	1	1	1																		
Gross Requirement	4	5	4	6	6	7	5	5	4	8	4	10	3	9	3	4	1	3	1	3	1	4	1	4
Available	4	5	4	6	5	7	5	7	5	8	5	8	5	8	5	8	5	8	5	8	5	8	5	8
Net Requirement/(Excess)	0	0	0	0	1	0	0	-2	-1	0	-1	2	-2	1	-2	-4	-4	-5	-4	-5	-4	-4	-4	-4
Recruitment			1	1	1	1																		
Temporary				1								2	1											

**Box
6–1**

Distributed Data Processing

Distributed data processing (DDP) is the processing of a single application on more than one physically and logically separate computer. The distributed application is any set of programs that share data (even through a batch interface such as the transmission of files of extracted data from a production data base to a decision support system). The computers may be physically separated by distances requiring telecommunications links, or they may be close enough that channel-to-channel connections or sharing of disk peripherals are available, but they must be running under the control of multiple independent operating systems (logically separate).

Conceptually, DDP is not particularly desirable. Shared access to data is much easier to control if the data exists in only one copy at a central site. Whenever multiple copies exist, there is a loss of control because the copies may wind up with inconsistent values. Also, the more copies there are, the easier it is for an intruder to get access to one of them.

Science fiction stories from the 1950s illustrate the dream of a single centralized data base serving the entire population. For example, stories by Isaac Asimov depict a giant "Multivac" spreading out over multiple square miles underneath the Washington, D.C., area.

Why hasn't this dream materialized? Why do we need distributed data processing?

There are two technical reasons and one organizational reason for distributed data processing. First, telecommunications costs have not dropped as fast as hardware costs. In some cases, transporting a data file to a staging point closer to its main users is more economical than letting the users connect via telecommunications lines to a central facility.

Second, the maximum processing capacity of even the largest mainframe computer run-

ning under control of a single operating system is limited. Moreover, this maximum capacity has tended to grow more slowly than the aggregate need for computing capacity. Therefore, some applications must run on multiple computers. IBM's internal electronic mail, electronic messages, and information data base system are of this nature. In some cases, an organization has multiple brands of computers. For example, an application software package that is particularly desired may not run on the main computer because it requires a different brand. (Thus, DDP may be an issue even for single-site installations.)

Third, the organizational reason, which has been the main reason for distributed data processing in the past, is that the management at a remote site (such as a factory, a bank branch, or a regional agency) has wanted control of its computing resources. Consequently, when the network and the central computer are not 100 percent reliable, locally controlled computer resources can continue to function in degraded mode while the problem is being fixed. Also, when the demand exceeds the capacity, local management wants to be able to arbitrate, rather than be subjected to, the decision of a remote headquarters.

In the late 1970s, the trend towards DDP was accelerated by the perception that minicomputers (and later microcomputers) had a better price/performance ratio than large mainframes. This perception was only superficially true. When all factors were taken into account, distributed processing and centralized processing tended to even out. For example, it was not as easy to balance the processing load of a collection of smaller machines (the machine at Location A might be nearly idle while that at Location B might be overloaded); it was more

Continued

Continued

costly to develop distributed systems; and data tended to be duplicated and therefore occupy more space.

As the technology evolved, the 1980s saw new applications, such as office automation and departmental systems, and new technologies, such as the personal computer. Now, the price of the personal computer has fallen so low that it is desirable to move as much processing to the PC, used as a workstation, as possible. Shared data must still be controlled at a more central point—a departmental file server or a central mainframe. However, an increasing number of systems that have user interaction are executed in what has been termed cooperative processing mode, partly on the PC, partly on the computer where the data resides.

In some cases, the PCs are attached directly, via a telecommunications link, to a single central mainframe. In other cases, the PCs are the workstations of a departmental minicomputer that maintains the communications link with the mainframe (three-tier computing). In most cases, however, the PCs are attached locally to each other via a local area network. To this local area network is also attached a file server that controls the shared data. A communications server is used as a shared gateway to the central mainframe.

The systems planning study team must address which of these architectures is best adapted to the organization's need and culture. Next, within the selected architecture, the team must estimate which part of the main applications will be executed where, where the data will reside, whether it will be replicated at multiple sites, and so on. Then, the team must evaluate the consequences of these assumptions on the hardware, telecommunications, and development costs.

- Add second-priority projects to the spreadsheet when resources become available from higher-priority projects. Adjust as required with temporary personnel.

- Summarize temporary personnel requirements to check that the total does not exceed the need determined earlier.

- Adjust the schedule as necessary by varying recruiting dates and temporary personnel and by changing project time lines until a satisfactory result is obtained.

Described in this fashion, the process seems relatively simple. However, there are many practical difficulties. At such an early stage little if anything is known about the specific requirements of each of the applications identified in the systems plan and the personnel requirements can only be roughly estimated. A frequent strategy is to refer to similar projects done in the past or in other corporations in the same industry. Experience is more useful than analysis in this case.

The most frequent error in personnel planning for such an exercise is to assume that executing the plan can start immediately with the first project. Very often the systems plan is associated with a change in the technical direction of the IS department, for example, towards relational data base, distributed computing, or even simply a new operating system. The lead time to get all the support functions in place for the first project is on the order of a few weeks, perhaps even months. Software and equipment may have to be installed, standards developed, and IS professionals trained.

An additional factor requiring lead time is the possible reorganization of the IS department to cope with a period of high development activity. Reorganization is especially necessary in IS departments that have gotten into the rut of *creeping maintenance*, defined as the gradual encroachment of day-to-day activities on new projects until practically all personnel are assigned to maintenance.

Finally, recruiting new or temporary personnel also requires long lead times.

In practice, it is prudent to provide for a two- to three-month buildup for the initial projects. Failure to provide enough time may result in having to report to management after only three months or so that the implementation of the plan is already behind schedule. Such a report can have disastrous effects on the credibility of the plan and the future of top management support for it.

Meanwhile, the plan will probably have identified one or two areas of quick return. These should be undertaken as high-priority items immediately without waiting for the support activities to take place. Early successes will increase the credibility of the plan and enhance both top management and user support.

HANDLING ORGANIZATIONAL ISSUES

As mentioned earlier, the implementation of a systems plan is often preceded by a reorganization of the IS department. A systems plan is often a manifestation of fresh thinking about how to tackle the problem of developing new applications. This freshness often carries over to the organization of the development teams and, indeed, the entire department.

The main objective of such a reorganization is to ensure that the resources that are assigned to new development (both the development teams themselves and the required support functions such as data administration, data base administration, and software support) remain assigned to new development and do not gradually get frittered away on maintenance of existing systems.

Even if no reorganization takes place, the analysis of personnel requirements described in the previous paragraph often leads information systems management to perform general personnel planning. Not only is it important to have the number of personnel available at the right times during the plan, but it is equally important that it should be the right personnel. Recruiting and training plans, career paths, and an assessment of existing personnel's managerial, professional, and technical qualifications should be undertaken during the development of the systems plan.

Summary

Poor infrastructure planning is at the root of many of the IS department's problems in the 1980s. The maintenance workload, often not planned for, tends to stifle systems development projects and contribute to the IS department's reputation for unresponsiveness. The accumulation of disparate hardware and software causes duplication of effort and makes development personnel less interchangeable. Finally, only recently have IS departments started to treat the technology needs of their personnel with the attention the problem deserves.

If a systems plan, developed as described in the previous chapter, is to succeed, it must be accompanied by proper infrastructure planning: for the development environment, for the production environment, and for personnel.

The decision that most affects the development environment is probably that of a data base management system. Today, the natural choice is a relational data base management system. Relational DBMS may not always be feasible in all environments, particularly those that already have a first-generation DBMS and those that rely heavily on application software.

The next decision is usually that of a teleprocessing monitor for transaction processing. Once the hardware and the DBMS are known, the TP monitor follows almost automatically.

Of more immediate importance to the development teams is the choice of methods and tools such as programming languages, application generators, fourth-generation languages, and CASE tools. All categories of tools are not equally suitable to all types of projects. For instance, the tools that shorten the coding cycle are less important on large projects where coding tends to be a smaller part of the total effort.

A plan for implementing these tools—a technology insertion plan—should accompany the choice of the actual tools.

Planning for production resources consists of making sure that the available hardware and software meet the needs of new systems as they are being implemented. Most of the capacity required is caused by on-line transaction processing and interactive end-user computing, but batch requirements cannot be neglected.

Telecommunications network plans are also part of the production environment, both for in-house communications and for electronic data interchange with customers and suppliers.

The planners must analyze the personnel requirements for developing the new applications and identify the sources of personnel: internal resources (analysts and programmers who are not required for maintenance), user departments, new hires, or temporary external sources such as consultants and programming houses.

Finally, due consideration must be given to organizational issues such as the best organization of the IS department for the implementation of the plan as well as training and career planning for its personnel.

Review Questions

1. List the three main components of infrastructure planning for a systems plan.

2. Why is the choice of a DBMS so critical?

3. Explain why tools that aim for programming efficiency are less important on large projects.

4. Discuss the relative importance of on-line and batch activities in determining the total hardware capacity required for the production environment.

5. Discuss the pros and cons of hiring new personnel, assigning user personnel as analysts, and using temporary personnel to fill personnel requirements for a systems plan.

Discussion Questions

1. What are the risks of trying to implement a systems plan without infrastructure planning?

2. Discuss the pros and cons of having multiple data base management systems or transaction processing monitors in a single IS department.

3. What are some requirements for implementing a homogeneous set of analysis, design, and programming tools or workbench?

Mini-Cases

Mid-Continental Electric Company. You are preparing a systems plan for Mid-Continental Electric Company. The applications to be developed over the next five years have been identified, and the required development resources have been estimated. The applications are described in Figure 6–2. Figure 6–3 indicates which current applications are being replaced by new applications and the number of analysts and programmers that are currently maintaining these systems.

Prepare a proposed calendar of application development covering all the applications in the plan. Assume that, as soon as an application project is started, the maintenance level on the applications being replaced is reduced by half. In addition, as soon as the new application is implemented, the maintenance level of the applications being replaced drops to zero. Also assume that maintaining one of the new applications for a year will require 5 percent of the total initial development effort.

The calendar should stretch over no more than five years and require no more than a personnel increase of 15 percent in any given year.

DRG International. James Muir, the corporate vice-president for administration, just called and asked you to meet with him and Philip Grey, the corporate director of MIS (who reports to Muir).

DRG International is a medium-sized manufacturer and distributor of restaurant supplies headquartered just outside of London. The business was started 20 years ago by its current president, Bill Jacobs. It has grown to its present 12 locations throughout the U.K. and Canada by purchasing poorly run distributors in other cities and turning them around. Bill is primarily an operations specialist and prides himself on running a "lean and mean" operation. The small staff at corporate headquarters is charged with overseeing the profit planning and performance monitoring of the remote locations, but for the most part, distribution center managers run their own show. Somehow, though, Muir feels as if he is the one who gets the blame for a distribution center's subpar performance. Once, for example, when there was a huge inventory loss at the Birmingham center, Jacobs chewed him out for not being close enough to that operation to be able to anticipate the problem.

On the advice of Philip Grey, Muir was able to convince Jacobs that DRG should standardize on the use of TLA computers. London had been a TLA user for five years, and Grey was pleased with both the hardware and the service he was getting from TLA personnel. The fact that London was TLA's world headquarters did not hurt when it came to getting service. One of Grey's arguments was that if DRG standardized on the hardware of one manufacturer, developing application systems that could be used by all units of the company would be much easier, with a resultant savings in development costs.

Last year, DRG acquired E-Z Ware Inc., a manufacturer of restaurant equipment located in Wilkes-Barre, Pennsylvania. At that time, DRG reorganized into two divisions, a distribution division headed by Frank Norris, based in London, and a manufacturing division under the leadership of Karl Gricar, who was the founder and president of E-Z Ware prior to its acquisition by DRG.

Muir wants to meet with you because Gricar has told Jacobs that he wants approval to lease a DAC mainframe computer to install a manufacturing control system. E-Z Ware has been a DAC user for many years, and its present computer does not have the capacity to handle the software package the E-Z Ware manufacturing people have selected. When Muir told Gricar about the DRG standardization policy on TLA hardware, Gricar's response was not helpful. "Look," he said. "I understand all that, but I've got a business to run. I asked our project team to find a package that would work on your TLA computers, but they came up dry. They found exactly what we need available on the DAC platform, so that's the direction we're headed. I know Jacobs will understand our position and support us."

When Muir told Grey about his conversation with Gricar, Grey was upset. "I think E-Z Ware should be forced to use TLA hardware. Otherwise, there's no use in having a corporate standard. Besides, you should know that the Canadian operation is getting large enough to justify their own hardware installation, and they're not too happy about using TLA because of some bias on the part of the general manager. If we don't hold fast and insist that E-Z Ware use TLA, we can forget about having a corporate standard."

James Muir feels he is getting in over his head a little bit and decides that he had better ask for some help. Thus, his call to you.

Figure 6–2 **List of Applications in Mid-Continental Electric Company's Portfolio**

```
SYSTEMS                        PLANNING TOOL                          CD-20
PLAN                        MID-CONTINENTAL ELECTRIC                   SCHED
               PROJECT SCHEDULE AND PERSONNEL REQUIREMENTS

PREPARED BY: ANNA TERHOOFT    DATE: 30APR89          VERSION:          PAGE 1
APPROVED BY: H. B. WALKER     DATE: 30APR89          STATUS:
```

PROJECT DESCRIPTION		WORKDAYS	MGR	ANAL	USER	PROG	FROM	TO
Budget Preparation	M	200	30		170		03/90	07/90
Crew Time/Field Rept.	M	900	135		765		07/89	12/89
Trans. Doc. Prep.	M	800	120		680		10/89	01/90
On-Line Table Maint.	M	1000	150		850		07/89	04/90
Job Closing	M	300	45		255		01/90	06/90
Forms & Report Review	M	1000	150		850		04/90	02/91
Enhanced On-Line Info.	D	300	45	255			12/89	02/90
	I	1400	210	420		770	03/90	09/90
Cooperative Proc. Arch.	D	200	30	170			09/90	10/90
	I	600	90	200		310	11/90	03/99
Training and Support		900	135	765			07/89	12/92
Detail Transaction DB	D	500	75	425			07/89	10/89
	I	1000	150	325		525	11/89	06/90
Work Reporting	D	1700	255	1445			07/89	01/90
	I	4900	735	1560		2605	02/90	02/91
Contract Management	D	700	105	595			03/91	05/91
	I	1500	225	400		875	06/91	12/91
Cost Accounting	D	650	100	550			01/90	05/90
	I	3450	500	1070		1880	06/90	03/91
Interim Commitment Rept.	D	100	15	85			07/89	09/89
	I	350	50	65		235	10/89	01/90
New FMIS Design	D	3450	525	2925			09/90	07/91
Source/Report Interface	I	11900	1785	3450		6665	01/91	08/92
Cost Acctg/Coding Block	I	600	90	230		280	01/92	08/92
Budgeting	I	2400	360	965		1075	10/91	06/92
General Ledger	I	7150	1050	3400		2700	09/91	12/92
Management Reporting	I	5950	890	2680		2380	10/91	12/92

```
KEY:    M-Manual System  D-Design  I-Installation
```

Figure 6–3 **List of Existing Applications to Be Displaced**

```
SYSTEMS                        PLANNING TOOL                              CD-20
PLAN                      MID-CONTINENTAL ELECTRIC                        SRSCH
                        SYSTEM REPLACEMENT SCHEDULE


PREPARED BY: ANNA TERHOOFT      DATE: 30APR89          VERSION:           PAGE 1
APPROVED BY: H. B. WALKER       DATE: 30APR89          STATUS:


                                                              CURRENTLY
                                                              ASSIGNED
     SYSTEM BEING REPLACED              REPLACED BY      PM     ANAL      PROG


     Work and Contract Management       Work Reporting    1     10        13
     Cost Accounting                    Cost Accounting   1     12         9
     Financial and G/L                  New FMIS          1     14        25
     Budgeting                          New FMIS                 2         3
     Responsibility Reporting           New FMIS                 6        10



     Personnel currently unassigned to maintenance:
          Project Managers:             4
          Analysts:                     6
          Programmers:                 13


     User personnel can be assumed to be available as required.


     Available time calculation:

          Workdays/year: 5 * 52                      =     260
               Less -
               4 week's vacation                     =     (20)
               Absences                              =      (5)
               Training and departmental             =     (25)
                                                          -----
     Net available:                                  =     210    workdays/year/person
                                                          =====
```

Questions for Discussion

1. What should be included on a discussion outline for your meeting with James Muir?

2. What steps should be included in a study to develop recommendations for discussion with Gricar and Jacobs?

Technique

Matrix Affinity Analysis

INTRODUCTION

Chapter 5 demonstrates the need for multiple representation techniques for systems planning. In addition to hierarchical diagrams, data flow diagrams, and entity-relationship diagrams, matrix affinity analysis is required for many of the planning activities.

Whereas hierarchical, data flow, and entity-relationship diagrams have their origins in other parts of the systems development life cycle, such as analysis and design, matrix affinity analysis is specifically associated with systems planning. Its incorporation into CASE tools is recent.

DEFINITION

Matrix affinity analysis is the representation of many-to-many relationships between objects listed in the rows and columns of a matrix. The relationships, represented as entries in the cells of the matrix, are analyzed so as to create natural clusters of entries in the rows and columns.

Each row or column represents an occurrence of some object type. Higher-level groupings can be indicated to the left of the rows or above the columns. Each cell at the intersection between a row and a column represents the existence (and possibly the type) of relationship between the object in the row and that in the matrix. With each relationship can be associated a strength, which serves to guide the affinity analysis. The strongest relationships serve as focal points for the analysis.

EXAMPLES

Figure 1 shows a matrix representing how business functions use data entities. The rows of the matrix are business functions, sorted according to the functional decomposition. Each row is a lowest-level function; higher-level functions are noted to the left.

The columns are data entities. The data entities are grouped into overall subjects.

The intersections are marked with U for functions that update (create, modify, or delete) the entity or with A for functions that access the data.

183

Figure 1 **Business Function/Data Matrix**

```
SYSTEMS                      PLANNING TOOL                          CD-20
PLAN                         SUBURBAN PUMPS                         PDMTX
                             PROCESS/DATA MATRIX

PREPARED BY: J. WEBER        DATE: 27OCT88          VERSION: 3      PAGE 1
APPROVED BY: JACK CROFT      DATE: 28OCT88          STATUS:  F
```

SUBJECT DATA BASES — EMPLOYEE · MANUFACTURING · MARKETING · MATERIALS · FIN

Application Systems	Department	Employee	Benefits	Payroll	Training	Product	Product Structure	Manufacturing Process	Work Center	Plant	Process Type	Equipment Type	Competitor	Sector	Region	Salesperson	Customer	Order	Agent	Finished Goods Inv	Warehouse	Vendor	Raw Materials	Raw Materials Inv	Purchase Order	Financial Info	Strategic Planning	Annual Planning
FINANCIAL																												
Purchasing						A																U	U	U	U			
Accounts payable																					A	A				U		
Accounts Receivable																				A	A					U		
Gneeral Ledger																				A			A			U		
Cost Accounting						U	A	A														U		A		U		
MANUFACTURING																												
Production Scheduling						U	U																					
Plant Process Control								U	U		U	U																
Inventory Control						A														U	U							
ADMINISTRATION																												
Personnel Planning	U	U	A	A	A																							
Payroll/Personnel	A	U	U	U																								
Training	A	A		U																								
MARKETING																												
Sales Analysis						A							A		U	U	A	A	A									
Profitability Reporting		A				A																				A		
Order Entry						A							A	A	U	U	U			A	A							
DECISION SUPPORT																												
Strategic Planning								A					A	A												A	U	A
Budgeting																										A	A	U

A–Access Only   U–Update

Figure 2 **Data Traffic Matrix**

```
SYSTEMS                          PLANNING TOOL                              CD-20
PLAN                          PRO-DEV CORPORATION                           TRAFC
                              DATA TRTAFFIC MATRIX

PREPARED BY:  E. WOJCHEKOWSKI    DATE: 15FEB93         VERSION: 2         PAGE 1
APPROVED BY:  GINNY HAWTHORNE    DATE: 15FEB93         STATUS:  D
```

	New York	Los Angeles	Hong Kong	Singapore	Paris	London	El Paso
New York		48.0	53.0				
Los Angeles	75.0		75.0	75.0	75.0	75.0	75.0
Hong Kong	6.0	75.0		27.0	15.7	31.4	2.7
Singapore	5.6	6.0	7.0		6.0	72.0	6.0
Paris	36.0	7.0	24.8	9.0		18.5	12.3
London	56.0	8.3	9.7	0.5	20.7		17.0
El Paso	5.4	19.0	19.0	7.8	24.1	8.6	

This example shows a matrix after affinity analysis has been performed: the matrix shows natural groupings of rows and columns, with associated clusters of cells. In this case, the clustering is more strongly associated with the *U* than with the *A* attribute.

Figure 2 shows a data traffic matrix between locations. Here, rows and columns are identical; the cell content is the number of characters (in millions) transmitted daily from the row location to the column location.

Figure 3 shows a matrix representing the tactical goals of the various departments of an organization. No clustering has yet been performed on this matrix. The relationships are represented by a simple mark signifying its presence. For instance, improving sales effectiveness is a goal of the human resource development department, the sales region, and order processing, but not of the legal department.

Figure 4 shows a more detailed process/entity matrix. The difference from Figure 1 is that a cell may contain several values: here, the cells indicate whether a function creates, reads, updates, or deletes the entity. (This type of matrix is widely known as a *CRUD* matrix.)

Figure 3 Organization/Goal Matrix

```
SYSTEMS                        PLANNING TOOL                        CD-20
PLAN                         PRO-DEV CORPORATION                    OGOAL
                           ORGANIZATION/GOALS MATRIX

PREPARED BY:  CHRISTOPHER HALL     DATE: 12DEC92        VERSION: 2     PAGE 1
APPROVED BY:  GINNY HAWTHORNE      DATE: 15JAN93        STATUS:  D
```

GOALS / ORGANIZATIONS

ORGANIZATIONS	Improve Sales Effectiveness	Identify New Target Markets	Improve Market Penetration	Add Distribution Channels	Exploit New Technology	Improve Information Systems	Streamline Shop Floor Operations	Enhance Employee Training	Enhance Customer Support	Improve Product Quality	Expand Product Line	Upgrade Product Warranty	Reduce Inventory Investment	Reduce Receivables to 45 Days	Improve Cash Flow Management	Locate Venture Capital	Enhance Corporate Image
Planning	x	x															
Accounting															x	x	
Cash Management															x		
Investments															x		
Purchasing													x				
Facilities							x										
Human Resource Development	x							x									
MIS						x											
Legal												x		x			
Manufacturing										x	x		x				
Quality Assurance									x	x							
Packaging											x						
Materials Management													x				
Sales Regions	x	x									x		x				
Customer Service									x								
Customer Education	x																
Order Processing	x		x								x						
Product Management			x	x							x						
Public Relations		x														x	x
Market Research	x	x	x	x						x	x						
Distribution			x	x													
Engineering					x			x		x	x	x	x				
Research	x	x		x						x	x						
Prototype Manufacture				x		x				x	x						
Testing Laboratory				x						x	x	x					

Figure 4 **Business Process/Entity Matrix**

```
SYSTEMS                    PLANNING TOOL                              CD-20
PLAN                    PRO-DEV CORPORATION                          BPENT
                    BUSINESS PROCESS/ENTITY MATRIX

PREPARED BY: CHRISTOPHER HALL    DATE: 12DEC92    VERSION: 2         PAGE 1
APPROVED BY: GINNY HAWTHORNE     DATE: 15JAN93    STATUS:  D
```

Entity	Plan Finances	Perform Accounting	Control Finances	Staff Organizations	Develop Individual Capabilities	Administer HR Programs	Plan Production	Research/Develop Products	Procure Materials	Produce Product	Plan Product	Market Product	Process Customer Orders	Manage Business	Manage Vendors	Manage Information
Employees	R	R		CRUD	RU	R	R						R			R
HR Plans, Procedures						CRUD									R	R
Third Persons				CRUD	R									CRUD		
Financial Plans	CRUD	RU	CRUD	R			R									
Income	R	CRUD	R											R		
Outflow	R	CRUD	R											R		
Investments	R	CRUD	CRUD											R		
Product Plans	R			R	R		R	R			CRUD			R		R
Materials		R					R	CRUD	RU	RU						
Finished Goods		R					R	CRUD		RU	R	R				
Facility Plans	R			R						R	R	R		CRUD		
Locations		R		R				R	R	R			RU	CRUD		
Equipment		R			R		RU	RU		R	R	R		R	R	
Vendors		R							R				R		CRUD	
Customers		R						CRUD			R	R	CRUD	R		
Third-Party Organizations	R	R	CRUD								R	R	CRUD	CRUD		
Systems Plan	R	R		R		RU								R		CRUD
Information Models																CRUD
Development Projects																CRUD
DP Operations																CRUD

C-Create   R-Retrieve   U-Update   D-Delete

WHERE USED IN THE LIFE CYCLE

The matrix representation itself is used throughout the life cycle, with the heaviest concentration in systems planning and requirements analysis. Affinity analysis, the organization of information according to naturally occurring clusters, is in practice only performed during systems planning. At other times, the matrix structure is simply used as a convenient and easy-to-understand form of documentation.

FORMAL RULES

Constraints

A matrix documents a many-to-many relationship. If the relationship were one-to-many (one column can be associated with many rows but each row can only be associated with one column), a hierarchical diagram would be appropriate.

Rows and columns must be homogeneous. Each row must represent an instance of the same type of object; so must each column, although rows and columns can be (and most often are) different.

Each instance of an object in a matrix corresponds to some object defined in some other document or in a CASE tool. The most frequently represented objects are the following:

- Entity or subject
- Business function or process
- Organizational unit
- User or executive
- Location
- Objective
- Goal
- Critical success factor
- Key performance indicator
- Problem or opportunity
- System or application
- Technology

Each of these objects has at least a definition and probably some additional attributes. Whereas the planners may first encounter the need for one of these objects when creating a matrix, the repository must ultimately contain a detailed description of it. A high-function CASE tool should be able to signal any discrepancy: objects in matrices that are not described elsewhere and objects that are not incorporated as a row or column in a matrix where it would be expected (for instance, an entity absent from the function/entity matrix).

Cells can only have predefined values; however, the set of possible values (the domain) of the cell depends on the objects being related. Consistency rules among cell values are also matrix-dependent. For instance, in a function/entity matrix, each entity can be expected to be created by at least one function.

Affinity Analysis

Affinity can be calculated between columns relative to rows, or vice versa. In the example of Figure 1, the function/data matrix, two columns (entities) are said to have total affinity if for each function where one is checked, the other one is checked too. They are said to have total lack of affinity if there are no rows on which they are checked off together. Thus, *Finished Goods Inventory* and *Warehouse* have almost total affinity, as do *Benefits* and *Payroll*. *Warehouse* and *Payroll*, however, have no affinity.

The formula used here is simply a count of the number of occurrences of two entities A and B on the same line divided by the total number of occurrences of one of them. Reverting to our example, the affinity of *Finished Goods Inventory* to *Warehouse* is 3/4, or 75 percent. (The affinity of *Warehouse* to *Finished Goods Inventory* is 3/3, or 100 percent.)

In this case, affinities were based on simply counting occurrences. Another possibility is to associate weights with the cell values and add up the weights instead. In the matrix in Figure 1, the normal procedure would be to associate a greater weight with the letter *U* than the letter *A*.

Once pairwise affinities have been computed, the analysis can be refined by associating more than two objects. For instance, the affinity of an entity C to a cluster (A,B) is defined as the average affinity of C to A and C to B, weighted by the number of occurrences of A and B respectively.

When all the affinities have been calculated, they are sorted in descending rank, and all those that are above a certain limit are taken into account. This constraint is often reformulated as follows: continue clustering until the desired number of clusters is reached. This number should neither be 1 (all affinities are taken into account, even if they are equal to zero), nor equal to the total number of objects (no affinities are taken into account, even if they are equal to 100 percent).

MECHANIZED TOOLS

CASE tools specializing in the planning phase (and sometimes those that specialize in analysis) may have an affinity analysis facility.

The corresponding matrix editor may or may not be strongly tied to the rest of the CASE tool, providing for integration between the matrices and the other CASE tool functions such as entity-relationship modeling, data flow diagramming, and hierarchical diagram (decomposition) editor. (It is with the decomposition editor that it is most desirable to have this integration.) Some matrix editors may create matrices automatically from the current inventory of the row and column objects; others can maintain a two-way connection.

Most matrix editors have a facility for checking consistency rules, for example, that each column or row must have at least one cell of a certain type or no more than one cell of another type. In general, no row and no column should be completely empty. Another typical example is the rule that each entity must be created at least once.

Some matrix editors can only create certain types of matrices; others are general purpose and can create any matrix, given the types of the rows and the columns.

As a last resort, a spreadsheet may be used to document matrix-like structures. In such cases, no additional functions such as affinity analysis, consistency checking, or integration with other CASE functions are possible.

CRITERIA FOR USE

There are no limitations on the use of matrices: they constitute an excellent tool for communicating and for spotting patterns or inconsistencies.

Traditionally, affinity analysis is used for two purposes:

- Grouping data entities into subject data bases and functions into systems
- Relating solutions (such as technologies, development projects, or critical success factors) to goals or objectives

This second type of analysis points out solutions that should be implemented together for maximum effectiveness.

Selected Readings

Martin, J. *Information Engineering, Book II: Planning and Analysis.* Englewood Cliffs, N J: Prentice-Hall, 1990.
The clearest exposition of the clustering algorithm used by most current CASE tools.

EXERCISES

1. Apply affinity analysis to the matrix in Figure 3. Attempt to do it by hand first, then with a CASE tool. Evaluate the results. Are there any surprising conclusions?

2. Create a matrix of the fifty states (or the countries of the European Economic Community, or a similar group of economic entities) against a set of about ten economic activity indicators (output by industry, for example, or growth in population; tax revenue; total agricultural, industrial, and service sector production; and corresponding productivity figures).

Analyze the affinity of the states (or countries) among themselves, using an automated affinity analysis program. Do you see any strong patterns? Does it make any difference whether you use absolute values or percentages?

Requirements Analysis

The four central sections of the book, Sections III through VI, describe the process of systems analysis and design. This section, Requirements Analysis, will help you understand how to start the systems development process. The section also introduces several tools and techniques helpful in collecting and documenting the facts that will serve as the basis for the analysis and, later, the design of a new system.

Lone Wolf Timber & Mining Company

◆

The Lone Wolf Timber & Mining Company is a conglomerate established in Billings, Montana, with mining and forestry operations throughout the Rocky Mountains. Lone Wolf also has several sawmills and paper mills in Montana and Wyoming, as well as part interest in a building materials manufacturing company in Portland, Oregon.

In the late 1960s, each of the mines of Lone Wolf had developed its own information systems. A few years later, a central accounting system was created for all the forestry and sawmills operations, and the individual mine systems were consolidated into a corporate system separate from the forestry systems. The paper mills, a recent acquisition, continued to have their own systems.

In 1989, the information systems and services (ISS) department of Lone Wolf initiated a project to consolidate all the billing, collection, and accounts receivable systems of all the operations. The objectives of this consolidation were to reduce maintenance, to simplify administrative operations, and, most importantly, to speed up invoice collection by providing on-line access to the system.

ISS decided to use the joint application development (JAD) approach to determine user requirements and design the user interface of the new billing and collection system (BCS). JAD had already been used a few months earlier to design the user interface and the data structures of a forest management system after the manager of systems development had attended an information-processing conference where JAD was discussed. At the conference, JAD had been presented as a new method for systems analysis and design that consisted of work sessions grouping up to ten key users and two or three information systems professionals, to arrive at requirements and design specifications through group consensus, with most of the emphasis on user participation.

When planning for the JAD sessions, Jeff Hamilton, the BCS project manager, contacted the project manager and several users of the forestry project to try to learn from the earlier effort's successes and failures. He found that the main success of JAD on the forestry project had been to reduce the need for "selling" the users on the benefits of the system. All those who had participated in the group sessions were knowledgeable and enthusiastic about the new system and had communicated their enthusiasm to their colleagues in their respective departments. Another benefit of JAD had been to accelerate some very complex design decisions requiring the input from multiple departments and locations. This benefit had been harder to achieve, however, because of the JAD session leaders' lack of forestry systems expertise, which had hampered the group in articulating the issues.

Jeff Hamilton also found that the JAD process had presented some problems, and he tried to devise means to avoid some of these problems. First, the users in a group session had difficulties creating documents from scratch. Hamilton therefore decided to rely heavily on prepared starting points communicated to the group well beforehand. Thus, the group could concentrate on critiquing rather than creating. He also prepared multiple alternative suggestions so that the group would never feel unduly pressured.

Hamilton also found that some earlier sessions had moved very slowly because group members had difficulty agreeing on terminology. He decided to prepare a project glossary at the outset of the sessions and to maintain this glossary, with new terms being defined or old definitions changed as required. Although this would not prevent all misunderstandings and delays due to explanations, it would accelerate the process.

Another problem had been found in the earlier project when technical subjects were broached: the group could only move as fast as its least knowledgeable member. Hamilton decided to reduce the impact of this problem by avoiding, to the extent possible, technical topics. He also ensured that those sessions during which technical subjects were likely to be brought up would be attended by at least one person with both technical and functional expertise who would be able to explain the topic better to the others.

Last, the previous project had encountered a problem when users from some departments had brought up requirements that were either inconsistent with those expressed by other departments or simply too costly. The forestry system team had found it difficult to say no when working in a group. Hamilton felt that this problem would not arise to the same extent on his project because all the users of BCS were in the same department, albeit from different locations.

When the BCS project started, two more problems were found. Both could fortunately be addressed quickly. First, the BCS systems development strategy was to base the system on application software packages, which would be completed with additional functions and interfaces to other systems as required. The JAD sessions were planned mainly to select the best package and to determine which additional features were absolutely required. However, the users in the group sessions showed a tendency to add too many features that were embellishments rather than requirements. This problem was partly corrected by organizing a presentation on the cost of changing and adding features to packages.

The second problem was caused by the solution to an earlier problem. The administrative support required to prepare the written materials prior to a session was underestimated. The project team found that it was usually necessary to produce 10 or 12 packets consisting of 50 to 80 pages of materials per day of workshop. Then, after the workshop session, these documents had to be edited and a session report issued. As a result, one additional analyst and two secretaries had to be assigned to the project team.

The benefits achieved by the use of JAD on the BCS project were those hoped for: quick results, maximum user adhesion, and a high-quality design, although at a somewhat greater cost than anticipated. The comment of one user who had attended JAD sessions for both projects was: "The forestry project went well, but I sometimes felt that I was spending too much time in group sessions rather than at my normal activities. On the BCS project, I rarely had the impression of wasting time, although my normal activities probably suffered as much as on the previous project."

PURPOSE OF SECTION

Requirements analysis is done in two parts. First, information about the requirements is collected; next, this information is organized to constitute a requirements specification.

How to collect information about user requirements is the focus of Chapter 7. Interviewing, which is covered first, is the most widely used information-gathering technique in systems analysis. Analysts interview future users of the system individually to find out what the present system does and what changes are needed. The information gathered during the interviews enables the analysts to design a new system that will eliminate the shortcomings of the current one.

An increasingly popular alternative to interviewing individuals is the group interview conducted by an impartial leader. A representative method, *described in the second part of Chapter 7,* is Joint Application Design (JAD), developed and taught by IBM. The advantages of JAD are that the analysis phase of the life cycle is shortened and that the specifications document produced tends to be better accepted by the users.

The requirements thus collected are of two types: functional requirements—what the system does—and quality requirements—how well it does it. Functional requirements, the traditional view, are covered in Chapter 8. The functional requirements specification consists of a description of the system's behavior as viewed from the outside, its data structure, and its flow of data (or process). Different strategies for eliciting the functional requirements are considered. The main questions addressed are in how much detail the current system is analyzed and whether the accent is on data structures or data flows.

Chapter 9 considers nonfunctional, or quality, requirements. Examples of quality requirements are performance, reliability, usability and flexibility. These requirements are considered from the angle of how they are likely to influence the design process.

Definition of Analysis

The term *analysis* applied to the first phase of systems development is somewhat of a misnomer. To analyze a system means to break it down into component parts and to study each part in isolation as well as in its interactions with other parts. To be useful, analysis must generally be followed by synthesis, that is, putting the parts together and determining how the system functions as a whole. Analysis consists of finding out *how* a system works, synthesis in *what* it does (and possibly why, how well, etc.).

The analysis phase produces a requirements specifications document that describes what the future system is to do but not how. The how will be determined during the design phase. The analysis phase would therefore appear to require a stronger component of synthesis than analysis, and a better term for *requirements analysis* might perhaps be *requirements determination* or *problem determination.*

The emphasis on analysis stems from two factors. First, the implementers of systems have not traditionally been experts in the area of the application being developed; rather, they have been technology experts—computer programmers or information systems analysts. Analysis is a powerful technique for learning about the application. Second, when the project consists of replacing an existing system, the easiest way to produce a requirements specification for the new system is to proceed by difference. Document the old system, make only those changes required to improve performance and eliminate operational problems, and—whoosh!—you have the specification of the new system.

This technique is still widely applied today although it tends to be de-emphasized when the project objective is to provide competitive advantage by finding new uses of information technology rather than to perfect old methods and procedures. Joint Application Design (conducting requirements determination in an intensely concentrated workshop) emphasizes the requirements of the future system rather than the analysis of the existing system.

KEY TASKS AND DELIVERABLES

The team should not start the requirements analysis unless there is a clear statement of the scope and objectives of the project. The systems plan or a feasibility study normally provides this statement. If not, or if the statement requires additional detail, the scope of the system must be circumscribed before work can start. Ideally, this step will tell the systems developers with some precision how much they can question existing rules or habits so that the team will know to what degree of abstraction the requirements should be carried.

The next phase is to build a logical model of the system (one that does not depend on details of implementation), usually by one of the following methods:

- Interviewing users to build a physical model of the present system, abstracting this to a logical model of the present system, and then incorporating desirable changes so as to create the logical model of the future system.
- Organizing a workshop with group methods such as JAD to create the logical model of the new system directly, without the intermediate steps of the physical and logical models of the present system.

In either case, the logical model of the new system becomes the requirements specification. Typically, it contains:

- An introduction containing the scope, goals, and objectives of the system.
- Data flow diagrams depicting the workflow of the new system, including the clear identification of business transactions.
- A project data model (as described in Section V).
- Information needs: which types of questions will be asked of the system and which data will support the answers.
- Interfaces with other systems.
- Sample report, screen, and form layouts, if required.
- Volume projections.
- Performance parameters such as processing frequencies and schedules, response time requirements, resource utilization constraints.
- Measurable criteria for judging whether the implementation has acceptable reliability, usability, and flexibility.

The final test of the system, the user acceptance test, should be conducted as a benchmark against this document. Therefore, all those factors that will determine whether the users are satisfied with the system should be documented and agreed upon.

There may be a final step in the requirements analysis—to have the users and top management sign off on the specification document. In most cases, if sufficient contact is maintained with the users during the work, this step is not necessary. The requirements specification approval can then be bundled with the approval of the design (see Chapter 19).

7

Interviewing and JAD

This chapter first examines the importance of reviewing the present system and under what conditions it should be done. Next, the chapter describes interviewing, by far the most widely used technique for reviewing present systems and determining future requirements. After presenting the rationale for an alternative technique, Joint Application Design (JAD), the chapter describes the roles of the various participants and explains how to prepare, organize, conduct, and use the results of a JAD workshop. The benefits and the risks of JAD are analyzed. Other techniques, such as questionnaires, observation, and sampling, are briefly discussed.

Learning Objectives

*   Recognize the value of reviewing the present system as a prelude to creating a new system.
*   Acquire skill in the five steps of the interviewing process: (1) prepare for the interview, (2) plan and schedule the interview, (3) open and close the interview, (4) conduct the interview, and (5) follow up for clarification.
*   Recognize the value of active listening and restatement at both the direct and emotional levels.
*   Understand the methodologies available for documenting the results of interviews and other data-gathering techniques.
*   Understand the advantages of Joint Application Design (JAD) and other similar techniques for collecting facts about a current system and for determining the requirements of a system under development.
*   Describe the various steps to be taken to prepare for a JAD session.
*   Understand the eight points about each application that should be covered in a JAD session.

REVIEWING THE CURRENT SYSTEM

Reviewing the present system is usually the first step in designing a new system. Some practitioners maintain that reviewing the present system is an unnecessary step, one that can lead to repeating in the future system the deficiencies of the present system. These practitioners are in the minority, however. Most agree on the value of reviewing the present system as a prelude to further design work for the following reasons:

- Reviewing gives the design team a good grasp of the business problems to be addressed by a new system and of the strengths and weaknesses of the present system in addressing those problems.

- It enables the design team to understand the environment in which the new system will operate.

- It ensures that no operating requirement or process will be overlooked in the specification of requirements for the new system.

- It anchors the new design in the old one: often, users can more easily understand implications of new designs when they are expressed as being "similar to before, with the following exceptions." It may also permit reusing satisfactory parts of the existing system.

- It enhances the cooperation between the project team and the users.

Some practical advice follows on how to exploit these advantages of reviewing the present system.

Understanding the Business Problem

The better the design team understands the business problem being addressed, the better the chances of developing a solution that uses information technology creatively. In many cases, the underlying business problem is not well articulated or well understood by the user. If the user's underlying business problem will be addressed by a new system, it must be clearly stated and understood by the project team. Gildersleeve states that a good problem statement begins with two things:

- A description of the present situation.
- A standard of desired performance.[1]

Rockart's critical success factors, referred to in Section II, can help define a standard of desired performance. Most business managers, at any level, monitor a relatively short list of items to assure them that their areas of responsibility are under control. For example, a supermarket store manager may monitor such items as sales per square foot, personnel cost per sales dollar, departmental margins, and this year's sales compared with last year's by day of the week. Such items would be the manager's critical success factors. If they are within a range of acceptability, the manager's mind is at ease. On the other hand, if margins in the produce department fall below the critical success factor target, the manager can initiate action to uncover the cause so that a correction can be made. Evaluating the quality of critical success factors can help analysts determine whether a particular manager has a good grasp of a unit's business problems. The approach also identifies information that a system must provide to satisfy a manager's information requirements.

Understanding the Operating Environment

One of the first things an experienced IS professional will do when beginning a new project is to take a plant tour—a tour of the relevant facilities that will be the subject of a review. It may be an actual plant in a manufacturing company, but it could also be an office, retail space, the registration desk of a resort hotel, or the emergency room of a city hospital on a busy Saturday night. The plant tour exposes the IS professional to the business environment that a new system will support. The professional is therefore more sensitive to which solutions will work and which will not. Understanding the business environment does not mean the internal environment only, because today's systems cast their nets much wider and include entities external to the organization. For example, imagine a project team member beginning a review of the department that handles customers' telephone inquiries for a large electric distribution company. The team member might sit beside a customer service clerk and listen to the types of questions customers ask and the information used by the clerk in responding to them.

Not all companies are ready to digest the latest in technology, and a project team sensitive to the operating environment can avoid expensive mistakes. For example, taking a tour of a bank's office in a lesser-developed country and seeing stacks of paper and disorganized files should sensitize a project team to two issues. First, such an organization might need to walk with the technology before running with it. In other words, a pilot test in a smaller unit may be wise; or improvements may have to be made to the manual procedures before mechanizing them. Second, if the project team were to recommend going ahead with a computerized system, they should realize that they may have serious problems with data conversion and should plan accordingly.

Considering All Requirements

A systematic review of the current system should identify all data used and all processes performed by the current system. This review will ensure that critical minor processes are not overlooked when requirements for the new system are specified. In addition, the project team can develop a list of strengths and weaknesses of the present system in meeting the business needs of its users. This list will help ensure that the new system retains the strengths of the present system where appropriate and corrects its weaknesses. A checklist of information usually gathered during a review of the current system is shown in Figure 7–1.

Anchoring the New System in the Old

The approach usually chosen to determine the requirements of the future system consists of constructing a model of the present system, interviewing management and hands-on users, then modifying the system with those changes that the analysis team deems necessary.

Figure 7–1 **Checklist of Information Usually Gathered during a Review of the Current System**

User responsibilities, priorities, goals, problems

Information sources
    Computerized/noncomputerized
    Reports/documents/screens
        Accuracy
        Timeliness
        Relevance
        Duplication
        Conciseness
        Uniformity
        Volumes

Information flow
    Action taken with information received
    Identification of bottlenecks and delays
    Identification of missing information
    Documentation of methods used to obtain information
        outside the formal system

User suggestions for improvement
    Responsibilities, work system
    Information sources
    Information flow

The analysis team should document not only the required changes but also all the possible changes that might be made in the future. The art of systems analysis is in large part the capability to choose those aspects of the present system that are unchangeable, those that are likely to change over the long term, and those that can be changed immediately. Box 7–1 describes which functions and features of a system are the most permanent and which are the most likely to change.

Enhancing User Relationships

Members of user departments may express some irritation at having their work interrupted, particularly if a project is perceived to be "yet another study." Usually, however, they welcome the opportunity to spend time familiarizing the project team with the present system. They like to have their problems taken seriously and are suspicious of analysts who jump to conclusions, in the same way we want to explain our symptoms to a physician before hearing the diagnosis. In addition, good ideas are often obtained from people who work with the present system every day. In many cases, they have had these ideas for a long time, but no one has ever taken the time to ask for them before.

Permanence versus Change

Any feature or function that depends on industry-wide standards or customs is likely to be fairly permanent. For instance, in an airline reservation system, it is not likely that one airline would be able to charge for cancellations (except on discounted tickets) without a radical change of mood in the industry. Similarly, a single insurance company is not likely to implement no-fault insurance on its own.

The next most unlikely changes are those that are tied to national or corporate culture. For instance, a closed-shop factory is likely to continue considering union requirements in its personnel scheduling systems for a number of years.

Organizational change is next on the list of unlikely changes. Most companies prefer not to reorganize too frequently; however, if management is convinced that reorganization will solve a problem, it will happen. It is therefore generally better to make information systems flexible enough that different distributions of tasks can be supported. It is also obviously better not to

code reporting relationships into the systems, thus avoiding heavy maintenance to cost centers, profit centers, and responsibility reporting if reorganizations do take place.

In contrast, management fiat is at relatively high risk of change. Rules such as the number of points charged for a mortgage loan, penalties for late payments, and cost-of-living salary raises are typical examples. A conscious effort should be made to avoid relying on these requirements as a permanent basis for the information system.

Finally, regulatory requirements are even more unstable than management decisions because the regulatory body, usually a federal or state government organization, often does not feel the effect of changing requirements with the same intensity as do the regulated companies. On the other hand, such changes tend to be unpredictable. In a heavily regulated industry such as electric utilities, considerable expertise is required to minimize future disruptions due to regulatory changes.

INTERVIEWING

Of the various techniques employed for reviewing present systems, interviewing is by far the most common. Other techniques—questionnaires, sampling, and observation—will be discussed later in this chapter.

An interview is a systematic attempt to collect information from a person. Interviewing is an important skill for systems analysts because success depends on an ability to identify work flows, factors that influence the operations of systems, and the elements (documents, procedures, policies, etc.) that make up systems. Without accurate and complete information, the new system would probably not contain the necessary features to meet the needs of the organization. In addition, poorly performed interviews can affect the attitudes of the users and have a negative effect on the entire project effort.

The interview process has five steps:

- Preparing for the interview
- Planning and scheduling the interview
- Opening and closing the interview
- Conducting the interview
- Following up for clarification

Each step is discussed in more detail in the following paragraphs.

Preparing for the Interview

Adequate preparation is essential for successful interviewing. Before undertaking an interview, the analyst should first have a good understanding of the organization, its industry setting, and the project's scope and objectives. Analysts become familiar with the organization by reviewing organization charts, annual reports, long-range planning documents, statements of departmental goals, and the like. Existing procedure manuals and systems documentation should also be reviewed. Finally, a physical tour of the facilities, as discussed above, completed before the interviews, is helpful in giving the analyst a feel for the organization.

Analysts performing a project for the first time in a particular industry will find the interviewing process more effective if they first familiarize themselves with the industry. Although first-time analysts should not pose as industry experts on the basis of their initial research, at least they will understand common industry terms and be somewhat familiar with the business problems of the industry. Users are more comfortable talking to analysts whom they do not have to educate in the problems of their industry. For example, in a banking setting, users would expect an analyst to understand that DDA refers to demand deposit accounting and that deregulation of the financial services industry and interstate banking are current items of concern in the United States.

Finally, as discussed in Chapter 3, management can pave the way for the interviewing process with an announcement that interviews will be taking place.

Planning and Scheduling the Interview

Analysts should plan interviews by preparing a list of topics and questions to be covered. This list will help ensure that important points are not overlooked and that the interview follows a logical progression. In some cases, a preinterview questionnaire (see Figure 7–2) is sent to the interviewee ahead of time. The questionnaire gives the interviewee time to consider the areas to be covered and, in many cases, to gather samples of documents and reports the analyst may wish to obtain.

The first task in scheduling interviews is to determine who should be interviewed. Most analysts will take a top-down approach to this task and

**Figure 7–2 Sample Preinterview Questionnaire
for a Supervisor of Order Processing**

```
CIS                              DESIGN TOOL                      CD-20
ORDERS                          SUBURBAN PUMPS                    PIQUE
                          PREINTERVIEW QUESTIONNAIRE

PREPARED BY: RHONDA TURNER       DATE: 27FEB88      VERSION:      PAGE 1
APPROVED BY: SUSAN BAKER         DATE: 05MAR88      STATUS:


   Position: Supervisor of Order Processing
   --------


   1. What are the steps performed to process an order?


   2. Are there different order processing methods used according to type of order,
      customer classification, geographical area, etc.?


   3. What data are used during the order-taking process? What data are generated?


   4. Are additional data needed? Under what circumstances?


   5. How large is a typical order, in number of items and dollar value? How large is
      the smallest order? The largest?


   6. How many orders are processed per day or week? What are the peaks and troughs?


   7. How often does a typical customer order?


   8. Are there ever difficulties with the workflow? If so, identify problems,
      bottlenecks, delays, frequent errors.


   9. What documents and reports are created? Who uses them?
```

start with higher-level user personnel. They may also use a copy of the organization chart when selecting personnel for interviews so that no critical areas or persons are inadvertently overlooked. Protocol also requires that interviews within departments or areas proceed from the top down. Heads of departments or sections are usually interviewed before employees who report to them. There may be a logical sequence for interviews that should be considered when the schedule is prepared. For example, analysts may get greater understanding of a process or transaction if they follow it from beginning to end, rather than starting in the middle. When time is short and many individuals must be interviewed, compromises are sometimes necessary to accommodate the individual schedules of the interviewees.

When contacting personnel to schedule interviews, team members should explain the purpose of the interview, the general areas to be covered, and the approximate amount of time required to cover all areas. In most cases, the interview takes place at the interviewee's work location. In some cases, however, another location must be found. For example, a work site may lack the necessary privacy or may be too noisy. An interview with a factory supervisor is probably best done in a location other than on the factory floor. An alternative location should be a relaxed environment conducive to a business discussion.

Opening and Closing the Interview

In addition to gathering targeted information, effective interviews are carefully opened and closed. Failure to open an interview properly may affect the body of the interview, and failure to close the interview properly may make a follow-up interview more difficult.

In opening an interview, an analyst will first introduce himself or herself, state the purpose of the interview, address any concerns sensed by the analyst or raised by the interviewee, and then explain that brief notes will be taken and shared with the interviewee after they have been organized. Often interviewees are concerned that an analyst is trying to find fault with the way they work. One way to set them at ease is to get them to talk about processes with which they are familiar. The analyst selects topics on the basis of an advanced questionnaire, if one was used, or on the basis of discussions with persons to whom the interviewees report.

The best interviews are those where the interviewees do most of the talking. Therefore, analysts look for ways to get interviewees to open up to them. With some interviewees, this is no problem; with others, it is. One of the most widely used approaches is active listening, which is described below. One technique to be avoided is a series of specific, closed questions. The result of this approach is usually that the interviewees give a brief answer to the question and then wait for the next one, almost as if they were being interrogated by a detective.

Note taking can become a distraction if not restricted to brief notations for later elaboration. The analyst's notepad is best kept out of the interviewee's line of vision. The purpose of an analyst's notes should be to help recall pertinent points and hypotheses formed during an interview. Many analysts will use broad headings for note taking rather than specific categories (see Figure 7–3 on page 206).

Taping an interview is usually not recommended. It tends to intimidate the interviewee; moreover, listening to the tape and culling pertinent information is very time consuming.

When all areas on the interview outline have been explored, analysts will often ask questions such as "Is there anything we've overlooked?" or "What other areas should I have asked you about?" This tactic encourages the interviewee to discuss issues that should have been covered. Another question often asked by analysts is "What one change would make your job easier or more effective?" This question elicits suggestions for improvement.

Closing the interview involves briefly summarizing the areas that have been discussed, highlighting the important facts and the analyst's understanding of them. This technique lets the interviewee know that the analyst has been listening carefully during the interview and also provides an opportunity for clarifying any misunderstandings. During the summary, as well as during the entire interview, the analyst should adopt a posture of objectivity and avoid personal comments, observations, or conclusions.

Finally, in closing, the analyst thanks the interviewee for the time and asks if a shorter follow-up interview can be scheduled at a later date if necessary.

Conducting the Interview

One of the main objectives of the analyst conducting an interview is to see that information flows easily from interviewee to analyst and is not shut off for any reason. The technique of active listening helps to maintain the information flow and facilitates adequate feedback from analyst to interviewee. The active listening technique has five key tools:

- Asking open-ended questions
- Using appropriate words and phrases
- Giving acceptance cues
- Restating the interviewee's responses
- Using silence effectively

Asking Open-Ended Questions. Open-ended questions cannot be answered with a simple yes or no response and thus encourage the interviewee to provide more information. Open-ended questions begin with such words as what, how, or tell me rather than such words as can, does, or when. For example, more information is likely to flow from a question such as "Tell me what happens when a customer calls" than a series of questions such as "Does your department handle customer calls? Can they be answered by any clerk sitting at a terminal? Do you expect the customers to have their account numbers ready?"

Figure 7–3 **Note Headings for a Data-Gathering Interview**

```
                              DESIGN TOOL                                    U716
                            SUBURBAN PUMPS                                    INOTE
                            INTERVIEW NOTES

PREPARED BY:                 DATE:                    VERSION:              PAGE 1
APPROVED BY:                 DATE:                    STATUS:


    Key Interview Topics                     Interviewee Response
    --------------------                     --------------------












    New Ideas
    ---------




    Interviewee Opinions
    --------------------
```

Some questions are best answered by a yes or no, so not all questions should be open ended. Experienced analysts try to find the right balance appropriate to each situation. An approach with no open-ended questions is almost never appropriate, however, and should be avoided.

Using Appropriate Words and Phrases. The analyst should avoid using words or phrases that are emotionally charged, distracting, or difficult to understand. For example, such emotional expressions as problem area, cumbersome process, or poorly controlled imply a foregone conclusion. Distracting statements contain excessive abbreviations or acronyms, name dropping, or controversial words and phrases. Finally, analysts should avoid colloquialisms, slang, and jargon unless the interviewee is certain to understand them. IS professionals are notorious for peppering their speech with the jargon of their profession, using such words or acronyms as data models, DFDs, DASD, and connectivity.

Giving Acceptance Cues. Humans communicate with more than words; they use body language as well, sending messages by tone of voice, posture, eye contact, facial expressions, and body movements. Such nonverbal cues play a critical role in the interviewing process. When used properly, they encourage an interviewee to provide information. When used poorly, they can have the opposite effect.

For example, failure to make eye contact in an interview can be interpreted as a lack of interest or concern for the other person. Good eye contact can communicate interest, attention, openness, and a regard for the other person's worth. On the other hand, too much eye contact can be misinterpreted as staring. In U.S. culture, for example, eye contact between strangers for more than a brief moment is considered a challenge. In some cultures, eye contact is considered an invasion of privacy.

Nodding the head to indicate understanding is an acceptance cue, as is a posture of attentiveness: sitting straight and leaning slightly forward. Contrast this posture with a person slouching in a chair with one arm flung over the back of the chair or leaning back with both hands folded behind the head. The following are other errors commonly made by inexperienced analysts:

- Sitting back in a chair with arms folded across the chest. (This posture implies a lack of openness to what is being said and may also indicate that the analyst is ill at ease.)
- Looking at objects in the room or staring out the window instead of looking at the interviewee. (Because this behavior suggests that the analyst would rather be somewhere else doing other things, the interviewee will often cut the interview short.)
- Taking excessive notes or visually reviewing notes. (An analyst who records rather than listening may arouse interviewee concerns over what is being written.)

Figure 7–4 **Effective versus Ineffective Restatements of an Interviewee Response**

Interviewee Response:	We continue to sell products to customers who have not paid their bills.
Effective Restatement:	The system processes orders to customers who are bad credit risks. (Encourages interviewee to expand.)
Ineffective Restatement:	Why don't you check the customer's credit status before processing the order? (Distorts interviewee's meaning.)

- Sitting too far away or too close. (Sitting too far away often communicates that the analyst is intimidated by the interviewee, while sitting too close may communicate an inappropriate level of intimacy and make the interviewee uncomfortable.)

Acceptance cues are used to convey understanding, not agreement. The communication of agreement that does not exist can cause future misunderstandings. Furthermore, the analyst must maintain an air of objectivity and neutrality throughout the interview.

Restating the Interviewee's Responses. Restatement is the most difficult of the active listening skills to master. It involves repeating something the interviewee has said in the analyst's own words as an indication that effective communication has occurred and that the analyst understands what the interviewee has said. Restatement must be made in such a way that the interviewee will acknowledge it and keep on talking. Effective restatements will encourage the interviewee to elaborate; ineffective restatements will create an unintended pause or halt in the interview process (see Figure 7–4).

Restatement is normally used under the following circumstances:

- When the interviewee is describing a problem. (At such times, the analyst's restatement communicates that the interviewee's problem has been heard and understood.)
- When the analyst wants to check his or her understanding of what has been said. (This technique is often used in response to complex statements or in group situations where several persons have commented on the same issue.)
- When the analyst wants to encourage the interviewee. (Restatement can prompt the interviewee to expand or elaborate on what has been said.)

Restatement can also overcome emotional barriers set up by interviewees who, for some reason, are uncooperative. Perhaps they feel that the interview squanders valuable time they could spend on more important tasks. Or

Figure 7–5 **Examples of Restatements at the Emotional Level**

Interviewee Statement:	The last time I was interviewed, the result was that I got this report that I cannot use without literally weeding it.
Restatement:	It seems as though you feel that some analysts do not listen carefully enough to your requirements and ideas.
Interviewee Statement:	I do not have the typing skills to become an on-line data entry operator in the new system.
Restatement:	You seem to feel that the new system might take away some of the challenge and excitement of your job.
Restatement Alternative (if the restatement does not evoke a response):	You do not appear to have been exposed to terminals or personal computers in your work.

perhaps they had negative experiences with systems analysts in the past. Whatever the reason, the challenge for the analyst is to establish rapport—to make the interviewees confident that their feelings are understood. This confidence, in turn, helps to break down emotional barriers and thus produce successful interviews. Figure 7–5 illustrates restatements at the emotional level. Although restatement at the emotional level is a powerful technique, it must be used judiciously. First, it should be used only when the analyst senses that the interviewee's strong feelings might jeopardize the interview. Second, even after restatement, the analyst will sometimes sense that the interviewee's attitude still does not permit effective communication. In such cases, the interview should probably be rescheduled at a later date. Third, the analyst should restate with such phrases as "it sounds as if" or "it seems as if" to avoid misinterpreting or misstating the interviewee's feelings. Finally, the analyst must remain neutral. For example, if the interviewee is critical of management, the analyst should neither agree with the criticism nor attempt to defend management. Instead, the analyst should simply convey that the interviewee's feelings are understood.

When using restatement the analyst must try to avoid the following common errors:

- Echoing the interviewee, i.e., repeating exactly what the interviewee has said rather than restating in different words. (Echoing becomes very obvious after the first few times it occurs and can make the interviewee uncomfortable.)

- Overusing restatement, which can be distracting to the interviewee.

- Altering or distorting the meaning intended by the interviewee. (A restatement should be as close to the interviewee's meaning as possible.)

- Raising the pitch of the voice at the end of a restatement. (This habit converts a restatement into a question answerable by yes or no instead of an invitation for the interviewee to expand on his or her comments.)

Using Silence Effectively. Silence as an interviewing technique is employed in two situations: either just after a question or after an answer that the analyst considers incomplete. Silence after a question gives the interviewee a chance to speak. Some people require longer periods of time to formulate an answer and become disconcerted if interrupted by another question or comment from the analyst. Silence following an incomplete answer can encourage the interviewee to elaborate as long as the analyst continues to maintain a posture of interest and receptivity. Long silences should be avoided, however; if the interviewee does not respond, the conversation should be resumed by the analyst.

Following Up for Clarification

After the initial rounds of interviews are completed and documented, analysis of the findings almost always results in the need to clarify certain aspects. For example, the analyst may have obtained conflicting information from two interviewees or may not have completely understood the way information on a particular report is used or by whom. If follow-up interviews are necessary, they are usually brief, consisting primarily of closed questions. Frequently, simple points can be settled by a telephone call or informal visit.

WHEN TO USE JOINT APPLICATION DESIGN (JAD)

As a method for gathering information about the requirements of a new system, JAD is an alternative to interviewing. In place of interviews, JAD substitutes a two- to four-day workshop, in which several qualified users meet with IS personnel. The method is designed to produce the same end product as the more traditional approaches but in a shorter period of time and at less cost.

JAD and related methods were developed in an attempt to reduce three of the problems associated with interviews. First, interviewing—preparing for the interview, conducting it, documenting the results, and combining the results into a homogeneous set of requirements—is time consuming. On a medium or large project, this phase could easily occupy a number of analysts full time for several weeks. JAD was designed to shorten the requirements analysis phase by weeks and, consequently, reduce the cost of analyst personnel.

Second, in the 1970s it became more and more apparent that most difficulties with operational systems—bugs, user dissatisfaction, high maintenance—were due to the analysts' poor understanding of the systems requirements. Moreover, poorly understood requirements could lead to a mistake such as forgetting a transaction type or a special case of billing logic applied to a category of customers. This kind of mistake is much more difficult to correct than a mistake in coding the program. The group technique of JAD is likely to eliminate more requirements errors than the one-on-one technique of classic analysis methods.

Finally, JAD promotes a participatory style of systems development. Most users who have participated in a JAD session feel some ownership of the system when it is delivered. Also, participation in a JAD session increases the users' understanding of the systems development process and of the demands that are placed on IS professionals.

JAD is not a life-cycle activity as such; rather, it is a technique that supports a life-cycle activity. As such, it has primarily been used in two areas—requirements analysis and user interface design. It can also be used in systems planning and in data analysis with minimal adaptations. Although JAD has its own deliverables, it can easily be adopted or adapted.

Because JAD is used extensively in the requirements analysis phase, the technique is detailed in this section. JAD can also be used in both user interface design and data design, but with more limited benefits. For instance, JAD is adequate for those systems in which the user interface is a simple menu and forms structure with a reporting or ad hoc query system, but it is not well adapted to the design of more sophisticated user interfaces.

SIX TYPES OF PARTICIPANTS

A JAD session has six types of participants: users, IS analysts, observers, scribes, a session leader, and an executive sponsor. The key participants are the **users,** those whose views determine the bulk of the requirements. Normally, any user who would be interviewed in the classic process is eligible for participation in a JAD meeting. Users can come from the top-level user management through supervisory personnel to clerks. Usually, an effort to have personnel higher than a clerical level will help ensure that the participants are knowledgeable, that they can see the forests as well as the trees, and that they have the authority to make decisions.

Obviously, the group should have as many users as necessary for a balanced view. One of the advantages of group methods is that the participants usually feel deeply committed to the decisions made by the group. If consensus is important, as many users as possible should attend. However, too large a group becomes unmanageable and defeats the very purpose of group methods.

The users invited to attend should have some familiarity with computer systems. If they do not, their fear (or just their ignorance) of the technology may prevent them from communicating effectively with the rest of the group. The problem of lack of familiarity usually does not arise when the proposed system replaces an already mechanized system. Most of the participants then have a fairly good sense of what can be expected of the new system, and little time will be spent on unrealistic ideas or basic explanations.

An **IS analyst** from the project team should also be present. In contrast to the interviewing approach, the analyst has a primarily passive role, listening to the users state their requirements and making sure that these requirements are understood and achievable. This passive role is difficult for an analyst who is used to interviewing and taking the lead in the design phase.

The analyst's role becomes even more difficult if user expectations are too high and the probable cost of the proposed system becomes excessive. Ideally, the analyst should be able to explain why certain functions are likely to cost too much. For instance, if the users decide that they need a response time of less than a second for certain transactions that involve a great deal of processing and data base I/O, the analyst should immediately be able to explain that this requirement might mean spending more on additional hardware than the organization would save.

The alternative to an immediate explanation is to accept the requirement and wait for a later stage to document its cost and prove that it would not be cost effective. Waiting is acceptable only if the number of unreasonable requirements is not very high. In other words, if the user requirements get out of hand during the JAD session, something must be done to moderate them on the spot.

In most cases, one analyst should suffice. If necessary, the analyst can be backed up by **observers** who are present to provide technical assistance and advice. There can also be observers from departments other than IS if the project calls for technical information from other sources.

One or two **scribes** should attend the meeting to note everything that is said and to publish the results of the session within a week or two after it is over. Normally, the scribe is from the IS department; if there are two scribes, it is a good idea to have one scribe from the user department. The two scribes can then divide the tasks so that one notes functional requirements, process descriptions, and data definitions and the other notes technical requirements, volumes, and performance and schedule constraints.

The **session leader** conducts the session according to JAD methods. A good session leader often means the difference between a successful session and a failure.

Because the essence of group methods is free expression and consensus, the session leader is responsible for providing a climate in which this is possible. The session leader must therefore have several important qualifications:

- The session leader should not report hierarchically to anyone in the group.
- The session leader should not play the classic role of a meeting chairman, for instance, by casting the decisive vote in case of disagreement.
- The session leader should be capable of promoting consensus rather than majority or authority decisions in case of disagreements or conflicts within the group.

Other important characteristics and skills are described later in this chapter.

The session leader role is best a full-time one because of the training required and because of the time needed to sell the concept of a JAD workshop to users, the IS department, and top management. An organization that cannot assign a person full time may retain a consultant. Several consulting firms specialize in training and providing session leaders.

Finally, an **executive sponsor** is required to kick off the meeting and to be present at its conclusion. The executive sponsor is a ranking user executive with some direct or moral authority over the IS personnel. The role of the executive sponsor is to assure the participants of top management commitment both to the project and to the JAD method.

PREPARING FOR THE WORKSHOP

The preparation for a JAD workshop, mainly under the direction of the session leader, can be divided into several steps. First, the session leader locates an executive sponsor and determines the workshop's scope. Then, the session leader helps identify the participants, becomes familiar with the application to be discussed during the workshop, and helps the participants gain familiarity. Finally, the session leader organizes the meeting. For a workshop to be successful, the session leader should perform each step in the following way:

* Locate an executive sponsor and determine scope.

    Once it has been decided to use JAD on a project, the session leader locates an executive sponsor. With the help of other management members, they determine the scope of the workshop. The scope is based on the systems plan or determined at the outset of the development project. The scope statement describes the areas (organizational, functional, geographical) to be covered, the business objectives of the system, the assumptions about future growth and other factors of change, and the general cost and performance constraints within which the system is to be developed.

    If the scope of the system is too broad to be covered in a single workshop or if the number of participants required to cover the entire ground is large, the system can be divided into several parts, each with its own JAD session. However, there is a risk of conflicting information or requirements arising from the several sessions. The most insidious of these risks is that terms may not have the same meaning for different groups of participants.

* Identify the participants.

    Next, the participants in the session are identified. Most experts recommend 8 to 12 users as the ideal number. The users should all be experts in some area of the business under study. In many cases, the best users to select are the people who user management feels can least be spared for the duration of the workshop. The role of the executive sponsor in negotiating their availability is likely to be critical. A useful plan is to ask hesitant user management personnel to get the opinion of some other company that has already practiced JAD. In general, testimonials tend to be glowing.

- Learn the application.

    Although the session leader does not need to be an expert on the application being discussed because he or she will not contribute content to the workshop, some familiarity with the application must be gained before the JAD session starts. In the method prescribed by IBM, the session leader interviews user personnel, focusing on the workflow within the area to be discussed at the workshop. An important difference from interviewing as presented earlier is that the interviewer makes no effort to critique or find areas for improvement; rather, he or she aims for a basic understanding of the business activity.

    Other methods can be used where applicable: studying existing procedure manuals and systems documentation, scanning general literature on the subject, and so on.

    IBM has a form called the Familiarization Guide for recording information from the interviews. One merit of filling in the guide is that its information can be communicated to the users and IS personnel in advance of the workshop. This information can solidify the common understanding of the area under study and serve as a guide to the discussions.

- Organize the meeting.

    The usual activities for organizing a meeting must take place. A **venue** must be identified, preferably off-site, so that there will be as few interruptions as possible. The room must be large enough to accommodate all the participants in reasonable comfort. The participants will have to spend two to four days in these quarters doing unfamiliar work, perhaps with an intensity not typical in their day-to-day activities. Plenty of refreshments should be provided, and it may be a good idea to relax the usual corporate dress code.

    Audiovisual aids must be available. The minimum aids required are two overhead projectors, a magnetic board or a white-board (if possible equipped with its own copier), and flipcharts. Slide projectors, PCs, and video projectors are also often used. See Figure 7–6 for the layout of a typical JAD room.

    Special technology to support the JAD process, or **group technology**, may be considered. Recent research has shown that great promise is borne by each participant having a workstation that can share its memory with the others, constituting a sort of electronic blackboard accessible to all. Although the state of the art is still somewhat experimental (and expensive), commercially available products will be offered within the next few years.

    A convenient **date** for meeting must be found. Thus, the meeting should be planned well in advance—several weeks at least. If a critical participant cannot make the meeting, it should be postponed rather than held without him or her.

Figure 7–6 **Typical Layout of a Room Suitable for JAD Sessions**

An **agenda** must be established and distributed in advance.

If possible, a half-day **orientation meeting** for the participants should be held some days in advance of the actual workshop. This meeting will help the participants understand their roles and adapt to them more quickly once the session starts.

CONDUCTING THE SESSION

At the beginning of the meeting, the executive sponsor briefly presents the objectives and expresses the interest of top management in the project. The session leader then conducts the meeting, guiding the participants through a structured analysis of the various activities identified earlier.

As taught by IBM, the analysis covers the following points of a proposed system:

- Planning
  What are the sources that tell users what work to expect and when?
- Receiving
  Where and how is work received? Where and how are resources (people, machines, materials, supplies) to do the work received?
- Receipt processing/tracking
  How are receipts reported and received work uniquely identified? Are other locations notified of receipts?
- Monitoring and assigning
  How will planned work be received, received work be processed, and priorities and resources monitored? What identification documents, instructions, and reports does the system provide?
- Processing
  How is the work done, by whom, on which machines? How does the system monitor and guide progress? How does it report?
- Recording
  How does the system record events about the work and notify clients, if required?
- Sending
  Where is the work sent after completion? What labels, directions, and other documents are required? Who is notified of completion? What billing or accounting data is produced?
- Evaluating
  What management information is required to indicate trends, summary data, measurements, or exceptions to plans, objectives, and budgets?

IBM's structured guide is well adapted to the automation of existing manual workflows or to the redeployment of aging systems. Used correctly, the guide can be helpful in integrating transaction systems with office automation—a major source of new systems development in the coming years.

The guide is perhaps less useful for analyzing new ways of using existing information (or identifying sources of new information) to gain competitive advantage. Also, management information systems and decision support systems are less amenable to any highly structured approach such as this one.

Value can be added to the approach if the session leader knows something about similar systems used by other corporations in the same industry and can tailor the questions accordingly.

During the workshop, the session leader should ensure that everybody is heard. The session leader can encourage less vocal participants to express their opinions and concerns, can stem the flow of discussion away from the more prolific participants, and can redirect the discussion back on track when it wanders.

The session leader should concentrate on how the meeting is conducted, not on the contents of the participants' remarks. The session leader should quickly gain everyone's respect. Finally, the session leader should be an effective negotiator, capable of devising satisfactory compromises or win-win solutions—those where no one loses.

DOCUMENTING THE RESULTS

After the meeting, the scribes organize the materials and deliver them to the IS analyst who attended the workshop. The analyst's responsibility is to prepare a specification document, which may include the following items:

- Management objectives
- Scope and limits
- Business questions the system will answer
- Information required to answer the questions
- Relationship with other systems
- Issues
- Data element definitions
- Screen and report layouts
- Menus
- Processing rules
- Operating procedures
- Performance and operational requirements

This list of items may be tailored to fit the organization's existing documentation standards.

ALTERNATIVE METHODS

Several firms have developed proprietary methods based on group techniques for requirements analysis. The best known are The Method, from Performance Resources, Inc; WISDM, from Western Institute of Software Engineering; and Rapid Analysis, from C&CE. The main difference between these methods is in the contents of the structured guides followed during the session. As described above, JAD's emphasis is on workflows, whereas WISDM emphasizes business functions and their associated inputs and outputs, and The Method emphasizes data analysis.

COSTS AND BENEFITS OF JAD

The main costs of JAD are the extensive training required for the session leader and the substantial time commitment of key users. When compared with the benefits that can be obtained, these costs should be easily borne.

Many companies report that JAD can shorten the total life-cycle time up to 15 percent. Perhaps more critically, the high degree of user participation in the JAD approach can increase the quality of the system: less rework after implementation, higher user satisfaction, and better responsiveness to management goals.

Care must be taken, however, not to raise false expectations from the method. After all, JAD produces only what can be expected from a two- to four-day concentrated effort. The team approach is powerful; it cannot, however, solve all business problems by itself, nor can it solve the technical and implementation problems of later phases.

JAD has been used successfully in several large organizations such as Texas Instruments, The Travelers, IBM, CNA, American Airlines, and TWA. As more experience is gained, we can expect increased acceptance of JAD and its integration into most systems development life cycles.

OTHER INFORMATION-GATHERING TECHNIQUES

Although interviews with user personnel are by far the most common way of gathering information on the present system, with JAD sessions gaining in popularity, questionnaires, observation, and sampling can be effective in certain situations.

Questionnaires

As mentioned previously, questionnaires are often sent to users prior to scheduling an interview. In some cases, a questionnaire is used without an interview—most often when analysts need to contact users in remote locations but cannot justify the travel and when the information needed is more than what can be obtained in a telephone conversation. In such cases, the combination of a questionnaire with telephone or mail follow-up for clarification is often appropriate.

Observation

Observation of the present system is often a fertile source of new ideas. For example, all of us have been frustrated at one time or another by choosing the incorrect line at a bank or an airline counter. Some of us even switch to another line when the one we originally chose seems to be moving too slowly, only to find that we would have been better off staying with our original choice. Many businesses now have a single waiting line for all customers so that all are served in arrival sequence. The new approach may well have been the result of someone who observed the lines with a fresh perspective and concluded that multiple waiting lines do not treat customers fairly. According to an article in *Fortune*, "the best intelligence is usually gathered in the field. Stephen Moss, of the Arthur D. Little consulting firm, an expert in streamlining factory operations . . . once tried to limit his staff's travel by having videotapes showing troubled factories sent to his office in Cambridge, Massachusetts. Unfortunately, he says, 'We couldn't see on the tape how workers were feeling or where the dust was piling up. Some of the most telling evidence just wasn't visible.' "[2]

Sampling

Sampling techniques are used when the population is too large to permit all members to be interviewed, given questionnaires, or observed. Conclusions on the attributes of the population as a whole are then drawn based on the results of a sample. When selecting the sample, analysts must take care that the sample is truly representative of the entire population. Otherwise, they may draw erroneous conclusions.

Summary

Most practitioners agree that the benefits of reviewing the present system outweigh the costs. After the review, the project team will grasp the business problems of the organization under study and the effectiveness of the present information system. In addition, the project team will appreciate the operating environment of the new system and will not likely overlook critical processing requirements.

Interviewing is by far the most common technique used in reviewing a present system. The five steps in the interviewing process are preparation, planning and scheduling, opening and closing, interviewing, and following up. Interviewing is an information-gathering technique, and analysts should learn such active listening skills as open-ended questions, appropriate words and phrases, acceptance cues, and restatement at both the direct and emotional level. Used properly, silence can also be effective. In most instances, not all information can be gathered during a single interview, and arrangements for follow-ups should be made.

The results of interviews and the other data-gathering techniques must be documented properly so that information thus obtained is easily accessible to all members of the project team. IS departments that have adopted one of the standard methodologies will have documentation formats available to them. Others will have to develop documentation standards applicable to the project.

JAD is a technique developed in the early 1980s to overcome some of the difficulties caused by the more classic approaches to requirements analysis. The two main difficulties addressed by JAD are the length of time taken up by interviewing and the lack of user participation and motivation generally associated with systems projects.

The technique itself consists of gathering highly competent users (about ten) for a two- to four-day workshop to discuss, conceptualize, and analyze. IS personnel are present, mainly to listen, to record what is being said, and to document the users' contributions. The workshop is led by an independent person to whom neither the users nor the IS personnel report. The role of the leader is twofold: to elicit decisions by consensus and compromise rather than by fiat or majority vote and to keep the meeting on track so that the system to be built is the one that is discussed.

The results of a JAD workshop need not be different from what they would have been with a classic approach. In general, each company can adapt JAD to fit into its own version of the systems development life cycle.

JAD has been used successfully in very large organizations, and its acceptance in the industry will probably increase.

Other data-gathering techniques that may be appropriate in certain situations include questionnaires, sampling, and observation.

Selected Readings

Gildersleeve, Thomas R. *Successful Data Processing Systems Analysis,* 2d ed. Englewood Cliffs, NJ: Prentice-Hall, 1985.
This text has good coverage of the topics of interpersonal relations and creative thinking with a chapter devoted to each. Gildersleeve is a practicing IS professional.

Rockart, J. F. "Critical Success Factors." *Harvard Business Review* (March-April 1979): 81–91.
The widely quoted article in which the critical success factors technique is described and discussed.

Wetherbe, James C. *Systems Analysis and Design,* 3d ed. St. Paul, MN: West Publishing, 1988.
As part of its coverage of systems analysis and design, this text has a section devoted to a framework for studying problems and opportunities and good coverage of alternative data-gathering techniques.

Joint Application Design, GUIDE Publication GPP-147, Chicago: GUIDE International, 1986.
This publication is the main source on JAD and the competing methodologies. For more details, one must attend a course given either by IBM or by the various consultants who provide proprietary versions of the method.

Gane, C. *Rapid Systems Development.* New York: Rapid Systems Development, Inc., 1987.
This book contains a chapter (8 pages) on impartial-leader group interviews. The chapter is concise, but points out all the essentials. This book

contains a number of other topics of interest, and it is highly recommended reading.

Doyle, M., and Straus, D. *How to Make Meetings Work.* New York: Berkley/Jove, 1976.
This book is not specifically about systems development, but it is very useful on how to make groups of people set and achieve common goals.

Wood, J., and Silver, D. *Joint Application Design.* New York: John Wiley & Sons, 1989.

August, J. *Joint Application Design: The Group Session Approach to System Design.* Englewood Cliffs, NJ: Yourdon Press, 1991.
Both these books are recent works on JAD. They are useful for filling in some of the details not covered in the basic GUIDE text.

Review Questions

1. What are the advantages of reviewing the present system? Why do some practitioners maintain that this review is unnecessary?

2. Why is interviewing such an important skill for IS professionals?

3. What are the five steps in the interview process?

4. Describe the recommended procedures for (1) preparing for the interview and (2) planning and scheduling the interview.

5. What steps are involved in closing the interview?

6. Describe the five key techniques of active listening.

7. Who should participate in a JAD session and what should the participants' roles be?

8. Describe the preparation steps for a JAD workshop.

9. Describe each of the eight points that IBM proposes be covered in a JAD workshop.

10. What is contained in the document prepared by the IS department after the JAD session? How does it differ from documentation that would be prepared after a series of interviews?

11. What are the information-gathering techniques other than interviewing? Under what circumstances are they likely to be most useful?

Discussion Questions

1. Note taking during an interview may distract, annoy, or even threaten the interviewee. How would you suggest the analyst overcome this problem? What do you think of tape recording the session?

2. The analyst walks a fine line between seeming to understand an interviewee's opinions and seeming to agree or disagree with them. Explain how an analyst can show understanding yet maintain neutrality.

3. The following questions have been outlined by a junior analyst for an initial user interview. Critique the questions and suggest ways in which they could be rephrased:

   a. "What information do you need that you are not currently receiving?"
   b. "I understand you are having trouble meeting deadlines. Is that true?"
   c. "Do you agree with the vice-president of marketing that implementing this new technology will significantly improve sales?"
   d. "What would you like the new system to do?"
   e. "Do you have any problems with the present system?"

4. Discuss the use of JAD-like techniques in other parts of the life cycle.

5. What are the disadvantages of JAD?

Mini-Cases

Foothills Industrial Supply, Inc. You encountered the following situations during a project at Foothills Industrial Supply. The project objective is to determine whether the company should replace its ten-year-old order entry/inventory control computer system with a more up-to-date system.

The inventory control manager has told you that he does not feel it is necessary to spend time with you personally or to make his people available for interviews. He has seen the system he wants—a software package used at his brother-in-law's company in Boston. He would like to quit wasting time, order a copy of the same package, and install it at Foothills.

In your initial interview with the sales manager, you first asked him what information he needed to make him and his organization more effective. He responded that he thought he was pretty effective already, and besides, it was your job to tell him what information was needed, not the other way around.

During your interview with the president, she confesses that data processing sends her several weekly and monthly reports but that she normally does not use them because they are too long. She tells you that she gets the information she needs by walking around the place and talking with people and by having the controller give her a hand-prepared summary of activity each day. She likes to find it on her desk the first thing every morning.

Question for Discussion

1. Describe how you would handle the situations at Foothills Industrial Supply.

Lord's Chemicals and Drugs. Assume you are a newly hired project manager in the IS department of Lord's Chemicals and Drugs, a pharmaceutical distributor located in Charlotte, North Carolina. Your first assignment is to lead a project to develop a new payroll system. Your proposed strategy on the project is to use joint application design, but when you suggest this to colleagues and users, the reactions are negative. Here is a sampling:

- From the IS department:

  "Last time we tried JAD, it took us longer than interviewing would have."

  "Our users do not understand information systems, so they create requirements that are impossible to implement."

  "All JAD does is create paperwork."

  "It won't be any use since all we want to do is put in a payroll package."

- From the personnel department, where JAD was tried three years earlier when the current payroll system was upgraded to include flexible benefits:

  "We never understood what JAD was supposed to accomplish."

  "The session leader did not understand what most of us were saying. He only understood the representative from the accounting department, so they designed a system that is not very practical for us in the personnel department."

  "The sessions got out of control and only those who spoke louder than the others were heard."

  "Workshop sessions take too much time, and our daily work suffers."

  "All they produced were more forms that nobody could use."

Questions for Discussion

1. What went wrong?

2. How would you persuade your colleagues from IS and personnel to give JAD another try?

Notes

1. Gildersleeve, Thomas R. *Successful Data Processing Systems Analysis*, 2d ed. Englewood Cliffs, NJ: Prentice-Hall, 1985.

2. Nulty, Peter. "Why Do We Travel So *#!?*! Much" *Fortune* (March 28, 1988): 84.

8

Functional Requirements

Following a brief overview of the purpose of functional requirements and their documentation, Chapter 8 discusses the four major approaches to functional analysis: structured systems analysis, essential systems analysis, business area analysis, and object-oriented analysis. After describing documentation alternatives, the chapter closes with advice on how to achieve further business integration as a by-product of this phase.

Learning Objectives

- Recognize the three perspectives addressed by a functional specification.
- Differentiate between alternative approaches to analyzing functional requirements.
- Understand techniques for documenting behavior, data structure, and data flow.
- Recognize opportunities to achieve further business integration.

FUNCTIONAL REQUIREMENTS DEFINED

The functional requirements of a system are the description of what the system is to do. Most authors add: ". . . but not how to do it." We will also add ". . . nor how well it is to be done." How to do it is determined during the design phase; how well it is to be done is the subject of Chapter 9.

There are two aspects to requirements analysis. The first is how to go about determining the requirements for a given system. The second is how they are documented in a specifications document. Such a document serves two purposes:

- It is a contract between users and project team, sufficiently detailed and understandable that the users will not be surprised by the eventual implementation.
- It is a guide for the designers and implementers, to make sure that they share a common view of what the system will do and that they will continue to share it until the system is ready.

The first aspect—that of the strategy for determining the requirements—has considerable variations in methodologies. There is more convergence on how to document the functional specifications. Even though the formats, the graphical representation schemes, and the syntax vary from author to author, there is consensus that a functional specification needs to address the following three perspectives:

- Data oriented
- Process oriented
- Behavior oriented[1,2]

In the 1970s, most methodologies favored one perspective almost exclusively over the others. During the 1980s, each methodology has evolved towards a fuller view, embodying at least two, often all three perspectives.

STRATEGIES FOR ANALYZING FUNCTIONAL REQUIREMENTS

The discipline of requirements analysis stems from the frequent misunderstandings between users and programmers in early IS departments. These misunderstandings were often based on users assuming that the programmers knew as much about the application to be mechanized as they. On their side, programmers often did not know enough about the application to realize that they were, indeed, making assumptions that should have been the subject of questions to ask the users.

In manual systems, these misunderstandings did not matter much; any discrepancy could be resolved case by case, perhaps gradually enriching the company's operations manuals. In computer applications, this approach is not reasonable: all the questions must have been asked beforehand and the answers incorporated into the program. Unanticipated combinations of events and conditions can potentially cause large errors that go undetected (the application not having been programmed to detect them) or that cause major rework of the application programs.

Thus, the role of analyst arose. The prime charge of the analyst is to understand the work of the users and all their tacit assumptions, so that a complete description of what the application is supposed to do can be produced before starting the design of the new application.

The earliest published analysis techniques for business information systems were created in the mid-to-late 1970s, under the name *structured systems analysis*. (Earlier methods were more oriented towards design.) These techniques were created by various authors such as Ed Yourdon, Larry Constantine, Tom DeMarco, Chris Gane, and Chris Sarson. They were later refined into *essential systems analysis* in the mid-1980s by Stephen McMenamin and John Palmer.

Around 1980, James Martin, a data base design expert, created Information Engineering, a coherent body of systems development techniques, the

Figure 8–1 **Structured Systems Analysis**

analysis part of which is called *business area analysis.* Martin thought that structured systems analysis was too oriented towards process and function descriptions and not enough towards data, which he thought must be at the foundation of any business system. The 1980s were a time of polemics between the two camps and of competition between data-driven and process-driven analysis techniques.

The late 1980s saw the emergence of *object-oriented analysis.* With its origins in object-oriented programming and design (see Section VI), object-oriented analysis purports to unify the data- and process-oriented approaches by putting near equal emphasis on both.

Each of these approaches has strengths and weaknesses. Structured systems analysis is time consuming if taken literally; it is most appropriate for naive users, inexperienced analysts, and manual systems. It provides a weak foundation for proper data base design.

Essential systems analysis is better adapted to a second round of mechanization, with more experienced users and analysts. It is still weak on the data side.

Business area analysis provides a much stronger foundation for data base design. Its danger lies in losing track of the purpose of the new system—to perform a given set of business functions—and creating a blue-sky design that will be too costly to implement.

Object-oriented analysis is an interesting attempt at synthesis between the mainly process-driven and the mainly data-driven approaches. It is still a young technique. Its graphical representation techniques are immature, and there is as yet little if any CASE tool support for object-oriented analysis.

Structured Systems Analysis

The overall flow of structured systems analysis is depicted in Figure 8–1. First, the current physical system is documented. The current logical system is abstracted from the physical by eliminating implementation-dependent details. Then, the current logical system is examined for shortcomings and problems.

These modifications give rise to the new logical system, which is still implementation independent. Finally (and this is really a design activity), implementation decisions are made and the new physical system is documented.

Current Physical System. The departure point for structured systems analysis is to observe the operation of the current system by documenting the **flow of data** through the organization. To do so, the analyst starts by looking at the flows of physical objects that carry information: documents, card files (in the 1970s, this was not absurd), and so on. Telephone conversations are material enough to count as physical data flows.

Each recipient and each source of a data flow is interviewed to ascertain how they **process** the data they receive before they reemit it (perhaps in another form): screening, sorting and collating, calculating, summarizing, transcribing. The processes are analyzed down to the level of a well-identified task accomplished by a single individual in a few minutes or perhaps hours.

Finally, **data stores,** points where documents or files are kept, permanently or temporarily while awaiting some further processing, are identified.

The documentation of the current physical system is then reviewed for completeness. Are there data flows that appear to come from nowhere or go nowhere? Does each process have all the data it needs to produce the output data flow? Are data stores used? Are they ever updated or purged? When the analyst is confident that the data flow is complete, he or she verifies it with the users and their management.

Current Logical System. Once the current physical system is completely analyzed, the current logical system can be established. This is done by removing all implementation considerations from the current physical system, leaving only what is done, not how it is done. All references to the following are removed:

- Who performs the process
- The medium on which data is transported
- Mechanical duplication
- Storing of data for no other purpose than to wait for some process to become available

Control variables, data or signals that indicate when something is to occur, are also eliminated

It is often difficult to decide whether a process is implementation dependent. Any process that would disappear if we could implement "perfect" technology—with instantaneous response and infinite capacity—should be eliminated from the logical system. Another way of evaluating what processes to eliminate is to ask oneself the question: "Can this process be changed in the future system without affecting what is accomplished?"

Once all the implementation-dependent processes are eliminated, the remaining processes are documented in full detail so that no ambiguity about the process is possible.

New Logical System. During the analysis, the project team has also gathered a list of desired changes to the current system. Indeed, the very fact that a project is being conducted indicates that desired changes have already been identified before the start of the project—otherwise why go to the expense of studying a new system at all?

The assumption of structured systems analysis is that many if not most of the current operational problems are caused by implementation shortcomings: order delivery times are too long because the order forms cannot be processed fast enough; stock-outs occur because the inventory records are being kept in batch instead of on-line; reports are inaccurate because the systems that produce them have inconsistent data bases.

If only operational problems caused by imperfect technology existed, the future logical system could be identical to the current one, and only the implementation need change. However, management may also wish to change the way business is conducted, providing new functions or changing processing rules.

New Physical System. The new logical system still carries the assumption of perfect technology—infinite capacity at instantaneous speed. The design of the future physical system reintroduces reality into the process by creating those processes and data flows that are made necessary by technological constraints. Obviously, this design will depend on the state of the available technology at any given time; more pertinently, it will depend on how much the technology costs and how much management is willing to pay to avoid the operational problems caused by imperfect technology in the current system.

Making these trade-offs is at the border between structured systems analysis and structured systems design. At this point, the view of systems design as a problem-solving process prevails. The problem is stated as follows: how to implement the new logical system while achieving the highest possible benefits (or the best return on investment or the highest net present value—whatever criterion management has set). Now is the time to generate alternative solutions—try out, on paper, alternative imperfect technologies—and evaluate which one gives the best result.

Essential Systems Analysis

In the mid-1980s, experience with structured systems analysis had pointed out a few areas for improvement. Two such improvements were incorporated into the technique known as essential systems analysis.

The first problem was that of excessive detail. Structured systems analysis prescribes that all processes be identified and documented. This thoroughness is justified for first-time mechanization of an application, because both users and analysts have little experience and may not be able to judge what processes are important for the new system. With experience, however, McMenamin and Palmer found that many processes were doomed to disappear or to be performed quite differently in a new system. Take, for instance, the creation of a new customer record. In manual, batch, and on-line data base environments, the implementation of the process is going to be totally different. Moreover, the process is not likely to be forgotten: it is quite easy to introduce a rule in the systems development methodology that provides for a file maintenance process (create, modify, and delete records) for each data store in the new system. Analyzing the current file update processes is not likely to increase the quality or the responsiveness of the new system.

Thus, essential systems analysis prescribes that the analysts **model only the essentials** of the system, those processes that contribute directly to the business objective of the application, such as entering an order, pricing it, delivering it, invoicing the customer, and collecting the cash. So-called *custodial activities* are added to the model in a later step.

The second adaptation made by essential systems analysis is that the detailed analysis of the current physical system and its abstraction into the current logical system may be curtailed, if not omitted. When appropriate, the analysts and the users establish together the logical future system direct-ly. They can do so fairly easily for a second round of mechanization, when converting from a batch to an on-line system, for example. The batch system is already to a great extent formalized and the risk of assuming away critical details is not nearly so great. The current system may still be analyzed, but only after the future logical system has been established; the purpose is to verify the completeness of the future logical system (see Figure 8–2).

The following steps are executed:

*   Identify the system's purpose: events and responses
*   Identify essential activities to respond to the events
*   Identify data flows required to produce the responses
*   Create custodial activities where required.

Essential systems analysis thus **omits the analysis of the current logical system.** The omission of this phase is appropriate when the application is being mechanized for the second time because of two reasons: first, both the users and the analysts have more experience and familiarity with the application, and second, most of the current data flows and processes are codified in software rather than in the minds of the users. (The structured systems approach of first analyzing the current system continues to be rec-ommended for projects that are not functionally innovative or where there is a high risk associated with omitting some current feature.)

A consequence of the differences between the two approaches just described is that joint application development (JAD, see Chapter 7) is more appropriate for essential systems analysis than for structured systems analy-sis. One-on-one interviewing is necessary in both cases, but is more critical in structured systems analysis. Finally, because much of the information about the current system may actually reside in the software itself rather than in people's minds or procedure manuals, studying the present system may

Figure 8–2 **Essential Systems Analysis**

very well entail delving into the program documentation (or the program code itself) to ascertain the processing rules and exceptions. This process is called **reverse engineering,** reconstructing the design by inspecting the product itself.

Another way of viewing the differences between the two approaches is that structured systems analysis proceeds bottom up and essential systems analysis proceeds top down (see Box 8–1).

Business Area Analysis

Business area analysis is part of information engineering, a systems development methodology created by James Martin and Clive Finkelstein in the late 1970s and early 1980s. Business area analysis is like essential systems analysis in that it concentrates on the system to be designed: the current system is reviewed after the analysis, to make sure that no significant processes or data requirements have been omitted. In contrast to essential systems analysis, however, business area analysis concentrates on data structures rather than data flows.

Business area analysis assumes that some data modeling has already been performed during a previous systems planning stage, for example, as described in Section II. Business area analysis proper starts with the analysis of the **scope** of the system being analyzed: which data entities, business functions, locations, and organizational units are involved.

Second, the **entity-relationship diagram** for the business area under analysis is created by extracting a subset of the overall entity-relationship model. The business events of the area under study are then identified and associated with entity types in a behavior model. (This behavior model is similar to the highest-level data flow diagram prepared in essential systems analysis.) For each entity, an entity life-cycle model is drawn: this model depicts how an entity is created, modified, and deleted by the various events associated with it.

Third, a preliminary **process model** is created. The process model is simply a functional decomposition of the business area (see hierarchical diagramming in Section I), carried down to a level of detail that is about the

Box 8-1

Top-Down versus Bottom-Up Analysis

The literature is replete with references to top-down and bottom-up approaches to systems analysis and design. The *top-down* approach implies proceeding from the general to the particular. A typical example is goal setting: the overall goal is set first, and then it is analyzed into the subgoals or intermediate stages that must be reached. Another metaphor for top-down problem solving is "dividing to conquer." The problem is partitioned into independent parts or subproblems such that solving all the subproblems constitutes a solution to the overall problem. The top-down approach is deductive.

In contrast, the *bottom-up* approach implies moving from the particular to the general. A typical example is how a novice analyst approaches a new application domain, gathering as many facts and fragmentary views as possible and gradually consolidating them into an overall understanding by abstracting away inessential details. The bottom-up approach is inductive.

Neither top-down nor bottom-up analysis is inherently superior to the other. Generally, top-down analysis is thought to require more experience and maturity on the part of both the analysts and the users. Bottom-up analysis provides a better opportunity for inexperienced analysts to learn by practice. It is also a better method when none of the participating users has an overall perspective of the domain being analyzed. Experience shows that top-down analysis is the easier of the two approaches for transaction processing systems and the more difficult for management information systems.

Top-down analysis also has the reputation of being less time consuming than bottom-up analysis. This reputation is the result of experienced personnel's tendency to work top down rather than bottom up; being experienced, they naturally use less time than inexperienced personnel.

Finally, when the analysis is over, the findings are invariably organized top down, i.e., hierarchically, as explained in the Technique for Section I. The need to use a top-down approach to documentation may explain the preference given to top-down approaches by most authors on systems analysis. We must recognize, however, that the structure of the final product does not need to reflect the process by which it is reached. The bottom-up approach is perfectly legitimate, especially when facing an ill-known domain. As in science, induction precedes deduction.

same as that specified for structured systems analysis. The difference is that no attempt is yet made to relate each business process with the data created by the previous process.

Fourth, a detailed entity-relationship model is created. James Martin recommends reverting to a bottom-up approach at this point, designing screens, reports, and input forms and identifying all the data elements used by the application. These data elements are then grouped by entity in a process that Martin calls **data synthesis.** Section V describes entity-relationship modeling and data analysis and synthesis further.

Fifth, **data dependencies** are analyzed. From the functional decomposition, each process is analyzed as to its input and output data entities. A process using data created by another process is considered to be dependent on it and the two processes are depicted as a sequence. The net result of this activity is a diagram that is very close in spirit, if not in form, to the data flow diagram of essential systems analysis.

Finally, entities and processes are associated with each other and with locations, organizational units, goals, and problems in a number of **matrices** that can be analyzed for completeness and consistency by the CASE tool.

Object-Oriented Analysis

Object-oriented analysis is just emerging as an alternative to both essential systems analysis and business area analysis. Object-oriented analysis uses the paradigm of object-oriented programming, which packages data and process together in **objects**. Objects are active components that exhibit behavior when stimulated by **messages,** or transactions.

Two other critical characteristics of the object-oriented paradigm are classification and inheritance. **Classification** is the organization of objects into classes and subclasses that share characteristics such as attributes and behaviors. For example, mammals are warm-blooded and viviparous; birds are warm-blooded and oviparous; amphibians are cold-blooded and oviparous. All these animals are vertebrates. **Inheritance** enables subclasses to have the same behaviors as the class they belong to by default. For example, ruminants are mammals: they are therefore warm-blooded and viviparous. (They can also have additional and/or modified behaviors: ruminants have a unique digestive system; penguins cannot fly.)

Object-oriented analysis goes about modeling an information system in the following way:

- Identify objects.

    Identifying objects is like identifying entities in systems planning or business area analysis. The set of objects of a system is that about which the system maintains data: material things, roles played by persons or organizations, events, interactions, and structures.

    A tactic often recommended is to derive objects from a written description of the system: most nouns in the text are likely to turn out to be objects.

    As objects are identified, their initial attributes and behaviors are documented.

- Identify structure.

    Objects tend to constitute natural classification schemes: this is the most important structure for object-oriented analysis. The classification structure corresponds to types and subtypes—Is-A relationships—as described in the Technique of Section I. In a classification structure, attributes and behaviors are assigned to the highest class possible, so that they can be shared through inheritance to the various subclasses.

A second important structure is the composition or assembly structure: an object may be composed of parts that are of interest to the application. For instance, an assembled product such as an engine is made up of subassemblies and parts such as pistons, valves, a crankshaft, etc. This type of structure is described as an Is-Made-Up-Of relationship in the Technique in Section I.

Classification and assembly structures are fairly easy to identify initially, but difficulties often appear when the analysis is pushed to a greater level of detail. Multiple classification schemes may overlap each other and exceptions (such as the penguin—a nonflying bird—and the bat—a flying mammal) quickly appear.

- Define subjects.

    Subjects are a way of abstracting objects into larger units, thereby avoiding excessive details when making schematics of the system. They are especially useful when presenting the systems requirements to users for confirmation.

    Subjects are groups of objects related by both classification and assembly structures, for which it makes sense to describe attributes and behaviors globally. Exceptions and detailed differences are glossed over and the subjects give a broad-brush picture of the object model.

    For simple domains, subjects may not be required.

- Define attributes.

    This activity corresponds to the identification of attributes and relationships in entity-relationship diagramming (see Section V).

- Define behaviors.

    This activity consists of identifying which events each object can react to and the responses that the object will generate. The behavior paradigm comes from the initial use of object-oriented programming, the modeling language SIMULA. In SIMULA, the programmer could describe the various components (objects) of a physical system, for example, a post office with windows, clerks, and customers. Each object type would have behaviors that were invoked when certain events happened. For instance, when a staffed window was free, the next customer in line would advance. The clerk would perform some service requested by the customer. If there was no one in line at a window, the clerk might leave it and go into the back office. Thus, each object was viewed as a bundle of possible behaviors, each of which could be set off by some event signaled to the object by a message. Once the object had received the message, it controlled its own behavior (rather than having the behavior controlled by a main program in a hierarchical structure).

    Thus, the behaviors in object-oriented analysis are those activities that are under the control of each object, independently of the object that requests the service or initiates the behavior. In business systems, there are three main types of behavior: create a new object (add a new order for a customer); respond to a request for information (is the credit limit of the customer exceeded?); or modify the information in an object (increase the amount due by the amount of the invoice).[3]

The emphasis of object-oriented analysis is to hide the particulars of how each behavior is implemented from the requesting objects. Only the stimulus (or message) and the response are visible.

STRATEGIES FOR DOCUMENTING FUNCTIONAL REQUIREMENTS

The previous paragraphs describe several different strategies for eliciting functional requirements. Which one is chosen on a given project depends largely on the scope and nature of the system development undertaken, on the competence and experience of the project team, and on the available CASE tools. Each approach purports to represent a codification of an intellectual process: such codifications cannot be totally rigorous (or they would be automated away—executed by a computer). It is better to leave some freedom to select, adapt, and improvise.

It is much easier to standardize the product than the process. The outcome of the functional requirements analysis is a requirements specifications document covering the three systems perspectives: behavior, data, and process.

There are variations here, too. Each methodology and each CASE tool has its own representation technique. In the days of manual development techniques, before we had CASE tools, it did not matter much which one was chosen. The essential criterion was that the technique chosen communicated clearly what it was intended to communicate. Most authors preferred graphical representation techniques as being more expressive than natural language—"a picture is worth a thousand words."

With the advent of CASE tools, the situation has changed. Now, the audience of the specifications document is not only human analysts and users, but the CASE tool itself. The requirements documentation should be readable by the design CASE tool, and the design specification should be readable by the implementation CASE tool. Expressiveness is no longer the sole criterion for the representation scheme: precision also becomes a factor. A good CASE tool should be able to assist the analyst in verifying that the specification is complete and coherent. In this regard, most CASE tools have yet to achieve maturity. Those that are expressive often lack somewhat in rigor; those that are more rigorous may lack in expressiveness.

In the following, we will concentrate on the expressiveness of the representation of the three perspectives of behavior, data structure, and data flow (process).

Figure 8–3 **Context Diagram Showing Stimuli and Responses**

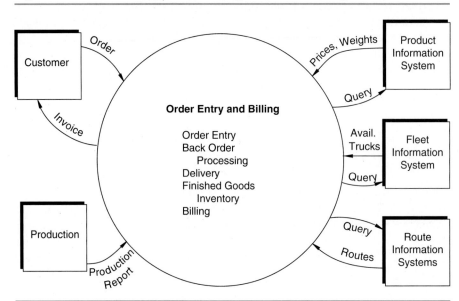

Behavior

A system behavior description contains a specification of the stimuli recognized by the system and the responses elicited by those stimuli. Most stimuli result from external events: a transaction, an event modifying the external world, a reading of a control variable such as the time of day or the day of the month. The system can also generate its own stimuli by alerting the operator to some state—perhaps a malfunction or an alert that some problem is about to arise ("disk nearly full" is one possible message).

There are two popular ways of representing system behavior. One is the context diagram in essential systems analysis. This diagram consists of a single process box—the system itself—connected via data flows to external entities (see Figure 8–3). Each data flow corresponds to a stimulus (input) or a response (output). There is only one exception: data flow diagrams do not represent control variables, so that a stimulus such as time will be omitted.

The second popular representation of behavior is the state transition diagram. Generally, it is associated with the state of an entity or an object (and may then be called entity life-cycle diagram), as in Figure 8–4. Each state is represented as a box on the diagram, and each stimulus (causing a state transition) as an arc between two states. On the entity life-cycle diagram, all the states of one entity, and that entity alone, are represented. Thus, a stimulus that affects the state of two entities would exist on multiple diagrams.

Figure 8–4 **State Transition Diagram Representing Entity States**

Successive States of a Customer Order

A state transition diagram does not necessarily represent the states of an entity; it could also represent the state of a process, as shown in Appendix 2. (These two views are unified in the object-oriented approach where the entity and the process are both objects.)

Data Structure

Until the mid-1980s, structured systems analysis used Ed Yourdon's concept of a "data dictionary" to document data structures. This technique consisted of identifying data stores as "buckets" containing data attributes, as illustrated in Figure 8–5. The convention used is that the plus sign signifies sequence or juxtaposition, curly brackets are repetitive groups, and parentheses are optional groups. The identifier or primary key is underlined. These data dictionaries are designed to be communicated to data base design specialists later in the development process and transformed into data base records and elements.

The superiority of entity-relationship diagramming over the simple enumeration of attributes for each data store is today universally recognized. Most CASE tools support this technique and have good support for underlying data entity and attribute descriptions. (The only attribute description in the Yourdon technique is the name of the data element.) Some CASE tools also have implementation class data dictionary functions (see Technique in Section VII).

Entity-relationship diagramming is treated in detail in Section V.

Data Flow

Practically all business systems development methodologies use data flow diagrams to depict processes (see the Technique at the end of this section for an explanation of the various symbols and rules for constructing data flow diagrams). The first step is to identify external entities and net input and output. Net input and output are those data that flow across the boundary of the system to and from its environment—represented by the external

Figure 8–5 **The Structured Systems Analysis "Data Dictionary"**

```
MARKETING SYSTEM                    DESIGN TOOL                           D065
ORDER ENTRY SUBSYSTEM              SUBURBAN PUMPS                        ORDER
                               ORDER DATA DICTIONARY


PREPARED BY: G. PILZ           DATE: 06SEP93          VERSION: 1        PAGE 1
APPROVED BY: DARRYL FIELD      DATE: 13SEP93          STATUS:  D


              ORDER = ORDER NO. +
                      CUSTOMER NO. +
                      CUSTOMER NAME +
                      SHIPPING ADDRESS +
                      (BILLING ADDRESS) +
                      ORDER DATE +
                      BILLING DATE +
                      {PRODUCT CODE +
                      QUANTITY +
                      UNIT PRICE +
                      EXTENDED PRICE} +
                      PRE-TAX TOTAL +
                      SALES TAX +
                      GRAND TOTAL
```

entities of the system. The scope of the data flow diagram should include all the external entities and data flows that are relevant to the development effort and exclude everything that is not. Entities that are excluded from the analysis are not studied or even represented on the diagram.

Having decided on a boundary between the system and the environment, all those data flows that cross the boundary are then analyzed. For instance, in Figure 8–6, there is one external entity, the customer. The net inputs are the customer subscription request and the payment, and the net outputs are the delivery of the paper and the bill.

The initial data flows must be labeled carefully. Any significant set of information that the user treats as a unit should be a separate data flow. Net input and output data flows usually correspond to business transactions requested or events initiated by the external entity and the system's responses to those transactions or events. The customer Subscription Request, made up of the Customer Name, Address, Date, Length of Subscription, and Subscription Rate, is a unit and thus serves as the label of a data flow. The names of the data flows should avoid such nonspecific words as *data* and *information*. One must also be certain that the data flow is not actually a group of disparate items. A data flow with a general name such as "miscellaneous" should be omitted or broken down into its constituents.

Figure 8–6 **High-Level DFD for a Newspaper Subscription System**

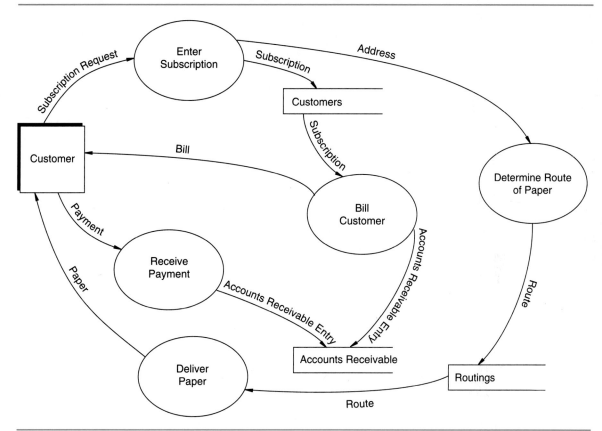

The user's vocabulary will usually include other units of information that correspond to data flows. Such units should be represented on the diagram, labeled as just described, and connected to some other data flow that logically precedes it or follows it. The two data flows can be connected by means of an empty process box, without attempting to label it initially.

Once all of the relevant units of information have been gathered from the users and represented as data flows, then the process boxes are labeled by identifying their inputs and outputs. An example is the Enter Subscription process, which transforms the Subscription Request from the Customer into two separate data flows. The name of the process must identify the entire process, and labels must consist of single-action verbs with a singular object. If there are two verbs, the process should be broken down further. Again, be wary of vague words such as *process* or *handle*.

If any internal data flows can be identified within the blank processes, the user should verify that they do exist. If so, the process should be broken down into several processes, and the required data flows put between them.

For each data flow, the key questions to ask at this stage are: What data components do I need to build this item? Where do these components come from? What intervening processes will be required to build them?

The data stores are then entered on the DFD to represent the data repositories the user has identified. For instance, the Customer data store in Figure 8–6 is a data store containing the required information about each of the newspaper's subscribers. The contents of each repository must be understood in detail so that flow into and out of it can be determined.

The data flow diagrams should above all concentrate on the main flows of data, those that support the business activity being modeled. Details of trivial error paths should be omitted. Some error paths require attention on the data flow diagram, whereas others do not. If the error does not require the undoing of past processing, it can be ignored for the moment. If it requires backing out previous updates, or a file to be converted to a previous state, then it can be included.

Likewise, control information is generally omitted. To uncover control flows, ask yourself what information travels over the pipeline; if there is none, the data flow is not documenting the flow of data. Hence, it is a control flow, and generally should not be included in the DFD. It is somewhat more difficult to remove flow of information that is used only for control purposes. To do this, you should ask how the destination process uses the information. If it modifies the information and creates it as an outgoing data flow or part of one, then it is a legitimate data flow. If it only serves to prompt the process into action, or to direct it to complete a task, then it is a control flow.

Finally, be prepared to iterate through the diagram several times, replacing your early data flows with improved versions. By repeating the process several times, a significantly better result can be achieved.

DEDUCING PROCESSING AND INFORMATION REQUIREMENTS: LESSONS FROM PRACTICE

In an era when information technology can create a sustainable competitive advantage, a premium should be placed on creativity in systems work. Mundane, run-of-the-mill solutions can no longer be accepted if an organization expects to remain competitive. Creatively designed systems are much more likely to help an organization compete more effectively. They can also contribute by promoting greater acceptance among the user community and by yielding a longer useful life. Both of these contributions provide a more favorable return on the investment.

The most creative systems result from a truly collaborative effort of users and IS personnel; a unique solution requires a deep knowledge of both the business problem and the capabilities of the technology. One of the values of the project team approach is that it encourages users and IS professionals to work together towards a solution. In the process, users learn more about

Figure 8–7 **Primitive Sophistication on the Costa de Careyes**

The error of today's architects is that they work in
offices with T-squares.
They might as well be working in factories.
They plan houses as if they were making the same Ford
car over and over. . . .

I cannot build a preconceived house . . .
I must understand the land . . .
feel the cold at night . . .
feel how the winds blow . . .
see how the sun moves and the birds fly . . .
think about the history of the place and the people. . . .

The personality of the owner is very important. . . .
I need someone who can help me—through his
personality—build a house.
The owner must consider architecture a work of art.
He is my collaborator.

I find these ideas to be extremely relevant to our systems development efforts. While some might say, "It's just common sense," we tend to forget why we do the things we do. Perhaps more importantly, we lose track of what to emphasize among all our activities. An important theme of this book is that the analyst must "go to the land" to get really in touch with the users, their problems, and their objectives. Working in some back room using memos and the telephone, the analyst will get only a secondhand view of the problem.

The back-room approach is not a substitute for firsthand data gathering. The analyst must touch, feel, and have extensive, personal contact with the environment. By doing so, the analyst will be able to obtain sufficient information to test the validity of preconceived notions. Furthermore, he will open the lines of communication with the user community. The most successful projects are truly joint efforts in which both analysts and users make significant contributions: Users bring to the problem an indispensable business expertise; analysts bring objectivity, technical expertise, and analytical skills. They need each other's perspective and cooperation to do the best possible job.[4]

Source: Allen Carter, "Primitive Sophistication on the Costa de Careyes," *Architectural Digest*, Vol. 33, No. 1 (July/August 1976), pp. 45—48. Reprinted from *Architectural Digest*. Copyright John C. Brasfield Publishing Corp., 1976.

the technology, and IS professionals come to understand the business problem from the user's perspective (see Figure 8–7).

Applying this attitude to the way that information and processing requirements are deduced, certain techniques have proven to be effective:

• Understanding the business problem.

Users often cannot express the business problem to an analyst in part because they tend to frame the problem statement according to what they believe the technology can handle. (Educating user members of the project team in the capabilities of the technology helps avoid this problem.) For example, a systems review with the executive vice-president of a small private bank catering to high-income individuals began with the vice-president's statement of the problem: getting monthly management reports prepared on a PC more efficiently. All of the bank's data processing was performed by a service bureau, and approximately 20 reports were prepared once each month. The problem, according to the vice-president, was to avoid a manual keying of summary data from the service bureau reports to the PC for combining into a management report needed by the bank's officers. An analyst could have tackled the problem by visiting the service bureau to see if information could be downloaded or combined in some way to make the process easier at the bank.

In the actual situation, however, the analyst got the executive vice-president to talk about the business. The analyst learned that the bank had been operating for about three years and had successfully attracted high-income customers because of its personalized services. The officers were struggling to continue growth in the face of increasing competition in a geographic area experiencing only moderate economic expansion. The systems project was defined more broadly: discovering how the bank might acquire an increasing share of the market through information technology. The original problem was solved with little effort. The real payoff to the bank, however, came from systems ideas that addressed its marketing problem.

- Avoiding early constraints on system boundaries or on the capabilities of the technology.

Early constraints can unnecessarily limit a systems solution to the detriment of the organization. For example, an analyst interviewing users of an aging inventory control system scheduled for replacement might find that users simply want the present system's features to be duplicated in the replacement system. If the study were constrained to inventory control, the users would end up simply getting a replica of the old system.

If, however, the analyst and users recognize the interrelationships of inventory control, accounts payable, and purchasing as components of the procurement cycle, they could produce a much more efficient system. Communications between subsystems would be performed within the computer system rather than by passing paper documents back and forth. In addition, if instead of accepting a paper purchase order as an output of the purchasing module, the team recognized that the technology could transmit orders directly to suppliers and thereby reduce the procurement lead time (and inventory levels), they would produce a more effective system.

- Viewing the problem from another perspective.

  Large organizations, in particular, tend to determine systems requirements solely on the basis of an internal perspective. Some of the best
  examples of creative systems design, however, have resulted when the
  project team has viewed the system from another perspective, for example, that of customers or suppliers. In other cases, creative design takes
  concepts from one industry and applies them to another. For example,
  the product costing approach so common in manufacturing can be
  applied to the health care industry.

- Determining the state of the art and attempting to extend it.

  A certain degree of similarity exists between the information and
  processing requirements for common applications in the same industry.
  (This similarity has made application software packages a commercial
  success.) Many experienced analysts prevent early obsolescence of their
  recommended systems by determining the state of the art for similar systems. Many will go further and attempt to extend the state of the art and
  establish a new standard. This technique is particularly useful for a company seeking a competitive advantage over its rivals. It is usually not
  enough simply to catch up with the competition; companies must
  attempt to surpass it.

  The state of the art for a traditional application can be determined
  by performing a literature search, by attending trade shows and semi-
  nars, and by talking with industry or technical experts from consulting
  firms, equipment manufacturers, or academicians who have had exposure to a number of organizations.

  As a rule, companies developing competitive systems do not publi-
  cize what they are doing. Therefore, analysts determining the state of
  the art typically focus on known systems and hypothesize on what the
  competition is doing.

  On the other hand, excessive broadening of a project's scope is dangerous. A fairly mundane project with well-defined objectives may grow
  out of hand, raising false expectations, exceeding time limits and costs,
  and giving the IS department a reputation for blue-sky thinking. In particular, if a systems plan exists, the boundaries and the variety of perspectives may already have been studied by the systems planning team
  in sufficient depth.

ACHIEVING BUSINESS INTEGRATION

The bulk of this chapter has described how to go about analyzing and documenting functional requirements, but has not described what is required of a
good business system being designed in the early 1990s. Most of our experience with business systems has been in mechanizing manual systems or
remechanizing the first generation of automated systems.

Figure 8–8 **Overall Business Processes**

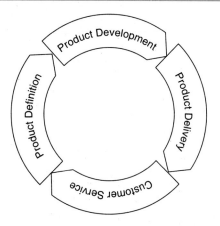

The danger in anchoring requirements analysis in current systems, which is still the norm for most projects, is that opportunities for improvement go undetected. As long as there is no acute operational problem, current ways of conducting business are unquestioningly reproduced.

To avoid this trap, information systems should be viewed in the context of the wider business processes. As shown in Figure 8–8, four categories of processes can be identified in most enterprises: product definition, product development, product delivery, and customer service. (This terminology is appropriate for a manufacturing setting, but the concept applies to services as well.) Each of these three "super"-processes spans multiple departments, but has a definite business outcome and a definite customer orientation. When analyzing systems requirements for a narrower business process, it is fruitful to step back from time to time and ask what the system under study contributes to the wider process and how it can make a difference—by decreasing the number of steps and the time taken by product development or delivery, or by providing information to some other business process enabling additional cost cutting or differentiated customer service.

Summary

The functional requirements of a system describe what a system is to do and how well, not how it is to be done. The latter is the task of the design phase. Functional specifications must be documented in terms the user can understand and also be in a form usable by designers.

Of the four most common approaches to requirements analysis, structured systems analysis is most appropriate for naive users, inexperienced analysts, and manual systems. It can be time consuming, however, and provides a weak foundation for proper data base design in comparison with the other methods. Essential systems analysis is better adapted to a second round of mechanization, with more experienced users and analysts, but is still weak on the data side.

Business area analysis provides a much stronger foundation for data base design, but can suffer from promoting idealistic designs that are too costly to implement.

Object-oriented analysis attempts to synthesize the process-driven approaches (structured systems analysis and essential systems analysis) and data-driven approaches (business area analysis). It is just emerging as an alternative to both essential systems analysis and business area analysis.

The strategy chosen to elicit functional requirements will vary from project to project. The final choice depends on the scope and nature of the system development effort, the competence and experience of the project team, and on the available CASE tools. The CASE design specification and its three perspectives (behavior, data structure, and data flow) must be expressed with precision so that it is readable by the implementation CASE tool.

It is important to view information systems in the context of wider business processes and to be alert for opportunities for wider integration. Otherwise, opportunities for improvement will be overlooked and shortcomings of the old system will be carried forward to the new one.

Selected Readings

McMenamin, S., and Palmer, J. *Essential Systems Analysis.* New York: Yourdon Press, 1984.
   The most complete and best-written book on process-oriented systems analysis.

Coad, P., and Yourdon, E. *Object-Oriented Analysis.* Englewood Cliffs, NJ: Yourdon Press, 1990.
   This is the first book to appear on object-oriented analysis (as opposed to object-oriented design and programming).

Olle, T. W., et al. *Information Systems Methodology: A Framework for Understanding.* Wokingham, England: Addison-Wesley, 1988.
   This book is the result of a working conference by a technical committee TC8 of the International Federation for Information Processing (IFIP). The working group tried to synthesize the commonalities and differences between dozens of methodologies, both commercially available and from a research setting. It has a very balanced view of what methodologies can and should achieve.

Review Questions

1. What are the two aspects of functional analysis?

2. What two purposes are served by the functional specifications document?

3. What is the role of the analyst in the functional requirements phase?

4. Distinguish between the future logical system and the future physical system.

5. What are the two improvements of essential systems analysis over structured systems analysis?

6. How does business area analysis differ from essential systems analysis?

7. What are the steps in object-oriented analysis?

8. Why is precision important when using a CASE tool for documentation of functional requirements?

9. What three perspectives should be captured in the documentation of functional requirements?

Discussion Questions

1. Discuss the comparative strengths and weaknesses of the four approaches to analysis: structured systems analysis, essential systems analysis, business area analysis, and object-oriented analysis.

2. Under what circumstances might reverse engineering be appropriate?

3. Discuss the pros and cons of reviewing the current system as a prelude to further analysis of functional requirements.

Mini-Case

Sterling Products, Inc. Sterling Products is a distributor of electronic components with headquarters in St. Louis and warehouses located in New York, Chicago, Los Angeles, Montreal, Vancouver, Amsterdam, Sao Paolo, and Singapore. The MIS group in St. Louis is interested in initiating a project to develop its first "corporate system," an inventory control system that would be used at all corporate locations.

Bob Gilman, Sterling's CIO, just returned from a trip to Amsterdam. One of the purposes of his trip was to lay the groundwork for a functional requirements study to be performed in Amsterdam by an analysis from St. Louis. Amsterdam has long been recognized as the best-performing branch of all the international locations. Bob is only too well aware that their endorsement of any system concept is important to its acceptance by other locations.

At present, the inventory control records of the Amsterdam branch are maintained on a manual Kardex file by a clerk who reports to Jan van den Pool, the manager of inventory control. Jan has been with the company for 22 years and claims he knows the characteristics of most of his 18,000 inventory items by heart. His perpetual records have been found to be extremely accurate over the years. Gilman discussed the notion of using a computer-based information system in Amsterdam, but came away with the feeling that personnel in Amsterdam were quite satisfied with the status quo.

On his return to St. Louis, Gilman asked you to spend a couple of weeks in Amsterdam as soon as possible to develop the functional requirements of a computer-based inventory control system. Gilman feels the mission is a critical one because he wants all company locations to begin using the software developed in St. Louis for the good of the company. As additional background for your trip, Gilman briefed you on the following:

- The Amsterdam branch manager is concerned that costs will rise if the new computer system is installed, and his bonus is based on local profitability. He's heard of problems experienced by some of the U.S. locations when they installed systems developed in St. Louis and would just as soon leave well enough alone.

- Jan simply cannot understand what a new computer system could do that his present system cannot do. It has worked well all these years, and he can see absolutely no reason to change.

- Despite Jan's denials, the salespeople are not satisfied with his performance. They claimed that stock outages were occurring with greater and greater frequency. Jan's response was that stock outages were occurring only on some items obtained in the United States or for items where the salespeople were not staying close enough to the customers to be able to anticipate shifts in demand. He told Gilman that if purchasing and sales paid more attention to purchase lead times and shifting patterns, there would be far fewer outages. Finally, he said that most of the problems could be solved not by a new computer system, but by having purchasing report to him.

- The Amsterdam location has a small Philips computer on which it runs accounting and sales analysis applications. The only systems professional on site is the general manager's nephew, who is studying computer science at a local university.

- Gilman estimates that, based on a quick review, inventory levels are about 40 percent higher than those of a comparably sized U.S. branch.

Questions for Discussion

1. What overall approach would you take to this assignment?

2. What analysis and documentation techniques would you choose?

Notes

1. Olle, T. W., et al. *Information Systems Methodology: A Framework for Understanding.* Wokingham, England: Addison-Wesley, 1988, 41.

2. Mills, H., Linger, R., and Hevner, A. *Principles of Information Systems Analysis and Design.* Orlando, FL: Academic Press, 1986, 7.

3. Coad, P., and Yourdon, E. *Object-Oriented Analysis.* Englewood Cliffs, NJ: Yourdon Press, 1990.

4. Weinberg, V. *Structured Analysis.* New York: Yourdon press, 1980, pp. 3–4.

9

Quality Requirements

The quality movement receiving so much attention in business is also becoming an important part of the software development process. After reviewing historical approaches to quality generally, the chapter discusses specific approaches used in IS. In particular the quality attributes of performance, reliability, usability, and flexibility are explored, along with quality attributes of projects: budget and schedule. The chapter closes with a discussion of documentation issues in a CASE environment, evaluation techniques, and metrics.

Learning Objectives

- Understand the importance of addressing the quality attributes: performance, reliability, usability, and flexibility.
- Place current views of software quality in the historical context of the quality control movement.
- Differentiate between quality as absence of defects and quality as meeting user expectations.
- Understand the quality feedback loop in systems development.
- Identify the quality attributes of systems development projects: budget and schedule.
- Understand the role of quality in arriving at design decisions.
- Appreciate the role of metrics in the assessment of system quality.

FUNCTIONAL VERSUS QUALITY REQUIREMENTS

Chapter 8 described how to discover and document functional requirements—what a system under development is to do. Once these requirements have been agreed upon by the steering committee and the users, the development team must decide among the many ways in which the system could be implemented. Each decision has some impact on how well the system will do what it is supposed to do. Let us take three examples to illustrate some of these consequences.

The system could be developed on a mainframe using a third-generation language such as COBOL. The cost and time to deliver this system is likely to be high. The performance of the system can probably be tuned so that it is adequate or even good. The user interface is likely to use 24×80-character alphanumeric terminals. On-line user training and help is likely not to be very sophisticated, and the system will not be very easy to use, especially for nondedicated users. The system is likely to be costly to maintain.

Management may want to cut cost and time to develop the system and dictate the use of a fourth-generation language or application generator. If the volume of transactions is high, more expensive hardware is likely to be required. The user interface is hardly likely to be more friendly than with a third-generation language. It may be difficult to integrate the system with other systems built using other technology.

If the system is to be used by high-level knowledge workers such as financial analysts or engineers, usability and maintainability may become critical, and management may decide to use intelligent workstations, cooperative processing, and object-oriented development techniques. Usability and maintainability will increase. Performance and time to develop will become much more uncertain because of the innovative architecture and development tools required.

The characteristics of performance, reliability, usability, and flexibility have been called nonfunctional attributes or just attributes to distinguish them from functions.[1] (They are also known informally among some systems developers as "ilities.") We prefer to call them *quality attributes*, or quality characteristics, or quality requirements, because they are closely related to current concepts of quality. Of course, meeting these quality requirements alone is not enough to produce a high-quality system: all the functional requirements must be met as well.

DEFINITION OF QUALITY

Historically, quality has been viewed as intangible: "Quality is in the eye of the beholder" and "I can't define quality, but I know it when I see it" are phrases we often hear. Since World War II, the view has emerged that setting goals is meaningful only if you can measure whether you have achieved them and that the goal of quality is no different.

This chapter's emphasis on the objective features of quality does not imply that the subjective aspects of quality—pride in one's work, professionalism, "doing it right"—are unimportant. Rather, we recognize that these aspects are better treated outside the framework of a formal methodology.

Historical Background

Until the end of the eighteenth century, quality was associated with painstaking craftsmanship, the time and care spent in obtaining a perfect fit between the individual components of each individual product.

The industrial revolution brought the imperative of a more objective approach to quality. Eli Whitney's pioneering efforts to standardize parts and Blanchard's invention of the pattern lathe were not enough for success. The final piece of the puzzle was John Hall's realization that we had to devise measuring tools that could check whether the result of the manufacturing process conformed to the specification within a margin of tolerance. The view of quality as *measured conformance to specifications* was born.

After World War II, Japanese industrialists (powerfully aided by two Americans, W. Edwards Deming and Dr. J. M. Juran) realized that it was possible to push the usefulness of quality control beyond simply scrapping or reworking substandard products. Any deviation from the quality standard set for the products was a symptom that something was wrong within the production process: fixing the process problem would lower the rejection rate permanently. At the same time, the Japanese realized that the workers themselves were the best placed to diagnose and correct process problems. This was in direct contrast to the Taylor-inspired organizational principle used in the West, which removed all competence from the workers and put it in the hands (or brains) of management and the technostructure (engineers, work analysts). The Japanese instituted *quality circles*, restoring some measure of competence and pride to the workers.

The Japanese model—a goal of *zero defects* ensured by quality control with a short feedback loop to the production process—has slowly been gaining currency in the West. Its application to software production has become a topic of research and experimentation in the 1980s.

In parallel, a complementary view of software quality has arisen, oriented more towards planning or designing specific quality characteristics into the end product. Quality emphasizes less the absence of defects (no dissatisfaction) than the presence of attributes that meet user expectations (satisfaction): performance, usability, flexibility, reliability.

To illustrate the role of user expectations, consider the buyer of a luxury car. He expects both mechanical perfection and luxury. He also expects those qualities to endure over the lifetime of the car. The buyer of an inexpensive car does not expect luxury; he does, however, expect mechanical perfection when the car is new. And although he may accept that doors no longer close as smoothly and that small squeaks and rattles develop after a while, he does demand continued mechanical reliability, as long as the car is maintained and worn parts replaced on schedule. Both the luxury car and the compact that conform to these expectations are quality cars.

Typically, the initial formulation of quality attributes is vague. The user may not even recognize his or her expectations of a software system, either through lack of experience with the class of system being built, or because the expectations are subconscious. A view of good design, propounded by F. Flores and T. Winograd, is that it is transparent until it breaks down.[2] Users of a hammer are not conscious of using it until it breaks; users of spreadsheet software are not aware of the CRT, the keyboard, and the mouse: they are manipulating figures, formulas, rows, columns, and cells— as long as the program does not respond unexpectedly. Thus, it is difficult to articulate beforehand what a user expects from a good design.

It is necessary to expend work to translate expectations into measurable goals such as response time, mean time required to learn to use the system, mean time to implement a change, and acceptable failure rates. These quantified attributes are known as requirements or specifications. Because the requirements process is difficult, meeting specifications does not necessarily mean meeting expectations. On the other hand, meeting specifications is quite binary: either you meet specifications or you do not. If the response time is specified to be less than .5 seconds for 95 percent of the transactions as measured over a 24-hour period, .49999 seconds meets the specification (as does .3 seconds); .50001 seconds does not.

Thus, we are faced with two slightly divergent views of quality; both are important to us.

Quality as Absence of Defects

Within the context of quality defined as the absence of defects, quality management relies on a feedback loop (see Figure 9–1) in which measurements of the quality (or lack thereof) of the product are used to diagnose weaknesses in the production processes, which can then be corrected and improved.

At the same time, the knowledge of the work force can be increased by feeding back the experience gained with the system. This part of the cycle is essential. What used to be taught through apprenticeship is increasingly codified as standard practices within a methodology and gradually incorporated into automated tools. Faced with a standard solution and the comfortable feeling of going by the book, the developer may not spot that the problem that the tool was designed to solve has changed and may have lost the skills to solve the new problem. The knowledge feedback loop can raise the understanding of the development process to a new level if the developer can learn to evaluate the impact of the choice of tools and techniques on the design rather than just the impact of the design on the problem to be solved. Thus, the cycle of decreasing craftsmanship associated with automation (CASE and prescriptive methodology) can be broken and indeed reversed.

To manage quality by continuous process improvement requires the production process to be well enough defined to be under statistical control. That is, the process must be repetitive and predictable: the quality goal (the standard by which it is decided whether the product fails inspection and whether to initiate correction of the process) must be met in most cases.

In the quality control of simple commodity products such as nails or light bulbs, the standard of performance is set by the market or the industry. A single point of measurement—at the end of the production run—is adequate. The manufacturer is competing on cost, and the marketplace sanction is sales volume. For more complex products, field reports and customer feedback may be required. Also, when the production process has multiple steps (as is the case with typical systems development life cycles, where

Figure 9–1 **The Generic Quality Feedback Loop**

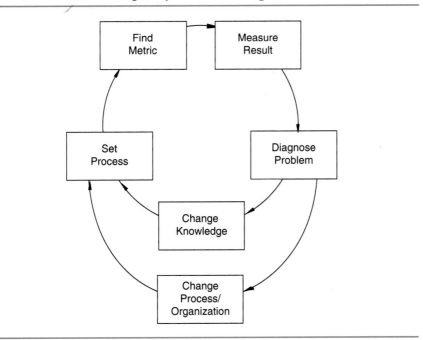

work is handed off from task to task, from group to group, as often as five or six times), it is often convenient to consider each step in the chain as a measurement point, so that defective parts are discovered before the final product is delivered.

Although this view is most appropriate to mass manufacturing, it can be applied to services such as systems development. There are some shortcomings in the approach of most IS departments, however:

- The metrics in use are informal and subjective.

- There is no systematic effort to tie symptoms of dissatisfaction to underlying problems in the development process.

- Most inspections concentrate on conformance to standards and internal consistency. There is a danger of "doing the thing right but not the right thing."

- Worker (IS and user) participation in the quality improvement process is not institutionalized.

- Satisfaction data may be collected as a new system is put into operation, but rarely over the rest of its life.

Quality as Meeting User Expectations

The second view of quality is more appropriate for products (services) that vary in some unique way every time they are created. This view focuses more on prevention and less on feedback and improvement. Here, quality means meeting user expectations—stated and unstated, conscious and unconscious.

What do users and management expect from a successful systems development project? They expect that:

- The project team meets its commitments (scope, budget, and delivery date).

- The delivered system meets the specified functional requirements completely and accurately.

- The system has quality attributes such as usability, reliability, availability, performance, security, responsiveness to problems, and maintainability. Quantified goals for each attribute are negotiated between developers and users at the beginning of the development process and monitored as work progresses.

- The system delivers the benefits that justify the development (cost reduction, delivery time reduction, increased competitiveness).

Achieving perfection for all of these expectations at once is impossible: they may be incompatible or simply ranked differently from stakeholder to stakeholder. More significantly, many of the characteristics are hard to design into the system; rather, they are emerging properties. Reliability and maintainability are typical examples; we cannot design a reliability module and a maintainability module. Rather, to achieve the desired level of these attributes, we must rely on previous experience and knowledge applied to each and every module in the system.

Moreover, some expectations are never formulated explicitly during the project. As an example, consider those subconscious expectations that arise from the mental model that users develop as they gain familiarity with the software: a "perfect" product would never surprise its user by reacting unexpectedly to his or her trying a new function or making an error. It is impossible to anticipate all the ways in which the unexpected will arise in a complex system, especially when the solutions are innovative.

Thus, the process shown in Figure 9–2 shows the role of quality requirements as design drivers on the one hand and as the source for quality metrics on the other. Measuring whether the requirements are met can be partly done during the project, through analysis and prototyping techniques. The real test comes once the system is operational and the actual achievements are measured against goals. By then, the feedback loop is double: there is a maintenance loop (not shown in the figure) to fix problems and evolve to meet changing requirements and a knowledge/process modification loop that draws the lessons from this project to be applied to the next one. The maintenance loop is used by maintenance analysts and programmers, the process modification loop by IS management or the IS methods group.

Figure 9–2 **The Quality Feedback Loop in Systems Development**

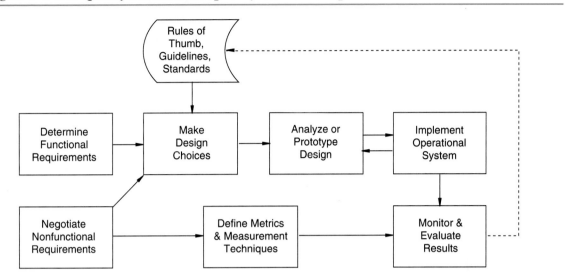

Today, most methodologies address quality requirements very partially, concentrating on performance and controls. For the rest of the "ilities," the developers are simply admonished to "make the system maintainable, reliable, user-friendly," and so on. The development process should include the following features:

- Early identification of quality requirements, including how they are to be measured.
- A process to arbitrate between conflicting requirements and achieve consensus on the corresponding decisions.
- Continuous management and measurement of user expectations (through prototyping wherever possible; through reporting and other change management techniques otherwise).
- A quality metrics feedback program.
- Emphasis on how the design decisions made during development are likely to affect quality attributes.

QUALITY ATTRIBUTES OF SYSTEMS

In the preceding, the four generic quality attributes were enumerated as performance, reliability, usability, and flexibility. Each of these attributes can be evaluated from several perspectives. To the four quality attributes, we will add two additional factors: achieving the intended benefits and meeting the systems development budget and schedule. These are not properly systems attributes; rather, they are attributes of successful development projects. However, during the design process, they are treated in much the same way as the quality characteristics, in that they underlie many of the design decisions. In fact, they are often traded off against the quality attributes: lesser quality is accepted if the project can be accelerated or its cost decreased.

Benefits

As explained in earlier sections, systems development projects are always undertaken for some reason: cost reduction, additional service, higher responsiveness. The ultimate quality mark of a system is that it achieves the intended benefits. To judge whether a systems development project has been successful from this angle, there must be a predefined metric—operating costs, customer retention, speed of delivery—that must be measured and compared between the current system and the future system. Ideally, the future system can be designed to measure all these achievements; the comparison with history may be more difficult, because the current system typically does not measure the relevant quantities and special measurement studies may be required.

Budget and Schedule

Both development schedule and project budget are fairly well circumscribed at the outset of any project. Management knows when it desires the new system to be operational—within weeks or months, a year or eighteen months at the outside. The overall level of spending envisioned by management may be less definite, but the order of magnitude of the project team size is usually set and thus also the order of magnitude of the cost. If nothing else, the feasibility study or systems plan has set the expected cost and schedule parameters.

As the requirements analysis proceeds, questions arise on the exact scope of the system. An experienced project manager weighs the consequence of including this or that functional requirement in the system or leaving it as it was. When the functional requirements have been completely or almost completely specified, the project manager can have some idea of whether all the requirements can be included with a reasonable chance of staying on schedule and within budget.

Generally, it will be found that the functions desired by the users exceed the time and budget allowed. The project manager can then either negotiate a more generous allowance or reduce the scope of the system. Most often, the functional requirements are divided into two parts, to be implemented as versions 1 and 2 of the application. Only version 1 is constrained by the current budget.

The advantage of this approach is that, if unforeseen difficulties arise later in the project, the project manager can negotiate with management for additional functionality to be transferred to version 2. Management's expectations as to the functionality delivered can be constantly managed as the project progresses.

The types of unforeseen difficulties that arise are usually that the complexity of some design task has been underestimated. The personnel available to carry it out may be less competent than anticipated or the problem may require more work. The additional work may be required either because some essential function had not been analyzed adequately in the requirements phase, or because some quality attribute is more difficult to achieve than anticipated—performance, for example. In this latter case, it is probably better to reduce the functionality of the system while maintaining the quality requirement.

Performance

Setting performance requirements and designing for performance is more fully explained in Chapter 18. All that is needed here is to realize that **response times, turnaround times, hardware resources,** and **throughput requirements** have to be set early in the requirements process, based on a thorough analysis of current and future volumes of transactions and files.

Performance requirements are the single most influential factor when deciding on development strategies and overall systems architecture. Hardware and throughput requirements also determine the continuing hardware costs of the system.

Reliability

Reliability is the quality of a system that responds to outside events—anticipated and unanticipated—in a consistent and appropriate manner. It implies the following attributes:

- The system's output has to be **accurate** and **complete.** Proper functional analysis and controls design will help ensure this.
- The system must be **available** when needed. Increasingly, this means 24 hours a day, seven days a week. There are usually periods within the day (or night) when the response time and throughput requirements of the on-line system can be somewhat relaxed, enabling such activities as data base backup and batch cutoff to take place.
- The system should be **bug-free.** Depending on how critical the system is, freedom from errors is a relative term. The requirement is much higher for the core functions of an air traffic control system than for a batch inventory system. When a malfunction does occur, it should be isolated and contained; it should not have an impact on any other activity or data than that directly involved.
- **Recovery** from errors should be simple and rapid.

Usability

Usability characteristics are those that make humans comfortable that they are effective when using the system. They are capable of executing their assigned tasks and can solve their problems by invoking the appropriate functions and features of the system.

There are two distinct aspects to usability. First, **ease of learning** implies that a novice user can become productive in a short time (ranging from minutes for an additional personal productivity tool given to a power user on a Macintosh to days for a first-time computer user on a mainframe decision support system). Ease of learning is achieved by good tutorials, training materials, and on-line help.

The second aspect is **ease of use** proper. This quality implies that as the user gains familiarity with the system, it does not get in the way. Simple tasks that are often executed can be done with a minimum of action—a simple keystroke or a click of the mouse. Similar actions elicit similar, predictable responses. When faced with a task or a problem that the user has never executed before, he or she can nevertheless intuitively discover a way to solve the problem, based on assumptions about what the system does. As the user gains experience, he or she can progressively undertake more and more complex tasks.

Ease of use depends most of all on a solid, natural metaphor or mental model underlying the application. The archetype of a good metaphor is that of electronic spreadsheets, which are so natural and comfortable to work with that very few accountants and financial analysts ever have any trouble using them.

Features making a system easy to learn and those making it easy to use may well be incompatible. For instance, a cascade of menus is easy to learn, but can quickly inhibit ease of use if the user is forced to navigate through five or six menus for the most trivial of activities.

Usability is further explored in Section IV.

Flexibility

Flexibility is defined as the ability of a system to adapt to variations in the environment. Flexibility can be achieved in the following three ways:

- Providing maintainability.

    If a system is easy to maintain, it is flexible: a change in requirements can simply be accommodated by correcting or adding to the system.

- Anticipating change.

    If change can be anticipated, it can be built into the system. A typical example is tax rates. It is known that tax rates change: a flexible system will store the tax rates in a single table that is easily and reliably modified by the users themselves rather than by the IS department.

Figure 9–3 **Design Drivers and Decision Context**

*   Providing access to system primitives.

    If a new transaction type is required, it may be possible to put it together by stringing together a number of more elementary operations. A good example is a data base utility that gives access to any field on any record of the data base, as desired. If an error or a change in processing rules results in wrong values being stored on the data base, this utility program can allow users to correct them without having to program and test a new transaction.

    This method of providing flexibility must be strictly controlled, since resorting to the primitive operations usually bypasses all programmed controls.

QUALITY CHARACTERISTICS AS DESIGN DRIVERS

The use of quality attributes as design drivers has been mentioned earlier in this chapter. Traditional systems development methods do not sufficiently acknowledge this, and few if any CASE tools help document the role these design drivers play in the design.

The lack of support for documenting why design choices are made causes maintenance problems in the form of architectural drift. A maintainer who does not know why a module, an interface, or a record was built the way it was may inadvertently modify something that should remain constant (because its rationale has not changed) or fail to modify something that needs changing (because the rationale has changed). As a result, the original developers' intentions become more and more obscure and the system becomes harder and harder to maintain.

A **design decision** is a choice between several alternative designs, each of which is evaluated according to a number of criteria. (The criteria have to be the same for all the alternatives evaluated.) These criteria can be expressed by domain (situation-independent) variables, project-specific variables, and management values (see Figure 9–3).

Relationship to Development Process

The development process of a system can be pictured as a series of transformations of one system representation into another (see Figure 9–4). Most of these transformations (in fact, all except the last one) require human intervention. These are the very points at which global decisions about the system are made, decisions that are based on the criteria just described.

Within each stage, CASE tools are used to detail the representation of the system; the CASE tool tracks how system objects relate to one another within the representation. The CASE tool cannot track objects across representations—how objects are split and recombined as a result of the design decisions made at the points of transformation—because the CASE tools do not have knowledge of the information models used at other stages. The repository must provide cross-CASE tools to track which decisions have been made and how they affect the design objects.

Evaluation Methods

Methodology cannot provide all the elements of a decision. Values and project-specific variables must be provided by the project team. So must the generation of actual relevant alternatives and their evaluation. However, the general terms of the alternatives and suggestions for how to generate relevant ones, the values of the domain variables, and a description of the nature of the situation variables can and should be provided by the methodology for all the major decisions to be made on a project—starting with the choice of approach or methodology.

Once variables have been defined and alternatives generated, the evaluation process takes place. There are several evaluation methods, the most important of which are:

- Optimization, useful for choosing settings of continuous variables with constraints when there is a single economic function to be maximized. In this case, the alternatives are not explicitly formulated as distinct courses of action because of the continuous nature of the variables.

- Cost/benefit analysis, useful when the main client value is cost reduction (if the main value is increasing profits through some other means, risk usually enters the picture).

- Risk analysis, a cost/benefit analysis modified by probabilities. The most difficult problem here is to get a reasonable evaluation of the probability of a risk materializing. The statistical data justifying the probabilities are usually negligible, especially when the purpose is to implement an innovative competitive system. Moreover, the use of probabilities requires mathematical background that may be hard to find.

- Gradual elimination by evaluation against criteria sorted in order of importance.

- Scoring methods, where criteria are assigned weights and ranges and the

Figure 9–4 **Transformations in the Development Process**

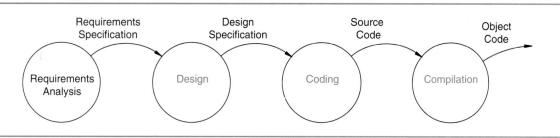

evaluation process consists in assigning values to the criteria by consensus of the evaluators. The weakness of this method is that it is sensitive to the subjective perception of weights and assigned variables.   It has been improved on by researchers, in particular Thomas Saaty, creator of a tool-supported method called the Analytical Hierarchical Process (AHP).[3]

•   And, of course, the time-honored intuitive method, also known as the "seat of the pants."

MEASUREMENT OF QUALITY

The point of quality requirements is that the system shall meet these require-ments at the end of the development process. Just as a function either is or is not accomplished by a system, so a quality requirement is or is not met.

To evaluate whether a requirement is met, we need a metric (a yardstick or way to measure the attribute) and a goal (the value of the attribute). For instance, to meet a performance requirement, the metric could be the response time of a transaction and the goal to attain less than 2 seconds for 95 percent of the transactions.

If no metric is set for the quality attribute, then the determination of the quality requirement becomes academic. Mass production did not succeed by inventing the pattern lathe alone, but John Hall's idea of setting specifica-tions and measuring conformance was critical.

Selecting Metrics

For some quality attributes, the metric is self-evident. Response time is a typical example. For other attributes, a satisfactory yardstick is not so obvi-ous: how does one measure ease of use? It then becomes necessary to mea-sure not the attribute itself, but evidence that the attribute is present. For instance, ease of learning can be measured by the average training time required before a novice user can perform a defined activity in a defined time with a defined error rate.

If all else fails, subjective measures are possible. If quality is meeting user expectations, a simple measure is a user survey, asking users to rate the degree to which they feel that the system does, indeed, meet their expectations. Such measures must be handled with some care; the exact wording of the question, the timing of the survey, and the method of rating can all introduce biases.

The selection of a metric for a quality attribute is not the affair of the project team alone. Both management and critical users must be involved in the definition and accept it wholeheartedly.

Setting Goals

Once the metric has been selected, the level that the quality attribute is to reach is negotiated. For instance, ease of learning in an order entry system could be defined by the training time required to be able to enter a ten-line order without errors in three minutes. The level at which ease of learning will be achieved could be set at four hours of training for a novice with keyboard experience.

The process by which the goals are negotiated is generally much more important than the actual values of the goals. Why four hours? If it took five hours, would the system be judged poor? Probably not, but if it took three days, the users would have the right to be disappointed.

The process of negotiating these goals is important for two reasons. First, it focuses the project team on the real success factors of the system, rather than the technical success that may be scored when bringing a system in on time and within budget—but that the users cannot or will not operate.

Second, it sets the level of user expectations. Many systems have had poor acceptance simply because the users had only a vague idea of the problems that would be associated with implementing and operating them and with the changes in organization and work that it would require.

Measuring Results

For quality attributes to be significant, not only must metrics be defined and goals set, but the actual result obtained must also be measured.

If at all possible, the measuring process should be part of the system as installed. For instance, throughput and response times should be monitored and reported by the system itself. Incident logs should be kept in combination by the operating system and the operations staff. If the system is an extensive one, hotline assistance may be implemented; all calls to the hotline should be logged and analyzed by cause. The reporting system should highlight all deviations from the norm. This type of measuring system is often called service level reporting.

When the measures are purely subjective, such as a satisfaction index, a periodic review may be the occasion for measuring. All applications should undergo a complete quality check a few weeks or months after having been put into service and periodically thereafter, perhaps every six months to two years.

TOTAL QUALITY MANAGEMENT
IN THE DESIGN PROCESS

What is to be done when a quality attribute is found to fall short of its goal? First, the symptom itself must be corrected. If ease of learning falls short, then either the training must be improved or the system simplified. If response times exceed the objective, the system must be tuned or resources added.

Most importantly, however, the IS department should try to draw conclusions for its next projects. Unsuccessful design techniques should be discouraged and better design techniques substituted. Successful systems or systems components should be documented and used as models by later projects.

The feedback of measured quality attributes to improve the process, rather than rework the product, is the meaning of total quality management.

Summary

The quality attributes of a system—performance, reliability, usability, and flexibility, also known as nonfunctional attributes—should be specifically addressed so they can be incorporated into the system specifications.

There are two views of quality control in the traditional sense: quality as absence of defects and quality as meeting expectations. Both can be applied to systems development.

The development process should include early identification of quality requirements, including how they are measured, a process to arbitrate between conflicting requirements, continuous management and measurement of user expectations, a quality metrics feedback program, and a systematic way of relating the effect of design decisions on the quality attributes.

Quality attributes of systems development projects are budget and schedule. Project managers must either negotiate a more generous allowance or reduce the scope of the system when, as   often happens, functions desired by users exceed the time and budget allowed.

Examples of performance requirements are   response times, turnaround times, capacity, and throughput. Performance requirements should be set early. Reliability attributes include accuracy and completeness, availability, freedom from errors, and simple and rapid recovery capability. Usability has two distinct aspects: ease of learning and ease of use. Flexibility includes maintainability, the ability to anticipate change, and access to system primitives.

Rationales for decisions should be carefully documented to avoid inadvertent or inappropriate modification later. Most CASE tools available today fall short in this respect.

Several tools are available to help the project team evaluate alternative designs. Among them are optimization, cost/benefit analysis, risk analysis, gradual elimination, and scoring methods.

Suggested Readings

Gilb, T. *Principles of Software Engineering Management.* Wokingham, England: Addison-Wesley, 1988.

A very thought-provoking book. Gilb advocates the setting of quantifiable attributes to judge whether a system attains its goal. He also advocates evolutionary delivery. His arguments are cogent and well stated.

Review Questions

1. When should the development team address the quality attributes?

2. What does software quality emphasize?

3. What is the advantage of a short feedback loop for software quality control?

4. What are the shortcomings of "quality as the absence of defects" as it is approached by most IS departments?

5. What do users and management expect from a successful systems development project?

6. What quality-related features should the development process include?

7. What are a project manager's options if a development project exceeds the allowable time and budget?

8. How are system performance requirements usually expressed?

9. In what terms is system reliability described?

10. What are the two principal aspects of system usability?

11. How can system flexibility be achieved?

12. What methods are used in evaluating quality attributes?

13. Why are quality measurements important?

Discussion Questions

1. What are the risks of not developing specific quality specifications for a new system? In view of the risks involved, how could an IS department justify not including quality specifications as a shop standard?

2. What are the risks in not properly documenting reasons why quality-related design choices are made?

3. Develop a real-world scenario where use of each of the evaluation methods described in the chapter for evaluating a quality attribute might be appropriate.

Mini-Case

Regalos de San Miguel de Allende is a start-up company offering artistic clothing and art objects produced in Mexico to customers in the United States. It plans to present its merchandise in a full-color catalog mailed to a list of upper-income prospects each month. Juan Gastillo and Marty Grand-champ, fresh out of business school, are partners in the venture.

It is anticipated that most of the orders will be received by telephone, with customers using an 800 number printed in the catalog. Some customers will order by fax, and a smaller number will order by mail.

Juan and Marty hired your consulting firm, Alex and Winston, to review the design of a computer system to support the order entry, billing, inventory control, and shipping processes for Regalos developed by the IS professional on the company's internal staff. In addition to making sure it will handle routine transactions smoothly, they are particularly interested in having the computer system support the image of quality they are trying to project for the company as a whole.

Questions for Discussion

1. What steps would you take in carrying out this assignment?

2. What specific quality-related attributes would be appropriate for a system of this kind?

Notes

1 Gilb, T. *Principles of Software Engineering Management.* Wokingham, England: Addison-Wesley, 1988.

2 Winograd, T., and Flores, F., eds. *Understanding Computers and Cognition.* Reading, Massachusetts: Addison-Wesley, 1987.

3 Saaty, T.L. *Decision Making for Leaders.* Pittsburgh, PA: RWS Publications, 1990.

Technique

Data Flow Diagrams

INTRODUCTION

Data flow diagrams were mentioned in Chapter 8 as the most frequently used graphical technique to represent how data is used by and flows through an information system. This representation technique is sufficiently widely used that all CASE tools possess a data flow diagram editor or the equivalent (information engineering-based tools use an approach that is slightly different from what is described here). In fact, it took the arrival of CASE tools to make the technique really useful: data flow diagrams drawn by hand are very costly to maintain.

DEFINITION

A data flow diagram (DFD) is a schematic representation of a complex process in as abstract a form as possible, disregarding material contingencies such as the media on which data is stored, the way the data is communicated, and the organizational unit or the computer that processes it. A DFD does not represent organizational structures or data relationships.

DFDs were developed in the 1970s by several authors more or less simultaneously and independently. Among the most influential are DeMarco, Gane and Sarson, and Yourdon and Constantine. As a result, several slightly different conventions have evolved.

DFDs were fairly quickly adopted by a large part of the IS community for two main reasons: DFDs are easy to prepare, and they force a certain level of abstraction, thus encouraging synthesis and innovation.

EXAMPLES

Figure 1 shows the data flow diagram for an order entry, shipping, and billing application. Orders arrive from customers. They are priced by referring to permanent product information. Availability of each product is checked against an inventory file. If the merchandise is available, it is reserved against the inventory and the order is stored for later processing. If the merchandise is not available, a back order is created. Back orders are reviewed periodically, and when the back-ordered merchandise becomes available, the back order is transformed into a regular order. Batches of

Figure 1 **Sample Data Flow Diagram**

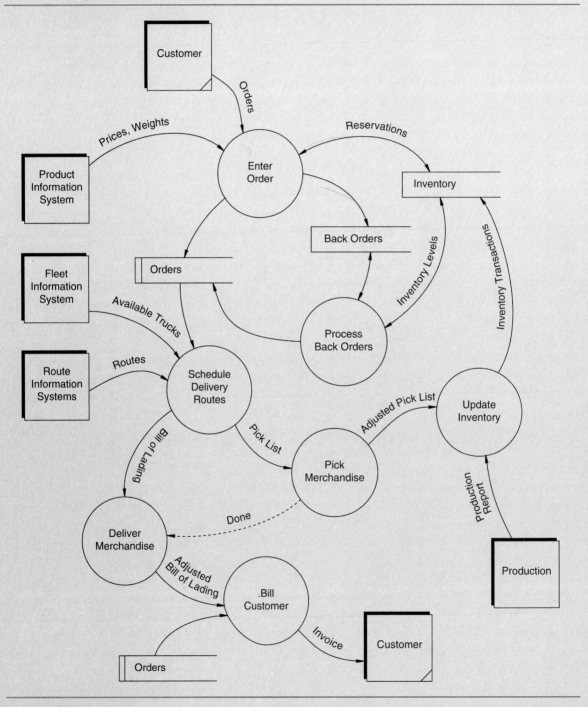

orders are taken from the store of orders and scheduled for delivery, using truck fleet and geographical route information supplied by the transportation department. Pick lists are prepared to enable warehouse workers to traverse the warehouse once, picking out all the items of a certain type to be shipped together in the same truck. Any exceptions (items that could not be located) are noted on the pick list, which then serves to update the inventory. When picking for a route is completed, the truck is loaded and deliveries made, using bills of lading (a list of what is to be delivered to each customer). The customer checks the delivery. Any exceptions are noted on the bill of lading, which then serves to prepare customer invoices for the products that actually reached the customer and to post accounts receivable.

Figure 2 shows an expansion of the Schedule Delivery Routes process of the Order Entry DFD. Orders are sorted by general geographical area using the route information supplied by transportation. Next, trucks are scheduled using fleet information from transportation, which indicates which trucks are available and what their capacities are. Orders are batched by truck so that each truck is loaded as fully as possible while called to do the shortest route possible. For each truck, the order items are sorted into warehouse location sequence and pick lists are created. For each truck, a bill of lading is printed for each order, in delivery sequence.

WHERE USED IN THE LIFE CYCLE

DFDs are principally a tool for documenting the results of the requirements analysis phase and for verifying the closure of the analysis. They are created at the end of the interviewing process or after a Joint Application Design (JAD) session.

As an example, the interviewing process could lead to drawing a DFD of the application as it currently works, with most of the implementation considerations factored out, yielding a logical view of the present application. This view would be analyzed with respect to the operational and informational problems diagnosed during the analysis. The required changes to the DFD would then be made, transforming it into a logical representation of the view of the future application.

The DFDs of the logical view of the future application are used as input in all the various design stages. During user interface design, the DFDs are used to determine which parts of the processing are to be on-line, batch, and manual and to identify which reports and screens are needed. In data design, the DFDs are used to check that all the processes are supported by data, that all the data in the data bases can be entered, and that each data item is used by some process. During process design, the DFDs are used to determine which processes have to be designed and which functions have to be incorporated into the various programs.

DFDs are used again in the implementation phase when all the ancillary processes and interfaces (such as table updating processes and error reports) are designed. This use of DFDs is quite similar to that in the design phase.

Figure 2 **Expansion of a Process Box (Leveling)**

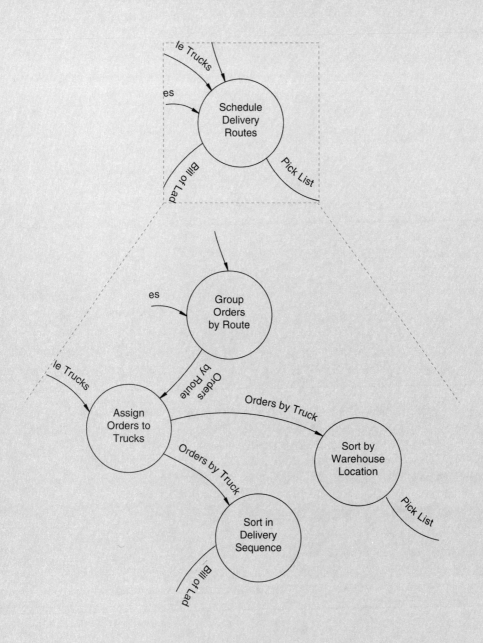

Figure 3 **Data Flow Symbols: Process and Data Flow**

One of the main merits of DFDs over other forms of process representations such as systems or procedure flowcharts is that DFDs force a certain level of abstraction. DFDs are therefore useful in those phases (such as requirements analysis) where abstraction is required and not so useful in later phases, where implementation decisions are documented.

FORMAL RULES

Symbols

The main component of a DFD is the **process box** (see Figure 3). The process box is a bubble or a rectangle with rounded corners. It contains the name of the process, in the form of a verb followed by an object. The presence of multiple verbs or multiple objects is a sign that there should probably be multiple processes that communicate between them.

Process boxes may be numbered. Numbering is useful for cross-referencing detailed DFDs to higher-level ones and to textual descriptions. In CASE tools that create and maintain DFDs, these cross-references can be maintained by the tool and do not necessarily appear on the DFD itself.

DFDs do not refer to the subject of the process verb, i.e., the person or program responsible for executing the function. Because responsibility for execution is an implementation decision, it is abstracted out of the DFD.

The next important component is the **data flow** (see Figure 3). A data flow is a line that connects a process to the rest of the system. Data flows carry the inputs and outputs of each process. A data flow is generally labeled (an exception will be noted later). Arrows indicate the direction of the flow; a double arrow indicates that the data is first retrieved, then updated.

Inputs to the system from the outside, and data from the system that is sent to the outside, originate or terminate in **external entities** (see Figure 4). These external entities are represented by square boxes, shaded on two sides. External entities can be persons, corporations, or other systems.

Figure 4 **Data Flow Symbols: External Entity and Data Store**

If the same external entity communicates with the system via several data flows (as the Customer in Figure 1), it may, for esthetic reasons, be represented several times on the chart. A useful convention is to note the number of occurrences of the entity beyond one by an oblique stroke in the corner of the external entity box, as illustrated in Figure 1.

Some data flows connect two processes or a process and an external entity. Others connect a process and a **data store** (see Figure 4). A data store is represented by a rectangle that is open at one end and that has a name. Data stores are used whenever it is functionally necessary to store the output from a process before sending it on to the next process. For instance, because it is necessary to have a number of orders before delivery routes can be scheduled, an Orders data store is required between Enter Order and Schedule Delivery Routes. In contrast, although invoices may be stored in the mailroom before being sent to the customer, there is no functional need for storage. Therefore, no Invoices data store is necessary.

Data stores provide the exception to the rule requiring that data flows be labeled. If the data flow between a process and a data store would carry the same label as the data store (in the singular instead of the plural), it is not strictly necessary to label the data flow (see Figure 5).

Some authors distinguish between data flow and control flow. Control information flows between processes and is represented by dotted arrows, as in Figure 5. Timing and other dependencies can thus be represented. Other authors do not distinguish control information, which must then be represented as an ordinary data flow.

Some authors permit the representation of the same data store at several places in the data flow diagram, using the same convention as for external entities—one or more oblique strokes in the corner of the data store. Others use a slightly different convention, multiplying the left side of the box (see Figure 6). Yet others insist that each data store can only figure once and that otherwise it becomes hard to check whether the DFD obeys the required set of formal rules. Our view is that imposing a single copy of each data store

Figure 5 **Data Store Symbols: Unlabeled Data Flow and Control Flow**

can make the DFD difficult to read. This difficulty arises especially when the data store represents a subject data base or part of a subject data base shared by many different processes.

Constraints

A process must have at least one input data flow and one output data flow. If the process has only one of each, it should also be critically examined to see whether it might be combined with a preceding or following process.

A data flow has at least one end connected to a process. On a top-level DFD, the other end must be connected to one of the following:

• Another process

• A data store

• An external entity

Figure 6 **Data Store Replicated in Several Places**

Option 1   Orders

Orders

Option 2   Orders

Orders

(On a lower-level DFD, it may be left dangling—see the section on leveling below.)

A data store must have at least one input and one output data flow. A data store with only one of each should be examined to determine whether the store is a functional requirement or just a physical, temporary storage that is conceptually unnecessary.

Leveling

Some authors, such as DeMarco, recommend that a single DFD not hold more than about seven processes, because the human brain can attend to only about five to nine objects, concepts, or chunks of information simultaneously. Others, such as Gane, insist that it is possible to concentrate successively on various parts of a DFD and that subdividing the DFD is not necessary, and may indeed be harmful. But even Gane admits that there are physical limitations to a DFD, especially when prepared on a CASE tool and viewed on a screen or sent to a printer. Therefore, it may be necessary to subdivide the DFD into more manageable pieces.

Leveling a set of DFDs consists of preparing a top-level (or level zero) DFD that depicts only very high level processes and data flows. Each process might require tens or even hundreds of pages of textual description to explain it completely.

For each process whose description would exceed a certain number of pages (which Gane puts at five on an average, ten at the most), a second-level DFD is prepared (see Figure 2). As the illustration shows, only the process box itself is expanded, not the surrounding processes, the external entities, or the data stores. Therefore, data flows that are disconnected at one end can arise. (If the data flow was not named on the higher-level chart, it must nevertheless be on the lower-level chart where the data store it is named after does not appear.)

A problem may arise when DFDs are developed top down. The analysis of a lower-level diagram may make new data flows appear to and from the outside of the process. These might typically be errors, exception reporting, and the like. Some authors advocate incorporating these data flows in the higher levels as necessary to make all the data flows balance. Others take the view that the higher-level diagrams are primarily planning and communication tools and that the system must balance downward, but not necessarily upward.

MECHANIZED TOOLS

Most CASE tools today have a facility for drawing DFDs. What differentiates the tools is mainly how the DFD diagramming facility ties in to other facilities. It should, for instance, be possible to cross-reference processes, data flows, and data stores to other components in the repository that give a more complete description (textual or lower-level DFD).

Another difference is the stringency with which the DFD diagramming tool will enforce the rules of data flow diagramming. The principal inventors

Figure 7 **Alternative Process Box**

of DFDs are far from agreeing on the rules; it is only to be expected that the tools should differ as well.

Today, the only rules that can be enforced relate to the internal syntax of the DFD. No convincing way of tying together data flow diagramming and data analysis has yet been developed. Therefore, no single tool exists that can analyze both data flows and data stores in terms of entities, access keys, integrity constraints, and processes using or updating these entities.

Finally, DFDs can be presented in many slightly different ways, as described below. The way chosen is largely a matter of preference and habit.

EQUIVALENT TECHNIQUES

The examples in this book use Yourdon's and DeMarco's round or elliptical boxes for processes.

Gane and Sarson use a square or rectangular box with rounded corners (see Figure 7). The top of the box contains a process number, usually coded in some hierarchical form to reflect the level and cross-reference to the parent DFD. The bottom of the box may contain the name of the entity—person, organization, or program—that executes the process. The executing entity's name is only for use in making the DFD represent physical systems rather than logical ones. In his later works, Gane does not refer to this possibility.

SADT, a proprietary set of tools and techniques from Softech, Inc., adds the important concept of control information flow in addition to data flow. Also, SADT has been adapted for use in real-time systems, such as the ones used in industrial control or embedded weapons systems. Today, real-time features are not normally required for business systems, but as business systems become more integrated and more complex, such additions may become important.

Adaptations to all of these methods have been proposed to accommodate the flow of goods or materials as well as data. In the order entry, shipping, and billing example in Figure 1, adding the flow of goods would be a marked advantage, especially in explaining DFDs to users.

Other methods of documenting processes exist. Although these methods may appear quite different from DFDs, they have fundamentally the same expressive power. Systems and procedure flowcharting represent basically the same concepts as DFDs, but they tend to show much more implementation detail. They are therefore less likely to force the analysts to look at the forest as well as the trees. They also put excessive emphasis on forms and documents (for procedure flowcharts) or files and reports (for systems flowcharts). In other words, they overemphasize the vehicles of information and underemphasize the information itself.

The appearance of HIPO (hierarchical input-process-output) diagrams (see Figure 8) is quite different from DFDs, but there is a rough equivalence between the two. This equivalence can be illustrated as follows: the H in HIPO corresponds to the leveling of DFDs; the I and the O correspond to input and output data flows of DFDs; and the P corresponds to the processes of DFDs. HIPO documentation is less visual, but can easily be made more detailed because it contains more descriptive text and more data structure information. HIPO is essentially suitable for communicating program structures and specifications to programmers. DFDs are much more suitable for communicating with users and management. HIPO diagrams are not good tools for abstraction. They are good for program packaging, because they tend to decrease coupling and increase cohesiveness naturally. Few CASE tools support HIPO diagrams; manual HIPO diagrams are very hard to maintain.

CRITERIA FOR USE

When invented, data flow diagramming made a major contribution to analysis techniques: it forced analysts to increase their level of abstraction. DFDs have become almost universally accepted as the prime tool for documenting the processes of an application.

Because of the simplicity of the symbols, users have little difficulty understanding a DFD and pointing out mistaken assumptions, omissions, and even possible improvements to the flow.

The danger in DFDs lies in two directions. The first is the temptation to use them to represent physical implementations, for which other tools are better suited. In particular, the much maligned systems flowchart is still a better tool than the DFD to document a batch systems flow. Also, DFDs do not contribute to data analysis, data design, and data base design. A similar danger lies in the exclusive use of DFDs to represent unstructured problems where the data flow is not known or does not even exist, as in many office automation, personal computing, and decision support environments.

The other danger is to mistake the documentation tool for an analysis tool. The syntactical rules of data flow diagramming ensure that some glaring omissions will not be made. They do not, in themselves, ensure that the system being analyzed will meet its objectives, that the users will be happy, or that the project will come in under budget. The analysis techniques of interviewing and JAD are better tools for that purpose.

Figure 8 **HIPO Diagram**

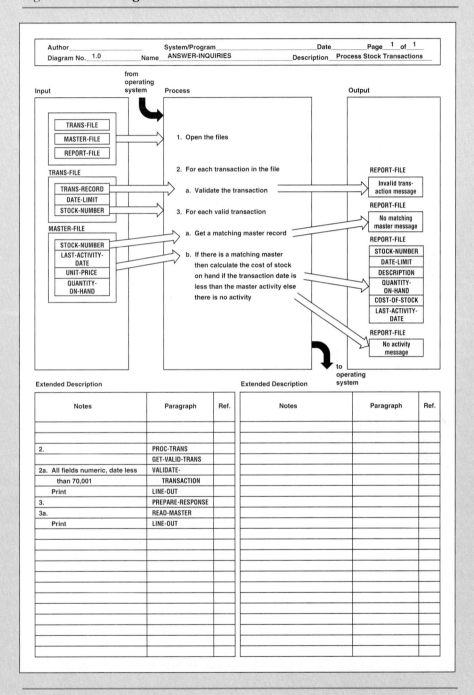

DFDs have shortcomings because the concept of a process is still ill-defined. In comparison, data analysis lends itself much better to formal treatment; it is therefore probably an inherently more powerful discipline today.

Despite its shortcomings, data flow diagramming is essential. No analyst can afford to be unfamiliar with the process. It is the best tool available for documenting a transaction processing system or a management information system at the desired level of abstraction.

Selected Readings

DeMarco, T. *Structured Analysis and System Specification.* New York: Yourdon Press, 1978.

Yourdon, E., and Constantine, L. *Structured Design.* New York: Yourdon Press, 1978.

Gane, C., and Sarson, T. *Structured Systems Analysis: Tools and Techniques.* New York: IST, Inc., 1977.
These three books make up the traditional view of structured analysis and design, which became popular in the late 1970s and which introduced the data flow diagram as an important analysis tool.

Gane, C. *Rapid Systems Development.* New York: Rapid Systems Development, Inc., 1977.
In this concise and to-the-point book, Chris Gane adds JAD-like techniques and entity-relationship modeling, thus extending the arsenal of analysis and design tools available to the systems professional.

EXERCISES

1. Draw a level-zero data flow diagram for the process of entering a university, completing its curriculum, and graduating with a bachelor's degree. Then draw a level-1 DFD for a student's view of the registration process, depicting the student's sources of information, the successive decisions to be made, and finally, the administrative steps.

2. Draw a DFD for the registration process from the viewpoint of the university administration. Contrast this view with the student's view in Exercise 1.

3. Draw a DFD for municipal dog licensing, tour organization, airline reservations. Keep the DFD you have created until you come to the exercises in entity-relationship diagramming in Section V.

User Interface Design

Section IV describes how to design user interfaces—those parts of the system that are on the boundary between humans and computers. User interfaces are designed in two steps. First, the flow of the interaction, or dialog, is designed, as described in Chapter 10: Designing Dialogs and Document Flows. Next, the detailed layouts of inputs and outputs are designed, as described in Chapter 11: Designing Forms, Screens, and Reports. Chapter 12 is devoted to the design of graphical user interfaces.

Videotex: A Success Story

In the early 1980s, Videotex was thought to be the magic medium by which the information revolution would reach into the home. At the touch of a button, users would be able to display the day's news, the weather forecast, the films playing at a nearby movie theater, the latest stock price quotations from Wall Street, and even bank balances.

Various systems were being experimented with before Videotex's full launch. Prestel in Britain, Télétel in France, and CAPTAIN in Japan were government-sponsored efforts; in the United States, Knight-Ridder, the Los Angeles Times, and Columbus-based Banc One were some of the prominent private corporations trying the concept.

Now, almost a decade later, only one of the efforts can truly be described as a success. In France, the system tested by the *Direction Générale des Télécommunications* (D.G.T.), the French telephone authority, went into production in 1984. At the end of 1987, more than 3 million Videotex terminals had been installed, with each terminal being used on the average of once every other day for a total of 90 minutes per month.

The technology that was initially developed for the Télétel system included a terminal that could be connected to standard television sets to provide color and graphic capabilities. The French authorities assumed that most people had television sets. With this terminal came a detachable keyboard that sent its signals via infrared waves—a sort of giant remote control. The keyboard had a full alphabet as well as a numeric keypad. Its special-purpose keys allowed users to sign on to the system, to leaf forward and backward in a sequence of related screens or pages, to back up one level and make another query, to retransmit garbled information, and to stop the session. Because the users of the system were presumed not to be trained typists, nor even computer literate, the keys were laid out in alphabetic sequence, instead of the more usual QWERTY style.

Later, the D.G.T. decided to add a low-cost choice of terminal. The so-called Minitel was a self-contained unit with a small (about 5 by 8 inches) black-and-white screen and the same keyboard layout as the larger terminals. Some models also had a handset so that they could double as telephone sets. This model was developed for the white and yellow pages application that was the telephone company's own principal motive for developing Videotex. This terminal has become the most popular, not least because of its low cost. In fact, in the initial stages, before the number of subscribers reached critical mass, the terminal was distributed free of charge. The telephone company was repaid by the success of the system: revenue from the increase in number of phone calls, revenue from the yellow pages advertisers, and reduced costs of printing directories and answering directory assistance calls.

After some resistance, the D.G.T. had to offer an additional option, that of a standard typewriter-layout keyboard, even though it meant reducing the benefits of mass production. But some of the most interesting initial applications were aimed at businesses and computer-literate people rather than the general public, and these users had an absolute need for standard keyboards.

Why was the French venture successful where the others were not? The main reason is probably that the technology and the initial applications were right for the users that the authorities had targeted. The low cost of the terminals, the reasonable response times, and the availability of transaction services such as home banking were crucial factors. In addition, the D.G.T. did not hesitate to invest large sums from which benefits would not be obtained for several years. The long term took precedence over quick profitability.

Some measure of serendipity was probably also present. One of the most popular applications initially, the so-called *carnet rose*, was a bulletin board dating service. It is improbable that the French government had counted on its success.

Initially, it was critical to provide a low-cost system, for instance by providing the Minitel terminal free of charge. Other endeavors did not succeed in reaching mass audiences, in part because they required expensive terminals or even personal computers and then relied on subscriptions to information services at an additional cost.

Another important factor was the availability of free transaction processing applications such as home banking. One of the initial service providers, the Crédit Commercial de France (France's ninth or tenth largest bank, with assets of $10 billion and 300,000 customers), converted its customer base from paper bank statements to electronic query. By avoiding the mailing of daily statements, it reduced its postage and paper handling costs so much that the home banking system was profitable even though it was free to the customers. Users had the perception that a system that processed their personal transactions was delivering much better value than a data base containing only generic information, such as the yellow pages, train timetables, and sports results. The home banking application, even more popular because it was free, contributed heavily to the early success of Videotex and gave the project momentum.

The Crédit Commercial de France was a precursor in another application. The first Videotex-based application that was operational in France, even before the experimental stage was over, was a cash management tool offered to corporate customers. The customers could obtain the detail of the previous day's activity via telephone first thing in the morning and transmit orders to the bank to transfer money from account to account as needed. The few hours gained in getting the information was enough to make this system a success.

Another major factor in the success was that the user interface was well constructed. When subscribers called the system, they were given clear and simple instructions on what to do to select a service. A cascade of menus led them to the application of their choice by using clearly labeled keys on the keyboard. Whatever service was desired, the conventions of calling up menus, leaving applications, and recovering from errors were identical. In addition, advanced users were given the option of typing in the name of the service that they wanted, to avoid going through multiple menu choices every time. (Prestel, the British system that was experimented with at about the same time, had a much reduced keyboard, with only a numeric pad and special keys. This limited keyboard reduced the possibility of typing in names directly and may have been a factor in the slower acceptance of Prestel.)

During the trial periods, it also became clear that colors and graphics were valuable in some applications but that, in most cases, the cost of transmitting colors and graphics was too high. Response time suffered, and the profusion of colors was counterproductive. The most successful applications used only two or three colors—for background, text, and response, for example—and graphics were limited to the initial display of the service provider's logo. As it turned out, the popularity of the black-and-white Minitel terminal de-emphasized the role of color, which had initially been thought to be much more important than it actually was.

The French system had a primitive graphics facility, relying on so-called alphamosaics, little squares of color the size of one-quarter of a character. Putting these squares side by side, service providers could develop graphic effects that looked satisfactory and were pleasant when watched from afar but that strained the eye when seen close up. By contrast, the system adopted in the United States has far more sophisticated graphics capabilities. Unfortunately, this capability also makes transmission either slow (on slow phone lines) or expensive (on higher-quality lines). The equipment required to handle the U.S. graphics is also more expensive than the Minitel. The proponents of Videotex in the United States may have thought that most homes would have personal computers capable of handling the complex graphics at no added cost, but a personal computer is still not part of the average American home.

One technological trick that the French used to improve response time while maintaining low cost was different transmission rates for sending and receiving. The French telephone network would normally support only aggregate rates of less than 1500 bits per second at the time of the initial implementation. Therefore, sending and receiving would have taken place at 300 bits per second (about 30 characters per second) each way, the highest speed for which standard components could be found and which would not exceed the aggregate capacity available. Instead, the French system was designed to deliver information from the application to the user at 1200 bits per second (resulting in information being displayed on the screen faster than the human eye can read it) and only 75 bits per second from the user to the application (still more than twice as fast as most people can type).

Other mass market systems have been successful. Bulletin boards, publicly available data bases, electronic mail systems, and services such as those provided by CompuServe and the Source are good examples. Automatic bank tellers and pay phones that read the magnetic strip on the back of a credit card are other, more specialized applications. But the Télétel system is certainly the most successful system to deliver multiple applications from different vendors to a large number of private individuals.

PURPOSE OF SECTION

As the story of the French Videotex system illustrates, user acceptance is a large part of the success of a system. User acceptance takes on particular importance when the system reaches outside the boundaries of the organization (see Figure IV–1) or when new classes of users—managers, engineers, analysts, office principals, and other types of professionals—will be in day-to-day contact with it.

Yesterday's back-office systems were designed to be used by specially trained clerks. Deficiencies in the system could be made up for by additional training or, in some cases, by coercion. Data entry clerks, employed exclusively to transcribe data from forms to a CRT, did not really have a choice of whether or not to use the system that they worked on. Doctors in a hospital do have a choice; so do engineers and managers. Even more importantly, so do customers. If customers feel uncomfortable with the automatic teller machines (ATMs) provided by one bank, they may well go to another bank that has fewer ATMs but longer lobby hours.

The purpose of this section is to show how to design those parts of an application where the users are in direct contact with the computer. Good

Figure IV–1 **Systems that Reach beyond an Organization's Boundaries**

An airline places a reservation terminal in a travel agent's office.

A hospital-supplies vendor places an order entry terminal on customer's premises (in hospitals and clinics).

An automobile manufacturer requires its suppliers to process orders and engineering changes from electronically transmitted data.

The entire transportation industry in the United States is increasingly relying on electronic order processing and billing.

Computers perform self-diagnosis and, in case of a problem, send a message to the computer maker to provide replacement parts. The part arrives at the computer user's premises the following morning with installation instructions.

Quarterly filings of financial reports are submitted to the SEC electronically by publicly traded corporations.

design will ensure that the users judge the system favorably and that the overall performance of the application meets the requirements set in the previous phase.

The user interface of an application is defined as the boundary between machines and persons. It includes all the points of interaction between the two, and it always relies on some mechanism for transforming data between human-readable and machine-readable forms. The most frequent of these mechanisms are input forms, workstations, and output reports.

Chapter 10 describes the design of the flow of data between the users and the system, whether in batch or on-line. Input forms and output reports are batch-oriented mechanisms; workstations are generally interactive.

Chapter 11 describes how to design the format of the elements of the user interface: input forms, output reports, and workstation screen layouts when traditional terminals are being used.

Chapter 12 describes the design of graphical user interfaces on intelligent workstations.

KEY TASKS AND DELIVERABLES

User interface design activities take place both in the design and implementation phases of the life cycle. The general rule is that all the interfaces must be identified and described in general terms in the design phase so that the effort required in the implementation phase can be estimated and the work planned accordingly.

In addition, during design, all the essential interfaces must be designed in detail (mocked up for reports and forms, prototyped for screens and dialogs). The detailed design of ancillary interfaces can be postponed until the implementation phase. The detailed design of essential interfaces is required to make sure that users and management understand enough of the system to come to an informed decision on whether to approve the design and go ahead with the implementation.

The key tasks and corresponding deliverables in the **design phase** are depicted in Figure IV–2. The general flow of activity follows these steps. First, those activities that are on-line and those that are batch are marked off on the data flow diagrams that were prepared in the requirements analysis phase. Then, for each on-line activity, each logical unit of work (conversation, dialog, business transaction) is identified and briefly described.

Required forms are identified for each batch activity as well as for those on-line activities that need forms. The forms are listed, and the purpose of each form is described. Generally, the purpose will be to support a business transaction or to provide updates to data stores.

For each logical unit of work, the analysis shows whether printed output (such as hard copy for audit trails, receipts, correspondence) is needed. Also, output reports from each batch process are identified. All outputs are listed, and the purpose of each output is described.

The analyst identifies and lists interface files, in particular those that will be sent to decision support and management reporting systems, and then describes the data contents of each in terms of entities, not attributes.

For each of the lists of logical units of work, forms, and reports, the analyst designs the detail of those elements that are essential in the sense described in Section III. For on-line conversations, the analyst describes the conversation flow fully, designs the screens, and creates a conversation prototype to show to the future users of the system. (If there are no tools for creating a prototype, the analyst may have to create screen mock-ups on paper.)

Next, form and report mock-ups for all essential forms and reports are created.

All of the deliverables in this phase have two destinations: printed out, they will become part of the design report that management and users will review and approve; in electronic form (by means of a CASE tool), they become part of the repository of design information that will be used by analysts and programmers to install the system. In addition, the interface file descriptions will be used in the data design segment of the design phase. Mock-ups of any preprinted forms and reports will be used in the forms procurement cycle of the implementation phase.

In the design phase, all of the interface design tasks described above are highly iterative. In addition, they are dependent on activities in parallel phases, data design and process design, which in turn depend on interface design. This lack of natural sequence among the tasks requires a high degree of coordination among the project members. The best approach for dividing the work is to assign subsystems to individuals or small teams, so that each individual can do all the design for a small part of the system. This approach is better than having some individuals specialize in report design and others in forms design or data element design, for example.

Figure IV–2 **User Interface Design Activities in the Design Phase**

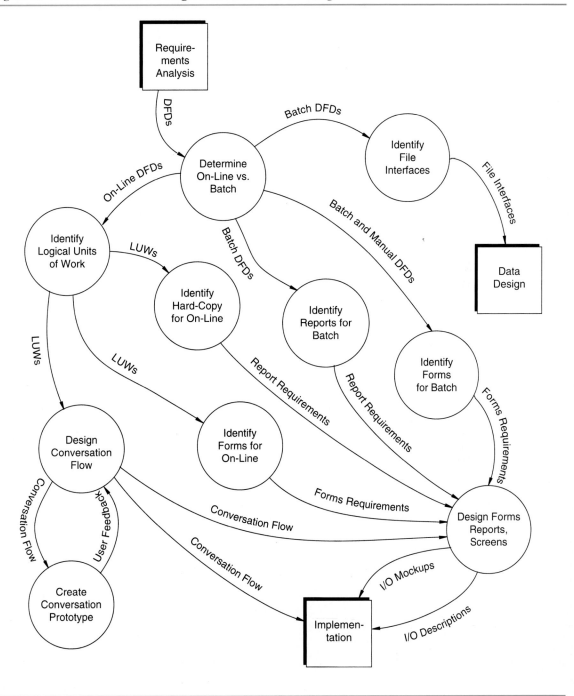

Figure IV–3 **User Interface Design Activities in the Installation Phase**

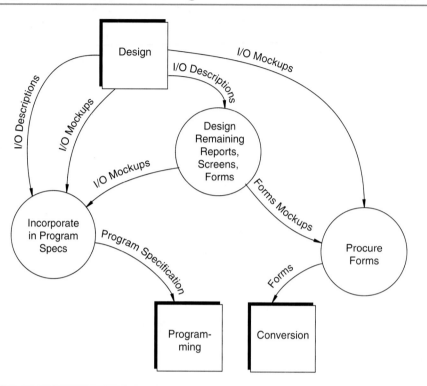

The key tasks in the **implementation phase** (see Figure IV–3) consist in completing the design of the nonessential, or ancillary, elements—reports, forms, and dialogs. The resulting documents will be shown to their users (but need not, in general, obtain management approval) and will also become part of the programming specifications. The reports and forms designed in this phase will in general not be preprinted, so they do not need to enter the forms procurement cycle.

The forms procurement cycle is generally performed during systems installation. It consists of communicating forms designs to one or more printers, evaluating bids, approving the typeset layout of the form, placing a firm order, and monitoring its delivery. It must be carefully planned by starting from the deadline for delivery (usually for the system test) and working backwards, allowing slack for unanticipated problems along the way. If the installation phase is very short, the procurement process may need to be started before the design phase is over.

CHAPTER

Designing Dialogs and Document Flows

Chapter 10 describes the various steps in the design of document flows and on-line dialogs. First, data flow diagrams from the requirements analysis phase are analyzed to determine which activities are to be manual, on-line, and batch. Next, how to design document flows (which are batch-oriented) is described. Then, the design of human-computer dialogs is presented: how to determine the scope of a conversation and select the dialog style. Dialog design also requires an understanding of the impact of the terminal technology both on dialog style and, more especially, on the type of on-line help to be provided. Some practical advice on clarity, consistency, performance, and respect for the user follows; the chapter ends with a section on how to document the conversation design.

Learning Objectives

- Understand the criteria for choosing between batch and on-line implementations of data flows.
- Identify logical units of work.
- Understand the different modes of user-computer interaction that are available to the designer and the criteria for choosing the appropriate mode.
- Apply these criteria to the design of on-line conversation corresponding to logical units of work.
- Understand the impact of technological characteristics of workstations on the design of dialogs.

ON-LINE VERSUS BATCH

The first step in user interface design is to start transforming the logical data flow diagrams established during the requirements specifications phase into physical data flow diagrams. This step requires identifying who—user, computer, or a combination of both—performs each activity.

287

Box 10–1

Good Design

A good design is one that the user does not even notice. When someone uses a well-designed object—say a hammer or a pen—there is no conscious perception of the tool. An ill-designed tool makes the user more conscious by causing awkwardness or irritation. It is when a tool breaks or does not function properly that its user consciously perceives it. (Picture what happens when a ball-point pen runs out of ink or a pencil point breaks.) This theory of design is well described in *Understanding Computers and Cognition.*[1] The book concludes that "design constitutes . . . a committed attempt to anticipate future breakdowns."

This view applies directly to the design of user interfaces, in particular to interactive workstation interfaces. (It is also applicable to less interactive media, such as reports. A well-designed report is one that presents information so clearly that its readers do not need instructions to interpret it. The report never offends with its poor appearance such as pale ink, unaligned characters, too many colors, and so on.)

By far the most important factor in interface design is knowledge of which tasks the user is to accomplish and how they are accomplished. This knowledge enables the designer to create what is called a metaphor. Users very quickly form mental models of the system they work

with: it is this mental model that prompts them to try various actions to perform their jobs or correct errors. If the mental model of a user is close to how the system actually operates, then that user will have few difficulties with the system. Another user, with a mental model that is very different from the system will have much greater difficulties in handling unanticipated situations. A good design strategy is to force a correct mental model on the user. Thus, the application should use as a metaphor something that the user already knows.

The best illustration of a useful metaphor is a spreadsheet package interface, such as that of Visicalc or Lotus 1-2-3. The reason the interfaces to these packages are said to be easy to learn, easy to use, friendly, and so on is that practically all the users understand the spreadsheet metaphor: "Lotus 1-2-3 is just like a paper spreadsheet, except for . . . ." The interfaces become totally invisible to the user as soon as he or she starts using them. The user acts as though there were a physical spreadsheet just behind the screen, on which figures and text can be written directly and which can be moved about behind the screen so that different parts of the spreadsheet become visible. The user "believes" that he or she is manipulating a concrete object directly.

The cost-effectiveness of computer-based systems is based on the computer doing as much routine work as possible. Humans intervene in a system for two main reasons:

- Technical requirements

    Humans must make data available to the computer system in the first place, through batch data entry or on-line transaction processing.

- Nonroutine work

  Despite the promises of artificial intelligence, humans outperform computer systems in making decisions in unanticipated situations, in recognizing patterns (or deviations from normal patterns), and in applying common sense. Typical areas for manual and interactive activities will therefore be analysis and forecasting (in decision support activities), system controls (in transaction processing), and professional work generally (in situations where the computer system is a supporting tool rather than a vehicle for automating the activity).

With routine work mechanized, users spend more time on challenging, nonroutine work.

In addition to this general principle, certain cues on a data flow diagram can help determine whether an activity should be manual, interactive, or batch. The three main cases to be considered are data flows from an external entity, data flows to an external entity, and data flows in which no external entity appears. In addition, a special case may arise when a data flow cycles from one data store through one or more activities and external entities and returns to the same data store.

Data Flows from an External Entity

Any activity that takes a data flow from an external entity and sends it with little or no processing to a data store should probably be interactive to help prevent errors and to increase the effectiveness of the system in meeting business requirements.

Interactive data entry as close to the source as possible is helpful in preventing errors because of two factors. First, the person originating the information may be present, so that any question that arises can be resolved then and there. For example, a new customer opening a bank account can check the spelling of the name. Second, manual transcription of data, which increases the distance between the source of the information and the data store, is error-prone. Transcribing a telephone order onto a form, to be keypunched later by a different operator, gives rise to mistakes both when the first operator writes to the form (transposition of digits in the customer number or product codes, for instance) and when the second operator reads the form (misinterpretation, such as mistaking a 1 for a 7).

The second reason for data entry at the source is to increase the effectiveness of the system in meeting the business requirements. For example, if the external entity is a customer, then interactive processing can often help in the sales process by indicating to the operator options to propose to the customer: special prices, new products or services, reminder of products that the customer usually purchases. This information can increase both sales and customer satisfaction.

An exception to the general rule that data flows from an external entity should be on-line is the possibility of obtaining the data in machine-readable form. The interface can then become batch. If the external entity is another

Figure 10-1 **Examples of Application of Electronic Data Interchange**

Industry	Applications
Automotive	Purchasing
Electronic Supplies	Order Entry
Textile Manufacturing	Shipping Information
Paper	Order Entry
Railroads	Order Entry and Invoicing; Bills of Lading
Trucking	Order Entry and Invoicing; Truckload Shipment Exchange
Ocean Shipping	Customs Paperwork; Shipment Brokerage
Pharmaceuticals	Order Entry and Invoicing
Medical Supplies	Order Entry
Optometry	Order Entry
Retail/Wholesale Distribution	Order Entry; Shipping
Health Insurance	Claims Processing
Insurance Underwriting	Policy Underwriting by Independent Agents
Internal Revenue Service	Electronic Filing of Tax Returns (Experimental)
Banks	Electronic Funds Transfer

system, passing data in a file (on tape, diskette, or via data communications) is effective. The rise of electronic data interchange (EDI) in the trucking industry is an example. Bills of lading and invoices are passed electronically between customers and suppliers. This cost-effective and safe way of entering data is extending beyond the trucking industry (see Figure 10–1).

Batch-oriented input to the system is also effective in situations where more unconventional input technology can be used. Optical technology (mark reading, bar codes, image scanners, optical character recognition) is the most widely used today; magnetic and electrical (mark-sensing) techniques have also been used, but they tend to be associated with particular industries. Magnetic ink character recognition (MICR) is, for instance, widely used in banks to read data on checks. Optical mark reading and character recognition can be used for manual input; the other techniques require that the input documents be specially printed. They will therefore usually be turnaround documents, printed by a computer (or a specialized output device) and then read back in (see Figures 10–2 to 10–6).

Optical reading is usually operator-assisted. Someone must feed in the documents; more importantly, there will be occasions when the input device cannot recognize a character because it is malformed or smudged; the operator must then be present to interpret the character.

Data Flows to an External Entity

An activity that prepares a data flow to an external entity will often be batch. Many of these data flows will be **transaction documentation** that goes with each individual transaction or that concerns each individual external

Figure 10–2 **Handwritten OCR Form**

This is an example of a form that can be completely handwritten, requiring no special equipment. It does, however, require great care and is not suitable for form-filling by occasional users.

Order forms are probably the most popular application for this technology. To motivate and train its sales force in the use of OCR, one company used OCR in an initial application to reimburse the salespersons' travel expenses. When the sales force had gotten used to the technology, the order entry system was implemented, with a very low initial error rate.

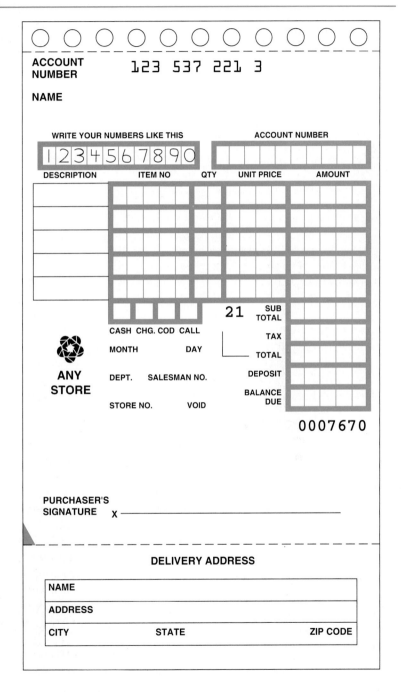

Figure 10–3 **Form for Mark-Sensing**

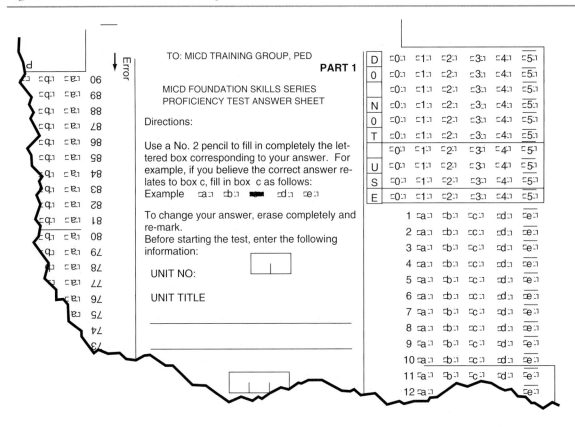

Here are some other special-purpose technologies that are quite popular. The first one is a vehicle for grading tests automatically. For each multiple choice question, the student fills in the box corresponding to the answer. Special mark-sensing (electrical or optical) equipment reads the marks and grades the student.

entity—customer, supplier, employee. These data flows are called reports, although they do not have the characteristics of management reports. The volume for each transaction is usually modest, say one or two pages per customer. The number of customers may be very large, however, and it is usually most cost-effective to print these reports in batch mode at the end of the day's processing. An exception to this rule arises when the data flow represents immediate feedback about the transaction, for example, in the presence of a customer.

Often, the external entity to which data is sent is labeled **management.** Depending on the use that management is to make of the data, reports or data files may be the most appropriate. For control purposes, reports are

Figure 10–4 **Printed OCR Form**

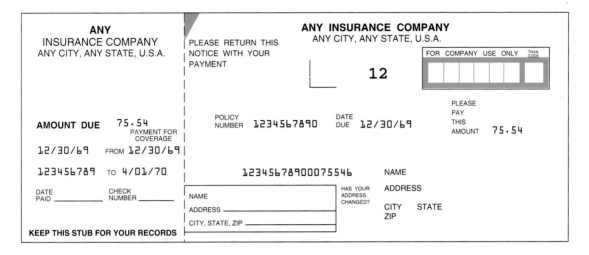

This is a typical turnaround document using OCR technology. To the left of the name is a line printed in machine-readable font, the so-called OCR A. In the upper right-hand corner is a field labeled "For company use only." This field is for entering handwritten machine-readable data.

usually the most appropriate. Such reports commonly contain exception data and overall totals that let management verify that the system—both mechanized and manual parts—is functioning correctly. The reports can also help determine whether management objectives for the application area are being met (comparing budgeted and actual sales or graphing statistics on customer satisfaction, for instance).

An example of another data flow to an external entity may be an **audit trail.** Audit trails are designed to enable users (or auditors, external or internal) to trace the chain of events leading from some event or events to a result, but traveling upstream, as it were, from result to event. For instance, an auditor may need to justify a customer's balance by reconciling it to all the transactions concerning that customer. Another example would be to justify that the prices applied to a given order (which may be months or even years old) were, at the time of processing, in accordance with company policy. Audit trails may be contained in reports or on files, depending on volume and retention requirements.

The main choice for output is between computer-readable files and printed reports. This choice is analogous to the choice of input medium: magnetic files are the least error-prone of media and they are also highly cost-effective. Sending data on files should therefore be the first choice whenever the external entity can make use of files. The main drawback is

Figure 10–5 **Magnetic Ink Character Recognition**

Here is an example of a check. The line at the bottom is printed in magnetic ink. It contains the customer's account number and the check number. Once the check is made out and deposited to the recipient's bank account, the amount of the check will be added, also in MICR characters. Thereafter, the clearing of the check (the processing that culminates with the issuer's account being debited and the check being returned) can be very largely automated.

that files cannot be read directly. Two computer tapes or two diskettes look exactly alike, and it is impossible to detect mislabeling or other errors of manipulation until the file is actually read by the receiving system.

Output flows to external entities within the system can often reside on a file to be called up and viewed through a screen-based terminal or workstation. This arrangement simplifies the report flow. However, in some circumstances, it is unacceptable to the recipient, who may not have a terminal. Moreover, the report may be too large (either in width or in length) to be suited to a terminal.

If management's requirement is more related to analysis and planning than to day-to-day control, it is probable that an output file is more responsive than a report to management's real need. What is to be avoided is to create printed output that will be directly reentered into a spreadsheet on a PC. Lotus Development Corporation did a study in the mid-1980s that showed that 80 percent of all Lotus 1–2–3 spreadsheet data was copied from computer-printed output!

The general rule that an output data flow to an external entity should be batch has an exception. An example of **on-line transaction output** is provided in international banking, where the network called S.W.I.F.T. handles interbank transfers (see Chapter 5). Although many banks accumulate these

Figure 10–6 **Universal Product Code**

The final example is this universal product code (UPC) bar code, universally adopted by the super-markets, which is found on the labels of practically all packaged food.

0 38900 00143

transfers and send them out in batches at the end of the day, others have their computers connected to the S.W.I.F.T. network and can both send and receive funds on-line as the need arises.

Data Flows that Do Not Involve an External Entity

Activities that neither receive data from, nor send data to, external entities can be manual, on-line, or batch depending on their characteristics. The choice of processing mode for most activities within the system depends on when and where the activity is performed.

When the Activity Is Performed. The general rule is that an activity set off by a transaction or an event is best processed on-line and that an activity set off by a schedule is best done in batch.

Event-driven activities are set off by transactions (external events such as a customer call) or by demands (internal events such as users deciding that they need certain information). Transactions are best processed on-line. Some demands are also best processed on-line, particularly inquiries that concern a single entity in a data base, such as the status of a shop floor work order or the schedule of a truck.

An exception to the general rule is that inquiries concerning more than one entity in the data base may sometimes best be performed in batch. Satisfying the request for information may require reading large portions of the data base. An illustration would be an auto dealer who is notified of a recall and who wants to find out how many customers may be affected (and the additional workload that the dealer may expect). The dealer might have to read the entire data base to find out the model and options purchased by each customer over the past several years. If several users make the same type of request every day, the file would have to be read multiple times in a 24-hour period to satisfy all the requests. Cost constraints may compel a batch solution, even though users would prefer to have the information immediately through on-line query.

Ad Hoc Inquiry and Data Storage

Ad hoc inquiry poses a problem. Because the inquiry is ad hoc, it is essentially unpredictable. (If it were predictable, it would become part of the exception reporting category.) It is therefore difficult to know the amount of detailed data to keep available for inquiry and the best form for the data. An extreme solution is to keep a trace of every single transaction that has entered the system ever since its beginning. This solution quickly becomes unmanageable for large systems. A credit card operation such as American Express, VISA, MasterCard, or Diner's Club can hardly be expected to keep records of individual purchases for much longer than it takes to bill them to customers. As an example, VISA processed 200,000,000—two hundred million—purchases between Thanksgiving and Christmas of 1986. If a marketing analyst in a credit card company wanted to track the buying habits of a customer over the past seven years by accumulating every purchase made in every store visited, the analyst would find that the data was not available. Some choice would have been made to accumulate statistical data by period, by customer category, or by category of expenditure,

at the expense of losing the details.

This dilemma illustrates an important application of information theory, the so-called data processing theorem. This theorem states that the output of a data processing operation cannot contain more information than the input. There are two immediate consequences. "Garbage In, Garbage Out" is one. The other is that, whereas you can obtain a total if you have the details, you cannot deduce the details from the total alone.

Determining what to accumulate and what to keep in detailed form requires experience and judgment. Unfortunately, judgment is not always enough. Requirements change and unanticipated needs arise—particularly in the services business, where new products (new forms of bank accounts tailored to the individual, new insurance policies, new combinations of travel, hotel and leisure services) can be created without much difficulty. The problems are to ensure that these new products meet a demand and to market them to the right targets. This can only be done if the right level of detailed data is available to marketing analysts.

Finally, processing that is driven by a schedule, such as the weekly payroll, the monthly closing of the accounts, the yearly renewal notices for magazine subscriptions, or periodic reporting to regulatory agencies, is practically always done in batch mode.

Where the Activity Is Performed. The location where the activity is performed may impose certain constraints on the technology and the processing mode. For example, an activity to be performed by a human agent in a place where there is no access to a workstation must obviously be done manually. This constraint is disappearing from many applications because of the increased availability of portable equipment, such as the laptop workstation where considerable progress has been, and is being, made.

A striking example is portable data entry equipment such as that used by Federal Express. This equipment can read bar codes that identify each individual package. Every time a package moves from one location to another, a hand-held scanner registers the fact. The package is thus tracked from the moment it is received until final delivery.

If a workstation is available at the location where the activity is performed, a choice still must be made between on-line and batch. If there is no on-line connection to the facility where the central application is run, the data flow must obviously be batch. In some cases, even if there is a possible communications link, it may not be cost-effective to use it on-line, for example, if response times are excessive.

Data Flow that Cycles through Several Activities

A turnaround document is one that is produced as output by a system, then completed manually, and reused as input to the same system. In many order entry and billing systems, the order is entered, then shipped, and only when the customer has actually received the order, is it billed. In this case, a turnaround document is often used. When the order is entered, a bill of lading is printed. The bill of lading goes with the shipment to the customer, who signs off that everything has been shipped or notes any exceptions on one of the copies of the bill of lading. This copy returns to the supplier, who can then call up the initial order, enter the modifications, and initiate the billing process.

This type of processing is indicated whenever the data flow diagram has flows with the same name or similar names flowing through several activities and returning finally to the same data store.

After the processing mode of each activity on the data flow diagram is identified, the data flow diagram is annotated as shown in Figure 10–7. During this analysis, some activities may need to be decomposed into several because there is a change of processing mode in the middle of the activity. (The annotated data flow diagram is an example of a work document used to help the analyst perform a specific task. It does not necessarily need to be stored as permanent project documentation, because the information that it contains will be reflected in other documents.)

At this point, the input/output medium for the data flowing in and out of the activity is selected. For on-line activities, it will usually be a CRT terminal; for batch or manual activities, forms, reports, or other technologies may be chosen. How to select the medium is described in more detail in Chapter 11.

DESIGN OF DOCUMENT FLOWS

Most of the system input and output flows identified above are likely to be paper-based. The overriding consideration for deciding how to implement these flows is that they should be as simple as possible. It is a good idea to distribute information—both files and reports—electronically.

Figure 10–7 **Data Flow Diagram Marked with Batch,
On-Line, and Manual Domains**

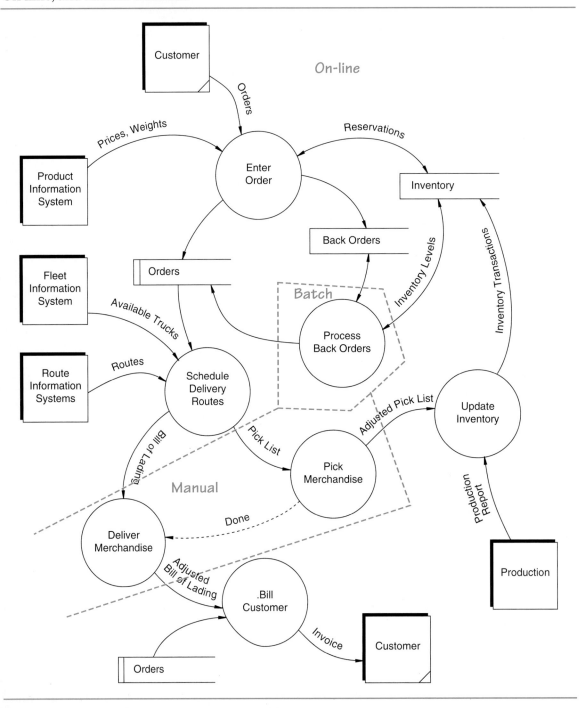

All outputs (except turnaround documents) should go directly to their recipients. A turnaround document should ideally accompany the merchandise to which it pertains to avoid loss or delays. This is obviously impossible in those cases where physical goods are not involved, such as in financial services. However, in the example of a check, which is a turnaround document on which the account number and check number have been printed and to which the amount will be added when the check is deposited, the paper flow is the materialization of the transaction. This case is quite similar to the cases where the documents accompany the physical goods.

Some systems produce large amounts of printed output that must be distributed to a large number of individuals or organizations. Billing individuals for services is a typical example. Direct marketing based on mailing lists is another. A large bank or a utility may need to print and mail several million statements every month. Handling this type of output can be very costly because it may require multiple stages of processing: bursting and collating the output forms, folding and inserting them in envelopes, and adding promotional inserts or canceled checks. Special equipment that automates these activities is available but may be expensive and occupy precious square footage. In some cases, the report and the envelope that is to contain it can be printed in a single operation, using specially designed mailers that are assembled as continuous forms. If the process cannot be automated or if the additional equipment is very expensive, the cycle billing technique that utilities have used for many years may be the answer. This technique consists of dividing the customer base into as many parts as there are days in the month, say twenty, and only processing one-twentieth of the invoices on any given day.

Input flows of forms—again with the exception of turnaround documents—should be as short as possible. Whenever input forms are transmitted from one activity in the system to another, there must be some control procedure to ensure that all the forms that leave their source actually arrive at their destination.

DIALOG DESIGN

The design of human-computer dialogs, or conversations, starts with determining the scope of the conversation, the logical unit of work. The next step is to choose the type of dialog—whether the dialog is controlled mainly by the operator or by the system. This choice is influenced not only by the functional requirements and the users' preferences but also by the terminal technology to be used. Finally, the level and style of operator help during the interaction is chosen. This choice is even more influenced by the technology than the overall dialog style.

**Box
10–3**

Logical Units of Work

From the technical side of systems comes the need for a notion of a logical unit of work. A logical unit of work is that portion of an activity that stands on its own, that has a meaning independent of other units of work.

Take, for example, a customer calling the Hawthorne Pasta Company with an order for 144 cartons of spaghetti and 160 cartons of rotini. This order is a unit of business. Recording that there is an order for 160 cartons of something unspecified has no meaning; nor has recording an order of 160 cartons of rotini for some unspecified customer. It is the entire order that is the logical unit of work, not a number such as 160, nor a single line. (Obviously, if the Hawthorne Pasta Company is out of spaghetti, a partial order for rotini only could be recorded; this would still be a logical unit of work.)

There are three reasons for logical units of work. First, logical units of work provide *closure* for the operator. Closure provides the operator with answers to such questions as *Where am I in my work? What have I done? What remains to do? What is completed and what remains open?*

Second, precise guidelines are necessary for *recovery* from a system malfunction. Logical units of work provide a means to recover. In the days of sequential files, it was fairly easy to know how to recover from a system malfunction: the program was just started over. The logical unit of work was the program that processed an entire input file. With direct-access files and on-line systems, it is more productive to have smaller units of recovery. It would in fact be very inconvenient to have to redo the entire day's processing if the system went down at 4:30 P.M.

The third reason is the *sharing of data* in files and data bases among several users. To avoid losing data in certain cases, each user must block off data that has been read from the file or data base with the intention of modifying it, so that no one else can modify it until the logical unit of work has been completed (see Figure 10–8).

The user of any on-line system that records activity against a shared data base must know what constitutes a logical unit of work, because it is the user's responsibility to signal the end of a logical unit of work by some action at the terminal (for example, by pressing the *Enter* key or responding *OK*) which is said to *commit* the transaction to the data base. Conversely, the user will then know that as long as the transaction has not been committed, there is always some way to back off, correct errors, or abandon the work without consequence.

Users of on-line systems must also be aware that if they pause for a long time in the middle of a logical unit of work, the corresponding records on the data base remain blocked; they cannot be unblocked until the transaction is either committed or abandoned. Blocked records cause problems for other operators who might be trying to get at the same data.

Transaction processing systems are the most sensitive to this type of constraint. Handling it has become a matter of routine programming discipline because most logical units of work, or *business events*, only take a few seconds or minutes to complete and because the risk of conflict is low. If a transaction requests a record that has been blocked, the user is not even notified; the system just suspends work on the transaction until the record is freed, and then proceeds. The operator notices nothing but a slight pause.

Decision support systems (DSS), where a given task of analysis can last for hours, usually provide the users with their own copies of the data, which they can then manipulate, update,

Continued

Continued

or even destroy without consequence to others. In general, DSS users are not allowed to update the data base that they share; they must go back through the transaction processing system that created the DSS data in the first place.

New types of systems are emerging where the transaction processing component is present, yet the units of work last much longer. Updating a drawing of a manufactured part or adjusting an insurance claim, for instance, typically takes minutes to hours. This kind of processing has been termed *casework* to differentiate it from data base transaction processing. The logical unit of work is a case, by analogy to a case in the medical and legal professions. In this context, any operator who requests a record or set of records on which someone else is already working must be notified that the data is unavailable. The system must thus provide for each user to "check out" (as when borrowing a library book) a case for the time required to

work on it, then "check it back in" (return the library book) when the work is done. This method is widely used in program development and maintenance when several analysts and programmers are working on the same project.

In summary, a logical unit of work is in general a business transaction that is accomplished or not as a unit. It can take several exchanges (or interactions) between the operator and the on-line program to accomplish. This collection of exchanges is often called a conversation. (The term *transaction* is better avoided, because it is ambiguous. Some system software products use it to mean an elementary exchange between the program and the operator. The program sends a blank form, a prompt, or some other form of data, and the operator responds by filling in the form or pressing a function key. This meaning of the word *transaction* is not necessarily the same as in the phrase *business transaction*.)

Determining the Logical Unit of Work

The first step in conversation design is to identify the logical units of work that make up an activity on the logical data flow diagrams. Usually, but not always, there is one logical unit of work for each activity. (If several activities make up a single logical unit of work, the logical data flow diagram may have been drawn to an excessive level of detail.)

In general, a logical unit of work is the processing of an elementary **business event,** that part of a business transaction that takes place within a single unit of time. Entering an order, entering modifications to a bill of lading so as to initiate billing, and entering the data on an accounting journal entry (making sure that debits and credits balance) are typical examples. The criteria for a good logical unit of work are that it must be a reasonably self-contained whole and that it must be completed within a short time span. The main characteristic of a unit of work is that, if the system should go down during the processing, the unit has either been completely processed or not at all. The unit of work is also the unit of data base update and the unit of recovery in case of incident.

Figure 10–8 **Example of How Data Can Get Lost When
Two Users Access the System Simultaneously**

ATM 1	ATM 2
3:33 Smith requests $90 withdrawal, authorized based on $100 balance	3:33
3:34 ATM 1 starts to deliver 9 ten-dollar bills	3:34 Jones requests $90 withdrawal, authorized based on $100 balance
3:35	3:35 ATM 2 starts to deliver 9 ten-dollar bills
3:36 ATM 1 completes delivery	3:36
3:37 Balance is updated: it is now $10	3:37 ATM 2 completes delivery
3:38	3:38 Balance is updated: account is $80 overdrawn

Generally, a logical unit of work concerns a single entity such as customer, product, supplier, account, employee—or at worst a very few entities. An exception might appear when a mass update is to take place, such as increasing the prices of a whole list of products by some percentage. Because this work does not involve a small number of entities, it is best processed in batch.

In many organizations, a new type of processing is emerging that is based on a much larger logical unit of work. The generic name for this type of logical unit of work is **case.** Examples of casework are the processing of an application (for life insurance, retirement benefits, or a mortgage loan); the design of a new product using computer-aided design and an expert system to estimate its manufacturing cost; and, closer to home, systems development activities such as the design of a conversation, the analysis of the impact of a request for maintenance, and the planning and conduct of a series of system test sessions.

Ease of Use

User friendly, easy to use, and *easy to learn* are terms that appear in advertisements for nearly every software package. But little is said about how these qualities are actually achieved. To understand what constitutes ease of use (the term used here, because it encompasses ease of learning and user-friendliness), one must understand the characteristics of different kinds of users and different kinds of usage patterns.

First, it is a myth that a user-friendly computer program is one that imitates an outgoing, friendly human by responding to the user with such items as "Hi there! I am Hal, your friendly computer, and I will help you add numbers together! By the way, have you heard the one about . . . ." This style of interface entertains no one but the programmer who implemented it. Computers are not humans; they are still far from being able to duplicate even the most primitive of human thought processes; and even if they could, it is not at all certain that they should give the impression that they have human qualities.

In reality, to design an easy-to-use system, the designer needs to know something about the user—his or her prior knowledge of the application and of computers—and about the pattern of usage—daily, intermittent, or infrequent.

Perhaps the easiest interfaces to design are those that address themselves to "perpetual beginners," where the designer can assume that the user knows little about the application, little about computers, and will only use the system very infrequently. In this case, extensive guidance and explicit instructions must be offered all the way. This type of user is the exception, and very few systems designed by IS professionals in a business organization will be of this nature. In most systems, the users (such as middle-level managers, engineers, analysts, or other professionals) know the application area and use it intermittently or daily. Or the users may be people (such as clerks) with little knowledge of the application area who use the system all day (see Figure 10-9).

For instance, data entry clerks have little prior knowledge of the application domain. They will, however, use the system with great frequency. Therefore, the user interface for data entry need not be especially well guided. Training and experience will soon make up for beginners' difficulties. The main criterion for a user interface for data entry clerks must be performance—speed and accuracy. Interfaces for such users are fairly easy to design; it is mainly a technical or technological problem.

On the other hand, highly qualified professionals such as engineers, financial analysts, or foreign-exchange traders bring considerable prior knowledge of their own application domain, far more knowledge than the designer of the user interface. However, they may know little or nothing about computers. Very often, the systems used by such people must provide a lot of initial guidance. Once the hurdles of learning the system have been overcome, the users may become impatient with too much guidance (if they use the system frequently). They also become impatient when they perceive that the computer does not "understand." This impatience frequently results from sketchy or ambiguous instructions, which cause a gap between the user's mental model of how the system works and the reality. Users who leave the system for a few weeks or months and then start using it again may also need an intermediate level of help for a short while.

If the metaphor presented to these users is a good one, the users will find the initial learning fairly easy and relearning after a period of non-

Continued

Continued

use even easier. The user may not recall all the details of the interface, but with minimal prompting, he or she will recognize the correct course of action. (Think of the difference between recall [open-ended questions] and recognition [multiple-choice items] in a test.)

An important characteristic of the dialog between the user and the computer system is the degree of initiative left to the user. Data entry clerks or transaction processing operators usually have little to say about how the work is to be done. Generally, the interface is computer-directed: the on-line program directs the sequence of operations in an invariable (or at least deterministic) manner.

Decision support systems, professional support systems such as computer-aided design, and office automation systems are, in contrast, user-directed. At any point in time, the user may choose between many different courses of action. The types of interfaces for these two categories of systems are very different.

Choosing the Type of Dialog

The choice of the type of dialog is mainly directed by the type of application and the degree of user-friendliness required (see Box 10–4). There are two main types of dialog between a computer system and the operator:

*   Program-directed dialogs

    The program has the overall initiative and directs the operator to enter commands and data in a predetermined sequence, leaving few, if any, choices to the operator. The sequence in which screens are processed can often be chosen by the operator, but each screen is usually fixed in format. Usually, the program is instrumental in determining whether the logical unit of work is completed.

*   Operator-directed dialogs

    The operator directs the program to perform various tasks in the sequence that the operator has determined to be appropriate in the particular case. The sequence of entering commands and data is often arbitrary. The operator may be totally responsible for determining whether the logical unit of work is completed.

Historically, transaction processing systems have implemented a largely program-directed dialog. Office automation, decision support systems, and case-work, on the other hand, tend to emphasize operator-directed dialogs. The choice between the two depends largely on how structured the operator's task is and how much decision power he or she has. The current trend is towards less specialized users with a wider range of options for performing their work and towards integration of computer systems in the tasks of knowledge workers. The trend is away from computers operated in the back office by data specialists.

Figure 10–9 **Users Classified according to Prior Knowledge and Frequency of Use**

This figure shows what types of users can be expected to use systems frequently, intermittently, or rarely and what prior knowledge they may be expected to have of the application they are working with. An arrow from a category of user pointing towards the knowledge of computers column indicates that some individuals in the population are likely to acquire a good knowledge of computers and become so-called *power users.*

		Degree of Prior Knowledge	
Frequency of use	**None**	**Application**	**Computers**
High	Data Entry Clerks	OA/Departmental Systems Workers	⟶
Medium		Professionals (Knowledge Workers)	⟶
Low	General Public	Professionals (Others)	

As a result, transaction processing is also becoming more operator-directed, although it remains, in general, more structured than casework, office automation, and decision support.

Within program-directed dialogs, the following modes of interaction are the most frequently used:

- Menu choices

  The operator is given a small number of alternative actions and chooses one by pointing to it.

- Form filling

  The program displays the equivalent of a form, with captions and fields where the operator keys in the data indicated by the corresponding caption. The fields are completed in fixed sequence, from left to right on each line and from top to bottom on the screen.

- Prompting

  The program displays a single question at a time and waits for the answer before displaying the next question.

In these types of dialog, operator help facilities are relatively easy to implement, because the program knows what the state of the processing is and because there are relatively few options at the operator's disposal. However, on-line help has often been absent from these systems in the past. A paper-based reference manual or operator training (with or without a manual) has usually taken the place of on-line guidance.

Operator-directed dialogs usually rely on one of the following methods:

- Command language

    Rather than ask a question, as in a prompted dialog, the computer indicates that it is ready, and the operator types in an activity description (usually in the form of a verb and one or more objects on which the verb is to act).

- Direct manipulation

    The prototype of this method is the Macintosh interface, where a number of objects are depicted on the screen; the operator selects the object to be manipulated and then indicates (by a menu choice or a command) the activity to be performed. Because these interfaces are often associated with graphics-capable workstations, they have often been called *graphical user interfaces* (GUI). The two are not synonymous, however: an example of direct manipulation without graphics is the spreadsheet, where the operator points to a cell, then enters or modifies its content.

Because the number of choices at any point is essentially the entire gamut of operator actions, providing focused help in a command-language based system is much more difficult. Even if complete help is provided, the user must usually remember either the exact form of each command or the topics along which the help facility is organized. Some systems do provide a menu-like table of contents for the help facility. This kind of help is tantamount to providing an on-line reference manual—not a bad solution, but not as helpful as more context-oriented help.

One of the major motivations for the direct manipulation style of interfaces is to have the interface itself provide the help by using the underlying metaphor of the interface to display most of the possibilities for action on the screen. Then the user can just point to icons or other objects of interest, rather than have to remember command and object names.

With the possible exception of direct manipulation, which has only recently become popular, all these techniques are well described in the literature, in particular by James Martin[2] and, more recently, by Ben Shneiderman.[3]

The choice between the different modes of dialog depends, as stated above, on the tasks that the user is expected to perform. It also depends on the technology that is to be used. For instance, a combination of menus and form filling is appropriate for simple transaction processing on traditional, so-called block-mode terminals (see Figure 10–10).

Prompting is most appropriate in two cases: either when the user is expected to be very naive (and the dialog short), as for an automatic teller machine (see Figure 10–11), or when the content of each question depends on the answer to a preceding question.

Figure 10–10a **Menu and Form Filling Conversation Example**

This is the main menu of a hospital patient care system. The operator has just chosen Line 1—Order Entry and entered it by the *?Line No.* prompt towards the bottom of the screen.

```
 PICS 0010  CP2              CONVERSATIONS                10/06/92    14:02
                                                           CCN 80432192



      01 ? Order Entry                    09 ? Review Messages
      02 ? Chart Review                   10 ? Signon
      03 ? Nursing Update
      04 ? Nursing Station Reporting
      05 ? Nursing Assignments
      06 ? PT Location
      07 ? PT Bed Swap
      08 ? PT Discharge




      _1  ? Line No.

    ?SIGNOFF     ?CANCEL     PAGE:    ?P   ?B   ?01   ?COPY    ?HELP    ?DONE    ?ENTER
```

Figure 10–10b

The system has responded by displaying the names of all the patients for which the operator has responsibility. The operator has just picked patient No. 2—Reginald Heathcraft.

```
 PICS 0060  CP2                ORDER ENTRY                10/06/92    14:02
                                                           CCN 32587112


    No.    Room/Bed Name                 Sex Age  SVC  C  Unit #  I  Physician
    01 ? CP203   1 Schwartzbinder, Malcolm  M  52  MED  S  123487  2  Knoll
    02 ? CP203   2 Heathcraft, Reginald     M  43  MED  S  218765  1  Grossman
    03 ? CP204   1 Smith, Joe               M  23  SUR  P  321862  2  Sampson
    04 ? CP205   1 Jones, John              M  28  MED  P  437906  1  Grossman
    05 ? CP206   1 Johnson, Cynthia         F  81  SUR  S  567215  2  Grant
    06 ? CP206   2 Wilson, Monica           F  78  SUR  S  286791  2  Sampson




      _2  ? Line No.
    ?SIGNOFF     ?CANCEL     PAGE:    ?P   ?B   ?01   ?COPY    ?HELP    ?DONE    ?ENTER
```

Figure 10–10c

This panel enables the operator to enter the name of the health care professional who has authorized the order, again by choosing from several alternatives.

```
   PICS 0444  CP2                ORDER ENTRY                   10/06/92    14:02
                                                                  CCN 38976332


   218765 Heathcraft, Reginald D.              Attending:  Grossman, Alvin, M.D.
   CP203-2 M 43Y Serious                       ***    PROVIDER IDENTIFICATION    ***

     01 ? Grossman, Alvin, M.D.
     02 ? Sampson, Stanley, M.D.
     03 ? Social Services
     04 ? Guerega, Barbara, R.N.









     _2  ? Line No.

   ?SIGNOFF      ?CANCEL      PAGE:   ?P   ?B   ?01   ?COPY    ?HELP    ?DONE    ?ENTER
```

Figure 10–10d

The operator has selected Line 2—Chemistry.

```
   PICS 0420  CP2                ORDER ENTRY                   10/06/92    14:03
                                                                  CCN 44498762


   218765 Heathcraft, Reginald D.

     01 ? Blood Service        08 ? Equipment              15 ? Pharmacy
     02 ? Chemistry            09 ? Gastroenterology        16 ? Physical Therapy
     03 ? Coagulation          10 ? Hematology             17 ? Radioligand
     04 ? Coronary Care        11 ? Hemodialysis           18 ? Respiratory Ther
     05 ? Diagnostic Prog.     12 ? IV                     19 ? Serology
     06 ? Dietary              13 ? Microbiology           20 ? Urinalysis
     07 ? EKG, EEG             14 ? Nursing Care           21 ? X-Ray
                                                           22 ? Other



     _2  ? Line No.

   ?SIGNOFF      ?CANCEL      PAGE:   ?P   ?B   ?01   ?COPY    ?HELP    ?DONE    ?ENTER
```

Figure 10–10e

The menu selection is Line 6—Potassium.   The operator has also marked the *?Comments* prompt with X, indicating that there is additional data to be entered.

```
PICS 04308 CP2                    ORDER ENTRY                    10/06/92    14:03
                                                                      CCN 34587609


   218765 Heathcraft, Reginald D.                        ***    CHEMISTRY    ***

     01 ? 2 Hr PP Glucose      08 ? Magnesium         15 ? COT
     02 ? Glucose              09 ? Uric Acid          16 ? Alk. P'tase
     03 ? Bun                  10 ? T. Protein         17 ? Cholesterol
     04 ? CO2                  11 ? Albumin/Globulin   18 ? CPK
     05 ? Chloride        .    12 ? Calcium            19 ? CPT
     06 ? Potassium            13 ? TID Bilirubin      20 ? CCTP
     07 ? Sodium               14 ? LDN                21 ? Acid P'tase



    _6  ? Line No.

     X  ? Comments   _ ?Stat   _ ?Today   _ ?Pre-Op   _ ?Label   _ ?Schedule

   ?SIGNOFF    ?CANCEL    PAGE:   ?P   ?B   ?01   ?COPY   ?HELP   ?DONE   ?ENTER
```

Figure 10–10f

The operator has completed the data entry of the comments and other indications such as the frequency, duration, schedule, and specimen requirements.

```
PICS 0421  CP2                    ORDER ENTRY                    10/06/92    14:05
                                                                      CCN 04659633
   218765 Heathcraft, Reginald D.              ***    PROCEDURE COMMENT    ***
          Procedure Potassium
          Comments: should precede X-ray at 11 a.m._____

          _____

          _____

  OD_____  2 day___  7:30_____  _____ _____ _____  3 Plasma
  Frequency Duration        Schedule   Start Date Stop Date  Other    Specimen
  ?OD   ?Q1H ?1    ?M ?Mon   ?7    ?:15                       ?AC      ?Urine
  ?RID  ?Q2H ?2    ?H ?Tues  ?8    ?:30                       ?PC      ?SterUrine
  ?TID  ?Q3H ?3    ?D ?Wed   ?9    ?:45                                ?24HrUrine
  ?QID  ?Q4H ?4       ?Thurs ?10                                       ?WndSwab
  ?QOD  ?Q6H ?5   ?15 ?Fri   ?11                                       ?Feces
  ?PRN  ?Q9H ?6   ?30 ?Sat   ?12                                       ?SpnlFl
  ?QOS       ?7       ?Sun    ?1
  ?Q12H      ?8              ?2
  ?Q15H      ?9              ?3
  ?Q30M ?10                 ?4   Back Procedure_____
  ?AD LIB                   ?5   Department____

   ?SIGNOFF    ?CANCEL    PAGE:   ?P   ?B   ?01   ?COPY   ?HELP   ?DONE   ?ENTER
```

Figure 10–11a **Example of a Prompted Conversation for Naive Users**

The customer inserts the
card in the slot.

```
WELCOME TO CASH NETWORK

 PLEASE INSERT YOUR

 CARD, STRIPE DOWN



                ==========>
```

Figure 10–11b

The customer enters four
numeric digits known
only to himself or herself,
and then presses the *OK*
key. After three unsuc-
cessful attempts, the
transaction is canceled
and the card remains in
the ATM. The customer
must retrieve it from the
bank the next day.

```
 ENTER YOUR PERSONAL

 IDENTIFICATION NUMBER



 IF CORRECT, PRESS    ===>

 IF ERROR, PRESS      ===>
```

Figure 10–11c

If the customer presses
any of the *7, 8* or *9* keys,
cash withdrawal is
selected.

```
    CASH WITHDRAWAL  ===>

    DEPOSIT          ===>

    TRANSFER         ===>

    BALANCE INQUIRY  ===>


 SELECT A TRANSACTION
```

Figure 10–11d

The customer enters the
amount, in whole dollars
with the decimal point or
in cents without the
decimal point. If the
amount is incorrectly
entered or if the the
customer pressed *Cash
Withdrawal* in error, the
Cancel key takes the
conversation back to the
selection screen.

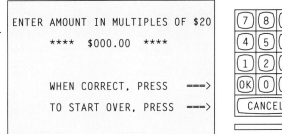

```
ENTER AMOUNT IN MULTIPLES OF $20

     ****   $000.00   ****


   WHEN CORRECT, PRESS    ===>

   TO START OVER, PRESS   ===>
```

Figure 10–11e

The customer can now
retrieve the cash. (In the
meanwhile, a screen may
have appeared, saying:
"Please be patient. The
transaction is being
processed.")

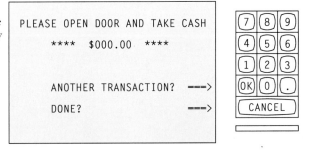

```
PLEASE OPEN DOOR AND TAKE CASH

     ****   $000.00   ****


   ANOTHER TRANSACTION?   ===>

   DONE?                  ===>
```

Figure 10–11f

The transaction is now
ended. Should the
customer wish to process
another transaction, such
as as a deposit or a
balance inquiry, the card
must be inserted again.

```
    PLEASE TAKE RECEIPT AND

      REMOVE YOUR CARD


     THANK YOU FOR USING

  *** THE CASH NETWORK ***
```

Figure 10–12 **Sample Dialog Showing Use of a Command Language**

The dialog shown represents the initial steps in installing Lotus 1-2-3® on a personal computer under MS-DOS. The user's responses to the prompts are in bold type. Note the cryptic nature of the commands and the unhelpful error message when the command *Copy* was misspelled. Also note that the last line contains the prompt *C >*. It is the user's "turn," but there is nothing to indicate which courses of action are possible. (The correct course of action is spelled out in the *Lotus 1-2-3 Installation Manual.*)

```
Current date is  Sat 2-27-1988
Enter new date (mm-dd-yy):
Current time is 10:28:21.94
Enter new time:

C>md \123

C>cd \123

C>cpoy a:*.*
Bad command or file name

C>copy a:*.*
A:123.CMP
A:LOTUS.COM
A:123.COM
A:1213.CNF
A:123.HLP
A:123.SET
        6 File(s) copied

C>
```

A command language is appropriate in very few cases. Typical examples of such an interface are operating systems such as UNIX and MS-DOS (see Figure 10–12). The problem is that a command language does not help the user recall how to perform a task. Consequently, command languages have been universally decried as "unfriendly" and hard to learn. There are exceptions: some command interfaces are well-designed and reasonably easy to learn. Many word processing programs and programming editors use this technique, and those operators who use the interface frequently like it.

A simplified form of command language is appropriate for data entry when the sequence of data is unpredictable, for example, in airline reservation systems. The operator enters data in the sequence in which the customer specifies his or her request. Each piece of data is entered either with a

Figure 10–13 **Sample Free-Form Dialog**

This is an example of a dialog on an airline reservation system. The operator enters cryptic input on an unformatted screen. The second screen shows the system response, which is in fixed form output but without captions or explanations. The third screen shows the operator's final action, actually reserving two seats in coach class on the 8:04 flight.

Need 2 seats in coach for flight number 3

prefix indicating what it means, such as *d* for departure time or *a* for arrival time, or in some unambiguous format, such as the standard three-letter abbreviation for the airport (see Figure 10–13).

Direct manipulation interfaces, also called graphical user interfaces or GUI, were created in reaction to the poor image of command-language interfaces. They tend to use technology that may not be available on older equipment—graphics, pointing devices (mouse, light-pen, tracking ball, graphic tablets), color, and local intelligence. In fact, the very logic of these interfaces usually requires that every user action—moving the cursor, clicking the mouse, entering a single keystroke—result in a change to the display. On fixed-function terminals that are driven by central, shared computers, this requirement is not economically feasible. These interfaces are described in more detail in Chapter 12.

Choosing the Technology, Dialog, and Help Styles

As mentioned previously, the type of terminal available to the user has an influence on dialog and help styles. The technology of terminals and workstations interacts with dialog styles and their associated help modes.

Types of Workstations. Three main types of workstations are available: unbuffered (character-mode) terminals, buffered (block-mode) terminals, and intelligent workstations.

Unbuffered terminals send each character entered via the keyboard directly to the processor to which it is attached. The processor sends the character back, in so-called echoplex mode, to be displayed on the screen. Thus, interfaces can be designed that are rich in function because they can respond to each elementary action performed at the keyboard. However, the price to be paid in number of instructions executed by the central computer to which the terminal is attached may be prohibitive.

Buffered terminals have a storage element, called a buffer, that contains as many characters as can be displayed on a screen. When the user presses a key on the keyboard, the character is sent to the buffer and is displayed on the screen at the location of the cursor (usually a blinking rectangle, the size of one character). To send the data to the processor, the operator has to press a particular key, usually labeled *Enter* or *Transmit*. The program in the central processor can then process all the data that was in the buffer. The data on the screen will stay there until the program sends its response, which will overwrite the buffer and change the contents of the screen.

Intelligent workstations such as PCs have not only a buffer but also a programmable processor in the workstation itself. Therefore, each character can be processed as it is keyed in (like unbuffered terminals). The workstation then sends a message, possibly already partly processed, to the central computer, where the rest of the processing (such as data base update) will take place.

One advantage of an intelligent workstation is that the user interface can be enriched (by processing character by character, by adding graphics, by providing much more user help) without overloading the central processor. Another advantage is that when the workstation is not being used to access a central application, it can be used for personal computing purposes—word processing, spreadsheets, maintaining personal data bases—or for gaining access to external data bases.

Styles of Dialog and On-Line Help. Different styles of dialog are suited to different types of terminals. The main difference in style is that the buffered terminal encourages so-called full-screen processing, whereas the unbuffered terminal is best for processing a line at a time. This makes the unbuffered terminal suitable for prompted (question-and-answer) and command-oriented dialogs. The buffered terminal is best suited to menu choices and form filling.

Fixed-function terminals, which include both buffered and unbuffered terminals, do not support on-line help very well. The text that is to help the user must be transmitted by the central computer to the terminal every time it is requested. This process is costly if the terminals are in a remote location, because it increases the load on the central computer and also on the communications network.

Intelligent workstations, on the other hand, can support on-line help of several kinds. In the most primitive kind, the user can invoke a **fixed help text** by pressing a function key. This text can fill more than one screen: all the help program needs to do is to provide *Next* and *Previous* function keys for the user to navigate within the help text. It can also provide a more elaborate menu system of its own, allowing the user to choose on a menu the subject where help is needed. When the help screen is no longer needed, the user can press an *Escape* key, returning to the place in the application where he or she left off.

A more elaborate form of on-line help is **context-sensitive help.** The program running in the intelligent workstation is capable of knowing where the user is and what he or she is trying to achieve at all times by sensing which field the cursor is in, what has already been filled in, and the like. It is therefore possible to display a more specific help screen, directed at what the user's problem is likely to be. For instance, if help is invoked while the cursor is in a field where a dollar amount is expected, the help facility could display: "Type in the dollar amount without leading zeroes. The decimal point is not required for whole dollar amounts."

Context-sensitive help can be augmented by artificial intelligence techniques that use a knowledge base to infer what the user is attempting to do, explain to the user what the consequences of previous actions were, and deduce the explanation most likely to satisfy the user on what to do next.

The most sophisticated form of help is **data-dependent help.** This kind of help enables the user to position the cursor in a field, press the *Help* key, and obtain a display of the possible data values in the field, for example, a list of legal two-letter airline codes (AA for American Airlines, UA for United, and so on). It is even better to provide a list of data values that are possible as a function of previously entered data. For instance, given a departure and an arrival airport, the help facility could display a list of those airlines and flight numbers that serve those airports. Or given the partial spelling of a customer name, the help facility could display the list of all those customers who match the partial spelling.

When this technique is adopted, the user should be able to point to the value that is to be entered and, with a function key, "escape" from the help facility back to the original screen, where the field for which help was invoked would be filled in with the selected value. With this technique, sometimes called the *sticky cursor*, the value on the help screen appears to stick to the cursor as one screen disappears and another one appears.

Even if data-dependent help cannot be implemented for every field, many transaction processing systems on buffered terminals can suspend a transaction, perform a query, and return to the original transaction. This technique, known as *suspend-and-resume*, should ideally be used with the sticky-cursor technique.

Box
10–5

User Dialog and Natural Language

All the dialog techniques described in this chapter require that their users undergo training or, at least, be given very specific directions. It has long been a goal of artificial intelligence research to reduce or eliminate this requirement by allowing users to communicate with computer systems in everyday English (or any other natural language, for that matter). The theory behind this research is that even top executives would use computers directly if they could communicate in their own language. The use of English would also reduce or obviate the need for programmers.

A number of reasonably successful products on the market use natural language technology. The two best known are Intellect from Artificial Intelligence Corporation and Clout from Microrim. Both are essentially capable of understanding loosely formulated queries against a data base, which must have been described to them previously. Intellect runs on large mainframes; Clout on personal computers.

A typical query to such a system might read:

"Print the names of all salespeople in New York who have sold more than $100,000 of widgets."

If appropriately instructed, the program might respond with:

"Do you mean New York City or New York State?"

A subsequent query might imply that the interest is still in salespeople in New York by asking:

"More than $50,000?"

Subsequent queries might be:

"How about Massachusetts?" "How about gismos?" "Print their addresses as well."

So far, only data base queries can be processed in this way. Other functions, such as decision support, office automation, or transaction processing, have not been addressed by natural language interfaces. The reason for concentrating on data base queries is that it is fairly easy to anticipate the sorts of questions that can be asked. Even so, these systems often fail to respond when users use unfamiliar terms, or they respond unexpectedly because the query was formulated imprecisely or erroneously. (For instance, if the query has to do with personnel who are outside the category "married, with children," the query should not be "not married and no children" but "not married or no children.")

Establishing a dictionary of terms for one of these systems can be a lengthy process. Extensive experimentation is usually required to ensure that the most common errors get caught. User training (to sign on to the system, to use the hardware, and to formulate queries correctly) is still required. Even so, the lexicon of the system is likely to be insufficient. It will lack the commonsense knowledge that is taken for granted in humans. An old chestnut is the story of the computer that was set to interpret results of physical examinations and rejected a draftee on the grounds that he was pregnant.

As for interfaces to other types of applications, it is probable that they will not be available for many years, if ever. The main problem seems to be that natural language is specifically adapted to communicating with humans, on human terms, about human problems. Human language is much more oriented towards negotiating an agreement between two individuals, one of whom, as a result of the exchange, commits to some course of action. (The negotiation may be pretty one-sided, as when a superior gives a direct order to a subordinate, but the subordinate will still make an explicit commitment, such as "Yes, sir!") Further conversations

Continued

Continued

can then take place to follow up on the commitment, if the result is not delivered or is late.

The nature of a dialog with a computer is totally different. The computer is already committed to perform a certain range of services and needs no negotiation, explicit or implicit, to actually do so. It may be that the request is not within the possibility of the program; no matter how hard the user tries to persuade the computer to do what he or she wants, the result will still be an error message. The further away from the prearranged possibilities of the computer the request is, the more cryptic the message.

According to this view, it is futile to attempt to use natural language to address the computer, not because the computer cannot "understand" it, but because natural language is not a good vehicle for communicating what the user wishes the computer to do. If a human being were asked to deliver the same type of information, natural language would be used to make sure that the person understood and accepted the task. A very restricted and formalized subset of natural language would be used to specify the information content of the request. (A branch of logic called first-order predicate logic deals with this type of language.)

Even if all the knowledge of the world could be infused into a computer, natural language is not a good vehicle for communicating that knowledge.

On intelligent terminals, a system could conceivably be built where it would not even be necessary to invoke the help screen. As soon as the number of possible choices is reduced to a certain number, the choices could all be displayed in a window to one side. If there is only one possible value, the operator could stop keying and let the program fill in the rest.

Again, for data-dependent help, artificial intelligence techniques can be useful.

Simple and context-sensitive help facilities are relatively straightforward to implement on intelligent workstations. Data-sensitive help is more difficult, both because the design is more difficult and because the data needed must be available instantaneously. The data must be stored either in the workstation or on a data server on a local area network to which the workstation is attached.

Coexistence of Multiple Terminal Types. It is not always possible to dictate that a given application will use a given type of terminal. Intelligent workstations, which are the most flexible, are also the most costly and, thus, may not be economically justified. The users may already be equipped with terminals, and it may not be possible, or desirable, to force the users to have multiple terminals of different types on their desks.

Some systems may therefore need to specify different classes of terminals for different users. Users may be at different locations or belong to different departments, and each location or department may have different types of terminals already installed. Sometimes, because the users are customers, the company cannot dictate which terminals they should equip themselves with.

This problem can be solved in two different ways: the application can be written for a fixed-function terminal, and the intelligent terminal only emulates, or imitates, a fixed-function terminal; or two different interfaces, one for fixed-function and the other for intelligent terminals, may be created. The first solution reduces the functionality available to intelligent workstation users. The second adds to the cost of the application.

ELEMENTS OF GOOD DIALOG DESIGN

The elements of good dialog design are clarity, consistency, performance, and respect for the user. The following practical guidelines were developed from experience with on-line business systems over the past two decades.

Clarity

The user should be given complete guidance on what the next permitted actions are by displaying menu bars (if the choices are not numerous) or pop-up/pull-down menus (if a menu bar is not sufficient or if space on the screen is scarce) or by invoking context- or data-dependent help.

The current state of the user process should always be displayed on the screen (this is known as WYSIWYG—What You See Is What You Get). If a user action has resulted in a data value being changed on the data base, the new value should immediately be displayed.

The effect of learning should be taken into account. Novice users appreciate a great deal of guidance, but after a certain time, would like to be able to shortcut some frequently used sequences of operations. For example, a cascade of menus can be intermixed with a command language that enables the user to go directly to some activity whose name is known. Or a dialog can be designed with shorthand keystrokes, where some function keys are reserved for the user to define as standing for a longer sequence.

Consistency

The same commands or function keys should have the same effect even under dissimilar circumstances. So-called modes, where a sequence of keystrokes can be interpreted either as a piece of data or as a series of one-letter commands depending on the context, should be avoided. This problem is easy to avoid with today's workstations with many function keys and pointing devices. Committing the transaction (end of conversation) should be an identifiable step, different from simply changing screens within the conversation.

The cursor movement should be uniform. If all the fields on the screen are a fixed length and must be filled in entirely, the cursor can skip automatically to the next field when a field is completely filled in. When the length of the information in a field is variable, as with a name, an address, or an amount, automatic cursor skip is not possible. The operator must indicate that the end of the data in the field has been reached and that he or she is ready for the next field. For example, the operator presses a function key, the *Tab* key, or the *Enter* key, depending on conventions. Mixing the two modes— auto-skip and tabbing—on the same screen should be avoided, where possible. (There is not always a choice, particularly with buffered terminals.)

Performance

The response time, defined as the time elapsed between the operator taking an action and the terminal showing that the action has been recorded, is critical in two main categories of actions. The first is the need for the terminal to display instantaneously every data character that the operator types in. This need can be a problem for unbuffered terminals. On these terminals, there is no direct connection between the keyboard and the screen. A character typed on the keyboard travels over the communication line to the computer to which the terminal is attached. The computer then echoes it back to the screen. If the computer is heavily loaded, there may be a perceptible interval between keying and displaying on the screen. The effect is to slow down the operator. It also tends to cause irritability and impatience. On buffered (block-mode) and intelligent terminals this problem does not arise.

The more traditional notion of response time is the time between the user signaling the program to begin a processing activity and the appearance on the screen of the first character of the program's response. (In some cases, it is the last character of the program's response that counts, rather than the first one, for example, if the transmission is lengthy—more than 10 or so characters—and slow—under 30 characters per second. Then, the user can read the response faster than it appears on the screen and therefore has the impression of waiting for the system. If the response is short or it is displayed at a high rate, the user does not feel slowed down by the system.)

On a block-mode (buffered) terminal, the operator usually fills in the entire screen before pressing the *Enter* or *Transmit* key. This method, typical of form-filling applications, can require a large amount of data to be processed before the program can display the result, thus causing a potential response time problem. This problem has two solutions. The first is to cut up the activity into smaller subactivities, getting partial results back. If it were to take 10 seconds to process a ten-line order in one single operation and 1.5 seconds to process each line, the operator would probably be more productive with the second solution, even though 5 seconds appear to have been wasted. Another solution is to display some indication that the screen has been received and to continue displaying signs of progress every few seconds. This solution helps the operator by showing that the reason for the delay is not a malfunction.

Response time requirements are relative. It is important that the response time be about the same for similar activities. It is also important that response times for what the user perceives as easy tasks be shorter than for difficult tasks. For instance, a user would expect that the response to a query to display the inventory status of a given item, identified by a code, would be substantially less than the creation of a table of amortizations for a 30-year mortgage loan.

It is also important that response times remain relatively constant over time. In one case, where the implementation of the system was gradual, a few users being added at a time, the response times in the build-up phase would have been on the order of one-half second, whereas the fully loaded system was expected to have response times of nearly two seconds. It was necessary to introduce a routine to slow down the system during the initial phases to avoid high expectations followed by disappointments.

Respect for the User

Respect for the user requires adopting a neutral tone in messages and directions. Computer anthropomorphism—the attribution of human qualities to a computer or a program—should be avoided at all costs. Messages, in particular error messages, should avoid loaded terms, such as "You committed an error." Experience has shown that novice users can panic when they see a message such as "Fatal error—transaction aborted." Although it is difficult, an error message should incorporate information that is useful to the user, showing the cause of the error rather than the effect and describing how to overcome the problem. For instance, "Order buffer overflow" is a poor error message. It should be replaced with something such as: "You can only enter 15 detail lines per order. If you have an order with more than 15 lines, please split it in two."

DOCUMENTING THE CONVERSATION FLOW

The best way to document a conversation flow is to prototype it. Prototyping entails designing each of the screens that can be used in the conversation and then adding indications on how to make the conversation progress from screen to screen. In most cases, a set of test data must also be specified so that the user can actually work the prototype with data that approximates real situations. This technique is described at the end of Section IV.

The main objective of such a prototype is to serve as a vehicle for showing users what a system will do. For subsequent phases of the analysis, additional documentation, in paper or electronic form, is required, in particular in the program design activity (see Chapter 16).

Most cases of transaction processing are based on a mix of menu selection and forms processing. From a menu, a user selects a form or set of forms; after processing the forms, the user returns to the menu to select the next form. In such a case, the conversation flow can be depicted as it would flow in normal sequence, if no errors are discovered and no on-line help is needed (see Figure 10–14). Exceptions to the linear flow can be noted on the side. Experience has proved that users understand a linear flow with exceptions much better than a flowchart with decision boxes and loops.

Another tool that can prove useful is the state transition network, which is used when it becomes difficult to keep track of the actions that

Figure 10–14 **Sample Conversation Flow Document**

The left part of the document shows the normal flow of a conversation to enter time cards for employees for payroll processing. The *Alternate Screen* column shows what other screens than the one immediately below the operator can choose, and the *Function Key* column shows the name of the function key to be pressed. (The assignment of these names to actual function keys such as PF1 through PF12 will take place later.) For each screen, the first function key listed (the one that does not have an alternate screen assigned to it) is the one that will cause the normal flow—the next screen in sequence.

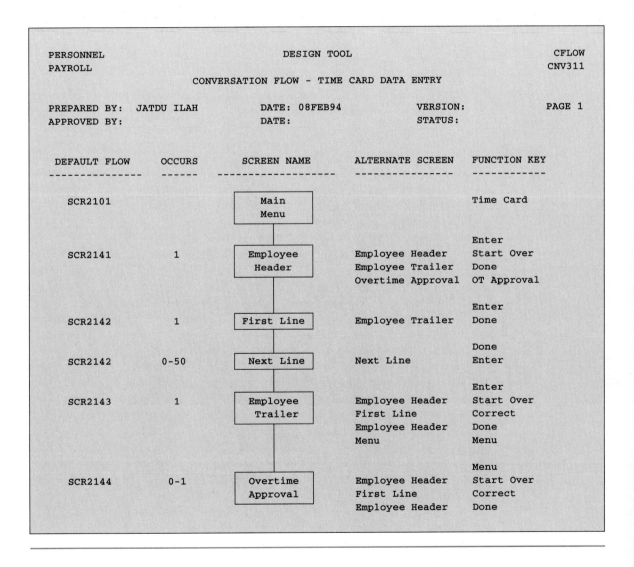

```
PERSONNEL                         DESIGN TOOL                              CFLOW
PAYROLL                                                                    CNV311
                    CONVERSATION FLOW - TIME CARD DATA ENTRY

PREPARED BY:  JATDU ILAH          DATE: 08FEB94              VERSION:        PAGE 1
APPROVED BY:                      DATE:                      STATUS:


   DEFAULT FLOW        OCCURS         SCREEN NAME       ALTERNATE SCREEN    FUNCTION KEY
   ------------        ------      -----------------    ----------------    -----------

     SCR2101                            Main                                Time Card
                                        Menu

                                                                           Enter
     SCR2141             1            Employee          Employee Header     Start Over
                                       Header           Employee Trailer    Done
                                                        Overtime Approval   OT Approval

                                                                           Enter
     SCR2142             1           First Line         Employee Trailer    Done

                                                                           Done
     SCR2142            0-50          Next Line         Next Line           Enter

                                                                           Enter
     SCR2143             1            Employee          Employee Header     Start Over
                                       Trailer          First Line          Correct
                                                        Employee Header     Done
                                                        Menu                Menu

                                                                           Menu
     SCR2144            0-1           Overtime          Employee Header     Start Over
                                      Approval          First Line          Correct
                                                        Employee Header     Done
```

are possible depending on where the user is in the dialog. The more oper-ator-directed a dialog is, the better chance there is of the state transition diagram being appropriate. Figure 10–15 shows a state transition diagram for a bank teller clerk who has several ways of identifying the account number or numbers of the customer who is being served. This diagram looks somewhat like a data flow diagram, but the flow is between states, not activities, and the lines of flow do not represent data, but control infor-mation. More details on how to prepare transition networks appear in Appendix 2.

A cascade of menus, where a choice in a top-level menu causes a lower-level menu to be displayed, is best represented by a hierarchy such as the one depicted in Figure 10–16.

Summary

In the design of the overall flow of a user interface, event-driven processing is generally best implemented on-line. Typical examples are transaction pro-cessing and ad hoc data base query. The main advantages of on-line pro-cessing are that it reduces error rates and may add value to the processing of transactions by making more information available to customers, suppliers, and employees.

Batch processing, on the other hand, is the best alternative for periodic processing such as management reporting and the preparation of activity files for decision support systems.

Forms and report flows should be as short and simple as possible to reduce the risk of manipulation errors. Because on-line work is more and more prevalent, the main emphasis of the chapter is on the design of conversations.

Conversation design consists in identifying logical units of work—busi-ness transactions or more extensive cases. Business transaction dialogs are usually program-driven. The conversations rely on menu selection and form filling. If the operator is not dedicated, on-line help is usually a major requirement. Buffered terminals or intelligent workstations are appropriate for this type of processing.

Casework, office automation, decision support, and other systems orient-ed towards professionals rather than clerks are usually operator-driven. Prompting, command languages, or more modern interfaces such as direct manipulation are usually appropriate. Context-sensitive help (and data-dependent help where possible) is usually required. Intelligent terminals are best for this type of work, with unbuffered terminals a possibility if the data traffic allows it without degrading response times.

Criteria for good on-line dialog design are clarity, consistency, perfor-mance, and respect for the user.

Figure 10–15 **Sample State Transition Diagram**

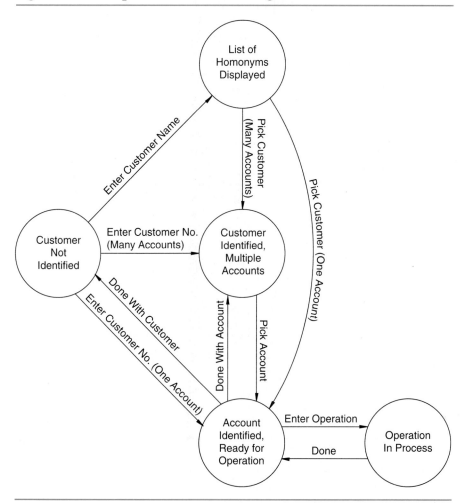

Selected Readings

IBM Corporation. *Systems Application Architecture: Common User Access Panel Design and User Interaction,* 1st ed. IBM Publication No. SC26–4351, 1987.

This document contains a detailed description of the standard that IBM recommends for screen and interaction design for developers of programs that are to run on IBM systems—whether mainframes, minis, or micros. The most striking characteristic of this book is that it illustrates how rich the intelligent terminal (or PC) environment is and how many choices are made explicitly or implicitly when designing even a very simple user

Figure 10–16 **Sample Hierarchical Chart Representing a Menu Structure**

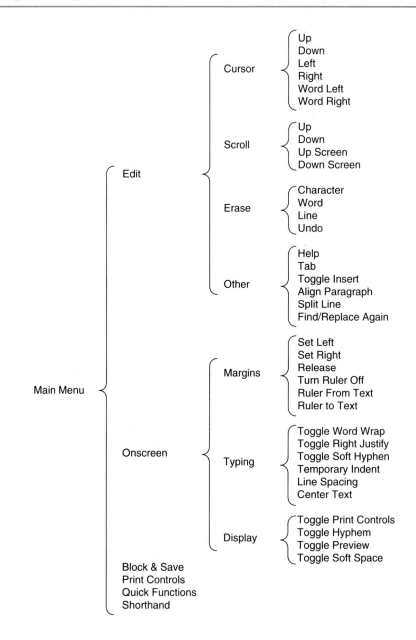

Figure 10–17 **Characteristics of Dialog Types**

Dialog Type	Data			Operator			Objective	Technical Requirements	Preferred Technology
	Source	Volume	Sequence	Decision Maker	Casual/ Dedicated	Training Required			
Menu	Operator	Low	Predictable	Yes	Casual	Low	Easy to learn	Fast response	Buffered Intelligent
Prompted	Operator	Low	Predictable	Yes	Casual	Low to Medium	Easy to learn/use Questions depend on context	Fast response	Unbuffered Intelligent
Form Filing	Customer Paper	Low to High	Predictable	Partly or No	Casual or Dedicated	Medium to High	Complete validation Assist business function	Fast response Good screen layout	Buffered Intelligent
Command Language	Customer	High	Random	Partly	Dedicated	Very High	Flexibility	High throughout	Intelligent Buffered
Direct Manipulation	Operator	Medium	Random	Yes	Casual	Medium	Flexibility Easy to learn/use	Good layout Graphics	Intelligent

interface. The problem with this manual is that it does not provide a high-level overview. This lack is partly made up for by the inclusion of demonstration diskettes.

Apple Computers, Inc. *Human Interface Guidelines: The Apple Desktop Interface.* Reading, Massachusetts: Addison-Wesley, 1987.
This document contains the same type of description as the IBM document above, but the description applies to Apple's Macintosh computers. The text is more concise and easier to read than the IBM document. It is, of course, mostly relevant to Apple users.

Winograd, T., and Flores, F., eds. *Understanding Computers and Cognition.* Reading, Massachusetts: Addison-Wesley, 1987.
This book describes Terry Winograd's theory of design as well as some of the reasons that natural language is not the best medium for human-computer interaction. This book is difficult but very rewarding.

Review Questions

1. What are the main criteria for deciding whether an activity should be performed on-line or in batch mode?

2. What are the advantages of operating on-line when doing transaction processing?

3. Why are management reports generally prepared in batch mode?

4. Describe the differences between transaction processing and casework.

5. What are the four criteria for good conversation design? Describe the most commonly used ways of meeting these criteria.

6. Describe the differences among buffered, unbuffered, and intelligent workstations.

Discussion Questions

1. Relatively few executives have terminals in their offices. For those who do, discuss user interface and dialog design requirements.

2. Discuss the differences in dialog design for untrained (naive), fairly frequent, and full-time users. Suggest how systems can be designed to fulfill the needs of all three categories simultaneously.

3. Review examples of businesses and local government organizations and identify examples of casework versus transaction processing. Discuss the differences. Are there gray areas that could be classified in either category?

4. Review systems or programs with which you are familiar (MS-DOS, spreadsheet, word processing package, automated bank teller, tourist information panels). Classify the type of dialog. Review the help facility. Critique. Conclude what sort of users these applications were designed for. Were the designers successful?

Mini-Cases

Sal's Pizza. Sal's pizza shop is so successful that it has decided to process its orders on-line. The requirements include telephone orders for take-out and delivery, as well as sit-down table service.

There are three sizes of pizza. Optional toppings are:

- Extra cheese
- Pepperoni
- Sausage
- Black olives
- Green peppers

Side orders are:

- Garlic bread
- Fried cheese

There are two sizes of the following beverages:

- Cola drink
- Diet cola
- Uncola drink

- Diet uncola
- Coffee

If the order is to be delivered, it must show the name, address, phone number, delivery time, and directions (e.g., Deliver to side door).

Question for Discussion

1. Design an interactive order entry dialog that will accommodate all the above requirements and handle multiple sizes, topping options, side orders, and beverages.

Offshore Data Entry Inc. Jim Mendenhall was sure he had an idea that would make him a ton of money and help people in less-developed countries at the same time. He had formed a company to perform data entry operations in the Caribbean for U.S. corporations. Wage rates there were around $30 per day, while comparable rates in the United States were around $80 per day, including fringe benefits. The wage rate differential was more than enough to permit U.S. corporations to send source documents to the Caribbean via air express, have the data from them keyed into terminals, and then have the data transmitted back to the United States via satellite-based communications. Local workers were diligent, trained in English, and eager to have the employment. U.S. corporations were looking for innovative ways to cut their costs in an increasingly competitive global economy. Jim expected to make a lot of money. Clearly, he thought, it was a situation where everybody wins.

On a marketing call to Atlantic Electric Company, he was surprised by the negative reaction he received from Dawn Fraser, a top MIS executive at the company. Dawn told Jim that her company had to be ever conscious of the image it was presenting to the public. It could not afford unfavorable publicity. Dawn said that although Jim's idea might make eminent economic sense, he would never get any business from Atlantic Electric. Her reasoning was that she did not think it was right to let technology take jobs away from American workers and give them to workers in other countries who might be willing to work for lower wages. She said she could just imagine the reaction from editorial-page writers, not to mention Atlantic's unions, if Atlantic Electric were to do business with Jim's company.

Jim came away from his meeting full of concern for the future of Offshore Data Entry Inc. He had invested a lot of his own money in the company with no returns thus far. He hoped he would be able to counter the objections of Dawn and others like her. If not, he would be out of business before he started.

Question for Discussion

1. Is there a way to reconcile the opposing views expressed in the case?

Notes

1. Winograd, T., and Flores, F., eds. *Understanding Computers and Cognition.* Reading, Massachusetts: Addison-Wesley, 1987.

2. Martin, James. *Design of Man-Computer Dialogues.* Englewood Cliffs, New Jersey: Prentice-Hall, 1973.

3. Shneiderman, Ben. *Designing the User Interface.* Reading, Massachusetts: Addison-Wesley, 1987.

CHAPTER 11

Designing Forms, Screens, and Reports

This chapter presents the general design factors that apply to forms, screens, and reports alike. The chapter then describes specifically the design criteria for input forms and reports—first, the overall format and then, the arrangement of component parts. The final section describes screen design and offers practical guidelines on specifics such as operator guidance, ergonomics, and paging and scrolling.

Learning Objectives

- Understand the criteria for good form, screen, and report design.
- Critique examples of form, screen, and report designs according to these criteria.
- Apply the criteria to design forms, screens, and reports, given a set of specifications.
- Relate the activities of form, screen, and report design to the other activities in the life cycle.

SIGNIFICANCE OF FORM, SCREEN, AND REPORT DESIGN

Input forms, output reports, and input or output screens carry practically all the information between users and the computer system. Forms and reports are also the most important vehicles for transmitting information to and from the outside world—customers, suppliers, regulatory agencies, and the general public. More and more frequently, screens are used in communicating with the outside: automatic teller machines, reservation terminals placed by airlines in travel agencies, on-line data bases.

Good form, report, and screen design practices are crucial in determining how the system is perceived by its users, and ultimately, how successful the system will be. The designer should strive for forms that are easy to fill in and reports in which users can easily locate the data they are interested in.

Ease of use of forms, reports, and screen layouts depends greatly on consistency in both layout and content (such as consistent captions). The designer does not work in a vacuum; the documents must be consistent with those that the users may receive from other systems. If the organization does not have formal standards for screen and report design, there is still likely to be an informal standard, a certain consistency in style from system to system, to which the designer should conform.

Decreasing Emphasis on Reports and Forms

With on-line data entry and query and with the use of electronic files to communicate activity data from transaction systems to decision support or management information systems, the emphasis is moving away from report design by the systems analyst. Often, the recipient of data will get the information in electronic form and use a report generator or a spreadsheet package to manipulate the information and present it in the best format.

This technique solves a dilemma that once made report design difficult: should reports be designed for a function or for an individual? In early systems, it was assumed that the analyst could determine objectively the data required for a given purpose—say, analyzing the trends in employee turnover and the reasons for it. In addition, this data would be independent of the personal tastes of whomever happened to be the manager in charge of performing the analysis.

Experience has shown, however, that different people have different styles and therefore need information presented differently. Some prefer graphic presentations, others a synthetic one-page summary, yet others a mass of details. When determining a user's information requirements, an analyst is influenced by the style of the individual who states the requirement. Consequently, many reports end up being designed for specific individuals rather than for an abstract, idealized function. Reports designed in this way work well until the person accomplishing the function is replaced by someone with a different style.

Many reports are designed to solve a specific problem and do not need to continue to be produced once the problem is solved. For example, a report that contains data analyzing the turnover of personnel has probably been requested because management has a problem with turnover. If the system meets its objective, then the report on turnover will become useless (or at least much less useful) as the turnover rate declines. The initial report will probably be replaced by a report on some other problem area masked by the previous problem (for instance, data helping management to analyze recruiting practices) or perhaps even caused by its resolution (for instance, data to analyze retraining requirements for experienced employees whose jobs change over time). Many of these problems can be solved by letting the users create their own reports from suitably prepared summary files.

The form and report design activities that continue to be required are for communication with the outside (order forms and invoices, for example) and for systems control purposes (error and exception reports, audit trails, control reports reconciling total inputs and outputs).

Increasing Emphasis on Screen Design

Conversely, screen design is taking on greater and greater importance. The most noteworthy consequence of this trend is that it greatly reduces the amount of information that can be presented simultaneously to a user— about 2,000 characters, including blanks (24 or 25 lines of 80 characters each). The designer may have to exercise considerable ingenuity to enable the user to leaf back and forth between multiple screens.

Another problem is that the contents of a screen are volatile and offer no audit trail. If erroneous information was presented on a screen, and later corrected, there may be no trace of what the erroneous information was or who used it to make what wrong decision.

On the plus side, more and more terminals have color and graphics capability, thus increasing the variety of information presentation techniques. To some, a picture is worth a thousand words, and a well-designed color graph can summarize large quantities of information. Most uses of graphics in business systems today are in the realm of decision support systems. In general, users design the graphics output that they want to produce them- selves, and IS analysts are seldom involved. The main considerations on the use of computer graphics are covered in Appendix 3.

Graphs are not always suitable, however. They are more difficult to print and duplicate (especially if they are in color). They can also introduce bias. Disraeli, the nineteenth-century British prime minister, once said: "There are three kinds of lies: Lies, damned lies, and statistics." (The quote has also been attributed to at least three other, less illustrious individuals.) We can perhaps add graphics as a fourth kind: "reports inform, graphics convince."

THE CHOICE OF THE MEDIUM

This section will cover the four main categories of input/output media: reports, screens, forms, and special-purpose media. Each is appropriate in different situations. There are no hard-and-fast rules, however. The range of choices is increasing with the availability of new technological alternatives. The analyst should use creativity in meeting information needs and imple- menting information flows effectively.

Printed reports are the usual choice for output when one of three condi- tions occurs:

- The output is to be sent to an outside organization: customer, supplier, or regulatory agency, for example.
- The output is too voluminous to be browsed on-line.
- The objective of the report is to have an audit trail or to exercise some systematic control over the application.

Screen-based output (with a hard-copy function where required) is appropriate in the following situations:

- Queries about a single entity in the data base.
- Low-volume output.
- Intermediate steps in a long interactive process (as in decision support systems).

The following situations indicate the use of preprinted forms for input:

- Input transactions from personnel or third parties who do not have access to workstations.
- Legally important documents.
- Turnaround documents.

Management information systems, decision support systems, departmental systems, and the like rarely if ever rely on preprinted forms, because their input usually comes in electronic form from other systems.

The following situations are examples of the use of special-purpose equipment:

- Bar codes can be used to track the whereabouts of physical goods (packages) or documents (files of people having applied for retirement benefits). Bar codes are also used for supermarket checkout and inventory control (universal product code).
- Magnetic ink character recognition (MICR) is used by banks for check processing.
- Optical character recognition (OCR) is used with turnaround documents (e.g., invoice stub returned with payment); order entry (handwritten figures on special forms); text storage and retrieval (a use emerging with the availability of OCR equipment capable of interpreting practically any printed or typed font).
- Mark sensing (electrically or optically) can be used to analyze responses to questionnaires and grade tests using multiple-choice questions.
- Voice output is appropriate for telephone queries (bank balances or directory assistance, where a human operator processes the call but stops short of communicating the result, which is spelled out as a series of numbers by a voice response unit).
- Voice input is used in industrial environments where users cannot conveniently reach a keyboard and where the vocabulary that the computer system must recognize is small. Baggage handling in airports is the best-known example. As bags pass operators on a conveyor belt, the operators call out the destination of each bag. A sorting system then ensures that each bag is conveyed to the plane with that destination.
- Microfilm is used for archiving large amounts of information.

Figure 11–1 **Sample Input/Output Design Standards**

Factor	Example
Size	Make all forms 8 1/2 by 11 or smaller.
Color	Send the green copy to accounting.
Data Positioning	Position important data on the left side of document or screen.
Media	Avoid preprinted computer forms; use stock only.
Codes	Tables of valid codes must always be printed on form or displayed on screen.
Dates	Use DD/MM/YY format.
Logo	Use standard logo on all external documents.
Heading	Include company name, page number, date, and report name in fixed positions.
Binding	Use three-hole paper.
End	Mark the last page of a report so that the user can check that the report is complete.
Distribution	Position distribution instructions at the bottom of the document.
Instructions	List the meaning of function keys at the bottom of the screen.
Identification	Give each form or report a company-wide identification number.

GENERAL PRINCIPLES OF FORM, REPORT, AND SCREEN DESIGN

The designer of forms, reports, and screens should observe the general principles of ease of use, one clearly identified purpose, and maximum benefits at minimum costs.

Ease of Use

As with the design of dialogs described in Chapter 10, the main consideration in the design of forms, reports, and screens is ease of use. Ease of use has different meanings for different types of media, however. For forms and input screens (which usually mimic forms), the term means easy to prepare; for reports and output screens (which closely mimic reports), it means easy to read and understand.

In all cases, consistency is a requirement—consistency within a system and consistency with other systems, even systems outside the organization. A document to be completed by a member of the general public should use familiar words and avoid industry or organization-wide jargon.

Figure 11–1 illustrates the areas that are the subject of standards in many organizations. In a company where all or some of these areas are left to habit or chance, the project team should investigate the habits and formalize a standard, at least for use by its own members. If the standards are well devised, they will probably spread to other project teams.

Fulfilling the Purpose

Obviously, any form, document, or screen should fulfill its purpose. What is less obvious is that each form, report, or screen should have only one purpose. This purpose should be clearly identified in the requirements specification document.

Single-purpose documents are easier to change when the organization and the objectives of their users change. A report could serve two users with different purposes for a while, but if one user changes the way the report is used, it may become incompatible with the needs of the other user.

Assume, for example, a report that serves both to inform the marketing department of customer activity, by listing the amounts of invoices for each customer, and to help the accounting department post payments to the correct invoice. If the company starts a new product line, marketing may well want two columns on the report, one for each product line. This makes the report useless to accounting, interested only in the invoice total so that a clerk can match it to the payment amount.

Combining a great deal of data on a single report to serve several users or many needs of a single user makes the report harder to design and fit within the carriage width and page length of the printer. Too much data also increases volume and causes maintenance problems. With today's ad hoc reporting techniques, it is probably more economical to produce a series of simple reports rather than a single complex report.

Benefits and Costs

Good design should consider the total benefits and the total costs of each document. The main benefit, against which costs are weighed, is the avoidance of errors—transcription, interpretation, or distribution.

The main costs involved are procurement costs (paper cost, cost of designing, printing, and possibly binding or padding); production costs (computer and printer time, cost of workstations, data communication costs); and handling costs (changing paper on a printer, bursting and collating multipart, multipage reports, distributing paper).

DESIGN OF INPUT FORMS

A form may be filled in by hand, on a typewriter, or by a computer printer, in which case it is a turnaround document. Turnaround documents are often completed by hand or by typewriter before they are reentered.

The data content of a form is dictated by the application requirements. Space should not be included on the form for data unavailable to the user when the form is filled in. If additional data is to be added to the form later by another person, that data must be clearly isolated and identified with a text such as "Reserved for office use."

The size of a form should be as standard as possible and should preferably not exceed 8 1/2 by 11 inches (or A4, i.e., 210 by 297 mm, in metric countries). Half-size forms are quite acceptable. Smaller forms should be used only in special circumstances (severe constraints on storage space, such as needing a pad of forms to be carried in a pocket, or industry habits and constraints, such as charge card slips).

The number of copies of a form should be limited, as each copy of a form adds to printing and handling costs. If the form is to be entered into a computer system, then the data can be made available on-line to other users instead of a paper copy. This technique may not always be applicable. For instance, a charge card slip needs to be created in triplicate, one for the customer, one for the merchant, and one for the credit card company. In most cases, however, the need for multiple copies of forms and reports should be questioned.

The layout of the form itself should follow the sequence of filling it in rather than the sequence of reading it. A form is customarily filled in left to right, top to bottom. (Just imagine how inconvenient any other sequence would be for someone using a typewriter.) If several different users fill in different parts of the form, these parts should be separated. It is also a good idea to isolate the data that will be entered into the computer system from additional detail (see Figure 11–2).

Related information is grouped together in a zone. Zones are kept separate from each other by physical location, by enclosing them in lines or boxes, or by highlighting with color or shading.

Detailed design techniques include the following:

- A descriptive title—short, but detailed enough to identify the form unambiguously.

- A preprinted sequence number, if it is necessary to account for all the forms, used or unused.

- Instructions, placed at the top of the form or the zone to which they apply. Very detailed instructions can be printed on the back of the form.

- Clear, brief captions and headings.

- Spacing. If space permits, the "3/5" formula enables a form to be filled in by hand or by typewriter equally conveniently. The "3/5" formula refers to 3 lines per inch in vertical spacing and 5 characters per inch horizontally.

- Alignment. On a form that is to be filled in by typewriter, columns should be aligned.

REPORT DESIGN

The following discussion applies to reports printed by computer either on a predetermined schedule or on demand. It does not apply to character-for-character hard copies of screens, such as those that can be requested by a terminal operator unbeknownst to the computer system to which the terminal is attached.

Figure 11–2 **Typical Form for Data Entry**

Note the disposition of the zones on the form: identification data on top, data entry zone to the left, human-readable zone to the right. Boxes are used to maximum advantage. Data entry fields use dogteeth and preprinted punctuation in amount fields.

The data content of the report should satisfy the data or information needs of its recipient. To reiterate, it is probably not a good idea to design combined reports that satisfy the needs of several functions for the same or different individuals. On the other hand, the report should be as complete and informative as possible.

The following purposes of reports are typical:

- To analyze trends.
- To identify exception items for action.
- To assist in management planning and control.
- To provide an audit trail.

Figure 11–3 **Example of Trend Analysis Report, Column Format**

| | PROJECTED SALES PER MONTH ($ 000) | | | | | | | | | | | |
	JAN	FEB	MAR	APR	MAY	JUN	JUL	AUG	SEP	OCT	NOV	DEC
SYSTEMS	27.0	29.0	30.0	32.0	33.0	35.0	37.0	38.0	40.0	41.0	42.0	43.0
SERVICES	3.0	4.0	5.0	6.0	8.0	10.0	12.0	14.0	16.0	18.0	20.0	20.0
COMPONENTS	0.0	2.0	2.0	4.0	6.0	8.0	10.0	12.0	14.0	17.0	20.0	24.0
	----	----	----	----	----	----	----	----	----	----	----	----
TOTAL	30.0	35.0	37.0	42.0	47.0	53.0	59.0	64.0	70.0	76.0	82.0	87.0

| | COST OF SALES PER MONTH ($ 000) | | | | | | | | | | | |
	JAN	FEB	MAR	APR	MAY	JUN	JUL	AUG	SEP	OCT	NOV	DEC
SYSTEMS	13.5	14.5	15.0	16.0	16.5	17.5	18.5	19.0	20.0	20.5	21.0	21.5
SERVICES	1.5	2.0	2.5	3.0	4.0	5.0	4.8	5.6	6.4	7.2	8.0	8.0
COMPONENTS	0.0	1.0	1.0	2.0	3.0	4.0	3.0	6.0	7.0	5.8	8.0	9.6
	----	----	----	----	----	----	----	----	----	----	----	----
TOTAL	15.0	17.5	18.5	21 0	23.5	26.5	26.3	30.6	33.4	33.5	37.0	39.1

| | OTHER EXPENSES PER MONTH ($ 000) | | | | | | | | | | | |
	JAN	FEB	MAR	APR	MAY	JUN	JUL	AUG	SEP	OCT	NOV	DEC
DEVELOPMENT	4.0	4.2	4.5	4.7	5.0	5.2	5.5	5.7	6.0	6.3	6.6	7.1
MARKETING	6.2	6.7	7.4	8.3	9.3	10.8	12.4	13.0	13.6	14.8	16.0	17.6
OVERHEAD	8.2	8.8	9.2	9.6	10.1	10.5	11.0	11.4	12.1	12.6	13.2	14.8
	----	----	----	----	----	----	----	----	----	----	----	----
TOTAL	18.4	19.7	21.1	22.6	24.4	26.5	28.9	30.1	31.7	33.7	35.8	39.5

- To provide detailed data for inquiries against permanent records.
- To provide totals for systems control.

Providing details for inquiry is normally best done on-line. In some cases, this method may not be possible, in particular where large amounts of historical data may be involved—for instance, all the detailed transactions in a bank over several years. A more appropriate method may be to print out the data for a given period and microfilm it for economical storage and retrieval. Even though the medium is no longer paper, the data still qualifies as a report.

Figures 11–3 through 11–7 provide examples of reports that exemplify some of the uses in the preceding list. Obviously, some of these reports are better designed than others, a consideration explored further along in the section.

In general, report designers should avoid preprinted forms for computer reports because of the cost of changing forms and aligning them properly on a computer printer. The exception to this rule is documents going outside the company, such as invoices and order forms. Multipart forms, whether preprinted or not, are also expensive to handle and should be avoided. Sin-

Figure 11–4 **Example of Trend Analysis Report, Bar Graph Format**

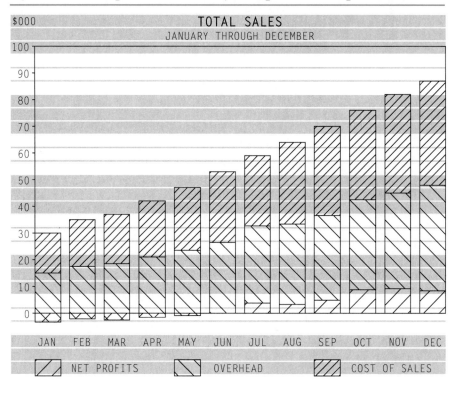

gle-part reports are often quite adequate for internal reporting, especially exception reports and reports to assist in management planning. However, preprinted forms such as invoices must often be multipart.

Recent evolutions in technology have brought to prominence the so-called laser printer, which uses electrostatic technology rather than the earlier impact technology. Because there is no impact, there is no possibility of printing multipart forms. On the other hand, because electrostatic printers are often capable of graphics, they can be used both to present graphic information and to print such elements as boxes or the company logo while the report is being printed.

Report designers should be familiar with the possibilities and the constraints of the available technology before designing a report in detail. The size of printed reports is limited to the width of the printer—132 positions per line, plus margins, for most mainframe-attached line printers. The length of a page is arbitrary, although it has to be a whole number of inches. The most frequently used page length is 11 inches, but 12 is also often seen.

Because of the trend towards preparing reports on a large computer and

Figure 11–5 **Example of Exception Reporting, Voucher Proof List**

```
                        JOURNAL VOUCHER PROOF LIST

                                07/31/93

BATCH JOURNAL    DATE    ACCT NO                          DEBIT       CREDIT    DIFFERENCE
NO    NO                 MAJ MIN                          AMOUNT      AMOUNT

01    06-408   07/31/93 111 401 COLLECTIONS ON ACCOUNT   $12,103.76
               07/31/93 521 000 DISCOUNTS ALLOWED        $225.03
               07/31/93 112 000 CREDITS TO A/R                       $12,328.79
                                                 JOURNAL NO. MISSING  01
      06-410   07/31/93 421 012 EXPENSE CLAIMS           $763.29
               07/31/93 111 104 EXPENSE CLAIMS                       $763.29

01    BATCH TOTALS                                       $13,092.08  $13,092.08

02    06-410   07/31/93 921 000 PAYROLL EXPENSE          $8,766.90
               07/31/93 212 110 ACCRUED PAYROLL                     $6,073.57
               07/31/93 212 120 INCOME TAX WITHHELD                 $1,109.43
               07/31/93 212 130 FICA TAX WITHHELD                   $480.40
               07/31/93 212 140 INSURANCE DED WITHHELD             $563.50
               07/31/93 212 150 BOND DED WITHHELD                  $300.00
               07/31/93 212 160 CREDIT UNION DED WITHHELD          $230.00

                         ENTRY DOES NOT BALANCE $8,766.90  $8,756.90    $10.00

               07/31/93 111 601 CASH COLLECTIONS                   $375.25
               07/31/93 411 100 CASH SALES               $375.25

02    *BATCH TOTALS           ERROR COUNT 01    $9,142.15  $9,132.15    $10.00

      **FINAL TOTALS          ERROR COUNT 01   $22,234.23 $22,224.23
```

then sending the data via communications lines to local, low-cost printers, reports are increasingly being designed for the reduced dimensions widely available on low-cost laser or dot-matrix printers, namely 8 1/2 by 11 (A4 in metric countries).

All efforts should be made to avoid routine printing of voluminous reports. The best alternative is to keep the data available on the computer and to let users, through the on-line system, query its contents or request ad hoc extracts. Another alternative is computer output to microfilm (COM), where a computer tape is fed directly into a device that produces microfilm or microfiche.

The frequency of a report depends on the frequency of the function that it helps accomplish. A weekly report to assist in the monthly closing of the

Figure 11–6 **Example of Management Reporting, Summary Responsibility Report**

| CURRENT MONTH | | | YEAR TO DATE | |
| UNDER/(OVER) | | | | UNDER/(OVER) |
BUDGET	AMOUNT	AREA NO. AND DESCRIPTION	AMOUNT	BUDGET
		AREA NO. 60		APRIL, 1994
		MANUFACTURING MANAGER		REPORTS TO NO. 40
(28)	5,064	61 MANUFACTURING MANAGER'S OFFICE	19,905	236
(2,798)	13,366	62 PUNCH PRESS DEPARTMENT	48,389	(4,414)
453	10,231	63 LATHE DEPARTMENT	43,704	(331)
(27)	7,619	64 DRILL PRESS DEPARTMENT	28,675	154
(1,295)	14,946	65 MILL & AUTOMATIC DEPARTMENT	57,015	(115)
(54)	4,164	66 PLATING DEPARTMENT	16,860	(55)
(54)	15,000	67 ASSEMBLY DEPARTMENT	63,516	(437)
198	14,178	68 TOOL & DIE DEPARTMENT	56,644	540
(24)	1,855	71 PLANT ENGINEERING	7,250	65
(2,414)	18,399	72 MAINTENANCE	65,498	(2,611)
323	38,525	73 OCCUPANCY	157,739	833
(5,720)	143,347		565,195	(6,135)

accounts is of little use. The frequency of a report is also tied to its data content. The recipient of a monthly report assumes that it contains data that is complete for the month in question. If there are delays in processing the month's transactions due to transmission times, workload on clerks, and so on, then the report must be delayed as well. An incomplete report is probably no better than no report at all, because it would destroy the consistency of one month's figures compared with another. The need to make sure that a report reflects all the activity of a given period, and nothing but that activity, is called cut-off; it is of great importance in accounting and in management information systems generally.

Most organizations have daily, weekly, monthly, and yearly cut-offs; some also have quarterly. One of the difficulties is that weekly and monthly cut-offs do not coincide, and various expedients have been adopted to counter this problem. A popular method is to align months on weeks, defining January and February as having 4 weeks, March having 5, April and May having 4, June having 5, and so on. Another method is to separate the two entirely and not try to reconcile them. In all cases, reports that detail the activity of a given period or the status on a certain date should state the period or date, preferably in the report heading.

Other elements that go in the report heading are the title of the report; the preparation date (the date that the report was actually created by the

Figure 11–7 **Example of Detailed (or Control) Report**

```
                                THOMAS MANUFACTURING-NORTH LOC                                   CO 003 LOC 001
                                                                                                      PAGE   13
                          CASH REQUIREMENTS REPORT FOR PAYMENT CUTOFF DATE 12/23/97

                                      DISCOUNTS LOST DATE 12/03/97
```

VENDOR NAME	VENDOR NUMBER	INVOICE NUMBER	TRAN TYPE	BK BATCH CD	DUE DATE ORIGINAL	REVISED	OVR RID	GROSS	AMOUNT DUE DISCOUNT	NET	ST CD
LEKTRO EAST SERV INC.	15943320	221730	INV	0107 25	12/12/97	12/13/97		420.50	.00	420.50	
		NET BALANCE FOR THIS INVOICE						420.50	.00	420.50	X
LEKTRO EAST SERV INC.	15943320	235822	INV	0107 25	12/23/97	12/23/97		276.00	12.00	264.00	
			D/C	0108 25	12/20/97	12/20/97		220.50CR	.00	220.50CR	
		NET BALANCE FOR THIS INVOICE						55.50	12.00	43.50	
LEKTRO EAST SERV INC.	15943320	472813	INV	0109 25	01/03/98	01/03/98		410.50	13.00	397.50	
			D/C	0108 25	12/29/97	12/29/97		2,175.00CR	51.25CR	2,123.75CR	
		NET BALANCE FOR THIS INVOICE						1,764.50CR	38.25CR	1,726.25CR	
		VENDOR TOTAL PAYABLE						420.50	.00	420.50	
		VENDOR TOTAL NOT PAYABLE						1,709.00CR	26.25CR	1,682.75CR	
		VENDOR TOTAL						1,288.50CR	26.25CR	1,262.25CR	ZZZ

```
* * * * * * * * * * * * * * * * * * * * * * * * * * * * * * * * *
*                                                               *
*   FINAL TOTAL PAYABLE              13,453.50    483.00   12,970.50   *
*   FINAL TOTAL NON PAYABLE           9,598.50     99.80    9,498.70   *
*                                                               *
*   TOTAL MANUAL CHECKS                   0.00      0.00        0.00   *
*                                                               *
*   GRAND TOTAL A/P FILE             23,052.00    582.80   22,469.20   *
*                                                               *
*   TOTAL CASH REQUIRED THIS PERIOD  15,003.50    480.00   14,523.50   *
*                                                               *
* * * * * * * * * * * * * * * * * * * * * * * * * * * * * * * * *
```

*** INDICATES TOTAL PAYABLE IS A DEBIT   2 VENDORS

XXX INDICATES VENDOR TOTAL EQUALS ZERO

ZZZ INDICATES VENDOR TOTAL LESS THAN TOTAL PAYABLE

X PAYABLE THIS CYCLE

computer system); the company, division, department, location, or person covered by the report; and the page number.

The body of the report contains column headings and data. In general, descriptive data (account number and name, product code, and description) are on the left of the report; the numerical data concerning the account, product, and so on are to the right. An exception to this arrangement is the report style that presents two sets of near-identical data, but for two different periods (say current month and year to date) or budget and actual data. Then it may be best to have descriptive items in the middle and numbers on either side, presented symmetrically (see Figure 11–6). This style can also be effective for a report that has many columns, such as a report where the months of the year are spread across the page. (The report in Figure 11–3 could be redesigned this way.) The body of the report also contains subtotals as appropriate.

The bottom of a report is in two parts. First, the bottom of each page, which does not have any particular function, may be used to provide instructions or explanations of codes. Second, the significant part, at the bottom of the last page of the report, contains grand totals or some other unmistakable indication that there are no more pages to the report.

Highlighting on reports is difficult. Impact printers can highlight by overprinting. Laser printers cannot overprint, but some have multiple fonts and graphics capabilities that can help highlight. By far the best technique, because it can be used with any technology, is to isolate the data to be highlighted in a separate zone on the page—for example, in a margin not normally used or in an area preceded and followed by a number of blank lines.

SCREEN DESIGN

General guidelines for screen design are similar to those of form design (for input screens) and report design (for output screens). What varies is the specific technology of screens (size, color, graphics) and the fact that screens are an interactive and volatile medium.

Operator Guidance

One of the advantages of interactive processing is that the program can give the user constant feedback. Not only can the program check the correctness of the data as it is entered, but it can also display guidance relevant to the specific context of the conversation.

Unbuffered terminals and intelligent workstations can provide this feedback character by character as each is keyed in. Buffered terminals are somewhat less interactive, because the guidance they display can change only when the operator presses the *Transmit* key after filling in the screen.

The following guidelines can help in designing operator guidance:

- Captions and instructions must be explicit for casual users; they can be more cryptic for dedicated users.

- When instructions are displayed, they should be placed consistently. Only those instructions that can be used in the specific context should be displayed. For instance, if the operator is at the end of a scrolled document, no *Next Page* instruction should be given.

- When an operator enters data in a wrong format or tries to make a choice that the program cannot process, the program should display a message to the operator. This message is unfortunately called an error message. As a result, the text of such messages often contains the word *Error* or *Wrong*. These words have a deplorable effect, especially on novice users. Error messages should be viewed as a form of context-sensitive help and worded positively. For example, instead of "Customer number error," the message should say: "This customer number is not on file. Please check that you have the right one and try again, or use the Alpha Search Facility to find the customer's number if you know the name."

- Constant operator feedback should be provided. If the operator enters a code or an identification key (customer number, product code, state code in an address), the translation of that code (customer name and address, product designation, spelled-out state) should be displayed as soon as it is entered. If the program can determine that a response will be long in coming, a message can be displayed warning the operator of the delay.

- Everything that has been said about consistency in this and the previous chapter applies to screen design—consistency of placement, captions, emphasis, and action items.

Highlighting, Aesthetics, and Ergonomics

Aesthetic and ergonomic factors are of great importance because of the bias of many naive users against the dehumanized aspects of computer systems and because of the widespread feelings of dedicated operators that CRT work may be hazardous or unacceptably strenuous.

The following factors should be considered when designing screens:

- The users of the system should be involved in selecting the equipment and designing ergonomically correct workstations. (If necessary, an expert in ergonomics can help.) Some of the most common factors are the height of the terminal and the keyboard, the screen glare, the combination of predominant colors on the screen (black on white, white on black, amber on black, green on black). Color should not be relied on to code hard information. Instead, color should be reserved to indicate the type of field: captions, fields that the operator can modify (data entry fields), fields containing output data, error messages, instructions, present status.

- No more than two levels of intensity and no more than three or four colors should be used. In lieu of levels of intensity, inverse video (a black-on-white field where the rest of the screen is white-on-black) or blinking fields may be used. Blinking is distracting and should be used very sparingly. If audio feedback (e.g., beeps) is used, short tones should be used for routine feedback (unavailable key or function, attempt to put alphabetic characters in a numeric field). Long, more aggressive signals are used for rare, emergency conditions, for instance, to accompany a message such as: "Ten minutes have elapsed since the last activity on this terminal. Please press a key within the next thirty seconds if you wish to remain connected to the application."

- For a sophisticated intelligent workstation that accommodates multiple sizes and fonts, no more than three fonts (normal, bold, italics) and four sizes should be used.
- Fields should be aligned judiciously. Data fields (both input and output) should be aligned vertically on the left-hand side and captions on the right-hand side. Numeric and alphabetic fields should be justified properly. If the screen has multiple columns, the cursor normally moves from left to right, top to bottom. (The normal movement could be changed with intelligent workstation or an unbuffered terminal, but it is not advisable to do so, as the application might want to change screen types.)

Paging and Scrolling

Both input and output on screens may occupy more space than is available on the screen (normally 24 lines of 80 characters). One solution may be to get a larger terminal, but this makes the application dependent on nonstandard technology. Other solutions are to use windowing systems, available on intelligent workstations, or to provide scrolling or paging.

The windowing metaphor consists in making a rectangle on the screen available to view a two-dimensional area (such as a table, a listing, or a menu) that is larger than the window. Using function keys, the data area can be moved around underneath the window so as to show different parts of the data area through the window at any time. A screen may have multiple windows showing different data areas at the same time.

Scrolling or paging is a reduced form of windowing. Take, for example, an order that may have up to a hundred detail items. The first few lines on the screen display the information that applies to the entire order (order number, customer number, name and address, delivery date, and so on). The bottom line(s) display function key assignments and system messages. The lines in the middle display a limited number of order detail lines (say, 15 at a time). Scrolling enables the operator to press a function key to shift all the detail lines up by one, losing the topmost line but displaying a new one at the bottom. The reverse operation would shift all the lines down by one, showing a new line at the top. Paging does the same thing as scrolling, but an entire page is moved up or down at a time.

A left-right scrolling or paging function is required if the screen design calls for a data area that exceeds the width of the screen (for instance, to browse the electronic image of a report that uses the full 132 character line width of most line printers).

Scrolling and paging are practically always required for output-oriented applications, such as data base query or on-line management reporting. Many, if not most, reports or query responses require more than the standard 2,000 or so positions available on a screen. Dedicated transaction processing may also require scrolling and paging when each transaction (logical unit of work) is made up of many individual items. Office automation and departmental applications practically always require paging and scrolling because the documents processed are of arbitrary length.

Summary

The design of input and output forms, screens, and reports should follow three main guidelines: be easy to prepare or understand, fulfill its purpose effectively, and be cost-effective.

The main factors for ease of use are clarity of the layout, sufficient space, consistent and logical sequence, instructions, and feedback. For online interactions, important aspects are consistency, constant feedback, and pleasant aspect of the screens with which the operator interacts.

For output, the best results are obtained with one report or output transaction for each purpose. Because they reduce the number of printouts, multipurpose reports may seem more economical initially, but they are ultimately likely to be less effective.

Proper choice of medium and technology as well as adequate consideration of handling and distribution costs will maximize the cost-effectiveness of the design.

Selected Readings

The bibliography for this chapter is largely the same as for Chapter 10. Most of the books listed contain aspects of both dialog and screen design.

IBM Corporation. *Systems Application Architecture: Common User Access Panel Design and User Interaction*, 1st ed. IBM Publication No. SC26-4351, 1987.

Shneiderman, Ben. *Designing the User Interface*. Reading, Massachusetts: Addison-Wesley, 1987.
  This book is mainly about the design of human-computer interactions, but it has useful guidelines and excellent illustrations that pertain to screen design (pp. 69–73 and pp. 311–351 in particular).

Martin, James. *Design of Man-Computer Dialogues*. Englewood Cliffs, New Jersey: Prentice-Hall, 1973.
  James Martin's book has several examples of good screen design techniques for a variety of applications and technical environments.

Garlitz, Wilbert O. *Handbook of Screen Format Design*, 2d ed. Wellesley Hill, Massachusetts: QED Information Sciences, Inc., 1985.
  This book is a complete and reasonably up-to-date description of the

main screen design techniques. It also contains chapters on the use of colors and graphics. Finally, it describes input forms design.

Review Questions

1. Which part of the user requirements document is the most directly used when designing reports, forms, and screens?

2. Which forms, reports, and screens must be mocked up or prototyped during the design phase? Which ones can be postponed until the implementation phase?

3. What types of guidelines are typically included in form, screen, and report design standards?

4. What are the three major goals of form, screen, and report design?

5. Describe the problems that might be encountered if inadequate attention were given to the following:
  - **a.**   Report data content
  - **b.**   Form makeup
  - **c.**   Number of copies
  - **d.**   Screen size
  - **e.**   Report security requirements

Discussion Questions

1. Why is the use of terminals for data entry and information display increasing at the expense of preprinted forms and computer-generated reports?

2. Review examples of forms used in everyday life (for example, restaurant order pads with a detachable receipt, credit card charge slips, individual income tax returns). Critique and improve. How would you design a screen replacing these forms, assuming that the function could be made interactive? Would alternative technologies (voice, OCR, mark sensing, bar codes, etc.) apply to these situations?

3. Identify screen design components of a PC-based product with which you are familiar, such as Lotus 1-2-3, a CASE tool, or a word processor.

4. It is often stated that if voice input and output were widely available, more executives would use computer technology. Discuss whether this is true.

Mini-Case

You are asked to prepare a mock-up of a report that will also serve as a turnaround document. A report definition form with the required data element descriptions is furnished as Figure 11–8.

The mock-up should be as realistic as possible. You should make up territory, salesperson, and customer names as well as realistic figures. The mock-up should ideally be prepared on a computer printer; if a printer is not available, use a printer spacing chart.

Figure 11–8 **Report Definition Form**

```
ACCTG                              DESIGN TOOL                         RDTDEF
BUDPREP                                                                R00262
              REPORT DEFINITION - SALES BUDGETING TURNAROUND REPORT

PREPARED BY: BEN DOVER            DATE: 15FEB92         VERSION: 2        PAGE 1
APPROVED BY: RL TURNER            DATE: 18FEB92         STATUS:


PURPOSE                     : Serves as a turnaround document for entry of sales budget
                              data. Report provides prior and current year sales and
                              gross margin by quarter within customer, salesperson and
                              territory. Sales and gross margin % change between prior
                              and current years are also reported. Budget preparers
                              enter for next year either:

                                 -  Budgeted sales and gross margin amounts, or

                                 -  Budgeted sales and gross margin % change from
                                    current year actual quarterly amounts.

                              For current year quarters for which actual amounts are not
                              yet available, amounts are projected based on the year to
                              date change between the prior and current years. Totals are
                              provided by customer, salesperson, territory and company.
                              Overall totals can be balanced to control totals to ensure
                              processing accuracy.



DISTRIBUTION                : Salespersons, Territory Managers

MEDIA                       : Paper

FREQUENCY OF PREPARATION: Quarterly

NUMBER OF COPIES            : 2

VOLUME OF PRINT             : 250 pages

RETENTION                   : 2 years

FORM                        : Stock

SEQUENCE                    : Territory, Salesperson, Customer

PAGE BREAK                  : Territory
```

Figure 11–8 *Continued*

```
ACCTG                         DESIGN TOOL                           RDTDEF
BUDPREP                                                             R00262
            REPORT DEFINITION - SALES BUDGETING TURNAROUND REPORT

PREPARED BY: BEN DOVER        DATE: 15FEB92         VERSION: 2      PAGE 2
APPROVED BY: RL TURNER        DATE: 18FEB92         STATUS:


X-REF TO     DATA ELEMENT                                          NO. OF
 SAMPLE      IDENTIFICATION     DATA ELEMENT NAME OR COMMENTS     CHARACTERS
--------     --------------     -----------------------------    ----------

    1        EL00200            Territory Number                      2
    2        EL00205            Salesperson Number                    3
    3        EL00206            Salesperson Name                     25
    4        EL00220            Customer Number                       5
    5        EL00221            Customer Name                        25

                                Prior Year $ Sales to Customer
    6        EL00361            - 1st Quarter                         7
    7        EL00362            - 2nd Quarter                         7
    8        EL00363            - 3rd Quarter                         7
    9        EL00364            - 4th Quarter                         7

                                Current Year $ Sales to Customer
   10        EL00371            - 1st Quarter                         7
   11        EL00372            - 2nd Quarter                         7
   12        EL00373            - 3rd Quarter                         7
   13        EL00374            - 4th Quarter                         7

                                Prior Year $ Gross Margin for Customer
   14        EL00381            - 1st Quarter                         5
   15        EL00382            - 2nd Quarter                         5
   16        EL00383            - 3rd Quarter                         5
   17        EL00384            - 4th Quarter                         5

                                Current Year $ Gross Margin for Customer
   18        EL00391            - 1st Quarter                         5
   19        EL00392            - 2nd Quarter                         5
   20        EL00393            - 3rd Quarter                         5
   21        EL00394            - 4th Quarter                         5
```

CHAPTER 12

Graphical User Interfaces

Graphical user interfaces are becoming increasingly significant in systems development. This chapter describes the most common types of graphical user interfaces and addresses the three major driving forces behind graphical user interfaces: users must be able to learn the interface through its self-learning features, and not as a separate operation; the application must present a consistent and useful metaphor to the user; and many applications must now have the ability to store and display images in addition to text. The chapter closes with design issues and standards of graphical user interfaces.

Learning Objectives

- Understand why the knowledge worker now needs the graphical user interface.
- Appreciate how self-learning systems provide the best training for this type of interface.
- Describe the evolution of the graphical user interface.
- Recognize the features of direct manipulation interfaces.
- Understand the need for image processing in today's applications.
- Be aware of the guidelines for designing graphical user interfaces.

INTERFACE REQUIREMENTS FOR KNOWLEDGE WORKERS

The new types of applications that are being developed today no longer support the piecemeal paperwork inspired by assembly-line techniques and Taylor's "scientific management." Instead of feeding data to heads-down clerks who enter it as speedily as possible into the computer without questioning its meaning, today's knowledge workers are in direct contact with the information system. They perceive the system as a tool to execute their daily activity rather than a machine to which they are responsible for feeding raw materials.

This trend affects not only professionals such as financial analysts, engineers, actuaries, and salespeople, but also shop floor workers (e.g., quality control, production scheduling) and traditional clerical workers such as receiving clerks and order entry operators.

As technology affects the nature of the work, enabling deep business process change (see Chapter 2), so does the changing nature of the work change the demands made on the technology—in particular the user interface, as already described in Chapter 10. The main new requirements are described below. They concern essentially the following aspects:

• The user interface must be learned as it is used, not as a separate operation.

• The application must present a consistent and useful metaphor to the user.

• In many applications, the ability to store and display images in addition to text is critical.

All these requirements are better satisfied by graphical user interfaces on intelligent workstations than on fixed-function terminals.

Self-Learning Systems

As applications serve knowledge workers more directly, they become more complex. The work of knowledge workers is by its very essence complex, consisting of nonrepetitive (although often similar) tasks and decisions. Every possible case cannot be anticipated and documented in an operator's reference manual or in training.

The complexity of these applications also dictates that they are delivered piecemeal, in successive versions with increasing functionality.

Finally, the learning curve is longer. There is a greater difference between expert and novice users. Some users never progress beyond the stage of competence; others become experts and take on, often quite spontaneously, the role of mentor or advisor to their colleagues.

The training needs for knowledge workers are thus quite different from those of traditional system users. A single concentrated course just prior to system conversion is insufficient. It would have to cover too much ground and most of the material would be forgotten by the time the user had a chance to use the various features of the system. Much more emphasis must be put on continuous training. Although no single approach applies to all circumstances, the following are typical elements:

• On-line Tutorials.

    An on-line tutorial steps the user through typical activities, demonstrating how the system can be used. Generally, the tutorial gives precise instructions to the operator on the actions to take, so that he or she gets actual hands-on experience. (A storyboard or demonstration mode may also be possible, where the system shows both its own and the operator's action.)

    The tutorial should be divided into chapters of increasing complexity. Ideally, the user should come out of the first chapter with the feeling that he or she could accomplish some useful, productive task, however elementary. Under normal circumstances, the user covers only a few chapters as initial training. The rest can be taken as the user encounters more complex situations.

Box
12–1

Ticket Stub Auditing at Northwest Airlines

Northwest Airlines has recently implemented an image processing system to help in the auditing of airplane ticket stubs. Most of Northwest Airlines' tickets are written, not by Northwest itself, but by independent travel agents. In many cases, Northwest Airlines does not see these tickets until they have been surrendered by passengers at the gate and transmitted to the airline's headquarters—well after the flight is over.

Of course, the passenger has paid the price of the ticket to the travel agent, who will retain part of it as a commission, previously negotiated with the airline. The rest of the money is owed to Northwest Airlines.

The travel agent is also responsible for seeing that the fare is applied in conformity with Northwest's tariff. These tariffs depend on whether the flight is a round trip, how many days in advance the reservation is made, whether the traveler has spent Saturday night on the road, and a host of other conditions. The complexity of the tariff is such that there is a substantial risk that the wrong price has been applied by the travel agent.

To correct pricing mistakes and discourage any possibility of fraud (by applying unjustified discounts to attract more customers), Northwest Airlines' accounting department audits the tick-et stubs when they are returned. Any anomalies are investigated and the travel agent's account adjusted, if required.

Until the automated auditing system was implemented, auditing was manual. Because of the millions of ticket stubs that were submitted, the auditing was done by random sampling; it was impossible to audit them all.

In the late 1980s, Northwest Airlines installed a system that scans in ticket stubs and uses OCR to recognize and interpret the pricing information on the stubs. An artificial intelligence program then helps determine whether there is any reason to suspect that a pricing error has been committed—eliminating from the auditing process all those tickets that are issued at full fare or where it is obvious that the discount rules have been applied properly. Thus relieved of examining all the manifestly good tickets, the auditing department can concentrate on the dubious cases. Moreover, it has instant access to a high-resolution image of the ticket and to the rules that could possibly have been violated.

The decrease in the cost of manipulating (and often losing—temporarily or permanently) ticket stubs and, more significantly, the increased revenue from travel agents have paid back the cost of the system in a matter of a few months.

- Practice Mode.

Many systems are capable of operating in practice mode, where the operator performs real activities but has no effect on the data of the system. This approach is different from a tutorial, since the user chooses which activities to execute and which data to enter. Practice mode can be used by a supervisor to demonstrate a particular activity; it is also useful for novice operators who are nervous about their lack of experience causing system errors.

- On-line Help.

   The various forms of on-line help were covered in Chapter 10: fixed help; context-dependent help (the most frequent), and data-dependent help.

The varying levels of user expertise with the system were evoked above. Ideally, the user should be offered different ways of operating the system, depending on his or her experience. For instance, beginners find cascades of menus to be of great help; experienced users prefer shortcuts such as short sequences of keystrokes—especially for routine activities. In the following, we examine gradually more advanced direct manipulation interface features.

The various direct manipulation interfaces that are on the market solve this problem rather well by providing pull-down menus (which are unobtrusive but easy to invoke), for which each frequently used command also carries a keystroke sequence. As the user grows accustomed to the menus, he or she can gradually start using keystroke combinations instead of pointing to a menu selection and clicking the mouse. (An additional benefit is that the hands need not then leave the keyboard; the user can avoid some of the slowing-down effect of mouse manipulations.) The Macintosh standard interface is particularly well designed in this regard (see Figure 12–1).

Some systems have two levels of menu displays: short and full. Short menus only display the most frequent actions and are appropriate during learning mode or for occasional users. Full menus can be displayed when the user feels more confident or requires more functionality. Full menus may intimidate the novice user, both by making the appropriate action harder to locate and by displaying arcane, possibly confusing terminology for less frequently used functions.

The window in which the current work is being performed may also have more than one level of options. An example is found in Microsoft Word (and other word processors) where the user may choose to display a *ruler*, providing a number of icons that help align the text with tab stops, justify paragraphs, and set line spacing. This provides a third alternative for some frequent actions, in addition to menu point-and-click and keystroke sequence (see Figure 12–2).

Word processors often have yet another way of providing paragraph alignment and font selection: the style sheet. A style sheet contains a number of styles of paragraphs likely to be used in a document: flush left, indented, bullet points, etc. A given paragraph can be associated with a style name that tells the software how to format it. The greatest advantage of this option is that when a style is modified, all the paragraphs using that style are automatically reformatted.

Finally, many systems have a "macro" capability. A macro is a recording of a frequently repeated sequence of keystrokes which the user can invoke with a single action. Again, most word processors have this capability. Thus, in the Macintosh version of Word, WordPerfect, Fullwrite, and other word

Figure 12–1 **Macintosh® Desktop**

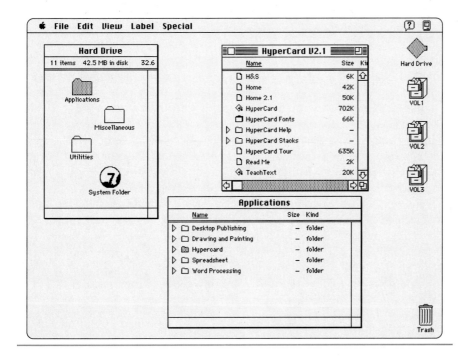

Figure 12–2 **Microsoft Word™ Ruler**

processors, some actions could be performed in any of five different ways; the user can select the one that best corresponds to his or her level of experience and understanding of the tool's capabilities.

The Direct Manipulation Metaphor

A critical success factor for systems serving knowledge workers is that they present a consistent and useful metaphor to its users. Early on-line business systems used **form-filling** as their metaphor: this was extremely successful because the metaphor was familiar to its users and thus both easy to learn and reassuring. Its drawback was that it was so limited: there is only so much a knowledge worker can do by filling in a form. Any activity that is not specifically planned in its least details and that does not have a specific form associated with it is impossible to execute.

A more powerful metaphor, one that did more than any other factor to ensure the success of personal computing, was the **spreadsheet,** created by Dan Bricklin with Visicalc in the late 1970s. Users of spreadsheets have the impression that there is a two-dimensional piece of electronic paper just underneath the screen of the workstation. Keys (and possibly a pointing device such as a mouse) enable the user to move spreadsheets that are larger than the 24×80-character screen so that different parts can be displayed successively. Each cell contains data—either explicitly entered or virtual, in the form of a formula allowing it to be calculated from other elements. The storing of formulas instead of actual data is what gives the electronic spreadsheet more power than its manual counterpart, but it is a very natural extension to the metaphor.

The next step in successful metaphors was the **desktop.** This metaphor was invented at the Xerox Palo Alto Research Center (PARC) and implemented commercially on the Lisa workstation. Lisa was not very successful, but the metaphor was taken up by Apple Computers and incorporated into the Macintosh operating system. The desktop is made up of folders that can contain folders within folders or other types of objects: programs and files, for example. An object can be manipulated "directly"—a metaphorical expression!—by selecting it (pointing a cursor to it by moving a mouse, a lightpen, a joystick, or a tracking ball), then specifying some action to be taken on the object. This action can be selected from a menu, specified by a command, or executed directly with the mouse (double-clicking or dragging).

The Macintosh interface has a main menu bar across the top of the screen. A **menu selection** is made by pointing to one of the menu items, causing a *pull-down* menu to appear (see Figure 12–3). The pull-down menu contains the second level of menu selection; the mouse is dragged vertically to select the appropriate option. If a third level of menu is required, a horizontal movement from the second-level item makes third-level selections appear. Three is the maximum reasonable depth of menus for this interface style.

Many menu items on the Macintosh can be selected by a combination of keystrokes rather than by moving the mouse. Each **command** calls for one or two auxiliary keys (shift, control, option, command) to be pressed together with a normal keyboard key. There is an attempt to make the keystroke combination mnemonic: Command–Q signifies *Quit* and Command–S *Save.*

The final possibility for selecting a course of action is caused by acting on the mouse. The mouse has a button incorporated in it (two buttons for IBM OS/2 and Microsoft Windows, three on Sun workstations). **Double-clicking,** depressing the mouse button twice, opens the selected objects. If it is a folder, the contents of the opened folder are displayed on the "desktop"—the screen. If it is an application, the program is brought into memory and given control. If it is a data file, the program that created the data file is brought into memory and given control after opening the data file itself, so that the user can start working on that file immediately. This is one of the

Figure 12–3 **The Macintosh Pull-Down Menu**

main distinguishing features of a direct manipulation interface: the user need no longer keep track of which program created which file, by naming conventions or other means.

To reinforce the illusion of direct manipulation, objects are represented not only by their names, but also by **icons.** Folders are represented by a rectangle with a tab, documents (files) by a rectangle of another size with a corner folded down, and the receptacle for deleted documents by an image of a trash can.

Dragging, pointing to an object, then depressing the mouse button while moving the mouse, moves the object from one folder to another, copies it from one disk to another, or deletes it (by dragging it to a trash can).

The Macintosh direct manipulation interface is **object-oriented.** The relationship is threefold. First, files are true objects in the sense that they are packaged with the program that created them and that can manipulate them. Opening an object also opens the applications. The object is invisible by other programs. If the application is unavailable (for instance, if a data file has been imported into a system that does not have a license for the software that created it), the file cannot be opened. This is akin to object orientation, where methods (or processes that can manipulate the object's data) are packaged with the object itself.

Second, objects are specified before actions. An object must be selected before the menu options become operative. This is akin to message passing in object-oriented systems; a message is sent to an object, specifying what the object is to do, rather than to a function, specifying what object to apply the function to, as do older interfaces such as the menu-driven, form-filling mainframe applications of the 1970s and early 1980s.

Third, the interface is actually programmed in an object-oriented language. This fact has no impact on the functions of the interface, which could equally well have been implemented in a third-generation language such as C. What is significant is that graphical user interfaces are much easier to implement in this technology. In fact, such interfaces are likely to be the main area of application of object orientation in the next few years.

A final comment may make it clear what a good metaphor can achieve. It is much more difficult to explain in words (without demonstrating, showing, or pointing) the use of a graphical interface to a novice than it is a traditional interface. The explainer usually has internalized the metaphor to a point where the manipulation has become instinctive. Thus, expert assistance over the telephone is ineffective when the recipient of the assistance does not have a sufficient level of fluency.

Image Processing

The third important new requirement for user interfaces for knowledge workers is the capability to display images. The underlying reason for this requirement is that knowledge workers often deal with complex objects that cannot be decomposed into simple parts, each of which can be processed independently by a computer program, as can fields in a record. Rather, the knowledge worker needs to see relationships and patterns, using undecomposable (as yet) mental operations. Two-dimensional representations support this type of activity better than one-dimensional strings of data: a picture is worth a thousand words.

There are three categories of imaging applications: WYSIWYG editing, scanned documents, and processable graphics.

WYSIWYG editing, the most primitive form of imaging, refers to applications where it is necessary to present on the screen as faithful an image of the end result (on paper) as possible. WYSIWYG stands for *What You See Is What You Get.* A word processor example illustrates the concept. Special features of a text designed to control its appearance in print are interspersed as control characters in the string of bytes representing the text. The text editor can display these characters on the screen so that the user can locate them and modify them. This mode is appropriate for fixed-format, alphanumeric terminals. The alternative is to display the text as it will appear on the printer and use direct manipulation techniques to locate and maintain the formatting commands. This is the option taken on most intelligent workstations (see Figure 12–4).

The technique is applied whenever the printer has functions that cannot readily be simulated on an alphanumeric screen. In practice, this means laser printers. Impact printers—dot-matrix or whole character—have essentially the same resolution as fixed-function terminals and WYSIWYG is not a major problem. Applications using laser printers today manipulate text (desktop publishing, electronic mail) or fairly simple images (line sketches to illustrate text, business graphics for presentations).

Scanned images refer to the capture, storage, and display on a computer of documents created either manually or on some incompatible technology. The archetypal example is the scanning in of entire reference

Figure 12–4 **Contrast between Formatting Control and WYSIWYG**

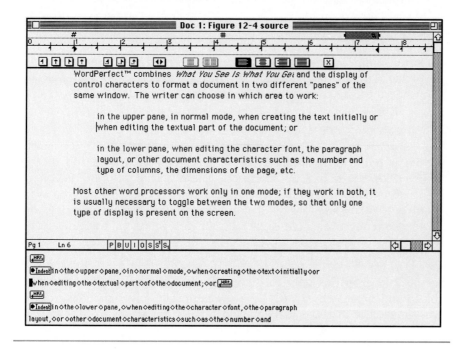

libraries onto optical disk to conserve space and ease duplication. Other applications include:

- Correspondence Management

    Correspondence received is scanned into a computer and filed according to criteria that makes it easy to retrieve. The advantage over paper filing is that it is more reliable (especially if additional documents are expected to be appended to an initial letter) and can be reviewed by multiple people at multiple sites simultaneously.

    When the correspondence is likely to contain photographs, drawings, or sketches, imaging becomes even more likely. Real-estate multiple listings with photographs and floor plans, insurance claims processing, and in a slightly different vein, health care (with X-ray photos) or computer-based encyclopedias are examples.

- Computer-to-Computer Facsimile

    Instead of preparing a document on a word processor and then printing it so that it can be fed to a facsimile transmission terminal, the facsimile is sent directly from the computer. On the other side of the transmission, the receiver may be a traditional facsimile printer with paper output or another computer, which can then store the document and reproduce it at will.

- Optical Character Recognition

    When the data on the scanned document needs processing, it may be cost-effective to translate it from scanned to processable form using optical character recognition. Great strides in OCR technology have been made over the past several years; there is equipment today that can recognize practically any typewritten font. This is useful for high-volume applications of documents that are prepared (or manipulated) outside the using enterprise. Airline ticket auditing is a recent example (see Box 12–1).

- Animation and Full-Motion Video

    Animation (or stop-motion video, showing several successive images without trying to imitate fluid motion) and full-motion video add another dimension to graphical interfaces. These techniques are becoming increasingly feasible as the cost of electronics is dropping and the available telecommunications bandwidth is increasing. Teleconferencing with video, attempted unsuccessfully with the videophone in the early 1970s, now seems poised for success. Other applications include marketing (animated catalogs) and computer-based training.

Processable graphics refer to drawings whose components can be recognized and processed as such by a program. The most immediate example is CASE. For instance, data flow diagrams are made up of such elements as processes, data flows, and data stores; the DFD editor recognizes these shapes and their interconnections. Changing the position of a process box automatically changes the position of the data flows in and out of the process; deleting a data store deletes all the data flows leading to and from it.

Other examples are computer-aided design (CAD) and computer-aided engineering (CAE). CAD and CAE tools can display and manipulate line drawings, electrical connection schematics, and the like, in two or (sometimes) three dimensions, thus eliminating the need for much tedious drafting by hand. In some domain designs, such as very large scale integrated (VLSI) circuit design, a large part of the design process itself—deciding where to locate each element and how to interconnect them—has been automated.

GUIDELINES FOR DESIGN

Graphical user interfaces have many more features than traditional alphanumeric terminals and are therefore more difficult to design. There are no hard-and-fast rules about how to create easy-to-use interfaces with useful metaphors. Moreover, the first graphical user interface implemented in an organization is sure to have a long-lasting impact. Because the interface is so complex, it is unreasonable to expect users to be able to assimilate more than one—unlike mainframe interfaces. Already, in traditional, nongraphical personal computer software, it has been found that most users refuse to have more than three or four programs. Even if the functionality of an additional program were attractive, most users prefer to make do with the old program, possibly at the price of awkward manipulations, rather than learn yet another interface. Thus, any errors committed during the design of the first interface, if not very quickly corrected, may prove to have a long life.

The most frequent mistake when designing a user interface for a graphics-capable workstation is to stay too close to old-style systems, simply emulating a menu-driven, form-filling metaphor.

The following guidelines follow primarily the terminology and the look and feel of the Macintosh interface. The concepts, if not the details, are applicable across other systems, such as IBM's Presentation Manager and Microsoft Windows.

The main elements of a graphical user interface are the following:

- Windows
- Alerts and warnings
- Pull-down menus
- Dialog boxes

Windows

A window is an area of the screen dedicated to a certain purpose. The initial window brought up when the application opens, in which the main activity of the application is conducted, is called the main window. From the main window, it may be possible to create auxiliary, or child, windows (see Figure 12–5).

The main design issue with windows is the choice between tiling and overlapping windows. Tiled windows occupy a fixed place on the screen and no window can impinge on another window's territory. Enlarging one window requires other windows to shrink (see Figure 12–6). Overlapping windows can be moved around by the user; they can be temporarily obscured, wholly or partially, by other windows , as shown in Figure 12–7. Tiled windows are more productive and overlapping windows more flexible, especially when large screens are unavailable.

Even with overlapping windows, the initial aspect—size and placement—of a window should be the same when it is opened. The user can then move and resize the window at will.

In fixed format screen applications, the screen is often divided into individual zones. Window systems have the advantage, because this concept can be implemented by zones within a window or separate zones in separate windows.

Opening, closing, resizing, and moving windows within a business application should be consistent with the rest of the interface, which will usually dictate how to do this. The options left at the designer's discretion are whether a window is to be resizable and/or scrolling.

A separate window is usually designed for each object or data entity processed by the application. Thus, in an order entry application, separate windows might be provided for customer, order header, order lines, ship-

Figure 12–5 **Main Window versus Child Window**

Figure 12–6 **Tiled Windows**

Figure 12–7 **Overlapping Windows**

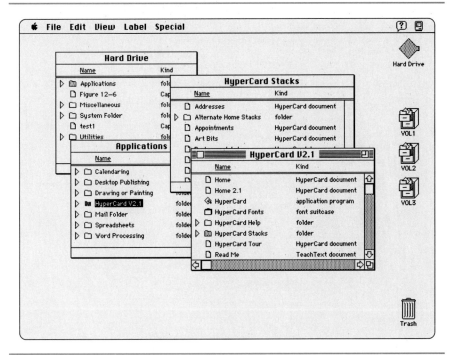

ping, and tax information, as illustrated in Figure 12–8. The window title bar contains an indication of the type of data displayed in the window as well as the actual entity that is being processed (the customer name, the order number, or whatever other information is required).

An auxiliary window can be provided for complex selections. If the value of a field can be one of about three to some hundred different values (for example, one of twenty warehouses from which an order could be shipped), a scrolling window can list all the possible values. The user can scroll to the appropriate message, select it, and click to make it automatically appear in the right field in the main window (see Figure 12–9).

A separate window is often provided for fields that need to be visible during an entire session. In an overlapped window environment, this window can be tucked out of sight most of the time, yet be quickly available when needed.

Alerts and Warnings

Alerts and warnings appear in windows that open automatically when some condition is reached that the user should be alerted to (see Figure 12–10). The user must take some action before the application can proceed. Usually, there is a choice between overriding the alert or making a correction so that the condition disappears. Another option may be to suspend the transaction

Figure 12–8 **One Window per Zone**

Figure 12–9 **Auxiliary Window**

Figure 12–10 **Warning Box**

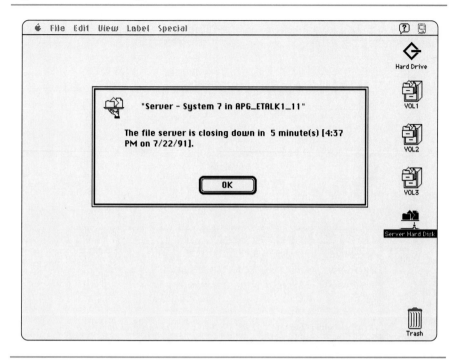

and open another window for the next one. Even if there is no choice of actions, the user is required to acknowledge the message before proceeding.

Pull-Down Menus

Pull-down menus were described earlier in the chapter. We will simply add here the need to adapt the content of the menu to the state of the computation. Only those options that are possible or that would have an effect should be selectable. All other options should either not be displayed or, preferably, be displayed in gray scale, indicating that they are inoperative (see Figure 12–11).

A frequent pull-down menu item is *Help*. This function could also be accomplished by giving the user the option to point to a field name or a window title and clicking on it.

Pull-down menus usually replace function keys as used on fixed-function terminals for controlling the flow of the application.

Dialog Boxes

A dialog box is a window that is dedicated to entering a data value or set of values that are logically connected. It is analogous to a prompt/response sequence on a fixed-function terminal, such as the one in Figure 12–12.

Often, the dialog box appears in response to a pull-down menu choice.

Figure 12–11 **Unavailable Options**

Figure 12–12 **Dialog Box**

If the menu option is *BackOrder*, for example, the dialog box might ask whether the whole order is to be back-ordered or only the missing items.

A dialog box could also be opened at the end of a conversation to confirm that the logical unit of work is complete and that it is safe for the system to proceed.

Summary

Today's knowledge workers perceive their system as a tool to execute their daily activity rather than a machine to which they are responsible for feeding raw materials. This trend affects both professionals and the traditional clerical and shop floor workers, changing the nature of their work. As work changes, so do the demands on technology—in particular the user interface.

As systems grow in complexity, the learning curve is likewise extending, so interfaces must be capable of teaching the user as the system is used, through self-learning techniques. Some common elements of self-learning systems are on-line tutorials, practice modes, and on-line help.

From the user's perspective, it is necessary to maintain a consistent system interface metaphor. This metaphor has evolved from form-filling in early on-line business systems, to spreadsheets in the early 1980s, and on to the most pervasive metaphor of today, the desktop. The desktop, an interface made up of folders that contain other folders within folders, programs, and files, has revolutionized personal computing. Each file can be regarded as an object that is bundled with the application it is written in. It is no longer necessary to know which application a certain file has been created in, because simply opening that file will open the application as well.

Today's user interfaces must also have the capability to display images. The new complexity of the knowledge worker's responsibilities makes it important for the system to be able to present relationships and patterns using images rather than strings of text or data. The three categories of image processing—WYSIWYG, scanned images, and processable graphics—have created a need for high-performance graphical user interfaces.

The components of graphical user interfaces include windows, alerts, pull-down menus, and dialog boxes. When designing the interface for a desktop-type application, it is imperative that the standard guidelines for these components remain consistent.

Selected Readings

IBM Corporation. *Systems Application Architechture: Common User Access Panel Design and User Interaction,* 1st ed. IBM Publication No. SC26–4351, 1987.

Apple Computers Inc. *Human Interface Guidelines: The Apple Desktop Interface.* Reading, Massachusetts: Addison-Wesley, 1987.

Johnson, E., and Reichard, K. *Power Programming . . . MOTIF.* Portland, OR: MIS Press, 1991.

These three books describe the three most popular graphical user interfaces in existence today. The Apple interface is the oldest one, dating to the early eighties. IBM's Common User Access (CUA) was announced in 1987. MOTIF, the UNIX environment offering, more recent, is emerging as the most popular nonproprietary solution.

Review Questions

1. Why are self-learning systems necessary training mechanisms for knowledge workers?

2. What are some typical elements of self-learning systems?

3. What are the components of the direct manipulation metaphor?

4. Describe the purpose of a macro.

5. What does it mean when the Macintosh's direct manipulation interface is described as "object-oriented"?

6. Why is it important for user interfaces to have the capability of displaying images?

Discussion Questions

1. What is the next step in user interfaces? Is this step feasible for the near future, or is the time horizon longer?

2. How closely is the quality of the graphical user interface tied to the underlying technology of the computer? Has the quality of interfaces increased with new technological developments? Are there areas where quality has declined?

Mini-Case

Sal's Pizza. Sal's pizza shop is so successful that it has had to hire a number of high school students to process orders part-time. This segment of the worker population has a high turnover ratio. The dialog you designed after Chapter 10 takes too long to master, and Sal's Pizza has decided to convert the application to a graphical user interface.

Questions for Discussion

1. Review the three main graphical user interface metaphors and decide which one is the most suitable for Sal's Pizza.

2. Design an interactive order entry dialog that will be easy to learn, using the selected GUI.

Technique

Tools for Prototyping

INTRODUCTION

As explained in Chapter 3, prototyping is a technique used to reduce uncertainty and risk when an application or the technology it uses is innovative. Prototyping consists of making small-scale trials of the application (or full-scale trials of small parts of the application) with a view to ascertaining the consequences of design options before they are implemented full scale. Thus, prototyping is practically always recommended for user interface design: even if the design does not appear particularly innovative to the development team, it probably will to the users.

When prototyping, the usual life cycle of analysis, design, and implementation is repeated on a small scale. Because design options are of less consequence than in full-blown implementation and because they are easy to modify, proportionately less time is spent on design and more on coding and testing. Equally important is the feedback cycle from the users of the prototype, who will indicate whether requirements or design changes are required.

DEFINITION

A prototyping tool is a set of programs that enable the project team to generate a prototype to demonstrate the actual application. The prototype typically works in a limited area and can be developed in substantially less time than it would take to build the entire application with traditional means. The purpose of prototyping is to make sure that the application will work as planned once it is actually implemented. Prototyping is therefore most appropriate when there is uncertainty.

EXAMPLES

A word processing package can show users prototypes of screen and report layouts.

A presentation tool such as IBM's Storyboard can show users the successive steps of a sample dialog, illustrating how screens are chained together, how errors are corrected, and how menus and forms are structured.

A fourth-generation language such as Focus can be used to generate an actual mini-application, with small data files, interactive screens, and executable programs. Thus, users can experiment with the conversation design to validate it or they can train on a "flight simulator."

A rule-based expert system or AI shell, such as AION, can be used to define complex processing rules and test their consequences. This type of tool is appropriate when the processing rules are so complex that the user cannot articulate them all in a single sitting. Many times, an AI shell can be useful when the user says: "I cannot explain what I need, but I will know it when I see it."

A program simulator that can generate data bases and/or transactions based on specifications entered by the design team can prototype application performance. A simulator can also exercise the teleprocessing monitor and/or the data base management system with volumes close to those that will be encountered during operations. Examples are IBM's Teleprocessing Network Simulator and DBPROTOTYPE II.

DOMAINS FOR PROTOTYPING

Prototyping is used for three purposes. The first is to ensure that the **user interface** is well designed—easy to learn and easy to use. This use of prototyping is by far the most frequent. It is no more costly than the traditional, paper-based approach for getting the users to sign off on the interface design, and it is tremendously more effective. This prototyping is part of the user interface design activity of the design phase.

The second most frequent use is for **performance modeling.** Performance modeling is done at a later stage of the life cycle than user interface prototyping and is used to evaluate the probable performance of a given technical design. Performance prototyping has been especially popular for evaluating physical data base design choices for prerelational data bases such as IMS. It is less useful for relational data base designs for two main reasons. First, relational designs offer fewer choices of implementation parameters; second, machines have become more powerful, thereby decreasing the amount of attention given to performance. Performance-oriented prototyping still has merit for applications where performance may be an issue and where the body of experience is insufficient to predict performance without prototyping.

The third type of use, **functional prototyping,** is just emerging. This type is concerned with developing the requirements specifications (outside the user interface) iteratively. Functional prototyping will increase as the level of ambition of the applications in development increases. In one example, functional prototyping was used to develop an application to manage leased equipment being moved from construction site to construction site by a contractor. Because the contractor was also part owner of some of the sites, the accounting rules were too complex to be enumerated by one person. The prototyping approach consisted of formalizing a number of rules, setting up a prototype based on those rules, and running a number of test cases. When a test case gave a result that experience had proved wrong, the rule base was refined to cover additional rules. When all the test cases were processed correctly, the rule base was translated into English. The English version constituted the specification for the accounting part of the system.

Although some of the tools may be the same, prototyping is not the same as iterative development. Iterative development consists in delivering subsets of an application in small increments at frequent intervals (weeks rather than months or years). With iterative development, the user can start realizing some of the benefits before the entire application is ready. The high-payback functions are typically implemented first, thus increasing the period over which economies can be made and consequently the total economics achieved. In iterative development, each component is developed with production in mind. The quality of the code, the documentation, the controls, the integration, and the performance are just the same as on a monolithic development project. The difference between iterative development and the traditional approach concerns primarily the delivery mode.

Prototypes of applications, on the other hand, are usually developed with the idea of throwing away the prototype and recoding it in a different language with different tools during an implementation phase. However, if a CASE tool is used for user interface prototyping, screen designs can often be reused. In the functional prototyping example cited above, it was deemed unnecessary to translate the accounting rules into a COBOL program, and the AI shell used for prototyping was integrated into the production application as well.

MECHANIZED TOOLS

By definition, prototyping requires mechanized tools. First, the very act of prototyping requires that a model system be run on a computer; a manual prototype is not adequate to demonstrate the running of a computer-based application and get significant feedback. If there are no tools, the prototype must be developed using a third-generation language such as COBOL, thus negating the benefit of quick and low-cost demonstration models.

On the other hand, the variety of tools that can be used for prototyping is immense. The considerations for picking the appropriate tool are the following:

- Availability

    Anything that can be done with standard tools on a PC (word processor, spreadsheet, micro-DBMS) is particularly effective.

- Functionality

    A user interface prototype must be able to show screens in a default sequence at least. If the application is operator-driven, this capability is not enough. For the user to give feedback, more choices need to be available. The prototype must be sensitive to data values and menu (or function key) choices. Any moderately programmable PC package (but not, for instance, a word processor) can perform the required functions.

Other prototyping situations require more capability. Functional prototyping is best served by AI techniques. Performance prototyping requires a modeling capability that cannot be developed easily from general-purpose tools.

- Reusability

    If a prototype is extensive, it is best if the prototyping tool will accept design or implementation documentation such as screen layouts and function key assignments. This requirement militates in favor of using a CASE tool. If the entire application (or substantial parts of it) will be developed in a fourth-generation language or with an application generator, it is usually appropriate to use the same application development tool for prototyping as well.

EXERCISES

1. Prototype the medical application given as an example of menu choices and form filling in Chapter 10. For each level of menu, implement only two or three choices—choosing any other will result in a message returned to the user: "This choice not yet operational." Implement a mini-data base of 8 physicians and 15 patients. Use the tool with which you are most familiar.

2. Choose another tool that can do prototyping. Implement the same prototype. Compare the two prototypes in terms of:
   a.   Cost to implement.
   b.   Closeness to real application.
   c.   Functional richness (and therefore probable quality of feedback).

Data Design

Section V deals with the creation of a data design, specifying the entities about which a system is to maintain data, their relationships, their characteristics, and their integrity constraints. The section covers approaches for both transaction processing systems and management information systems.

Data Modeling at Bailis, Kronberg, Kendall & Son

◆

When the firm of Bailis, Kronberg, Kendall & Son, a New York–based financial services company, decided to replace its outdated portfolio management system, the first step of the project team was to establish a data model for the application. A working group was created, made up of the project manager, one IS analyst with a data base background, and one financial planner with stockbroking experience.

The group met for one full day a week for four weeks. For each session, an additional functional expert was brought in: marketing, international markets, futures, and income tax specialists all enhanced the team's understanding of stocks and bonds and of the services required by Bailis, Kronberg's customers.

At the end of four weeks, the group had prepared a one-page conceptual schematic of the data entities. This schematic depicted customers; contracts that these customers had signed with the firm to provide various types of services (stocks and bonds purchasing, money market accounts, portfolio management, dividend and interest collection, tax services, and so on); accounts holding the assets about which the contracts were signed; assets such as stocks, bonds, and options; and third parties involved in the various transactions, such as the person or institution from whom the stocks were purchased and the agents through which delivery was to take place.

Once this analysis had been completed, the team contacted the IS department of First Mechanics' Bank, one of the main business partners of Bailis, Kronberg. First Mechanics' Bank's IS department had recently applied data modeling to a systems plan for all the bank's loan systems (commercial loans, mortgages, consumer loans, and so on). The Bailis, Kronberg project manager wanted to cross-check the portfolio model with the model of a similar business problem.

The comparison was especially relevant because the customer bases of both companies were quite similar. Both had a number of individual customers and a few medium-sized corporations, who used the brokerage firm's services to invest their pension funds and had commercial accounts with the bank.

First Mechanics' Bank's team had made a much more detailed data model, with 150 entities (compared with the 15 or so in the Bailis, Kronberg model). The bank's data modeling project had taken a team of three analysts four months to complete.

The result of the comparison was that few discrepancies were noted. The major discrepancy was in the definition of a customer. Whereas the bank had considered a customer to be either an individual or a corporation (or similar institution), treating joint accounts as an exception, the brokerage firm considered individuals and corporations as entities that were neither customers nor suppliers (or third parties to the various transactions) and created "role" entities for them. For instance, an individual could have a customer role and a supplier role. The same individual might have a role as a sole account-holder for one account and as a joint holder of another account. In addition to individuals and corporations, trusts were established as a separate category.

The Bailis, Kronberg team was very satisfied with the comparison and felt that the model developed for the portfolio system was now anchored in solid, understandable concepts. The model subsequently served as a starting point for data base design in the various portfolio management subsystems that were developed over the following three years. At the end, despite some evolutions in the design, the management information system (the last installed) was able to benefit from the ease with which all the operations processing systems were integrated with one another.

First Mechanics' Bank also benefited from the discussions with Bailis, Kronberg. They were able to develop a high-level view of the data structure of the bank, which had hitherto been missing. This high-level view later proved useful in discussions between users and IS teams by resolving elusive vocabulary misunderstandings early in the development projects for demand deposit and credit card application.

PURPOSE OF SECTION

The purpose of Section V is to show how to create a data design for a computer-based application. A data design consists of a description of the following:

- The entities about which the application needs to maintain information (Chapter 13).
- The relationships that these entities bear to one another (Chapter 13).
- The specific elements of data that are maintained for each entity (Chapter 14).
- The integrity rules that the data should obey at all times (Chapter 15).

A data design serves three goals. First, it should enable the users of the application to understand the underlying structure of the information. Second, it should permit data base designers to implement this data structure to yield the right balance between high performance and flexibility. Third, it should constitute a solid foundation for the future maintenance of the application by embedding in its structure only those characteristics that are unlikely to change.

The data design constitutes a static view of an application. The user interface design and the process design depict the behavior of the application; the data design depicts its structure. The data design is therefore by nature more abstract, less implementation-oriented, than the other parts of the design. This abstraction makes the data design more difficult for clerical users to understand, but easier for top management, which tends to have a bird's-eye view of the organization and its systems.

Because data design is remote from implementation considerations, it tends to provide a longer-lasting foundation for applications than the design of processes. The structure of processes depends on contingencies—both technological (such as the typical batch file update process) and organizational (such as piecemeal clerical work). In the past, however, data design has been equated with data base design, and has, as a result, been affected by technological contingencies. Section V does not teach data base design. In fact, it attempts to avoid data base design considerations altogether.

The handling of data is the hallmark of commercial information systems. Transaction processing, management information systems, and decision support systems all rely heavily on the concepts of files and data bases. Conversely, the data structures used by systems software and embedded software (in space shuttles, weapons systems, or air traffic control) rely much less on files and records, and much more on structures such as arrays, queues, stacks, and sets. These structures are what computer science tends to deal with. As a result, much of what is taught and researched in computer science is not usable in information systems unless adapted and completed.

KEY TASKS AND DELIVERABLES

The approach to data design depends on the type of system being designed. Transaction processing systems use one approach; management information systems and decision support systems use another.

Transaction Processing Systems

Data requirements analysis is difficult to distinguish from data design. Data requirements analysis starts very early in the development life cycle; in fact, it is the basis for identifying systems projects in an information plan. It is performed in the requirements analysis phase as well.

If data requirements analysis is performed globally during **systems planning** for the entire organization or for one of its strategic business units, the output is a corporate or systems group data model. This model identifies the main entities that the information systems are likely to maintain data about.

In the development of transaction processing systems, the part of data design that occurs in the **requirements analysis** phase is relatively simple and global. The various entities that participate in the transactions are identified: What is the transaction about? Who supplies it? From where? To whom? To where? For what return? This analysis is either based on a subset of the corporate or systems group data models or developed from scratch by creating a preliminary project data model.

Until this point in the life cycle, the emphasis is on representing entities that the users of the system are familiar with and on indicating their natural relationships. Thus, this stage has a top-down approach. Only later are the contents of the entities and the precise nature of the relationships analyzed. This later stage is what is properly called data design and takes place in the design phase, in parallel with process design.

In **data design,** the two input data flows are the business functions and the preliminary project data model (entities and relationships) identified during requirements analysis. The activity of data design interacts with user interface design. The user interface designer needs to know which attributes are available and how they can be represented; the data designer needs to know which attributes are present together on screens, forms, and reports, and therefore need to be related.

The output of the data design activity is a finalized, detailed, normalized project data model. This model resides on a data dictionary in electronic form and on hard-copy documentation in graphic form. It details the physical representation of all the data elements and the users' views (not necessarily the physical representations) of the entities and relationships. This project data model then allows the data base designers to perform various volume analyses (data and transaction volumes) that will enable them to make the right physical data base design decisions. The project data model is independent of the data base management system (DBMS) used; it does not even assume that a DBMS is used.

Data base design activity, not covered in detail in this book, creates a logical data base design that represents the application programmers' views of the data base (also called the subschemas) and a physical data base design that represents the data base management system's view of the data base (also called the schema). The outputs of this activity become inputs to the implementation phase. The logical data base design becomes part of the programming specifications, and the physical data base design is used by the data base administration department to create the actual data base.

The flow of data design activity for transaction processing systems is depicted in Figure V–1, and the deliverables from the activity are shown in Figure V–2.

Management Information Systems and Decision Support Systems

The process of designing management information systems (MIS), decision support systems (DSS), or departmental systems is somewhat different from what was described above. For MIS or DSS, underlying transaction systems already exist and can supply the base data for the system that is being designed. These underlying transaction systems have a data model, either explicit or implicit.

If the underlying data model has not been formalized, the **requirements analysis** phase of the management information system under study must elicit it. The best method is a bottom-up approach, collecting documentation about how the existing transaction systems work—identifying data elements on files, reports, screens, and forms and building an entity-relationship model from them.

The **data design** phase in this case consists in ensuring that all the information to be delivered by the new system can actually be derived from the existing data models. New entities may have to be created by storing processed forms of the base data (accumulated data, data that has been properly cut off) or by adding new data from other sources (competitive or total market data, for example, which usually are not available from transaction processing systems).

If the MIS or DSS being developed needs to store its own data, the **data base design** activity would create the description of the new data base to be created. It is more probable, however, that data base design will consist of a number of requests to expand or modify the existing data bases in the underlying systems. Figures V–3 and V–4 show the alternative flow and deliverables for MIS/DSS.

Figure V–1 **Data Design Flow for Transaction Processing Systems**

Figure V–2 **Tasks and Deliverables of Data Analysis
for Transaction Processing Systems**

Phase	Deliverable
Systems Planning	Corporate Data Model
Requirements Analysis	Preliminary Project Data Model
Data Design	Fully Normalized Project Data Model
Data BaseDesign	Data Definition Language for New Data Base

Figure V–3 **Data Design Flow for Management Information Systems**

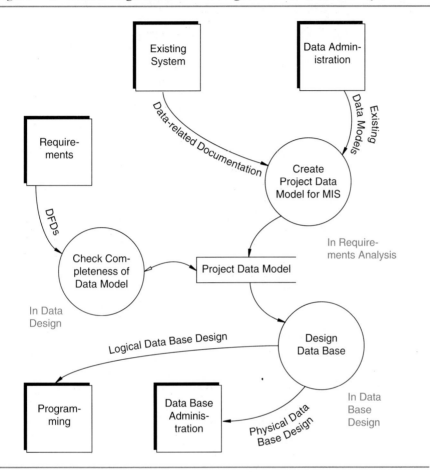

Figure V–4 **Alternative Tasks and Deliverables for Data Analysis**

Phase	Deliverable
Systems Planning	Corporate Data Model
Requirements Analysis	Preliminary Project Data Model
Data Design	Fully Normalized Project Data Model
Data BaseDesign	Data Definition Language for New Data Base

13

Entity-Relationship Modeling

After outlining the benefits of entity-relationship modeling and providing the definitions of the terms *entity, relationship,* and *attribute,* Chapter 13 describes the two possible approaches to the work. The first approach is top-down analysis, used mainly for data design in transaction processing systems. It consists of four main steps: creating the initial project data model, analyzing relationships between entities, selecting attributes to be included, and assigning these attributes to entities.

The second approach to entity-relationship modeling is bottom-up analysis, used mainly for MIS/DSS systems. It consists of three steps: analyzing the present system's forms, reports, and files; creating business function data models and user views from the existing data; and consolidating the user views into a final project data model.

In both approaches, entity-relationship modeling concludes with normalization: checking that the model conforms to a number of rules of good behavior.

Learning Objectives

- Delineate the scope of the data analysis activity, depending on the scope of the application under development.
- Analyze an initial data model to design the entities, relationships, and attributes that the users and the programmers of the application will know about.
- Update the data model to produce a final data model.
- Check that the final data model is fully normalized.
- Analyze the impact of possible future changes to forestall them whenever possible.

BENEFITS OF ENTITY-RELATIONSHIP MODELING

The key benefits of entity-relationship analysis, from management's perspective, are threefold. The analysis is a good vehicle for users to understand the system; it provides a more solid base for future evolution; and it reduces the cost of the system by eliminating the storage of redundant data. The net result is a more responsive system.

Information Modeling

Some have claimed that information systems are models of the world. They do not describe everything about the world, but they have enough of its characteristics that one can draw warranted conclusions about the world by looking at the model. (This is the very purpose of modeling.)

An example of such a model is a personnel data base. The personnel data base contains information about real-world entities (employees)—information that enables the users of the data base (the personnel department) to get answers to questions about those entities. In reality, when personnel clerks query a personnel data base, the only direct information they obtain is about the contents of the data base. The assumption is that those contents are an accurate representation of the real world that justifies conclusions about the flesh-and-blood employees.

The view that data bases are a model of the world applies to most management information systems. A set of accounts—balance sheet, profit and loss statement—is a model of the financial state of the business at the time the accounts were closed. (This example applies to both manual and computerized accounting systems.) Many so-called subject data bases are models of real-world entities such as customers, suppliers, products, inventories, employees, and so on.

In all of these examples, the data in the model may or may not be an accurate representation of the state of the world. The main objective of the whole profession of certified public accountants is to find out whether the figures in a set of accounts fairly represent the state of affairs. A data base may or may not be up to date: an employee may still be on the data base for some time after termination. A customer may not be recorded as a poor credit risk until bankruptcy has already been declared and the company has found out about it. It is always possible, in this type of system, to seek out independent confirmation of the data base content by going out and examining the real world that is represented (see Figure 13–1).

On the other hand, many modern transaction processing systems do not model an independent physical reality. For instance, in a computerized hotel reservation system, the main entity, the reservation, is totally abstract. Its only embodiment is in the system. No amount of searching of physical reality will reveal whether it exists and has such-and-such an attribute. The customer who made the reservation may believe that it exists, but if the hotel reservation system does not have it, the belief may not be justified. Just imagine what happens when a customer who believes that he or she has a reservation tries to check into a hotel that is already full (see Figures 13–2 and 13–3).

More and more systems are of this nature—a trend caused by the increasing integration of technology into the operations of the organization. More and more of the data manipulated by the system only exists in the system and does not correspond to a physical reality. As a result, in these systems, users cannot examine the records post facto to determine whether they are in accord with reality. The only way to determine the accuracy of the data is to look at the way the system works to see whether the control procedures guarantee that all transactions that should be processed are processed and to ensure that the processing is in agreement with the rules. Over the past decade or so, this technique has radically changed the way auditors work. The emphasis has moved from checking the figures on the balance sheet to checking how the figures were arrived at.

Figure 13–1 **Data Base as a Model of the World**

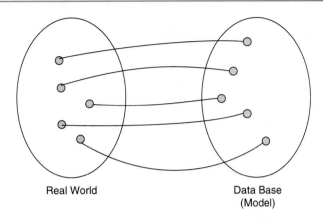

Real World

Data Base
(Model)

Figure 13–2 **Overlap between Data Base and World**

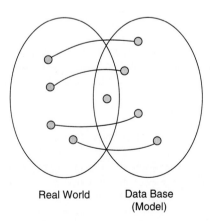

Real World

Data Base
(Model)

Figure 13–3 **Modern Trend: Data Base and World Are Intertwined**

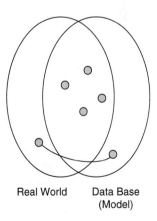

Real World

Data Base
(Model)

If the users **understand the data model** that underlies an application, two benefits are likely to result. First, the model is more likely to be correct than if it were established by an IS professional alone. Second, the users will be able to use query and reporting tools to generate the output that is the most appropriate for their purposes, thus reducing the workload of the IS department in modifying or creating report-writing programs.

An entity-relationship model also provides a much more **stable foundation** than an analysis of the functions performed within the organization. Functions can be organized more arbitrarily than data, in accordance with management's wishes of the moment. For example, whether customers have a single address to which goods are delivered or several addresses is not for management to decide. On the other hand, whether billing is done daily or weekly or whether the billing function reports to marketing or accounting is much more arbitrary.

The third benefit of data analysis is the potential **reduction of data redundancy.** In nonintegrated applications, the same data might be stored in several different files. For instance, product information might be stored both in a manufacturing system (for storing manufacturing cost information) and in the marketing system (for storing sales prices, terms, and conditions). A customer address could be stored in the order entry application file for delivery and billing and in the accounts receivable application for collection of delinquent accounts.

The problem with data redundancy is not so much the waste of space, but the inherent loss of control over the information. In some older systems, redundancy is not carefully controlled. Thus, a customer's change of address may not be posted at the same time in both the order entry and accounts receivable files. If the new address gets changed in both applications, nothing guarantees that the new data is the same in both: Murphy's law, applied to data, says that if the same data is to be stored in two different places, at some point that information will become inconsistent. It may then become impossible, or at any rate very difficult, to determine which piece of data is correct.

Data analysis helps reduce data redundancy. Even if data redundancy is required for performance reasons, data analysis helps reduce its impact by providing a means of anticipating inconsistencies and resolving them before problems arise.

ENTITIES, ATTRIBUTES, AND RELATIONSHIPS

The basic objects of data modeling are **entities.** An entity is some object that has a real existence and that is of interest to the system being designed. Examples of entities are Jane Brown; the Acme Window Cleaning Corporation for whom Jane Brown works; the route segment from New York to Dallas; American Airlines' 9:00 A.M. flight from New York to Dallas; American Airlines' 9:00 A.M. flight on February 29, 1992, from New York to Dallas; seat 17C on any airplane; seat 17C that Jane Brown occupied on American's 9:00 A.M. flight on February 29, 1992, from New York to Dallas.

Each of the above entities has properties or **attributes** that are of inter-est. Jane Brown was born on August 8, 1956; she is 5'7" and weighs 140 pounds. The Acme Window Cleaning Corporation is based in Irving, Texas. Seat 17C on a Boeing 727 is an aisle seat in the nonsmoking section.

Also, there are associations or **relationships** among the different entities that are apparent in the previous examples. The route segment from New York to Dallas is related to American Airlines' daily 9:00 A.M. flight. This daily flight is related to the actual instance of the flight on February 29, 1992. Another example is the fact that Jane Brown works for Acme. This relation-ship can also have an attribute: the position that Jane holds, for example.

As explained in the Technique at the end of this section, a relationship between two entities has a degree, or cardinality, at either end. For example, each employee holds one position and one only; a position may be held by one or more employees (or none, if it is vacant). Jane Brown occupies one seat and one only; she is the only one on her flight to occupy that seat..

Data modeling does not work directly with entities such as Jane Brown, but with abstractions such as employees, passengers, flights, and so on. These abstractions, called **entity types,** exist because similar information is recorded about similar entities. All persons have a date of birth; all flight legs have a departure and a destination; all employees work for some depart-ment and occupy some position. The rules for processing an entity type apply to all the instances of that entity. For example, all employees are paid; no flight leg can have the same departure and destination. Business systems are possible only because there are rules that apply across the board to all instances of an entity type.

An entity type is characterized by the **attribute types** and **relationship types** that apply to it. Attribute types and relationship types are abstractions of attribute instances and relationship instances. An example of an attribute type is the property "birth date" of a "person" entity type. An example of a relationship type is the "department to which an employee is assigned," where "department" and "employee" are entity types (see Figure 13–4).

Entity, attribute, and relationship types are at a higher level of abstrac-tion than the corresponding instances. There are many levels of abstraction. For instance, a flight leg from New York to Dallas is more abstract than the flight that took place on a given day and at a given time between those two cities, but less abstract than the entity type "flight leg."

Entity, relationship, and attribute types are described in the design of a system. Entity, relationship, and attribute instances, on the other hand, do not materialize until the system is operational. The test of the proper level of abstraction—type or instance—lies in whether general rules of processing apply. If rules apply, then the object is a type rather than an instance.

One difficulty is that many attributes and relationships can also be seen as entities. Many data modeling objects appear initially to be relationships but are revealed by later analysis to be entities. For instance, there is an obvious relationship between a part and a subassembly—the relationship of composition ("is made of"). An engine is made up of a block, pistons,

Figure 13–4 **Entity-Relationship-Attribute Model**

valves, a camshaft, and so on. It may be necessary to record attributes about a relationship, for instance, the number of valves and the number of pistons. The thing—apparently a relationship—about which these attributes are recorded is in reality an entity, although it is a very abstract one in this case: it might be called the "made-up-of" entity.

Other modeling objects appear to be attributes, but may also turn out to be entities in some other application. For instance, a street in a customer address appears to be an attribute, but for a municipal survey application, the street in question is obviously an entity. In most cases, these difficulties can be solved intuitively. However, intuition can be dangerous, because it is often an excuse for perpetuating hidebound thinking and shallow analysis.

In other words, although the rules of data modeling appear to be quite formal and susceptible to some degree of automation, there are many gray areas. Therefore, data modeling requires more judgment than is commonly assumed.

TOP-DOWN ANALYSIS

The two main approaches to entity-relationship analysis are top-down and bottom-up. The top-down approach starts from entities and relationships that are identified intuitively or from experience, then are gradually refined. The bottom-up approach starts from more detailed information, such as the data elements used by existing systems—on forms, reports, and computer files. Then these elements are grouped according to usage and affinity, so that entities and relationships fall out naturally.

Most of the books and articles on data modeling emphasize the top-down approach. Data modeling, especially in the early stages (systems planning or business area analysis) is usually performed by experienced personnel who try to shorten the time of the study as far as possible so that top management's commitment does not flag halfway through the study.

Figure 13–5 **Initial Project Data Model**

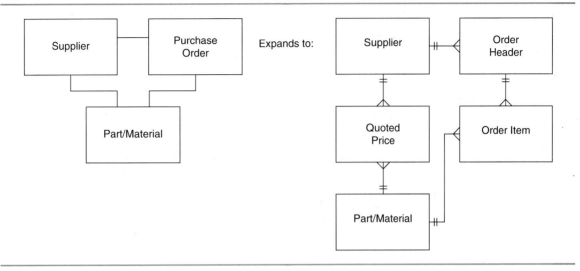

There are four steps in top-down analysis of an entity-relationship model: creating the initial model, analyzing the relationships in the model, selecting the attributes to be included in the model, and assigning these attributes to entities.

Creating the Initial Project Data Model

If a **systems plan** exists, it will generally contain a data model. As described in Chapter 5, this model was developed by considering the business entities and data classes required to support the business functions of the organization. This overall data model is generally documented according to the guidelines for entity-relationship models described in the Technique at the end of this section. Such a data model can serve as the starting point for entity-relationship modeling.

However, the global data model is usually too extensive. It is designed to meet all the data requirements of the entire enterprise or at least of a strategic business unit. The model must be reduced to the proper scope; all those data entities that are irrelevant to the functions covered by the application must be eliminated, which is fairly easy. The requirements specification is reviewed function by function, and the data classes required by each function are marked on the model. All those entities that remain unmarked at the end of this process can be deleted from the model; the result is the initial project data model. For example, in the design of a purchasing system, the corporate data model from Figure 3 in the Technique at the end of this section would be pared down as shown in Figure 13–5.

If no data model exists, then it must be created from scratch during the **requirements analysis** phase. Unless JAD is used, the best technique is to write a description of the business activity that the system will cover based on the scope statement of the project and the early interview notes. Data flow diagrams (DFDs) can also be used if they have already been established. Any noun in the description is likely to be an entity; any verb that denotes a state, such as is, has, belongs, is likely to represent a relationship or an attribute (a relationship if both sides of the verb are nouns, an attribute if one side is an adjective or a number).

Figure 13–6 is a written description of a purchasing system. It has much more detail than does the initial model illustrated in Figure 13–5: the written description contains attributes as well as entities and relationships that are not represented on the schematic. Thus, even if an initial data model exists, it is useful to enrich the extract by going through a system description and identifying other entities and relationships. Because the system description becomes more and more detailed and accurate during the requirements analysis phase, a project data model that conforms to the description is likely to be fairly accurate at the end of that phase. However, at this point, the requirement is to establish a starting point, not a final document; if errors occur, the rest of the analysis and design process will catch them.

As work progresses in the requirements analysis phase, the data model is developed in parallel with the DFDs, so that, at the end of the phase, the two are synchronized; there should be about as many entities as there are data stores. There are exceptions: a data store may store information about more than one entity type, and an entity may appear on the DFD in several different data stores. The appearance of an entity in several data stores is often justified by the fact that DFDs reflect the dynamics of the system, whereas the data model is more static. The DFDs may depict several successive versions of the same data (such as Orders Entered but Not Picked, Orders Picked but Not Billed, Orders Billed), whereas the data model contains only one (Orders).

Entities that are not stored in any data store are likely to be outside the scope of the system being developed and should probably be removed from the data model.

An initial data model for an application is perhaps even easier to establish in a group such as a **JAD session.** The session leader or recorder can draw boxes for entities and arrows for relationships as information is contributed by members of the group, correcting misunderstandings or imprecisions as they arise. The session leader asks questions, in particular on the nature and the degree of the various relationships that are being depicted: "Can a supplier have several orders in process simultaneously?" "Can the same part be supplied by several suppliers?" "What is the relationship between a part and a substitute part? If part A can substitute for part B, does that mean that part B can also always substitute for part A?" If the group is unable to reach consensus, the session leader elicits concrete examples and counterexamples.

Figure 13–6 **Description of a Purchasing System**

```
PURCHASING                       DESIGN TOOL                        CD-20
                               SUBURBAN PUMPS                       PDMDS
                           DATA MODEL DESCRIPTION


PREPARED BY: ANN LYNN          DATE: 12NOV93          VERSION: 2      PAGE 1
APPROVED BY: JACK CROFT        DATE: 15DEC93          STATUS:  D


Once a year, suppliers submit price quotes for parts for the following year. A
supplier is free to submit a quote for any part that is on the master parts list at
that time, but no late bids are accepted. The price quoted remains in effect for the
entire year.

When parts are required, the purchasing department locates the supplier that can
deliver in the time needed at the lowest price, grouping parts ordered from a single
supplier on a purchase order. (This process will continue to be manual, but the
purchasing agents will have on-line access to the supplier-parts data base.)

When the shipment is received from the supplier, the goods delivered are checked
against the order and any exceptions noted; the order is transferred from "Not
Received" to "Received, Not Invoiced." When the invoice is received, it is matched
against the receiving report on the "Received, Not Invoiced" order.  After resolving
any discrepancies, the order is transferred to accounts payable.

If an invoice is received before the shipment, it is held in suspense.

As soon as a shipment is received, it is summarized in a history file by supplier (for
timeliness) and by supplier/part (quality, price, and completeness of order).  This
will be used by purchasing agents when deciding between two suppliers who both qualify
from a price viewpoint.
```

Although there is a danger of the discussion ranging beyond the scope of the application, the group technique is very useful in systems planning. It is also useful early in the requirements analysis phase, when it may help adjust the scope of the project to cover more (or different) problems than initially planned.

During requirements analysis, the designers emphasize the identification of entities and relationships; however, they can also begin to enumerate the essential attributes for each entity. This early attribute analysis has two benefits. If the designers document user knowledge as early as possible, they will not have to return to the users with the same questions later. Also, considering attributes may refine the entity-relationship analysis. For instance, someone in the group may identify an attribute and associate it with one entity; and someone else, with another. This difference may signal the need for a

Figure 13–7 **Transforming Relationships into Entities**

new entity or relationship. For instance, if someone associates a price with a product (the normal situation) and someone else with a customer (a special rebate or a quote), there may be two price attributes—list price and quote price. A new entity such as a quote may be needed.

Analyzing Relationships

The previous steps of the entity-relationship modeling approach are best described as analysis. The next step, the first step of the data design phase, is the first formal step in the top-down methodology. Identifying entities, relationships, and attributes remains intuitive. Consequently, two different individuals using the method just described could come up with quite different results for the same problem. The analysis of relationships is the first step towards unifying the results and applying a real methodology.

The designer applies the following six transformation rules to the initial project data model:

- Any relationship that has an attribute is transformed into an entity.

    In the university/course/student data model shown in Figure 13–7, any student who takes a course will ultimately obtain a grade in that course. What appeared initially as a relationship between the student and the course (the static verb *takes* or *has registered* for indicating a relationship) becomes an entity. Naming this entity is somewhat problematical, as there is no English noun for such a complex notion, but a combined form such as Student-Course might do. Alternatively, the entity can be named to reflect the main information that it will contain, such as Grade.

- Any many-to-many relationship is decomposed into two one-to-many relationships.

    In the supplier-parts diagram of Figure 13–5, a supplier can supply many parts, and a part can be supplied by many suppliers. This structure is fairly common, but it would result in difficulties in any of today's

Figure 13–8 **Subdividing Entities into Subtypes**

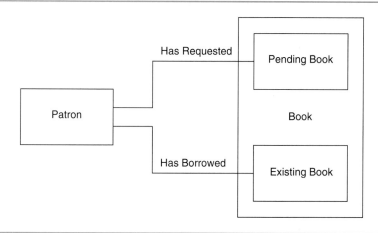

data base systems (as well as non-data base files). In this case, a supplier-part entity must be created. This entity type will have an instance (a record or row) for each possible part that each supplier can furnish.

It is quite probable that the previous rule, that of creating an entity for each relationship that has an attribute, would have eliminated this problem. The price quoted by two different suppliers on the same part is quite likely to be different. Therefore, the supplier-part relationship has "price" as an attribute and should be transformed into an entity.

• "Or" relationships are reduced by subdividing the entity into subtypes.

In the library example of Figure 13–8, either a book is owned by the library or someone has requested that it be purchased. This example indicates that there are in reality two subtypes of books, Existing and Pending. The two entity types share many attributes and many relationships, but some are distinct. In such a case, the designer should create a subtype representation where all the common relationships are on the outer box and all the distinct relationships are on the inside boxes.

Note that the concepts of subentity and superentity correspond to the notion of object hierarchies as discussed in Section III.

This inside-outside representation technique will not work if an entity is divided into subtypes according to more than one criterion. For instance, employees may be paid weekly or monthly; they may be married or single (significant for benefits processing). The two subdivisions are orthogonal, i.e., totally independent of each other. Some of the employee relationships depend on one of these criteria, some on another, and some are common to all employees. There are no hard rules for representing this case; two suggestions are given in Figures 13–9 and 13–10.

Figure 13–9 **Possible Representation of Multiple Subtypes**

The preceding examples concern the one-side of relationships. If an entity has two many-sided relationships that are mutually exclusive, a superentity on the one-side of the relationship can be created. For instance, in a bill of materials, a part is either purchased from any of several suppliers or made in-house. In that case, in-house plays the same role as a supplier for some business functions, and it may be opportune to create an Extended Supplier entity, whose instances will be all the normal suppliers and the in-house source. One of the attributes of the Extended Supplier entity (in reality of the Extended Supplier-Part relationship) might be the price if the company practices transfer pricing (an accounting system whereby all the goods or services furnished by one department to another are priced competitively with the market, and each department is free to purchase from or sell to the inside or the outside).

•   Optional relationships may be transformed by creating superentities.

An optional relationship (usually qualified as zero-to-one or zero-to-many) may be a variation of the subentity/superentity phenomenon. It may be that certain instances of an entity always have the relationship and others never do. In that case, if one of the attributes in the relationship indicates which is which, subdividing the entity may be possible. For instance, some loans may be secured by collaterals, such as a mortgage, and others not. Whether there is security depends on the type of loan—mortgage, home equity, guaranteed letter of credit, and so on (see Figure 13–11). From some viewpoints, all loans are the same; from others they are different.

Figure 13–10 **Alternative Representation of Multiple Subtypes**

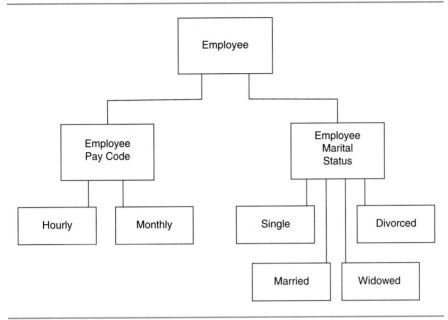

Figure 13–11 **Creating Superentities for Optional Relationships**

Figure 13–12 **Transforming One-to-One Relationships**

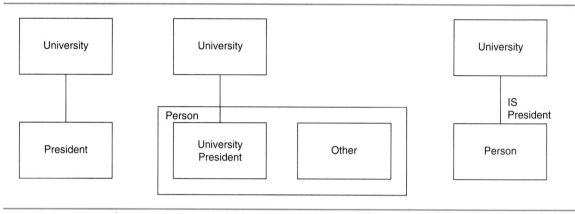

In other instances, the optional relationship may be accidental. At any time, each instance of the entity may or may not participate in the relationship. For example, in the library illustration (see Figure 13–8), some patrons may not have borrowed any books, and some books may not be on loan to anyone. These are legitimate zero-or-one-to-zero-or-many relationships.

- One-to-one relationships are examined for modifications.

A one-to-one relationship is an anomaly. If a relationship is truly one-to-one, then for every entity of one sort there is one and only one of the other sort. Therefore, the two entities ought to be collapsed into a single entity that combines the attributes of the two. For instance, for the relationship between a state and its constitution, most analysts would instinctively create two entities. A state is a geographical area, and a constitution, a legal document: the two entities are clearly distinguishable. From another viewpoint, however, each state must have a constitution, and no two states share the same one. In information processing, it is quite possible to consider the clauses of the constitution as attributes of the state rather than as an independent entity.

This example is farfetched. Very few business systems deal with constitutions. If they did, however, a system could deal with constitutions of countries as well as states. It becomes much less certain that constitutions of countries can be considered attributes of a country. What happens to a country such as the United Kingdom, whose constitution is not a single body of law but a series of acts and various customs and legal precedents? Could some countries not have a constitution? Or would some have two, for example, during a civil war?

In most cases, one-to-one relationships appear to be between two entities that have different natures, such as the relationship between a university and its president (see Figure 13–12). However, such relation-

Figure 13–13 **Sample Hierarchy: Taxonomy of Biology**

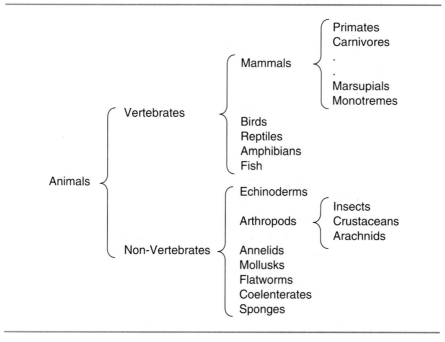

ships are really between an entity and a subset of some other entity. The quality of being a university president is not an essential one; rather, it is an attribute that a certain person holds at a given time. When a university gets a new president, the ex-president goes on existing but without the title of university president.

In practically all cases, a one-to-one relationship hides a superentity/subentity structure of some kind. It is safer to keep these one-to-one relationships as they are rather than to collapse the two entities and the relationship into a single entity, which may be difficult to uncollapse later.

• Some hierarchical relationships are represented with very specific techniques.

A hierarchy of entities exists whenever an entity (the *parent*) is related to another entity (the *child*) by a one-to-many relationship and whenever the child does not have any other parents. The child can itself be a parent of other children. A parent can have children of multiple types.

The traditional hierarchy representation is the tree diagram or Warnier chart (see the Technique for Section I). Examples are the taxonomies of biology (see Figure 13–13), hierarchies of menus (see Figure 10–16 in Chapter 10), the organization chart of an enterprise (see Figure 13–14), the bill of materials making up an assembly (see Figure 13–15). These examples have identical or near-identical entity types at the various levels of the hierarchy.

Figure 13–14 **Sample Hierarchy: Organization Chart of an Enterprise**

All these examples show a diagram of the entity instances rather than the entity types. For data modeling, other techniques are required to depict a single entity type that plays the dual role of both parent and child in a relationship. One solution is to connect an entity to itself, as in Figure 13–16. The relationship connector is of the one-to-many type, indicating that a parent may have many children and that each child has at most one parent. Another solution is to adopt the previous technique and transform the relationship of the entity to itself into another entity. This solution is appropriate when the relationship bears attributes, as in a bill of materials (see Figures 13–17 and 13–18). (Another reason a bill

Figure 13–15 **Sample Hierarchy: Bill of Materials**

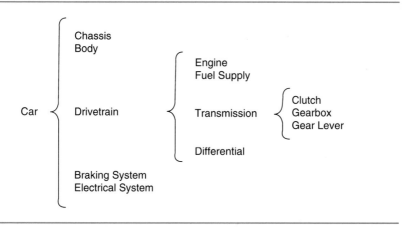

Figure 13–16 **Data Model for a Hierarchy**

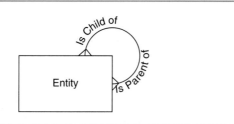

Figure 13–17 **Data Model for a Bill of Materials**

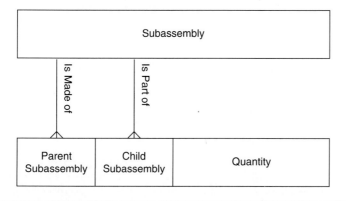

Figure 13–18 **Examples of Entities and Relationships in a Bill of Materials**

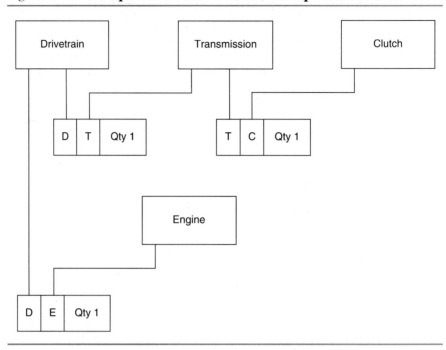

of materials should be represented as illustrated is that a subassembly may actually have several parents. For example, a nut, washer, and bolt subassembly may be used in several parts of an engine. The bill of materials is therefore not a strict hierarchy, as a child may have several parents. However, the data model representation can use the same techniques—either an entity related to itself with a many-to-many relationship, as in Figure 13–19, or a parent-child entity representing the relationship.)

Representing a hierarchical relationship by a parent-child entity has a twofold advantage. First, data about the relationship can be captured. For instance, in the bill of materials example, the number of parts of a certain type that enter into a subassembly can be indicated. Second, the data base designer will not inadvertently omit the possibility of navigating the data base in both directions, from product to elementary parts as well as from elementary parts to subassemblies and products.

The representation may seem somewhat artificial. It is certainly more difficult to understand intuitively than the other examples in this section. Thus, the technique is not appropriate for communicating with users. A much more appropriate technique for that purpose is the relationship between an entity and itself described earlier (see Figure 13–19).

Figure 13–19 **Simplified Data Model for a Bill of Materials**

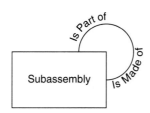

Once the designer has applied all these transformations, the data model consists of named entities and relationships that are, at worst, one-to-many. It is still in accord with the DFDs established during the requirements analysis phase. In fact, this whole process could have been part of the requirements analysis phase and can certainly be done independently of user interface design and process design.

Selecting Attributes

As the design has progressed, some preliminary work on data attributes has already been done. Now is the time to enumerate all the attributes of each entity completely. This step can only be accomplished with reference to the user interface and the process design activities. For each interface—screen, report, form—the designer assigns each data element to the entity that it characterizes. Then, for each process or activity, the designer checks that all the data logically required to obtain the output data flow is present as an input data flow or in a data store.

This approach is sufficient in many transaction processing systems that support clerical activities, rather than managerial, marketing, or professional ones. In other cases, there are two pitfalls to be avoided.

The first one is the inclusion of data that will not be used. Especially in marketing-oriented systems, there is a temptation to store information about a customer that might prove useful in selling, analyzing sales statistics, planning promotional campaigns, etc. Unless this information is actually used in taking orders, it will almost certainly become outdated. For instance, an insurance company might wish to store information about a policyholder's family, so as to propose new forms of coverage as the children grow older. However, in the ordinary course of paying annual premiums, the average policyholder will not report family events such as births and deaths to the insurance company. It is up to the insurance agent to maintain a relationship with those policyholders who may be of future interest. The computer application may help the agent by maintaining a sort of scratch-pad area in the policyholder file for the agent to note interesting facts. If the policyholder should change agents (as a result of a move, for example), the new agent would have to renew the scratch-pad area. This information is not guaranteed to be complete and reliable, and should probably not be used for personalized mass mailings directly to the customers.

Two criteria can be used to determine which data can reasonably be kept up to date:

- If an organization does not update a data element as a direct result of day-to-day business activity, then the value of that data element will become incorrect.

- If no person or application depends on the value of the data element to achieve a stated objective, then the value of the data element will become incorrect. If a data element on a utility's customer file is "profession" and is used only to derive statistics of electricity usage by profession, there will be a high percentage of incorrect "profession" codes on the file.

The second pitfall to be avoided is the inclusion of data that is not owned by anyone. If no one is assigned specific responsibilities for keeping the information on the data base up to date, the data base will become out of date. Each group of data elements on each record, each attribute of each entity, should be the responsibility of a specific individual within the organization. If the information is used by only one function, then the individual accomplishing that function is its owner. If several users or applications use the data, then one of them must be designated principal owner and take the responsibility for keeping the data accurate. Unless this safeguard is established, the data will become inaccurate over time. The risk of such inaccuracies is particularly high for subject data bases (see Chapter 5).

Most user departments do not view a file or a data base as a composite object over which control is shared. Therefore, the data structure may have to be presented to users as though each subject data base were divided into as many parts as there are functional groups responsible for maintaining it. The implementation may still be a single data base, but the users will have multiple views of it.

Assigning Attributes to Entities

The assignment of attributes to entities should be the most economical possible. In other words, no elementary application event or transaction should require a given element to be updated in more than one place. This technique will ultimately ensure the objective of minimum data redundancy. If a given event can update the same data element in two or more places, a situation will eventually arise where one place has been updated and the other has not, thus causing an inconsistency.

Two examples of how data redundancy might occur are useful.

Inheritance of a Modifiable Attribute. An order item must contain the order number (to group the entire order together in a single delivery), a

Figure 13–20 **Inheritance of an Attribute Value: The Unit Price**

Order #	Line	Product Code	Qty	Order Date
11764	01	751A	5	June 3

Product Code	Description	Price
751A	2" Widget	1.85

New Price:
1.79 on June 5

product code (to know which product has been ordered), and a quantity. Should it also contain the unit price of the product? If it does, the unit price has been *inherited* by the order item from the product.

The intuitive answer is that the order item should not contain the unit price, because it would be redundant information: the price is already recorded on the product data base in a product record. It is common information to all those order items for the given product (see Figure 13–20).

A deeper analysis would pose the question: What happens if there is a price change? Obviously, the product data base must be updated to reflect the change. But are current orders—not yet delivered, or delivered but not yet billed—affected by the change? Is the price change retroactive? If the price is guaranteed when the order is taken, then the price attribute of the order item is subtly different from that of the product entity. The price on the order is no longer the current price of the product, whatever that happens to

Figure 13–21 **Binding the Inherited Unit Price at Order Time**

Order #	Line	Product Code	Qty	Order Date	Price
11764	01	751A	5	June 3	1.85

Product Code	Description	Price
751A	2" Widget	1.85

New Price:
1.79 on June 5

Figure 13–22 **Binding the Inherited Unit Price at Delivery Time**

Order #	Line	Product Code	Qty	Order Date
11764	01	751A	5	June 3

Order #	Line	Product Code	Qty	Order Date	Bill Date	Price
11764	01	751A	5	June 3	June 10	1.79

Product Code	Description	Price
751A	2" Widget	1.85

New Price:
1.79 on June 5

be, but the guaranteed price for this order. It can only change if the specific guarantee represented by that specific order changes (see Figure 13–21).

Another possibility is that prices are those in effect at delivery date. Thus, undelivered orders should not contain the price, but orders delivered and not yet billed should (see Figure 13–22).

In all cases, any sales statistics data (for the MIS component of the application) must be based on the amount actually billed. This amount cannot change as product prices change but could change only as a result of the individual invoice being renegotiated with the customer.

A possible way out is to maintain a price history on the product data base, with each price accompanied by its effective date (see Figure 13–23). Then, the application logic could examine the date of the order, the date of delivery, and other fields to determine which of the multiple prices on the data base is to be used when printing the invoice.

This solution could be generalized to any modification of data attributes. The result would be the storage of the initial state of the data base together with all its modifications, each at the date at which it had occurred. Every time a piece of data was needed, the program could go back to the initial state and trace all the modifications to that piece of data. Although this solution is theoretically possible, it is hardly economical.

This discussion illustrates an important point. If the multiple versions of each price were to be stored, according to entity-relationship analysis canons, the price would become an entity and would be in a one-to-many

Figure 13–23 **Avoiding Inheritance by Storing Multiple Values of the Price**

Order #	Line	Product Code	Qty	Order Date	Bill Date
11764	01	751A	5	June 3	June 10

Product Code	Description
751A	2" Widget

Product Code	Effective Date	Price
751A	Dec 2, 1991	1.74
751A	Mar 6, 1992	1.85
751A	Jun 5, 1992	1.79

relationship with the product. Any other attribute that can change over the life of an entity could be processed the same way (see Figure 13–24). *Whether or not to do so is a totally arbitrary decision.* As a result, any attribute could potentially need to be isolated in its own entity. The difference between attributes and entities becomes very blurred.

Figure 13–24 **Storing Each Modifiable Attribute as an Entity**

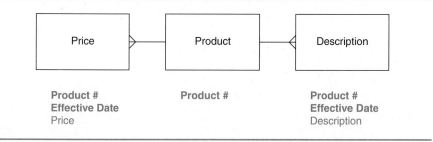

Price   Product   Description

Product #
Effective Date
Price

Product #

Product #
Effective Date
Description

Figure 13–25 **Storing Street as a Separate Entity**

Customer #
Name
Street Number
Geographical Location
   of Street
City
ZIP Code

**Geographical Location
of Street**
Street Name

Inclusion of an Attribute that Is a Noun, Not an Adjective. Redundancy might occur in another way. An address of a customer, employee, or supplier is usually considered as a single attribute or group of attributes, decomposed into street, city, state, zip code. The subdivision is mainly to allow the address to be printed on multiple lines. The street itself does not have any significance if taken without the city. It is obviously redundant to store both the zip code and the state, or both the address and the zip code, or both the city and the state. However, if the customer address changes, all of it changes at the same time. Never does the state change without a change of zip code and city. Nor does any element in the address change for several customers in the same elementary transaction. Or is this true?

After World War II, free municipal elections were held in France. Practically all the new municipal councils decided to honor one or more war heroes by renaming the largest streets or central squares. Left-wing municipalities usually decided to honor communist resistance heroes, such as Roger-Salengro and Gabriel Péri; right-wingers preferred Generals Leclerc and de Gaulle. Here is a case of an elementary transaction—a street name change—affecting multiple records in the data base. Conceptually, it would be possible to devise a data base where all the addresses on the same street used the same street name record so that a change of street name could be done in a single update. This issue does not arise in most transaction processing systems, because it is so exceptional and because the customer is usually responsible for a change of address.

In reality, we do not question that the street name is an attribute of a customer, whereas we could more rigorously consider it an attribute of a geographical location (see Figure 13–25), which is an attribute of a customer. This argument is not to encourage this sort of analysis on every single data attribute. Rather, it is to show that the data structure of a system is

Integrating Data, Text, Voice, and Graphics

This book covers only traditional data bases, containing formatted records of string and numeric variables. Many applications imaginable today would benefit from enriching the data base with other forms of information. For instance, an insurance company might like to have a data base with the data about a customer, his or her various policies, a textual description of a claim (such as an auto accident), copies of the correspondence exchanged, voice annotations made in the margins of the text by the claims adjuster, a map of the scene of the accident, and a picture of the damaged automobile.

Today, it is quite possible to store this kind of information on magnetic or optical media. There is a cost associated with the equipment required to transcribe the information—optical scanners and audio digitizers, for instance—and an even higher cost associated with the storage of all the bits required. For instance, a voice annotation of 30 words would require 10,000 to 50,000 bits of storage, whereas the same information in text form would need less than 2,000 bits.

More of an obstacle is that efficient processing mechanisms are not available to process the relationship between two pieces of data in two different forms. Algorithms are reasonably proficient at processing two-dimensional information, such as that found on graphs, maps, and other schematics, but even these algorithms are usually not available within data base management systems designed to process one-dimensional records. Very few robust algorithms are available that can relate the content of one form of representation (say, voice or image) to another (say, line drawings or numerical data). It is very hard for a program to know that the sound made when someone says "eight" is related to a figure 8 in a photo or to the binary pattern 00001000 in a record.

Most of today's applications of the integration of classical forms of data and richer types such as voice and image are therefore in office automation, which manipulates envelopes or objects without regard to the meaning of their contents. An electronic mail system is indifferent to the content of the messages passed from one subscriber to another. Each recipient of a message must interpret its meaning and its relationship to, say, another message from someone else on a different day.

determined by those functions and events that fall within its scope. If street name changes are forgotten in the scope, nothing serious is likely to befall the application. However, if price changes are forgotten or if the right questions are not asked about about how price changes are applied, something might be seriously amiss by the time the system is ready.

This example also illustrates the relative arbitrariness of the distinction between an attribute and an entity. A data element such as a street could be considered as either, depending on the functions or events that the designers consider to be of interest to the system.

BOTTOM-UP ANALYSIS

Bottom-up analysis is done either when the project is initially identified (during systems planning or during a feasibility study) or during requirements analysis. Normally, it is done in the latter phase, because it tends to be too time consuming in the planning stages.

Starting Points

The best starting point for a bottom-up analysis of data structures is the existing system, if one exists. If the analysis is done during a systems planning project, the best starting point is to look at the information on **forms and reports** that the organization exchanges with the outside world—suppliers, customers, employees, regulatory agencies, industry organizations, and competitors. The analyst can then list all the elements of information on the various forms and reports and try to relate them as attributes to the entities (people, organizations) with which the information is exchanged or to the entities (transactions) represented by the form (orders, invoices, payments). Interviews with middle management will help clarify the meaning of the pieces of information on the forms and their mutual relationships. As in top-down analysis, a useful question to ask is "How many Xs can Y have?" Another is "How can the value of X change?"

If bottom-up analysis is done as part of the analysis of a management information system, or of the MIS component of a transaction system, then the analyst should look at the transaction processing system's data stores (files, data bases) and at any existing management reports. In this case, the starting point is the **file and data base records.** The analyst can presume that each record represents an entity. If the file is a direct-access file or a data base, the name of the entity is probably closely related to the name of the key field. If the key is made up of several fields, the entity is probably related to other entities whose keys are the components of the composite field.

The analyst can also analyze data attribute (or data field) names. If two fields in two different records have the same or similar names, there may be a relationship between the two entities of those two records. Or the information may be stored redundantly, as in the case of the unit price stored both in the order file and the product file. If a field in one record has a similar name to a key in another record, there is almost certainly a one-to-many relationship between the record with the key and the record with the field.

If a record contains repeating fields, each repeating field is probably a separate entity. For instance, if a file contains one amount field per month, then there should be a monthly amount entity containing the month number (date) and an amount field. Even better would be to have a period amount entity, containing the code of the period type (yearly, quarterly, monthly, weekly), the identifier of the period (month number, week number, and so on) and the corresponding amount. If an employee record contains a list of deduction codes, then there should be an employee entity with a one-to-many relationship to an employee deduction entity.

Figure 13–26 **Business Function Data Model**

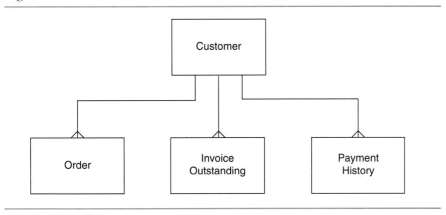

Reviewing existing management reports will probably introduce some new concepts. In particular, management tends to group figures into time periods and significant categories such as customer types, market segments, and geographical areas. Another added concept is that of trends—comparing similar figures for different time periods. In many instances, the patterns are seasonal, and the current period is compared with the same period of last year, rather than, say, this month with last month. Finally, many management reports eliminate the normal and focus on exceptions. This focus does not necessarily introduce new entities and attributes; it merely changes the emphasis.

The understanding that comes from reviewing management reports and management information needs does not necessarily add new entities, relationships, and attributes. It does, however, help the analyst focus on those that are important to management. This fresh perspective on the data will also be helpful in the user interface and process design stages.

Business Function Data Models and User Views

Data design can now proceed from the collection of presumed entities and attributes collected during requirements analysis. If the bottom-up approach is used for a transaction processing system, the designer now analyzes entities and relationships for each process box on the data flow diagrams. Each box represents a business function, and each uses data elements or attributes. For instance, a process such as checking customer credit typically requires the total amount of the order that the customer is trying to place, the outstanding balance, and a list of payment incidents over the past few months or years. This analysis should lead to a partial data model, called a **business function data model,** applicable only to the function itself (see Figure 13–26).

Next, the designer consolidates the business function data models of all the functions normally performed by one user (a single person or an entire department). The resulting data model, also called a **user view,** is a superset of all the business function data models. A problem can arise during this consolidation if there are contradictions among the various business function data models. Such contradictions generally indicate the presence of homonyms—pieces of data called by the same name by different individuals but having different information contents. In other cases, the designer may discover synonyms—the same data called by different names by different people.

One of the most difficult problems occurs when the existing systems and habits of the industry have created very general-purpose entities that hide the details. An example is the bank account. The word *Account* in a bank covers a multitude of different concepts. Each type of account usually corresponds to a particular product or service—checking, money market, loan, or trust, for example. Each of these has different processing characteristics, different attributes, and different relationships. In addition, accounts may have relationships between them. For instance, a loan may be guaranteed by assets that exist in another account, such as a savings account. The loan contract may specify that the amount deposited in the savings account should not be allowed to fall below the outstanding balance on the loan account. This clause is logically an attribute of the loan entity, but it is the savings processing that must enforce it. In such cases, it becomes absolutely necessary to strip away the general behavior of the entities and analyze each subtype in detail. Here is an example where bottom-up analysis is more likely to point out the right direction than top-down analysis.

Project Data Model

Once the user views have been documented, the project data model can be established by consolidating all the user views of the application and doing a top-down analysis of relationship degrees as described earlier. The end result will be the data model for the transaction systems that underlie the MIS or DSS being analyzed. In addition, there will be an analysis of management information requirements such as criteria for summarizing, accumulating amounts by periods, comparing periods for trend evaluation, and exception reporting.

NORMALIZATION

With either approach, top-down or bottom-up, the work done so far should have produced a structure of entities and relationships that obeys certain rules of good behavior. There should be no relationships of degree many-to-many; there should be no repeating groups; and each identified attribute should be associated with the entity that it characterizes in reality. No attribute bound to one entity should inherit its value from another entity through a relationship. For example, the unit price of an order item is inherited from the product entity only until the order pricing is definitively committed to. At that point, the unit price becomes bound to the order item and does not change even if there is a price increase on the product data base.

If this work has been done with sufficient understanding of the business area being modeled, the data model is almost certainly in normalized form. Although most authors consider normalization as a separate step in data modeling, we prefer to regard it as a result of applying common sense and rigorous analysis all along the process. It may be worthwhile to check that the data model actually is in normal form, however. It may be easy, especially for relatively inexperienced personnel, to overlook something.

The rules of normalization are set out in Box 13–3. They are expressed in the traditional form. As a result, they are better adapted to the process of normalizing a set of arbitrarily designed entities than to the verification of a data model established as described above. Each step of normalization corresponds to a normal form. For instance, after Step 1—the creation of a new entity for repeating groups—the data model is said to be in first normal form.

For verification purposes, these four steps should be followed:

• Check that there are no many-to-many relationships.

   This check prevents repeating groups of any importance. There may still be repeating groups of data within an entity, but there will be no other entity dependent on each of these repeating groups. In other words, the repeating groups will not carry any relationships. Avoiding repeating groups with relationships is most important to reduce redundancy and make maintenance and evolution easy. On the other hand, no great risks are associated with repeating groups that do not carry relationships. For instance, if a customer may have up to four different addresses, they may be stored with the customer entity as Address-1, Address-2, Address-3, and Address-4. Some addresses would be left blank for those customers who have fewer than four.

   A customer order can be used as a counterexample. At a high level, an order item could legitimately be considered as a many-to-many relationship between customers and products. Each customer may order many products; each product may be ordered by many customers. The risks of storing an order as a repeating group of lines within the customer, however, are great. It will in particular become difficult or costly to answer questions such as "Which customer has product so-and-so on order?" In addition, if each customer could have only one order at a time, the data structure would be different than if the customer could have several orders simultaneously. The data structure of the repeating groups in the customer record might even influence the design of the product data base. The data design would become too tightly integrated and be too costly to change. Enforcing first normal form in this example would eliminate most of these problems.

• Check for inherited attributes.

   This check consists in reviewing attribute names that are the same or nearly the same in two or more entity types. If these are true attributes (that is, neither of them is an identifier such as customer number, order number, product code, or social security number), a determi-

Definition of the Five Normal Forms

First Normal Form

A relation is in first normal form (1NF) if it contains no repeating groups.

Repeating groups are sometimes called multivalued dependencies. Each attribute must have a single, well-defined atomic value, not a set of several values.

Second Normal Form

A relation is in second normal form (2NF) if it is in. 1NF and all its attributes depend on the whole key; there are no attributes that depend on part of the key.

This definition only makes sense for entities that have a composite key. If the key is a single attribute, then everything that depends on the key depends on the entire key.

Dependence is defined as follows: if one attribute such as the key has a given value, then the value of the dependent attribute is wholly determined (at a given time). For instance, a unit price is dependent on the product code, not on an order quantity or a marital status.

Third Normal Form

A relation is in third normal form (3NF) if it is in 2NF and all its attributes are nontransitively dependent on the key; there are no attributes that depend on a nonkey attribute that in turn depends on the key.

This definition helps remove so-called hidden keys, attributes that appear as normal attributes in a relation, but that are in reality a key of another relation with a one-to-many relationship to the relationship being considered. An example would be the zip code and the city in an address. If the zip code is known, the city can be determined.

Boyce/Codd Normal Form

A relation is in Boyce/Codd normal form (BCNF) if it is in 2NF and all its determinants (attributes on which other attributes depend) are candidate keys (attributes that could have been chosen as keys).

This definition is slightly more stringent than the previous one. It introduces the concept of a candidate key. As we shall see in the next chapter, a candidate key is an attribute (or a set of attributes) that identifies a relation uniquely. In some cases, there are several candidate keys for the same relation—any one of them can be chosen. It is fairly clear that what has to hold for the key actually chosen also has to hold for every candidate key not chosen.

Today, 3NF and BCNF are usually considered to be the same by adding the word candidate wherever the word key is mentioned in the definitions of 2NF and 3NF.

Fourth Normal Form

A relation is in fourth normal form (4NF) if it is in BCNF and it incorporates at most one multivalued dependency.

The problem of 4NF would arise if a relation (before being reduced to 1NF) had two or more independent repeating groups, and only one relation, incorporating both repeating groups, were separated out into a new relation. Such a separation is so counterintuitive that most authors pass over 4NF; it rarely arises in reality.

Fifth Normal Form

A relation is in fifth normal form (5NF) if it is in 4NF and all relations with three attributes or more that cannot be decomposed into two

Continued

Continued

relations have been decomposed into three (or more) relations where possible.

For example, consider this company regulation: If a part used by a department can be supplied by multiple suppliers that supply some other part to the department, then that department must necessarily procure the part from each of those suppliers. The relation that says that a supplier *S* supplies part *P* to department D should then be decomposed into three independent relations, between *S* and *D*, between *S* and *P*, and between *P* and *D*. This example was inspired by Chris Date's *Intro-*

duction to Database Systems.[1]

In summary, 3NF is usually considered to be enough. In some cases (illustrated by the zip code/city example), 3NF is not ideal, and 2NF is better. Some data bases can even contravene the 1NF principle without dire consequences. Consider, for example, the case of China, where the overwhelming majority of families have one child and one only. It would be quite admissible, for efficiency purposes, to consider that the family relation should contain all the data about the first child; only second and further children would justify creating a separate record.

nation should be made as to whether the value of the attribute in one of the entities is inherited from one of the other entities. Inheritance occurs when, at the creation of one entity, some attributes are copied from another entity that already exists. For example, when an order is entered, all the characteristics of the product ordered as an item on an order line are copied from the product entity.

Inheritance should occur only at the exact time when the attribute value becomes bound to the inheriting entity. The product price, for instance, should be copied to (inherited by) the order item entity when the price is irrevocably agreed on. The color or weight of an order item should be copied as soon as the actual product is shipped. After that, the color and the weight can no longer be changed by an event in the order entry system.

- Check for redundancy of attributes.

    Attribute redundancy (the same value of the same attribute of the same entity stored in several places) occurs when a single event causes the same update to be made in several entities. The meaning of *same* here is the same attribute name, the same value before update, and the same value after update. For instance, if the event were renaming 6th Avenue to Avenue of the Americas in New York, this change would have to be made to all the places where the street name was, precisely, "6th Avenue" and the city "New York."

    If this type of redundancy is found, hidden inheritance may be the problem. To resolve it, a new entity type must be created from which the existing entities can inherit the value at the proper time. If the event that would cause such an update is too rare or remote from the application, it may be decided not to resolve the redundancy.

These two analysis techniques will check that the model is in second normal form.

- Check for derived data.

    In some cases, one attribute in an entity is a simple function of other attributes in the entity (or inherited by the entity). An example is the extended price on an order item, which can be deduced very simply by multiplying the unit price by the quantity. To store the extended price is useless and can indeed cause errors, because it can only change as the result of some other attribute (price or quantity) changes.

    In other cases, there is a more complex function. For instance, the monthly payment on a mortgage can be calculated from the principal, the length, and the interest rate. The base attributes are unlikely to change except in the event of refinancing or an adjustment in a variable rate at the end of a fixed period. Furthermore, the calculation is a resource-consuming one. Thus, it is legitimate to store the result, the monthly payment amount, even though it is theoretically redundant.

    Another case is that of the zip code. The zip code is strictly speaking a function of the city and street address, and there are publicly available data bases that can yield the correct zip code every time the address is printed. Again, the cost of doing so may be prohibitive considering the risk and cost associated with redundant data. The person or organization whose address is stored is perfectly willing to supply the redundant data every time the address changes.

The application of this analysis will ensure that the structure is in third normal form.

Ensuring that a data model conforms to fourth and fifth normal forms is not frequently a problem. Infractions against fourth normal form arise when there are two different repeating attributes in the same entity and both have been split out into the same separate entity (which is in a one-to-many relationship with the original, owning entity). If the designer has named the relationships so as to convey their business meaning, this infraction will not occur. Nor is it probable that violations of fifth normal form will occur. In fact, if the analyst thoroughly understands what the entities are, their behavior, their real-world relationships, and their patterns of change, the data model is likely to be fully normalized before checking begins.

A simple way to express that a data model is fully normalized is the following: Each attribute in an entity depends on the key, the whole key, and nothing but the key.[2]

Analysis of Probable Changes

The final step in creating the entity-relationship model is to consider the future. This step is generally omitted, because few IS development departments worry about creating maintainable systems early enough in the life cycle. However, from experience, change analysis is the single most powerful way to make maintenance easier. Change is inevitable, both in the world and in the systems dealing with the world. Thus, a data designer should anticipate changes to the designs, because these changes are far more likely to have a major impact on the system than a simple functional change.

Generally, files and data bases are shared by many users and many programs. It is more likely for many programs to need maintenance if a data base structure changes than if a single function changes. For instance, in 1988, there was a change in the formula for computing FICA withholding on employer-provided life insurance. This instance constitutes a logic change, not a data structure change. For properly built payroll systems, the modification was not difficult to implement. Implementing a flexible benefits program where none existed before would be much more difficult, because new files and new record types would be required. In many cases, programs that do not process flexible benefits at all would still feel the impact of the new data base structure.

If the designer can anticipate that a given change will occur, both the old and the new function can be built into the system and the actual change can be made with very little disruption. However, anticipating every change in this way is not possible. Furthermore, some changes are too remote to be worth the added cost of building them into the system. Nevertheless, those systems that have been analyzed and designed with change in mind are much easier to maintain.

Changes to the **degree of relationships** should be the main objective of the analysis of probable changes, not because such changes are frequent, but because they can be very disruptive unless planned for. Moreover, they are easy to accommodate early in the process.

A typical example is a system designed so that any customer can have only one order recorded in the system. This design might result in the order header information being made part of the customer entity. But the customer may need to place another order before the first one is delivered and, therefore, have two order headers. Or the customer might want delivery on part of the order at one date and another part at another date. If this is realized after the design is completed, the data structure will need to be changed radically.

The questions that must be asked when analyzing possible changes in relationship degrees are usually of the form: "How many Xs for each Y?" "Now?" "In the future?" The objects (Xs) are typically locations (delivery address, distribution depots, manufacturing locations, departments versus office buildings) or transactions (orders per customer, parts per supplier or per purchase order). The Ys are more typically persons or organizations.

A very helpful tactic for anticipating change is to **look to the industry leaders** to see how they are organized; if they are truly leaders, they represent the future direction of the industry. Another tactic is to look at other countries. Differences in legislation lead to different forms of organization. For instance, a few years ago, branch banking was the exception in the United States, the norm in Europe and Japan. Changes in banking law have made branches more and more common in the United States. Systems built in the seventies with the assumption that the U.S. banking industry might move to branch banking have been much more resilient than those that did not make the assumption.

The last approach to anticipating change is to **analyze what can cause changes:** management fiat, regulatory agency action, the economic environment, changes in human behavior patterns. These types of change are enumerated in the sequence of how easily the change can be made, not necessarily how easily a system can be changed to accommodate it. It is needless to justify expensive features enabling an application to change in order to accommodate a change in human nature or even a cultural change (such as computer literacy) that may take a generation to become prevalent.

Summary

Entity-relationship modeling consists in creating graphic representations of the data entities about which data will be stored and about the relationships between those entities. In addition, a list of the data attributes for each entity is created. This documentation (schematic and lists) is called a data model or an entity-relationship model.

In some cases, an existing corporate data model shows global entities and relationships without much detailed information. Such a model is a valuable starting point for creating an initial project data model during the requirements analysis phase. The initial project data model is suitable for communicating data structure information between analysts and users. The schematics are usually understandable without very much specialized competence.

In the absence of preexisting, higher-level data models, the analyst must build the project data model from scratch during requirements analysis. This work is often done in a group session, with middle-level user management as one of the key participants. Another approach is more akin to interviewing; the analyst collects all the documents that the organization exchanges with the outside world and identifies natural groupings of data from this knowledge.

In data design, the initial project model is refined by applying various analysis techniques to the initial model. Mainly, this work consists in making sure that all relationships are of degree one-to-many, if necessary by splitting or combining entities. Any exceptions to the one-to-many rule must be justified. Then, all the required data attributes are assigned to the various entities that have been identified.

The previous applies best to transaction processing applications. In MIS or DSS applications, bottom-up analysis is often more realistic. This has the benefit of formalizing a third level of entity-relationship model, the user view. The user view differs from the project data model in that its scope is reduced to that of one user or a series of users who perform the same functions. The user view is of most benefit in MIS/DSS applications, where different users usually have a greater variety of perspectives on the data than do the operators of a transaction processing application.

Because many systems built today have characteristics of both transaction processing and MIS/DSS, a combination of the two approaches is usually the best solution.

The analyst then creates a final project data model and checks it for adherence to third normal form. Any discrepancies are resolved or justified. Finally, the model is reviewed with respect to changes that may be expected to occur in the data structure over the lifetime of the application. If possible, these changes are reflected in the data model itself, so that should a change occur, it will be easily implemented.

The project data model derived in this fashion should have the following property: each attribute stored about an entity is truly a characteristic of that entity and that entity alone. This property eliminates data redundancy, with its attendant storage cost and risks of integrity loss.

Selected Readings

Practically all the books in this bibliography are primarily about data base design as opposed to data design, because data design has not been sufficiently recognized as a discipline independent of data base design. Data design must be done by people who understand the application; data base design must be done by people who understand data base technology. Only rarely do people have both qualifications.

Date, Chris. *An Introduction to Database Systems,* 4th ed. Reading, Massachusetts: Addison-Wesley, 1986.
> *This book is excellent, covering both relational and nonrelational technology. It is fairly technical, however, especially in Part Two. Recommended for a deep understanding of the issues of data design seen from the data base viewpoint.*

Gane, Chris. *Rapid System Development*. New York: Rapid System Development, Inc., 1987.
> *This book is written from a very functional, application-oriented perspective by one of the early proponents of data flow diagrams as a tool for analyzing processes. As a result, Gane maintains proper balance and perspective.*

Rock-Evans, Rosemary. *An Introduction to Data and Activity Analysis*. Wellesley, Massachussetts: QED Information Sciences, Inc., 1989
> *Covers data analysis, functional decomposition, and some data flow diagramming. This book is different in that it has a chapter on how to locate problems in the current systems and how to overcome them in the design of the new system.*

Martin, James. *Information Engineering*, 3 vols. Englewood Cliffs, New Jersey: Prentice-Hall, 1990.
> *This book is written by the foremost advocate of basing the analysis of systems on data structures, almost to the point of neglecting processes. Although lacking in balance, it is a good book on information engi-*

neering techniques, in particular those underlying some of the CASE tools on the market.

Finkelstein, Clive. *An Introduction to Information Engineering: From Strategic Planning to Information Systems.* Sydney, Australia: Addison-Wesley, 1989.

A recent book by one of the two creators of the Information Engineering concept (the other being James Martin). Finkelstein has created "Business Normalization," an interesting concept that is akin to object-oriented class hierarchies.

Inmon, W. H. *Information Systems Architecture.* Englewood Cliffs, New Jersey: Prentice-Hall, 1986.

Despite its title, this book is essentially about data design. It also covers process modeling, but in contrast to Gane's book, it is heavily inspired by data analysis. The book contains some nonstandard terminology and abbreviations, but once you have overcome the initial effort to interpret them, it has a wealth of interesting examples.

Shlaer, Sally, and Mellor, Stephen J. *Object-Oriented Systems Analysis.* Englewood Cliffs, New Jersey: Yourdon Press, 1988.

The title of this book is somewhat misleading; it has nothing to do with object-oriented design and programming as embodied in certain modern languages such as Smalltalk. It is, in fact, one of the only books that deals more with data design than with data base design. It has excellent examples of how to identify entities and attributes and how to analyze cardinalities of relationships.

Ross, Ronald G. *Entity Modeling: Techniques and Application.* Boston, Massachusetts: Database Research Group, 1987.

This book is one of the most complete about data modeling. Ronald Ross is also the editor and publisher of the Data Base Newsletter, *a periodical for both data designers and data base designers.*

Rumbaugh, James, *et al. Object-Oriented Modeling and Design.* Englewood Cliffs, New Jersey: Prentice-Hall, 1991.

Under the name of object modeling, this book has an excellent two-chapter treatment of advanced entity-relationship modeling. The rest of the book treats other aspects of requirements modeling and design as well as an introduction to object-oriented programming languages. The graphical conventions are nonstandard.

Review Questions

1. What is the difference between a corporate data model and a project data model? What is shown on each that is not shown on the other? Use examples to illustrate.

2. What differentiates the top-down approach from the bottom-up approach?

3. Is it always possible to dissociate a many-to-many relationship into two one-to-many relationships?

4. Draw an entity-relationship diagram for a family tree such as that established by a genealogist. (Use your own family as a starting point.) Are there entities that could conveniently be subdivided into subentities or grouped into superentities? How is the relationship of cousin represented? Is the model likely to change in the future?

Discussion Questions

1. Why is it difficult to analyze MIS needs in a top-down fashion?

2. In relation to the genealogy exercise above, discuss whether the cousin relationship can be seen as a user view. Show that a bottom-up design is more likely to have elicited the relationship between cousins than a top-down design.

3. Using group dynamics techniques, establish an initial data model (which can contain many-to-many relationships) for a business such as a local cable TV distributor. Consider customers, locations, equipment (decoders and remote controls but not the actual cable, which we assume has been drawn already), and suppliers (TV stations).

4. Group the class into two projects. Let one refine the data model using relationship analysis techniques. Let the other use the rules of normalization successively from 1 to 3 (4 and 5 will probably not arise). Are there any differences in the results? Discuss why or why not, as the case may be.

Mini-Case

You are an analyst for Condor Telephone Company. You have been assigned to analyze and design a new service order entry system for Condor.

Figures 13–27 through 13–30 are documents describing the scope of the new system and some of the functions to be performed. Initially, only the service order entry part of the application is to be implemented; service scheduling and billing will come later.

Question for Discussion

1. Create a complete project data model for the service order entry project. This model will include all the entities, relationships, and attributes required to perform the functions as described. When completed, you should check that the data model is in third normal form.

Notes

1. Date, Chris. *An Introduction to Database Systems*, 4th ed. Reading, Massachusetts: Addison-Wesley, 1986.

2. Kent, W. "A Simple Guide to Five Normal Forms in Relational Database Theory." *Communications of the ACM* (February 1983): 120.

Figure 13–27 **Scope of the Condor Telephone
Company Service Order System**

```
MARKETING                       DESIGN TOOL                          CD-20
ORDER ENTRY             CONDOR TELEPHONE COMPANY                     SCOPE
                        ORDER ENTRY SYSTEM SCOPE


PREPARED BY: DENNIS CASH        DATE: 27AUG88      VERSION: 1        PAGE 1   ·
APPROVED BY: J. MALINOWSKI      DATE: 05SEP88      STATUS:  F


The Service Order Entry System processes orders from customers to perform telephone
equipment and service installations.

There are six types of service requests:

     - new connect
     - complete disconnect
     - transfer existing service to new location
     - temporary disconnect
     - restore service after temporary disconnect
     - change to existing service/equipment

The most frequent case is that orders are called in to the Business Office where a
service representative (SR) takes the order. For existing customers, the SR asks the
customer for one of his telephone numbers and looks up the customer data. If a new
location is involved, the SR makes a note of it. (Each customer may have any number of
locations.)

If it is a new customer, all the relevant data (name, location, service request) are
first obtained. Before scheduling the installation, a credit check is performed. The
SR must obtain credit data, either from another telephone company where the customer
currently has or has had service, or, if the customer has never had telephone service,
other credit references such as charge cards, etc. The required data is obtained from
the customer over the telephone, and provisional arrangements are made for the
installation.

If the service is on existing equipment, the customer records are reviewed to
determine the exact location and complete description of the equipment being serviced.
```

Figure 13–28 **Order Entry Function Description**

```
MARKETING                        DESIGN TOOL                      CD-20
ORDER ENTRY               CONDOR TELEPHONE COMPANY                 FUNCD
                                 ORDER ENTRY

PREPARED BY: DENNIS CASH         DATE: 27AUG88        VERSION: 1    PAGE 1
APPROVED BY: J. MALINOWSKI       DATE: 05SEP88        STATUS:  F

Service Representatives will respond to Customer Service Requests by phone. To
initiate a Service Order, the following data will be captured:

     - Customer Data (name, address, historical data)
     - Service/Equipment Data (service type, equipment)

For existing customers, the Service Representative will look up the customer data
during the contact and verify that all the information stored about the customer is
current. Any errors will be corrected and reviewed with the customer.

For new customers, a temporary customer number will be assigned by the system, and the
Service Representative will enter all the required data.

This function must be completed before service and equipment charges are reviewed and
credit application information is obtained.
```

Figure 13–29 **Credit History Function Description**

```
MARKETING                         DESIGN TOOL                          CD-20
ORDER ENTRY                CONDOR TELEPHONE COMPANY                     FUNCD
                               CREDIT HISTORY


PREPARED BY: DENNIS CASH        DATE: 27AUG88       VERSION: 1         PAGE 1
APPROVED BY: J. MALINOWSKI      DATE: 05SEP88       STATUS:  F


For all new customers, credit application information must be
obtained. The following is needed over the past five years:

     - Address
     - Previous telephone service
     - Employer
     - Major credit cards

The system will generate a letter to any telephone company with which the customer has
had service, requesting a credit check.
```

Figure 13–30 **Equipment Inventory Check Function Description**

```
MARKETING                        DESIGN TOOL                      CD-20
ORDER ENTRY               CONDOR TELEPHONE COMPANY                FUNCD
                          EQUIPMENT INVENTORY CHECK

PREPARED BY: DENNIS CASH        DATE: 27AUG88        VERSION: 1       PAGE 1
APPROVED BY: J. MALINOWSKI      DATE: 05SEP88        STATUS:  F
```

When customer data and possibly credit data has been obtained, the following is done:

- For new equipment, inventory is checked to see whether the equipment is available.

- For existing equipment, the location and the precise nature of the equipment to be serviced is ascertained. This is particularly important where the customer has several pieces of equipment installed at the same location.

- All charges are reviewed: the one-time service charge, the charge for future services (such as a reconnect of a temporary disconnect), and the equipment rental charge in case of a new equipment or permanent disconnect.

The service charge varies by type of service and type of equipment. The charge for temporarily disconnecting a PBX is higher than for a residential telephone; the charge for reconnecting is smaller than for disconnecting.

14

Data Element Design

Chapter 14 describes the design of four different characteristics of data elements: names, data types, the use of data elements as keys, and the use of data elements as codes. In this part of the design, the methodology has no fixed sequence. The analyst can carry out the work in any order, although data naming should probably be carried out first.

What is critical is that data element design has to be performed by an analyst. It cannot be left to each individual programmer. Also, the analysts must observe great discipline in documenting the work. A mechanized data dictionary (see the Technique at the end of Section VII) is invaluable.

Learning Objectives

- Assign meaningful names to data elements.
- Group data elements in meaningful data types.
- Design the representation of data elements and coding schemes that users and programmers will be aware of, and ensure that this representation remains independent of the physical representation used on external data files.
- Use the coding schemes designed for users and other data elements to assign keys (identifiers) to entities in a manner consistent with data base design and user query and reporting requirements.
- Use tables to represent coding schemes.

NAMING DATA ELEMENTS: HOMONYMS, SYNONYMS, AND QUALIFIERS

A large part of the implementation effort of a system is devoted to programming. Whereas each programmer works alone on a single program or module, all the data definitions are shared by all the programmers. Therefore, good data-naming discipline must be followed. Data items—elements, groups, records, files—are named by analysts or data administrators in the data design phase. Most programming standards call for the programmer to use these names exclusively.

Poor naming usually results in three types of problems. **Homonyms,** the worst problem, may have an effect even on the design of the system, because it can be a major obstacle in communicating with users. In ordinary usage, homonyms are words that look alike but differ in meaning. In data design, the term refers to using the same name for two pieces of data that are in reality different. Homonyms may occur when one department adopts a technical term as a shortcut and another department uses the same term, or a very similar one, to mean something different. For instance, the arrival date of a shipment in a data base that tracks shipping history with various transport firms might in fact consist of several dates: arrival of ship in harbor, release of goods from customs, or availability in the warehouse. If these three dates were in fact used by different departments and possibly stored in different entities, the homonym problem (ARRIVAL_DATE meaning three different things) would be severe.[1]

Homonyms can also cause problems when an attribute is the identifier or key of an entity and at the same time is used in another entity to implement the relationship between the two. For instance, a supplier number might appear in a purchase order entity and in the supplier entity. These two attributes have the same type. They do not have quite the same meaning, however. In the supplier entity, the supplier number means "identifier of the entity to which all the attributes in this entity apply." In the purchase order, it means "identifier of the supplier who placed the purchase order that is identified by the purchase order number elsewhere in this entity."

Once a case of homonyms has been found, the problem is solved by qualifying the data names, i.e., by appending to the common name a word or phrase that is different for each homonym. For example, the three arrival dates in the transportation example could be named HARBOR_ARRIVAL_DATE, CUSTOMS_ARRIVAL_DATE, and WAREHOUSE_ARRIVAL_DATE. The usual technique is to put the qualifier first and the common part last. The qualifier often refers to the entity in which the data element resides: for instance, in the supplier and purchase order example, the name for the two versions of the supplier number might be ORDER_SUPPLIER_NO and SUPPLIER_NO.

Another problem is **synonyms.** Synonyms are two different names for the same thing. The problem is much less serious than homonyms. However, some discipline is required to make sure that all synonyms, or aliases, are recorded in the data dictionary. When maintenance is performed on a data element that has synonyms, it is necessary to search for uses of both the primary name and the synonym within the system to make sure that all the possible consequences of a modification to a data item have been evaluated.

Very often, especially in old programs, data names are difficult to understand because of **excessive abbreviation.** Part of the reason is that early programming languages were limited to eight-character names. In addition, most programmers do not care to use long names, which are time consum-

Figure 14–1 **Frequently Used Data Name Abbreviations**

ACCR	Accrual; Accrued	INVC	Invoice
ACCT	Account; Accounting	INVN	Inventory
ACCUM	Accumulated	MO	Month
ADDR	Address	MTD	Month-to-Date
AMT	Amount	NO	Number
BAL	Balance	ORD	Order
BOM	Bill of Materials	PO	Purchase Order
CGR	Compound Growth Rate	PROD	Product
CLI	Client	QTY	Quantity
CO	Company	RECD	Record
CORP	Corporation; Corporate	RECV	Received; Receiving
CR	Credit	SEQ	Sequence
CUM	Cumulative	SER	Serial
CUST	Customer	SUPP	Supplier
DEPT	Department	TRANS	Transaction
DIV	Division	WK	Week
DT	Debit	YR	Year
EMP	Employee	YTD	Year-to-Date
FYE	Fiscal Year End		

ing and error-prone. Some IS departments even impose the use of abbreviations because of the data entry cost associated with long names!

The arguments against verbosity and length are still valid to some extent. Most programming standards acknowledge, however, that the value of explicit naming more than makes up for the cost. As a compromise, a set of standard abbreviations is often agreed on; this solution encourages brevity without sacrificing clarity. A sample list of abbreviations is given in Figure 14–1.

The best solution for all these problems is to give the responsibility for naming standards (or even for the actual naming) to a special section within the IS department, called **data administration.** On large projects, a data administrator may be assigned full time during the data design phase of a project. In smaller departments or on smaller projects the function of data administrator is usually performed by one of the analysts part time. In no case should individual programmers be given the freedom to name data elements.

The coordination of data naming should be ensured by a single individual or a closely knit group, such as data administration. Coordination can prevent problems not only within the system being developed, but also in future, related systems.

DATA TYPE ANALYSIS

Data type analysis can help prevent maintenance problems because it promotes *data hiding.* The principle of data hiding is that the user of any data element should have to make as few assumptions as possible about how the data element is represented in memory or on disk. The user, whether a person or a program, should be concerned with the meaning of the data, not with its form. Unnecessary information about the data should be hidden.

Definition of Data Types

A data type is a class of data items that is homogeneous enough that all the data items of the type support the same operations. This concept of data types originated because the primitive data processing operations, those that are built into the hardware or the programming language, are constrained to work on data items that are homogeneous. For instance, it is possible to compare two variables containing numbers, perform arithmetic operations on them, and assign them new values. Assignments and comparisons may also be performed on text variables.

Another way to say that two data attributes are of the same type is to say that they have the same domain of values. This definition of a data type is slightly less powerful than the previous one. It is important, however, to specify the domain of each data type in the data model.

The following two examples illustrate the problem of incompatible data types. First, if an employee file contains the social security number of each employee stored as a number with nine digits, the hardware would allow a program to add the social security numbers of two employees and store the result. (An additional digit might be needed to accommodate a possible carry.) Most programming languages would also allow this addition. However, the result of this addition has no meaning whatever. The semantics of the application (payroll, personnel, or other) do not contain an addition operation on social security numbers.

The second example is the comparison of two fields, such as a name and a street address, that appear to have compatible types. Both are alphanumeric; in a given application, they might have the same length, say 30 characters. But to compare them, although possible from a syntactical viewpoint, makes no sense. What difference would it make to a user to know whether a customer has a street address that is the same as the customer's name?

As shown in these examples, data type analysis consists in identifying those attributes that will support the primitive operation of comparison. Two data attributes that may have the same values or that have values that can be ranked as greater or less than each other are of the same type.

If two attributes can be compared, then the contents of a variable of the type of the attribute can generally be moved into another variable of the same type. This operation is called assignment.

If the data type is numeric, then arithmetic operations may possibly be defined on it as well. As the social security number example above showed, this possibility is not as evident as one might think at first. The term *numeric* does not always mean that the variable represents a number of things, an amount, or a quantity. The term quite often refers to a variable that is arbitrarily constrained to taking on only a subset of all the possible characters in a representation scheme.

Examples of Data Types: Date

Type analysis makes no assumption whatever about how data will be represented on files, screens, forms, and reports. Thus, for example, a date is a date, regardless of whether it is represented in any of the following forms:

*   January 15, 1980

*   15 January 1980

*   15JAN80

*   1-15-80

*   80015

*   15/1/1980

Date is a data type according to the definition used above. Two dates, regardless of their functional significance (date of birth, delivery date) can always be compared to see which one comes first. How a program would compare dates depends on the representation chosen. The result, however, is independent of this representation. January 15, 1980, always precedes January 13, 1981, even if the program had to deal with 1-15-80 and 81013.

Other frequent data types are listed in Figure 14–2. Most of these are simple data types that cannot be further decomposed. Entity identifiers, codes, and quantity or amount fields are typical examples. Some data types are complex; they are made up of more elementary data types. For instance, a date can be decomposed into year, month, day within the month, day counted since the beginning of the year, day of the week. Is a year a date? Whenever the precision required by the application is a year, then it could be considered a date. Is a month a date? Yes, if it is accompanied by a year and the precision is a month. The same reasoning applies to days within months. Every year, April 15 is the IRS income tax filing deadline. The data type of April 15, however, is not a date, because it is not clear which April 15 is referred to. April 15 without a year cannot be compared with January 15, 1990.

Thus, there can be several subtypes of date according to the precision desired. Comparison operations can be extended, provided an appropriate meaning is assigned to "equality" between two dates with different precisions. Conventionally, October 1988 might be considered to be equal to, or at least compatible with, October 2, 1988.

Time is an example of extending the precision of date. If the precision of an application demands that events be timed to the hour, minute, or second, then the date (year, month, day) is no longer enough; the time needs to be added. An example of a date in this case might be January 15, 1980, 10:55.7546 A.M., GMT. This date is equal to January 15, 1980, 2:55.7546 A.M., PDT.

Figure 14–2 **Frequently Used Data Types**

Type	Operations Available	Notes
Address	Assign, Compare =	Complex
Amount	Assign, Compare >, <, +, −	Precision must be indicated
Color	Assign, Compare =	Enumeration
Corporation Name	Assign, Compare =	Text
Date	Assign, Compare >, <	Math with Duration
Dimension	Assign, Compare >, <	Math if same unit
Duration	Assign, Compare >, <, +, −	See Date
Frequency	Assign, Compare =	Enumeration
Identifier or Key	Assign, Compare =	Only if same entity type
Period	Assign, Compare =	Complex (2 Dates)
Person Name	Assign, Compare =	May be complex
Precision	Assign, Compare =	Used with Amount, Price. . .
Price	Assign, Compare >, <	Math with Quantity
Quantity	Assign, Compare >, <	Math if same unit
Rate	Assign, Compare >, <	Math with Duration
Size (Surface)	Assign, Compare >, <	Math if same unit
Speed	Assign, Compare >, <	Math with Duration
Time	Assign, Compare >, <	Math with Duration
Unit	Assign, Compare =	Used with Size, Volume. . .
Volume	Assign, Compare >, <	Math if same unit
Weight	Assign, Compare >, <	Math if same unit

The following examples illustrate typical complex data types:

- Names—first, middle, and last names.
- Addresses—number, street, city, state (or other geographical subdivision), zip code (or other postal code), country.
- Periods—start date and end date.
- Weights—a code representing the unit (pounds, ounces, grams, metric tons, etc.) and the quantity expressed in that unit.
- Amounts—currency code plus amount in that currency.

Defining Operations on Data Types

For any data type, comparison and assignment are always permitted. Other operations have more complex rules. Usually, mathematical operations such as addition and subtraction are available for many numeric data types, but not for all. Also, the operations of addition and subtraction may be defined in various ways for different types. Here are some examples of difficulties and ways to resolve them:

- Two quantities or amounts can only be added directly if they use the same unit of measure. A weight of two ounces cannot be added to a length of two yards. A weight of two ounces can be added to a weight of two pounds only if both numbers are converted to a common unit. A number of nails cannot be added to a number of machine tools. However, the dollar cost of a pound of nails *can* be added to the dollar cost of a machine tool. But if one of the cost figures is expressed in pounds sterling and the other in yen, the amounts cannot be added without prior conversion.

- A date can be subtracted from another date to yield a duration. This duration can be expressed in years, months, weeks, down to milliseconds, depending on the required precision.
- A duration can be added to a date to yield another date.
- Two durations can be added to yield another duration. A period, defined as the time elapsed between a start date and an end date, has the same unit of measure as a duration. However, two periods cannot be legitimately added unless the definition of the addition operation contains an explanation of how the addition is to be made for two periods that are not consecutive.
- A quantity can be multiplied by a unit price to yield a total cost, by a unit cost to yield total cost, by a unit weight to yield total weight, and so on. A rate or speed can be multiplied by a duration to yield total distance, output, or another result.
- Numbers that are in reality a ratio, such as unit price, rate, or speed, cannot be added. Neither can averages be added. (It is useful to remember elementary mathematics.)
- Nonnumeric data (such as names, addresses, text) and numeric data that does not represent quantities (such as entity identifiers and codes) cannot be added, subtracted, or multiplied. Other interesting operations may be defined on them. An example is concatenation, the stringing together of two partial texts to make up a longer text, often done with elementary fields such as title, first name, middle initial, a period, and last name to arrive at a single name field for printing on an envelope.
- Some attributes can require a null value, as in optional attributes. For instance, an employee file might have an attribute for storing the kind of discharge that each employee has received from the armed services. This attribute would be null for all those who had never served. Unfortunately, the term *null values* can have other meanings: does not exist, does not apply, do not know, do not care, not assigned yet, and so on. It is important to inventory all these meanings and describe the possible values of the data type accordingly.
- Multicurrency systems have to take into account the variability of the conversion factors over time. Whereas the ratio of an inch to a millimeter is constant, the ratio of the Swiss franc to the dollar is not. In many cases, currency translations must use the exchange rate in effect on the date of the transaction, which must therefore be known. If the conversion concerns the amount of an asset or a liability, the rate at the time of

translation is usually used. For accounting purposes, this time means the closing date, e.g., December 31, rather than the date at which the translation was performed, perhaps some time in February.

Documentation Requirements for Data Types

The results of the data type analysis is a document or an entry into a data dictionary containing for each data type:

- The name.
- The description.
- The domain (including null values).
- The different representations on files (usually one form only), input (usually one form only, the shortest possible), and output (several forms, in particular if there are several possible precisions or if there is a need to conserve space on certain media).
- The operations—arithmetic or other—that can be performed on the type (including the notions, if any, of sequence or order).
- The restrictions, if any, on those operations (such as adding quantities only if the product codes are the same).
- The elementary data types that make up a complex data type.

If the type is a coding scheme where all the possible values are known, these values have to be specified. For example, the data type "day of week" is described as Sunday, Monday, Tuesday, Wednesday, Thursday, Friday, Saturday. An addition operation can be defined on this code: adding one day transforms a "day of week" into its successor (by definition, the first element, Sunday, is the successor of Saturday). A comparison operation yielding either equality or inequality can also be defined.

In many cases, some of the data types that are required for a new application already exist. This is almost universal when the system being designed is a management information system or a decision support system that builds on some existing transaction system or when the system is designed to replace or extend an existing computer-based system. Even in these cases, the existing data description may need to be modified to make the definition more precise, to add new representation formats, or to extend the domain (see the Technique at the end of this section).

Once all the required data types exist on the dictionary, the entity descriptions can be completed. Each attribute of an entity must have the following elements:

- Attribute name (a composite name usually containing the type name as one component).
- Data type name, pointing to all the data type characteristics.
- Additional definition.

- Representation (if the data type allows more than one).
- Unit of measure and precision (if the data type allows more than one).

KEY ANALYSIS

An important design step is the choice of data elements to be used as keys to an entity.

Purpose of Key Analysis

The key can have one of the following three objectives:

- To ensure that each instance of an entity can be uniquely identified and differentiated from any other instance of the same entity type.
- To implement relationships between two entities by storing the key of a parent entity in a child entity.
- To indicate to the data base management system (DBMS) that the data element is likely to be used as a search argument to retrieve specific instances of the entity.

An entity type really represents a set, in the mathematical sense, of entity instances—all the employees of an organization or all the customers of a business, for instance. In set theory, every member of a set must be distinguishable from every other member. The use of a key is the most frequent way of guaranteeing **uniqueness** in a data base or file.

The idea is to create a key attribute and assign it a different value for each instance of the entity. Two people might have identical attributes on the personnel file of an organization. Two Edward Kennedys, both graduates from Northwestern University, might be hired by the same CPA firm on the same day. They might even have been born the same day. One might be squat and the other lanky; one might have blue eyes and the other brown, but these attributes would not be on file. A distinct employee number for each would guarantee that the two would look as different to any computer program as to friends and colleagues.

The second reason to use key attributes is for the **implementation of relationships** in relational data base systems. Two entity instances that have a relationship between them, such as a customer and all the orders of that customer, must have attributes that can be related uniquely. Thus, an order can be associated with only the customer who placed it. A reasonable way to relate the two is to store the customer number of the owner of the order in the order entity (see Figure 14–3). A data element used in this way is called a *foreign key*—the customer number stored in the order entity is a key of another, or foreign, entity.

Foreign keys are not the only way that relationships can be stored. Any functional relationship between two attributes can be used as well. For instance, a fiscal year entity might have as attributes the first and last dates of

Figure 14–3 **Relationship Implemented by Foreign Key**

Customer #
Name
Address
Category
. . .

Order #
Customer #
Date
Delivery Date
. . .

the fiscal year. These dates would be especially useful for companies that close their accounts on a date other than December 31. An accounting entry or other transaction can be related to its fiscal year by determining whether the date of the transaction falls between the two dates of the fiscal year (see Figure 14–4). (A code indicating the fiscal year could also be stored with the transaction, which could then be used as a key to the fiscal year entity.)

The third important reason for keys is that data base management systems often assume the existence of an identifying key and use it for efficient **data retrieval.**

Because uniqueness, implementation of relationships, and data retrieval can all be achieved through the use of keys, a great deal of confusion reigns about key design. However, each requirement can be met by other means as well:

- Uniqueness can be ensured by making certain that a combination of attributes of an entity—maybe all of them—make up a unique relation. (Some micro-based systems do this, in particular Rbase.) In addition, some entities could easily be assigned any one of a number of attributes as a key—employee number, social security number, or, in a futuristic vein, fingerprint characteristics.

- Relationships can be evaluated by relating attributes rather than keys or by using so-called pointers (a nonrelational technique).

- Direct access to a record can be achieved without keys or with nonunique keys. Also, attributes that are not the primary or identifying key can be used as access keys (sometimes called secondary keys). In fact, identifying keys and access keys are nearly totally independent, at least from a logical standpoint.

The access key is properly a concern for physical data base design and thus will not be discussed further in this book. In most modern data base management systems, the access keys can be changed with very little impact on applications and files. Usually, only performance is affected.

Figure 14–4 **Relationship Implemented by a Processing Rule**

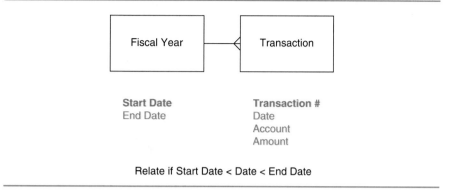

Relate if Start Date < Date < End Date

Choosing the Identifying Key

The choice of an identifying key for an entity is usually fairly simple. The main entities within an organization already have unique keys associated with them, and there are usually many good reasons for not changing them.

If keys need to be selected for the entities in the project data model, one of the simplest and best solutions is simply to remember that an identifying key is an identifier, nothing more. *The value of the key must be unique for each instance of the entity, and it must not change over the life of the instance that it identifies.* These two criteria are easy to fulfill if the key is a simple **serial number.** In fact, some authors, in particular E. F. Codd, advocate that serial number keys, which he calls *surrogates*, be the only type of key allowed and that the DBMS be made responsible for assigning and managing all such keys.

Other techniques are possible, however. Most of them are used in a large number of installations. Two of the techniques have few problems: they are both based on concatenating a key with another attribute. A third technique, which should be avoided, consists in using a composite key with meaningful attributes.

A frequent situation is when a one-to-many relationship exists between a parent entity and a child entity, especially when the child is created by splitting out multiple occurrences of a data group (to reach first normal form). For example, a customer may have several locations where goods can be delivered. There is a strict one-to-many relationship between the customer and the location: each location must belong to one customer and only one.

The most usual (and economical) technique for designing a key for the child entity is to give the child the **parent key with a sequence number.** In the customer location example, the key of the location would be the customer number with a location number appended to it. Thus, each customer would have locations numbered from 1 to N; the uniqueness would still be ensured by the fact that no two locations would have both the same location number and customer number (see Figure 14–5).

Figure 14–5 **Key Constituted by Parent Key with Sequence Number**

Customer #
Name
Category

Customer #
Location #
Address

There are only two types of difficulties caused by this technique. First, the technique fails if the relationship is an optional one on the parent side. If a location could belong to no customer (or have a null customer number, meaning "not applicable," "do not know," or "do not care"), there would be a high risk of nonuniqueness as well as of later changes in the key value. Moreover, null values in the key are against the rules for most data base management systems. The solution here is to assign serial number keys, or surrogates, to both entities.

Second, a location could be sold or transferred to another customer, and thus, the key could conceivably change. For instance, a fast-food restaurant might transfer from one franchise to another and still be operated by the same operator. There are two solutions. The transfer can be considered as two separate transactions: one transaction deletes the location from one customer, and another transaction adds it to the other customer. Or the location entity could be assigned a unique location key that does not contain the customer number.

The next valid technique for concatenating keys, an extension of the previous technique, can be used when the entity in question has a child relationship to two other entities. This is frequently found when the entity to be identified started life as a relationship, until it was discovered that it had

Figure 14–6 **Key Constituted by Concatenated Keys of Parents**

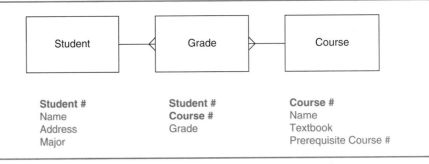

Student #
Name
Address
Major

Student #
Course #
Grade

Course #
Name
Textbook
Prerequisite Course #

Figure 14–7 **Example of a Composite Key: Automobile Serial Number**

```
FLEET SYSTEM                        DESIGN TOOL                          D072
ALL SUBSYSTEMS                     SUBURBAN PUMPS                        GPDEF
                  GROUP DEFINITION - VEHICLE IDENTIFICATION NUMBER

PREPARED BY: G. PILZ           DATE: 12SEP85        VERSION: 3         PAGE 1
APPROVED BY: DARRYL FIELDS     DATE: 15NOV85        STATUS:  F


DESCRIPTION            :    Unique identification number for all vehicles in the
                            transportation fleet. Assigned by the vehicle
                            manufacturer.

SYNONYMS               :    VIN        V.I.N.


RESPONSIBILITY         :    Transportation Department

MAJOR DATA ELEMENTS:

DATA ELEMENT           TYPE      LENGTH    OCCURS    MAN./OPT.    COMMENTS
------------           ----      ------    ------    ---------    ------------------
  NATORG                N          1         1           M        Nation of Origin
  MFR                   A          1         1           M        Manufacturer
  MKTYPE                N          1         1           M        Make and Type
  RESTRSYS              A          1         1           M        Restraint System
  SERIES                X          1         1           M        Series
  BODYTYP               N          2         1           M        Body Type
  ENGTYP                X          1         1           M        Engine Type
  CKDIGIT               N          1         1           M        Check-digit
  MODYR                 A          1         1           M        Model Year
  ASSPLANT              A          1         1           M        Assembly Plant
  SEQNO                 N          6         1           M        Plant Sequential
                                                                  Number

Example: 1.G.1.A.Z.37.3.6.B.R.123456
```

an attribute. The usual solution is to create the key as the **combination of the keys of both parents.** Figure 14–6, the case of a student's grade, illustrates this solution. The key to the grade entity is the combination of student ID and course code. This solution works well in this particular case because the student can get only one grade for each course. The same technique is frequently used in bill of materials processing (see Figure 13–17).

The last technique is one that should be avoided. Composite keys that have some significance other than the unique identification of the entity should not be assigned. An example of a composite key is an automobile serial number (see Figure 14–7), made up of 11 different codes.

Although composite keys are known to cause problems, they are still popular for two main reasons. First, if a key can be decomposed into components, it is easier to remember. An easily remembered key helps in filling in forms, because it eliminates having to look up the correct value in lengthy lists or catalogs. Ease of remembering is less important nowadays because many on-line systems have implemented on-line catalogs, so that customer numbers, for example, can be looked up by customer name. It can still be of importance in systems where back-office workers enter data from forms filled out in the field. With composite keys, the field-worker, typically a sales representative, may be able to remember the keys of many products without having to look them up in a printed list.

Second, composite keys may also be assigned for file sorting purposes. If a customer key contains the customer category, the geographical area, and the number of the assigned sales representative, then the file can be sorted on any of these criteria and significant statistics can be printed. This use of composite keys was especially important when most systems were card-based and when all the information concerning a customer had to be crammed into 80 characters. This problem justified many "trick" data representation techniques that should no longer be used today. Data storage space is no longer limited. Nor is it expensive enough to justify an identification key that contains data.

If user pressure leads the analyst to choose a composite key, each component should have an unchanging value. If the value of the key changes for an entity, most systems (and good systems practice) require that the instance of the entity identified by the old value of the key be deleted and another instance with the new value of the key be created.

Permanent values are those that cannot conceivably change over the lifetime of an entity. For a person, they include the date of birth, but not the name, and not even the sex. In many countries, the social security number contains a digit that indicates the sex of the person. A problem would arise quite needlessly if a person had a sex-change operation.

Another example of a nonpermanent value is the registration number of a motor vehicle. This number will change if the vehicle is sold, and in many countries the same registration number can be assigned successively to different vehicles belonging to the same owner. In the United Kingdom, registration numbers can be sold and bought by individuals almost at will, and vanity plates are flourishing.

In summary, the identifying key should have the following two properties:

- The key should ensure uniqueness of identification.

- The key should not be subject to modification.

In some cases, several **candidate keys,** attributes or combinations of attributes, may meet these criteria. For example, an employee might be identified by an employee ID or by the social security number. The number chosen does not much matter. What does matter is that if several candidate keys exist, they must all satisfy the integrity requirements of the entity that they identify. In particular, each candidate key must continue to be unique and not change its value.

Implementing Relationships with Keys

There are two main techniques for implementing a relationship between two entities. The first technique is used when the key of an entity consists of the concatenation of two keys or one key and a serial number. As shown in the customer location example in Figure 14–5, a one-to-many relationship that is mandatory on the parent side can be implemented by including the key to the parent entity in the key of the child entity, as part of a **concatenated key.**

The second technique is the **foreign key.** The key of the parent entity is stored as an attribute in the child entity. Because this attribute is not a key of the child but is nevertheless the key of some parent, it is called a foreign key. The term is also used to gloss over the fact that storing this value in both the child and the parent entities appears to be a redundancy—a piece of data stored in two places.

The foreign key technique does not cause difficulties. The data that appears to be redundantly stored is in reality two different pieces of data: the key to the parent, as stored in the child, does not have the same meaning as the key of the parent, as stored in the parent.

The foreign key technique can be illustrated by a customer order. The relationship between the order and the customer who placed it is implemented by storing the customer number in the order entity as a foreign key (see Figure 14–3). This technique is preferable to having the key to the order entity made up of a customer number combined with an order number assigned within the customer. It would be inconvenient and unnecessary to keep track of the next order number to be assigned for each customer.

In this case, therefore, the customer number is a normal attribute of the order. It is because the order must belong to one customer that null values are not allowed in the customer number of the order entity, not because the customer number is a key.

When foreign keys are used, the relationship is always implemented on the child side and not on the parent side. Implementing the reverse relationship would require multiple values of the child key in the parent. A customer entity would have to store several order numbers. This solution is contrary to the precepts of first normal form and to accepted relational data base practice. Also, if the relationship is zero-or-one-to-many, the foreign key could have a null value (a child with no parent).

Both of these techniques—concatenated key and foreign key—are quite standard and offer no particular difficulties. Other methods are possible but are much less frequently used and are liable to be difficult to apply. Two methods are described briefly here: the use of a common attribute that is not a key, and the use of a relationship between two attributes that is a relation other than strict equality.

Figure 14–8 **Relationship Implemented by Nonkey Attribute**

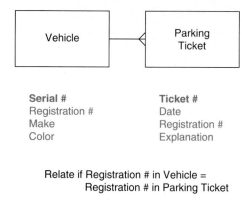

Relate if Registration # in Vehicle =
Registration # in Parking Ticket

One of the infrequent methods is relating two entities through **nonkey attributes.** If a state has an integrated motor vehicle registration and parking fine collection system, motor vehicles can be identified by the serial number. Until processed, the parking tickets contain the vehicle registration number as an attribute. This attribute implements the relationship between a vehicle and its fines (see Figure 14–8). In this case, a relationship is implemented via a data attribute that is not a key of either entity.

Problems can arise because of the choice of a nonkey attribute. A motor vehicle might have a null registration number (as it is being sold or disposed of), or it might change license plates over its lifetime. The nonkey attribute itself is not the cause of the problem; rather, the cause is that the license plate number is not a good candidate key. The number can change or be nonnull, although it cannot be nonunique. If the candidate key is as good as the actual key, as with an employee identifier and a social security number, the choice does not matter—although the integrity checks must be enforced for candidate keys as well as for actual keys.

Another little-used method of implementing relationships is by **processing rules** rather than by attribute values. In all the techniques based on keys or candidate keys, the equality between two attributes of the same type found in two different entities is what could implement the relationship between those two entities. Equality between attributes may not always be the best way to implement relationships, however, as shown by an example from computer-aided design. If the application is to draw floor plans of buildings, the relationship between a point on the floor plan and the building being drawn is, functionally, a yes/no relationship: either the point is inside the building or it is outside. (Consideration must be given to points that are exactly on the boundary.) The floor plan shape would most probably be represented on the CAD data base as a series of coordinates. The point would be represented as two coordinates. To determine whether the

Figure 14–9 **Relationship between a Point and a Two-Dimensional Surface**

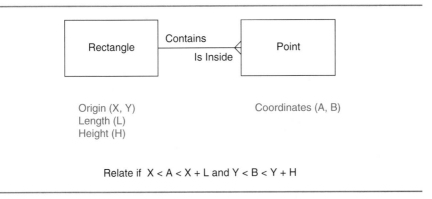

Relate if X < A < X + L and Y < B < Y + H

the point is inside or outside would require a complex series of comparisons. Yet the relationship is plain in another representation as a two-dimensional figure on a display (see Figure 14–9).

In summary, a relationship can best be implemented by storing in a child entity an attribute with the value of the key of the parent entity. This attribute may be a partial key of the child entity. If this technique is used consistently, then the logic of normalization works well. If not, the rules of functional dependence must be modified to incorporate candidate keys as well as identifying keys.

Documentation Requirements for Implementing Relationships

Both identifying keys and the ways relationships are implemented must be noted in a data dictionary. For each entity, the set of attributes making up the key must be identified, as must the well-qualified candidate keys, those that have the required attributes of uniqueness and nonchangeability.

The description of each relationship contains information on how the relationship is implemented and its cardinality, or degree. A good data dictionary will automatically annotate each entity in a relationship with the way the relationship is implemented. If not, all the uses of foreign keys or attributes that are candidate keys of other relationships must be identified.

The illustrations in this chapter show how relationship descriptions are depicted graphically. Figure 14–10 illustrates how the documentation might look in textual form.

CODES AND TABLES

A code is an attribute that is designed as an abbreviation, a symbol, or a placeholder for some other attribute. Abbreviating data has several advantages: abbreviations take up less space on disk, they take less time to fill in

Figure 14–10 **Documenting Keys and Relationship Implementations**

```
LIBRARY                        DESIGN TOOL                      CD-20
SYSTEM                       COUNTY OF DUSABLE                   ERIMP
                     ENTITY-RELATIONSHIP IMPLEMENTATION


PREPARED BY: ADS              DATE: 27NOV92        VERSION:           PAGE 1
APPROVED BY: JCG              DATE: 06DEC92        STATUS:  D


ENTITY              Patron
KEY                 Patron-Number
ATTRIBUTES          Patron-Name
                    Patron-Address
                    Patron-Telephone-No

ENTITY              Book
KEY                 ISBN-No
ATTRIBUTES          Book-Title
                    Book-Author-Name
                    Book-Edition
                    Number-of-Copies
                    Purchase-Requestor
                         IS FOREIGN KEY Patron-Number in Patron

ENTITY              Has-Borrowed
KEY                 Patron-Number
                         IS FOREIGN KEY Patron-Number in Patron
                    ISBN-No
                         IS FOREIGN KEY ISBN-No in Book
ATTRIBUTES          Date-Borrowed

ENTITY              Is—Waiting-For
KEY                 Patron-Number
                         IS FOREIGN KEY Patron-Number in Patron
                    ISBN-No
                         IS FOREIGN KEY ISBN-No in Book
ATTRIBUTES          Date-on-Waiting-List
```

fill in on forms, they are less prone to transcription errors, and they cost less to transmit over communications lines. Also, abbreviated codes used in keys such as product codes, customer numbers, and employee identifiers help ensure uniqueness and stability.

A good code is complete, well defined, not error-prone, expandable, concise, and convenient.

- Complete

    All the possible values must be represented. A state code that only provides for the 48 contiguous states is incomplete.

- Well defined

    If programmer, programmer/analyst, analyst/programmer, and analyst are four job classifications, then the coding guidelines must be clear enough to classify any individual within the population to be encoded.

    Also, a well-defined code represents a single concept. A code to be applied to cities could have the following values:

    0 County Seat

    1 State Capital

    2 Largest City

    3 Geographical Center

    Which code would fit Atlanta? Would a fifth code, County Seat and State Capital and Largest City, have to be created? What about other possible combinations? It would be far better to have four independent codes, each having a value of Yes or No (0 or 1).

- Not error-prone

    The code must be easy to transcribe and check. When a code is too long, it is easy to miss one of its digits or to transpose two digits. A solution is to "chunk" the code, dividing it into smaller units. An example of chunking occurs with telephone numbers. The series of seven digits is decomposed into two chunks of three and four digits.

    Three other features that decrease the tendency to make errors in a code are to avoid mixing numeric and alphabetic digits arbitrarily, to make the code meaningful or easy to remember, and to use a self-checking digit. These features are discussed later in the chapter.

- Expandable

    A two-digit numeric code provides for 100 possibilities, a three-digit code for 1,000, and so on. A two-digit state code is adequate: it is unlikely that there will ever be more than 100 states. However, the number of products, locations, warehouses, and so on is very likely to increase. The size of the code that is chosen must be able to accommodate the increase. If the code has to be expanded to include more digits, the entire IS department could be paralyzed. A chain of department stores saw all its new development projects curtailed for nearly three years while the store code was expanded from 3 to 4 figures. A bank stopped developing new systems for 18 months when it became necessary to increase the account number from 12 to 13 digits.

- Concise

    A five-digit code for a population of 100 is probably excessive.

- Convenient

- Convenient

   A code that is subdivided into distinct parts, each with a meaning, may look satisfying, but may not be as convenient as a straightforward code. A subdivided code might require looking up several tables to find its meaning.

   For instance, there may be a choice between a three-digit product code and an eight-digit code subdivided into four parts: brand, product category, product, and packaging. The three-digit code is more convenient because it is shorter. The eight-digit code has more meaning and each component may be easy to remember. However, there is a risk of assembling meaningful components into a code that does not correspond to a real product.

   Just like composite keys, codes that are subdivided are usually not advisable, especially if the codes are not strictly independent. For instance, if food category 34 is canned vegetables and category 35 is frozen TV dinners, then product 01 might mean carrots in one category and beef Stroganoff in the other.

   A compromise, which is also a help in locating codes when they are being looked up, is to assign significant ranges. For instance, customers from 00000 to 19999 might be independent grocery stores; 20000 through 79000, supermarket chains; and 80000 through 99999, delis. It is difficult to ensure that the initial classification stays complete and coherent, but the device is often useful. Under no circumstance should ranges determine the processing that is to be done by a program. A distinct code is required.

A code can be meaningful (mnemonic) or not. Some interesting examples can be found in the air travel industry. Air carriers have an industry-wide symbol consisting of two letters: AA for American Airlines, PA for Pan American, TW for Trans World, and UA for United Airlines. When, in the 1960s, the newly independent ex-French colonies in Western and Equatorial Africa created an airline, they called it Air Afrique. What to do, as AA was already spoken for? The code that was chosen was RK, no more than vaguely reminiscent of Air Afrique.

Another meaningful code in air travel is the airport code: JFK for Kennedy Airport, LAX for Los Angeles, SFO for San Francisco. However, ORD for O'Hare field in Chicago (O'Hare used to be Orchard) and YUL for Montreal Dorval are not meaningful.

These examples illustrate both the attractiveness of a mnemonic code and its shortcomings. Almost invariably (with the exception of country and state codes, which have not varied much recently and are not likely to), the mnemonic code winds up having obscurities or ambiguities. If such codes are used, they should be used only as shorthand for information access. Primary keys, relationships, or processing options should preferably not be based on them.

Should keys be alphabetic, numeric, or a mix? Numeric codes have the advantage of being better adapted to turnaround documents and to international systems (Arabic numerals are more widely recognized than the 26-letter Latin alphabet). Alphabetic mode is required for all mnemonic codes.

Mixed, or alphanumeric, codes are the most economical: each digit can take 36 different values (0 to 9 and A to Z). Because each additional digit multiplies the code capacity by 36, a three-digit alphanumeric code has a capacity of 46,656, or almost half the capacity of a six-digit numeric code. By contrast, a pure alphabetic code of three digits has a capacity of 17,576. A drawback of long alphanumeric (non-mnemonic) codes is the difficulty of ensuring that offensive combinations are not assigned. Avoiding such combinations is especially difficult in an international environment. Another drawback is that codes that mix numeric and alphabetic elements freely are error-prone. For example, a code such as M1XC4D3 is much more difficult to transcribe correctly than MXCD143 or 143MXCD.

Lowercase characters are not used as separate values in codes. On data entry, it is useful to accept lowercase input, but the program should convert the input to uppercase. Special characters, such as hyphens, asterisks, underscores, commas, and periods are not part of the code. They may be included as separators on output to preserve the appearance of the code (as in telephone numbers and social security numbers). Special characters should be optional on data entry: the program should accept separators but should not require them.

A self-checking code contains an extra position with a redundant character or digit in it. The value of this extra character can be calculated from the other characters. Data entry equipment can perform the calculation as the operator enters the code and can check that the result is the same as the check digit. If it is not, then there must be a transcription error somewhere. With the advent of on-line transaction processing, self-checking codes have become much less popular. The on-line program can check all the codes entered against master files or tables and provide feedback to the operator whenever the code appears to be illegal or illogical.

Documentation Requirements for Codes

Whenever a code has been designed, it is usually appropriate to create a table to translate between the code and its meaning. In most installations, a centralized data administration or data base administration function maintains a table system and will explain the requirements. The data administrator may also locate an existing code similar to the proposed one, so that a new table will not have to be created without need.

The central table maintenance system has the following goals:

• To avoid creating codes that already exist.

• To print out or display code lists for users.

• To be read by programs that require the codes (thus avoiding embedding the codes in programs and having to change every program whenever the code changes).

A shortcoming of many existing table maintenance systems is that each table entry has only two fields, the key (or code) and the value. However, in many cases, there is a need for more than one value field. For instance, the department code might translate to a long text for reports and a short text for screens. To accommodate both, an additional table may have to be created. It then becomes difficult to keep the two tables synchronized. The lack of additional fields can also cause difficulties with a hierarchical set of tables, where one table could contain regions and another table sales territories (a subdivision of regions). Usually, the region to which each territory belongs must be known. The resulting structure looks very much like the beginning of a data base and may not be handled by a simple table maintenance system.

Summary

When entities, relationships, and the principal attributes of a data model have been defined, design decisions are made for each of the identified data attributes. Each attribute in each entity is named uniquely and related to its data type.

Each data type, unless it already exists, is described with respect to its functional definition, its value domain, its physical representation on various media, and any restrictions on the operations that can be performed. This documentation decreases the number of programming errors and data base integrity problems during implementation and operation of the system.

For each entity, a key is chosen to identify it uniquely. A good key has no meaning outside of identifying the entity uniquely (and perhaps implementing a parent-child relationship). In addition, a good key never changes its value for any given entity over the entire life of that entity.

For each relationship, an implementation is chosen. In most cases, relationships are implemented via foreign keys.

Finally, all codes are inventoried and documented. If possible, existing code tables are used to decrease the risk of inconsistencies.

Even though the cause of all this work is the implementation of a single system, one of the main purposes of data element analysis is to ensure coherence of definitions and consistency of data values across all the systems of an organization. Thus, much of this work is ideally performed by a data administration section, which covers the activities of the entire IS department, not only the current project. If there is no data administration section, then one of the analysts on the project plays the same role, covering only the project.

Selected Readings

This chapter is essentially about data element design. In the literature, it is usually treated as a subtopic of data base design or data analysis. The bibliography of the previous chapter therefore applies to this one, in particular:

Date, Chris. *An Introduction to Database Systems,* 4th ed. Reading, Massachusetts: Addison-Wesley, 1986.

Martin, James. *Information Engineering,* 3 vols. Englewood Cliffs, New Jersey: Prentice-Hall, 1990.

Review Questions

1. Explain why homonyms present a more serious problem than synonyms.

2. What is the domain of each of the following data types?
   a. Date of birth.
   b. Annual interest rate for a bank loan (for example, mortgage, credit card).
   c. A nation's gross national product, expressed in U.S. dollars.
   d. Zip code.

3. What are the two characteristics that a primary key should have?

4. Use the example of a lending library to design a set of keys for each of the following entities:
   a. Book (or title).
   b. Individual copy of a book.
   c. Library patron.

5. How would you implement the relationships between patrons and the books they have borrowed, the books they are waiting for to be returned, and the books they have requested to be purchased?

6. Review and evaluate various codes encountered in everyday life from the viewpoint of the characteristics of a good code described in the chapter. Consider, for example, postal codes, telephone dialing codes (international and area codes), vehicle registration numbers, social security numbers, and taxpayer identification numbers.

7. Why do some writers suggest prohibition of the use of social security or other national identification number as the primary key in computer data bases? Should it be permitted to be included at all?

Discussion Questions

1. You suspect that, in an insurance company, the life insurance department and the group health insurance department use the words "policy" and "customer" slightly differently. Discuss how you would go about finding out whether there is a difference and what the difference is.

2. Analyze the following data types:
   a. Instant—used to time-stamp events in a real-time data collection system.
   b. Period—defined by a starting and an ending instant.
   c. Duration—defined as the length of a period

3. Document which operations can be performed on what types, independently of their representations. Consider only primitive operations; if an operation can be performed by a succession of simpler operations, do not include it.

4. The text affirms that there must be a primary key to make each entity unique. But if two entities have exactly the same attributes and are indistinguishable from the system's viewpoint, would it be immaterial to give them an artificial identification number? Should you distinguish between two entities that have the same properties? Discuss this problem using the following examples:

a. Two employees with the same name, the same job, the same salary.

b. Two gearboxes destined for two cars of the same make and year, produced by a parts supplier and waiting in the car manufacturer's inventory to be inserted into two cars on an assembly line.

c. Two trucks of the same make, year, color, and price—but with different serial numbers—owned, operated, and maintained by the same transportation company.

d. Two 1 1/2 inch No. 8 roundheaded galvanized wood screws.

5. Review the parking ticket example of a relationship implemented using an attribute that is not a candidate key. What are the trade-offs between using the license plate number and the serial number? Consider both the likelihood of making errors and the consequence if an error is made.

Mini-Case

Complete the data element analysis for all the entities defined during the entity-relationship analysis of the Condor Telephone Company mini-case at the end of the previous chapter.

Note

1. Gane, Chris. *Rapid Systems Development.* New York: Rapid Systems Development, Inc. 1984.

Specification of Integrity Constraints

Chapter 15 describes the reasons for errors in a data base, two types of integrity constraints designed to prevent errors, and two transaction validation techniques to enforce integrity. The focus of the chapter is on processing rules to prevent errors, not on how to recover from them.

Learning Objectives

- Analyze the entity-relationship model and the functional requirements to find what logical rules the data must observe in order to be valid.

- Design the processes to enforce these rules.

DATA BASE INTEGRITY

The objective of imposing integrity constraints on the data base is to ensure that the data base contains as few errors as possible. If the data base is designed to model the real world (as in a personnel or customer data base), the state of the data base must change as the real world changes. If the data base is the real world (as in an airline reservation system), it must reflect all the activities that users believe to have been posted.

Reasons for Errors in the Data Base

Any data base will always contain some errors. (Most countries now have laws that allow the public to scrutinize records concerning themselves and have material errors corrected.) However, many errors can be avoided by having the system routinely examine all the transactions and the state of all the data on the data base to catch the most obvious mistakes—those that would make the data base absurd and those that are not permitted by management policy.

For example, if an employee file contains the marital status of each employee, there must be a transaction to modify the marital status as it changes from never married to married to divorced or widowed. The rules must not allow an unmarried person to become divorced or a widowed person to become never married (except to correct an error). Another example is that it should not be possible to delete a customer master record if there is still an order in that customer's name.

Some more subtle errors cannot be caught by today's computer programs. For example, a mail-order house might receive an order for skiing equipment in July. This order might be an error due to a mistranscribed product code, or it might be a legitimate order from a customer preparing to go on a skiing vacation in the southern hemisphere.

An analyst could imagine such errors and insert routines in the processing to catch transactions that deviate from the normal pattern. The system could then flag these transactions for manual verification before they are released. But however thorough the analyst may be, some error types will always slip through. A computer program is not capable of diagnosing those errors that the analysis did not specifically anticipate: the program has no judgment, no intuition, no common sense.

Types of Errors

Three main types of errors can arise. The first type is errors in flow: data is lost, incomplete, or not transmitted on time. The second type is errors in processing: a program has a bug or a person makes a mistake. The third type is errors in data content. It is the third type that we are concerned with here. How to prevent or minimize errors in flow and in process is treated in Section VI, which also discusses how to recover from errors.

Errors that creep into the data base are usually one of the following types:

- The data does not reflect the actual state of the world. For example, no one has recorded the fact that Bud Green got married last month. Or someone recorded Patricia McCreary as having left the company on January 15, although she did not leave until January 31. Or the M. P. Schwartz who died and is to be taken off the welfare rolls is the one who lived on 53rd Street, not the one on 35th Street.

- The data is inconsistent. Inconsistencies arise only when redundant data is stored. For example, Bud Green is recorded as being married in the personnel file but not in the departmental project control file.

- The data base is in an illegal or impossible state. This type of error occurs primarily when one entity in a mandatory relationship, such as the "1" end of a one-to-many relationship, has been deleted. For example, there are payroll deduction records for Patricia McCreary, although the master record for Patricia was deleted when she quit. Or there are orders for products that are no longer carried. Or suppliers have been deleted although money is still owed them.

The consequences of the third type of error can range from benign to catastrophic. An order for a nonexistent product could be discovered when the bill of lading or the invoice is printed or when the customer complains about not receiving the whole order. The error may affect only the single order for that customer: no great damage is likely to result. However, a batch program might assume that the error will never occur and therefore react unpredictably when it does occur. For instance, the inventory record of some other, existing product might be posted with the quantity ordered or the accounts receivable might be out of balance. If the error materializes during an on-line session, the entire computer may come down, stopping the work of all the users who are connected to the order entry application as well as to other applications that happen to be running.

To recover from the error can also be difficult. If the error has not been anticipated, hasty action could cause further errors. If the error discovered in one invoice is thought to have invalidated the work done for all the other invoices of the same run, the error correction may be to redo the whole batch. However, if some unprinted invoices were already posted to accounts receivable, customers who properly receive only one invoice may be dunned for two.

Even more insidious can be the effect of errors in files used for management or decision support. Redundant but inconsistent data is especially insidious, because a given user will normally have access to only one of the versions. Two users who believe they are working on the same data may not understand why they have discrepancies. Errors that would easily be spotted on an individual record may get drowned in the process of summarizing and averaging.

Lack of relationship integrity is also insidious, because such an error may never be discovered. Take the example of an employee whose master record is deleted but whose deduction records remain in the system. The deduction records are normally used by the payroll application, but the program only processes deductions for current employees (i.e., those who have a master record). The persistence in the data base of deduction records is not noticeable in this application. Imagine, however, that the human resources department decides to analyze the cost of certain benefits programs paid for by deductions (flexible benefits, group life insurance, stock options). An employee might use the personnel file to extract all the deductions of a certain type without worrying about master records. No error will be encountered, but the results will be wrong. If the error occurred for only one employee, the impact will not be great. However, if the error has affected all those who have left the company over the past several years, the impact could be substantial.

There are so-called pointer audit programs that can read an entire data base and check for integrity errors such as having detail records without masters. The technique for using these audit programs is described later in the chapter.

THE REFERENTIAL INTEGRITY PROBLEM

The most important type of integrity constraint on a data base is called referential integrity. The term *referential integrity* refers to making sure that actual instances of relationships between actual instances of entities follow the degree rules documented during entity-relationship analysis.

Implementing Relationships

Relationships between entities can be implemented in a number of ways. In nonrelational data base systems, pointer chains are often used. With pointer chains, the disk address of one record is stored in another record; then the address of a third record is stored in the second record; and so on. It is possible to build different types of pointer chains, such as open-ended or circular, one-way or two-way. The data base management system is responsible for maintaining these pointer chains, and part of the job of the data base designer is to specify to the data base management system which pointers are to be implemented. As a return service, the DBMS also ensures integrity. If the designer has documented to the DBMS the rule that a relationship is mandatory, then no program can violate this rule by attempting to delete a parent record without having deleted the children first.

Storing address pointers causes some inflexibility, however. In particular, the existence of pointers makes it difficult to extend the data base to encompass new entities and relationships. Also, any program that reads the data base needs to know something about the characteristics of the pointer chains; and so changing the implementation of a data base may require changing most of the programs that refer to the data base. Relational data base overcomes the lack of flexibility of traditional data bases by using foreign keys, explained in the previous chapter, to implement relationships. A foreign key in one entity provides a reference to the identifying key of another entity. In return for the flexibility allowed by the foreign key scheme, the application must check the integrity of the relationships that are not known to the data base management system.

Checking for Referential Integrity

Referential integrity is ensured when all references between data base records (or entities, in the data analysis vocabulary) are correct.

One-to-Many Relationships. Most of the relationships in a well-analyzed data model are one-to-many (where the "1" means exactly one, neither more nor less, and the "N" can stand for various possibilities—0 to N with N arbitrarily large; or 1 to N with N arbitrarily large; or either 0 or 1 to N with N limited to a theoretical maximum). For instance, in an order entry system, a customer might have any number of orders, and an order must have at least one order item, with no upper limit; in a library lending system, it might be decided that no patron can have more than nine books on loan.

Whenever one of the sides of the relationship has some imposed minimum or maximum, then every delete or create operation on an instance of the entity on that side must first make sure that the proposed operation would not violate the rule. In other words, if every X must be owned by a Y, then no transaction can suppress any Ys without first checking that they do not currently own any Xs. No transaction should delete a customer who still has products on order, a supplier who is still owed money, or departments with employees still attached. The converse, checking that maxima are not exceeded, can be illustrated by the following example: Do not let a library patron who already has borrowed nine books borrow another book; at least one book must be returned before another is borrowed.

Another check must often be performed: when a record containing a foreign key is created or modified, the foreign key points (or continues to point) to an existing record. Therefore, the value of the foreign key must be equal to the primary key of some instance of the parent entity in the data base. For example, when creating an employee record, the department number to which the employee is assigned must be the number of an existing department. If an employee is transferred from one department to another, causing the value of the foreign key to be modified, the same rule holds.

If the relationship is optional on the parent side, then the foreign key may be null. If the key is not null, it must have the value of the primary key of some existing entity. For example, an employee record might contain as a foreign key the number of the department of which the employee is in charge. Some employees are not in charge of any department and the foreign key is null. An employee cannot be put in charge of a department unless that department exists. An employee who is in charge of a department can be demoted, however, by assigning a null value to the department number in the employee record. The relationship no longer points to a department that the employee manages.

In most cases, the application of these create/delete/modify rules and the strict application of the prohibition against changing the value of a key are sufficient to guarantee referential integrity.

Referential integrity is easy to enforce in transaction processing systems developed according to a life cycle, by a project team, with appropriate standards, training, and management structures. Enforcement is much more difficult in an end-user environment, where users may not be aware of the total model of the data base. There are two solutions to this problem:

- The first solution is to use the DBMS facilities to refuse update authorization to end users. They can only read the data base; they may be able to modify a local copy that no one else shares, but they cannot modify shared files or relations.

- The second solution is to use a relational DBMS that implements referential integrity. Such a DBMS would require descriptions of how each relationship is implemented and its degree. The DBMS could then perform all the integrity checking required whenever a program attempted to create or delete a row.

Until data base systems with referential integrity checking become widely available, the technology requires that all creations, deletions, or modifications on a shared data base be implemented in an application that also performs integrity checking. This application must be specified, designed, written, tested, documented, and maintained in accordance with professional practice and cannot be left to the typical end-user environment.

One-to-One Relationships. A special difficulty arises when a relationship is strictly one-to-one. If the referential integrity rules were applied strictly, it would not be possible to create or delete a record. The "do not delete" rule would prevent deleting either of two related entities, because deleting one would leave the other in an invalid state. Similarly, creating one before the other is impossible, because the first one to be created would point to empty space.

The solution to this problem is to defer checking on the integrity until the entire operation (double deletion, double creation) is completed. This solution amounts to considering the double deletion or creation as an atomic operation, different in nature from the successive creation of two entities. This operation can be validated as a whole before attempting to call the data base management system to perform the creation. The logical unit of work, or business event, is what is important, not each elementary data base operation. This approach is legitimate, because the definition of logical units of work specifies that whatever happens, a unit of work is either wholly processed or not processed at all (see Section IV).

OTHER INTEGRITY CONSTRAINTS

There are many other types of integrity constraints on a data base. The most frequently encountered are the following:

- Domain constraints
    The value of each attribute must remain within the domain of that attribute, both when the attribute is modified and when the domain specification is modified.

- Nonkey dependency constraints
    The range of possible values of some attributes (their subdomains) may be dependent on the value of some other attribute, either in the same entity or in another one.

- Consistency of redundant information
    If information is stored redundantly for any reason, then any modification to one instance must be reflected in the other.

- Constraints on derived data
    If the constraint is expressed on derived data, such as an extended amount, a total, or a balance, the derived data must be recalculated or adjusted every time the base data is changed.

The domain of a piece of data is a function of the data type. The ideal solution is to have an integrated data dictionary that automatically takes care of **domain checking**—making sure that each data value that is input to the system belongs to the proper domain. Otherwise, the project standards must enforce the discipline of checking the domain of every single piece of input data, whether on a screen, an input form communicated to a batch program, or a file from some other system or outside source. This solution is neither difficult nor constraining.

More difficult than domain checking is checking the data base integrity when the domain specification changes. Such a change has a retroactive effect: not only does the processing rule for new elements change, but the entire data base may need to be checked for values outside the domain.

There are two kinds of domain specification changes. The first occurs when the domain is enlarged. In this case, the data base does not need to be reviewed. The second occurs when the domain is narrowed. Then the data base should be examined to determine what to do with existing records that do not meet the constraints. For instance, if the criteria for membership in a club is expanded from all-male to both male and female, no great difficulty is likely. However, if a club previously open to residents and nonresidents of a community should decide to require residence, then a number of existing members would no longer qualify. This problem can only be solved by striking their memberships or by instituting a so-called grandfather clause, which states that the criteria for membership are those in effect when membership was applied for.

Nonkey dependency constraints are similar to relationship (key) constraints, but they apply to ordinary data elements rather than to foreign keys. Suppose, for example, that employees in the "executive" category cannot have a payroll code of "hourly." This rule might have been implemented as a referential integrity constraint, using appropriate subentities for executive employees and for hourly employees. The crucial difference between nonkey dependency constraints and referential integrity constraints is that the former must necessarily be checked by the application: even a DBMS with referential integrity will not do the checking (see Figure 15–1).

In theory, **consistency of redundant information** is fairly easy to achieve. All that is required is to group in a single logical unit of work the updating of all the places where redundant information is stored. By definition, either the logical unit of work is incomplete (nothing has been committed) or complete (the redundant information has all been updated). In reality, ensuring consistency may be easier said than done. In the case of distributed processing, the redundant information might be on another computer in a remote geographical location, and the user would have to wait too long before both locations are updated. Or the remote location might not be reachable because of a breakdown in a communications link.

A special case of redundancy arises when both detail and summary records are stored. The constraint is that the summary record must at all times contain the exact total of all the detail records. A practical problem is that updating a summary record on-line each time a detail record is created or updated may cause a performance bottleneck. For instance, suppose that the application is accounts receivable and that the double-entry accounting system is implemented in the system itself. Then every payment recorded

Figure 15–1 **Nonkey Dependency**

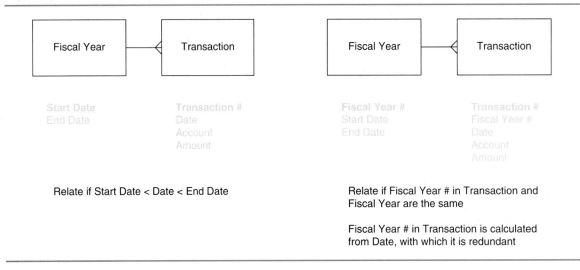

Relate if Start Date < Date < End Date

Relate if Fiscal Year # in Transaction and
Fiscal Year are the same

Fiscal Year # in Transaction is calculated
from Date, with which it is redundant

individually as a credit on the accounts receivable balance file would update the cash on hand balance—a single figure on a single account. Every accounts receivable clerk would contend for the same cash balance record. What is more, by the law of logical units of work, each clerk would reserve this record at the beginning of each transaction and relinquish it at the end to ensure that no other transaction can interfere until the transaction in process is done. Thus, the system could in effect process only one transaction at a time. All operators except one would always be waiting for the cash balance record to become available. Changing the system to update the single cash balance record at the end of the day would avoid the bottleneck, but all throughout the day, the data on files would appear to be inconsistent.

A solution is to declare that the cash on hand figure is not redundant with the accounts receivable balances by making it "last night's balance" rather than "current balance." This is one example of a concept known as closing or cut-off—classifying all recorded activities by a well-defined period regardless of when the system processed the transaction. Closing is used both in accounting and in management information or decision support systems. One of the merits of cutting off is to avoid having users working on figures that keep changing as the business is conducted. It is hard to analyze trends when the figures do not stay stable for more than a few minutes at a time.

Constraints on derived data are more difficult to deal with. An example of such a constraint is the rule that a check should be rejected if the issuer's account has a debit balance. This rule requires either that redundant data be maintained (the customer's balance as well as all the transactions) or that the balance be recalculated for every transaction. Neither is wholly satisfactory. Whenever this dilemma arises, the cost of recalculating derived data every time it is needed must be analyzed versus the cost and risks of maintaining derived, and therefore redundant, data.

ILLEGAL TRANSACTIONS VERSUS TRANSACTIONS THAT CAUSE AN ILLEGAL STATE

During the design phase, constraints are specified on the state of the data base: all relationships in the data base must be of degree such-and-such; all data values in the data base must be in the proper domain; no keys in the data base can be null, and so on.

In contrast, there are two techniques for implementing the validation of integrity constraints. In most cases, it is reasonably easy to transform the constraint on the data base into transaction constraints, rules that any transaction must obey to be allowed to update the data base. In other cases, a technique akin to the casework approach described in Chapter 10 is better. This approach consists in trying to do all the updates required by a complex, multitransaction business event before validating the effect of the updates. If an error is discovered after all the individual updates have been performed, then the entire set of transactions is rejected.

The **transaction constraint approach** was described in the paragraphs on referential integrity above. For the degree constraint to be satisfied, it was enough to prohibit certain things from happening. (This was roughly the idea behind prohibition. It was thought that to stop a state of drunkenness from occurring, it would be enough to prevent certain transactions, namely, the sale of alcoholic beverages.)

Analyzing transaction constraints consists of describing all the legal states of the data base, listing all the events (state transitions) that can be requested, and authorizing only those that result in a legal state. Most often, this analysis is done intuitively on the basis of elementary logic and referential integrity rules:

- No attribute can have a value outside its domain.
- An entity that already exists cannot be created.
- An entity cannot be modified or deleted unless it exists.
- Children must be deleted before parents.
- Parents must be created before children.
- Children can be transferred to new parents only if the parents exist.

These rules must be applied to the business event as a whole (the logical unit of work) rather than to the individual transactions as seen by the data base management system.

The **casework approach** may be the best in applications where many different elementary transactions might occur in arbitrary sequence within a logical unit of work. In this case, analyzing each transaction separately can become onerous, because each of them might change something that would make another transaction illegal. The only disciplined way to apply the constraints transaction by transaction would be to sort the transactions into a predetermined sequence or force the operator to enter them in that order. This solution may not be the best for today's complex systems. It may be simpler to make a copy (in memory or on a working space on a disk) of all the entities touched by the update, do the update without worrying about validity, and check whether the result obeys the integrity constraint. If it does, then all the elementary transactions are correct and the working copy of the data base entities is copied back into place, with all the updates posted to it. If the result does not obey the integrity constraint, then all the elementary transactions are rejected and the working copy of the data base entities is discarded. No attempt is made by the application to determine which transaction made the difference.

Thus, an elementary transaction can create a temporary illegal state, as long as a subsequent transaction (which might also be illegal) changes the state back to a legal one. On occasion, two wrongs do make a right. This technique is usually appropriate when the logical unit of work is not completely determined in advance but rather at the initiative of the operator, as is typical of casework applications.

An extreme example of the casework approach is the data base audit program. This program reads the entire data base and examines whether it conforms to specific integrity constraints. The program is run whenever there is reason to suppose that errors have slipped through, for instance, because the validation criteria in the updating application were incomplete or because some program bug was destroying integrity. Data base audit programs can be vendor-supplied utilities, or they can be written by the development team. The former are usually limited to checking pointer integrity, whereas the latter can do as extensive a check as desired.

DOCUMENTATION REQUIREMENTS FOR INTEGRITY CONSTRAINTS

Many of the integrity constraints, particularly referential integrity and domain constraints, can be deduced directly from the documentation of the entity-relationship model and the descriptions of data types. Others need to be added explicitly, usually at the level of an entity or a relationship description.

Nonkey dependencies, or mutually exclusive values of two attributes, within a single entity are documented on the data dictionary within the entity description. For instance, if the flight leg entity of an airline schedule contains a flight departure time and a flight arrival time, the constraint that the flight departure time should always precede the flight arrival time is described in the flight leg entity description.

If the two attributes with a nonkey dependency are in different entities, the constraint is best documented in the description of the relationship between two entities. For instance, if a customer credit rating of "poor" entails that the customer cannot place a COD order, this constraint should be documented in the description of the customer-order relationship. When such a dependency exists between two attributes in two different entities, a relationship must always exist between those two entities.

Integrity constraints on derived data are stored with the data description of the derived data, where the derivation rule is also stored. If the derived data is not stored in an entity, it nevertheless does characterize an entity; it is in this entity that the description belongs. For instance, if a check should be rejected whenever a bank customer has a debit balance, this debit balance is recalculated whenever the check is processed. If the balance were to be stored, it would be stored in a customer account entity. Derived data of this type is sometimes called virtual data and considered a virtual extension of the entity.

In addition to a description of the constraints themselves, which are documented on the data dictionary, it is useful to start documenting the way in which integrity checking is performed. This documentation will be completed during the process design phase.

In general terms, the designer should document which integrity rules for each logical unit at work might be transgressed by the transaction and therefore need to be checked. In most cases, the documentation is a simple description in English (see Figure 15–2). In other cases, when the rules are more complex, the designer should create a state transition network diagram (see Appendix 2 and Figure 15–3). These documents will eventually be incorporated into the program specifications to be developed later.

Summary

To make sure that a data base remains in a valid state as transactions are posted to it, the transaction processing programs must enforce a number of rules. The main constraints on the data base concern referential integrity—making sure that the specified degree of relationships continue to hold true. Specifically, in a one-to-many relationship, the normal rule is that children cannot exist without a parent, whether a child has been created and not the parent or the parent has been deleted, leaving orphans.

Other integrity constraints include:

- Domain integrity: all data element values must belong to the data type's domain.

- Nonkey dependencies: the values of some data elements may be constrained by the value of other data elements.

- Redundant data rules: if the same data appears twice in the data base, they must have the same value.

- Constraints on derived data: derived data, such as a total or a balance, must be recalculated every time some transaction affects it.

There are two main approaches to maintaining integrity. The first is to assume that the data base is in a legal state prior to any transaction, and to either allow or not allow the transaction, depending on whether it will cause

Figure 15–2 **Sample Description of Integrity Rules**

```
PERSONNEL                       DESIGN TOOL                        CD-20
PAYROLL                        SUBURBAN PUMPS                      VRULES
                            INTEGRITY RULE CHECKING

PREPARED BY: H. WETTERGREN      DATE: 27FEB90       VERSION: 1.1      PAGE 1
APPROVED BY: JIMMY WEBER        DATE: 04MAR90       STATUS:  D


TRANSACTION:  EMPLOYEE RECAP RECORD UPDATE

TRANSACTION TYPES:        C - Create
                          M - Modify
                          D - Delete

DOMAIN CHECKING:

Check that each data element value belongs to its domain as specified in the data
dictionary.

Null values are not allowed for Create transactions.

Null values are allowed for Modify transactions (except Employee-ID).

Delete transactions contain only the Employee-ID.

TRANSACTION INTEGRITY CHECKING AGAINST DATA BASE:

Employee to be created must not already exist.

Employee to be modified or deleted must already exist.

Employee to be deleted must have a Gross-Year-To-Date equal to 0 on the data base.

If an employee segment is to be deleted, then all its dependent segments (skills, job
history, pay history, accumulated benefits) must be removed from the data base and
copied to the personnel history file.

If an employee is created or an employee's Social-Security-Number is modified the new
Social-Security-Number must not match any other Social-Security-Number on the data
base.

TRANSACTION INTEGRITY CHECKING AGAINST EMPLOYEE-LEVEL RULES:

At the end of the processing of one employee, the employee's Gross-Year-To-Date must
exceed the sum of the employee's FICA-Withholding, Federal-Tax-Withholding, and
Benefits-Withholding. If this does not occur, all the transactions concerning the
employee are rejected.
```

Figure 15–3 **Sample State Transition Network Diagram for Integrity Rules**

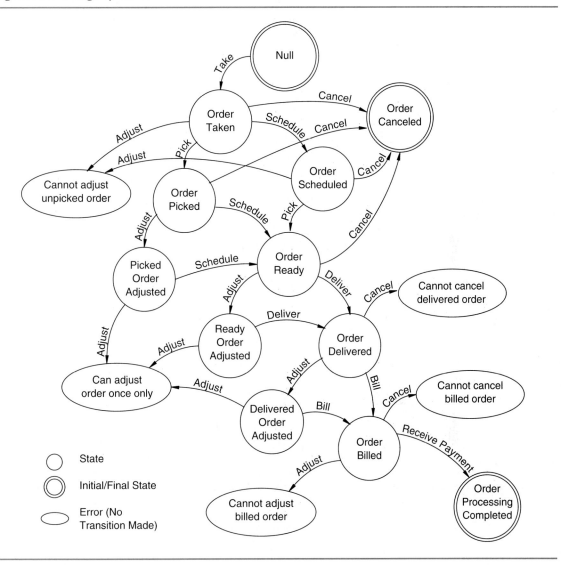

a transition to another legal state. The state of the data base is never checked, only the type of each transaction. This is the normal approach for transaction processing systems.

The second approach, used when the transactions are too complex or too unpredictable, is to perform the update as though every transaction were legitimate and then check the resulting state of the data base. If the state is correct, then all the transactions are accepted; if not, they are all rejected.

Selected Readings

Ross, Ronald G. *Entity Modeling: Techniques and Applications.* Boston, Massachusetts: Database Research Group, 1987.
  This book is one of the few to address the practical ways in which data integrity can be ensured.

Review Questions

1. What are the three main types of data content errors?

2. Define and give examples of referential integrity constraints.

3. Define and give examples of nonreferential integrity constraints.

4. Describe the difference between the transaction constraint approach and the casework approach. Which is the most frequently used?

Discussion Questions

1. What can be done to reduce the number of errors that result when a data base is not in agreement with the actual world?

2. What can be done to minimize the risk of inconsistencies on the data base?

3. Analyze the features required for a relational DBMS to ensure relational integrity. Give examples of syntax expressing the various referential integrity rules described in the chapter. How would you solve the problem of a strict one-to-one relationship, where two entities have to be created together or not at all?

Mini-Case

For the Condor Telephone Company, translate all the referential integrity constraints on the data model developed at the end of Chapters 13 and 14 into constraints that must be met by each transaction type outlined in the scope description.

In addition, add constraints on the service requests, depending on the status of the equipment. For instance, a customer cannot reconnect equipment unless it was previously temporarily disconnected. Use a state transition diagram or similar schematic to document this constraint.

Entity-Relationship Diagrams

INTRODUCTION

Entity-relationship diagrams have become the most popular technique for representing data designs for data-oriented systems, transaction processing, and management information systems. Entity-relationship diagrams are used pervasively, from information systems planning (where they may be little more than conceptual sketches of the main data entities and relationships) through functional design (where rigorous analysis techniques are used) to physical data base design (which may be aided by expert systems).

Entity-relationship diagrams are used throughout the text to illustrate data structures and relationships, in particular in the following chapters:

- Chapter 5: Establishing the Systems Plan, where a sample corporate data model is presented.

- Chapter 8: Functional Requirements, where the technique is related to other representation techniques such as data flow diagrams and functional decomposition charts.

- Chapter 13: Entity-Relationship Modeling, which describes the formal analysis techniques to be used when creating entity-relationship diagrams.

DEFINITION

An entity-relationship diagram depicts the types of objects about which data is maintained in the system, the types of relationships that hold among these objects, and in some cases, the types of attributes (data elements) that are stored about each object.

An entity-relationship diagram is one technique used to represent a model of the data base that stores the system's data. (There are other, usually less graphic techniques.)

EXAMPLES

A library lends books to its patrons. Each book is characterized by its title, author, publisher, edition, and ISBN number. Each book in the library may exist in several copies. Each patron can borrow a certain number of books.

Figure 1 **Entity-Relationship Diagram for a Lending Library**

If a patron requests a book for which there are no copies available (all are out on loan), he or she is put on a waiting list. If a patron requests a book that the library does not have, the library may decide to order the book. The patron is to be notified when the book arrives (see Figure 1).

A university enrolls students in courses. Each course has a name and a number. Each course may be given several times in a given semester. Each course is given by a professor—not necessarily the same for the different schedules of a single course. For example, Professor McCarthy may give Accounting 101 on Tuesdays at 9 A.M., and Professor O'Brien may give Accounting 101 on Thursdays at 3 P.M. Courses have prerequisites; for instance, Accounting 210 requires that Accounting 101 has been taken previously. The system has registered the courses each student has already taken, together with the grades obtained (see Figure 2).

A manufacturing company manufactures washing machines from raw materials, stores the manufactured machines in one of several regional warehouses, and sells the machines to customers. Each customer order is delivered from the warehouse closest to the customer. Deliveries are always complete; there is no back-ordering system. Each order can request several different products. Payment on orders is due ten days after delivery.

Raw materials and parts are obtained from suppliers. For each type of raw material and for each different part, the company maintains a list of suppliers, with the prices that the supplier has quoted. Two suppliers may sup-

Figure 2 **Entity-Relationship Diagram for a University**

Figure 3 **Entity-Relationship Diagram for a Manufacturing Company**

ply the same materials at different prices. Every time more materials are needed, the company calls one or more suppliers to find out the delivery lead time and places the order with the supplier who charges the least and who can deliver within a specified time.

The washing machines are made of parts that can be manufactured in-house, from raw materials (sheet metal for the body), or purchased (nuts, screws, washers, and bolts). A rough corporate data model for this manufacturer is shown in Figure 3.

WHERE USED IN THE LIFE CYCLE

Entity-relationship diagrams (ERDs) are initially created in the project identification phase. Depending on the methodology chosen for project identification, they may be more or less central to the process. In general, if systems planning (identification of a long-term strategy for implementing projects that have been identified early) is implemented, ERDs are a critical part of the phase. If project identification is ad hoc, with each project being identified as its need is felt by the users, the use of ERDs is more informal.

The ERDs established during project identification are refined and detailed during the requirements analysis phase to incorporate the different uses of the data that different users will make.

The updated ERDs established during requirements analysis are refined in the data design activity of the design phase. They are given their final form here; they are then communicated to the implementation phase where programmers and data base administrators use them as input to their work.

FORMAL RULES

Entities, representing the objects about which data is to be stored, are depicted as rectangular boxes. Straight lines between the boxes indicate the relationships among these entities. Each end of the relationship may have a symbol indicating the degree, or *cardinality*, of the relationship. For instance, some relationships hold between one of each of the two entities. In a data base about universities, each university has one president and one only (see Figure 4).

Each university has many students registered. If students are not allowed to register in several universities at the same time, this would be represented by a crow's foot (indicating "many") on the student end of the relationship and a double bar (indicating "one") on the university side (see Figure 5).

Each university delivers a number of different degrees. Some degrees (such as a B.S. in mechanical engineering) are delivered by many different institutions. This type of relationship is known as many-to-many (see Figure 6).

In the above examples, the name of the relationship has also been indicated. Each relationship can be read in either of two ways and has therefore two possible names. The name is always a verb; it is written closer to the subject of the verb than to the object. The relationship names in the last example can be read as:

"Each university delivers one or more degrees."
"Each degree is delivered by one or more universities."

In all these examples, the cardinality at either end is at least one. There is no university without a president, and there is no university president without a university. This may not always be the case. For instance, in the relationship between a customer and an order in the manufacturing example, each order is placed by a customer (and one only), but there may be customers who do not have an order. This situation may be represented by drawing a small circle at one end of the relationship (see Figure 7).

An entity may have a relationship to itself. In the real world, one instance of the entity type has the relationship to another entity of the same type. For instance, on a family tree, each person has a relationship to other persons in the same family, as illustrated in Figure 8.

Figure 4 **One-to-One Relationship**

Figure 5 **One-to-Many Relationship**

Figure 6 **Many-to-Many Relationship**

Figure 7 **One-to-Many Relationship (Optional)**

Figure 8 **Entity with Relationship to Itself**

Figure 9 **Either-Or Relationship**

In the manufacturing example, a part could have a relationship either to a number of suppliers or to materials from which the company makes it. This is an either-or relationship, and it could be represented in either of two ways.

The bracket encompassing the two relationships that the part has indicates an alternative (see Figure 9).

Figure 10 is slightly more complex, but it is a more powerful way of representing alternatives. In reality, this diagram states that what the finished product views as an entity (a part) is made up of two subentities, a purchased part and a manufactured part, each of which has a different set of relationships.

Simplifications may be made to the entity-relationship diagram. In the early stages, before a detailed analysis is made of the entities, the degree symbols may be suppressed. They may be evident or they may not be critical to the understanding of the diagram. The degree symbol can often be omitted early in the life of a project (especially during systems planning).

Usually, only one relationship exists between two given entities. In that case, it may be possible to omit the relationship name, especially where the nature of the relationship is evident from the context (as between customer and order, between order and order item, or between order item and product). If multiple relationships exist between two entities, they must be designated. In general, only one of the two possible names are given, to be read in the active voice and in the one-to-many direction (if it is a one-to-many relationship). An example of multiple relationships between two entities is given in the library example where a patron may have borrowed one book and be on the waiting list for another (see Figure 1).

MECHANIZED TOOLS

Most CASE tools on the market have some facility for drawing entity-relationship diagrams. Those tools that have the most powerful ERD features are the ones that adopt a data-driven development methodology; they may be some-

Figure 10 **Relationship with Entities and Subentities**

what weaker for data flow diagramming. This characteristic may be a deterrent to installations that have implemented other methodologies (process-driven or more classically structured, such as Gane & Sarson, DeMarco, or IBM's IPT).

The ideal facility would be able to store formal descriptions of entities, relationships, and attributes and transform these into diagrams for display. The tool should also store data descriptions for programming languages (such as COBOL) and data description language (for describing data base structure to a DBMS).

Ideally, the form used for storing the information about entities and relationships should be one that captures most of the structure. To capture structure, it is better to store the information as data rather than as schematics. However, most input and output should be in the form of schematics. Transforming a description into a schematic is not very difficult, whereas creating a formal description from a schematic is much more difficult. The process generally requires a fairly strict methodology. Thus, the products that rely on such a methodology are generally more powerful than general-purpose graphics tools.

The tool also needs to be able to download data descriptions from other tools such as data dictionaries or program libraries. Most tools that are interactively oriented only, with no batch facility, cannot do this.

Finally, the tool should provide support for both the informal, high-level diagrams established early in the development process and the detailed, formalized diagrams used in the design phase. It should support both bottom-up and top-down development.

EQUIVALENT TECHNIQUES

Many different conventions exist for drawing entity-relationship diagrams. The technique described in this section follows the majority, as exemplified by James Martin in *Information Engineering* and Chris Gane in *Rapid System*

Development. Many of the minor variations (in particular on the incorporation of relationship names and degree symbols) have also been described.

The main variation that has currency today is the notation introduced by Peter Chen. Chen's notation includes the use of a diamond shape to represent relationships or *associations*. (Martin's notation is to represent relationships by lines between entities, if they are one-to-many, and by entity rectangles, if they are many-to-many or if they carry attributes. The logic behind this convention is that such relationships will ultimately wind up in the relational data base as tables.)

Chen's notation is widespread in the United States but is not as popular overseas. It has declined in popularity in the United States as well, as the use of information engineering-based CASE tools has increased.

Other variations are:

- Including attributes alongside each entity. (Some authors recommend including only the key to each entity—its identifying attribute, such as its social security number. Others recommend including all the known attributes or data elements.)

- Using ovals instead of rectangles.

- Using arrows and double arrows, or noting degrees with numbers, instead of the cross and crow's feet symbols.

- Distinguishing between different types of entities with different box shapes: entities that exist independently of others (customer, product), entities that cannot exist except in connection with some other entity on which it depends (order, depending on customer), and intersection (product).

- Forbidding many-to-many relationships. (This is appropriate in the design stage where one of the design steps is to make sure that the relationships are either one-to-one or one-to-many. However, in earlier stages where the ERD is used to communicate with users rather than with data base designers, the many-to-many relationship is a useful form of shorthand.)

- Using data attribute names rather than verbs to designate relationships. (A relationship such as that of a customer and an order can be implemented by including the customer number of the owner of the order as an attribute of the order. Again, this technique is appropriate in later stages where the main purpose is to communicate with data base designers rather than with users.)

- Including narrative. (A useful guideline is to include enough narrative with the top-level models—before the design phase—that users can understand all the implications and conventions of the diagram without formal training. Typically, for a one-page diagram, this might be a one- to three-page typed narrative.)

- Letting relationships bear attributes.

- Using representations that depend on the data base management system being used. (This variation is obviously appropriate only when the physical data base design is done. To use the technique earlier is harmful, because it forces the designer to make implementation decisions before design decisions. The peculiarities of these representations are the strongest for the hierarchical type of data base, such as IBM's IMS.)

An obvious alternative is to use a nongraphic representation such as that provided by a DBMS data definition language. Each entity is described by noting its name and data contents (attributes). Each relationship is described by noting the two entities that participate in it and the degrees at either end. An example of such a description for the library example is shown in Figure 11.

This technique is equivalent to the graphic technique: one can be generated from the other. However, it is much less effective in communicating the data design to a user or a programmer. ERDs represent a case where the cliché "A picture is worth a thousand words" actually holds true.

CRITERIA FOR USE

The use of entity-relationship diagrams is particularly helpful in two areas: communicating with users to make sure that the analyst understands the application area and serving as a basis for proper design.

The first goal is served by using the graphic technique, by providing intelligible names for the entities, and by depicting relationships (and naming them wherever necessary).

The second goal is served by including the cardinality, or degree symbols, on the graph. The majority of bad design decisions come from inadequate analysis of many-to-many relationships and from the analysis of which attributes implement those relationships. As described in Chapter 13, this activity constitutes the substance of data design.

Other items that would be useful for good design would tend to overload the diagrams and therefore make them less suitable for communicating with users. With appropriate CASE tools, a complex diagram could be maintained, showing only the simple parts of it to users. This is not, however, a feature of most current CASE tools.

Selected Readings

The readings at the end of Chapter 13, Entity-Relationship Modeling, are all relevant to this technique. In addition, the following books explore different aspects or different representation techniques that may be of interest to students who want to study data modeling more deeply.

Nijssen, G. M, and Halpin, T. A. *Conceptual Schema and Relational Database Design: A Fact Oriented Approach.* New York: Prentice-Hall, 1989.

Figure 11 **Sample Nongraphic Representation
of Entities and Relationships**

```
LIBRARY                         DESIGN TOOL                     CD-20
SYSTEM                        COUNTY OF DUSABLE                  ERIMP
                        ENTITY-RELATIONSHIP DESCRIPTION


PREPARED BY: ADS              DATE: 27NOV92        VERSION:          PAGE 1
APPROVED BY: JCG              DATE: 06DEC92        STATUS:  D



ENTITY           Patron
KEY              Patron-Number
ATTRIBUTES       Patron-Name
                 Patron-Address
                 Patron-Telephone-No


ENTITY           Book
KEY              ISBN-No
ATTRIBUTES       Book-Title
                 Book-Author-Name
                 Book-Edition
                 Number-of-Copies


RELATIONSHIP     Has-Borrowed
ORIGIN           Patron
    DEGREE       {O,N}         N<=Number-of-Copies
TARGET           Book
    DEGREE       {O,N}         N<=Lending-Limit
REVERSE-NAME     Is-On-Loan-To


RELATIONSHIP     Is-Waiting-For
ORIGIN           Patron
    DEGREE       {O,N}
TARGET           Book
    DEGREE       {O,N}
REVERSE-NAME     Is-Reserved-By


RELATIONSHIP     Has-Requested-Purchase
ORIGIN           Patron
    DEGREE       {0,1}
TARGET           Book
    DEGREE       {O,N}
REVERSE-NAME     Is-Ordered-For
```

> *This book describes a technique known as binary relationship modeling. It differs from entity-relationship modeling in that it emphasizes individual attributes ("facts") rather than entities. It is the relationship between one attribute, such as Name, and another, such as Social Security Number, that constitutes an entity.*

Flavin, Matt. *Fundamental Concepts of Information Modeling.* Englewood Cliffs, NJ: Yourdon Press, 1986.
> *Flavin espouses the Chen convention of representing relationships. This book is a classic among structured systems analysis practitioners.*

Chen, Peter. *The Entity-Relationship Approach to Logical Data Base Design.* Wellesley, MA: QED Information Sciences, Inc., 1977.
> *Peter Chen was the first author to write about entity-relationship modeling.*

EXERCISES

1. Make an ERD for the following application:

A bank has a number of customers of two types: individuals and companies. Each customer may have several accounts of various types: checking, savings, mortgage, consumer loans, trust. In addition, the bank can sell a customer certificates of deposit (redeemable only at the bank) and treasury bonds (redeemable in other banks and at designated federal facilities). Treasury bonds may be sold by the customer to some other person or company without the bank's being informed about it.

Other services that are offered are automatic transfers between accounts and automatic bill payment. An automatic transfer between two accounts can be, for example, transferring the amount of the monthly mortgage payment from the savings account every month or depositing the revenue from the trust account (bond interest and stock dividends) into the checking account. Automatic bill payment consists of the bank's transferring an amount of money to another customer in the same bank or a customer of another bank.

The trust account activity is different from the others because it contains stocks and bonds rather than money. For each trust account, the bank must keep track of which stocks and bonds the customer has and how many of each. Also, for tax purposes, the purchase price and the commissions paid must be tracked.

2. Investigate the following applications and make the corresponding entity-relationship diagrams (use the same application as in the exercise on data flow diagramming you did in Section III):

    a. Municipal dog licensing.

    b. Organized tours for groups of people—making arrangements for travel, hotels, and events.

    c. Airline reservations.

3. Draw an entity-relationship diagram for an application for which you have not already established a DFD. Is it easier to do entity-relationship diagramming first, then data flow diagramming? Or is it easier to do the DFDs first, as in the previous exercise?

Process Design

Section VI describes the third and final component of design, that of the system processes. How to design programs that satisfy the user's functional requirements is explained in Chapter 16. Chapters 17 and 18 describe how to ensure that these programs also satisfy the control and performance requirements, respectively.

Finally, Chapter 19 describes how the design is translated into a plan for implementing the system, how to analyze its costs and benefits, and how to gain management approval for proceeding.

The New York State Retirement System

♦

In the early 1980s, the state of New York needed a new system to manage its retirement program. The new retirement system would take two and one-half years to develop. It would contain 800 COBOL modules with a total of several hundred thousand lines of code, and the development team would number between 40 and 50 analysts and programmers.

The system would handle all state employment retirement functions, from the membership application through the retirement itself, the payment of pension and other benefits, and the final disposition by death or other termination. The system would write 200,000 pension checks per month and handle employees from 2,000 different state agencies.

The project team had several challenges. First, the users of the system were to be the retirement case officers themselves—the operational decision makers—rather than clerks; the users would therefore place greater demands on the human interface of the system. Second, because the system was to be so large, the team would have difficulty coordinating the designs of the various subsystems. Third, the underlying technology was unfamiliar: the system would be one of the first of its size to use relational data base for transaction processing.

The first challenge to be addressed was designing a system for the case officers rather than for data entry clerks. The job characteristics of these professionals were the following:

- The two major events in the life of a retirement plan member were the initial registration (at employment time) and the retirement itself. Each of these events could open up a series of processing steps lasting up to six months. A single officer would be assigned to the case for the entire six months.

- Frequently, the case officers would have to interpret regulations and make judgments according to a sense of fairness. At the end of a case, the officer's supervisor would review the work and approve the decisions made by the case officer before clearing the case for final disposition.

- The regulations and the processing were so complex that new case officers required an apprenticeship period, with more supervision and more on-line help available than more experienced officers.

- Each case officer would handle many cases concurrently. The caseload of each officer would therefore have to be managed.

- The main problem of the previous system was to control all the paperwork, making sure that each member's file was complete, that copies of relevant documents could be found, and that the necessary letters were sent to members. The new system would therefore require a strong office automation component.

The designers created a human interface based on a dialog structure illustrated in Figure VI-1. The first screen is a sign-on screen: the user enters an identification and a password so that the system can establish access to the caseload of the user. Next, a case selection screen prompts the operator for the case to be worked on. Depending on the type of case (such as membership application, transfer, or retirement), the system displays a guide to the different activities that the user can choose. From this point on, the user is free to select any of the activities by picking one of the case-general or application-specific screens.

Case-general screens include activities required for all cases regardless of their type: opening, reviewing, and closing a case; maintaining a list of things to do or a list of personal notes that the case officer makes as the case progresses; and so on. The application-specific activities depend on the type of event processed: the forms to be filled out, the calculations to be made, and the decisions to be taken are different for each type.

At any point, the user can suspend the processing to invoke help functions; execute queries against the member data base, the caseload, or existing correspondence; or adapt and combine standard paragraphs into a letter informing the member of decisions or requesting more information.

The second challenge was to coordinate the team's design and development of a large number of program modules. This challenge was primarily met by creating a highly standardized application architecture. For the on-line part of the system, four standard screen styles were designed (see Figure VI–2). Every screen had to conform to one of four styles: case open/close; form with one line per data item; report with a header and detailed lines; and text used for help and word processing.

Another element for standardizing the on-line part of the system was to provide five different styles of on-line programs for the following processes: data entry and update; queries; displaying lists for browsing; opening and closing cases; and selecting a case activity. Each style of on-line program had its specific structure so that the programmer had only to complete the needed details—which screen was to be displayed, which record was to be read on the data base, and so on.

Finally, batch architectures were also standardized (see Figure VI–3). In the structure shown, batch transactions are received from the retirement system's 2,000 employers, each with its own system to track employment, transfers, terminations, and retirements. These transactions are first validated, then posted to the permanent data bases. Reporting is done either from an activity file or from the permanent data base, depending on the content of the report. Various logs and control reports are issued at critical points in the processing for manual balancing and reconciliation.

The third challenge was the use of relational data base technology for high-volume transaction processing. The project team selected DB2, IBM's relational DBMS, but not before the team had developed and run a performance benchmark to ensure that the software could process between five and ten transactions per second. During the rest of the project, the benchmark results helped the team evaluate whether a design decision would have a negative effect on performance. In the final implementation, the system required a somewhat larger processor than initially anticipated; however, this was mostly due to requirements that arose after the benchmark was conducted. Today, the performance of the system is generally satisfactory and improving with every new release of the software.

PURPOSE OF SECTION

The purpose of Section VI is to explain how to design the programs that implement the functions of the system and that fulfill the control and performance requirements established during the requirements analysis phase. The section concludes with a chapter on the cost/benefit analysis performed at the end of the design.

The section emphasizes the role of the system's technical architecture in making the design easier. The technical architecture consists of three layers. The first is made up of the hardware, the systems software, and the distributed processing approach of the entire installation. This layer is described as the production environment in Chapter 6. The second layer is made up of the development environment—a subset of the standards and tools used by

Figure VI–1 **Dialog Structure**

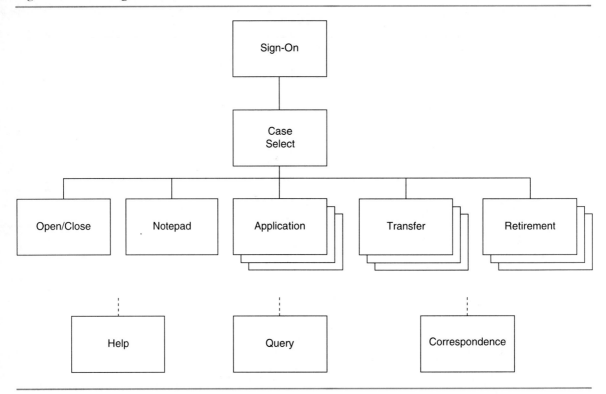

the IS development personnel across applications. The third layer, known as the application architecture, is made up of the overall structure of the on-line and batch processes, the common style of user interfaces, and the standard program designs adopted by the project team. The New York State retirement system illustrates one particular application architecture well adapted to the casework style of user interface.

Some IS departments do not establish a technical architecture at each of these three levels. Instead, many installations let the project team choose its own tools, which can result in excessive tool proliferation. Other installations do not encourage an application architecture and allow each project team member to solve the same design problem in different ways. This practice wastes time spent devising solutions and makes maintenance more difficult. This section therefore concentrates on frequently used architectural elements in transaction processing systems.

Figure VI–2 **Standard Screen Styles**

Screen 1 (top left):

```
SCREEN NO                    NEW YORK STATE              MM/DD/YY
                           RETIREMENT SYSTEM            CASE NUMBER
                             SCREEN TITLE                CASE NAME
OPERATOR NAME


      CASE NUMBER: 999.99.9999
            NAME: XXXXXXXXX X. XXXXXXXXXXXXXXXXXXXXXXX
         ADDRESS: 9999 XXXXXXXXXXXXXXXXXXXXXXXX XX
                  XXXXXXXXXXXXXX. XX 99999-9999
          STATUS: XXXXXXX
LAST ACTIVITY DATE: MM/DD/YY
           NOTES: XXXXX XXXXXXX XXX XXXXXXXXXXXXXXX XXXXXXXX XXXXXXX
                  XX X XXXXXXXXXXXXXX




PF1=HELP  PF3=END  PF4=TOP  PF5=BOTTOM  PF6=RIGHT  PF7=LEFT  PF8=NEXT  PF9=BACK
PF10=PRINT PF12=CANCEL
MESSAGE TEXT: _____
```

Screen 2 (top right):

```
SCREEN NO                    NEW YORK STATE              MM/DD/YY
                           RETIREMENT SYSTEM            CASE NUMBER
                             SCREEN TITLE                CASE NAME
OPERATOR NAME

XXXXXX  XXXXXXXXX  XXXXXXXXXXXXXXX    XXXXXXX  XX  XXXXXXXXXXXXXXXX
9999    99,999.99  XXXXXXXXXXX        XXXXXXX  X
9999    99,999.99  XXXXXXXXXXXX       XXXXXXX  X
9999    99,999.99  XXXXXXXXXXXX       XXXXXXX  X
9999    99,999.99  XXXXXXXXXXXX       XXXXXXX  X
9999    99,999.99  XXXXXXXXXXXX       XXXXXXX  X
9999    99,999.99  XXXX                XXXXXX  X
9999    99,999.99  XXXXXXXX            XXXXXXX  X
9999    99,999.99  XXXXXXXXXXXXXXX     XXXXXXX  X   99 XXXXXXXXXXXXXXX
9999    99,999.99  XXXX                XXXXXXX  X


PF1=HELP  PF3=END  PF4=TOP  PF5=BOTTOM  PF6=RIGHT  PF7=LEFT  PF8=NEXT  PF9=BACK
PF10=PRINT PF12=CANCEL
MESSAGE TEXT: _____
```

Screen 3 (bottom left):

```
SCREEN NO                    NEW YORK STATE              MM/DD/YY
                           RETIREMENT SYSTEM            CASE NUMBER
                             SCREEN TITLE                CASE NAME
OPERATOR NAME



      XXXXXX: _____
    XXXXXXXX: _____
                           _____
         XXX: _____
XXXXXXXXXXXXXXX:  _____
     XXX XXXXXXX: _____
                           _____
         XXXXXX: _____


PF1=HELP  PF3=END  PF4=TOP  PF5=BOTTOM  PF6=RIGHT  PF7=LEFT  PF8=NEXT  PF9=BACK
PF10=PRINT PF12=CANCEL
MESSAGE TEXT: _____
```

Screen 4 (bottom right):

```
SCREEN NO                    NEW YORK STATE              MM/DD/YY
                           RETIREMENT SYSTEM            CASE NUMBER
                             SCREEN TITLE                CASE NAME
OPERATOR NAME

Aaslufasdf luyoiunb

Ert yuiop asdfgh jk KLzxcvbnmpo luytrewqlkj hgf dsammbvcxz plok mi IJNUHB·Y.
gv tfcrdxe:

   SZW:    Aqwazsexdr. cftvgy bhu njimkolpqwer tio y uopaas df
           ghjklzxcvbn mpoiuytr.

   EWQ:    Lkjhgfdsam nbz bvcx pl okm ijnuhbygvtfc tf CRD.  Xredszw. waq
           qawzs xe dcrf vtgby: tgbyhnujm ujmik olploktijn uhb ygvtfcr
           dxes zwaq(p) oli kujmyhn tgbrfvedc wsxqaz (mmbvcxzlkj
           hgfsdapoiu: exhaustively ytrewqd zxcv bnmasd fghj kl qwe
           rtiyu.


PF1=HELP  PF3=END  PF4=TOP  PF5=BOTTOM  PF6=RIGHT  PF7=LEFT  PF8=NEXT  PF9=BACK
PF10=PRINT PF12=CANCEL
MESSAGE TEXT: _____
```

Figure VI–3 **Standard Batch Architecture**

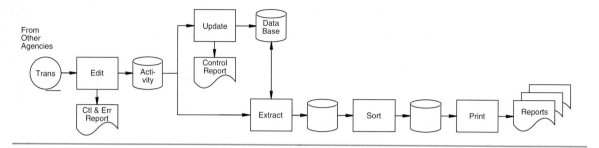

KEY TASKS AND DELIVERABLES

Based on data flow diagrams, conversation designs, and the data model for the application, program design identifies all the programs required to accomplish the processing specified. The design is documented on a system flowchart that depicts the sequence of batch programs, the relationships between on-line programs, and the interfaces between programs through messages and files.

The next level of documentation concerns the decomposition of the largest programs into modules, i.e., the appropriate units of work for estimating and assigning work to individual programmers. A structure chart, a Warnier or Jackson diagram, or HIPO documentation depicts the control structure of the program.

Controls design consists of analyzing and documenting the risks that must be controlled, assessing their potential impact, and selecting the appropriate control techniques. A controls memorandum documents the analysis and serves as a supplemental input to the program design activity, so that control functions can be incorporated in the appropriate modules. Because many of the risks that the controls are designed to cover arise only as the programs are being designed, controls design and program design must be conducted with some degree of parallelism or iteration.

Performance analysis consists in estimating the resource consumption of the processes and the data bases and the impact on the performance requirements. Where required, the process and data designs are modified. The output from this activity is a document summarizing the estimated resource requirements of the application to be used as input to the cost/benefit analysis.

Once the design is completed, all the outputs from the user interface, data structure, and process design tasks flow into the final activity of the design phase: installation planning, economic analysis, and management approval. Only at the end of the design can the project team develop the plans for building the system, testing it, training the users, converting files, and starting live operations. These plans help determine the total development cost and

Figure VI–4 **Data Flow Diagram for Process Design**

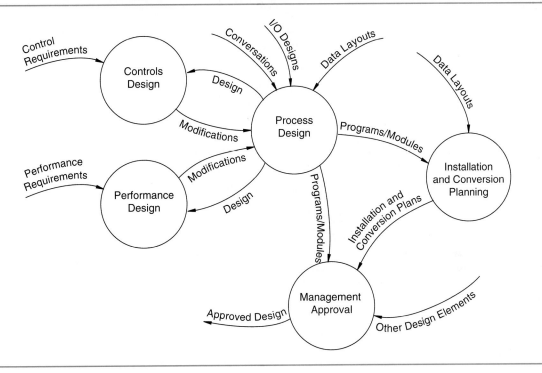

the cost of operating the manual part of the system. The performance design determines the cost of operating the automated part. An economic summary is provided to management, weighing the development and operating costs against the benefits determined during the feasibility study and the requirements analysis, possibly modified by decisions made in the design phase. Management can then decide whether to go ahead with the installation of the system: this is the last major go/no-go decision point in a project.

16

Program Design

This chapter describes how to design on-line and batch programs. Included are examples of on-line programs of increasing complexity, from the simple inquiry to on-line update. Backup, recovery, and restart are discussed in detail. Also described is the standard batch architecture, consisting of a succession of programs to validate transactions, update data bases, extract data, and prepare reports. A discussion of interfaces explains how to communicate data between systems. Finally, the need for cut-off processing is described.

Learning Objectives

- Understand the principles of on-line program design.

- Describe the considerations underlying the design of single-exchange and multi-exchange conversations for inquiry, data entry, and update.

- Be aware of the need for restart and recovery procedures in on-line systems and of the main methods of implementing them.

- Describe the standard batch processing architecture for validating, updating, and reporting, as well as some of the common variations on this standard.

- Understand the process of extracting and printing report data and apply it to specific cases

- Be aware of the impact of the requirements to interface to other systems and to do cut-off processing.

ON-LINE VERSUS BATCH PROGRAM DESIGN

The main distinction between systems architectures of today is between batch and on-line processing. The architectural difference is that in on-line processing, a number of processes go on at the same time, and the sequence of activities is unpredictable. It is generally impossible to reproduce the exact sequence of events that led to a given result because many operators interact with the system simultaneously and independently. (Consequently, some bugs in on-line systems are extremely hard to find if they depend on a coincidence of several independent events happening in a specific sequence.) To each user corresponds a thread of control; the on-line monitor intertwines these threads to maximize the use of resources and minimize response time, while ensuring the integrity of shared data. This type of process is called *transaction-driven* or *event-driven*.

In traditional batch processing, only one thread is going on. Each record of the principal input file is read, processed completely, and replaced by the next record in sequence. Contrary to on-line processing, two successive executions of the same batch program with the same input files will yield identical results, unless there has been a change in the hardware or the systems software.

Sometimes, the very nature of the problem dictates a batch solution. For instance, to produce a management report with detail lines, subtotals, and grand totals, all the detail lines in a group have to be processed before the subtotal is printed; then the next group is processed with its subtotal, and so on, until the end of the file when the grand totals are printed. The input file is in the same sequence as the report, and the technique used is called control break processing. Processes that depend on the input file being in a specific sequence are called *file-driven*.

At other times, the problem calls for batch processing but the sequence is less significant and there is no control break processing. Take, for instance, the processing of insurance premiums. A file of policyholders is read, and each policyholder is billed for a premium that depends on the specific policy, neither on the previous one nor on the next one. The process appears file-driven in the sense that there is an input file and a single thread of control; nevertheless, this processing is much more akin to on-line processing than the previous example and is therefore better qualified as event-driven.

Another example of transaction-driven batch processing can be found in the insurance industry. Assume an insurance company with 2 million policies, all billed every six months. Rather than read the entire file of 2 million policies every day to extract only those policies that fall due (on the average 1 in 180 or so), the company could create a file for each day of the year that contains the numbers of the policies that fall due on that day. It could use the day's file as input, and therefore read only the full data base records for the specific policies contained on the input file—an average of less than 26,000. This method is possible because the processing is not dependent on sequence—just as in event-driven processing. The same type of logic is also applied in utility billing and bank statement preparation. In these cases, the activity is spread over the period of a month.

For on-line programming, the design strategy is transaction-oriented. Each transaction type is considered as a separate entity, and all the functions required to complete the transaction are analyzed within that transaction.

For batch processing, the design strategy is not to group functions by transaction but by type of data transformation they accomplish. Thus, validation functions are grouped together for all transactions, as are data base updating, report extraction, and report printing functions. Within each transformation type, the processing is then broken down by transaction.

Figure 16–1 **User View of On-Line System Functional Hierarchy**

These transaction and transformation strategies are due to Ed Yourdon.[1] Each strategy is normally assigned to on-line and batch systems, respectively. However, it is possible, although uncommon, to organize on-line processing along data transformation lines and batch processing along transaction lines (see Box 16–1).

ON-LINE PROGRAM DESIGN

On-line program design is largely determined by the user's view of the user interface. Some technical decisions remain to be made, however, including decisions on how to use the functions of the teleprocessing (TP) monitor. How to implement these decisions is naturally dependent on the specific TP monitor and is therefore beyond the scope of this text.

A day in the life of a user of an on-line system is depicted in Figure 16–1. The first step is the initialization of activity through a sign-on procedure, which starts a session. In traditional, mainframe-based, centralized transaction processing systems, a session is made up of multiple conversations, each corresponding to a unit of work that stands on its own (a business transaction). Each conversation is made up of several exchanges between the program and the operator. On some days, the user may see a system crash: the work will be interrupted while the cause of the crash is located, the data is recovered, and the processing restarted.

Session Sign-On

As a user signs on to the application, a number of activities must take place. First, it is necessary to *identify* the user: name, account number, terminal location, for example. Then, if the application is sensitive, it may be necessary to *authenticate* the identification. An example is the PIN or Personal Identification Number that users of automatic bank tellers are asked to key

**Box
16–1**

Strategies for Program Design

The strategies for program design that underlie the content of Chapter 16 come from two sources, Edward Yourdon[2] and David L. Parnas.[3]

Yourdon's contribution is to distinguish two substrategies for designing programs: transform analysis and transaction analysis. Briefly, in transform analysis, processes are factored according to their action on the data: validate, calculate, post, print. In transaction analysis, processes are factored according to the business functions that they accomplish: for instance, in an order entry program, new orders, back orders, credit checking, and order status inquiry. Depending on the approach chosen, the top level of the program (the mainline) will generally have a file-driven or an event-driven structure. The modules called by this top-level structure will be factored according to the strategy—either by transform or transaction function.

Parnas's work, published earlier than Yourdon's, does not distinguish between these two substrategies. Instead, Parnas points out the qualities that good modular design should have. The design should group functions into modules (a unit of work for a programmer or a maintainer) that have high cohesiveness and low coupling. These qualities will increase the maintainability of a program made up of such modules and therefore decrease its total life-cycle cost.

A highly cohesive module is one that contains processing instructions that are closely related to each other, that accomplish a single goal, and that are likely to change or stay unchanged as a unit. These characteristics preclude grouping functions solely on the basis of their being performed at the same time, for example, the processing of control totals and the closing of files at the end of the program, which should be in separate modules.

Parnas also advocates low coupling. Two modules have low coupling if each does not depend on the internals of the other. High coupling occurs if a single design or implementation decision affects both of the modules: if the design decision is changed, both modules will change. For instance, the design team may decide to incorporate into the customer number a check-digit of a certain type, say Modulo-11. If the checking is done in two different modules in the system (e.g., in an order entry module and in an accounts-receivable payment posting module), an error in the algorithm or a decision to change the number to Modulo-10 would be reflected in two different places, causing both debugging and maintenance changes.

Another, more universal, example of high coupling is the sharing of data structures—record layouts, data base relationships and pointers, program working storage. Very few IS professionals realize that COBOL is conducive to high coupling because it encourages programmers to share data structures among multiple programs. When a data structure changes, one, many, or all programs that use the data structure may be affected. The worst problem is that some programs appear to see parts of data structures without needing to see them. For instance, a module that changes customer addresses may see the entire customer data base record, including, say, billing conditions. If the billing condition data elements were to change, the address change module would probably not notice; it might simply be recompiled with the new record layout. However, it is impossible to predict this reliably without further analysis.

Conflicting assumptions about the meaning of individual data items can cause many bugs. Conflicting assumptions occur especially fre-
Continued

Continued

quently for codes such as status information, for fields that may have a null value, and for fields that have a choice of formats (such as a date or an amount whose precision could vary). A problem arises when a module that uses the information is unaware of all possible values the data element can take and is therefore surprised when the data element contains a value that appears illegal or meaningless. When such an error occurs within the working storage of a single program, it may be relatively easy to find the source of the error because no other program is involved. When the problem occurs on a file, the culprit may be much more difficult to find, especially if the file can be updated through end-user facilities such as relational data manipulation languages.

There is always a temptation to factor into a single module functions that have the same purpose, the same name, and even similar algorithms but are performed on different data structures. Two functions that fit this description could be the sorting of an array or a table in memory and the sorting of an external, sequential file. Two business-related functions would be insurance processing for homeowner and automobile insurance. In both examples, the objective and the general logic of the process is the same. However, the actual implementation is likely to be quite different. Reading and writing files of arbitrary length is not at all the same as manipulating an array of known length in main memory; and the premium calculation, the claims processing, and the management statistics about two different kinds of insurance are

likely to take into account a vast number of different elements. To factor them into a common module would require multiple processing switches directing the procedure to account for such items as the driver's record (for auto insurance) or the neighborhood (for homeowner insurance). Too many of these switches would increase the coupling of the module and decrease its cohesiveness.

Thus, each module should see only the data that it uses. Parnas calls this "information hiding." Later authors have pushed the argument further, stating the requirement as: "Each module should hide one design decision, and one only." Therefore, any change to a design decision should be limited to one module.

This doctrine cannot be strictly enforced. Some design decisions are all-encompassing and cannot be confined to one module. In addition, many design decisions are made subconsciously and are not seen as decisions. For instance, the decision to represent an amount as packed decimal rather than floating-point is probably so natural to a commercial application programmer that it does not appear to be a decision. In CICS, the design of the work area that enables data to be held in memory over the course of a multiple exchange conversation must be known to all the screen processing modules. And it is illusory to think that programmers and end users can be insulated from knowledge of file layouts and that all I/O must go through centrally controlled modules. End-user computing, decision support, and ad hoc query would then become cumbersome, if not impossible.

in before any transactions are accepted; this number is akin to the password used in many on-line applications. The third step is to *authorize* the user to perform certain functions. Authorization can be given by reference to a file containing the facilities that each user is allowed to request. Or the system can, by default, allow the user access to all the functions of the application. A user authorization file might also contain some of the user's characteristics, such as personalized tailoring of screens (color preferences, for example) and the characteristics of the terminal used (number of lines, monochrome versus color).

Technically, sign-on (or log-on) processing can be done by the operating system, by the application, or by a combination of both. Usually, a system-wide sign-on process will perform all the identification and authentication interactively, and the application will perform the authorization processing without user interaction. In this way, a user can switch back and forth between applications with different authorization requirements without having to provide identification and authentication every time.

If the operating system performs identification and authentication, the project team building an application need not design these functions. On the other hand, the team must make sure that the authorization processing that the application is to perform obeys the constraint of the system sign-on facilities.

Additional authorization processing may be performed by the DBMS at program execution time, for instance, when the data base contains sensitive information that certain users are not allowed to see. For instance, a payroll clerk might be allowed to see salaries of everyone in the data base except managers and above.

The authorization file, if it exists, must obviously be well protected. Protection is even more critical for the file containing authentication data such as passwords. In addition to being password-protected, with access reserved for security personnel, these files are often encrypted, so that a computer operator will be unable to gain access to its data through a utility program that bypasses the operating system.

In some cases, the application or the operating system will monitor each user, so as to cause an automatic sign-off after a certain interval of inactivity. Thus, if a user leaves the workstation, passersby cannot easily gain access to a restricted application.

Depending on the architecture of the transaction processing monitor and the application, resources may need to be allocated to the operator at application sign-on time. For instance, the application may maintain running control totals of transactions by type, so as to have a check at the end of the day against a preestablished total and against the transaction files processed in batch during the night. If a single, application-wide control total is maintained, it may have to be shared by a large number of users and therefore constitute a bottleneck. A better technique may be to assign a control total work area to each operator and consolidate all the operator totals at the end of the shift.

Conversation Design

This section covers only the design of programs interacting with block-mode terminals. In this operating mode, a user fills in an entire screen (usually a form-oriented layout or a menu choice) and presses an *Enter* or a *Transmit* key. The system then processes all the data on the screen and sends a response to the user at the terminal.

Programs running on an intelligent workstation and programs interacting with character-mode terminals are covered under cooperative processing in Box 16–7, at the end of this chapter.

Single-Exchange Inquiry Conversations. Some business transactions require only one exchange between the operator and the system—for example, an inquiry to list all the open orders for a customer whose customer number is known. The programming technique for this type of transaction is simple. The logic of the inquiry dictates that certain tasks be performed in a certain order: validate the format of the data entered by the operator, read the data base record(s) requested, and format and send the response. If there is a format error or if the record requested does not exist on the data base, an error message is sent instead of the formatted screen. Such a transaction can usually be processed within a single module.

Very few inquiry transactions are as simple as this one. In general, the data structures are more complex, requiring several successive inquiries to get the answer. These inquiries can be strung together independently, as illustrated in Figure 16–2, which shows a series of single-exchange, unrelated conversations that nevertheless accomplish a single objective.

Forms of processing other than inquiry, such as data entry and on-line data base update, are also more complex. Even though they may be single-exchange, they have file access and data integrity control requirements that require special consideration.

Conversational Inquiry. A more functional way of implementing the three single-exchange inquiries of Figure 16–2 would be to design a three-step, conversational inquiry, as shown in Figure 16–3. In this design, the user does not need to remember and reenter the customer number from the first to the second exchange and the order number from the second to the third. The design does complicate the program somewhat, however. Now the program must keep track of data between two operator actions. Depending on the teleprocessing monitor, this can be done in either of two ways. In **conversational mode,** the teleprocessing monitor does not automatically release resources when a message is sent to the terminal. Therefore, the whole conversation can be written as a single module, as shown in the pseudo-code in Figure 16–4, using its own working storage to transmit customer and order numbers from one part of the conversation to the next.

Figure 16–2 **Single-Exchange Inquiry Application Flow**

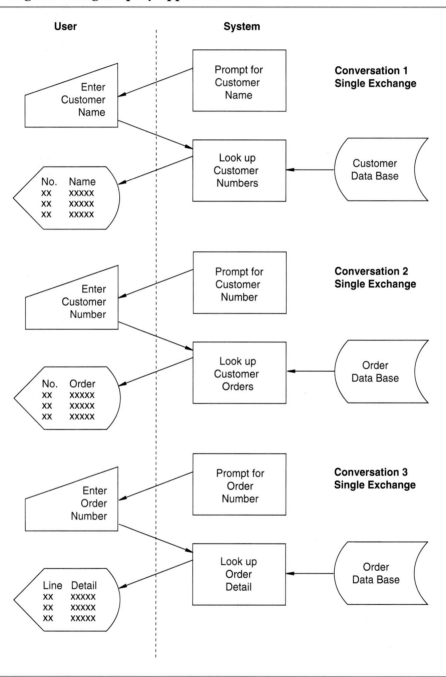

Figure 16–3 **Multi-Exchange Inquiry Application Flow**

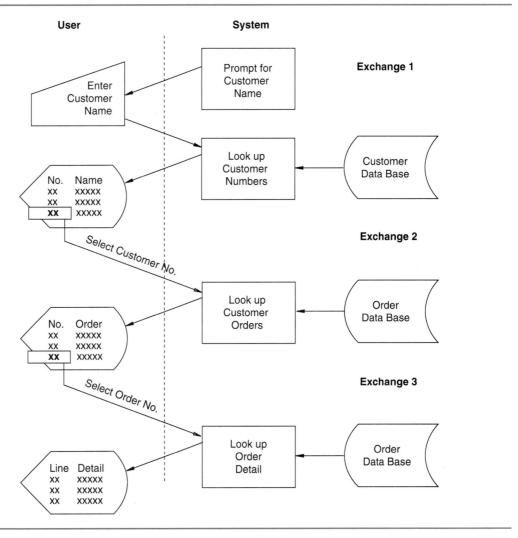

In **nonconversational mode** (or pseudo-conversational mode), the teleprocessing monitor cannot send several messages from the same program. As soon as a message is sent, the program that sends it terminates, and the teleprocessing monitor waits for a new message to appear. No data in working storage is kept between the two successive programs. In this case, the programmer must write three distinct programs and use the teleprocessing monitor's facilities (for instance, a temporary file) to pass data from one to the other. This method is obviously more complex, because the programmer

Figure 16-4 **Multi-Exchange Inquiry Pseudo-Code (Conversational)**

```
SALES                            INSTALLATION TOOL
ORDER ENTRY                        SUBURBAN PUMPS
                               ORDER DATA BASE QUERY


PREPARED BY: F. LAGARDERE      DATE: 27SEP90        VERSION: 1        PAGE 1
APPROVED BY: J. WEBER          DATE: 05OCT90        STATUS:  D


Dowhile Operator_Signed_On
        Write_To_Terminal Prompt_For_Customer_Name
        Read_From_Terminal Partial_Customer_Name
        Dowhile Customer_Name Matches Partial_Customer_Name
                Get_From_DBMS Customer_Number
                              Customer_Name
                Move_To_Next_Line Customer_Number
                                  Customer_Name
        Enddo
        Write_To_Terminal Customer_Number_Screen
                          Prompt_For_Customer_Number
        Read_From_Terminal Selected_Customer_Number
        Dowhile Selected_Customer_Number Matches Order_Header_Customer_No
                Get_From_DBMS Order_Header_Data
                Move_To_Next_Line Order_Header_Data
        Enddo
        Write_To_Terminal Order_No_Screen
                          Prompt_For_Order_Number
        Read_From_Terminal Selected_Order_Number
        Get_From_DBMS Order_Data for Selected_Order_Number
        Move Order_Data to Order_Detail_Screen
        Write_To_Terminal Order_Detail_Screen
        Read_From_Terminal When_Operator_Done
Enddo
```

must manage the acquisition and release of temporary storage areas (on files or in memory). Figure 16-5 illustrates the sample pseudo-code.

Why use nonconversational mode for conversational activities, then, as it is much more complex? There are two answers. First, there may not be a choice: the most popular teleprocessing monitors, IBM's CICS and IMS/DC, are both essentially nonconversational. Second, and more important, conversational mode can have severe performance implications. In general, the processing between an operator pressing *Enter* and receiving a response takes a few seconds or even less. For the operator to respond to the message takes considerably longer: 10 to 15 seconds for typical end-user work; 30 to 60 seconds for on-line data entry and data base update; 5 minutes to an hour if the operator leaves the terminal to get a cup of coffee or go on lunch break. Any

Figure 16–5 **Multi-Exchange Inquiry
Pseudo-Code (Nonconversational)**

```
SALES                          INSTALLATION TOOL
ORDER ENTRY                      SUBURBAN PUMPS
                              ORDER DATA BASE QUERY


PREPARED BY: F. LAGARDERE      DATE: 27SEP90         VERSION: 1        PAGE 1
APPROVED BY: J. WEBER          DATE: 05OCT90         STATUS:  D

Module 1
            Read_From_Terminal Partial_Customer_Name
            Dowhile Customer_Name Matches Partial_Customer_Name
                    Get_From_DBMS Customer_Number
                                 Customer_Name
                    Move_To_Next_Line Customer_Number
                                 Customer_Name
            Enddo
            Write_To_Context_Data_File Customer_Number_Screen_Data
            Write_To_Terminal Customer_Number_Screen
                            Prompt_For_Customer_Number


Module 2
            Read_From_Terminal Selected_Line
            Read_From_Context_Data_File Customer_Number on Selected_Line
            Dowhile Customer_Number Matches Order_Header_Customer_No
                    Get_From_DBMS Order_Header_Data
                    Move_To_Next_Line Order_Header_Data
            Enddo
            Write_To_Context_Data_File Order_Header_Data
            Write_To_Terminal Order_No_Screen
                            Prompt_For_Order_Number


Module 3
            Read_From_Terminal Selected_Line
            Read_From_Context_Data_File Order_Number on Selected_Line
            Get_From_DBMS Order_Data for Order_Number
            Move Order_Data to Order_Detail_Screen
            Write_To_Terminal Order_Detail_Screen
```

resources used by a conversation, main storage in particular, will then be unavailable to the rest of the system for the duration of the operator's absence. Most teleprocessing monitors were created when storage was at a premium and therefore take measures to conserve its use. Today, many systems use virtual memory or memory-swapping techniques; the resource consumption of idle tasks is therefore a less critical issue than before.

The trend is towards less expensive memory and intelligent workstations, which should make conversational mode become more attractive.

However, this evolution is likely to take a long time. Most mainframe-based systems today are still being developed using nonconversational monitors.

Inquiry with Terminal Paging. A common case of conversational inquiry arises when the response to an inquiry may not fit on a single screen. For example, suppose an inquiry screen requests the operator to enter a customer's name and returns a list of customer numbers for that name. If the name is Brubaker, a single screen may suffice to hold all the Brubakers in the data base, but if the name is too common, such as Smith, it may not. A similar problem probably arises when displaying the order.

This problem can be resolved by scrolling or paging. Scrolling is invoked by a function key that causes the program to drop the topmost line on the screen, roll all the remaining lines one line up, and thereby provide room for one fresh line at the bottom. An alternative to scrolling is paging, which consists of keeping the screen header intact and refreshing all the detail lines, 120, 16, 20, or whatever there is room for at the time (see Figure 16–6).

Two techniques are possible for paging. The inquiry program can prepare all the data at the initial request, display the first page, write the entire result of the inquiry to some temporary storage medium, and let a general-purpose paging routine take over if the user wishes to navigate from page to page. This technique is costly in hardware resources, but less costly to develop and maintain.

The alternative is that the inquiry program reads only the data base records required for the first page. If the user requests page two, the same inquiry program reads the next few records, and so on, until the user is satisfied. This technique is more economical of hardware resources, because a number of accesses to the data base may be avoided (if the user finds the answer on the first page) and only the data base keys required to start the following page need to be passed from one exchange to the next. It takes more time to program, however, especially if there are many types of multi-page inquiries, because the paging routine has to be rewritten for each inquiry type.

On-Line Data Entry. On-line data entry is practically always implemented with a multi-exchange conversation because one of the main objectives of data entry is to validate the input and have the operator correct errors as they occur. The error correction cycle requires saving the data that has already been entered so that the user needs to reenter only the erroneous data and not the entire transaction.

There are two types of on-line data entry: intelligent data entry at the source and media conversion. With intelligent entry at the source, the operator has all the information required, or can get it easily, and can correct practically any type of error on-line. In media conversion, the operator has only a document of the transaction at his or her disposal. If errors were committed when the document was created, the operator has no way of knowing what the correct information should be. The difference between

Figure 16–6 **Terminal Paging**

Box
16–2

Distributed Processing

The design of a distributed application, one where data and processes are distributed over multiple processors that run independently of each other, is beyond the scope of this book; only elementary considerations and illustrations of some of the difficulties associated with distributed processing will be covered.

A simple form of distributed data processing is one where the on-line activity is done at remote locations (close to the customer or the warehouse) during the day and where results are consolidated centrally at night. No communication between sites is required to complete a given on-line transaction. The problems associated with this type of distributed processing are fairly simple to solve: It is sufficient to design efficient data uploading and downloading mechanisms and effective controls so that all data that should be transmitted actually will be. A typical design consideration is whether to download to each site in the morning the entire data base required by that location or only the records that have changed as a result of the night's activity.

The problems become more complex when a transaction at a given site requires access to data from another site. A typical design consideration in this case is whether the user or operator must know where to look for the data or whether the system will keep track of it. The latter is the ambition of distributed data base management systems, which are not universally available today. Another consideration is how the transaction will be handled if the remote site that has the data is unavailable because of hardware or network failures. Can the application work in degraded mode? This question is much more critical than with a single-site application because the probability of some link's

failing in a distributed network is much higher. (The risk of the *entire* network's failing is much lower, however.)

The most difficult case to design for is one in which a given transaction requires that several locations in the network update data locally and that these updates be synchronized: either all the updates are performed or none of them are. This synchronization is generally considered to require a procedure called *two-phased commit*. A "commit" is the action that an on-line user takes to indicate to the system that the business transaction being processed is essentially complete and correct and that it can be posted to the data base. This technique ensures that transactions do not get partially posted and, thus, that they do not endanger the integrity of the data base.

The two-phase commit procedure consists of a transaction at a given site asking all the other sites involved in the transaction whether they are ready to commit (phase 1). When a positive acknowledgment has been received from each one, the transaction sends the order to perform the actual commitment (phase 2).

Two problems are associated with the two-phase commit. One, it is time consuming and resource consuming. Even a two-second response time is unlikely to be achieved if a telecommunications network is concerned (rather than a local area network, for example). Two, there are no standard protocols that allow different DBMS software to cooperate in two-phase commit transactions. Therefore, either a homogeneous network where all the DBMS systems come from the same vendor and have a two-phase commit protocol must exist, or a custom protocol must be developed. The latter is costly; the former is hard to find.

Figure 16–7 **Data Entry Application Flow**

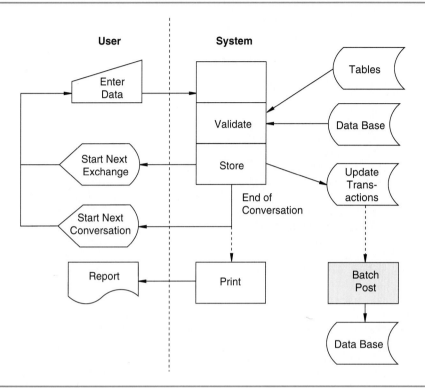

the two is therefore in the amount of validation performed. Intelligent data entry implies as much validation as possible; media conversion tries to catch only transcription errors by the operator.

The architecture most commonly used for either form of data entry is depicted in Figure 16–7. This schematic shows that each exchange consists of accepting the input data, validating it for errors, and storing it on a transaction file. The transaction file will later be used in a batch job to update master files and to do whatever other processing is required. At the end of the conversation, the program acknowledges to the operator that the work is completed and the transaction written to the output file.

Hard-copy output may be required for different reasons—for instance, to print out a receipt, a confirmation, or a temporary justification to a waiting customer. Such output is generally deferred until after the conversation. During the conversation, the program accumulates the data necessary to print the report. At the end, it communicates the data to a report-writing program that can print the output while the operator starts a new transaction. This technique is called spooling or asynchronous printing. The TP monitor may

Figure 16–8 **On-Line Update Application Flow with Immediate Posting**

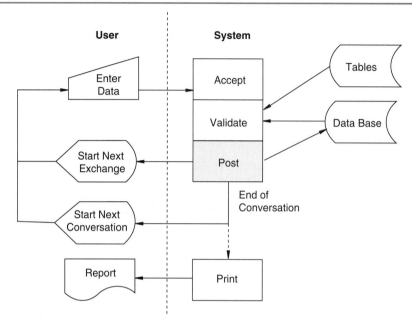

not be able to accommodate spooling, in which case the operator will be slowed down by waiting for the printing to be completed before starting the next transaction. No hard-copy output should be necessary for media conversion. Proof lists, if required, are a batch function.

A slight problem may arise in this architecture. If data is stored as it is validated and the user either decides to abandon the transaction or discovers an error in already entered data, it may be difficult to correct or eliminate those records already written to the transaction file. It must be possible to update records already written, thereby introducing many of the complexities of online update into the program. A better alternative is to create a "cancel" record that can be inserted or sorted before the erroneous records, thus signaling to the batch processing routine that these records are not to be processed.

On-Line Update. On-line updating is quite similar to on-line intelligent data entry, with the added requirement to post the transaction to one or more master data bases. There are three alternative architectures for on-line updates: immediate posting, end-of-conversation posting, and asynchronous (or postconversation) posting (see Figures 16–8 through 16–10). In all three cases, validation and reporting are similar to data entry: validation is usually done immediately, as data are entered, and on-line reporting, if any, is asynchronous. When the posting is performed is different for each of the three approaches. In immediate posting, the data base is updated and transaction

Figure 16–9 **On-Line Update Application Flow
with End-of-Conversation Posting**

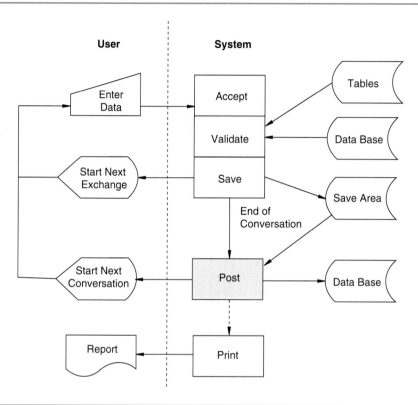

records for batch processing created as soon as a correct screen is received. In end-of-conversation posting, the processing takes place once all the screens of the conversation have been validated and the operator is satisfied that the logical unit of work is complete. The operator is notified when the posting is complete. Asynchronous posting is similar to end-of-conversation posting, except that the operator may start a new activity before being notified that the previous transaction has been posted.

The biggest problem with on-line posting is that each data base record to be updated must be reserved for the duration of the updating process, lest some other user try to update the same information simultaneously. How this might occur with an automated teller machine is shown in Section IV. Another example might occur when an airline passenger is told at 12:10 that a seat is available and lets a few minutes pass before making the reservation, say at 12:17. In the meanwhile, another passenger may have taken the same seat from a different agent by reacting more quickly, say, only a minute after being told at 12:12 that it was available.

Figure 16–10 **On-Line Update Application
Flow with Deferred Posting**

The advantage of immediate posting is that the reservation of the record to be updated and the actual updating usually occur within a very short time, often less than a second. This short span decreases bottlenecks occurring when some other user wants to update the same information (or, depending on the DBMS, information that is stored in its general vicinity). Another advantage is that transactions are simpler to design.

Immediate posting is not always possible, especially when the validity of the transaction depends on the state of several master data base records or when the sequence of updates is at the operator's discretion, as in most customer-contact applications, such as airline reservations. The resulting applications are more complex to design.

Asynchronous posting can be advantageous when the application can tolerate slightly deferred updates and some rejected transactions that appeared correct when entered. Because less processing takes place on-line, the response time can be improved. Also, the system may be operated in degraded mode if the master data base should not be available (for example, it is being backed up, restored, or converted to a new format).

To illustrate the difference between immediate posting and end-of-conversation posting, consider what happens in the following order entry situation. In this system, reservations for the ordered quantities are made against an inventory file. If one item is not available, the entire order is put in as a back order. To avoid overreservations, back-order items are not reserved against inventory.

In immediate posting, each order line is processed completely as it is entered, and the ordered quantity is reserved for the item if it is available. If an item is unavailable, all the previously processed order lines must be backed out and the corresponding reservations undone.

In end-of-conversation posting, each item is first checked for availability, but no reservation is made. At the end of the conversation, if all the items are available, all the reservations are made and the order is declared good. There is some risk that another order might have decreased to zero the quantity available between the time the availability was checked line by line and the time the reservation was actually made. If so, the order would be rejected even though it appeared acceptable initially. The only way to avoid late rejection would be to block the product records for each item ordered so that no other user could interfere with them between checking the availability and making the reservation. For a large order entry system with perhaps hundreds of orders being processed at the same time, this solution is not reasonable, and immediate update is probably preferable.

In other cases, blocking the records is of lesser consequence and end-of-conversation posting is the preferred alternative. It may be the only alternative if the sequence of exchanges with the conversation is variable and if the transaction cannot be validated until all the exchanges have been completed. It may also be the only possibility when the data base integrity constraints specify that two entities depend on each other—for instance, that all departments must have at least one employee and all employees must work for at least one department (see Chapter 15). In this case, the creation on the data base of a new department and at least one employee must be an "atomic" action: either both are created or neither. If the creation takes two successive exchanges and there is a system error or hardware failure between the two, the data base might well wind up in an illegal state.

Backup, Recovery, and Restart in On-Line Systems

On-line systems are particularly vulnerable to hardware and software failures, because these interrupt an activity in the middle, and it is very difficult to know where to restart. In single-threaded batch jobs, recovering from failures is easier, because the process can normally be restarted from the beginning.

The difficulties caused by recovery and restart procedures were long a major deterrent to on-line updates. For many years, prudent designers advocated updating in batch; the most that should be done on-line was so-called memo update. Memo update consists in having a scratch-pad area in each record that can be updated to provide a running value; this value is erased at the end of the day and recalculated by the batch update program running overnight.

Most TP monitor and DBMS combinations now have good enough restart and recovery facilities that memo update is no longer a requirement. The advantages of on-line update are great enough to justify the slight additional effort required to use these vendor-provided restart and recovery facilities.

There are still many decisions on restart and recovery to be made by the designer. The main incident to be guarded against by restart and recovery procedures is the failure of the system at an arbitrary point during the on-line session. When the system fails, there is no way to tell how much work has been actually completed and recorded on the data base or other external files. Because the contents of memory may be lost, any work that has been done only in memory is deemed not to have been done at all.

The principle of all restart and recovery procedures is to place the external data base and other files in a known state of integrity (recovery), inform the users of the system of this state, and ask them to resume processing at this known point of integrity (restart).

The simplest way to accomplish these tasks is to take a **backup copy** of the data base every night; if the system goes down, the copy is restored and the users are asked to reenter all the day's transactions. This way of ensuring recovery is not popular with users. Imagine how a user might react when the system loses power or has a bug at 4:55 P.M.! Manual reentry can, however, be used for very low-volume applications, where no single user is likely to enter more than a few transactions every day. For instance, an on-line time-reporting package where, each individual worker enters time-sheet data once a day or even once a week might use this kind of restart recovery.

Instead of every day, the data base might be backed up several times during the day to minimize the work lost in case of failure. This solution usually fails because of the volume of data to be backed up. Some data bases are so large that it takes all night to back them up.

A more usual practice is to take a daily copy of the data base and then accumulate all the modifications posted to the data base on a separate log. The log will contain each modified record as it looks after the update. The technique is called **after-image logging** (see Figure 16–11). Whenever the data base is updated, the log must be written to first, and the transaction must wait for the actual physical I/O to be completed.

If the system goes down, the backup copy can be restored, and a special recovery program can read all the after-images and write them to the data base. Validation and other processing should be unnecessary, as anything written to the log has gone through all the validations already. When the log has been completely posted, the data base is in the same state as when the system went down.

There is still a problem, however. Those conversations that were stranded in the middle may have been partially completed (because some updates were already made), but the working storage component of the transaction program is lost. If the program maintains a running total, say, to provide a control total or a credit check, the operator entering that transaction would have to reconstitute the state of memory before continuing. Accordingly,

Figure 16–11 **After-Image Logging and Forward Recovery**

Data Base

1. Anne	Chicago	1,000.00
2. Brian	Milwaukee	750.00
3. Charles	St. Louis	850.00
4. Dorothy	Abilene	2,500.00
5. Ernest	St. Paul	500.00
6. Francis	Madison	750.00
7. Genevieve	Dubuque	1,250.00
8. Helen	Hammond	650.00
9. Imogen	South Bend	650.00

Transactions

1. Delete Brian
2. Create James in Decatur with $250.00
3. Add $250.00 to Genevieve
4. Move Charles to Peoria
5. Switch cities for Charles and Genevieve
6. Double Genevieve's money

New Data Base

1. Anne	Chicago	1,000.00
3. Charles	Dubuque	850.00
4. Dorothy	Abilene	2,500.00
5. Ernest	St. Paul	500.00
6. Francis	Madison	750.00
7. Genevieve	Peoria	3,000.00
8. Helen	Hammond	650.00
9. Imogen	South Bend	650.00
10. James	Decatur	250.00

(2) → Process

(1) Back Up

Back-up Data Base

1. Anne	Chicago	1,000.00
2. Brian	Milwaukee	750.00
3. Charles	St. Louis	850.00
4. Dorothy	Abilene	2,500.00
5. Ernest	St. Paul	500.00
6. Francis	Madison	750.00
7. Genevieve	Dubuque	1,250.00
8. Helen	Hammond	650.00
9. Imogen	South Bend	650.00

After Image Log

2. - deleted -		
10. James	Decatur	250.00
7. Genevieve	Dubuque	1,500.00
3. Charles	Peoria	850.00
3. Charles	Dubuque	850.00
7. Genevieve	Peoria	1,500.00
7. Genevieve	Peoria	3,000.00

Normal Processing
- -
After Incident

(3) Restore

Restored Data Base

1. Anne	Chicago	1,000.00
2. Brian	Milwaukee	750.00
3. Charles	St. Louis	850.00
4. Dorothy	Abilene	2,500.00
5. Ernest	St. Paul	500.00
6. Francis	Madison	750.00
7. Genevieve	Dubuque	1,250.00
8. Helen	Hammond	650.00
9. Imogen	South Bend	650.00

(4) → Apply Images

Reconstructed New Data Base

1. Anne	Chicago	1,000.00
3. Charles	Dubuque	850.00
4. Dorothy	Abilene	2,500.00
5. Ernest	St. Paul	500.00
6. Francis	Madison	750.00
7. Genevieve	Peoria	3,000.00
8. Helen	Hammond	650.00
9. Imogen	South Bend	650.00
10. James	Decatur	250.00

many log systems are designed so that incomplete business transactions, or logical units of work, are not restored using after-images.

This result is easy to achieve if the TP monitor is truly conversational, i.e., it knows when a conversation starts and when it ends. The most popular TP monitors, however, are pseudo-conversational. With these monitors, the same result can be achieved if all updates are done in an end-of-conversation routine, rather than exchange by exchange. From the standpoint of data base recovery, all the significant activity then takes place in the end-of-conversation routine. Since after-image recovery process recovers those exchanges that were completely processed when the system failed, the data base can be returned to a consistent state. This characteristic is one of the reasons why end-of-conversation posting is popular.

The same effect as forward recovery using after-images can be achieved differently and sometimes more economically. Instead of storing the modi-

Figure 16–12 **Before-Image Logging and Backout Recovery**

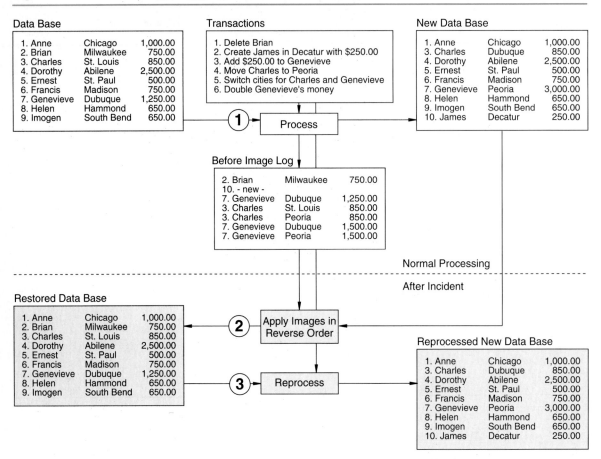

fied images of the data base records, the log stores the images of the records before they were updated. This is called **before-image logging.** These images can be used to roll back the data base: the log is read in reverse sequence and the before-images are substituted, gradually working backwards to the point where each transaction in process at the time of the crash has been undone (see Figure 16–12). At that point, those transactions that were in process are restarted from a transaction log. This technique saves the time required to restore the data base from a backup copy. Still required is knowledge of the starting point of each business transaction; thus, multi-exchange conversations in nonconversational systems still pose a problem.

An additional refinement is installed in systems where on-the-fly recovery is required. This term refers to recovery to the point where the operator

Figure 16–13 **Transaction Restart**

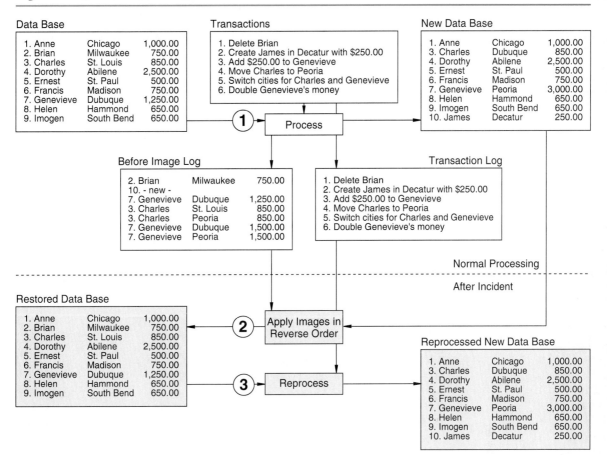

does not have to reprocess anything at all, except possibly the contents of the screen being filled in at the time.

On-the-fly recovery is made possible by logging transactions as well as either after- or before-images. When the data base has been restored to a known state, an automatic **transaction restart** facility can bring the system up to date by simulating the work done by the operators at the time of failure, up to the point where there is no more data on the log. Then, each user takes over, very close to the point where the work was interrupted (see Figure 16–13).

The designer must understand the various recovery methods, know which tools are available either in the DBMS or the TP monitor to implement recovery, and be able to choose the appropriate method based on cost of implementation versus risk and cost of possibly lost work. Also, restart and recovery considerations help govern the choice of update method in a non-conversational system.

BATCH PROCESSING

On-line processing has gradually overshadowed batch since the mid-1970s. On-line applications have taken over practically all transaction processing. Many management information systems also rely heavily on on-line query or on-line ordering of reports. Some practitioners even surmise that batch processing will eventually disappear because it is an unnatural way to conduct business.

Although batch has decreased in importance relative to on-line, it is still far from defunct. Many applications where the processing is initiated by a date rather than by an arbitrary event (such as bank statements or parking sticker renewals) are better done in batch and will continue to be. Why should an operator intervene in a process than can be completely automated?

Other processes require substantial amounts of data to be read before the result can be obtained. Much management control reporting is of this nature. Other applications include taking backup copies of files for restart and recovery purposes, reviewing a data base to audit its integrity, materials requirements planning for a production run, and so on. These applications are file-driven; they may be executed on-line, but many of them are not because they are too costly.

In any case, whether or not file-driven programs are executed on-line, the technique used to design them is the same—and it differs substantially from transaction processing.

Standard Batch Architecture

The standard batch application architecture evolved in the late 1950s and early 1960s and has changed little since then. Figure 16–14 shows its three main components: validation, update, and report separated by sorts.

There are many variations on this architecture. Some batch applications need to update multiple master files or data bases, and the central run may be duplicated. Others have multiple reporting runs. Validation may not be required for date-driven or file-driven processes. Sorting transactions before posting may not be necessary. The essence of the architecture is still the same.

Validation

Batch transaction validation is quite similar to on-line validation. There may be an additional level of validation, called batch control. Batch control consists of grouping transactions together in batches and checking that each batch is complete. The number of transactions is counted or the transaction amounts are totaled and noted on the batch header. When the program has processed an entire batch, it can determine whether the total accumulated during the processing corresponds to the one noted on the batch header. If not, the program signals the discrepancy.

Each transaction is validated, field by field, to determine whether the value of the field belongs to the domain.

Next, all the integrity constraints applying within each transaction record are validated, then those that apply across multiple records, and finally those

Figure 16–14 **Standard Batch Architecture**

that apply to the state of the data base (for example, a nonexistent entity cannot be modified or a parent cannot be deleted without deleting the children, and so on—see Chapter 15).

Invalid transactions are generally rejected and an error report generated. In some systems, the invalid transactions are kept in a suspense file that can be corrected on-line (or in batch, for that matter) and resubmitted for the following validation run. In some cases, when a transaction against a master record is invalid because of the state of the master record, the master record can be modified and the invalid transaction recycled without change the next day. It will automatically become valid when the master record changes.

In some cases, the validation against the master data base or master file is not done until the update run. This method is typical of sequential master files, where access for validation requires the transactions to be sorted in the same sequence as the master file.

Some validation programs do not reject transactions; rather, the problematic transactions get posted to the master file, to a suspense account, for example. One of the integrity criteria of an accounting system is that the total amounts of credits and debits must always balance. It is therefore difficult to reject a credit transaction of, say, $187.65, especially if there is no debit transaction of the exact same amount (an accounting entry may have multiple debits and/or multiple credits). If the accounting entry itself is out of balance, a dummy transaction is generated to a specific suspense account to make up for the difference. Error correction does not consist of modifying the transactions and resubmitting them; rather, it consists of creating new accounting entities that will balance those in the suspense accounts.

Update

In the standard batch architecture, the valid transactions are sorted in the same sequence as the master file or the data base to be updated. The master file and the transactions are both read sequentially, and each transaction is posted to the corresponding master file records before these are written out to a new generation of the master file. If there are no transactions for a given master record, then the master record is written to the new master unchanged. As each master record and each transaction is processed, all the information needed to prepare the reports of the application are extracted to

Box 16–3

Process-Driven Design

Most of Chapter 16 deals with the identification of which programs will make up an application, which functions will be performed by each of these programs, and how the programs relate to each other through data interfaces. The question of how each program is structured is usually left to the implementation phase. There are two exceptions: (1) when the program designer is inexperienced and needs to check that the program he or she designed will actually work and (2) when the program is so complex that it has to be decomposed to estimate its complexity and to incorporate it into the implementation plan.

The traditional way of structuring a program is to group related processing functions into related modules: A mainline module acts as "traffic cop" and passes control to each subordinate module in turn.

A typical example of process-driven design is found in on-line conversational transactions, where processes are grouped by their objectives: validation, update, reporting.

Another typical example is in the standard sequential file update structure (see Figure 16-15). Functions are grouped mainly according to the file operations performed, and the central pivot of the program is the comparison of the sort key of the master file and the transaction file.

A third typical example is represented by the report printing program (see Figure 16-23). The

key elements are the determination of control breaks and page breaks.

In the standard sequential file update and the report printing program, it is easy to spot what appear to be illogical structural elements. For example, in the file update, the reading operation takes place just after the writing operation (and there are two initial file read operations in the housekeeping section). In the report printing, precautions must be taken so that control breaks are not processed at the start of the program when no detail lines have yet been printed.

These seemingly illogical structures are, of course, highly logical; the program would not accomplish its functions if they were not there. Experienced programmers do not think twice about them and incorporate them naturally in their programs, as required. Experience has told them that these structures are the best way to make a process-driven program work. Novice programmers, on the other hand, usually have trouble the first few times they encounter these situations. They have to simulate the flow of records from the input files before understanding that structures that appear more natural at first have bugs in them.

In the authors' experience, process-driven design is not problematic in most transaction-driven or event-driven applications. It is less well adapted to file-driven applications.

a report file. This file, which consists of one record per report per item (master or transaction) to be reported on, will later be sorted by report number, and within report number, by sequence within the report. Sequential update is a classic example of a file-driven process. Boxes 16–3 and 16–4 describe two popular sequential update architectures.

There are many variations on this architecture. The main variation is that sequential processing can be replaced by direct-access update. In this case,

Figure 16–15 **Structure Chart for Process-Driven Update**

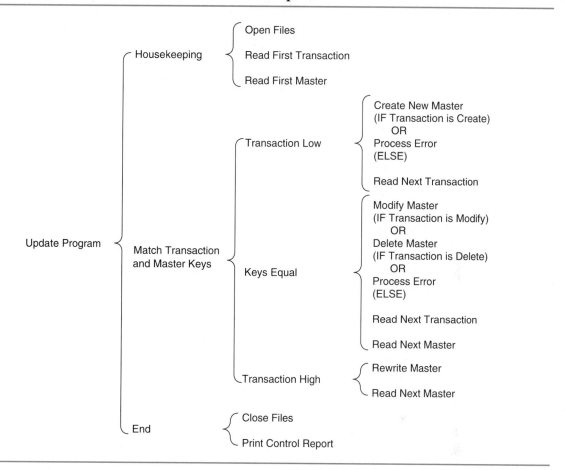

the transaction file does not require sorting, and each transaction is posted as it arrives. The master file or data base is not rewritten to a new generation; it is updated in place. The validate run and the update run can often be combined (see Figure 16–16). In direct-access update, the process is transaction-driven.

Figure 16–16 **Alternative Batch Architecture**

Data-Driven Design

Process-driven design of programs (see Box 16–3) is the norm in the United States. Data-driven design is much more common in Europe; Jean-Dominique Warnier generalized its use in France starting in the 1960s, and Michael Jackson popularized it in the United Kingdom in the 1970s. Since then, both Warnier and Jackson methods have been acknowledged in the United States and have been adopted by some advocates.

The premise of data-driven design is that the program structure should match the data structure. Warnier's view is that the output structure should dictate the program structure, which in turn dictates the input structure. In Jackson's slightly different view, the correspondence or lack of correspondence (called structure clashes) between input and output structures determines the program structure.

Designing a program, thus, consists of designing a hierarchical data structure. The structure of the program does not depend on which entities are on which files. If a program has two transaction files or updates two master files (which are in the same sequence), the program looks no different than if it had a single file. (As an example, the two programs described in Box 16–3 are shown designed according to Warnier's principles in Figures 16–17 and 16–24.)

As an exercise, the reader should try to modify the update program so that the add and modify transactions are in two different files. The reader will quickly realize that the process-driven program's structure changes much more than the data-driven one.

Is data-driven design better than process-driven design, then? Not necessarily. In transaction-driven processes, the two do not yield substantially different results, mainly because the data structures are not complex. In sequential update, data-driven design has the reputation of being easier to debug and of being less dependent on file organizations. However, sequential update has gone out of fashion. In reporting problems, data-driven design also provides clearer and more logical structures, although, if the data structure is straight, with no fan-out at lower levels, its advantage over process-driven design is minimal. (Report writers have the least trouble with this type of structure.) For more complex data structures, such as the one represented in Figure 16–24, data-driven design is most certainly advantageous from a debugging standpoint. (This argument applies to reporting as well as to other file-driven processing, such as the daily cut-off processing of an on-line data base.) There is still disagreement on whether data-driven or process-driven programs are easier to maintain. It is possible to find cases of maintenance requests that would wreak havoc with either of the structures.

Many reports require every master file record to be read because the criteria for including data are independent of the transaction file. For these reports, the transaction-driven update run cannot be used. A separate, file-driven run must read the entire file or data base sequentially to prepare the report records.

A random-access update followed by a sequential read of the master file or data base for extraction of reports is well adapted to relational data base

Figure 16–17 **Structure Chart for Data-Driven Update**

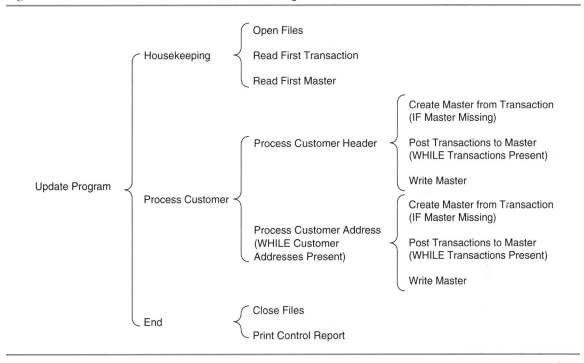

technology, where the master relation does not necessarily have to be maintained in key sequence.

The report extraction process just described works well for routine production reports such as proof lists, routine management reports, and documents that are to be sent to outside entities. The process does not work as well for ad hoc reporting using a report writer. Most report writers can produce only one report per pass of the master file. In this case, each report is a distinct run, consisting of either a single run of the report writer (if the report is in the same sequence as the file) or a dual run with a sort interposed (see Figure 16–18).

The extract run parallels the hierarchical structure of the file or the hierarchical view of the relations making up the master records. (In structured programming, every program is a hierarchical, or tree, structure. Data-driven design, as explained in Box 16–4, chooses to use the hierarchical view of the data as the program structure.) For each detailed record in the master file, the current headers are maintained in memory. These headers change only when a control break is encountered. For example, if the file contains detailed sales records and is sorted by sales region, product, and customer category, then the layout of the work area that is passed to each extract

Figure 16–18 **Ad Hoc Reporting Architecture**

Alternative 1: One report per pass

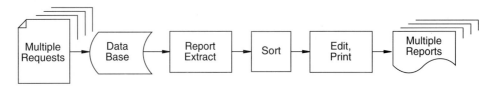

Alternative 2: Multiple reports per pass

module contains a complete *information set:* sales region data, product data, and customer category data as well as the detailed sales record (see Figure 16–19). The header information may be on the master file, or it may have to be looked up on a direct-access file or data base. When all the detailed sales records for a given customer category within a product within a region have been exhausted, the next customer category information set is fetched and delivered with the first of the detailed records within that category.

Figure 16–19 **Information Set for Simple Hierarchy**

Country	Region	Salesperson	Product Type	Sales Data	
U.S.					Country Record
U.S.	N.W.				Region Record
U.S.	N.W.	147			Salesperson Record
U.S.	N.W.	147	01	xxxxxxx	Product Type Record

Figure 16–20 **Information Set with All Detail Records in Storage**

Country	Region	Salesperson	Product Type	Sales Data	
U.S.					Country Record
U.S.	N.W.				Region Record
U.S.	N.W.	147			Salesperson Record
U.S.	N.W.	147	01	xxxxxxx	Product Type Records
U.S.	N.W.	147	13	xxxxxxx	
U.S.	N.W.	147	15	xxxxxxx	
U.S.	N.W.	147	17	xxxxxxx	
U.S.	N.W.	147	24	xxxxxxx	
U.S.	N.W.	147	63	xxxxxxx	
U.S.	N.W.	147	64	xxxxxxx	
U.S.	N.W.	147	69	xxxxxxx	

In relational data base technology, the same effect can be obtained by using the base relation containing the detailed sales data and by joining customer category, product, and sales territory relations to it.

In some cases, the extraction criteria require that a collection of detailed records be examined to determine whether or not to extract. Perhaps someone has requested a report showing all orders with more than 20 items. Then, the entire order (header and detail lines) would have to be read to find out how many lines it contains. The extract program must then provide sufficient space to contain all the records in a detailed group. Only when all the records in the group have been read can the extract modules be called (see Figure 16–20). When the hierarchy is a complex one, as in the employee data base shown in Figure 16–21, this approach is the standard one.

**Box
16–5**

Object-Oriented Design

Chapter 8 described object-oriented analysis as a modern method of representing systems requirements. Object-oriented analysis is valuable in itself because it models the real world more closely than other forms of analysis. It also has the advantage that an object-oriented specification can be translated much more easily into a design than can specifications that use other techniques. Object-oriented design can close the gap that exists between the users' view of system requirements and the technicians' view of the system implementation.

Although object-oriented analysis is beneficial in itself, its potential is best achieved when it is followed by object-oriented design and programming. The converse, object-oriented design not preceded by object-oriented analysis, is problematical.

Object-oriented design and programming purport to eliminate the controversy between process-driven design and data-driven design by combining the two. An object is a piece of data to which is attached all the processing that the data can undergo. For instance, a number is stored together with the rules of addition, multiplication, printing, rounding, and so on that apply to it. The programmer can never have access to the data other than through one of these processes, also called methods.

There are two main benefits to object-oriented design. First, data representations are hidden inside the modules (now called objects), thus making them more cohesive and less subject to intermodule coupling (see Box 16–1). Second, storing code together with the data structures it operates on avoids redundancies. For instance, if several programs had the need to validate an account number, the traditional approach would often result in the repetition of the code,

with slight variations perhaps, in many programs. More significant is the mechanism of class inheritance, where superclasses (or superentities in the vocabulary of Section V) enable subclasses to share common characteristics and routines that are stored only once. The net effect is a sort of "third normal form" for code as well as for data: code is stored where it is needed, everywhere it is needed, and only where it is needed. Applications written in object-oriented languages are usually considerably more concise and flexible than their traditional modularized counterparts.

Even though an object-oriented design is often superior to a traditional design, most systems being built today are not object-oriented for lack of tools and environments in which object-oriented languages can operate comfortably. The object-oriented paradigm is relatively new: it traces its origins to the late 1960s in a modeling language called SIMULA. The ideas of SIMULA were picked up by a team at Xerox PARC (Palo Alto Research Center) and incorporated into a language called Smalltalk. In the 1980s, additional object-oriented languages made their appearance on the market. The most successful of these newcomers is C++, an extension of C, the UNIX-oriented language. Another interesting language is Eiffel, described in a book by Bertrand Meyer, *The Construction of Object-Oriented Programs.*

A common trait of today's object-oriented environments is that they are limited to workstations. There is no mainframe object-oriented language; nor do object-oriented programs on workstations integrate easily with other programs on other workstations or servers. Thus, object-oriented design and programming today is mainly applied to graphical user interfaces on

Continued

Continued

personal computers and workstations. (This is probably the domain where object orientation is the most beneficial.) Other successful applications have included graphic processing software and simulation applications.

There have been experiments with the building of information systems in custom-made object-oriented environments in traditional languages on a mainframe (under PL/1 in particular). Although the results showed that object orientation has great potential, especially in creating easy-to-maintain applications, the lack of an industrial-strength toolset was a severe handicap during development. Other difficulties encountered during these experiments were the lack of proven testing methodologies and the difficulty of controlling a

design that had many more, although much smaller, modules.

The field of object-oriented design and programming is very fertile. A great amount of research and experimentation is being carried out. New books and journals appear almost daily, and theoreticians and practitioners engage in passionate debates. There is no doubt that object orientation is here to stay. The authors believe that, for the next few years, the main impact will be on systems software development on workstations. From there, the paradigm will spread to user interface building, and then to the workstation end of cooperative processing. Finally, it will spread to the mainframe environment (if such an environment still has an independent existence at that time).

If just one report requires that multiple detailed records be contained in the work area passed to the extract module, then all the reports in the run must be extracted with the same work area structure. A sample structure of an extract run using the information set approach is illustrated in Figure 16–22.

Reporting

Once all the report records have been extracted, they are sorted in sequence by report number, and, within report number, in whatever sequence the report is in. This process determines the overall structure of the report printing program as illustrated in Figure 16–23.

Writing report programs is fairly simple: there is generally only one input file and one output file. Maintaining running totals and tracking control breaks is not very complex. As a result, report programs or modules are often given to beginning programmers, whereas validate and especially update/extract runs are given to more experienced personnel.

The only difficulty in report writing is keeping track of page breaks. In Michael Jackson's terms, there may be a structure clash between the output (physical pages of reports) and the input (control groups in a hierarchy; with an arbitrary number of lines in each detail group). If the hierarchy is complex, as in Figure 16–24, page breaks can become quite difficult to manage.

Figure 16–21 **Information Set for Complex, Fanned-Out Hierarchy**

Records:

Level 1 Key	Level 2 Key	Level 3 Key	Data
A 1	000	000	Root Data
A 1	B 1	000	1st B segment
A 1	B 2	000	2nd B segment
A 1	B 3	000	3rd B segment
A 1	C 1	000	1st C segment
A 1	C 1	D 1	1st D segment
A 1	C 1	D 2	2nd D segment
A 1	C 1	E 1	1st E segment
A 1	C 2	000	2nd C segment
A 1	C 2	D 1	1st D segment within 2nd C
A 1	C 2	E 1	1st E segment within 2nd C
A 1	C 2	E 2	2nd E segment
A 1	C 2	E 3	3rd E segment
A 1	C 2	E 4	4th E segment
A 1	F 1	000	1st F segment
A 1	F 2	000	2nd F segment
A 1	F 3	000	3rd F segment
A 1	F 4	000	4th F segment
A 2	000	000	2nd A segment

Some common styles of reports require special techniques either for extraction or for printing. Three of these special techniques are calculating totals before printing details, responsibility reporting, and printing multiple columns in phone-book style.

Total before Detail. When each detail report line contains the percentage of the total control group represented by that detail line, the total of the control group has to be calculated before the detail is printed. The simplest way of dealing with this requirement is to extract two detailed records for each line to be printed and add a sort criterion with a value of 0 in one of the records and 1 in the other. This sort field must be inserted just after the argument that serves as the basis for the total (see Figure 16–25). When the report program reads a record with 0 in the field, it totals it; when a 1 record is encountered, the total is already known, and the line can be printed.

Figure 16–22 **Structure of Extract Program**

Begin
- Open Files
- Read First Master

Constitute Information Set
- Move Master to Information Set (IF No Control Break)
- Read Next Master

Extract Reports

Process Report 1 (WHILE Detailed Records in Infoset)
- Apply Extract Criteria to Detailed Record
- Write Extracted Record

Process Report 2 (WHILE Detailed Records in Infoset)
- Apply Extract Criteria to Detailed Record
- Write Extracted Record

Process Report 3 (WHILE Detailed Records in Infoset)
- Apply Extract Criteria to Detailed Record
- Write Extracted Record

. . . . .

Process Report N (WHILE Detailed Records in Infoset)
- Apply Extract Criteria to Detailed Record
- Write Extracted Record

End
- Close Files
- Print Control Report

Responsibility Reporting. Responsibility reporting consists in creating a report for each organizational entity (cost center, profit center, section, etc.) at a certain level of detail (say, by account) and then rolling up the organizational entity into the next one, while maintaining the same level of detail reporting.

This type of report is best handled by a specialized extraction technique. It requires maintaining a hierarchical file of the organizational entities, as illustrated in Figure 16–26. When a detailed record to be extracted is encountered, the extract program creates one report record with the original department or section number in it. This process will create a report line at the lowest level. In addition, one report record is created for each entity that is directly above the detail one in the hierarchy, with the corresponding entity number replacing the detail department or section number.

The report records are sorted by organizational entity as the major key. The report-printing program will then encounter all the records required for each organizational entity in sequence by entity.

Figure 16–23 **Structure of Report Printing Program**

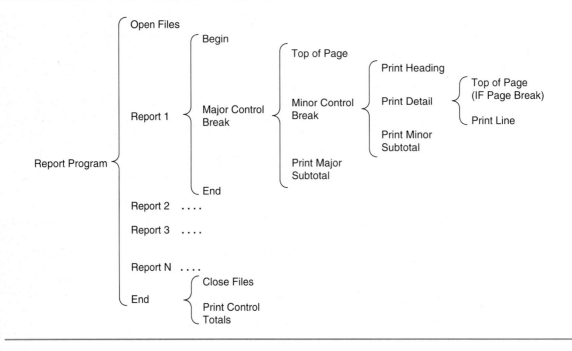

Phone-Book Style. When a report only requires a small number of print positions (usually less than 40), the number of pages required to print it can be reduced by half or more just by repeating the column multiple times across the page (see Figure 16–27).

The temptation is to print the report line by line so that the elements are in sequence from left to right, top to bottom. This format is by far the easiest for the programmer. It is also by far the most inconvenient for the reader, especially if the report is to be used as a reference, such as a phone book in which the reader searches for an item by using the alphabetical sequence.

The desirable sequence for reading such a report is top to bottom, left to right. This arrangement implies that the reporting program must accumulate all the data required for an entire page before starting to print the first line. An added complication occurs at the end of the report, when the information to be printed does not fill an entire page. Special logic must then be provided to balance the length of each column.

INTERFACES TO OTHER SYSTEMS

Interfaces to other systems are frequently part of the design of the system. Interfaces are of three types: shared master files, interface files, and interface messages.

Figure 16–24 **Complex Report Structure**

Shared master files or data bases present no particular problem except when several different programs or applications can update the same data. Then, carefully designed audit trails are required, because understanding the concurrent interaction of multiple independent programs can become very difficult. If the master file is a data base, a good audit trail is usually sufficient. If the master file is a traditional file, then it cannot be updated simultaneously by several programs running at the same time. Care must be taken in the design so that the file will never be needed by another program during the update run.

Figure 16–25 **Total before Detail**

```
MARKETING                          DESIGN TOOL                        D220
STATISTICS                        SUBURBAN PUMPS                      R394
                         SALES CONTRIBUTION REPORT MOCKUP


PREPARED BY:  ANNE LYNN          DATE: 27AUG90        VERSION: 4       PAGE 1
APPROVED BY:  JACK WEBER         DATE: 05SEP90        STATUS:  D



               CONTRIBUTION TO SALES BY PRODUCT TYPE AND SALESPERSON
                            PERIOD: MAY 19XX

            Salesperson 147 JOHN Q. DOE


                    Product 01         123,250          22.0%
                    Product 13          61,600          11.0%
                    Product 20          76,550          13.7%
                    Product 72         175,740          31.4%
                    All others         122,860          21.9%
                    ------------       -------          ------
                    All products       560,000         100.0%
                    ============       =======          ======
```

Interface files are files written and closed by one system and then opened and read by another system. A typical example would be the accounts receivable information produced by an invoicing application. The use of one application to generate transactions for another application is one of today's prime sources for batch processes, along with reporting and file backup. No particular design considerations are required here.

Interface messages achieve the same goal as interface files, but are generally on-line. They are used when one application has to request another application to process some transaction without delay. An example can be found in international banking, where money transfers and other transactions are carried on the S.W.I.F.T. interbank network. Some commercial banks have applications that produce requests for international transfers. If the bank's computer is connected to the network on-line, a message can be sent by this application. (In other banks, transactions to be sent on the network are accumulated all day on an interface file, which is read by the system at the end of the day using interface files rather than messages.)

Interface messages are also used when one application needs data from another application, perhaps on another computer, as in distributed processing.

Message interfaces present two design requirements. The first is that the sending application must make sure that the receiving application has actual-

Figure 16–26 **Hierarchical Responsibility Reporting**

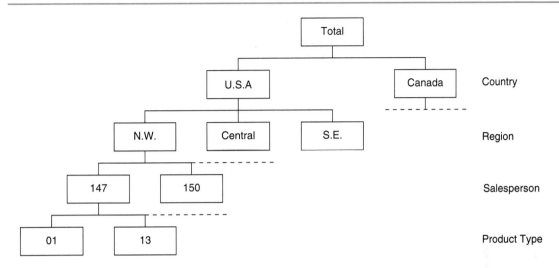

The problem is to print an analysis of sales by product type at each level, salesperson, region, country, and grand total.

From a detail record such as the sample below . . .

U.S.	N.W.	147	01	$123.25

. . . extract the following:

Country	Region	Salesperson	Product Type	Sales Data	
All	All	All	01	$123.25	for grand total
U.S.	All	All	01	$123.25	for country total
U.S.	N.W.	All	01	$123.25	for region total
U.S.	N.W.	147	01	$123.25	for salesperson total

Figure 16–27 **Phone-Book Style Report**

MARKETING STATISTICS	DESIGN TOOL SUBURBAN PUMPS MARKETING DIRECTORY MOCKUP		D220 R398

PREPARED BY: ANNE LYNN   DATE: 27AUG90   VERSION: 2   PAGE 1
APPROVED BY: JACK WEBER   DATE: 05SEP90   STATUS: D

Reading Sequence 1   2   3

NAME	EXT.	NAME	EXT.	NAME	EXT.
LAUTERBURG, STEVEN C.	5371	LAYTON, MARY T.	7599	LEARY, WILLIAM F.	7053
LAVERY JR, RONALD C.	6698	LAZARE, ED	5106	LECAROS, ARNOLD	4639
LAVEY, STEPHEN P.	5112	LAZOR, MARTIN S.	5117	LECLERC-LIND, RENEE A.	4544
LAVOIE, JOHN P.	5117	LAZZARI, MICHAEL J.	5106	LEDEBUHR, CHARLENE M.	4700
LAW, ERIN M.	5113	LAZZARI, PETER F.	5117	LEDERER, JEFFREY T.	4310
LAWICKA, VALERIE D.	4159	LE CAVALIER, SHARI L.	7876	LEDERER, MURIEL N.	2384
LAWLER, JAMES E.	5113	LE FEVRE, ALAN W.	7275	LEDERER, THERESA L.	5117
LAWLER, JOHN E.	5353	LE PENSKE, SANDI J.	1237	LEDYARD, PAUL	9951
LAWLER, SUSAN E.	5113	LEAHY, MARGARET A.	6134	LEE, BEVERLY A.	3941
LAWNICZAK, ADABETH L.	1510	LEAHY, MARY JO	5101	LEE, DEBRA A.	6088
LAWRENCE, MICHELE D.	3280	LEANDER, MARY L.	2171	LEE, GILBERT C.	5112
LAYMAN, DANIEL R.	4926	LEARN, CYNTHIA J.	5018	LEE, GREGORY A.	7500

ly received the message and acknowledged it. In certain cases, it must also wait for the response. If the receiving application "times out," i.e., does not acknowledge receipt within a specified time, the sending application must decide what to do—abandon the transaction or use a backup procedure to write it to a file for later processing.

The second requirement is that, as with shared master files, a carefully designed audit trail must be built. When exchanging sequential files, the file itself constitutes a good audit trail (although file control totals, as described in the next chapter, are still required). When exchanging messages, both the sending and the receiving systems must log these messages so that discrepancies can be researched and accounted for.

CUT-OFF PROCESSING

Cut-off processing is the processing required to synchronize two applications that use the same data but have different rhythms. For instance, taking deposits and disbursing funds in a bank; preparing and selling hamburgers in a fast-food restaurant; making automobiles in a Detroit factory; drilling, pumping, and refining oil in an oil company are essentially continuous activities. The accounting for these activities has a yearly rhythm (for audited financial statements to stockholders), a quarterly rhythm (for some regulatory report-

Box 16–6

Impact of Fourth-Generation Tools and Prototyping

If a fourth-generation tool is used to prototype an application, many design considerations do not apply. A prototype does not normally require the attention given to integrity and performance that an operational application needs. Moreover, most good fourth-generation tools have design decisions built into them. These decisions concern the structure of the application, the controls, and the general performance criteria.

These built-in decisions eliminate some design work; on the other hand, they reduce the number of options available to a designer. This lack of options is not much of a problem for prototyping. In contrast, problems arise when such a tool is used to develop a full-fledged transaction processing application, where several users share the same data and when there is a mix of on-line and batch preprogrammed and ad hoc activities (as is often the case in departmental applications).

One technique used by a fourth-generation language to avoid having two people update the same record simultaneously is simply to cancel one of the transactions when there is a collision and to request one operator to start over again. This solution is perfectly acceptable as long as the problem happens very infrequently. However, it cannot be used when volumes increase and users start requiring the same records more and more frequently. Another technique used by some fourth-generation tools is that a full pass of the master file is required for every report extracted. This technique is acceptable for small master files that can be read quickly or for situations with very few reports. It can become prohibitively expensive when volumes are high.

Even if a fourth-generation language is used for prototyping only, there may be a temptation to make the prototype the basis for the operational system and to carry over some of the design decisions (and even code) from the prototype. This carryover might be tantamount to a "creeping decision" to use a tool adopted only for prototyping purposes to implement the operational system.

In summary, a fourth-generation tool simplifies program design, but it also reduces the designer's degree of freedom to satisfy integrity and volume requirements.

ing), a monthly rhythm (for internal accounting reports), and perhaps even a daily rhythm (for customer and cash requirements accounting in a bank).

The data supplied by transaction processing to management information systems and decision support systems must be cut off. Management reports or summary files that feed decision support systems have their data neatly classified by period; once a transaction has been assigned to one period, it cannot normally be reassigned to a different period.

It is not possible here to give exhaustive descriptions of all the cut-off processing requirements that a corporation may have. Some of these requirements, however, are often encountered and are often mishandled by inexperienced analysts. The discussion will be limited to the daily cut-off between

Cooperative Processing

Cooperative processing is the name given to a reduced form of distributed processing. It refers mainly to the case where the user's workstation handles part of the application and another processor—usually a PC, but possibly any other size computer—handles the other part.

Cooperative processing has two main purposes. The first is to present the user with a better interface, which uses the modern techniques of graphic interfaces, pointing devices, windows, and WYSIWYG (What You See Is What You Get). The second main purpose is to reduce the load of processing on shared resources, in particular, the processor that has access to data.

The conventional view of cooperative processing is therefore to separate the application into two parts: a user interface part, running on a PC, and a data server part, running a DBMS on a mainframe, a mini, or another PC. Little is known about the long-term effects of cooperative processing on user satisfaction, on maintain-

ability, and on cost-effectiveness.

However, two considerations come to mind. One is that the best on-line help is data sensitive. To achieve data sensitivity, the data should be at the workstation rather than on another processor, contrary to the objective of data sharing. The other consideration is that multiple-exchange conversations need to be known to the data server if proper control over the shared data is to be maintained. (The alternative is to go to two-phase commit, but the cost hardly seems worth the advantage.) The division of the application into conversations and exchanges is part of the user interface, which therefore must be known both to the workstation and the data server.

Thus, even though the general guideline is to separate user interface and data manipulation, compromises must be made to preserve the integrity of the application. Experience is insufficient yet to determine where these lines of compromise should be drawn.

the on-line system and the batch activities. Weekly, monthly, and yearly cut-offs are subject to similar considerations.

Assume that the application is a demand deposit accounting application in a bank, and that there is a requirement to process daily statements. Moreover, the account balance and all the transactions of the last two weeks are maintained on-line for customer inquiry purposes.

If the on-line system is only available during office hours, the cut-off process is relatively simple. At five o'clock, the on-line system is shut down; a batch process is started to extract transactions for the daily statements; and fresh balances and transaction histories are reloaded to the data base. The data base has to be re-created because it is not economical to carry more than two weeks' transaction history. Therefore, every day, the oldest transactions are dropped and the most recent ones are added.

This form of cut-off is the easiest to design. However, even in a simple case such as this one, there are several important requirements. One is to design the system so that the on-line processing can start even though the batch programs may not have been completed. A frequently used control step is to check, during the on-line start-up process, that the date of creation of the data base is equal to the system date less one. Although this control step is useful, it must be possible to override it to handle unexpected delays in the overnight batch process.

Another important requirement is to design the system so that it is possible to run two cut-off processes in a row. If the batch process could not be run on one night, it must be possible to run two cut-off processes in succession on the following night.

An example of a more complex (and less common) requirement is illustrated by a bank that acquires a series of automated teller machines, requiring the system to be up 24 hours a day, 7 days a week. The extraction of statements must not disrupt the on-line processing. The cut-off process will have to be run by the transaction processing monitor concurrently with other transactions, so that any possible simultaneous updates can be controlled. The requirement to reload the data base with a fresh transaction history is more difficult to meet. The procedure in this case is to create a fresh copy of the data base, switch from the old copy to the new copy, and reprocess any transactions that came in while the fresh copy was being prepared and that therefore were posted only to the old copy. This is very similar to recovering on the fly.

RECENT TRENDS IN BATCH PROCESSING

On-line systems are more and more often run well beyond office hours. Automated teller machines must be available 24 hours a day; so must airline and hotel reservation systems and often also computer-integrated manufacturing systems. In such systems, batch programs cannot be assumed to run under a single thread of control because they must share the master files or data bases with the on-line system. One solution often adopted is to write the batch functions as though they were "operatorless" on-line transactions.

Summary

The main architectural characteristic of programs is whether they are on-line or batch. On-line programs are event- or transaction-driven; batch programs are generally file-driven, although they may also have transaction-driven characteristics in some cases.

On-line programs should provide for sign-on activities and the actual transactions to be carried out. Sign-on activities are required to authenticate the user and to authorize him or her to work with the application. The designer must know the operating environment of the application to decide which part of the sign-on is done in the application and which is done by the operating system or other general facilities.

Conversations fall into several patterns. The most frequent patterns are single-exchange inquiry, multiple-exchange inquiry, on-line data entry, and on-line update. Single-exchange inquiry is the simplest and presents no general design problems. Multiple-exchange inquiry is more complex; the program must provide for data to be kept in memory or on disk between two successive exchanges. The techniques for doing this depend on the functions and the architecture of the TP monitor being used. On-line data entry introduces the additional notion of validating, posting, and, if required, reporting on the transaction. The designer must choose at which point in the conversation these activities take place: at each exchange, at the end of the conversation, or after the conversation is finished. In on-line update, additional consideration must be given to the best way of ensuring that the updated data base remains in an acceptable state of integrity.

Backup, restart, and recovery must be provided for. The designer chooses between the various methods—backup with after-images or backout with before-images being applied to a point of integrity. The designer also chooses whether to provide on-the-fly restart of transactions.

Batch processing generally uses a standard architecture of validation, sorting, update/extract, sorting, and reporting. Validation is very similar to on-line validation in that it is transaction-driven. Updating can be file-driven (in a sequential update, more and more infrequently encountered) or transaction-driven (in direct-access update). Extracting and reporting is always file-driven. The standard reporting architecture calls for reading the master file (or the master relation) once, extracting all the information required for all the reports in the same pass. Some special considerations apply to particular kinds of reports: processing totals before details, responsibility reporting, and printing a report in phone-book style.

Interfaces to other systems also have to be designed. They are of three types: shared data bases, files created by one application and used by another, and messages sent from one application to another. Of the three, sending messages between systems is the least frequent and requires the most care in design.

A particularly frequent requirement for interfacing to other systems results from the need to perform cut-off processing, i.e., assigning transactions to periods that are significant to MIS and DSS users. The need arises whenever there is an interface between two applications or two parts of an application that do not have the same processing cycle, on-line, daily, weekly, monthly, quarterly, or yearly. Most important, cut-off processing must provide flexibility in the overlap of these cycles.

Selected Readings

Best, Laurence J. *Application Architecture.* New York: John Wiley & Sons, 1990.
   This is a very original book. Rather than concentrating on how to structure individual programs, it describes the typical large mainframe appli-

cation architecture that has arisen from the collective experience of many thousands of information systems departments.

Martin, James. *The Design of Man-Computer Dialogues.* Englewood Cliffs, New Jersey: Prentice-Hall, 1973.
As described in Chapter 10, this book, although fairly old, still has extremely useful information, both on user interface and program design.

Blackman, Maurice. *The Design of Real-Time Systems.* London: John Wiley & Sons, 1978.
This is a very complete book for on-line systems.

Date, Chris. *An Introduction to Database Systems*, 4th ed. Reading, Massachusetts: Addison-Wesley, 1981.
This book has an explanation of recovery and restart as well as two-phase commit.

Jackson, Michael. *System Development.* Englewood Cliffs, New Jersey: Prentice-Hall International, 1983.
Michael Jackson is perhaps best known for his work on how to design the internals of a program. This book extends his work to the design of application architectures. His methods in this field have not reached the same degree of recognition as in program design; nevertheless, his book is very interesting and has a number of novel approaches. It is recommended for those who want to explore the subject to great depth.

Review Questions

1. Explain the difference between a single-exchange conversation and a multi-exchange conversation:
  a. From the user's viewpoint.
  b. From the viewpoint of program design.

2. Compare development effort and resource consumption of the two types of terminal paging:
  a. Preparing all the data at the initial request and letting a generalized paging module display those pages that the operator is interested in.
  b. Preparing only the data strictly necessary to answer each request for a fresh page as the user makes it.

3. Describe the advantages and disadvantages of performing some functions after the end of the conversation (asynchronously).

4. Describe the recovery and restart process involved in restoring the data base and posting after-images to it. Describe the process using the current state of the data base and backing out the updates to a known point from before-images. Contrast the two in terms of performance, user impact, and risk to the integrity of the data base.

5. Is batch processing likely to disappear?

6. What are the components of the standard batch (sequential update) architecture? How does the batch architecture change if the master file is not processed sequentially?

7. Why is it usual to extract data for reports in a first program and then print the reports in a second program?

8. Describe the three main ways of interfacing to other systems. Which is the easiest to control?

9. Name some reasons for the need for cut-off processing.

Discussion Questions

1. Contrast nonconversational and conversational modes of processing. Why is conversational processing likely to increase over the next few years?

2. What additional work does the use of nonconversational mode impose on the program designer and the programmer?

3. Discuss scrolling and paging applied to intelligent workstations (given that the text of the chapter only refers to block-mode terminals). In particular, discuss whether scrolling is preferable to paging, or vice versa:
  a. For the user.
  b. For the developer of the workstation portion of the program.
  c. For the developer of the host portion of the program.

4. What are the merits of transaction restart on the fly? In what type of application would you expect to see it used?

5. How does distributed processing affect restart and recovery procedures?

6. How does the use of fourth-generation languages affect program design?

Mini-Case

Figure 16–28 depicts a conversation flow for order entry for the Condor Telephone Company. This conversation implements the ordering of telephone equipment and services for private individuals.

The conversation flows as follows: a menu choice has permitted the user to display a screen requesting either a customer number (in practice, one of the customer's telephone numbers) or a customer name (if the number is not available). The name may be partially entered. If the number is known, the order header panel is displayed by the program. If not, the program displays a list of names with their respective telephone numbers matching the partial name entered on the first screen. The operator picks one and continues with the order header screen as before.

When the order header is entered, each order line is entered in turn. There can be no more than ten lines per order. (Remember, these are residential customers.)

Finally, when the order is all entered, the operator presses a function key and the order is finalized; the program goes on to display the menu choices again.

Figure 16–28 **Order Entry Conversation at Condor Telephone Company**

```
MARKETING                          DESIGN TOOL                              U525
ORDER ENTRY                  CONDOR TELEPHONE COMPANY                       CNV016
                           CONVERSATION FLOW - ORDER ENTRY


PREPARED BY: KATHY KRALL         DATE: 15JUN93          VERSION: 1.1       PAGE 1
APPROVED BY:                     DATE: NNAUGNN          STATUS:  D



                (PER CONV.)
DEFAULT FLOW      OCCURS    SCREEN NAME        ALTERNATIVE SCREEN        FUNCTION KEY
------------      ------    -----------        ------------------        ------------
SCN0050             1       MENU                  SCN0051                  Line 1
                                                  SCN0052                  Line 2
                                                  SCN0053                  Line 3
                                                  SCN0054                  Line 4


SCN0060             1       ORDER ENTRY PROMPT    SCN0099                  F11

SCN0061             1       ORDER ENTRY HEADER    SCN0061                  F14
                                                  SCNO099                  F11


SCN0062           1-99      ORDER ENTRY HEADER    SCN0063                  F3
                                                  SCN0062 (Previous)       F7
                                                  SCN0062 (Next)           F8
                                                  SCN0098                  F11


SCN0063             1       ORDER CONFIRMATION    SCN0050                  F3
                                                  SCN0060                  (Enter}
                                                  SCN0061                  F14


Suspend-and-resume screens:

SCN0098           0-99      PRODUCT QUERY         Resume                   F3

SCNO099           0-1       CUSTOMER QUERY        Resume                   F3
```

Questions for Discussion

1. Design the on-line conversation (excluding the menu choices) implementing this function. The following assumptions are made:

  a. The environment is nonconversational: you must design the data to be held from one exchange to the next.

  b. Each order line concerns an item of equipment or a service. If it is an item of equipment, then the inventory must be checked for availability and updated by subtracting the item from stock.

    c. If it is a service, the service department schedule must be checked. If the service request can be accommodated, it must be entered on-line on the schedule. Last-minute adjustments to the schedule are frequent, however, and it is not unusual to overbook the service department on a given day.

    d. No back ordering of unavailable equipment is possible. The customer must call again to reorder when the item is in stock.

    e. The phone company covers a township with 65,000 inhabitants in an area that is popular with corporate transferees.

2. Your design should cover validation, file look-up, error processing, file update, and printing a hard copy of the order for customers who are physically present (less than 5 percent of the total number of orders). Although many orders are for new customers, vou should consider that the customer has already been created on the data base; this step is not necessary during order processing.

Notes

1. Yourdon, Edward, and Constantine, Larry L. *Structured Design.* Englewood Cliffs, New Jersey: Prentice-Hall, 1979.

2. Yourdon, Edward, and Constantine, Larry L. **Structured Design**. Englewood Cliffs, New Jersey: Prentice-Hall, 1979.

3. Parnas, David L. "On Criteria to Be Used in Decomposing Systems into Modules." *Communications of the ACM* (April 1972): 221–227.

Controls and Security

Chapter 17 examines the importance to management of controls over information systems and the main sources of errors. Also described are general controls and application controls. The general control objectives recognized by industry are described. Next, specific examples illustrate the most frequently used transaction processing control techniques for transaction origination, data entry, processing, reporting, data base, and system interfaces. Finally, privacy issues and the rights of the individual are discussed.

Learning Objectives

- Recognize the importance of controls in protecting the organization from the risks associated with a system failure.

- Understand general systems controls as a set of overall controls and standard operating procedures in the IS department.

- Understand application controls as specific features built into computer systems to protect the application from inherent risks as well as risks associated with the system's hardware and software.

- Recognize three typical sources of computer system errors: human errors, technical failures, and natural forces.

- Describe the generally accepted application control objectives useful in identifying overall risks related to the organization and transaction processing risks related to the application.

- Apply transaction processing control techniques that pertain to how transactions flow through a typical data processing system.

- Give examples of transaction processing control techniques, including controls over transaction origination, data entry, and processing.

- Become aware of societal concerns regarding privacy and the rights of individuals when designing information systems.

MANAGEMENT CONTROL OVER
INFORMATION SYSTEMS

As information and information systems become more significant in the long-term success of an organization, management must have greater assurance that the IS function is properly controlled. The importance of having adequate controls can best be appreciated by understanding likely results of inadequate controls:

- Normal business operations may be curtailed with the resultant loss of revenues and customer goodwill. If the disruption is so serious that normal operations are suspended for an inordinately long period of time, then permanent termination of operations may follow.

- Erroneous management decisions may be made because of inaccurate or untimely information supplied.

- Excessive costs may be incurred when information systems are less efficient or effective than possible.

- Fraud and embezzlement are made easier.

- Legal or regulatory penalties are possible from late or misleading information.

Organizations have learned to deal with such risks by making sure their IS function is well controlled. Proper controls over IS functions fall into two categories, general controls and application controls.

General controls are the controls and standard operating procedures in place in the IS department governing all aspects of the unit's operations. They typically cover such areas as the organization structure, personnel policies, physical security, and information access.

Application controls are specific features built into computer systems to protect the organization from risks inherent in the application itself or in processing by the computer system's hardware and software.

To ensure adequate protection against risks, management should at least enforce the following rules:

- Adequate overall written control procedures should be provided for all general controls. Systems development documentation should describe the appropriate application controls.

- Management should verify that controls are used in daily operations by having periodic compliance tests made under the supervision of audit personnel.

- Periodic reviews of IS controls should be made by a qualified third party. Control reviews are usually performed by external auditors during the course of the annual audit. A more in-depth review may be warranted in many instances, especially in those organizations whose information systems are in one of the three strategic quadrants described in Chapter 1.

- Finally, management should be responsible for maintaining or supplying information to such people as investors who rely on information to make decisions and individuals who expect protection for their rights to privacy. Litigation may be the price paid for lack of diligence.

SOURCES OF ERRORS

Controls are made a part of computer-based information systems to protect the organization from risks associated with a system failure. Controls can not only **prevent** errors but also **detect** and call attention to errors that do occur in order to **correct** them quickly. Corrective action will normally consist of reversing the effect of the error on data bases, transactions, or reports, and then examining the design specifications for systems controls to determine changes necessary to prevent similar errors from occurring again.

To understand how to prevent, detect, and correct errors, it is useful to analyze the three most usual sources of errors: human errors, technical failures, and natural forces (see Figure 17–1).

Human Errors

As illustrated in the figure, human errors resulting in system errors occur when authorized users make mistakes or when unauthorized users accidentally or intentionally gain access to the system. For example, a clerk taking telephone orders for software could capture information incorrectly, fail to ask for needed information, or enter information into the system more than once. The clerk could enter an incorrect product code, for example, and the customer would receive the wrong software package. The clerk could fail to enter the customer's telephone number, resulting in an incomplete customer data base record. Finally, if in the backup procedures (used when the computer system is down), clerks write orders manually and save them for later entry to the computer, a clerk could inadvertently enter the same order twice or forget an order.

Errors can also occur when unauthorized users gain access to the system either accidentally or intentionally and introduce errors. For example, a disgruntled employee familiar with the order entry system described above could enter fictitious orders or alter existing orders.

Technical Failures

Technical failures occur when a system's hardware or software do not function as expected. Although hardware malfunctions from time to time, computer program bugs are the most common type of technical failure. Even though a program has been well tested and in operation for some time, errors can still arise when circumstances not encountered before cause a new path to be taken with unforeseen, erroneous results. Ted Glaser, a prin-

Figure 17–1 **Generic Causes of Errors**

cipal designer of the IBM705, one of the earliest computers, was fond of saying that "there is no such thing as a completely debugged computer program. What we call a debugged computer program is simply one that has
not experienced an error in a reasonably long period of time."[1]

Natural Forces

System errors, or more accurately system disruptions, are often the result of
natural forces such as fire, earthquakes, or flood. Organizations have learned
to protect themselves against business disruptions caused by natural forces.
This protection becomes particularly important as organizations become
more dependent on computer-based systems to conduct normal business
operations. Imagine the effect on our daily lives if such computer-based systems as electric power dispatching and control, air traffic control, and supermarket checkout systems suddenly ceased to function.

A case in point was the fire that destroyed much of an Illinois Bell telephone switch in Hinsdale, Illinois, in May 1988. Not only did the fire leave numerous residences and businesses without telephone service, but it also disrupted data transmission networks over long-distance lines in the western suburbs of Chicago. Most of the damage was caused, not by the fire, but by the water used to extinguish it. Similar incidents could have occurred in computer rooms.

GENERAL SYSTEMS CONTROLS

General systems controls are the set of overall controls and standard operating procedures in the IS department, while application controls are specifically designed for a particular application. General systems controls include organizational and administrative controls, systems development controls, and controls over computer operations. Their primary functions are to ensure that the IS organization operates as planned, provide a firm base for application controls, and safeguard information and system resources. General systems controls usually incorporate a set of policies and procedures in such areas as the following:

- The organization structure should clearly define the functions within IS responsible for the development, maintenance, and operation of information systems. The systems development and operations functions should be clearly separated from each other—for example, to lessen the likelihood of erroneous or fraudulent changes to transactions or programs. Responsibilities of users for entering transactions and verifying application controls should also be set forth; IS personnel should be prohibited from carrying out such activities.

- Standard operating procedures for performing the various functions within the IS organization should be clearly defined, documented, and maintained.

- Personnel policies for positions within the IS organization should be developed and adhered to. For example, adequate screening procedures should be established to ensure that only those persons with the necessary qualifications are hired for or promoted to the various positions within the IS organization. Orientation of new employees should include all security practices applicable to the employees' positions as well as the organization's policies on personal and professional ethics.

    Terminated employees should be removed from sensitive positions immediately and should relinquish confidential or proprietary documents (e.g., customer lists, program listings) along with keys and identification cards. Physical and system access privileges should be restricted in keeping with the turnover of responsibilities to a replacement. Some of the best documented examples of system sabotage have been committed by recently terminated employees.

Turning a Computer into a Better Vault

Just as the outlaws of the Old West spurred security companies to design better vaults, modern-day electronic bandits are inspiring the development of advanced computer security gadgetry. The most sophisticated new equipment includes biometric machinery-products that verify the identity of would-be computer users by analyzing their unique physical characteristics. Among the offerings is an eye-scanning device that detects the unique blood vessel patterns in the retina, a sort of "eye signature." Made by EyeDentify, an Oregon firm, it is designed to restrict access to computer databases. To use a computer equipped with the scanner, you first have to look through a scope. The scanner then takes a reading of your retina. It grants computer access only to authorized users whose blood vessel patterns have been recorded and stored in its electronic memory. Other biometric devices work on the same principle. For example, Palo Alto-based Identix Inc. produces devices that use fingerprints to control access to computers. Your fingerprint is read by a rectangular sensor about the size of a large index card. A Boston company, Ecco Industries, manufactures voice-based identity verification equipment. How far can biometric technology go? Some companies are experimenting with lasers to scan people's cells for genetic characteristics to determine who should be granted computer access. Other access control equipment relies more on the way people do things rather than on their biology. For example, there are devices that read signatures based on writing patterns, speed and pen-to-pad pressure. Similarly, there is an identity verification gadget designed to distinguish a "keyboard signature"—an individual's typing speed, acceleration patterns and finger-to-key pressure. In addition, there are systems that rely on identification cards, much like the banking industry's automated teller machines.

While these new devices are becoming more popular, the use of passwords is still the most common means of controlling computer access. Many companies assign a password—typically a one-word code—to their computer-using employees. To gain access to computer data, employees type these passwords on the computer keyboard. However, the password system also has been advanced. There are circuit-bearing "smart cards" for traveling employees who use a personal computer to communicate with the company's main computer. These cards flash the password needed to gain access to the main computer. What's more, they flash new passwords continuously, a feature designed to thwart intruders who try to gain computer access by guessing or stealing the code. Typically, the passwords change one to four times a minute. Such access controls are sufficient for many companies, but some corporations—firms involved in top-secret U.S. Defense Department contracting, for example—provide an extra layer of protection. They install cryptographic ciphers, equipment that turns English into a gibberish-like code.

The devices, used when sensitive data is transmitted from one computer to another, are intended to thwart industrial spies who try to intercept messages. Another device translates the code back to readable form. Meanwhile, the work goes on to develop even more sophisticated computer protection. "Companies are still trying to build a better vault," said Richard Rueb, executive director of the Newport Beach-based Information Systems Security Assn.[2]

- Physical security procedures should be established to minimize losses caused by such physical threats as fire, storms, floods, and access by unauthorized persons.

   Adequate fire detection and fire suppression equipment is critical. Although most computer equipment will not burn, fire or heat can cause severe damage. The computer room and the data set libraries, in particular, should be closed to all except those who have responsibilities directly related to computer operations or data storage management. Visitors, vendors, and others who have reason to be in restricted areas temporarily should be properly authorized and escorted at all times by a responsible member of the IS department.

- Information security should be provided by software that restricts access by unauthorized persons to information residing within the computer system. The software should provide positive identification (authentication) of each person logged on for system access and should monitor the activities of that person throughout the time that the terminal is connected and active. Usually there are several levels of access controls implemented in a system. An on-line computer system, for example, might restrict any sort of access to those persons who are able to supply a valid password to the system when logging on. From that point on, various system functions would be made available to the terminal based on an internal authorization list. Some users would be authorized to inquire against the file, some would be authorized to inquire and post certain transactions, and some would be authorized to perform all system functions.

- Finally, contingency plans permit operations to continue when they are disrupted for any reason. Most installations store duplicate copies of programs and data off-site. Thus, duplicates can be made available to an alternate processing facility so that system operations can be quickly resumed. The contingency plan should be tested by realistic exercises at least twice a year.

As information systems become more critical to the strategic mission of organizations, general systems controls become increasingly complex and important. A complete discussion is beyond the scope of this text, but additional information can be obtained from the sources cited in the selected readings.

APPLICATION CONTROLS

General systems controls and application controls are not mutually exclusive. Application controls are built on the foundation provided by the general systems controls. Once a specific set of control requirements for a particular application has been determined, the analyst will see which of those requirements are already provided by the general systems controls. Requirements not already met will be incorporated into the set of requirements for

Figure 17–2 **Specification of Control Techniques**

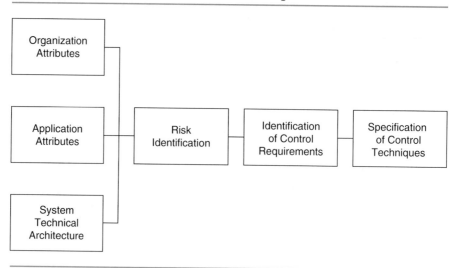

the new system in the same way as any other system processing, data, or reporting requirement and treated exactly the same way: designed, programmed, tested, and implemented.

Application controls deserve separate consideration from other user requirements for two main reasons. First, users tend not to think of control requirements when they are interviewed in the requirements analysis phase. Second, systems techniques introduce sources of errors that users may not be aware of. The IS professional therefore has a special responsibility to provide for complete and reliable control mechanisms.

Specification of Application Controls

Application controls are built into information systems to protect the organization if the system fails to operate properly. The thrust of controls design, therefore, is to first identify risks associated with the system and then specify adequate controls to protect the organization against them.

With a knowledge of the organizational and application characteristics as well as a knowledge of the processing system, an analyst can identify specific risks (see Figure 17–2). Once the risks are reviewed with appropriate users (including audit personnel), an analyst can identify control requirements and from them specify control techniques for the design specifications of the system. When controls are designed, experienced systems analysts will consult with both internal and external auditors for two principal reasons:

•   To make use of their expertise in the identification of risks and related controls requirements.

Figure 17–3 **Overall Control Objectives**

Authorization should be according to criteria established by the appropriate level of
   management.
Transactions (or business events) should be *classified* to permit preparation of
• Financial statements in conformity with generally accepted accounting
   principles and management's plan.
• Internal operating reports according to management's plan.
Report and data base contents should be periodically *substantiated* and *evaluated.*
Access to assets and proprietary data should be allowed only according to
   management's criteria.
Company operations should result in *efficient* and *effective* utilization of resources.

• To reduce the likelihood of having control deficiencies pointed out by
  the auditors reviewing the new system in operation.

Application Control Objectives

Over the years, a set of generally accepted control objectives has been
developed by various organizations and professional bodies such as the
American Institute of Certified Public Accountants and the Institute of Internal Auditors. An example of broadly stated control objectives used by one
organization is shown in Figures 17–3 and 17–4. Figure 17–3 contains overall
application control objectives, useful for identifying risks related to organizational and application characteristics. Figure 17–4 contains transaction processing control objectives, more useful for identifying risks related to the
way the computer system operates.

Overall Application Control Objectives. A list of overall control objectives might consist of such items as the following. **Authorization** refers to
the fact that responsibility and authority for tasks are often delegated to specific positions within the organization. For example, a salesperson in a
department store may be authorized to approve a personal check up to $50,
but a supervisor's approval is required for larger amounts. Systems controls
enforcing the authorization policy should prevent the acceptance of checks
over $50 when, for example, a clerk does not enforce the policy. The con-
trols should also detect any infraction in order to inform the clerk and avoid
future errors.

   Proper **classification** of transactions is necessary for accurate systems
information. For example, both sales and adjustments contain monetary
amounts, but systems information will not be accurate if sales are somehow
misclassified as adjustments.

   Periodic **substantiation and evaluation** of information contained in
systems reports and data bases ensures that the information is accurate and
reliable. For example, certain data bases become inaccurate because they do

Figure 17–4 **Transaction Processing Control Objectives**

Business events should be *recognized* and submitted for acceptance on a timely basis.

All and only those business events meeting management's criteria should be accurately converted to transactions and *accepted for processing* on a timely basis.

All accepted transactions and/or recognized business events should be *processed* accurately, on a timely basis, according to management's policies.

Results of processing should be *reported* accurately and on a timely basis.

Data bases should accurately reflect the results of processing.

Interfacing events between systems should result in transactions that are reflected by each system in the same processing period.

not lend themselves to updating through the natural course of events. A personnel data base might contain different attributes on each employee. Information such as employee address or postgraduate courses taken may not be accurate at some point if the employee has no convenient way of notifying the employer when such items change. To make sure such information is accurate, organizations often distribute to each employee yearly reports of information on the personnel data base and ask for any necessary corrections. Ex-spouses are often removed as life insurance beneficiaries through just such a process.

As more and more confidential or proprietary data is contained in computer data bases, **access** to information assets and proprietary data should be restricted to those persons authorized by management. For example, one of the most valuable assets of a mail-order house is its list of potential customers to whom catalogs and product descriptions are sent. Management would want to be sure that its customer list did not fall into the hands of a competitor. In addition, a mail-order house that advertises in newspapers and magazines typically codes responses to evaluate the effectiveness of ads in various media. Summary information showing the relative returns from ads would also interest a competitor and should therefore be protected by restricting access to such information.

Efficient and effective utilization of resources is even more important as the competitive environment intensifies. Management has a right to expect that systems controls will help realize this objective. For example, large electric power companies employ hundreds of clerks to answer customer inquiries on account status and process orders using on-line computer systems. Many such systems provide by-product information to help ensure efficiency and effectiveness. Standard times are established for handling various types of on-line transactions. Actual times taken to handle transactions are developed by the system, as well as totals of the various types of transactions. If, for example, certain transactions take more time than what management expected, ways to correct the departure from standard are devised,

Figure 17–5 **Typical Transaction Processing System Flow**

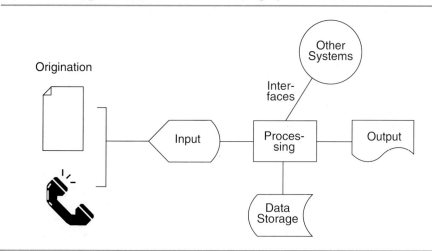

such as additional training for clerks. This technique falls under the general category of computer monitoring, and certain ethical issues should be considered before the technique is used. For example, if someone is monitoring the time employees take to process system transactions, the employees should be informed of the monitoring and the reason for it—to identify the need for further training.

Transaction Processing Control Objectives. The control objectives related to the system technical architecture, or transaction processing control objectives, have to do with the way transactions flow through a typical data processing system, such as the one illustrated in Figure 17–5. Figure 17–6 superimposes the transaction processing control objectives from Figure 17–4 on a typical data processing system's transaction flow to show how each control objective relates to the transaction flow.

•   When an event occurs that should be recorded as a system transaction, the first requirement is that it be recognized. For example, if you purchase a quart of milk at the local convenience store but the clerk decides to pocket your money rather than ringing up a sale on the cash register, an unrecognized business event has occurred. Or, if you call your insurance agent to say you have purchased a new car and the agent forgets to transmit the new information to the home office, a business event occurred that was not properly recognized.

•   Only business events meeting management's criteria should be accepted for processing. Not all recognized transactions are accepted for further processing by a computer-based information system, only those that meet a predetermined set of criteria. Reasonableness tests on transaction

Figure 17–6 **Transaction Processing Control Objectives**

amounts are often set by management to avoid the processing of incorrect transactions. For example, a reasonableness test on a transaction recording the issue of inventory items from stock may relate that quantity to the average quantity issued over some time period in the past. Thus, if ten were the average quantity, a transaction containing an issue quantity of 1,000 would not be accepted for processing until it had been reviewed and either accepted or corrected.

• Transactions that are accepted for processing should be processed on time, accurately, and according to management policies. Processing rules that conform to management policies are embodied in the system's specifications. Controls are necessary to verify that management objectives are being met. It is not unusual to read stories in the business press of companies that have been victims of inadequate transaction processing controls in their computer systems. The typical story is one of customer bills going out late or payments being improperly credited to customers' accounts as a result of a "computer glitch" and the resultant cost to the company in clean-up efforts and a tarnished image.

• Reporting results on time and accurately is important because management relies on information to control operations and make decisions. Standards for accuracy and timeliness will vary by application. In some cases, management may be willing to sacrifice some degree of accuracy in exchange for obtaining information sooner. Once standards are set for accuracy and timeliness, however, the transaction processing controls must see that they are met.

- Data base controls ensure that changes to the data base can be explained by the known effect of transactions accepted for processing. Controls are necessary to protect against program bugs that cause unwanted changes to occur, against changes caused by a person who has managed to gain unauthorized access to the data base, or against a technical failure of some sort.

- The higher the level of management, the more likely it is that information needed for decision making is drawn from several information systems. All too frequently, however, individual subsystems were designed and installed over a period of many years with imperfect interfaces between them. The purpose of interface controls is to ensure that information passed between systems is accurately received so that there is consistency in information between related functional subsystems.

Business risks are systematically identified by an analysis that can best be thought of as a subset of the process of determining functional requirements. Lists of overall control objectives such as the one illustrated in Figure 17–3 can help uncover control requirements otherwise overlooked. Other techniques include involving audit personnel as well as persons with specific knowledge applicable to the industry and application.

For example, the text referred earlier to a mail-order business that placed a high value on its customer list maintained in a computer data base. When analyzing control requirements, the business was interested in finding a way to make sure that the customer data base would not fall into the hands of a competitor and that, if it somehow did, management would know it as soon as possible. It had already established traditional physical security controls over copies of the data base and password control over access through on-line terminals. It also developed an encryption routine, a program that made the data base contents unintelligible unless translated by the encryption program. Even with these measures, management wanted to know if security had been breached by having employees, for example, copy and sell the data base and the encryption program specifications. The solution was to intersperse records on the data base containing fictitious names and the home addresses of various members of management. If the head of the internal audit department, for example, received from a competitor a mail solicitation at his or her home addressed to the fictitious name "Robert T. Kendall," he or she would know that a competitor had somehow obtained an unauthorized copy of the company's data base.

EXAMPLES OF TRANSACTION PROCESSING CONTROL TECHNIQUES

In selecting transaction processing control techniques, analysts are able to use experience gained from establishing effective controls over computer-based information systems. While business functions change from system to system, basic transaction processing flows tend to resemble the one illustrated in Figure 17–5. Examples of specific control techniques used in practice are discussed under the headings of functions listed in Figure 17–6.

Controls over Transaction Origination

Controls over transaction origination provide assurance that all business events that should be entered in a system are recognized. These controls usually tend to be manual controls rather than controls built into the computer system itself. They include such techniques as written procedures explaining the way source documents are to be prepared.

A common technique is to use prenumbered forms and have all forms accounted for in numerical sequence as either properly completed and containing a transaction or voided. Most people use this same technique to balance their personal checkbooks.

Another common technique is to log all incoming mail and phone calls to ensure that all requests originating outside the corporation are ultimately taken care of. To be effective, requests should be logged as soon as received by someone not charged with responding to them.

Controls over Data Entry

Data entry is entered into a computer system in one of two modes: in batch mode (wherein a number of transactions are accumulated and entered at the same time) or in real time (transactions are entered into the system as they occur). Batch entry can be either off-line (with transactions keyed into computer-readable formats before entry into the system) or on-line (with transactions entered directly into the system). Real-time entry of transactions is always associated with on-line entry. Illustrations of the three basic forms of data entry are shown in Figure 17–7. The three main control techniques applying to data entry are transcription error controls, batch controls, and validation controls.

Transcription errors can occur as the clerk prepares the manual document or as the data entry clerk enters it onto the data entry equipment or on-line terminal. These errors are minimized by techniques such as check digits and double data entry (where two operators enter the same data independently and the data entry equipment signals an error if the two do not agree).

A check digit is a digit added on to a code such as a customer number. Its only purpose is to guarantee that the code has been transcribed correctly. It is calculated as a function of the rest of the code the first time the code is assigned (when the customer number is created). Thereafter, it becomes part of the customer code itself. There are several algorithms that yield good check digits. The quality of such an algorithm consists in detecting whether a single digit has been altered or two contiguous digits have been transposed.

Batch control techniques can help minimize the loss or duplication of transactions. Batch control techniques are used to provide assurance that all data to be entered into the system is actually entered. User departments break transactions down into "batches" of numbers of transactions (say, 100)

Figure 17–7 **Three Types of Data Entry**

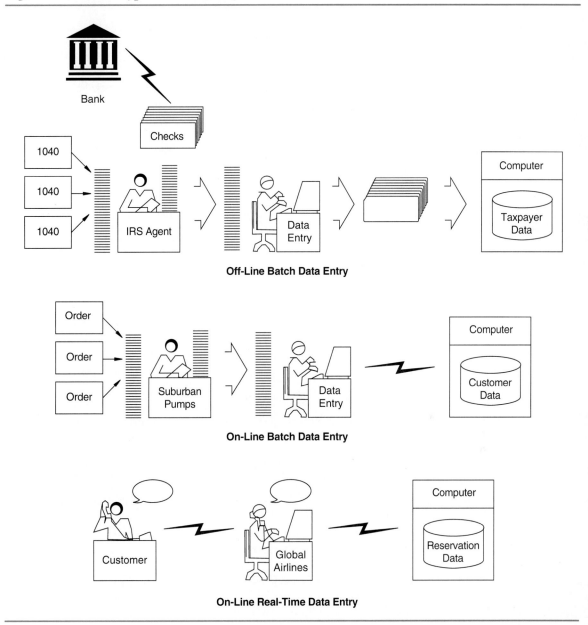

Off-Line Batch Data Entry

On-Line Batch Data Entry

On-Line Real-Time Data Entry

and establish control totals on the batches before submitting them to the data entry department. A control total is generally a "hash" or meaningless total of a numeric field on the source document such as the amount field. Sequential numbers are assigned to individual batches as the batches are prepared and entered into a log in the user department. As batches of source documents are entered into the computer system, the data entry program adds the individual control field amount in each transaction and compares the total to the total for the batch as computed by the user department. If the two totals do not agree, the entire batch is rejected and returned to the user department, which traces the error, corrects the batch, and submits it for reentry. A batch control report lists batches in sequence by batch number. Thus, users can verify that all batches submitted were entered. The batch control report also lists the details, i.e., each transaction, the batch total, and the total calculated out-of-balance batches. With this information, the user department can track down the error, correct it, and resubmit the batch. The entire process is illustrated in Figure 17–8.

Validation of transactions is required regardless of whether data is entered in batch mode. Complete validation attempts to ensure that transactions with invalid data do not even enter the system, much less endanger the integrity of the data base. The types of validation performed were described in Section V. In particular, it is necessary to check that every elementary data field has a value belonging to its domain and that the referential integrity of the data base would not be compromised if the transaction were executed.

The following are examples of domain checking: determining that amounts have numeric data; seeing that these numeric data stay within reasonable ranges (an age less than 10 or greater than 85 for a new employee might be questioned); making certain that coded fields take on only possible values (sex must be either male or female); and ensuring that consistency is respected (a male patient should not be admitted to a maternity ward).

Referential integrity involves such tasks as making certain an existing customer is not created; requiring that a customer must already exist before it can be modified; preventing the placement of an order by a nonexistent customer or for a nonexistent product; and preventing the deletion of a customer if there are still orders to be filled.

In on-line systems, as much validation as possible is built into the transaction processing conversation. The operator must have access to the information needed to enter all the required information correctly. As each data element is entered, or as each exchange of a full screen is processed by the on-line program, the program verifies all the constraints and responds to any errors with a message highlighting the error: an error message in a reserved area of the screen; a visual cue, such as displaying an erroneous field in red or high-intensity mode; or a discreet audio beep.

Where possible, a batch validation program applies tests to all data fields. Every field on each transaction is subjected to the appropriate validation tests. Transactions with invalid data are rejected by the system and listed

Figure 17–8 **Batch Balancing Flow**

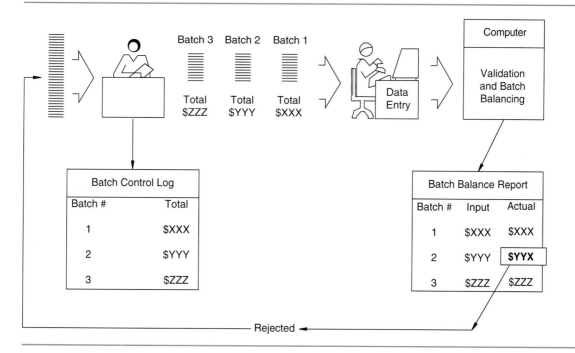

on an error report, which is returned to the user department for correction and subsequent reentry.

When validating transactions, all fields must be tested for errors, rather than rejecting the transaction based on the first error encountered. The latter procedure might require several cycles before all errors are found and a transaction accepted.

Controls over Processing

The overall purpose of processing controls is to provide assurance that transactions are processed correctly and that system files or data bases accurately reflect the results of that processing. In the past, these controls were established to ensure that card files were complete and in the correct sequence and that operators did not make errors of manipulation. An operator could easily misplace a card and cause a processing error. When card files were replaced with tape files, these controls seemed unnecessary: it is impractical to excise a record from a magnetic tape—and even more difficult to remove a portion of a disk permanently enclosed in a disk drive. Unfortunately, however, operator errors continued to plague correct processing even on tape systems. Yesterday's tape could easily be taken instead of today's; they do look alike from the outside. Moreover, a new culprit had been added: the program. Because the

Figure 17–9 **Run-to-Run Controls**

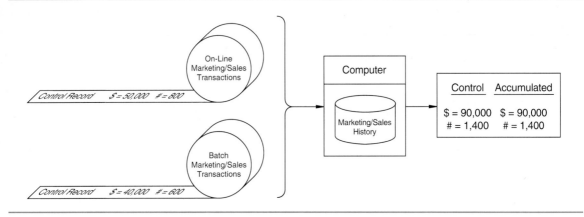

program can remove records or alter them in subtle ways under the influence of bugs, processing controls are now more required than ever.

The nature of processing controls differs depending on whether a sequential or direct processing method is used.

Sequential Processing Controls. In a sequential processing system, transactions are accumulated and sorted into the same physical sequence as the master file. Each master record is read, and if a transaction is present for it, processed. If no transaction is present for a master record, processing may still take place, usually initiated by the passage of time (e.g., end of month). If there is no master file record for a transaction, the transaction is rejected as an error unless the transaction is to insert a new master record. Three types of controls are typically used with sequential file processing.

• **Run-to-run controls** ensure the accuracy or completeness of information received by a program. For example, following validation, the program that validated the transactions develops control totals of valid transactions by transaction type. Control records are written at the end of the transaction file containing the control totals by transaction type. The file processing program accumulates a similar set of control totals as the transaction file is read. When all transactions have been read, the program compares the control totals at the end of the transaction file with the total accumulated by the file processing program. Any difference signals an error, usually caused by a program malfunction (Figure 17–9).

• **File balancing controls** ensure that records are not lost because of processing and that changes in critical fields in the file are a function of the known effect of valid transactions entered. Control fields in the file are selected; totals are accumulated on them during each processing cycle and written in control records at the end of the master file. At the

Figure 17–10 **File Balancing Controls**

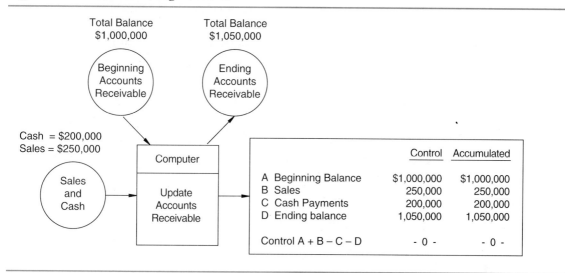

completion of each processing cycle, the beginning balance of a file control field is added to the net transactions processed and compared with the independently developed ending balance of the control field. An out-of-balance condition signals an error. Figure 17–10 illustrates the way this technique is employed for an accounts receivable file. At the end of a processing run, the beginning balance in the accounts receivable file is obtained from the control record. Sales transactions posted are added to it, and cash transactions processed are subtracted from it. The total should equal the ending accounts receivable balance obtained by accumulating accounts receivable balances from individual accounts.

In addition, a standard technique is to maintain a control record at the end of the file containing these totals. Any program that reads the file (not only the update run) can therefore validate that the file is not corrupted and that the program itself processed all the master records correctly.

•   **Generation data sets** are a common file backup technique for sequential data files. In Figure 17–10, for example, the updated accounts receivable file is considered the "child"; the input master file is considered the "parent"; and the version of the master file combined with a transaction file to create the parent is considered the "grandparent." Most systems maintain three generations of data sets to protect against the inability to use the current version of the master file. For example, in the above illustration, assume that in the next file maintenance cycle it was not possible to read the child version of the master file then being used as the input master file. The backup procedure could re-create the child by rerunning the program that originally created it using the parent version of the file together with the associated transaction file. The grandparent version of the file is held in case the parent file cannot be used or in case an error in the parent file is discovered when the child file just created is read for some other purpose. Usually at least one copy of all backup files is stored in another location to protect against disaster at the primary computer center.

Direct File Controls. In direct file processing, transactions are processed in the sequence of their arrival. Master files are updated only if a transaction is processed against them. In contrast to sequential file processing, the entire master file is not re-created during each processing cycle. In direct file processing, analysts are typically working with a data base management system in which updates occur in place. In other words, the updated master file is written in the same physical location on the disk as the original version. Thus, the old version of the master file is destroyed.

Processing controls are more complicated in a direct processing environment. For this reason, some systems are designed to update in place on a memo basis only and capture transactions thus entered for later updating sequentially after the close of business. Many demand deposit applications in banks, for example, are still handled this way. The most common controls in a direct file processing application are system logs and data base balancing. These are also described, from a restart/recovery viewpoint, in Chapter 16.

- A **system log** is used to record file processing activity so that the file can be re-created if necessary. The most common techniques record an image of every updated master record before and/or after its update. Also recorded are the transaction data, the date and time the change was made, and the program and on-line user who made the change. The log is written on a secondary storage device, often in two copies to guard against loss, and backed up as well. System logs are used to re-create the data base by reposting transactions against a copy data base from a point in time when the data base was known to be correct.

- **Data base balancing** is done from time to time to be sure that changes in the data base control fields (e.g., accounts receivable balance) are the result of beginning data base balances plus or minus the known effect of valid transactions. In contrast with sequential file processing, the entire data base may not be re-created each processing cycle. Periodically, however, the entire data base is read and control totals taken. Re-creation of the file to correct errors, if necessary, would be done using the system logs.

Controls over Reporting

Controls over reporting primarily verify that reports are correctly printed and delivered on time. Many IS departments have a control group to review output for accuracy and completeness before it is delivered to the user. For instance, if a continuous report were being printed as the printer ran out of paper, the control group would see that printing had resumed where it was interrupted and that no pages were missing. The control group would also ensure that system output is delivered on time to authorized users and would control access to output until it has been turned over to the users. User departments are generally responsible for verifying application control totals and batch control totals and for correcting validation errors.

Data Base Controls

Data base controls are generic controls established to protect the organization from loss or misuse of information in permanent files. These controls include the following:

- Integrity checks, most often performed during transaction processing, but on occasion during a separate run.
- Files and procedures for recovery and restart.
- Control over access to the data base.
- Physical protection against destruction or theft.

These controls are explained elsewhere in this chapter and in Chapters 15 and 16.

Systems Interface Controls

Systems interface controls resemble the data entry controls except that data entering one computer system is the output of another computer system. Control totals should be established on transactions passed from one system to another to prevent a loss of data in the exchange.

In addition, validation tests may need to be added. Even though transferred data was validated when it first entered a computer system and has been controlled since then, there may be different error tolerances between systems and, therefore, a revalidation of certain fields may be necessary. An example is that of a weekly file produced for a monthly run; between the first and the last week of the month, the contents of the master file might have been changed and the data from the first week might no longer be associated with a master file record. The validation does not necessarily point out errors in the transactions only; an error in a transaction may only be symptomatic of an error in a master file.

Another, more frequent error may occur when an interface file is produced by a third party, as in electronic data interchange. A customer may produce an order file or a vendor an invoice file. In all probability, the customer's or vendor's systems and files are not synchronized with those of the organization.

PRIVACY ISSUES AND THE
RIGHTS OF THE INDIVIDUAL

IS professionals need to be aware of individual and privacy rights, because the systems design largely determines how these rights can be protected.

Individual rights relate to the responsibility of organizations to be sure stored information is given freely, accurately, and confidentially. Everyone routinely supplies information to various organizations: banks, tax authorities, applications for consumer credit, and so on. Then why is the issue of privacy of greater concern with computer-based information systems than with paper-based systems? According to Deborah G. Johnson[3] concern has increased because more and more organizations maintain computer data bases and thus can exchange information on individuals so much more easily than with paper documents. An error in the information exchanged is a matter of concern. Because organizations base decisions about individuals on information contained in computer data bases, an individual could be harmed if the information is not correct. For example, the individual could be denied credit, turned down for employment, or perhaps even arrested.

The issue is complicated because with multiple exchanges between computer-based systems, erroneous information is not restricted to a single organization but could be multiplied many times over. Imagine the difficulty an individual would have correcting an erroneous credit rating report if the report had been shared with countless organizations. It would be difficult even to find out which organizations were keeping records on the individual.

Organizations could be held responsible in the courts if an individual could prove harm as a result of decisions made on erroneous information. Systems analysts have certain ethical responsibilities to society that should dictate the way systems are designed. Systems professionals also have a responsibility to their organizations to design systems that minimize the likelihood of lawsuits.

Another issue arises mainly in government organizations. Information from different sources could be pooled and conclusions drawn about individuals that might threaten their civil liberties. In particular, there is a fear that law enforcement agencies might obtain revealing data about personal habits, religious beliefs, or other knowledge that would not qualify as evidence in the courts. Some agency could use this information to interfere in citizens' private lives, much as Big Brother in *1984*.

A Special Advisory Committee on Automated Personal Data Systems to the Secretary of Health, Education, and Welfare identified five principles that established a code of fair information practices. The Committee worded the principles as follows:

- There must be no personal record-keeping systems whose very existence is secret.

- There must be a way for an individual to find out what information about him is on record and how it is being used.

- There must be a way for an individual to correct or amend a record of identifiable information about him.

- There must be a way for an individual to prevent information about him that was obtained for one purpose from being used or made available for other purposes without his consent.

- Any organization creating, maintaining, using or disseminating records of identifiable personal data must guarantee the reliability of the data for their intended use and must take precautions against the misuse of the data.[4]

These principles have become widely accepted as the foundation for much social policy and possible legislation on privacy. Systems analysts should keep the principles in mind when designing data bases and their related controls.

The attention given to privacy and individual rights varies from country to country. In some countries, legislation has been enacted; in other countries, legislation is pending. Thus, the issue is particularly thorny when an application transfers personnel data from one country to another, causing a so-called transborder data flow. Because the area is in a state of evolution, analysts should be sure they are current.

Summary

Management and IS professionals must be certain that the organization's information systems include the necessary controls to protect the organization from risks. Such risks range from erroneous decisions made because of incorrect information to loss of assets and the interruption or cessation of operations.

Errors are usually attributable to one of three sources: human errors, technical failures, and natural forces. Controls are instituted to prevent errors and to detect errors that do occur so that corrective and preventive measures can be taken.

General controls are the set of controls and standard operating procedures in the IS department. They serve as the foundation for application controls. Application controls are tailored to the specific requirements of each application and incorporated in the system's specifications, much the same as other functional requirements.

Once risks are identified for a particular application and its organizational setting, application controls can be specified. Audit personnel can be helpful in this process and should be consulted.

Two sets of application control objectives are used to help identify specific control techniques: a set of overall application control objectives and transaction processing control objectives. Each set of control objectives has a set of associated control techniques that practitioners have used to satisfy the objectives.

Finally, the issues of privacy and individual rights focus attention on the risks organizations may face because of inaccurate or misused information they maintain on individuals.

Selected Readings

Davis, G., Adams, D., and Schaller, C. *Auditing and EDP*, 2d ed. New York: American Institute of Certified Public Accountants, 1983.

In this authoritative and recent book, controls are seen from the external auditor's viewpoint.

Johnson, Deborah G. *Computer Ethics.* Englewood Cliffs, NJ: Prentice-Hall, 1985.
This book covers ethical issues for IS professionals, including codes of the various professional societies, privacy, power, liability for malfunctions in computer programs, and issues of computer program ownership.

Review Questions

1. Describe the difference between general systems controls and applications controls. The two are not mutually exclusive. How do they relate?

2. When do human errors result in system errors?

3. What are common types of technical failures?

4. Why is it increasingly important for organizations to protect themselves against disruptions of their computer systems by natural forces?

5. Explain the approach taken in designing application controls.

6. Why do experienced systems analysts consult with both internal and external auditors when controls are designed?

7. Briefly summarize the overall application control objectives.

8. Briefly summarize the transaction processing control objectives.

9. Explain how and why user departments use batch control techniques over data entry operations.

10. Which data validation test would apply to the following examples?
   a. A transaction that listed bananas at $390 per pound.
   b. A transaction containing an "o" instead of a zero in a quantity field.
   c. An undergraduate student attempting to register for a graduate-level course.
   d. A student undergraduate classification of "5" where the permissible classifications are "1" (freshman), "2" (sophomore), "3" (junior), or "4" (senior).

11. Describe the purpose of the following transaction processing control techniques:
   a. Controls over transaction origination.
   b. Controls over data entry.
   c. Controls over processing.

12. Summarize the control techniques over sequential file processing and direct file processing.

13. What are the privacy and individual rights issues related to designing computer-based information systems?

Discussion Questions

1. Software may provide information security by restricting access to computerized information on a need-to-know basis. Consider a bank with four departments: new customer accounts, checking, savings, and loans. What controls would you recommend on departmental employees' ability to read and/or modify data base information? (For example, should a checking department employee be able to read savings account information? Modify savings account information?)

2. Compare and contrast file processing controls for sequential processing and direct processing controls. Discuss why direct processing controls are more difficult than sequential processing controls.

3. Imagine that you have become associated with a new organization that needs to establish general systems controls over all aspects of its IS department's operations. Outline the areas that should be considered and recommend appropriate controls.

4. For the same organization, outline general application control objectives and transaction processing control objectives for an on-line point-of-sale system designed for a discount retail store. Assume that a perpetual inventory system interfaces with the point-of-sale system.

5. Discuss the possible ramifications to individual privacy of multiple exchanges of data base information between computer-based systems.

6. If personal privacy is a widely-held value, give several examples of how companies could "play" to this value for competitive advantage.

7. Under what set of circumstances, if any, would you agree to design and install a computer-based system containing data on patients who had previously filed medical malpractice suits that physicians could access prior to accepting an individual as a new patient?

Mini-Case

Genesee Supply Corporation. Assume that you are an independent consultant engaged by Genesee Supply Corporation to assist it in the design of an order entry, billing, and accounts receivable system. Genesee is a medium-sized distributor of industrial supplies with sales of approximately $80 million per year and 185 employees. The company has had a minicomputer installed for several years. Applications include the present order entry, billing, and accounts receivable system (installed about ten years ago), payroll, inventory control, financial planning and reporting, and sales analysis. The MIS department is headed by Ricardo Diaz. He has two programmer/analysts and four operations personnel in his department. The controller, Marsha Hunt, is in charge of all accounting operations, including billing and accounts receivable.

During the course of your project, you interviewed both Ricardo and Marsha in order to understand the general systems controls in place at Genesee Supply and the applications controls in place for the present order entry, billing, and accounts receivable system. The results of the interviews will be used as one of the inputs into the process of specifying the controls required in the new system. Their responses to your questions to describe the general systems and applications controls, respectively, were as follows:

Ricardo (re: general controls): "I believe that controls can choke an organization. People become too involved in controls and end up not doing their jobs. We have very low turnover and our employees are loyal and motivated. If something is wrong with a system, they will notice it. They are familiar enough with our routines to fix errors when they occur. Every year our external auditors review our operations and submit their suggestions. However, we never have adequate resources to implement the suggestions. I go over the auditor's recommendations with the president and explain to him how we're covered, and then we don't worry about controls for a while. I can tell you this: we've never lost a file, we've never had a program bug we couldn't fix, and we've never had a fraud or embezzlement. That's more than a lot of companies can say."

Marsha (re: application controls): "I happen to be a fanatic on accuracy. Every transaction that is entered into the system is proofread from a report prepared by the computer back to the transaction document to be sure there were no errors. The data entry clerk does proofreading for new accounts added to the master file and for each transaction, cash, bills, etc. As far as balancing the file is concerned, we keep a control account balance of accounts receivable. After each posting run, we reconcile the change in the control total to the total amount of bills for that day less the total amount of cash and adjustments for the day. Cash flow is a problem for us, so you can be sure we're paying attention to receivables controls!"

Question for Discussion

1. In each case, what additional information (if any) do you feel you should obtain?

Notes

1. Personal communication with the author.

2. White, George. "Battle Against Computer Crime Out of the Trenches." *Los Angeles Times.* Los Angeles, CA; v107, n248, Section 4, August 7, 1988, Copyright The Times Mirror Company; Los Angeles Times. All Rights Reserved. 1988 Los Angeles, CA.

3. Johnson, Deborah G. *Computer Ethics.* Englewood Cliffs, NJ: Prentice-Hall, 1985.

4. Hare, W. H., chairman. "Records, Computers and the Rights of Citizens, A Report of the Secretary's Advisory Committee on Automated Personal Data Systems." Washington, D.C.: U.S. Department of Health, Education and Welfare, 1973.

18

Designing for Performance

Chapter 18 describes how to design systems to meet the most frequently specified performance requirements, while minimizing the cost associated with these requirements. First, the main measures of performance are defined. Next, practical ways of attaining stated requirements are described. Finally, techniques for estimating systems resource requirements, which ultimately translate into costs, are covered.

Learning Objectives

- Understand the definition of the three most generally used measures of performance: response time, throughput, and availability.

- Describe some of the most frequent ways of designing a system to ensure that the performance requirements are met.

- Be aware of the various steps involved in estimating the resource requirements of an application as it is being designed.

DEFINITION OF PERFORMANCE

An example can illustrate how difficult it is to define the meaning of "meeting performance requirements." In the example, three transportation systems basically perform the same function: they move people from one point to another. However, the three must meet widely varying performance requirements. The performance of a 747 airplane is described by its capacity to carry 385 passengers at 550 miles per hour for a maximum distance of 6,000 miles without refueling. The performance of a sports car is described by the horsepower rating of its engine, its maximum speed, its acceleration, and quite secondarily its fuel consumption. The number of passengers is also a secondary consideration. The performance of the Queen Elizabeth II is characterized by the time it takes to cross the Atlantic Ocean, the number of passengers it carries, but perhaps more importantly, the ratio of service personnel to passengers and the availability of luxuries.

As explained in Chapter 9, the nonfunctional characteristics of a system—usability, flexibility, reliability, and speed—are the measures of *how well* a system performs, as opposed to *what* it does: an application that performs well is one that accomplishes its quality goals within given time and resource constraints. This chapter concentrates on meeting the time and resource constraints; it does not cover the other characteristics.

Meeting the time and resource requirements is just as important to the success of the system as is meeting the functional needs. For example, a small insurance company was replacing a card-based system in the early 1970s with a system based on sequential processing of tape files. The system had been entirely designed, programmed, and tested. As the time for system testing approached, the team decided to call in a consultant to help estimate the time that would be required for the application to run. The consultant found that the daily update would take 18 hours of processing time on the existing equipment and that the monthly billing run would require 125 hours of processor time. Design changes, which would take about three months to implement, would reduce the figures to 11 and 25 hours, respectively. Even these figures were considered excessive, and the system was abandoned. The new computer was returned to the vendor, and the two principal designers of the system found jobs elsewhere.

In early days, performance requirements were mainly considered to be made up of quantifiable volumes of input and output to be processed. Today, much more attention is given to the performance requirements of the users of the system. For instance, the psychological effect of excessive on-line response times is considered on a par with the economical effects. If the response time to a transaction is too long, the operator loses concentration and requires more time to enter the next transaction. Excessive irritation at frequent delays can also cause increased fatigue. As hardware becomes less and less costly compared with the cost of human resources, the balance of performance preoccupation shifts from optimal use of hardware to optimal use of personnel.

USUAL MEASURES OF PERFORMANCE

The three most commonly used measures of performance are response time, throughput, and availability.

Response Time

Response time is the first measure of computer system performance that usually comes to mind, just as speed is for transportation. It is also the most frequent subject of complaints by users because it is the most noticeable characteristic.

Response time is defined as the time that elapses between the initiation of an activity and the availability of the result. In an on-line system, the response time is usually the time taken by the computer to process a single exchange. More specifically, the user response time on a block-mode terminal is the time elapsed between the operator pressing the *Transmit* key and the first character of the response appearing on the screen. (Sometimes, the

Figure 18–1 **Components of On-Line Response Time**

last character of the response is used instead.) In a batch system, the expression "response time" is rarely used; instead, the turnaround time is defined as the time elapsed between the user making a request for processing (such as an ad hoc report) and receiving the output (such as the printed report being delivered to the user's office).

Both of these response times are viewed from the user's perspective. They may include components over which the IS department has no power, such as mail-room delays for the delivery of printed reports or delays encountered on the public data transmission network for on-line transactions from a remote terminal. Often, an IS department considers response time and turnaround time to include only the part of the time spent in the department. (This part is often called the *system response time.*) This difference in definition is obviously a source of conflict; the response or turnaround time objectives that are set in the requirements specifications are those that the users see.

On-line response time is made up of several components, as illustrated in Figure 18–1. Figure 18–2 illustrates the components of batch turnaround time. When the operator presses the *Enter* key, the data in the terminal buffer is sent over a communications line to the computer. The telecommunications access method readies the data in a buffer and signals to the teleprocessing monitor where the message comes from. The teleprocessing monitor determines which user program is to process the message, usually by looking at a code at the start of the message or because it knows that the terminal was previously attached to an unfinished conversational program. The user program performs work, such as validation, calculations, etc., and it probably also requests data from the DBMS (or from a traditional file access method).

Once the user program has finished its processing, the reverse sequence is gone through. The teleprocessing monitor deactivates the program and signals to the telecommunications access method that there is a message in a

Figure 18–2 **Components of Batch Turnaround Time**

buffer waiting to be sent to the terminal. When the first (or, alternatively, the last) character of the message has negotiated its way back to the terminal through the transmission network, the time elapsed since the operator pressed *Enter* constitutes the response time.

The previous discussion applies to block-mode terminals. Character-mode terminals have an additional category of response time, called character or screen response. This is the time it takes for each character to appear on the terminal once it has been keyed in. In many systems, this time is so short that it appears instantaneous, but in others, it can become substantial. If the operator systematically types faster than the system can display characters on the screen, the application may become unusable.

The response time is a function of the volume of information or processing at each stage and of the speed or capacity of each component. For instance, a **volume** of 2,000 characters per message takes longer to transmit than one of 200. It does not necessarily take longer to process at the access method, TP monitor, user program, or DBMS stages, however. Obviously, a short message requiring 80 data base records to be read will use more data base access time than a long message requiring 10 records to be read.

Another factor is the speed with which each stage is processed. This speed is a function of the **capacity** of the resource. In business data processing, transmission lines vary in capacity from 1,200 bits per second to hundreds of millions of bits per second. Transmission speed is a function of technology and distance; the hundreds of millions cannot be achieved over long distances with the present state of the technology. On the other hand, DBMS speeds depend on the disk technology—the faster a disk rotates and the quicker the reading arm travels, the shorter the response time—but also on the functions performed by the DBMS and the organization of the data base. If the data base does not have an index to the field that is used as a search argument, a more extensive search is needed and response times go up. This fact has often been cited as an argument against relational data base management systems in the past; the problem can be overcome by proper design and also by the DBMS adding more efficient searching mechanisms.

What is less obvious is that it is not enough to add up the processing time used by each resource at each stage to process the transaction. Whenever a resource is shared by several users, one user may have to wait for the previous user to be finished with the resource before being able to use it. This is called **queuing,** by analogy to customers waiting in line at a supermarket or a service station. The art of performance design is to strike a compromise between short queues and economy of resource. A comparison with a supermarket can illustrate the need for a compromise. If management's objective is to avoid customer waiting time altogether, enough checkout lanes and enough cashiers would need to be present at all times to handle the largest possible crowd. As crowds are not permanently present, most of the registers and most of the cashiers would be idle most of the time. Management therefore effects a compromise: customers must wait in line part of the time and cashiers must be idle at other times. Statistics enable management to know how many lines to provide and what the average customer wait time will be.

Similarly, in on-line systems, rules of thumb provide guidance on how much resource to provide to keep queuing times at a tolerable level. A branch of mathematics called queuing theory has established that the time spent waiting for a resource varies as the inverse of its free capacity ($1 - u$, where u is the degree of utilization of the resource). This yields a graph such as the one in Figure 18–3. The curve in the figure has a characteristic elbow beyond which queuing rises dramatically for very little additional utilization. The goal of response time design is to get as close to the elbow as possible without going beyond it, thus striking the optimal balance between performance and economy.

Throughput

Throughput refers to the capacity of the system rather than to its speed. Throughput can be defined as the amount of work that the system can process in a unit of time. In on-line systems, this capacity is generally expressed as the number of transactions per second or per hour; in batch systems, it is usually the number of jobs per 24-hour period or per month.

In the requirements analysis stage, the system throughput requirement is usually stated as follows: "The system must be capable of performing all the processing associated with so many orders per day or paychecks per month."

One of the problems associated with throughput is that there is no universally satisfactory method of measuring it across applications. Capacity cannot be expressed in a single unit which might assume that one order is equal to 1.75 paychecks or .05 management report.

The throughput of an on-line transaction processing system is a function of the number of operators doing work and the time it takes each operator to process a transaction. As long as response times stay acceptable, most of the operator time is devoted to what is conventionally termed *think time.* This is the time that elapses between the first character (or the last, depending on which convention is used for response times) of a

Figure 18–3 **Queuing Time as a Function of Utilization**

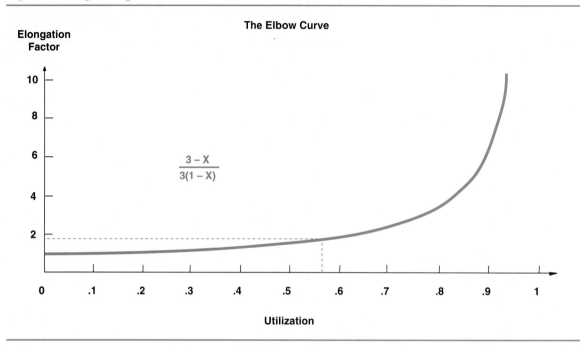

Elongation Factor

The Elbow Curve

$$\dfrac{3-X}{3(1-X)}$$

Utilization

response appearing on a terminal and the user pressing *Enter* for the next transaction. For dedicated operators, the think time is everything that is not response time; it is composed of time spent thinking about what to do, getting the information required, and keying it onto the terminal. For intermittent operators, think time also includes time spent away from the system on other tasks. Breaks and other brief periods of inactivity must also be taken into account.

Typical think times range from 10 seconds for trained users doing interactive work, such as end-user computing or on-line programming, testing, and debugging, to 60 seconds for complex on-line transaction processing, such as order entry in the presence of a customer.

As suggested in the discussion of response times, when many users share the same resource, response times go up. This increase results from each user consuming a certain percentage of the available resource over the cycle of response time plus think time. When this percentage is added up for all of the users sharing the resources, the total utilization of the resource is obtained. If this utilization does not reach the elbow on the curve in Figure 18–3, the response time is made up mainly of processing time. If it goes beyond the elbow, queuing increases and response times are degraded. Apart from the consequence on the productivity of the user, high response times add to the total time required by each operator to enter a transaction.

If the operator has a think time of 60 seconds, then, degrading the response time from, say, 2 seconds to 33 seconds will increase the time required by 50 percent. Such an increase would mean that the same workload would require 50 percent more operators, 50 percent more terminals, etc. If the cumulative resource usage of all the operators combined exceeds the available capacity, the relationship with response times becomes immaterial.

For batch systems, the throughput is generally expressed in number of batch jobs per time period. This unit of measure is a problem because the variability of batch jobs is much greater than that of on-line transactions, ranging from seconds to hours or even days. Stating the performance requirements during the analysis phase and making sure they are met during design can be done in one of two ways. The first is to assume that, because batch tends to be a decreasing part of the requirement, any resource (such as a mainframe processor) capable of handling the on-line load can also handle the batch load. This method is the most frequently used and the least satisfactory.

The alternative is to estimate batch processing requirements based on input/output requirements. When the process design is completed, file volumes are known and total input/output requirements can be estimated. Instead of concentrating on whether the processor resource is available, as is usually done in on-line systems, the analyst can determine whether the I/O subsystem can handle the workload. There are rules of thumb relating the I/O subsystem capacity to the size of processor normally needed for a balanced configuration. If the I/O subsystem capacity needs to be increased for the batch processing load, the processor capacity probably needs to be increased accordingly.

Availability

Not only must the system be capable of processing the requisite number of transactions within a given response time, but it must also be able to do so when required. Availability is especially important for on-line transaction processing systems that are integrated into the operations of a company. If an airline reservation system fails, passengers can no longer be checked in at the gate and flights are delayed. If a bank's ATM system has frequent outages, customers will no longer rely on it. If a computer fails on board the space shuttle, the flight may have to be canceled. The failure of even a small part of the air traffic control system could have dire consequences.

The availability of a system is generally expressed as a percentage. The time that the system will be available to process work is divided by the time period that is of interest—24 hours a day, 7 days a week for an ATM or an airline reservation system; 8 hours a day, 5 days a week for an on-line order entry system manned from, say, 9 to 5 on weekdays.

Availability is tied to schedule and reliability. If the daily schedule calls for the on-line system to be operational at 9 A.M. and it takes 30 minutes to start it, then all the elements required for the start-up phase (the data base, for example) must be ready at 8:30. If the data base needs to be backed up and the backup takes 3 hours, then the backup process must start no later than 5:30 A.M.

Here is where reliability comes in. If the schedule dovetails so nicely that the entire 24-hour cycle is accounted for, as it is with the 100 percent availability requirement of airline systems, for example, then the reliability of the system is what determines availability. The reliability of a system is characterized by two statistical measures: the mean time between failures (MTBF) and the mean time to recover (MTTR). The mean time between failures can be quite short as long as the mean time to recover is also short. For instance, a system that is capable of recovering from program incidents on the fly, by backing out uncommitted transactions and restarting them, has a short MTTR, and an application with a fairly high frequency of program failures can have acceptable availability.

HOW TO DESIGN FOR PERFORMANCE

Designing for performance is done in three steps: identifying the performance requirements, estimating the likely performance consequence of each design decision, and choosing the design decision that minimizes total cost while meeting the performance requirement.

Understanding the most frequent solutions to performance problems depends on some general characteristics of the design decisions. First, a performance design decision usually falls into one of the following classes: changing the design so that it uses fewer resources, increasing the resources available, or relaxing the performance requirement.

Second, to satisfy the principle of maximum return when design changes are contemplated, most of the work is done on those parts of the design where the performance impact is the greatest.

- If a transaction response time is predicted to be excessive, it is usually not useful to optimize the application code. The telecommunications access method, the teleprocessing monitor, and the DBMS frequently consume ten times more CPU time than the application code. Therefore, improving the application code even by a factor of two is likely to have very little impact on the response time (which is mainly made up of I/O time and transmission time) and even on the total CPU consumption.

- It is better to concentrate on the 20 percent of transaction types that typically make up 80 percent of the total volume than to work on rarely executed transactions.

Although many sources of performance problems exist, the following discussion addresses the most frequent sources of problems and their suggested solutions for each of the three classes of performance measures: response time, throughput, and availability.

Response Time Problems

The two greatest contributors to response time problems in on-line environments are message transmission times and data base I/O times. Message transmission time is only relevant for remote terminals. Terminals that are within 2,000 feet of the host machine can usually be attached locally, and transmission speeds are so high that there is no need to worry about their impact on response times. There are various ways to minimize the impact of **message transmission times:**

- Decrease transmission volumes by not transmitting repetitive or useless information.

  This solution implies technology at the terminal that automatically transmits only the part of the screen that has changed or that can store screen formats (text, instructions, headings, etc.) so that they do not need to be transmitted from the host.

- Increase transmission capacity by increasing line speeds.

  Today, the maximum recommended speeds are 4,800 bps over switched lines, 19,200 bps over leased lines, and 56,000 bps over digital transmission facilities. When using a third-party network, such as a value-added or packet-switched network, transmission speeds vary with many other factors, in particular with the number of nodes where the message has to be received in its entirety before it can be forwarded to the next node. The number of nodes traversed can actually vary from transmission to transmission.

  In some cases, transmission capacity may be increased by adding more transmission lines to reduce line sharing between multiple terminals.

- Relax the performance requirement.

  This solution may seem like admitting defeat, but that is not necessarily the case. First, many response time requirements identified in the analysis stage are unreasonable. For instance, some studies have shown that subsecond response time increases productivity; such short response times are certainly more pleasant for the users. However, with today's transmission technology, it is probably useless to hope for subsecond response times over an analog network. Many transaction processing applications have been quite successful with 2- to 5-second response times.

  Another consideration is that users expect response times to be high for what is perceived to be difficult or nonroutine transactions. Quite high response times are therefore acceptable for a small number of transactions that perform complex tasks.

  The worst feature of high response times is that the user does not know when to expect the response to arrive. In fact, the user generally does not even know whether the system is operational while waiting for the response. A proven measure to minimize the impact of poor response times is to give the user immediate feedback, such as: "Your query is noted. Processing will take some time. Please stand by." Even better is to display an estimated percentage of completion of the task at regular intervals. This solution is usually confined to intelligent workstations.

A final consideration is that in dedicated-operator processing, such as data entry, telephone order processing, or reservations, consistency of response time is the most important factor. An occasional longer wait than normal breaks the operator's rhythm and concentration. It would be better to have all response times be 2 seconds, rather than 1.5 seconds 80 percent of the time and 3 seconds 20 percent of the time.

The impact of **high I/O times** can be minimized by the following steps:

*   Decrease the volume of I/O operations performed.

    The volume of I/O may be decreased by redesigning the data base to introduce a controlled amount of redundancy (by storing parent data in the child records, for example) or by providing more indexes. Another solution is to keep larger volumes of data in main storage. As the price of main storage continues to drop, this solution will become more and more attractive.

    A different strategy can be to cut a complex, high-I/O transaction into several smaller transactions, each requiring substantially less I/O (see Section IV).

*   Increase I/O capacity by using faster disks or channels or by spreading the I/O over more resources (decreasing resource sharing and queuing).

    The effect of this type of measure is limited by the fact that disk performance tends to span a very narrow range. The main cause of disk performance problems is "seek time," the time it takes for the read/write arm to move to the track where the data is. Seek time usually varies within a range of no more than 1 to 2 on a given category of equipment.

*   Relax the performance requirement.

For batch turnaround times, the time required to get the request to the IS department, schedule the work, print the output, and transmit the report back to the user usually overshadows processing times. The same applies for end-of-period processing such as the monthly or yearly accounting and management information applications. Organizational measures are the ones that are the most likely to be effective.

Throughput Problems

Where the performance problem is one of total throughput rather than response times, the measures to be taken are somewhat different. (Throughput depends on the total capacity of the system, and capacity problems tend to cause high response times. The reverse may not be true: high response times are not necessarily caused by capacity problems.)

For a throughput problem, the performance bottleneck must be identified. The bottleneck is caused by a single resource that cannot handle the total processing load—the one whose consumption would exceed 100 percent with the estimated workload. Often, removing one bottleneck causes another bottleneck to appear. However, it can be difficult to guess which resource will cause the next bottleneck before the prior bottleneck is actually removed.

The bottleneck is likely to be the central processing unit, the main memory, or both. In either case, for on-line systems, it is not easy to solve the problem by redesign, nor is it realistic to expect the user to decrease the volume of activity. Therefore, most solutions will entail getting a larger processor or main memory. The requirement for upgrading the processor or the memory must be defined before the economic evaluation of the application takes place (see Chapter 19); the cost impact can be very high.

For batch processing, the system may be redesigned so that total throughput can increase. The main step to be taken is to avoid nonproductive work. Several examples in other chapters have pointed out designs that minimize the number of times a file is read sequentially. Reducing the total volume of output by reporting only exceptions or reducing the reporting frequency might be other steps to be taken.

Availability Problems

The last measure of performance to be considered is availability. There are two main ways to increase availability. One is to increase the MTBF (mean time between failures), the other is to decrease the MTTR (mean time to recover).

Increasing the MTBF can be achieved through the following types of measures:

- Design the application to be independent of schedules.

    If the cut-off process is designed so that the on-line application can restart regardless of the state of the daily batch processing, the number of availability incidents due to late starts will be minimized.

- Design the application for continuous operation so that it does not have to be stopped to do cut-off processing.

    This solution may not be possible in all environments. In particular, few data base systems are capable of maintaining the data base description while the on-line system is running, continuing to update the data base.

- Increase software reliability through good design, programming, testing, and debugging practices.

    Improving software reliability is easier said than done. However, some interesting results have been obtained by various approaches to develop zero-defect software. These approaches rely on continuous monitoring of quality throughout the entire process so that bugs are not allowed to arise.

- Increase hardware reliability by duplicating critical components.

    This is the approach chosen by several manufacturers of so-called fault-tolerant equipment, who make machines that continue to operate in the presence of failures. A well-known example was the system of computers on board the Apollo flights, where four computers all processed the same data, and a fifth processor continually monitored the four to make sure that they were obtaining the same results. In the commercial world, Tandem and Stratus are the best known for fault-tolerance equipment.

Reducing the MTTR can be done by resorting to the following types of measures:

- Use the duplication technique described in the previous paragraph to achieve a shorter MTTR, rather than MTBF, by providing for spare parts on site.

  The spare part concept can extend to the entire processor: if a company has two processors, one doing more essential work than the other, then one of the processors can serve as backup for the other.

- Decrease the time to recover from a malfunction by designing the recovery process adequately.

  This technique is described in Chapter 16.

ESTIMATING RESOURCE REQUIREMENTS

The resource requirements of an application must be estimated for two main reasons: to verify that response time (or turnaround) requirements can be met and to check whether there are enough hardware resources available in the installation to execute the new application. Ultimately, the resource requirements of an application translate into hardware and systems software costs. Although these costs are decreasing relative to total systems costs, they are still substantial.

There are two ways to estimate resource requirements. The first, **the analytical approach,** is to decompose the application into its components and to estimate what is required for each component. This approach is the easiest, given enough data about the environment. It is also the most uncertain, especially with innovative applications or recently released systems software. The description of the analytical approach emphasizes the general logic to be followed. The specific details of the calculations and the base resource consumption figures are dependent on the particular hardware and software in use. The details also change rapidly over time, as new hardware and software technology becomes available. Possible sources of current performance data are vendors, industry associations, specialized firms, and the press.

The alternative to the analytical approach is **benchmarking,** or prototyping, the application. Benchmarking consists of creating and running an application with the same volumes, I/O, and processing characteristics as the application being designed. This approach works quite well in modern DBMS-oriented applications because the resource consumption is more a function of the data base structure and activity than of the complexity of the application code. At the stage reached before the economic evaluation of the application, the data design is usually much more firm than the process design. Benchmarking also requires less knowledge of the internals of the systems software (such as TP monitor and DBMS). Benchmarking is much more expensive than the analytical approach, however, and it may also require specialized software to simulate a large population of terminal users and a high-volume data base.

The following example describes a simple order entry application such as the one for Condor Telephone Company (see the mini-case in Chapter 16). In the example, the conversation consists of two exchanges: an order header exchange (used to enter the customer number, order number, delivery dates, etc.) and a detail line exchange (used to enter an average of 3.7 order item lines per order).

The following assumptions are made:

- An input screen contains an average of 200 characters.

- An output screen contains an average of 1,200 characters.

- Each order detail screen requires 45 disk accesses, as specified in Figure 18–4.

Transmission Time

In the simplest case, the transmission time is equal to the number of characters transmitted (here, 1,400) divided by the effective line speed in characters per second. The effective line speed is always somewhat slower than the rated line speed because of transmission overhead, such as parity bits and control characters, and electronic switching delays. It is prudent to assume that the effective line speed is between 60 and 75 percent of rated line speed.

Thus, a line speed of 9,600 bits per second might correspond to an effective line speed of 700 to 1,000 characters (each composed of eight bits) per second. For a volume of 1,400 characters, the time required would be between 1.4 and 2 seconds (see Figure 18–5).

If the network topology requires that the data transmission should flow over several nodes, the transmission times must be calculated for each segment and added up, as each node must receive the message completely before passing it on. Some applications call for a protocol converter between the user and the processor. The protocol converter is used for connecting two equipments that do not use the same transmission disciplines (because they are from different manufacturers, for example). If the application had a protocol converter to which the terminal was connected via a dial-up line of 1,200 bps and if the protocol converter was attached to the host via a 9,600 bps line, the total time required would be between 7 and 10 seconds (see Figure 18–6).

Transmission via satellite has the same requirement. Although transmission speeds are much higher, the transmission does not bounce off the satellite like a mirror; the message is received and retransmitted. This buffering adds an overhead of about 250 milliseconds to any transmission time. In addition, the satellite is usually far enough from the earth that the speed of

Figure 18–4 **Disk Accesses Required to Process a Four-Line Item Order Exchange**

```
MARKETING                        DESIGN TOOL                              CD-20
ORDER ENTRY                    SUBURBAN PUMPS                             DASDA
                           DISK ACCESS ESTIMATE


PREPARED BY: PETER NG        DATE: 13DEC94           VERSION:            PAGE 1
APPROVED BY: JEANNE ZMUD     DATE: 13DEC94           STATUS:
```

	Primary Index	Secondary Index	Record	Total
	-----	-----	------	-----
Alpha search for customer no:				
- max		20	12	
- avg		6	4	10
Read 2 customer records	1		2	3
Search for product no:				
- avg		6	6	12
Read 4 product records	4		4	8
Write 6 order records	6		6	12

Grand Total				45
				======

transmission (the speed of light, 186,000 miles per second) is a factor. Communications satellites are in orbit about 22,000 miles above ground, thereby imposing a minimum trajectory of 44,000 miles for any message, tacking on another 250 milliseconds or so. This phenomenon can sometimes be observed in overseas phone calls, or even on domestic television when the image is carried via satellite and the sound through ground telephone lines.

Even though satellite transmission channels are very fast, typically exceeding a million bits per second, the half-second incompressible overhead makes satellite transmission unsuitable for applications with many short exchanges; it is much better suited to applications such as file transfer, where there are long bursts of data transmitted in one direction.

In some applications, the time required to establish the connection must also be added. For instance, credit card authorization terminals are used by many retail stores. These terminals are not permanently connected to the authorization center; the costs would be staggering. Instead, a code in the

Figure 18–5 **Calculation of Transmission Time**

```
MARKETING                         DESIGN TOOL                        CD-20
ORDER ENTRY                     SUBURBAN PUMPS                       TCEST
                       TELECOMMUNICATIONS TIME ESTIMATE

PREPARED BY: PETER NG            DATE: 13DEC94            VERSION:         PAGE 1
APPROVED BY: JEANNE ZMUD         DATE: 13DEC94            STATUS:

                       Line Speed:    9600 bits/second
                  Character Length:    8 bits
                       Line Speed:    9600/8 = 1200 characters/second
          Useful Line Speed Factor:    60% to 75%
             Practical Line Speed:    1200x60% to 1200x75%
                              say:           700 to 1000 characters/second
    Time to Transmit 1400 Characters:    1400/1000 to 1400/700
                              say:           1.4 to 2.0 seconds
```

magnetic stripe on the back of the card indicates to the system how to reach the authorization center. The terminal waits for the dial tone, dials the number, waits for the phone to ring and be "picked up" by the authorization center computer at the other end before transmitting the card number and the amount to be authorized. This sequence takes several seconds and is the main component of the response time of that particular application.

Figure 18–6 **Calculation of Transmission Time—Multi-Node Network**

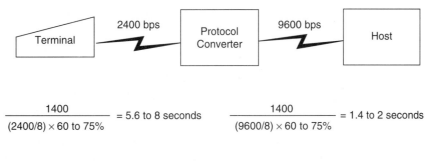

$$\frac{1400}{(2400/8) \times 60 \text{ to } 75\%} = 5.6 \text{ to } 8 \text{ seconds} \qquad \frac{1400}{(9600/8) \times 60 \text{ to } 75\%} = 1.4 \text{ to } 2 \text{ seconds}$$

Total: (5.6 + 1.4) = 7   to   (8 + 2) = 10 seconds

Figure 18–7 **Number of Machine Instructions per Function**

```
MARKETING                        DESIGN TOOL                               CD-20
ORDER ENTRY                    SUBURBAN PUMPS                               PATHL
                                PATH  LENGTHS


PREPARED BY: PETER NG         DATE: 13DEC94          VERSION:            PAGE 1
APPROVED BY: JEANNE ZMUD      DATE: 13DEC94          STATUS:


                                 Operating              TP
                                  System             Monitor            DBMS
                                  ------             ------             ----

Sign-on                          50,000
Read message                     10,000             10,000
Load program                                         4,000
Read DB record by primary index   5,000                                35,000
Read DB record by secondary index 5,000                                75,000
Read next DB record               5,000                                20,000
Update DB record                 10,000                                20,000
Create DB record                 10,000                                45,000
Write record to log               2,000              4,000
Write message to terminal        10,000             10,000
```

Processor Time

Most of the processor time is devoted to teleprocessing monitor and data base management systems functions. Figure 18–7 shows some representative estimates of the number of machine instructions executed for various functions. These estimates, called path lengths, vary enormously from manufacturer to manufacturer and for each systems software component; they also vary over time, as new releases of the software add new functions and therefore new overhead. (The data in Figure 18–7 should not be used in a real situation.)

In transaction processing systems, a conservative estimate is that application logic adds 20 percent to the number of instructions required by the systems software.

Once the number of instructions per transactions has been estimated, the time it takes the CPU to execute these instructions can be calculated. Many manufacturers supply instruction execution rates, expressed in MIPS, or millions of instructions per second, for their various models. For those manufacturers that do not, the press publishes estimates. These execution rates are by necessity rough approximations only. As some types of instructions take longer to execute than others, the average rate depends on the

Figure 18–8 **MIPS Ratings of IBM Mainframes**

Model	MIPS
9221-120	0.5
9221-130	1.3
9221-150	2.2
9221-170	3.3
9121-190	4.8
9121-210	8.1
9121-260	7.5
9121-320	10.1
9121-440	15.6
9121-480	31.2
9021-330	46.3
9021-340	61.5
9021-500	79.0
9021-580	62.0
9021-620	79.0
9021-720	112.0
9021-820	142.0
9021-900	202.0

particular mix of instructions. This mix varies with the software environment, the operating system, and even the hardware: some models may be optimized for engineering and scientific applications, and others for program development, batch, or transaction processing.

The MIPS rating of processors can therefore be used to estimate execution times only in a given hardware and software environment. In a different environment, the MIPS rating of the hardware could change by as much as 20 percent; and the instruction count is certain to vary by much more than that. The MIPS rates illustrated in Figure 18–8 cannot reliably be used to compare the power of the machines among themselves, or to other machines whose MIPS rating is provided in the press. MIPS has been translated to "meaningless indicator of processor speed." The uncertainty on MIPS ratings is at least 30 percent. In addition, the uncertainty on the estimated number of instructions is very high.

In the case study, the total processor time comes out to 0.25 seconds on a 9221–170 processor from IBM.

Disk Access Time

To calculate disk access time, it is first necessary to estimate how many disk accesses are required. Each transaction does a certain number of file or data base operations. In the example of the order entry application, each order line must be written to disk, and each perpetual inventory record to be

Figure 18–9 **Calculation of Number of Disk Accesses**

```
MARKETING                       DESIGN TOOL                        CD-20
ORDER ENTRY                    SUBURBAN PUMPS                      DASDA
                            DISK ACCESS ESTIMATE


PREPARED BY: PETER NG          DATE: 13DEC94          VERSION:        PAGE 1
APPROVED BY: JEANNE ZMUD       DATE: 13DEC94          STATUS:


                              Primary      Secondary
                               Index         Index       Record       Total
                               -----         -----       ------       -----
Read Customer Table              1                         4            5
Read Product Table 4 Times       4                         36          40
                                                                       -----
              Read Total                                               45
                                                                       =====


Write 6 Order Records            6            36           24          66
Write to Log                                               9            9
                                                                       -----
              Write Total                                  .           75
                                                                       =====
```

updated must be read, then written back to disk. In addition, the teleprocessing monitor generates a number of I/O operations of its own to retrieve context data saved from the previous exchange, load processing programs, and log transactions and data base images.

The DBMS does more than one I/O operation for each file access requested by the application. Usually, the DBMS will read one or several index entries to find the address of each input record to be read, and it will create index entries for the records to be written. Sometimes, a verify operation is requested after a record is written. What was just written to disk is read and compared with the original, so that hardware errors can be detected while they are still easy to correct.

In relational data bases, if there is no index on the attribute that serves as the selection argument, the entire relation may have to be read. If the volume is low, the relation may be kept in memory; if not, lengthy disk access times can be anticipated. In the example, if the order entry system were to be implemented using relational technology, indexes would in all probability be available, thus bringing the relational data base performance closer to that of a nonrelational one. In other cases, it may be impossible to obtain enough knowledge to estimate the number of disk accesses reliably. The prototyping approach may then be the only viable alternative.

Figure 18–10 **Calculation of Estimated Disk I/O Times**

```
MARKETING                        DESIGN TOOL                        CD-20
ORDER ENTRY                    SUBURBAN PUMPS                        DASDA
                              DISK I/O ESTIMATE


PREPARED BY: PETER NG          DATE: 13DEC94          VERSION:       PAGE 1
APPROVED BY: JEANNE ZMUD       DATE: 13DEC94          STATUS:


IBM 3380
        Avg. Seek Time                                     16     ms
        Avg. Latency                                       8.33   ms
        Read time for 1 block of 6,000 characters          2      ms
                                                       -------------
              Total per access (no write check)            26.33  ms


        Rotation time for write check                      16.67  ms
                                                       -------------
        Total per access (with write check)                43.00  ms


        Total disk time
             45 x 26.33 + 75 x 43  =  3,500 ms  or  3.5 seconds
```

Thus, knowledge not only of the application logic but also of the data base organization and the internals of the teleprocessing monitor is required to estimate the number of disk accesses. An example is shown in Figure 18–9.

Once the number of accesses is known, the time for each access must be determined as a function of the performance characteristics of the disk device. A disk access consists of three phases: seek, latency, and data transfer. Seek time refers to the average time needed for the arm that bears the read/write mechanism to be positioned on the disk cylinder. Latency refers to the average time required before the beginning of the record to be read rotates to a position where it is exactly under the read/write mechanism. On the average, if the movements of the arm are randomly distributed with regard to record locations, latency is one-half of the time it takes the entire disk to rotate one full rotation. (However, for a verify operation, it is one full rotation minus the length of the record, because the disk has to come full circle before the read/write head can read the record it just wrote.) Finally, the data transfer time is the time actually spent reading or writing data; it is a function of the length of the record and the speed of the disk.

As Figure 18–10 shows, the estimated disk I/O time for the order entry application is about 3.5 seconds.

Figure 18–11 **Calculation of Total Response Time**

```
MARKETING                        DESIGN TOOL                          CD-20
ORDER ENTRY                     SUBURBAN PUMPS                        RTEST
                          TOTAL RESPONSE TIME ESTIMATE


PREPARED BY: PETER NG            DATE: 13DEC94         VERSION:        PAGE 1
APPROVED BY: JEANNE ZMUD         DATE: 13DEC94         STATUS:



                              Service        Elongation        Total
                               Time            Factor          Time
                              -------        ----------        -----
Transmission                    1.4             1.2             1.7
                       to       2.0                             2.4


CPU                            0.25             2.0             0.5


Disk                            3.5             1.2             4.2
                                                               -----
             Total                                              6.4
                                                       to       7.1

                                                      say:      7.0 sec
                                                               ========
```

Calculation of the Response Time

In on-line systems, all the activities within a transaction are executed in strict sequence. Therefore, all the components of response time have to be added together. There is one exception: asynchronous processing as described in Chapter 16 does not enter into the response time calculations.

In the case study, the total response time was calculated to be 5.15 to 5.75 seconds. This calculation, however, assumed that all the resources were available and that there was no waiting or queuing. Even under the best of circumstances, it is prudent to allow at least twice the CPU time and a 20 percent factor on the other times. This factor corresponds to a CPU utilization of 60 percent and to network and I/O utilizations of about 30 percent. A conservative estimate for the response time for the application in the example is therefore 7 seconds (see Figure 18–11).

Although the calculations used to arrive at 7 seconds may seem rigorous, the result is in reality not very reliable—certainly not within a second or two. However, the result can be used to determine whether the order of magnitude of response time is compatible with what is expected. In addition, each of the components of the response time has been analyzed, so that it is easy to concentrate on those components that make up the largest portion—in this case disk I/O times and network transmission times.

Total On-Line Resource Consumption

If the throughput of the application is of concern, then the resource usage must be computed for each transaction by component (including any asynchronous processing but excluding wait times) and must be multiplied by the transaction rate. If there are 60 users, each entering a transaction every 50 seconds, a transaction rate of 1.2 transactions per second would result. If the CPU usage was estimated to be 0.25 processor second per transaction, as in the example, the total processor utilization would be less than 40 percent—a perfectly acceptable figure if no other activity is going on in the system. In fact, the processor would have enough capacity to accommodate three transactions per second, achieving a maximum utilization of 75 percent (generally thought to be the rule-of-thumb figure for most transaction processing systems).

Other Resources

Once the required CPU capacity has been determined, the memory required to run the application can be estimated. Again, rules of thumb are available to account for operating systems, teleprocessing monitor, and DBMS requirements. To these must be added the application requirement—usually a minor factor nowadays. If the system has virtual memory (as most mainframes do), the real memory required for the application code is usually about one-half the size of the amount of virtual memory required. An example is detailed in Figure 18–12.

Similar calculations would have to be made for the I/O components and the network. As these calculations depend on the topology of the network and on the architecture of the processor and the operating system, no further details are given here.

Resource Consumption in Batch Processing

Calculating the resource consumption of a batch process follows the same logic as for on-line systems, with a few minor exceptions. Network time is usually not applicable; however, printing time and time spent reading and writing batch-oriented peripherals such as magnetic tape must be added. In general, operating system overhead figures for batch are more difficult to obtain, and estimates may not be very reliable.

Calculating elapsed times (turnaround, the batch equivalent of response time) becomes more difficult. Contrary to on-line programs, batch programs may overlap sequential file operations with processing. Direct access file operations cannot be overlapped with processing but could overlap sequential file operations.

As a consequence, the elapsed time of a batch program is somewhere between a maximum (represented by the addition of CPU time, direct access

Figure 18–12 **Calculation of Memory Requirements**

```
MARKETING                           DESIGN TOOL                          CD-20
ORDER ENTRY                        SUBURBAN PUMPS                        MEMEST
                        TOTAL MEMORY REQUIREMENTS ESTIMATE


PREPARED BY: PETER NG              DATE: 13DEC94          VERSION:        PAGE 1
APPROVED BY: JEANNE ZMUD           DATE: 13DEC94          STATUS:



                    Operating system base:            6.0 MB
               Teleprocessing monitor base:           2.0 MB
                               DBMS base:              4.0 MB
                    Application programs:
                        2.4 MB virtual / 2 =          1.2 MB

                  Workarea per user:   .17 MB
                   Number of users:      30
                   Total workarea:
                           .17 MB x 30 =              5.1 MB
                                                      -------
                        Grand total:                 18.3 MB
                                                      =======
```

time, and sequential file time) and a minimum (represented by the largest of the overlappable components—either CPU plus direct access time, or file processing time for the largest sequential file). The calculation of batch turnaround time is shown in Figure 18–13.

Summary

Many performance problems can only be solved through proper design of the applications. Others can be solved by increasing the resources used to run the application. Both types of problems must be addressed in the design phase of the application rather than at implementation time, when it is too late to solve them.

The main measures of performance of an application are response time (called turnaround time for batch processing), throughput, and availability. All of these measures relate to processing capacity; the way of solving problems is to decrease the amount of resources consumed by the processing, increase the amount of capacity available, or relax the performance constraint. In any case, the greatest effort should be expended on those parts of the process where the payback is likely to be the highest, i.e., where the resource consumption is the highest.

Figure 18-13 **Calculation of Batch Turnaround Time**

```
MARKETING                        DESIGN TOOL                          CD-20
ORDER ENTRY                     SUBURBAN PUMPS                        BTEST
                    TOTAL BATCH TURNAROUND TIME ESTIMATE


PREPARED BY: PETER NG          DATE: 13DEC94          VERSION:        PAGE 1
APPROVED BY: JEANNE ZMUD       DATE: 13DEC94          STATUS:


System time for batch program:
        CPU + direct access time                     5.00 min
        Transaction file input                        .75 min
        Master file input                            4.50 min
        Master file output                           4.50 min
                                                    ----------
Pessimistic hypothesis of no overlap:
        (no allowance for other jobs)
        5.00 + .75 + 4.50 + 4.50                    14.75 min

Optimistic hypothesis of total overlap:
        max (5.00, .75, 4.50, 4.50)                  5.00 min


Assuming the transaction and master
files are on the same data path:
        max (5.00, .75 + 4.50 + 4.50)                9.75 min
```

Response times can probably best be reduced by increasing the transmission speed to and from remote terminals and by designing the data base so that the number of I/O operations is minimized. It may also be possible to divide complex transactions into simpler transactions, each with a shorter response time. Finally, excessive response times may be made more tolerable by simply informing the user of the progress of the transaction.

Problems with batch turnaround time are usually best solved by organizational measures, because most of the delays are likely to be in waiting for a job or printed output to be transmitted to the next stage of processing.

Many of the design hints described in earlier chapters (Chapter 16 in particular) have the objective of reducing resource consumption, thereby enabling the available capacity to meet the throughput requirements.

Availability can be increased by various means: proper scheduling and cut-off processing, an increase of the mean time between failures (increasing reliability), and a reduction of the mean time to recover (decreasing recovery times).

Estimating resource requirements is an important part of performance design. It serves to check that both response time and throughput performance requirements can be met.

Response times are calculated by adding the time required by each resource—line transmission, processor, and disk access—and then calculating a queuing factor, which is a function of the utilization of each resource involved.

Resource utilization is calculated by multiplying the amount of the resource used for each activity by the number of times the activity is executed in an interval. If resource utilization is less than 100 percent, then the throughput requirement may be met. However, high utilization may cause long response times beyond the required maximum.

Selected Readings

Most of the available literature is about performance modeling, rather than benchmarking and performance improvement. For the two latter topics, the reader is referred to current magazine articles in such publications as Datamation, Byte, and, most importantly, *EDP Performance Review*.

Sauer, Charles H., and Chandy, K. Mani. *Computer Systems Performance Modeling*. Englewood Cliffs, NJ: Prentice-Hall, 1981.
   This book is a representative example of most of the literature on the analytical approach to performance prediction. It requires some mathematical background, in particular in probability theory.

Review Questions

1. Describe briefly the three main measures of performance. What is the functional requirement that underlies each unit of measure?

2. What are the three courses of action open to an analyst when the design does not meet some performance requirement?

3. Describe some possible ways to make excessive response times meet the requirements.

4. Describe some possible ways to resolve availability problems.

5. Summarize the process of calculating response times in an on-line environment. Explain how the result ties in to the calculation of throughput.

Discussion Questions

1. At what points in the life cycle is performance-related work performed?

2. Why is it important to do detailed performance analysis at the end of the design? What are the risks incurred if this activity is glossed over?

3. Discuss the response time requirements for different types of applications (transaction processing, query, DSS, office automation) and different types of users (dedicated, heads-down operators; frequent professional or managerial users; infrequent professional or managerial users; members of the public).

4. In some cases, an application is implemented in stages, with volumes only gradually increasing. This kind of growth is typical when the system has to be installed and users have to be trained in multiple locations.

Although the first few months of operation show satisfactory response times, a problem may arise when there is a gradual degradation of response times as volumes increase and resource utilization creeps past the elbow in the curve. Discuss approaches to deal with this problem.

Mini-Cases

Condor Telephone Company. You have just performed the response time calculations for the order entry application example described in this chapter, and your preliminary results show response times of upward of 7 seconds for many of the exchanges of the application. You are attending a meeting of the project steering committee and have informed the committee of these figures.

The reactions of various members of the committee range from benevolent to vocal:

> Ed Schramm, VP of administration, to whom the IS department used to report before being attached to a newly created chief information officer: "That is way too high! All the on-line applications that I have seen have response times of 2 seconds. You can read any book you want on the subject, they all say that 2 seconds is the absolute maximum for human operators. You must bring the time down dramatically."

> Barbara Cahill, CIO: "This application is not heads-down data entry. I admit that 7 seconds sounds high, but we don't have the budget to buy the hardware required to bring the response times down to 2 seconds. I would guess that we can fine-tune the design and reduce the times to about 5 seconds, which ought to be enough."

> Grant Hougham, head of the Customer Service Department (the main user of the application): "I don't understand. I was sitting at the same table as two of your programmers the other day, and they were telling me that a scientific study had proved that response times below 1 second got the best productivity and user satisfaction. They also told me that our installation was well on its way to achieving that goal for on-line program development. Why can't my people in the field offices, who take customer orders over the phone, get the same kind of service?"

The committee does not reach consensus. The meeting breaks up with the chairman asking you to prepare an evaluation of what it might take—redesign, additional hardware resources, or whatever else—to reach each of these three goals.

Questions for Discussion

1. For each of the three goals, prepare a strategy and an assessment of the following:
   a. The probability of success.
   b. The economic impact.

2. Pick one of the three goals as your preferred choice; prepare to defend it and to marshal arguments against the other two alternatives.

Penchant Products, Inc.   Assume that you are Ralph Boardman, VP of administration for Penchant Products, Inc. You have just received the memorandum depicted in Figure 18–14 from Nancy Hanson, who reports to you.

Question for Discussion.

1. What course of action will you take in response to this memorandum?

Figure 18–14 **Penchant Products Internal Memorandum**

Penchant Products, Inc.

Interoffice Memorandum

```
     To:  Ralph Boardman, Vice-president, Administration
   From:  Nancy Hanson, Director of MIS
Subject:  Hardware Upgrade Requirements
   Date:  June 29, 1992
```

The MIS Department has completed a system performance review on the computer equipment installed at Corporate Headquarters. The review was conducted by our personnel with assistance from our current hardware vendor, Digital Computers, Inc. (DCI).

The results of the review showed that:

1. CPU utilization is running at 89% of capacity.

2. Maximum memory utilization is 80%.

3. Disk I/O was determined to not be a bottleneck.

4. Terminal response time is satisfactory except during the peak hours of 9:30-11:30 am and 1:00-3:00 pm.

Inasmuch as we are planning to add two significant new applications in the coming months (Sales Forecasting in November followed by Production Planning in December), my recommendation is that we place an order now for an upgraded CPU, the DCI 1400-2. This recommendation has the support of the entire review team, based on the following rationale:

1. The DCI 1400-2 CPU is the next upgrade available from our present CPU which has been operating well since 1987.

2. I have been pleased with the service and support received from DCI over the years. This fact, coupled with the investment we have in our existing programs leads me to strongly recommend staying with DCI.

3. If we purchase the DCI 1400-2 and amortize the costs over five years, our monthly cost will be less than our current lease payments. Thus, we will be getting much more computing power for our money.

I look forward to discussing this with you at your earliest convenience.

Nancy Hanson

Installation Planning, Economic Analysis, and Management Approval

Chapter 19 describes the activities required to complete designs for management's approval. The end products of user interface design, data design, and process design must be sufficiently detailed to allow realistic estimates of the effort, cost, and time necessary for implementing the system. In addition, the chapter describes how to plan the installation and how to present anticipated costs and benefits of the system to management. Finally, the chapter describes the process of deciding whether to proceed with the installation of the system, cancel it, or postpone it.

Learning Objectives

- Understand the criteria used to determine when design is complete.
- Understand why the management checkpoint after systems design is the most important checkpoint in the entire systems development life cycle.
- Describe the planning activities involved in developing plans for testing, user training, file conversion, and detailed installation.
- Become aware of the importance of preparing cost/benefit analyses at this stage.
- Know the components of a cost/benefit analysis.
- Understand the structure of the overall economic summary.
- Understand how intangible benefits are treated in the cost/benefit analysis.
- Recognize the contents of the management report as well as the order of presentation.
- Appreciate the preparation activities and presentation skills appropriate for the management review meeting.

COMPLETING THE DESIGN

Although management can review a system at many points during the development life cycle, the most important checkpoint is at the end of design, prior to implementation. At this point the system can be described in sufficient detail for users to understand what the new system will do for them. The technical design has also reached the stage where IS professionals can prepare a reliable estimate of the time needed to implement it. With this information, an economic analysis that will set forth the costs and benefits of proceeding with implementation can be prepared. Experience shows that approximately 25 to 30 percent of the total project effort is expended in the project steps through this point (see Section I). If management decides not to continue with implementation, the major portion of the project effort will have been avoided.

If the users do not understand the functions and features of the new system before implementation, they may ask for changes after programming has begun. At this point, changes are more costly. If the project steering committee decides that a proposed change should be postponed until after implementation, the new system will not function as the users expect. Thus, users will not likely accept the new system. James McKeen reports that systems projects in which more time was spent making sure users understood the requirements were more likely to be implemented within their budget and accepted by the users.[1]

If the IS department attempts to estimate the time required to implement the system before technical design has been completed, time and cost estimates may be inaccurate. Management has a right to be upset when told that an approved system implementation project is going to require considerably more time and money than originally estimated. In some instances, management's reaction to such news has been to press the IS department to meet the original targets, creating a "crisis" project characterized by overtime for the project team and by a compromise on quality. Crisis projects are also the ones most likely to result in operational disasters.

The design can be considered complete, therefore, when the project team prepares the following end products in sufficient detail to estimate realistically the effort, cost, and time needed to implement and operate the proposed system.

The **functional specifications report** summarizes the system's functional design for final management review and approval. It describes the following components of the system:

- Processing functions
- Reports
- Screens
- Input forms
- Procedures (manual and automated)

The **technical specifications report** summarizes the system's technical design for final management review and approval. It covers both computer and manual processing and includes the following:

- Application architecture
- Design of the data base and files
- Major program logic
- Testing and conversion procedures
- Hardware and systems software requirements

PLANNING THE INSTALLATION

An important step is to identify the effort required to install the system. For each of the tasks, the required skill level, estimate of effort, and timetable must be included. Some of the major components in the installation plan are the test plan, the user training plan, the file conversion plan, and the detailed installation plan.

The Test Plan

Testing is an essential step in the development of a new system. It provides assurance that the system will operate in accordance with its design specifications. A program is not considered complete until it has been thoroughly tested, and a system is not considered complete until its constituent programs have been tested together as a system.

The test plan outlines the procedures for all types of testing, including unit tests, integration tests, system tests, and acceptance tests. Standards for using program libraries and test files are identified. Any special software required for testing is identified as well. This software might include such programs as test data generators for volume testing and programs that can automatically compare test results with anticipated results.

Users should be involved at this stage to ensure that any acceptance testing criteria important to them are considered in the test plan. For example, users may wish to have assurance that the system operates in accordance with specifications when large volumes of transactions flow through the system. Users may also wish to have the system pilot tested in a small, controlled environment prior to making it available to the larger community for which it has been designed. Pilot testing is particularly appropriate when a critical system, one that affects many users or locations, is contemplated. A hospital system designed to perform real-time monitoring of intensive care patients' vital signs would no doubt benefit from careful pilot testing—first in a simulated setting and next with one or two patients.

The User Training Plan

Because users who are expected to use the new system must accept it, the proper training of users on the new system is critical. In addition, users should understand the way the new system will help to achieve an organization's goals and objectives. This understanding can make users more receptive to the necessary training.

Before training begins, a plan must be prepared. The training plan should identify the time required both to prepare training materials and to plan and conduct training sessions.

The usual approach to training is one of "training the trainers." Resources are used to train a cadre of personnel from the user departments and/or from the organization's internal training department. The personnel trained in the initial training sessions then conduct training sessions for the other users. This approach is preferable; it minimizes the drain on project team resources, and users prefer training sessions conducted by persons who are recognized as users or professional trainers.

The Conversion Plan

The conversion plan explains the method of converting to the new system. The plan consists of two key elements: the method of preparing initial system master files and the approach to shifting operations from the old to the new system.

System master files or data bases are often converted from master files maintained by existing computer systems. In such cases, all that is necessary is that the project team be sure the format and content of the new files are consistent with system specifications. In some cases, the existing files can be used without change. In most cases, however, a file conversion program is written to translate files from the existing system into the format required by the new system. Validation and file maintenance programs from the new system should be used to perform at least a portion of these tasks, if possible. This procedure will ensure that the new system's beginning files will have passed through the same validation and control routines as will be used by the new system.

Usually, the new system will require some additional data, which must be collected and added to the converted files before the system is operational. During this phase, synchronization is very important in both sets of files—the old ones, which are still operational and therefore continue to change, and the new ones, which are not yet part of the standard change process. All changes posted to the existing file must be logged and processed before the new files can be operational.

If files are not available on an existing computer system, the first option is to use programs from the new system. Additions to the file could be created and passed through the new system's validation and file maintenance programs. This approach is almost always the preferred approach unless for some reason it cannot be used. For example, if the project team is approaching the date of conversion with the file maintenance program behind schedule and on the critical path, it may be more expedient to write a special file conversion program. In any case, controls over the conversion will have to be established to ensure the accuracy and reliability of the beginning system master files.

The project team should also decide on **the basic approach to conversion** at this time. Some of the factors that the team should consider are whether to run the new system in parallel with the old and whether to convert to the new system in phases.

Parallel Operations. Fundamentally, the project team must be sure that the conversion approach selected protects the organization from an intolerable interruption in operations in the event the conversion does not go well. The most conservative approach is to continue to run the old system after converting to the new system, running both systems in parallel. The results of the new system's operations are reconciled to the results of the old system. When the members of the project team have confidence that the new system is operating as planned, they will recommend to the project steering committee that operation of the old system be suspended. If the new system has too many problems, operation of the new system will be suspended, and the old system will be used until the problems with the new system are corrected.

Running the new system in parallel with the old provides the most protection in the event the conversion has to be suspended. Parallel operations also require a significant effort from the project team and users. Project team members are typically very busy at this point, attempting to make final adjustments to the new system and "putting out fires." Users are also attempting to adjust to the changes in their routines that the new system has created. Thus, running two systems requires an additional resource commitment that must be recognized and planned for.

If a parallel operation is chosen during conversion, the outputs of the new system may not be directly reconcilable with results of the old system. For example, the system control scheme or the way certain calculations are made may be different. In addition, the new system and the old system will usually not match business functions on a one-to-one basis. For such reasons, procedures must be established to reconcile the results of the new system with those of the old system. If possible, computer programs should be written to perform such reconciliations automatically.

Sometimes, in parallel operations, difficulties occur that necessitate suspending the new system's operation. Organizations generally try to avoid this undesirable occurrence by planning a thorough system test of the new system and allowing ample time for all parties to be satisfied with the new system's operations before beginning the conversion.

Phased Conversion. Converting the system in phases is another way of reducing risk during the transition period. If the system is to be installed at several locations, it can be pilot tested at a selected location. In addition to

Figure 19–1 **Example of Phased Conversion**

giving the project team an opportunity to observe the system in operation in a controlled environment, pilot testing can help promote user acceptance. If users at the pilot location are pleased with the new system, word will usually spread to their counterparts at other locations within the organization. Bad news about the new system will probably spread even faster. For these reasons, the site for the initial conversions in a phased approach should be selected with care. The site for a pilot test should be one where management and support personnel are eager to learn about the new system.

Another option for a phased conversion is to convert a large system in modules. For example, an integrated system for inventory control, accounts payable, and purchasing using electronic data interchange (EDI) for purchase orders and invoices might be converted in the sequence illustrated in Figure 19–1.

The Detailed Installation Plan

The detailed installation plan is the way the project team estimates the amount of effort and the elapsed time required to install a new system. The plan lists the segments, tasks, and work steps required for the system installation phase. For each task, required skill levels are specified. The work plan should be sufficiently detailed to be used in the cost/benefit analysis prepared at this point in the project. A more detailed plan for controlling the installation project is prepared after management's approval to proceed with the installation.

Sample work plans containing checklists of project segments, tasks, and work steps are usually included in commercially available standard development methodologies. Such checklists should be used only as a guide, however. Standard work plans must almost always be tailored to the specific

Figure 19–2 **Description of Software Package**
Used to Prepare Work Plans

```
SYSTEMS                            DESIGN TOOL                          CD-20
PLAN                               SUBURBAN PUMPS                        PMF&F
                    FUNCTIONS/FEATURES OF PROJECT MANAGEMENT SOFTWARE

PREPARED BY:  J. WEBER             DATE: 27AUG88          VERSION: 1.1     PAGE 1
APPROVED BY:  JACK CROFT           DATE: 05SEP88          STATUS:  D


The following functions and features for project management software are to he used as
a guideline for evaluating commercially available packages and selecting the one that
best fits the needs of Suburban Pumps for the implementation of the systems plan.

1.  Work plan preparation

       o    A hierarchy of phases, tasks, and detailed activities compatible with our
            systems development methodology

       o    Enough flexibility to accommodate changes in the methodology

       o    An existing data base of estimating factors which we can use in the absence
            of our own

       o    A means of updating the estimating factors based on historical data

       o    Critical path (or PERT) analysis

       o    What-if functions to assist in rescheduling in case of project overruns

       o    Presentation of printed output by project, subproject, and individual

       o    Bar chart (GANTT chart) presentation of overall work program

       o    Variable degree of detail in reports (summarized by phase, task, subtask...)

2.  Time reporting

       o    ...

       o
```

requirements of each project. Some steps will probably be added, and others
will probably be deleted. In addition, as illustrated in Figure 19–2, some
commercially available software packages aid analysts in developing work
plans. Some of the packages have data bases compiled from the experience

gained from working with other projects. These data bases can aid in estimating the effort required on specific work tasks. The detailed installation plan for a system might well contain all of the segments illustrated in Figure 19–3. A bar chart (Figure 19–4) summarizes the estimated workdays and time frame for each segment of the project and gives management an overview of the sequence and timing of the major segments of project effort.

COST/BENEFIT ANALYSIS

A cost/benefit analysis is performed at this stage in the project. The system's functions and features have been designed in sufficient detail to permit the benefits of the new system to be identified, and the technical design has been completed to the point where its installation and operating costs can be estimated with acceptable accuracy.

The preparation of cost/benefit analyses is so common now that it almost constitutes a standard practice. In some situations, however, a key member of management may suggest that this step be omitted, usually on the grounds that the system is so important that it must be implemented no matter what the cost. If possible, the project team should press for a cost/benefit analysis anyway. Even though cost may not be a crucial issue, management should be aware of the costs and benefits before proceeding. In addition, members of management are replaced from time to time, and the project team is well advised to press for a review of costs and benefits to protect itself from criticism by successor management.

For example, in one company, the IS department had adopted as standard practice the preparation of cost/benefit analyses and post-implementation audits. Top management, in this case, was preoccupied with other issues and had left the details of IS operations to middle management. Later, the business environment turned sour, and top management turned its attention to finding ways of reducing costs. It found that IS expenditures had increased markedly over the period and asked that the current level of expenditures be justified. Because the head of IS had prepared cost/benefit analyses over the years, he was able to demonstrate quickly that although expenditures had indeed gone up, they were more than justified by the cumulative savings in affected user departments.

Components of the Cost/Benefit Analysis

A cost/benefit analysis includes the costs of operating the old and new systems and the costs of installation.

Operating costs of the present system are obtained by adding all costs associated with the operation of the present system, including personnel, hardware, software, communications, other IS department costs, and other costs incurred by user departments.

Figure 19–3 **Standard Activities of Installation Phase**

```
PERSONNEL                     PROJECT MANAGEMENT TOOL                    CD-20
PAYROLL                            SUBURBAN PUMPS                        IPLAN
                                 INSTALLATION TASKS


PREPARED BY:  GLORIA HUNTER        DATE: 15JAN92        VERSION: 1       PAGE 1
APPROVED BY:  JACK WEBER           DATE: 22JAN92        STATUS:  F


PROJECT ORGANIZATION
     Organize and manage project
     Establish standards
     Establish project training program
     Administer training
DETAILED DESIGN
     Complete design of screens and reports not done during design
     Complete data base design
     Design and document programming work units
     Prepare common test data for unit tests
     Perform structured design reviews
USER PROCEDURE DEVELOPMENT
     Develop user and IS operations manual contents
     Plan training program
     Produce user and operations manuals
     Produce training materials
     Conduct training
SITE PREPARATION
     Plan site modifications (user and IS)
     Procure required hardware, software, and supplies (e.g., preprinted forms;)
     Supervise construction, delivery, and installation
CONVERSION PREPARATION
     Complete conversion plan
     Develop conversion procedures
     Convert files
     Plan system test
PROGRAMMING
     Code
     Unit test
     Document
     Conduct structured review
     Supervise programming
SYSTEM TEST
     Perform integration test
     Perform system test
     Check results and issue change requests
     Implement changes if approved
CONVERSION
     Convert system
     Monitor production
     Transfer to routine production
ACCEPTANCE
     Measure degree of compliance with requirements specification
     Negotiate and implement required changes
     Formalize user acceptance
```

Figure 19–4 **Sample Bar Chart Summary**

PERSONNEL
PAYROLL

PROJECT MANAGEMENT TOOL
SUBURBAN PUMPS
INSTALLATION BAR CHART

CD-20
IBAR

PREPARED BY: GLORIA HUNTER
APPROVED BY: JACK WEBER

DATE: 15JAN90
DATE: 22JAN90

VERSION: 1
STATUS: F

PAGE 1

SEP OCT NOV DEC JAN FEB MAR APR MAY JUN JUL AUG SEP OCT NOV DEC JAN FEB

PROJECT ORGANIZATION

DETAILED DESIGN

USER PROCEDURE DEVELOPMENT

SITE PREPARATION

CONVERSION PREPARATION

PROGRAMMING

SYSTEM TEST

CONVERSION

ACCEPTANCE

Operating costs of the proposed system are obtained by estimating the costs of operating the proposed system. The same categories are used for these estimates as were used in determining the costs of the present system. Because the proposed system costs are estimates, user departments should be involved in the prediction of those costs under their control. For example, an estimate that the new system will operate with 80 percent of the clerical staff required under the present system has more credibility with management if it is made by user personnel rather than IS personnel.

Estimates of operating costs for the proposed system will often include net changes in revenue (usually increases) associated with the system's installation. For example, suppose a resort condominium complex proposed the installation of a marketing system to attract previous renters. The objective is to increase by 5 percent the percentage of renters who return in subsequent years. The increase would offset the costs of operating the proposed system.

Installation costs are the one-time costs associated with installing the system. They include personnel costs as reflected in the installation work plan, incremental hardware costs for program testing and conversion, and any other resources required to move from the present system to the proposed system.

OVERALL ECONOMIC SUMMARY

Present system costs, proposed system costs, and installation costs are projected in an overall economic summary, as illustrated in Figure 19–5. The overall economic summary should be presented in a format familiar to management. The project team should involve others in the organization who can give guidance on the proper format. The illustration in Figure 19–5 is a simple payback analysis, which is used by many companies.

Some organizations may adopt more sophisticated analysis techniques such as return on investment (ROI) or net present value to analyze capital investment proposals. Using ROI, an organization simply divides the average annual benefits by the average investment. Figure 19–6 shows the overall economic summary from Figure 19–5 using ROI rather than payback analysis. ROI analysis assumes that the benefits from the investment in the new system are realized evenly over its useful life.

Present value is widely used as a capital investment analysis technique and receives complete coverage in finance courses. If present value analysis were used for the overall economic analysis of the system of Figure 19–5, it would appear as illustrated in Figure 19–7. What has been done is to multiply the cost and benefits for each year of the useful life of the project by a factor obtained from a table of present values. Present value tables discount amounts by a factor that takes into account both time and interest rate. For example, the value today of a dollar to be received one year from now is

Figure 19–5 **Sample Overall Economic Summary**

```
PERSONNEL                       DESIGN TOOL                        CD-20
PAYROLL                         SUBURBAN PUMPS                      ECONS
                           OVERALL ECONOMIC SUMMARY

PREPARED BY:  GLORIA HUNTER     DATE: 15JAN90          VERSION: 1    PAGE 1
APPROVED BY:  JACK WEBER        DATE: 22JAN90          STATUS:  F


Benefits/Costs                   1991  1992  1993  1994  1995  TOTAL   AVG
                                 ----  ----  ----  ----  ----  -----   ----
     Tangible benefits approximation

          Cost avoidance opportunity    160   160   160   160   160    800   160
          Cost reduction opportunity     10    10    10    10    10     50    10
          Quantifiable intangible benefits 30   30    30    30    30    150    30
                                         ----  ----  ----  ----  ----  -----  ----
               Total quantifiable benefits 200  200   200   200   200   1000   200

     Cost approximation

          Development costs              180     0     0     0     0    180    36
          Continuing costs (net increase) 30    30    30    30    30    150    30
                                         ----  ----  ----  ----  ----  -----  ----
          Total costs                    210    30    30    30    30    330    66

Net continuing benefit (cost) *          170   170   170   170   170    850   170
Less taxes (50%) *                        85    85    85    85    85    425    85
Net after tax benefit (Cost) *            85    85    85    85    85    425    85
Depreciation *                            40    40    40    40    40    200    40
Estimated cash flow approximation        109   109   109   109   109    545   109

* Does not include development cost


ACCEPTANCE
     Measure degree of compliance with requirements specification
     Negotiate and implement required changes
     Formalize user acceptance
```

Figure 19–6 **Sample Overall Economic Summary Using ROI**

```
MARKETING                       DESIGN TOOL                           CD-20
ORDER ENTRY                     SUBURBAN PUMPS                        ECONS
             COST/BENEFIT OF SUMMARY SALES REPORTING MODIFICATION

PREPARED BY: MARYANN UNGER      DATE: 08JAN92        VERSION: 1.1     PAGE 1
APPROVED BY: GLORIA HUNTER      DATE: 22FEB92        STATUS:


                                                                    Amount
                                                                    ------

1. One-time Change Costs
----------------------------------
Personnel expense -
                   50    workdays analyst                            6,000
                  100    workdays programmer                         8,000
                   30    workdays clerical                             960
        Machine hours cost -
                   20    CPU hours                                  12,250
        Equipment and supplies -
                         Paper and office supplies                    100
                   25    reels magnetic tape                          625
                                                                  ---------
                                               Subtotal             27,935
                                                                  ---------


2. Recurring Costs and Savings
----------------------------------
Clerical savings - Annual -
                   25    workdays/month                             (9,600)
                         Supplies                                     (100)

3. Intangible Costs and Benefits
----------------------------------
             Information available earlier (not quantified)            (0)
                                                                  ---------
                                               Subtotal             (9,700)
                                                                  ---------

4. Payback Period
----------------------------------
         27,935/9,700 = less than 3 years

5. Return on Investment over 4 Years
----------------------------------
             9,700 * 4 - 27,935 / 27,935 = 40%
```

Figure 19–7 **Sample Overall Economic Summary Using Net Present Value**

```
MANUFACTURING                    DESIGN TOOL                            CD-20
QUALITY CONTROL                 SUBURBAN PUMPS                          ECONS
                           OVERALL ECONOMIC SUMMARY

PREPARED BY:  JOE DAVIS         DATE: 15MAR93            VERSION: 1     PAGE 1
APPROVED BY:  PIERRE FAVIER     DATE: 04APR93            STATUS:


CLASSIFICATION                  Period 1 Period 2 Period 3 Period 4 Period 5 Period 6
------------------------------  -------- -------- -------- -------- -------- --------

Continuing cost and benefits
(assuming 7% inflation)
     Present system                      1,480    1,584    1,694    1,813    1,940
     Proposed system                     1,353    1,448    1,549    1,657    1,774
                                         -----    -----    -----    -----    -----
     Net reduction (increase)              127      136      145      156      166

Installation costs                280       21        0        0        0        0

Net savings (costs)             (280)      106      136      145      156      166

Estimated savings using
   present value method

     Present value of savings   (280)       96      112      109      106      103
     (cost) based on 10% cost
     of capital

     Total net present value     248

Cumulative savings (cost)       (280)    (174)     (38)      107      263      429

Cumulative present value        (280)    (184)     (71)       38      144      248

Estimated payback period: 3-4 years
```

$.909, assuming 10 percent could be earned on money invested today for one year. (The value of a dollar today is one dollar.) Net present value is the difference between costs and benefits computed on a present value basis.

Most companies have an assumed interest rate factor that is used for evaluating investments based on the company's opportunity cost—the amount the company feels it could earn if this particular investment were not made. In such cases, the company's opportunity cost is the basis for selecting the interest rate used in present value calculations. In any event, if the net present value technique is to be used for the overall economic summary, the project team should consult the company's finance or budget department to obtain the appropriate rate. By doing so, the team will be assured of using assumptions that are consistent with those used in other capital investment analyses reviewed by management.

The finance or budget department can also supply the project team with the standard assumptions it uses for such factors as inflation, wage increases, standard volume increases, and the like. Using standard assumptions about the future will result in financial projections in the project report that are consistent with what management is accustomed to seeing in financial projections. In some cases, management is more comfortable seeing the overall economic summary expressed with a range of values, i.e., as most likely and least likely scenarios rather than as specific estimates.

Experience has shown that the overall economic summary should not be extended beyond a period of about five years. Beyond that, the accuracy of the estimates becomes less reliable, particularly in the present environment of rapid competitive and technological change.

Questions often arise about the proper way to show IS department costs if the organization charges costs for development and/or operations back to the using department. Differences in the figures can arise depending on whether incremental costs or allocated costs are used. For example, if a relatively small system were to be installed on a large CPU with ample additional capacity, the incremental cost to the organization to operate the new system might be very low. If, however, the IS department allocated costs to user departments, the user departments would have to account for the allocated costs in their budget. Depending on the method of allocation, the costs to the user departments could be considerably higher than the incremental costs to the organization. The procedure usually followed by the project team in such cases is to prepare two overall economic summaries, one using incremental costs and the other using allocated costs.

When the overall economic summary is prepared, it is often possible to place economic values on intangible benefits (or costs), employing various estimating techniques. For example, if a proposed billing system is designed to produce bills five days sooner than the present system, it should be possible to estimate the net effect of a speedup in cash flow and a possible reduction in write-offs for uncollectible accounts. If the system is expected to increase market share, the net effect of such an increase should be estimated. However, such estimates should have the strong support of users so that they will have credibility with management.

After all quantifiable costs and benefits have been identified, additional benefits often remain that are too difficult to quantify. Examples of such intangible benefits are more timely management information, better customer service, and more accurate information. Such intangible benefits should be identified separately and discussed as a part of the overall economic summary, for they can have a significant bearing on management's decision to proceed with the installation of the proposed system.

PRESENTING THE ANALYSIS TO MANAGEMENT

Presentation of the analysis of the project effort usually takes two forms: a written report of the work performed to date and a meeting at which the report is presented and discussed in order to reach a decision on a future course of action.

The Management Report

The management report is prepared to summarize the relevant considerations affecting management's decision of whether to proceed with the installation of the system. It usually contains the following items:

- An executive summary presents the key system objectives, features, and benefits, including the bottom line of the economic analysis, a high-level contrast of the new system with the old system, and the project team's recommendation for the next steps to be taken.

- A summary of system functions and features—drawn from the more detailed functional specifications report—should present key differences between the present and proposed systems in more detail than did the executive summary.

- A summary of the system's technical architecture, processing, data base design, and security and control design—drawn from the more detailed technical specifications report—should be presented in terms understandable to the management audience being addressed.

- An overall economic summary.

- A bar chart summarizing the installation schedule.

- A discussion weighing the costs and benefits of installing the system against other options that should be considered. A typical case is one where management can choose to stay with the present system, install the proposed system, modify the present system in some way, install only certain modules of the proposed system, or postpone the installation. The project team should identify and discuss other viable options that management may wish to consider before making a decision.

The project team should be sure that the final report addresses the five elements of feasibility (technical, operational, economic, schedule, and motivational).

The Management Review Meeting

After management has read the report, analysts meet with the project steering committee to reach agreement on the proposed course of action. The level of management approval required will vary from organization to organization and from project to project. With some projects, only the steering committee's approval is required to proceed with the installation.

The written report should have been distributed to those persons attending the meeting well enough in advance to give them a chance to absorb its contents. The presentation itself is shared between users and IS personnel. Users cover the functions, features, and benefits of the proposed system and that portion of the economic analysis for which they will be responsible. IS personnel cover the technical features of the proposed system, the installation plan, and that part of the economic analysis for which they will be responsible.

It is worthwhile to hold a practice session of the presentation before knowledgeable persons who have not been closely associated with the project. Members of the audience should play devil's advocate, critiquing the project team's presentation. They should attempt to anticipate the questions management will ask to see how effectively the project team is able to respond. Finally, they should evaluate the relevancy and readability of visual aids.

After the project team has decided who will be giving the presentation, they should agree that any questions from management will be answered by the person in front of the group at that time. Presenters should refer questions they are unsure of to the project team leader, who may either answer the questions, or refer them to another project team member. It is disconcerting to ask a question of a presenter only to hear the answer come from someone sitting on the sidelines.

At the conclusion of the presentation, the project team should seek formal approval of its recommendation. Management may approve the installation of the proposed system; it may choose one of the other options identified by the project team; or it may suggest new options the project team will be asked to evaluate. When approval is given to move ahead with the proposed system, the project has reached the beginning of the implementation phase (see Section VII).

FREEZING THE SPECIFICATIONS

Once installation is approved, the system's specifications should not be changed. If the project team has done a thorough job, user requirements have been carefully identified, and the need for changes to the specifications should be unlikely. Some changes cannot be avoided, however, and analysts must decide whether to include them in the new system specifications or to add them after the initial conversion. Changes imposed on the system from the outside—changes in tax law or legal reporting requirements, for example—cannot be postponed.

The further along the project team is in the installation the more costly it is to make changes. If changes cannot be avoided, and they are significant enough, analysts can revise the installation schedule and economic summary; management can review the changes and consider their effect.

Summary

The design is considered complete when the users understand and are satisfied with the functions and features of the proposed system, and when the IS professionals are satisfied with the system's technical feasibility. At this point, IS professionals can comfortably estimate the time and resources required to implement the system. The functional specifications report and the technical specifications report should be complete at this point.

Planning the installation includes preparation of plans for testing the system, training the users, converting files, and developing a detailed installation plan to control the work of the project team. Various conversion strategies and options include the pros and cons of running the new system parallel with the old. A fallback plan is necessary in the event that the new system does not function well enough to continue it. Also valuable are phased conversions and pilot tests.

A cost/benefit analysis should be prepared regardless of whether management feels it is necessary. Even if the new system need not be cost justified, management should be made aware of its cost. In addition, managers sometimes move on, and their replacements may ask for the cost/benefit analysis of a converted system.

The cost/benefit analysis should use the organization's usual techniques for analyzing capital expenditures. The most common techniques are payback, return on investment, and net present value. The typical components are current system operating costs, proposed system operating costs, and the costs of installation. The project team should also use the standard assumptions of the organization for such factors as inflation and wage increases. Extending the economic analysis beyond five years is probably not wise because of the effect of business and technological change on factors used in the analysis.

Intangible benefits should be identified separately and presented to management as additional factors in deciding whether to install the new system.

The project team should submit to management a written report that summarizes work completed and recommends the next steps. After reviewing the report, management will decide whether to accept the recommendations.

If approval of the implementation phase is obtained, the system's specifications should be considered frozen. If subsequent changes become necessary, the target dates or resource requirements approved by management may have to change. Depending on the magnitude of the changes, reapproval of the project may be required.

Selected Reading

Gildersleeve, T. *Successful Data Processing Systems Analysis*, 2d ed. Englewood Cliffs, NJ: Prentice-Hall, 1985.

This text contains a detailed section on alternative techniques for preparing cost/benefit analyses. In addition, it has a useful discussion on ways to place values on intangible benefits.

Review Questions

1. Why is the management checkpoint at the end of design considered the most important of all the management checkpoints in the systems development life cycle?

2. Describe the end products of systems design.

3. What are the main components of the installation plan?

4. What is the purpose of testing? When is testing complete?

5. To what extent should users be involved in preparing the test plan?

6. How is user training related to their acceptance of the system?

7. What are the two key elements of the conversion plan?

8. Describe the procedure(s) for preparing the initial system master files.

9. Compare the advantages and disadvantages of parallel system conversion.

10. Describe two options for a phased conversion approach.

11. Why should the project team press for cost/benefit analyses for new systems?

12. How is the overall economic summary prepared? What is the maximum time frame recommended for the summary? Why?

13. How should intangible benefits of the new system be treated in the cost/benefit analysis?

14. What is the purpose of the management report?

15. How should the project team prepare for the management review meeting?

16. How flexible are the system specifications once management approval has been secured?

Discussion Questions

1. Why is the approval of the major portion of project expenditures delayed until after completion of the technical design?

2. Discuss the opportunities for user involvement during installation planning, economic analyses, and management approval.

3. What is the difference between tangible and intangible benefits? Provide examples of each. For the intangible benefits, is it possible to attribute economic benefits to them? If not, how would you cover them in the cost/benefit analysis?

4. Why is the project team's recommendation to management presented "up front" in the executive summary of the management report?

Mini-Cases

Techline University. Techline University is planning to install a new student registration system. Although Techline has served its students with an on-line registration system for quite some time, the new system design will provide notable improvements. For example, the new system will permit students to request classes by using a touch-tone telephone. Currently, they have to wait in long lines for a data entry clerk to key in class request data.

Another design improvement is that the system will check the student schedule for time conflicts. In addition, the new system will provide reports for better administrative planning, for example, predicting the need for additional classes long before the need arises.

Question for Discussion

1. The project team is preparing a conversion plan. Make recommendations for the following:

    a. A procedure for creating the new system's master file.

    b. A recommended approach to conversion.

United Charities of Colorado. United Charities of Colorado owns an HCL 1000 minicomputer. The machine was purchased five years ago for $250,000 and is used principally for administrative applications. One of the largest applications is a volunteer data base containing over 60,000 names of individuals who have indicated their willingness to serve charitable organizations in the state. The system has proven to be very helpful in matching willing workers with organizations that need assistance. It operates in an on-line mode to give quick answers to queries from either volunteers or organizations. The executive director is convinced that the system's overwhelming acceptance is due to its ability to generate an immediate response, and that in addition to providing a much-needed service, the public relations by-product has been quite valuable to United Charities.

As the application has grown, and as other applications have been added to the HCL, response time has degraded to the point where it will be unacceptable in a few months' time.

Bob Fitzmorris is the HCL salesperson who handles the United Charities account. He sold them the HCL 1000 and has worked with them ever since. For the past three months he has been working with Sylvia Shaw, United Charities' MIS director, on a plan to upgrade to an HCL 2000. The plan the two of them have worked out will cost about $75,000 net and should provide adequate capacity for growth over the next five years. During the course of the study, Bob was pleased to have been told by his company that the price of the HCL 2000 was being reduced by 30 percent, effective immediately. It gave him a more competitive product to sell and would save some of his customers money. The savings was certainly welcomed by Sylvia.

Last night, Bob received a call from Jan Sakayama, a friend of long standing and a research engineer at HCL's lab in Santa Rosa. During the course of an hour-long conversation, Jan told Bob that HCL was close to announcing a replacement for its current line of computers. The new line would make the HCL 1000 and 2000 obsolete. Jan said she really should not be discussing these plans with anyone on the sales force because it was important for the company's survival that the inventory of 1000 and 2000 models be sold prior to the announcement. Afterwards, their value would drop much beyond the recent 30 percent reduction. She asked Bob to hold what he had been told by her in the strictest confidence.

Question for Discussion

1. What, if anything, should Bob do with the course of action he and Sylvia had agreed upon for United Charities?

Note

1. McKeen, James. "Successful Development Strategies for Business Application Systems." *MIS Quarterly* (September 1983): 47–65.

Program Structure Charting

INTRODUCTION

Chapter 16, Program Design, uses structure charts to depict the functionality and architecture of programs. Structure charts gained their popularity with the "structured revolution" of the 1970s as a substitute for the then current program flowcharts. Structure charts (and other techniques introduced at the same time, such as pseudo-code and structured English) had the advantage over flowcharts that they forced the program designer to abide by the rules of structured programming and avoid the "harmful GOTO statement."

DEFINITION

A program structure chart is a specialized version of a hierarchical diagram (see the Technique in Section I) that depicts the relationships among the functions executed by a program. Program structure charts afford a more graphical view of a program than does code or pseudo-code. Program structure charts can easily be prepared to show less detail than code or pseudo-code. It is therefore a tool that can be used by analyst and programmer alike, regardless of the prevailing division of responsibilities.

EXAMPLE

Figure 1 shows a program structure chart that contains examples of the three main logical constructs of a structured program: sequence, iteration, and condition. The sequence is implicit in the disposition of the diagram, which is read left to right, top to bottom. The iteration construct is illustrated by an UNTIL clause. The condition construct is illustrated by four IF clauses.

WHERE USED IN THE LIFE CYCLE

Program structure charts are used in the late stages of design and in programming. During design, program structure charts are prepared to display the functions performed by each program and their relationships. The charts can serve to verify that the design is exhaustive, i.e., that all

Figure 1 **Illustration of a Program Structure Chart**

the functions identified during the requirements analysis are performed. They can also help check that the design is consistent and, in particular, that the data required to perform each function can be made available to the program. Finally, the program structure charts serve as the basis for estimating the programming effort and assigning work to analysts and programmers during program specification and programming. During the design phase, only high-level charts are prepared. Iteration and condition constructs are only indicated when they are essential to the understanding of the chart.

During programming specification and programming, program structure charts are used to specify the way a program functions in successively greater detail, until all the control functions (iterations and conditions) are described. Generally, a first level of detail is prepared by an analyst for the programming specification; then a programmer takes over and documents to the lowest detail. The limit between the two is determined by installation standards or, in many cases, by the experience level of the programmer.

FORMAL RULES

A program structure chart consists of a number of *statements* tied together by three constructs: *sequence, iteration,* and *condition.* The tool on which the illustrations in this chapter are based depicts statements in Warnier-style hierarchies, left to right, top to bottom. Each statement can be accompanied by an iteration or a condition specification in parentheses under the statement (see Figure 1). Each bracket to the right of a statement represents the span of control of the iteration or the condition and contains all statements that are executed inside the loop or are executed when the condition is true.

There are three forms of loops: UNTIL, WHILE, and FOR (see Figure 2). An UNTIL loop is performed by executing the loop, then testing for the condition specified in the UNTIL statement. If the condition is true, the execution continues in sequence; if false, the loop is performed again. An UNTIL loop is always executed at least once.

Figure 2 **Iteration Constructs**

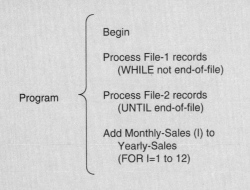

Program
{
Begin

Process File-1 records
(WHILE not end-of-file)

Process File-2 records
(UNTIL end-of-file)

Add Monthly-Sales (I) to
Yearly-Sales
(FOR I=1 to 12)
}

A WHILE loop is similar to an UNTIL loop, but the condition is tested before the statements in the loop are executed. If the condition is true, the loop is executed; if false, the loop is skipped and the next statement in sequence is executed. A WHILE loop may not be executed at all, unlike the UNTIL loop.

A FOR loop is controlled by a variable inside the loop, so that the loop is executed a specified number of times (at least once). An additional construct can be simulated with the FOR statement, namely, a FOR EACH iteration. This iteration specifies that the loop is to be performed for each occurrence of some item on a file, in a table, or in an array. The most useful way to use FOR EACH is to document a loop that is repeated for each row in a relational table. The FOR EACH statement can then be qualified further with a WHERE statement similar to the WHERE statement in SQL, the most popular relational data manipulation language (see Figure 3).

Figure 3 **The FOR EACH Construct**

Program
{
Begin

Process Customer
(FOR EACH Customer
WHERE Billing-period =
Reference-period)
{
Print Invoice

Update Accounts Receivable
}

End
}

Figure 4 **IF and ELSE Constructs**

The conditional statements that are allowed are the simple IF and the repetitive IF (or CASE) statement. Each may be used with an ELSE condition. Figure 4 illustrates the use of IF and ELSE.

When using program structure charts in the programming phase, the rule normally followed for creating brackets is that the parent of a bracket (the statement to the left of it) is necessarily qualified by a loop or a condition. An exception may be made if there is a lengthy sequence of unqualified statements that are logically tied together: an owning bracket may then be created with a statement to the left of it, which simply names the function that the related statements accomplish. A statement with an iteration condition attached to it must always be the parent of some lower-level bracket.

Subprograms and common routines cannot be represented on the same program structure chart as the the statements that call these subroutines. A fresh structure chart should be created for each subprogram. If the subprograms are few and simple, a possible artifice is to create a bracket (the last one on the second level) to contain them (see Figure 5).

When using program structure charts in the design phase, the rules are less stringent. In particular, lower levels may be omitted, as may iteration and condition clauses that do not add to the understanding of the functions performed by the program. For instance, such iteration clauses as UNTIL

Figure 5 **Subprogram**

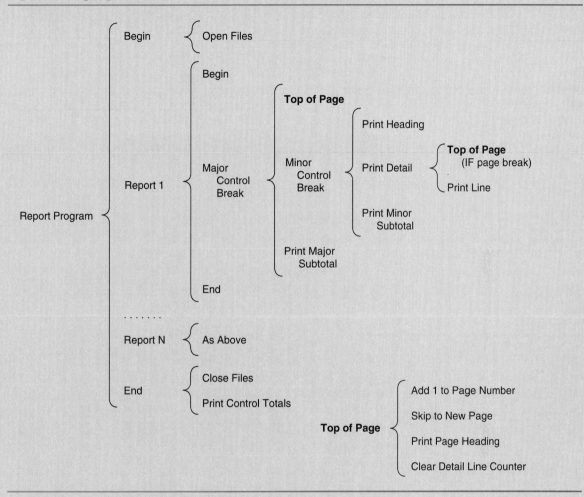

End-of-File following a READ statement are not necessary. A program structure chart in the design phase is to be considered an unfinished structure chart, to be detailed in a later phase.

EQUIVALENT TECHNIQUES

Two main forms of documentation are equivalent to the Warnier-style program structure charts described here. One is the Jackson-style chart. This is a hierarchy of boxes containing the program functions marked with a symbol

Figure 6 **Jackson-style Program Structure Chart**

to signify iterations and conditions (see Figure 6). In addition, some methods recommend adding indications of data used and created by each function (see Figure 7).

The second form of documentation is pseudo-code (see Figure 8).

As explained in Section I, these two alternative techniques are both hierarchical in nature and have about the same expressive power as Warnier-style charts. The main disadvantage of the Jackson-style chart is that it is more difficult to describe iterations and conditions fully. The main disadvantage of pseudo-code is that it does not depict the overall structure of the program quite as graphically.

EXERCISES

1. Create program structure charts for a program that counts paragraphs, lines, words, and characters in a text file and prints the totals out at the end of the program. Use two or three different documentation techniques. Compare and contrast the various techniques.

2. Create a detailed program structure chart for each program in the Condor order entry application described in the mini-case of Chapter 16.

3. Create a detailed program structure chart from the pseudo-code examples given in Figures 16–15 and 16–16. Once each detailed chart is created, simplify it so that it corresponds to a level of detail appropriate for the design phase rather than the programming phase.

Figure 7 **Jackson-style Program Structure Chart with Data Used/Created**

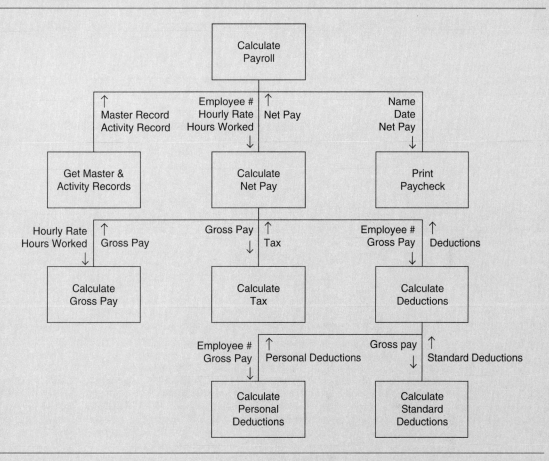

Figure 8 **Pseudo-Code**

```
Open Master_File Activity_File History_File
Dowhile Records_on_Activity_File
   Get Activity_Record
   Get_Corresponding Master_Record
   Do Net_Pay_Calculation
      Gross_Pay = Hourly_Rate * Hours_Worked
      Tax = Gross_Pay * Tax_Rate
      Net_Pay = Gross_Pay – Tax
      Deduction_Total = 0
      Dowhile Personal_Deductions
         Deduction = Gross_Pay * Deduction_Rate
         Write Deduction, Deduction_Code to History_File
         Deduction_Total = Deduction_Total + Deduction
      Enddo
      Dowhile Standard_Deductions
         Deduction = Gross_Pay * Deduction_Rate
         Write Deduction, Deduction_Code to History_File
         Deduction_Total = Deduction_Total + Deduction
      Enddo
      Net_Pay = Net_Pay – Deduction_Total
   Enddo
   Print Name, Date, Net_Pay on Pay_Check
Enddo
Close Master_File Activity_File History_File
```

Implementation

This section covers the remainder of the systems development life cycle, once the planning, analysis, and design phases have been completed. Chapter 20 describes the tasks of program specifications, programming supervision and testing: unit tests, integration tests, systems tests, and acceptance tests. Chapter 21 describes how to convert the files for the new systems and how to prepare the users for the day when the new system goes into operation. Finally, Chapter 22 describes how systems are maintained and enhanced during the rest of their life cycles, until they are replaced by new systems.

IBM's Multiples Marketing Program

◆

A glass and concrete building outside Atlanta houses IBM's Multiples Marketing Program. This organization assists IBM customers who are installing a system—hardware, software, or both—at a large number of sites.

The Multiples Marketing Program could help manufacturers of agricultural or automotive equipment to install ordering and inventory systems in their dealerships around the country. It could help insurance companies to install workstations at their agents' offices or airlines to place reservation systems at travel agencies. In fact, it could be used by any corporation that has distributed processing requirements for many sites or that is installing a system linking it to its customers.

The program is called "Multiples Marketing" because it deals with multiples of systems—one hundred at a minimum—and because it emphasizes advice to the customers of the program on how to market their systems to their own customers or users. The need for a well-thought-out approach to marketing is evident in many cases. For example, if a car manufacturer wants to place a system at its dealers, any dealer is free to refuse to install the system. If the dealer is or feels coerced, the installation will not be a success. Even if the users are internal and therefore not free to refuse, a poorly presented system increases the risk of failure.

The program therefore offers customers assistance in developing a marketing plan to sell the system to its prospective users. Techniques to make the prospective users want to use the system are developed. Responsibility for marketing the system is assigned to the organization that is the most closely associated with the user. This is often the marketing or the sales organization when the system is being distributed to customers.

Project planning and control assistance is also given. In IBM's words, the two phases are: "plan the work" and "work the plan." The Multiples Marketing Program provides assistance in the first phase, establishing a project schedule by adapting and detailing the Master Project Schedule shown in Figure VII–1. The project control process is also designed. However, executing the plan and controlling it remain the responsibility of the customer.

Systems installation is prepared by planning for the logistics of installing new hardware at all the locations. The plan calls for the user to do as much of the installation work as possible and for the role of the central installation team to be limited to problem situations. This approach reduces the bottleneck that would be caused by a central installation team flying around the country and spending several days at each site.

An administration group is created centrally to handle all the logistics of ordering equipment, monitoring delivery schedules, and tracking problems. For large numbers of installations, the responsibility of logistics should not be assigned to the systems development team, which will be occupied with technical problems during the installation.

The program also offers help in setting up other support functions, such as training, documentation creation, and a response line or help desk. The overall objective of these functions is to help the end users of the system develop two essential attributes for the success of a system: self-sufficiency and ownership.

By far the most interesting aspect of the Multiples Marketing Program, however, is the usability lab. Two usability lab rooms are installed in the same building as the rest of the program. The rooms have a workspace for an operator and an observation center separated from the workspace by a one-way mirror. The observation center is equipped with video and audio recording equipment, as well as with two computer terminals. One terminal shows exactly what is being shown on the screen in the workspace; on the other, an observer can log events as they happen.

A usability lab session usually lasts about a week, during which two to four volunteer users, one at a time, test the system (or a prototype of it) under conditions that are as realistic as possible. The user is instructed to "think aloud" as he or she is doing the work. This running commentary provides a valuable guide for the observation team to pinpoint why difficulties arise. The last day of the week is reserved for evaluation. The observation team and sometimes the users come together to summarize what problems were encountered and what is required to solve them.

The usability lab has proven extremely valuable to those organizations that have used it. Some have even set up their own labs in-house. According to several users, the usability lab has made all the difference between a smooth installation with good user acceptance and a problem-fraught one where the central help desk is smothered by irate customer calls or where users reject the system after experiencing early frustration and failure.

PURPOSE OF SECTION

The purpose of this section is to round out the topics of analysis and design by summarizing the part of the life cycle that comes after the design has been completed and approved. Instead of covering the full detail of such familiar activities as programming and testing, the section illustrates some of the main types of problems that arise during programming, testing, installation, and maintenance. These illustrations will help explain many of the design practices described in earlier chapters.

Many of the problems encountered after the design of a system is complete result from the need for IS professionals to work as a team rather than as individuals. Whereas programming is essentially a solitary exercise, systems development cannot be: systems are too large to fall within the scope of a single individual. Although most IS professionals may have been trained to solve the technical problems that they are faced with, they may not have been exposed to the problems of teamwork. They may have had little experience with imperfect communications; noninstantaneous access to information; frictions with users, with management, and within the team.

To help address these problems, this section describes some of the management techniques that have been found useful on large projects.

KEY TASKS AND DELIVERABLES

Detailed program design and coding is the first of the activities to take place once the design has been completed. This activity can be viewed as the last point at which design decisions are made. Usually, all the important design decisions have already been made, either because they have been explicitly made during the design phase, or because there is a department-wide stan-

Figure VII–1 **Multiples Marketing Program Master Schedule**

Master Project Schedule

	1	2	3	4	5	6	7	8	9
Application Software	Plans & Req'mnts	FS +	Design	Devel Proto-type	Develop Programs	System Test	User Pilot Test	Pkg | Buffer	Ship
Milestone	1	2	3	4	5	6	7	8	9
Usability Evaluation		Plan	Develop Script		Usab. Test				
User Documentation	Plan & Design		First Draft / Review		Second Draft	Re-view	User Test | Print	Buffer	Ship
User Training	Plan & Design		Develop Training Course			Test/Review | Up-date	User Test	Buffer	Train End Users
System Installation		Plan	Site Planning	Develop Install. Guide	Usability Test	Up-date Guide | Re-view	User Pilot Test	Install Hardware / Install Application	
Support Center			Plan	Design		Train	User Test	Support Users	
Marketing	Determine Goals		Develop Plan		Organize to Plan	Set Timetable	User Test	Set Expectations	
Administration	Plan		Design System & Create Data Base			Train	Implement System		

dard that dictates how details will be implemented in each program. Only those decisions that have no impact on the team as such are left to individual programmers.

The next activity is testing. The first tests of a program or a module are run by the programmer writing it: this is called *unit testing*. Later, several modules or programs making up a larger unit, such as a subsystem, are integrated and tested: this process is known as *integration testing*. Finally, the entire system—both its automated and its manual parts—is tested with the participation of the users. This is called *system testing*. Normally, after a satisfactory system test, the system is put into service. In some cases, the first weeks or months of service are also considered to be part of the test of the system: this process is called *acceptance testing*.

A very effective view of testing is to consider it as part of a quality control scheme, as depicted in Figure VII–2. This schematic shows the main phases of the development cycle and the corresponding phases of tests. Quality control appears in three different ways. First, the arrow pointing from each phase back to itself indicates the need to check that the document produced at the end of the phase is internally consistent and has been prepared according to the rules, methods, and standards of the phase. The

Figure VII–2 **Testing and Quality Control**

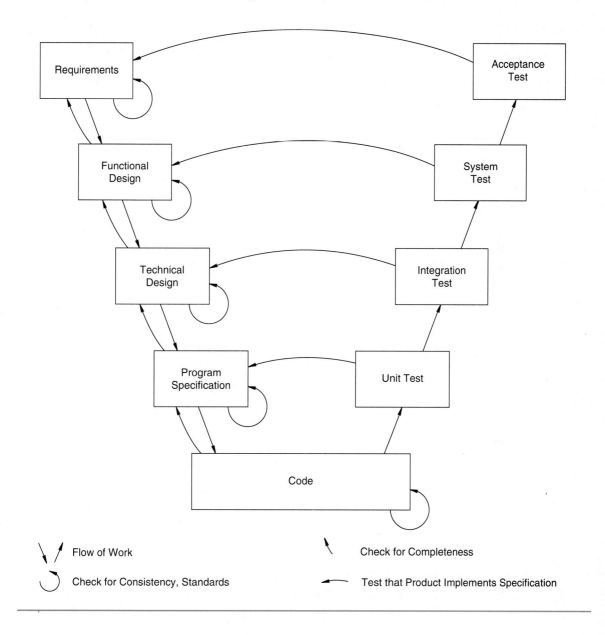

Figure VII–3 **Test Phases and Objectives**

Test Phase	Objective
Unit Test	Check that each module or program behaves as specified in the programming specification
Integration Test	Check that the system behaves as specified in the technical specification (process design)
System Test	Check that the system behaves as specified in the functional specification (user interface design)
Acceptance Test	Check that the system behaves as specified in the requirements specification

arrow pointing to each previous phase indicates the need to control that all the decisions made in that previous phase have been carried over to the next phase—that nothing has been forgotten or deformed. The arrow pointing from each test phase to the corresponding development phase indicates that the objective of the test is to verify that the component, subsystem, or system being tested actually implements the specification produced in the development phase.

The term *installing the system* refers to two kinds of activities: building the data bases required for the system to operate (conversion) and preparing the manual component of the system (user procedures and training). These activities can be performed in parallel with programming and testing.

The key deliverable of the implementation phase is an operational system, which includes the following components:

- Programs and program documentation from the programming step.

- Test plans, test results, and user sign-offs from the testing steps.

- User and operations documentation, training materials, and a trained body of users and operators from the implementation step.

- Master files and data bases, if applicable, from the conversion step.

Maintenance, the last phase in the systems development life cycle, is what happens to the system after it has become operational. It includes changes to the programs as well as to the user procedures. The inevitable changes to organizations and the way they conduct business must be reflected in the organization's business systems. More importantly, the systems of an organization should never be allowed to impede changes that the organization wishes to make. As a result, maintenance is a critical activity of the IS department. In fact, many IS departments have more than 75 percent of their analysts and programmers assigned to maintenance.

The key deliverable from the maintenance phase is a system that continues to be operational: all the programs, tests, and other documentation must be kept up to date as the system evolves.

Programming and Testing

Chapter 20 describes various programming team organizations, management styles, and planning methods. It covers the programming specification, the documentation package prepared for a programmer by an analyst. Structured walk-throughs and programming supervision activities are detailed. It then outlines the importance of proper testing practices. It describes unit testing (the tests run by a programmer on a single program) and integration, system, and acceptance testing (the tests run on a collection of programs and procedures). The chapter concludes with a description of other, less frequently used methods to find errors in a system.

Learning Objectives

- Understand the most frequent forms of organization of the programming team, the way it is supervised, and the way it relates to the rest of the project team.

- List the contents of a completed program specification and describe who is usually responsible for preparing each part.

- Recognize the role of structured walk-throughs and describe how a walk-through is planned, performed, and followed up.

- Understand the different components of testing productivity: sharing test data, reusing test data for maintenance, testing with the objective of finding bugs, using a test plan and precalculating results, referencing the test to a specification, and using proper tools.

- Describe unit testing in terms of objectives and responsibility, planning the test cases and test cycles, preparing test data, and running and exploiting the test.

- Describe integration, system, and acceptance testing in terms of objectives and responsibility, planning the test cases and test cycles, preparing test data, and running and exploiting the test.

- Be aware of other methods for removing defects from programs, such as program proving and statistical testing.

ORGANIZING AND MANAGING THE PROGRAMMING EFFORT

On most projects, programming and related activities consume large amounts of time. Therefore, programming management is a critical aspect of the wider concept of project management.

The principles of programming management are no different from the principles of project management: plan the work, identify the resources to do it, monitor its execution, and evaluate the result. But because of the technical specialization of programmers, programming management is usually not the responsibility of a single person. The planning and evaluation phases are by necessity done by the overall project manager. Usually, a programming supervisor with authority over all the project's programmers assigns and monitors the work.

If the project is large enough, the programming supervisor may be assigned to the project full time. In this ideal situation, the programming supervisor is integrated into the team structure, understands the project's overall context, and can develop a sense of ownership. A "we and they" attitude between analysts and programmers is less likely to develop.

On smaller projects, the programming supervisor may only be assigned part time to the project. This situation is more difficult to manage. The analysts will tend to suspect that the programming supervisor, and by association the entire programming team, have divided loyalties. Also, the reporting relationships and communications between analysts and programmers tend to become more formal.

These difficulties may be solved by assigning the required number of programmers directly to the project team and having an analyst—usually the most technically oriented—play the role of programming supervisor. This solution is often adopted by IS departments organized along application lines rather than by technical specialty. However, the arrangement is not without drawbacks. The main one is probably that the programmers lack permanent leadership, from the perspective of their technical specialization as well as their careers. Also, the analyst chosen to play the role of programming supervisor is generally chosen for his or her technical know-how and may not have the leadership and administrative qualifications to be a full-time programming supervisor.

The structured walk-through, or peer review as the technique is also called, is an idea from the 1970s. It has had some success, but is not practiced nearly as universally as it ought to be. During a structured walk-through, the work of one programmer or one small team is reviewed by other people who have not been involved with the work. The reviewee "walks through" a completed unit of work (for example, a section of code or an entire program), explaining how it is supposed to work, while the reviewers try to point out problems such as errors, omissions, or nonstandard practices. Structured walk-throughs can very effectively increase code quality and decrease the number of bugs. They are difficult to implement, however, because most people's work habits do not make it easy for them to bare their work to others and to receive criticism, however constructive. Nor is it easy for most people to give constructive criticism. The rule of structured walk-throughs that is the most difficult to follow is the one that forbids reviewers from suggesting solutions to the problems found; that is the province of the programmer who did the work initially.

The use of structured walk-throughs can make the technical role of the programming supervisor somewhat less critical; when properly applied, it certainly promotes team cohesion.

Structured walk-through techniques originated in programming. They have later been extended to encompass both design and requirements analysis activities as well. How a walk-through is conducted in the programming phase is explained later in this chapter; it is easy to adapt the rules to other situations.

PLANNING THE PROGRAMMING EFFORT

However the programming effort is organized, the main difficulty with managing the programming portion of a project is making sure that the work gets done on time. In *The Mythical Man-Month*,[1] Fred Brooks points out that time and personnel resources are not interchangeable. In fact, one of his laws states, "Adding people to a project which is late makes it later." (Incidentally, this law holds for the entire project, not only for the programming phase.) To prevent the project from becoming late in the first place requires monitoring progress very closely, so that underlying causes of problems can be corrected before major delays occur.

An almost universal characteristic of programmers is their incurable optimism. Most programmers believe that the next program they write will be bug-free, or almost, and that it will only require a few tests. As a result, when asked how far along they are, programmers tend to respond: "I am almost (or 90 percent, or 95 percent) finished." The impression is often that the last 10 percent of a program takes as long to finish as the first 90 percent. The remedy for this is to create frequent measurable milestones: no module should take longer than about two weeks to write and debug fully. (Milestones should not be based on coding alone because it is easy to cut down the time spent on coding at the expense of time spent testing.) At the end of the two weeks, the module is either done or it is not. If another week goes by before completion, there is a problem, as the variance is then 50 percent. In this way, systematic problems can be diagnosed and corrected within the first few weeks of the programming effort.

The following maxim is also useful to remember. Underestimating the time required for a unit of work will result in late delivery. Overestimating, however, will not make the delivery early; it will make the worker perform below full capacity. Even with a mix of over- and underestimating, the project will tend to slip, because there is no automatic compensation between the two. Frequent milestones will help for two reasons. First, it is easier to give reliable estimates for short tasks than for long tasks. Second, people can work above capacity for a short time without side effects, thereby catching up when minor delays occur for a single milestone.

THE PROGRAMMING SPECIFICATION

The analyst documents the work to be done in a program specification, which is communicated to the programmer. The specification, based on the process design done in the design phase, is created in the implementation phase. As described in Section VI, the amount of detail in the design phase is sufficient when the implementation can be planned and a cost/benefit analysis can be completed with reasonable precision.

In the implementation phase, the detailed design must be continued to a level sufficient for the programmer to understand it. Also, the design must add ancillary functions that are not of direct day-to-day concern to the user, such as table updating programs, file printouts for audit trails, and other utilitarian functions. (These functions must all have been identified in the design phase for planning purposes, but their content had not been detailed at that time.)

Level of Detail

A difficult question is the degree of detail required in the specification, i.e., the division of labor between analyst and programmer. A specification can be more or less detailed, more or less close to the actual code that will implement it. In fact, just as the design documents created earlier, the programming specification can be viewed as an arbitrary point on the continuum between requirement and operational system. The difficulty is that if the specification is not detailed enough, the programmer will flounder; if it is too detailed, the programmer will feel reduced to a role of coder who simply transcribes into programming language what the analyst has specified in a variety of English that strangely resembles COBOL.

A problem is that the right level of detail varies with the experience and competence of each individual programmer. Generally, the programmer to be assigned to a specification is not known when the specification is created. Therefore, the role played by the programming supervisor is critical in directing analysts to a level of detail that is appropriate for the general population of programmers to be assigned to the project.

As programmers code and test the programs assigned to them, they complete the specification with the results of their work to the level of source code and test results. The specification of a finished program is invariable (unlike the state of the specification prepared by the analyst for the programmer).

Content

The specification of a completed program contains the following:

- The context of the program: its place and objectives in relation to other components of the system.

    The context specification takes the form of a schematic that shows which other programs call this one; which programs this one calls; and which files, screens, or other I/O are read and written. A short statement states the objectives of the program.

- The I/O interfaces: file, record, and element descriptions from the data dictionary, as well as screen and report mock-ups.

- The calling interfaces: input and output parameters as well as return codes for the calling sequences that call this program and the parameters and codes this program uses to call other programs.

- The functions of the program: the processing to be done to accomplish the objectives, including the handling of exceptions and errors.

- The unit test plan: a list of each test case, cross-referenced to the function description to be tested and to the input and output test data.

- The program design in graphic or pseudo-code form.

    In some installations, the design may be omitted if it is established by the programmer and if it is fully documented in the code, i.e., if the COBOL program actually reflects the pseudo-code accurately and understandably.

- The source code of the final version of the program.

- The unit test input and results, cross-referenced to the test plan.

- A checklist of milestones and review sign-offs.

In most cases, the analyst is responsible for at least the first four items on this list—context, I/O interfaces, calling interfaces, and functions. The programmer is always responsible for the last three—source code, test results, and checklist. The middle two—design elements and test plan—are the responsibility of the analyst in some installations and of the programmers in others. A test for checking whether the programmer has a good understanding of the program is to have the programmer prepare the test plan. The analyst can then check the programmer's understanding of the program by reviewing the test plan for completeness and relevance.

The design section of the specification is the least important one, at least if the guideline of not exceeding two weeks' worth of work in a single program or module has been observed. If the program is substantially more complex and cannot be subdivided, this section takes on much more importance and may need to be completed by an analyst or by a senior programmer.

Traditionally, all these documents have been typed or handwritten pages, put together in a three-ring binder, and maintained as the primary maintenance documentation of the system. An emerging approach is to use electronic documentation for large parts, if not all, of the specification. This trend started with the emergence of data dictionaries in the 1970s. Data dictionaries made it possible to exclude the detailed I/O interfaces of the program from the specification; only the file (or screen/report) names were given. Programmers could obtain up-to-date details by consulting the data dictionary.

Electronic documentation can easily be extended to other parts of the specification. The concept of the data dictionary can be enlarged to that of a *repository* for all the elements of the system: data descriptions, source code, test files, and textual documentation.

STRUCTURED WALK-THROUGHS

In addition to quality control practices such as standards and proper supervision, structured walk-throughs are believed to have a major impact on quality in programming. A structured walk-through is a peer review of any activity—programming, design, requirements analysis, or other—to pinpoint errors, weaknesses, and omissions while they are still easy to correct.

This section will deal with structured walk-throughs during programming and unit testing. This is the area where the practice first emerged in the 1970s, as part of the "structured revolution."

Participants

A walk-through is performed by one or more peers of the author of the product to be reviewed. For a program, the peers are programmers; normally, they should be at least as experienced as the author, but they should not be in the author's direct chain of command.

Some reviewers may play specific roles, reviewing the program from different vantage points. One role is that of standards enforcer, who has responsibility for pointing out areas where standards are not being followed. (Remember, however, that a standard is the way that something should be done unless there are valid reasons to do otherwise—standards are not absolutes.) Another role is that of future maintainer, played by a programmer adopting the viewpoint of a person who will maintain the program.

The customer should also be represented. In programming activities, the customer is typically the analyst; in technical design, the customer can be the functional analyst; in functional design and requirements analysis, the customer is a representative of the users. Often, in technical design, DP operations are represented as well.

The author of the product to be reviewed participates by presenting the product to the reviewers and by making sure all the comments are understood.

One of the participants is designated to take notes and produce a detailed list of points after the walk-through. This role is very time consuming and probably precludes any actual review work during the meeting. This role should therefore rotate among reviewers from walk-through to walk-through.

Finally, the meeting leader's role is among the most important. This role is similar to that of the leader of a Joint Application Design session (see Chapter 7). The meeting leader should be the most highly qualified and respected of the participants but should not be in their direct line of hierarchy. His or her role is to introduce the meeting, keep it on track, and make sure that it is followed up.

Preparation of the Walk-through

The walk-through meeting needs preparation: the participants and their roles must be identified; the meeting must be scheduled; materials must be distributed in time to be reviewed before the meeting (see Figure 20–1).

Normally, the programming supervisor is responsible for identifying the participants. Some care must be taken to distribute the roles evenhandedly so that no one has the feeling of doing too much or too little, or of being saddled with the thankless job too often.

The meeting is fairly easy to schedule because the participants usually have few schedule constraints and because the meeting is short. Ideally, a walk-through takes less than an hour; it should never exceed 90 minutes. The meeting should be scheduled with the first clean compile and before unit tests have proceeded too far. A clean compile is of great help to the reviewers because it provides neat, legible documentation, including cross-references. If testing has proceeded too far along and if the review reveals a need for heavy modifications, all the tests will have to be redone.

Before the meeting, each reviewer should receive all the materials required: a copy of the program specification, a compilation listing, and any other materials that help explain the context of the program. The author is responsible for packaging the product to be reviewed. As the walk-through should take no more than an hour or so, the amount of materials to be reviewed is strictly limited. A guideline is that about 100 lines of code can be reviewed in a single meeting. In an installation that has strong standards, a somewhat higher number of lines of code can be reviewed. If more than the allowed quantity of code is to be reviewed, the programmer may have to divide the program into separate parts, each of which stands relatively well on its own. (This is a desirable practice in any case: divide to conquer!)

Each participant should review the distributed materials before the meeting. Generally, preparation time of one hour is adequate for a one-hour walk-through. If a single participant comes unprepared, the others may feel that they are wasting precious time while the unprepared person is brought up to speed.

Conduct of the Meeting

The leader starts the meeting. If any participants are unfamiliar with the ground rules or need reinforcement, the leader explains how the review is conducted.

Figure 20–1 **Walk-through Control Sheet**

```
                    INSTALLATION TOOL                              A455
_____           SUBURBAN PUMPS
_____        WALK-THROUGH CONTROL SHEET                     _____

PREPARED BY: _____    DATE: _____    VERSION: _    PAGE 1
APPROVED BY: _____    DATE: _____    STATUS:  _


Coordinator's checklist:

  [ ]  1.    Confirm with author that material is ready and stable

  [ ]  2.    Issue invitations, assign responsibilities, distribute materials

             Date: _____   Time: _____   Duration: _____

             Place: _____


                                                    Can          Received
             Responsibilities       Participants    Attend?      Materials?

             _____    _____   _____    _____
             _____    _____   _____    _____
             _____    _____   _____    _____
             _____    _____   _____    _____
             _____    _____   _____    _____


Agenda:

  [ ]  1.    All participants to follow the set of rules (see A552)

  [ ]  2.    New project:  first walk-through

  [ ]        Old project:  item-by-item checkoff of previous point sheet

  [ ]  3.    Creation of new point sheet

  [ ]  4.    Group decision to be taken

  [ ]  5.    Forward copy of this form to management after completion


Decision:   [ ]  Accept as is    [ ]  Revise    [ ]  Revise and redo walk-through
```

The author of the program then describes the product to be reviewed. For a program, the description progresses level by level, then line by line. Each control structure, such as a DOWHILE-ENDDO or an IF-THEN-ELSE-ENDIF, is reviewed before the code inside it is tackled.

As the author walks through the code, the reviewers ask questions and make comments. This is the substantive part of the walk-through. It is important that the meeting leader make the reviewers speak out and keep the meeting from turning into a confrontation. Disagreements may occur, but it is critical to keep them on a nonemotional level.

For two reasons, the purpose of the walk-through should be error detection, not correction: first, the meeting must be kept short; second, the author's sense of ownership should not be challenged. If the author sees an immediate solution to the problem, it can be proposed to the group. Alternatively, the author may request that a reviewer outline an idea for a solution. If the discussion becomes too detailed, the meeting leader should stop the discussion and ask that the interested parties continue it after the meeting.

Follow-Up

The follow-up to a walk-through consists of documenting its results and implementing solutions to the problems identified during the meeting. The documentation is the primary responsibility of the meeting leader. It has two parts: first, evidence that the walk-through was conducted (see Figure 20–2) and second, a detailed list of points to be addressed based on the notes taken by the designated reviewer. These detailed notes are normally given only to the author, although in some installations, they are given to the other participants as well. It is usually not a good idea to send the notes to the programming supervisor or to anyone who has the responsibility of reviewing programmer performance. Structured walk-throughs should encourage the viewpoint that errors committed during development are normal, that a peer review is one of the best ways of detecting them, and that the programmer should be judged only by the end result.

The author of the program is naturally responsible for implementing solutions to all the problems found during the review. Evidence that all the problems are covered can be furnished to the initial reviewers in a subsequent review or in an annotated copy of the points discovered during the review. In any case, the programmer should keep a written log of the disposition of each of the points raised (see Figure 20–3).

THE ROLE OF THE PROGRAMMING SUPERVISOR

Because the programming effort is such a large part of the project, one of the most important roles of the programming supervisor is to identify problems early. Three types of problems tend to arise frequently:

Figure 20–2 **Sample Walk-through Point Sheet**

```
MARKETING                    INSTALLATION   TOOL                    A557
ORDER ENTRY                     SUBURBAN PUMPS                       OE550
                          WALK-THROUGH POINT SHEET


PREPARED BY:  J. WEBER        DATE: 27AUG88          VERSION: 1      PAGE 1
APPROVED BY:                  DATE:                  STATUS:  I

CREDIT CHECKING MODULE

No.      Point                              Disposition            Review
---      ---------------------------        --------------------   ------


1.       Working-storage prefix is not
         standard.

2.       CASE statement without an "ALL
         OTHERS" part.

3.       Calculation of aged balance
         will be incorrect in leap
         years.

4.       Test data to be extended to
         test leap years.

5.       Unnecessary code in line 132-
         150. Case of Credit Code = 7
         has been eliminated in line 45.

6.       If Credit Code is tested before
         Customer Category, program
         would be simpler (to maintain).

7.       Error in logic line 165: NOT
         (A OR B) means NOT A AND NOT B.

Disposition to be reviewed in next walk-through.
```

- The programming team does not have the required resources: poor response times, infrequent turnaround on tests, inadequate technical assistance.
- A particular programmer does not perform well, through lack of training, personal characteristics, or incapacity.
- A particular programmer may perform well in isolation, but has a problem functioning in a team.

Figure 20–3 **Disposition of Points Raised**

```
MARKETING                    INSTALLATION   TOOL                        A557
ORDER ENTRY                     SUBURBAN PUMPS                           OE550
                           WALK-THROUGH POINT SHEET


PREPARED BY:  J. WEBER        DATE: 27AUG88        VERSION: 2        PAGE 1
APPROVED BY:  RHONDA HILL      DATE: 27AUG88        STATUS:  F


CREDIT CHECKING MODULE


No.     Point                           Disposition              Review
---     -----------------------------   --------------------     ------

1.      Working-storage prefix is not    Pass. Too costly.         OK
        standard.

2.      CASE statement without an "ALL   ALL OTHERS included.      OK
        OTHERS" part.

3.      Calculation of aged balance      On investigation, old     OK
        will be incorrect in leap        formula proved correct
        years.                           (see test).

4.      Test data to be extended to      4.Included.               OK
        test leap years.

5.      Unnecessary code in line 132-    5.Deleted.                OK
        150. Case of Credit Code = 7
        has been eliminated in line 45.

6.      If Credit Code is tested before  6.Pass.Too costly.        OK
        Customer Category, program       Additional comments
        would be simpler (to maintain).  inserted

7.      Error in logic line 165: NOT     7.Pass. Error was in      OK
        (A OR B) means NOT A AND NOT B.  specification (analyst
                                         has corrected).

Disposition to be reviewed in next walk-through.
```

The programming supervisor is responsible for monitoring these problems. For the first one, lack of machine or technical assistance resources, the programming supervisor must first determine whether there is a real problem or whether the complaints of poor service cover some other, hidden phenomenon such as lack of training or poor organization.

The programming supervisor must negotiate agreements on the levels of service to be provided by the supplier of the resources—normally some other group in the IS department, but on occasion a service bureau or a consultant. This service level agreement should cover such items as on-line response times and system availability, compile and test turnaround with results accessible on-line, frequency of library maintenance, availability of disk data space, turnaround for printed output, and access to specialists when problems arise.

The performance objectives in this agreement should ideally be monitored continuously. In many cases, however, they are measured only when there is a complaint. Measuring often makes the cause of the complaint disappear—for instance, when programmers complain of long response times, they can usually be measured the next day and found to be quite acceptable. The problem is only partly psychological; many disturbances are transitory and disappear by themselves. The most consistent psychological factor is that one freak problem is taken to be systematic. A programmer who has to wait too long for a compilation twice in a row might be tempted to see the degradation as permanent. The next time a compile takes too long, the previous incident will reinforce that impression, even if turnaround has been consistently good for several days. Regular monitoring and publication of the results help prevent such exaggerations.

When a programmer fails to perform as expected, the problem is more difficult to resolve. The programming supervisor must be a good people manager to handle all the problems that can occur.

Sometimes, the problem can be easy to solve. If a programmer repeats the same mistake, the problem may simply be a lack of training.

More difficult is the case of a programmer with personal or family difficulties. Some people are unable to perform well under pressure when this happens; others take refuge in their jobs and use them as an outlet for the pressure they feel, thus being even better than usual. Many large corporations have a counseling service for employees with problems; the programming supervisor should become familiar enough with these services and with some practical examples of situations where the service has helped to be able to direct programmers who need assistance to the appropriate counselor.

THE IMPORTANCE OF TESTING

Proper testing practices are necessary to deliver a product that fulfills the user's requirements and runs without major incidents. Proper testing practices can also reduce the cost of the systems development project and contribute significantly to higher productivity.

Testing vies with coding for the most time-consuming activity in systems development. Often, unit testing is counted as part of coding, because they are done by the same person and are therefore difficult to distinguish. In that case, coding is probably the most expensive part of the cycle. But if unit testing is included with other kinds of testing—integration, system, and acceptance tests—then testing is the most expensive and therefore has the most potential for cost reductions.

Box 20–1

Why Is Testing Necessary?

Early in the history of computing, it was realized that however much effort was put into the coding of a program, it would still malfunction on occasion. Testing became a major part of computer programming almost immediately.

Testing has been the main way of finding errors or defects in a system, so as to remove them before the system goes live. There are two basic causes for errors. First, if a requirement is considered as a problem and the program or system as its solution, the two do not have a common structure. The very languages in which the problem and the solution are expressed are totally dissimilar—from natural language to a series of binary bits. The number of transformations between one and the other leaves the door open to errors at every stage.

The second factor is the very large number of interacting system elements to keep track of: data elements, processing modules, interfaces, data structures, and program structures. No single human brain can manage the ensuing complexity; as a result, errors cannot be totally eliminated by simply thinking about the implementation or reviewing it.

This potential is even higher because of the poor testing discipline that prevails today. The following are the main areas where testing productivity and quality could be improved in most installations:

- Sharing test data among team members.

- Reusing existing test data to test modifications during maintenance.

- Testing to find bugs rather than to prove that the program or system works.

- Testing from a test plan and precalculated results rather than from operational or randomly generated data.

- Testing against a documented specification.

- Using proper tools: test data generator, output file comparators, testing harness, symbolic debugger, static analysis tools, etc.

Some of these elements exist in most installations; in very few installations are they all present. Most of the emphasis tends to be on finding causes of errors once the errors are discovered (*debugging*) and altogether too little on planning the tests so that they will be exhaustive yet of manageable size. This emphasis is probably partly because debugging is much more fun than planning. Most IS professionals feel intense satisfaction when they understand some improbable concurrence of conditions that lead to an unexpected result. Of all the activities of the life cycle, debugging is the most like puzzle solving—both challenging and rewarding.

UNIT TESTING

Objectives and Responsibility

The objective of unit testing is to check that each individual unit of work—program or module—that makes up the system is a correct implementation of its specification. It is generally done entirely by the programmer, who plans the test, creates test data, executes the test, and evaluates the results. The programming supervisor and possibly the analyst will later review the programmer's work to verify that the testing of the program has been done properly.

The resources available to the programmer to perform this work consist of the programming specification and a testing environment with whatever tools are required to create test data files, run the test, print the results, and find bugs. In addition, the programmer may be able to use a common test data base (already loaded with test cases) and programs that have previously been written and tested.

Planning the Tests

When planning tests, most analysts and programmers tend to ignore the real objective of a test. The objective is not to check that something functions as planned. The objective is to find where the program does not function as planned. Many programmers declare their programs tested based on a small number of test cases, all within the normal range of data. But most program bugs arise when input data values are exceptional, when users take unexpected actions, or when combinations of conditions produce strange effects. In addition, performance and control requirements are part of the systems specification: they also need to be tested. To test that response time is acceptable, a useful technique is to run higher and higher volumes through the system, noting at what point performance becomes unacceptable.

As a result, it has been said that a test that does not uncover a problem is not a successful test. Therefore, the last test of a program or a system is always unsuccessful.

To start testing, the programmer uses the programming specification to create a test plan. The test plan usually contains a number of test cycles. For each test cycle, a number of test cases or conditions to be tested are created. For instance, for an order entry system, several different orders are created, each order being designed to test one or more conditions. One order might test that the logic works for single-line orders. Another order would be required to test multiple-line order logic using a single screen (no paging), and a third might have more lines than can fit on the screen to test the paging logic. For reasons of economy, many conditions may be tested in each test case. For instance, the one-line order might be for a residential customer and one of the multiple-line orders might be for a corporate customer. As many independent conditions as desired may be tested in a single test case (see Figure 20–4).

Figure 20–4 **Test Case Control Sheet**

```
MEDICAL RECORDS                   INSTALLATION TOOL                              T935
ADMISSIONS                         GENERAL   HOSPITAL                          APR0100
                               TEST CASE CONTROL SHEET


PREPARED BY: CRAIG MINDRUM        DATE: 27DEC92            VERSION:            PAGE 1
APPROVED BY:                      DATE:                    STATUS:



DATA ELEMENT                 TEST CASE 1      TEST CASE 2      TEST CASE 3

Patient Name
Room Number                  1                2                2
Bed Number                                    11               11 (error)
Patient Address
Patient City
Patient State
Patient Zip
Patient Phone
Patient Soc Sec
Division                     01               03               07
Patient Birthday             Feb 22, 1899     March 1, 1899    March 29, 1999 (err)
Admitting Priority           A                B                C
Patient Sex                  M                F                F
Smoker                       Y                N
Married                      Y                N                Y
Occupation
Employer
Business Phone
Birthplace
Maiden Name                  None             None             None (error)
Spouse Name                  Jones            Jackson (error)  Jackson
Father Name
Mother Name
Religion

(Arbitrary values to be picked where not filled in)
```

Each of the test cases is initially developed from the programming specification, and each condition is cross-referenced to the specification. Cross-referencing consists in annotating the specification with the case number and the condition number (see Figure 20–5). When all the different elements of the specification have been cross-referenced, the basic test plan is complete.

One verification remains to be made. The test plan should also be cross-referenced against the program itself to check that each branch of the code is

Figure 20–5 **Annotated Program Specification**

```
MARKETING                    INSTALLATION TOOL                      T235
ORDER ENTRY                    SUBURBAN   PUMPS                    OE12010
                   PROGRAM DEFINITION - CREDIT CHECKING


PREPARED BY:  FRANK GERMAIN        DATE: 01MAR89        VERSION: 1.T      PAGE 3
APPROVED BY:                       DATE:                STATUS:
```

		Test case
2.1.3.7	If the customer-rating code is equal to 7, do credit processing as outlined in paragraphs 2.1.4.g through 2.1.4.k.	007
2.1.3.8	If the customer-rating code is equal to 8, do credit processing as outlined in paragraph 2.1.4.1.	008
2.1.3.9	If none of the above, perform program error processing as described in paragraph 2.9, with error message number 78 (see attached list of error messages). Then exit the execution of the program with a return code of 0016 (hex 0010).	199
2.1.3.10	Once the credit has been checked, test the order-reject switch. If it is on, process the next order; if it is off, go to Section 3.	All
2.1.4	Detailed processing rules.	
2.1.4.a.	Add the order total calculated in paragraph 1.2.3 to the current balance of the customer.	001,101 102,104 003
2.1.4.b.	Add the order total calculated in paragraph 1.2.3 to the 30-day-or-more balance of the customer.	002,103
2.1.4.c.	If the balance calculated in 2.1.4.a exceeds the credit limit of the customer, perform order-reject processing as described in paragraph 2.7 with error message 12. Add 1 to the control counter for number of orders rejected. Set the order-reject switch and return.	001
	If the balance calculated does not exceed the credit limit, then add one to the control counter for number of orders accepted.	101 102
2.1.4.d.	If the balance calculated in 2.1.4.b exceeds the credit limit of the customer, perform order-reject processing as described in paragraph 2.7 with error message 13. Add 1 to the control counter for number of orders rejected. Set the	002

exercised at least once. Traversing each branch is not so much to ensure that all the instructions written get executed at least once as to ensure that the test plan does, indeed, cover all the conditions that can arise and that the analysis of the test plan against the specification was complete. If the analysis was complete, and there are still branches of the program that are not traversed during the tests, then those branches will logically never be traversed under any circumstances and can be suppressed from the program. This might be a sign that the programmer has misunderstood part of the specification.

Next, the test plan is finalized by grouping the test cases into test cycles. Test cycles are designed to get as much output as possible from each test run so that many errors can be found for each test shot. (Remember that the primary objective of testing is to find the errors in the program, not to check that the program runs correctly.) For a simple program or module, a single cycle may be enough, but generally, several are required. For instance, one of the conditions to be tested may include the absence of transactions: the program should run correctly even though it has nothing to do. This test must obviously be done in a separate run. Another frequent case to be tested arises when the program checks the input file control totals. At least two runs are necessary, one with a correct control total and one with an incorrect control total on the input file. On-line query programs have as many cycles as there are different transaction cases to be tested. A document must be prepared noting the composition of each cycle (see Figure 20–6).

Preparing Test Data

When the program to be tested is an on-line transaction taking input from the screen and writing output to a sequential file or querying an existing data base, the input test data preparation is fairly easy. The test cases in a cycle are documented on paper, and the programmer (or a clerical operator) uses them as a script for executing the test.

In most cases, however, the program requires input from one or more files (or data bases). Normally, these files do not exist, and the programs that create them as output are probably not yet completely written and tested. Therefore, the programmer must create files or relations on data bases that contain the required conditions, using a specialized program, called a test data loader.

There are generic test data generators on the market, whose only purpose is to help programmers create test files (see Figure 20–7). Other solutions include using fourth-generation languages, application generators, or even regular programming languages to create a mini-application to load the required files (see Figure 20–8). In both cases, a specialized program takes a sequential file with alphanumeric characters only and transforms it into the required file or data base structure, with data in the format required by the program to be tested (for example, alphanumeric, binary, floating point, or decimal). In principle, every field on the test file to be created must be specified by the programmer on the input file. Some test data generators have

Figure 20–6 **Test Cycle Control Sheet**

```
MEDICAL RECORDS                   INSTALLATION TOOL                    T925
ADMISSIONS                        GENERAL   HOSPITAL                   APR0100
                               TEST CYCLE   CONTROL SHEET

PREPARED BY: CRAIG MINDRUM        DATE: 27DEC92          VERSION:       PAGE 1
APPROVED BY:                      DATE:                  STATUS:


Cycle 6: Confirmation processing
--------------------------------


Purpose:   Test for proper processing and printing of patient admission confirmations.

No.      Condition                                            Test cases
---      -----------------------------------------------      ----------
A.       Proper printing break processing                     001,002
                                                              003

         Only one confirmation should print for every patient
         admitted. Page breaks should occur properly.


B.       Patient age calculation                              001,002
                                                              003

         Correct patient age to be calculated from birth
         date.


C.       Admission date and time generation                   001,002
                                                              003

         Admission date and time generated from system timer.
         This requires that part of the test be run without
         the system date/time simulator.


D.       Patient number generation                            001,002
                                                              003,101
         Patient numbers are generated by the system on a     102,103
         consecutive number basis. This test requires         201,202
         shutting the system down and restarting it in the
         middle of the cycle twice: once cleanly and the
         other time in the middle of a transaction.


E.       Proper admitting division classification             001,002
                                                              003

         The proper division, corresponding to the division
         code entered, will be printed on the confirmation.


F.       Correct patient type processing                      001,102

         The patient type of Inpatient or Outpatient will be
         printed correctly.
```

Figure 20-7 **Test Data Generation**

features that can generate random values or calculate values (for instance, by generating transaction numbers that increase by one for every new record). These features may sometimes be useful for reducing the effort required to create complete test data.

   In some cases, there may be a data base of shared test data that can be used. A test data base usually exists for system and acceptance test purposes. It may also be a copy of an operational data base for the system being replaced. In the latter case, the programmer may use this copy as the basis for creating a test data base or file. Normally, the data on a shared test data base need to be adapted to the test conditions for each individual program. The best procedure is to extract those test data from the shared test data base that are relevant, copy them to a temporary file, and modify them as required using a test data generator, an application generator, or some other utility (see Figure 20-9). The programmer always works on a copy, never on the original data.

   In modular programming, the program may not have input and output files. Rather, it receives messages from the calling module and sends messages to subordinate modules. It is of course possible to postpone testing until the entire set of modules has been written, making up a program that

Figure 20-8 **Loading Test Data with a 4GL**

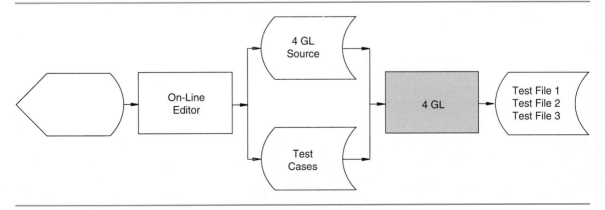

Figure 20–9 **Loading Test Data from a Shared Test Data Base**

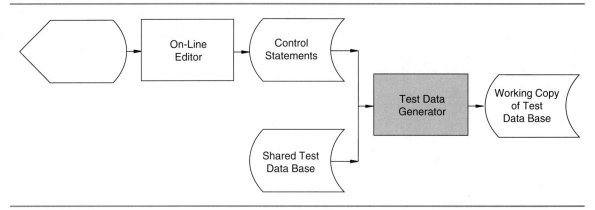

has only external file I/O. Testing in this manner is generally counterproductive, both because of the waiting involved and because it is tantamount to doing integration testing at the same time as unit testing.

The solution to this problem is stub testing. Instead of waiting for the calling module to be available, the programmer can create a stub, a simple program that makes a call with the appropriate parameters to the program to be tested. These parameters can be hard-coded into the stub or read off a file prepared with a test data generator (see Figure 20–10). By the same token, stubs can simulate modules called by the program to be tested. A called stub posts updates to the parameters passed to it and returns control to the calling module without doing any actual productive work (see Figure 20–11).

Before executing any tests, a last activity must be completed: calculating the expected results of the tests. Every expected output for every test case in every test cycle must be calculated and documented before the test is run. This discipline is required because the human brain tends to anticipate positive results: when checking the result of a calculation, a programmer quite frequently makes errors that make the result seem right. Also, precalculating results can allow this data to be loaded to a file and the comparison between actual and expected output can be mechanized with a file comparator, thus providing much greater accuracy.

Figure 20–10 **Stub Testing: Calling Stub**

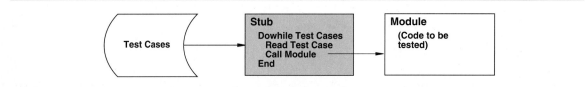

Figure 20–11 **Stub Testing: Called Stub**

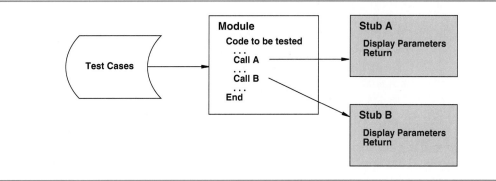

Executing the Test

Executing a batch test is not a great problem. It is no different than submitting a compilation, except that more job control statements have to be prepared. (In good installations, much of this job control preparation is automated to relieve the programmers of the burden of being experts on job control.) With modular programming, the module itself as well as all the required stubs must also be linked together, requiring some additional knowledge of job control.

The test run is made up of a series of steps: loading the test data, executing the program, and printing the results (see Figure 20–12). Whether the test data is reloaded for each execution of the test is a compromise between execution time and storage space. However, if the test run modifies the input data in place or when the test data is wrong, there is no choice: the test data must be reloaded.

Figure 20–12 **Test Run**

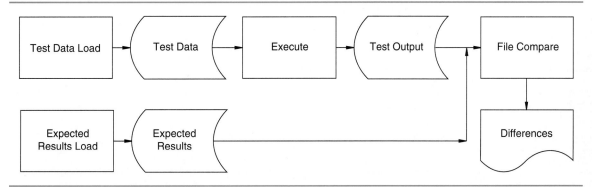

The problem is more difficult with on-line programs. On-line programs do not stand alone; rather, they are executed in the environment provided by an on-line monitor. Some on-line monitors have associated batch simulators. These make it possible to treat each test cycle as a batch process by simulating the on-line environment to the program. The program believes that it communicates with a screen; in reality, the screen images are intercepted by the simulator, which turns them into batch test files (see Figure 20–13). The advantage of this procedure is its repeatability.

Without a batch simulator, the test must be performed on-line, which is much more time consuming for the programmer. On-line testing usually requires a test version of the on-line monitor, so as to avoid any risk of interference with production work. Also, some monitors require that all the programs that are to be run be linked to the monitor before it is started up. This requirement implies a great deal of planning and discipline. Moreover, in most environments, the programmers share the on-line monitor. The environment in which the test is executed therefore has an element of randomness, making it extremely difficult to trace causes of some errors.

Another element of randomness is that the person who executes the test may do things in a slightly different sequence, committing different errors of data entry on different executions of the test cycle. This problem can be avoided by the use of a tool known as a transaction capture facility, which records every keystroke by an operator and reproduces the sequence later on.

Checking screen output against the expected results is more difficult than for output files, because screen contents are volatile. Unless the program writes a copy of the screen to a file, an automated comparator cannot be used.

Evaluating the Results

Test results are normally in the form of output files, reports, screens, or updated data on data bases. To be exploited by the programmer, these results must be printed out, made available for on-line browsing, or compared with the expected results and the differences printed out.

When the results are not as expected, other forms of output may be generated. The best known is perhaps the storage dump, which presents an unformatted printout of the contents of memory when an execution is interrupted because of some serious problem—for instance, trying to perform a numerical operation on nonnumeric data. For many reasons, a dump is the least desirable result of a test run. First, it is difficult to use. Second, as it usually interrupts the execution of the test, subsequent test cases must wait until the next execution. Third, it is often the sign of a serious problem in the program.

The dump used to be the main tool of debugging; fortunately, it is increasingly replaced by more powerful tools. One series of such tools is implemented by the compiler, which, as an option, may be able to print out the names of the routines as they are executed together with the contents of critical data areas. This feature is called a trace option. If the compiler does

Figure 20–13 **Batch Terminal Simulator**

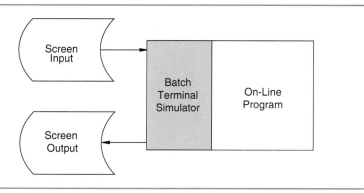

not have one, the programmer can fairly easily introduce trace points to display messages or selected data. These trace points must be removed before the final test of the program.

Another compiler option is to print a cross-reference between data areas and program code, indicating which parts of a program use a given data element or record, thereby potentially modifying it. The cross-reference is very useful for forming hypotheses about why a data area contains unexpected values.

Even more sophisticated is the tool known as a symbolic debugger, which enables a program to be executed on-line, with a window on the terminal reserved for programmer interaction. The programmer may cause the program to execute in step mode, one instruction at a time, inspecting the contents of data areas and the instructions affecting them as the test is proceeding. The programmer may also modify erroneous data areas (and in some cases, program instructions) to enable the rest of the program to execute.

When a discrepancy between the test result and the expected result is found, the program or possibly the test data is corrected and the test cycle is repeated until all the results are correct. To aid in controlling this process, the test plan is annotated with the results from each execution of each cycle, together with the actions taken (see Figure 20–14).

After the final test, a walk-through or a review by the programming supervisor or the analyst checks the completeness and the accuracy of the tests. At this point, the unit test data should be "frozen" and kept until the program needs modification, when it may serve as the basis for regression testing—testing not only that a modification works, but also that what has not been modified continues to work. Because additional bugs are likely to be discovered during integration, system, and acceptance testing, the unit test data will probably be used very soon after the unit test is completed.

Test walk-throughs are organized very much like programming walk-throughs, as described earlier in this chapter. A test walk-through is organized at the completion of the testing plan, at the completion of testing, or both.

Figure 20–14 **Testing Log**

MEDICAL RECORDS
ADMISSIONS

INSTALLATION TOOL
GENERAL HOSPITAL
TEST LOG

T940
APR0100

PREPARED BY: CRAIG MINDRUM   DATE: 27DEC92   VERSION: PAGE 1
APPROVED BY: HARRY ENDERBY   DATE: 27NOV93   STATUS: F

CYCLE NO	DESCRIPTION	CYCLE COND DEFINED	TEST DATA PREPARED	EXPECTED RESULTS PREPARED	RESULTS TEST 1	TEST 2	TEST 3	TEST 4
1	Load Initial Patient Number	04SEP93	20SEP93	22SEP93	ABEND	EOJ, no report	OK (24OCT93)	
2	Inpatient Processing	04SEP93	20SEP93	22SEP93	ABEND	processed invalid patient	OK (27OCT93)	
3	Outpatient Processing	04SEP93	26SEP93	28SEP93	data format error	ABEND	accepted invalid division	OK (01NOV93)
4	Admission Update	04SEP93	26SEP93	28SEP93	conv ctl problem	slow response time	OK (26OCT93)	
5	Daily Admission Extract	05SEP93	26SEP93	28SEP93	OK (17OCT93)			
6	Confirmation Processing	05SEP93	02OCT93	17OCT93	ABEND	invalid date processing	report format errors	OK (17NOV93)
7	Periodic Reporting	05SEP93	02OCT93	17OCT93	some reports not generated	OK (06NOV93)		
B	On-Line Inquiry Processing	06SEP93	02OCT93	21OCT93	slow response time	OK (08NOV93)		
9	On-Line Update Processing	08SEP93	07OCT93	23OCT93	slow response time	invalid ID updated	ABEND	OK (03DEC93)

INTEGRATION, SYSTEM, AND ACCEPTANCE TESTING

Integration, system, and acceptance testing have objectives similar to unit testing; they all seek to demonstrate that a given specification—technical design, functional design, or user requirements—is met by the implementation of the system. They are all quite different from unit testing, however, in that they are generally conducted by separate testing teams. Both technical and functional analysts may participate, but tests are best conducted by people who have not been too closely involved with design and implementation decisions. This precaution is less imperative for integration testing than for acceptance testing.

Definitions

Integration testing consists in testing that programs and modules communicate with each other in accordance with the technical design specifications developed in the design phase. This means that calling and called modules agree on the contents of the messages that are passed back and forth and that output files from one program can actually be used as input files to the next. The integration is gradual. The test team starts with one module to which it adds a few other modules, then some more, increasing the scope gradually until the entire system has been put together. On small, relatively simple systems, integration testing can be conducted as part of the system test.

System testing exercises not only the computer system itself but also the manual procedures, restart and recovery, and human-machine interfaces, which must all operate according to the functional specifications. The basis for the system test data is selected live data that is adapted and extended to make it as complete as possible. The objective is not to generate large volumes but to have representative samples. Users must be involved in the system test.

Acceptance testing is the final hurdle before the users declare the system ready to go. For small, simple systems, this may occur at the end of system testing. On larger systems, a separate acceptance test with user-prepared test data and realistic volumes is conducted. One of the most popular ways of conducting acceptance testing has been parallel testing: running the old and the new system at the same time and checking that the results are the same. Parallel testing is becoming less popular. Running in parallel is becoming more and more expensive as systems grow in size. Comparing the outputs of the old and the new system is also becoming increasingly difficult, because many modern systems implement changes in the business process and create new information.

In other cases, acceptance testing may simply be the first few weeks of operation, during which the project team is on call and during which a fallback to the old system may still be possible. In this case, user acceptance frees the project team for other duties and gives final production status to the new system.

Planning the Tests

Planning integration, system, and acceptance testing starts earlier than the planning for unit testing. The strategy for each, and indeed whether they are separate tests or just separate objectives of the same test, is determined in the installation planning segment at the end of the design phase.

The approach to detailed planning is similar to that described for unit testing. Test cases are identified based on the specification being tested against and cross-referenced to it. Test cases and cycles are determined based on the functions of the system and the natural cycles of the business. There is likely to be a greater number of cycles in system testing than in unit testing, however. A typical financial accounting and control system might require as many as 20 or 30 system test cycles. Some of the functional requirements that have to be tested in separate runs are file loading; budget preparation; daily posting; monthly, quarterly, and yearly closing, each with a preliminary and a final run; error corrections; and restart and recovery.

Preparing Test Data

The volume of test data increases with each subsequent testing cycle. One imperative of integration and system testing is to keep the data as low in volume as possible, while still remaining complete. Keeping the volume low reduces the time required for preparing expected results and checking the actual output.

The system test data should be prepared in such a way that it can be saved and can serve as regression test data for successive versions of the system in maintenance. To serve in regression testing, the test data must be complete; it must also be documented so that future maintainers understand the purpose of each test case. (One frequently used technique is to include a description of the case in text areas of the data records. For instance, instead of putting "John Smith" in the name field of a customer record, one might put "Residential customer with $250 credit limit.")

Acceptance tests require higher data volumes than system tests because one of the objectives is to stress test the system, i.e., to evaluate whether it meets volume requirements. If parallel testing is adopted, the normal daily volumes will be encountered. It may then be necessary to add artificially created transactions to test peaks. For instance, the New York Stock Exchange may want to test a future system based on the volume of transactions experienced on October 19, 1987, rather than on a run-of-the-mill day. Artificially high volumes can be created using random test data generators or just plain duplication, as the objective of this test is not to evaluate the functional output; rather, the expected result that serves as the yardstick of a successful test is response time or throughput.

For other integration, system, and acceptance tests, files with expected results must still be prepared before executing the test. Using live data here has the advantage of possibly decreasing the time required to create the expected results files. It must be emphasized again and again that live data alone cannot be expected to constitute complete coverage of all the test cases.

Executing the Tests

The greatest difficulty in executing integration, system, and acceptance tests comes from the large volumes of on-line transactions, which require human resources, terminals, and computer power to be available in large quantities. The problems with unpredictability of the environment and nonrepeatability of the exact sequence of steps continue to exist. For large-scale on-line systems, a batch terminal simulator facility is extremely useful.

The testing cannot be entirely based on simulators, however. Both the reaction of users to terminal dialog and the behavior of the communications network (including human operations, troubleshooting, etc.) must be addressed before acceptance testing is over.

Evaluating the Results

In general, the same comments apply as for unit testing. The role of walk-throughs of integration testing and especially system testing, both plans and results, is even more important than for unit testing.

New questions arise in connection with program changes made necessary by problems found during integration or system testing. These changes must be analyzed and controlled at least as rigorously as for maintenance. When a change is made, each modified program must be unit tested afresh. In fact, as the error is probably in the specification, the test plan must usually be revised. When the program is unit tested, the integration or system tests must be redone. There are two approaches: one is to run all the test cycles again (time consuming but reassuring); the other is to rerun only those cycles that are predicted to be affected (less safe, but more economical). No one approach is superior; in fact, the best is probably to make the decision every time the case arises, based on an assessment of the actual costs and risks involved (see Figure 20–15).

Normally, the question of debugging tools arises much less in integration, system, and acceptance testing than in unit testing. Testing in later phases is not designed to debug programs; abnormal results such as memory dumps needing advanced program tracing or on-line debugging should not arise. Most of the diagnostics required can be performed by looking at printed output, possibly going so far as to browse a file or data base with an on-line query facility.

There is, however, a dearth of tools to deal with the great administrative complexity of the execution of the test cycles and the modifications made necessary by bugs. The best that can be done today in most environments is probably a mix of manual bookkeeping and PC-based tools such as spreadsheets. Even though it is time consuming to prepare expected results and to keep scrupulous track of all the test runs, omitting these steps is likely to be even more time consuming.

Figure 20–15 **Strategies for Testing after Bug Correction**

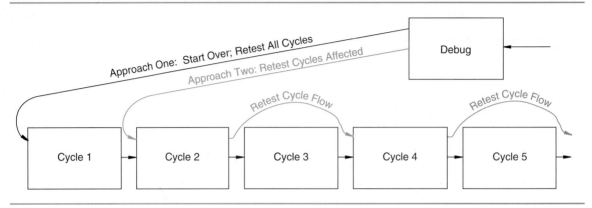

OTHER DEBUGGING TECHNIQUES

Although testing and walk-throughs are the most common techniques for removing defects from systems, other techniques exist. The two most important are static program analysis and statistical testing. Two others are described in Box 20–2.

Static program analysis consists in using a series of automated tools to analyze the structure and content of a program, beyond the syntax checking done by the compiler. For instance, the analyzer can point out data items that are not referenced and code that cannot be reached. It can find dowhile loops that might never terminate and show errors in logic by a procedure known as *pretty-printing*—indenting code so that the various logical blocks of the program stand out clearly. It can also help enforce standards by extending the syntax checking to incorporate coding rules that are edicted by the installation. Static program analyzers exist in large numbers for Fortran; there are few available for commercial languages such as COBOL and PL/I.

Statistical testing proceeds from another idea altogether. As the objective of testing is to remove bugs, testing should continue until only a small number of bugs remain. (It is, according to popular wisdom, impossible to eliminate bugs altogether.) This logic is flawed because it is impossible to tell how many bugs remain in the program—or is it? Statistical testing is an effort to predict, at all points during the test, how many bugs are left. An independent team injects a controlled number of known errors into the program, in addition to the unknown bugs already there. This process is called seeding. The proportion of seeded bugs discovered by the testers indicates the proportion of unseeded, or natural, bugs. For instance, if a program is seeded with 20 errors, and testing has discovered 45 errors, 15 of which were seeded, the 30 unseeded bugs discovered represent, on the average, 75 percent of all the unseeded bugs. Therefore, there remain, statistically speaking, 10 bugs to be discovered.

**Box
20–2**

Alternative Testing Techniques

Techniques for locating and removing errors or defects are constantly being improved. One important current of research in recent years has been the attempt to treat programs as mathematical entities susceptible to proof: if mathematical techniques can prove a program correct, then it should not be necessary to test it. Another research theme can be described as the clean-room approach: as in semiconductor manufacturing environments, no "polluting particles" (read: errors) are allowed to creep into the system during the development process.

These two techniques do not dispense with testing. Proving that a program functions correctly falls short for two reasons. First, it is only possible to prove that the program does what it is supposed to do, not that it does what the user actually needs. Second, it is only possible to prove that programs behave correctly, not the human beings who use the system. So although program proving may help locate some bugs, it is of little help in ensuring that the system will achieve its objectives and that its human interface is good. One can only prove that the program performs the task right, not that it does the right task. An additional, practical difficulty is that the proof itself is generally long and cumbersome; if it is done by hand, the proof itself becomes error-prone.

The clean-room approach could theoretically eliminate testing altogether if it is applied successfully at every stage. The phrase "no defects allowed" means literally that. However, for the two reasons outlined above, some errors will continue to creep in and testing remains necessary. In the clean-room approach, however, testing is used much the same way as in statistical quality control: it serves as the measure of the quality of the product and as a criterion for accepting or rejecting the product. If the product is rejected, it is reworked. Some successful experiments have been conducted combining the clean-room approach with the statistical testing approach.

Statistical testing of this type requires a completely separate testing team: the authors of the program would soon recognize the majority of the seeded errors if they were to do the testing. Moreover, it requires a separate seeding team, which has to exercise considerable ingenuity in inventing errors to be seeded. Finally, if the statistical foundation for the method is to work, no unit testing by the author of the program can be allowed. The technique has been used together with so-called clean-room methods in systems programming; it has not gained popularity in commercial programming.

Summary

Programming management does not differ significantly from other aspects of project management. A variation is often introduced by the role of the programming supervisor, who performs part of the programming management (usually the assignment of the work and the supervision of its execution, but not the planning and the evaluation).

The programming supervisor may be attached to a project full time; this is the form of organization that causes the fewest problems. A programming supervisor who splits his or her time between several projects runs the danger of being viewed as having conflicting loyalties. Having no programming supervisor and having programmers report directly to the analysts on the project team is unsatisfactory because it endangers the long-term prospects of the programmers.

Programming management relies on dividing the work into units that can be planned, assigned, executed, and followed up individually. These units should take no longer than about two weeks, so that programmers do not work too long without measurable milestones of progress.

The programmer works from a program specification, which includes descriptions of the context of a program, its interfaces to files and to other programs, the functions to be executed, the test plan, the actual design and implementation of the program, the test results, and a checklist of milestones and review sign-offs. This specification is begun by the analyst and completed by the programmer. Where the frontier goes between the two is installation dependent.

Although formal specification languages are useful for eliminating some of the programming work, most program specifications are written in natural language. Thus, the programmer and, later, the maintainers can understand not only what is being done, but also why functions are being performed.

Once the program is written, but before it is tested, a structured walk-through of the program may take place. A structured walk-through is a review of the program by a number of the programmer's peers, under the leadership of a meeting leader who plays the role of facilitator and sees that the rules are followed. A structured walk-through is similar to a joint application design session, but it is much shorter, ideally only an hour. It is therefore much easier to organize and conduct.

During the session, the reviewee explains the work to the group, which in turn asks questions and points out errors. Some reviewers can be designated to play specialized roles, reviewing the work from a specific vantage point such as the enforcement of standards and the ease of later maintenance. The focal point of the review is to identify problems, not necessarily to solve them on the spot.

During the session, notes are taken on the problems encountered and on the comments made, so that the author of the product can later follow up and implement solutions to all the points raised.

Throughout the programming phase of a project, the programming supervisor is responsible for solving any problems that may arise on the programming team, such as insufficient technical resources, the failure of programmers to perform adequately, and behavior that is detrimental to the team effort.

Testing makes sure that the system performs in accordance with its specifications, i.e., that it does what it is supposed to do and does not do what it is not supposed to do. Modern systems require that testing be done at four levels: unit testing, integration testing, system testing, and acceptance testing.

Unit testing is usually performed by the programmer who has coded an individual program or module. When the programmer is satisfied that testing has been completed successfully, the results are reviewed by the programming supervisor and possibly by the analysts for their concurrence. The programmer prepares a test plan before beginning the unit test, building test cases cross-referenced to the program specifications. Test cases are grouped into test cycles to test a number of cases in a single test run.

Test data must be created containing information necessary to test the conditions identified by the test plan. Specialized programs are available to assist the programmer in developing test files or data bases. Among these are test data loaders and test data generators. The programmer is responsible for specifying the data to be included in each field of each test data record, even though some of the tedium of developing test data can be performed by the specialized programs.

Shared test data bases are often used. In these cases, the programmer must still ascertain that the test data covers all of the conditions to be tested.

The final step before beginning a test is the calculation of predetermined output from each test case and test cycle. This step not only ensures that errors are not overlooked, but also makes it possible to place expected results in computer-readable form so that a file comparator can compare test results against expected results. A file comparator program makes this comparison much more accurate than a manual comparison.

Although executing the test in a batch environment is fairly straightforward, conducting a test of on-line programs is more difficult. If the on-line monitor has an associated batch simulator, it can facilitate the testing process. If not, the programmer must perform the test on-line—a time-consuming process. In addition, evaluating test results can be a laborious and error-prone process, unless testing tools and techniques such as a transaction capture facility or automated comparisons of test result screens with expected result screens are used.

When test results differ from expected results, additional tools are available to assist in debugging. The storage dump, once the most common tool, is being replaced by such compiler features as trace options, cross-references between program data areas and code, and symbolic debuggers.

Integration testing verifies that modules work together correctly by joining them together gradually, testing their operation at each step, until the entire system has been assembled.

System testing tests the entire computer system together with the surrounding manual procedures, restart and recovery procedures, and human-computer interfaces to be sure all components function in accordance with the specifications. User involvement is required during system testing.

Acceptance testing is the final step in the process. This step, which requires heavy involvement by the users, attempts to run the system under volume and stress conditions as close to the expected operating environment as possible. The acceptance testing team is often composed of personnel who have not been too close to the system's design and installation in order to achieve maximum objectivity in evaluating the acceptance test results. When the acceptance testing team is satisfied that the system will perform as planned, the acceptance testing step is considered to be complete and ready for implementation. An alternative technique is to consider the first few weeks following implementation to be the acceptance test with the project team standing by to deal with problems as they occur. This latter technique is usually employed only if the old system can be easily reintroduced in the event serious problems are experienced with the new system.

Selected Readings

Brooks, F. *The Mythical Man-Month.* Reading, Massachusetts: Addison-Wesley, 1975.
This book has become a classic on project management. Brooks managed the creation of IBM's Operating System (OS/360), which required a thousand work-years of effort, in the 1960s. This book describes the errors that he learned from.

Weinberg, G. *The Psychology of Computer Programming.* New York: Van Nostrand Reinhold, 1971.
Weinberg's book is one of the earliest works on the nontechnical aspects of programming. This book has been extremely influential in promoting the thought that programmers do not work in a social vacuum (although they might want to). It coined the term egoless programming. Although some of the examples are somewhat dated, the principles and the practical advice contained in this book are remarkably valid 20 years later.

Yourdon, E. *Structured Walkthroughs,* 2d ed. Englewood Cliffs, NJ: Prentice-Hall, 1979.
This well-written and consistently useful book is the main reference on structured walk-throughs by one of the best-known authors on structured techniques in systems development.

Dunn, Robert. *Software Defect Removal.* New York: McGraw-Hill, 1984.
This book is a quite complete treatment of testing and debugging methods. It gives practical advice on how to use many of the tools and techniques described. And last, but not least, the book is well-written and a pleasure to read.

Cho, Chin-Kuei. *An Introduction to Software Quality Control.* New York: John Wiley & Sons, 1980.
Cho describes in more detail than the previous book some of the more recent testing methods based on sampling approaches. He also refers to correctness proofs.

Review Questions

1. What is the purpose of a structured walk-through?

2. From a programming management standpoint, what is the value of restricting the size of programming assignments to about two weeks?

3. Why must the programming supervisor be careful to direct programming specifications to the correct level for each programmer?

4. What are the usual contents of a complete set of program specifications?

5. What is the right time to schedule a structured walk-through? Why?

6. What are the key roles played by the various participants in a structured walk-through?

7. What three problems are identified most frequently in the programming phase of a project?

8. List some of the areas where testing quality could probably be improved in many IS departments.

9. Explain the purpose of each of the four testing phases:
   a. Unit testing
   b. Integration testing
   c. System testing
   d. Acceptance testing

10. What is stub testing? Under what circumstances would it be used?

11. What is the value of using a batch terminal simulator for testing on-line programs? What are their operating characteristics?

12. Why do many IS professionals consider the storage dump to be the least valuable of the possible outputs from a test?

13. What is the value of having a trace option in the compiler? A symbolic debugger?

14. Why should test data volumes be kept low in the integration and acceptance testing phases?

15. What are static program analyzers?

16. Explain the concept of statistical program testing.

Discussion Questions

1. Discuss the pros and cons of alternative forms of organizing teams for the programming phase of a project.

2. Given the numerous problems that could confront a programming supervisor, why is it said that his or her main difficulty is in ensuring that the work gets done on time?

3. Discuss the pros and cons of using a specification language.

4. Discuss the pros and cons of giving the notes from a structured walk-through only to the author of the program. Could there not be, for example, some training value to other programmers if the results of the walk-through were shared with them as well?

5. Under what circumstances should the use of a test data generator be considered?

6. What are the advantages and disadvantages of using a common test data base?

7. Discuss the pros and cons of conducting formal walk-throughs for the planning and evaluation of the integration and system testing phases.

8. What is the value of having key participants in the acceptance testing phase who have not been closely involved in the systems design?

Mini-Cases

Walton Products. Walton Products is in the programming phase of a new order entry system to be installed in each one of its 70 U.S. and Canadian branch offices. Carl Martin, the programming supervisor on the project, is determined not only to bring the project in on time and within budget, but also to deliver code of a higher quality than Walton Products had ever seen before. To help him accomplish these objectives, he decided to introduce the practice of conducting structured walk-throughs of each program. Carl had heard a speaker discuss structured walk-throughs at last month's DPMA meeting, but had no other experience in employing the technique.

He told Marge Krawlik that her program would be the guinea pig for this new technique and asked her to be ready to discuss it with the rest of the programming team on the next Friday. Carl then sent the following memo to the other six programmers on the team:

> I would like each of you to plan to attend a structured walk-through of Marge's program this coming Friday. The meeting will be held beginning at 8:30 in the staff conference room and will continue until we are collectively satisfied that her work is of the highest quality obtainable. The success of the order entry system is critical to the future success of Walton, and we must all work together to see that our product is the best that we can produce as a team.

Marge wondered why she had been singled out. She felt that Carl suspected that her work was not up to par but that he did not want to deal with the issue personally. Her worries were intensified when other members of the programming team jokingly commented that they could not wait until Friday when they would have a chance to go over her program with a fine-tooth comb.

Questions for Discussion

1. How successful is the walk-through on Friday likely to be?

2. How likely will members of the programming staff be to want to adopt structured walk-throughs as a shop standard?

3. What steps could Carl have taken to increase his chances of a successful meeting?

Crawford Corporation. Heather Paulson has just been hired as the director of MIS for the Crawford Corporation. One of the primary reasons for her employment is that the president of Crawford is not satisfied with the overall quality of the MIS operation. Projects never seem to come in on time and within budget, and users are constantly complaining that the computer systems are not operating satisfactorily.

The systems and programming group consists of 40 professionals. Stuart Hendren has seniority over the three programming supervisors in the MIS department. He has been with Crawford for over 20 years, having started as a computer operator before becoming a programmer and now a programming supervisor. Stuart has been in the habit of using live data in test data bases for new systems that he and his team develop as well as those that they maintain. Heather's training was in an environment where test data bases were constructed for various test phases along the lines discussed in this chapter. She has decided that one of the first things that must be changed in the department is the practice of testing with live data. Stuart is a man of strong opinions, known to be reluctant to accept suggestions from anyone.

Question for Discussion

1. If you were Heather, what approach might you take in trying to convince Stuart of the advantages of using specially prepared test data bases rather than live data for each phase of testing?

Note

1. Brooks, F. *The Mythical Man-Month.* Reading, Massachusetts: Addison-Wesley, 1975.

21

Installing the System

Chapter 21 covers the remaining activities that must be performed before the system can be delivered to its users. After an introduction on preparing users for change, the chapter describes how to document the user procedures and train the users, how to document the data processing operating procedures, and how to convert the files to be ready for use by the new system. The chapter concludes with a discussion on the cutover and follow-up activities after the initial weeks of operations.

Learning Objectives

- Describe the various types of user and operations documentation prepared during systems implementation.
- Understand how to prepare for and conduct end-user planning.
- Be aware of the issues to be resolved with DP production before the application can be put into production.
- Understand the issues raised by the need to convert the files some time before cutover and maintaining both old and new files.

PREPARING USERS FOR CHANGE

Today, increasing emphasis is placed on the behavioral aspects of systems implementation. Many failures or operational problems encountered in the past were caused by insufficient user preparation. In addition, today's systems tend to reach a much wider spectrum of users.

The diminishing cost of hardware makes it possible to design systems that are much more responsive to human needs. In the implementation phase, this orientation must be followed up by reemphasizing the nontechnical activities. The Multiples Marketing Program owes much of its success to the central tenet that to be a success, the system must be adopted and owned by its users rather than pressed on them by some external agent.

The marketing plan for the system should therefore be aimed at establishing in the user's mind, first, that there is a need for a system, and second, that the system being implemented meets that need. This effort should start at the very beginning of the systems development cycle.

User participation throughout the development cycle is another key to adoption. The more the users participate, the more they will feel ownership when the day comes to start running the system live. Many IS departments now tend to involve users in the early stages, when analyzing requirements and designing the user interface. Later, they consider that users cannot contribute anything during the technical design and programming phases and do not involve them again until the system test, or worse, the acceptance test. This approach is to be rejected; the participation must be permanent.

Permanent participation can be achieved in two different ways. One of the most popular today is the combination of prototyping and iterative development. If the user interface design phase is interspersed with delivery of operational systems components, the users continue to feel permanently involved. In addition, their training is gradual enough that they do not feel the shock effect of a more massive change. End-user development can be seen as the ultimate form of iterative development. All other things being equal, systems developed by end users have a much higher acceptance rate than do those developed by the IS department.

Prototyping is always possible, at least in the user design phase. Iterative development, however, may not be appropriate in all cases. Many systems developed to gain a competitive edge or to change the way in which management uses information are too complex for iterative development. They must be designed first, in their totality; once designed, a critical mass must often be implemented as a unit. For example, implementing a frequent-flier program in only certain parts of the country or for only certain flights or ticket types may not be possible. The part of the system that accumulates mileage may be implemented a little before the part that handles the awards, but not by a wide margin: a really frequent flier can tot up enough miles in a month to be eligible for a companion ticket.

In many cases, these systems are complex enough that a number of activities performed by users can be staggered all along the project. Typical user participation in the installation might include the following:

- Planning and preparing test data for the system test and the acceptance test.
- Preparing training materials and conducting user training.
- Detailed forms design and procurement.
- Converting files, particularly correcting errors discovered in existing files before conversion.
- Planning physical installation of equipment in user locations: terminals, printers, telecommunications equipment, electrical cabling, and remodeling.

User participation in system and acceptance testing is critical. This is the best possible vehicle for training a core set of users to become self-sufficient as early as possible. In general, the system test will reveal a number of operational difficulties; if users can be made to diagnose and resolve these difficulties, they will understand the system much better, develop ownership, and be trained to meet unanticipated difficulties and changing requirements.

USER PROCEDURE DEVELOPMENT AND USER TRAINING

User procedure development concerns the manual aspects of the system. The general flow of manual work has already been identified in the requirements and design portions of the project. Now is the time to create the documentation explaining how this flow is to be implemented.

On-Line versus Paper-based Documentation

User procedures can be documented in various forms. The current tendency is to provide more and more documentation on-line for users who interface through the system via workstations. Explicit prompting, help screens, and other design features explained in Section IV can help. Perhaps the biggest advantage of on-line documentation is that it largely eliminates the administrative task of distributing corrections and updates to bulky users' manuals and making sure that they actually get updated.

Where users do not have access to workstations, the user documentation must be paper-based. It is then important to reduce its bulk and make information in it easy to find. The documentation must also be easy to modify when the procedures change: a loose-leaf organization with pages numbered within chapters is probably the best. This makes the manual easy to update and to disseminate selectively, each user receiving only those parts of the documentation required for his or her specific tasks.

Types of Manuals

There are three generic types of user documentation: reference manuals, training documentation, and task guides. Traditionally, the **reference manual** has been the main type of documentation. A reference manual typically contains a description of all the components of a system: manual procedures, input forms, output reports, screens, equipment, and so on. The description of each component outlines its purpose, its relationship to other parts of the system, the possible values of the data, and some guidelines for interpreting the report or filling in the form. Manual procedures are described as flows of documents, starting with who prepares each document and in what way, how it is transmitted from one department or section to the next, what is done to it at each stage, and how it is finally disposed of (see Figure 21–1).

The reference manual is usually organized in sequence by component type and component name: first all the input forms by form number, then all the reports by report name, etc.

Figure 21–1 **Sample Reference Manual Page**

```
DEMAND DEPOSIT ACCOUNTING          INSTALLATION  TOOL                      U715
TELLER POSITION                    FIRST MECHANICS BANK                    RFMAN
                                   REFERENCE MANUAL INDEX


PREPARED BY: RUBY CORTEZ          DATE: 15MAR91          VERSION: 1.1      PAGE 1
APPROVED BY: STEVE JACKSON        DATE: 03APR91          STATUS:  D

                            INDEX TO REFERENCE MANUAL
                            =========================


                      TOPIC                      SECTION      ITEM      ENTRY
------------------------------------------------  ----------  ---------- ---------
General System Description                          100

    Policy Guidelines                                           .10
    Security and Safety                                         .20
    Description of the Workstation                              .30
    Description of Transactions                                 .40
    Flow of Transactions and Data                               .50
    Daily and Monthly Processing Schedule                       .60

Detailed Procedures                                 200

    Opening and Closing the Teller Position                     .10

        Physical Access                                                   ..1
        Logging On to the Terminal                                        ..2
        Adjusting and Closing the Position                                ..3
        Replenishing Cash                                                 ..4
        Troubleshooting                                                   ..5

    Deposits and Withdrawals                                    .20

        Customer Identification                                           ..1
        Balance Inquiries                                                 ..2
        Cash Deposits                                                     ..3
        Check Deposits                                                    ..4
        Cash Withdrawals                                                  ..5

    Other Customer/Non-Customer Transactions                   .30

        Bulk Coin Deposits                                                ..1
        Intrabank Transfers                                               ..2
        Interbank Transfers                                               ..3
        Traveller's Checks                                                ..4
        Banker's Checks                                                   ..5
        Foreign Exchange                                                  ..6
        Account Maintenance                                               ..7
        Credit Card Expense Advance                                       ..8
```

The complete reference manual for any but the smallest system is therefore likely to be extremely bulky and difficult to use. In fact, many installations have found that users do not refer to the reference manual at all, preferring to ask other employees or call the IS department when they have difficulty. As a result, some IS departments do not prepare reference manuals.

Instead, they tend to rely on **training documentation,** hard copies of overhead foils, handouts, and the notes taken by each participant. Training documentation is certainly needed, but it should not substitute for other forms of user documentation. Training documentation distributed at a given session is a picture of how the system works at a point in time. Usually, updated overheads are not sent out to already trained personnel. Moreover, training documentation usually treats only the basic cases. The trainers rely on users understanding how to process more complex tasks through a combination of experience on the job and formal documentation.

The most widely used form of documentation today is not a reference manual, but a **task guide.** Less complete than a reference manual, the task guide lists the most frequent tasks or situations that a given employee may encounter and explains how to deal with them. Exceptions and advanced topics are relegated to the reference manual, which still remains a necessity, although large parts of it can be replaced with on-line help. Rather than describing the flow of work from one position to another and detailing the role of each link in the chain, the task guide concentrates on what a single individual is called on to do. This approach is very appropriate in on-line systems, where manual procedures are less often based on forms transmitted from one employee to another and where each on-line user performs a fairly complete and complex set of tasks. For example, a task guide for a bank teller might be organized as illustrated in Figure 21–2.

Most users find that a good task guide is sufficient for everyday work. The reference manual is still needed, but only to resolve exceptions. In the bank teller example, for instance, the reference manual might be the source for how an international wire transfer is handled, a transaction not frequent enough for each teller clerk to know about. Often, only one or two users have a reference manual, and other workers come to them when the task guide does not explain how to perform a task under specific conditions. The same function is handled by a central help desk when the users are dispersed in multiple locations.

Contents of Procedure Manuals

The procedure manuals must contain a description of all the tasks that are required to run the system. The main categories of procedures are summarized as follows.

User procedures cover functional tasks performed by users, such as processing documents, filling out forms, and distributing or using reports in batch systems; interactions with terminals for data entry, error correction, and reentry; and conversation flows in on-line systems.

Figure 21–2 **Sample Task Guide**

```
DEMAND DEPOSIT ACCOUNTING        INSTALLATION   TOOL                          U716
TELLER POSITION                  FIRST MECHANICS BANK                         TGUID
                                    TASK   GUIDE


PREPARED BY: RUBY CORTEZ         DATE: 15MAR91          VERSION: 1.1          PAGE 1
APPROVED BY: STEVE JACKSON       DATE: 03APR91          STATUS:  D



                        INDEX TO TASK GUIDE
                        ===================


                TOPIC                        SECTION      ITEM       ENTRY
------------------------------------------- ----------  ----------  ---------
Who Should Read this Manual?                   1000


In Case of Hold-up                             2000


Tellers                                        3000

     How do I find an account number?                    .010
     When must I verify a customer's identity?           .020
     What transactions can I process for a
             non-customer?                               .030
     How do I handle cash deposits?                      .040
     How do I handle check deposits?                     .050
     How do I handle cash withdrawals?                   .060
     Can I accept penny jars?                            .070
     What if the customer has forgotten his/her
             checkbook?                                  .080
     What if I run out of cash?                          .090
     What must I do before leaving my position?          .100
         Temporarily                                                 ...1
         At the end of the day                                       ...2
     What happens if I make an error?                    .110
     What do I do with counterfeit bills?                .120


Assistant Branch Managers                      4000

     Assigning tellers and positions
     Opening and closing the teller position             .010
     Requirements for temporary tellers                  .020
     Telecommunications help desk                        .030
     End-of-day cash discrepancies                       .040
     Clearing items from suspense                        .050
     Handling overdrafts                                 .060
     Account opening and maintenance                     .070
     Checkbook orders                                    .080
     Foreign exchange regulations                        .090
```

Computer operations procedures cover tasks performed by DP personnel, including scheduling the application, manipulating tape and disk files, processing output such as bursting and collating printed reports, and so on. In the on-line environment, computer operations procedures also cover network supervision, control, and troubleshooting. Vendor-provided documentation is usually available to describe the operation of the processor, its peripherals, and its terminals.

Security procedures ensure that only authorized personnel gain access to the application and its data and that only security personnel modify the authorizations.

Performance procedures describe how to monitor actual response times, turnaround, throughput, utilization, and the performance of both user and DP personnel.

Control procedures ensure that valid and complete data enter the system and are processed accurately and without loss. Controls are ultimately the users' responsibility; however, many controls are actually performed by DP personnel to monitor the automated portions of the system.

Recovery/restart procedures are required to restore the system to normal use after the system has had an emergency or abnormal termination. Most of the activities concerned with recovery/restart are performed by DP operations personnel, in particular restoring files from backup copies and transaction logs and restarting the on-line system. However, users must also know about restart, in particular where activities must be reprocessed. For instance, if an invoice has to be reprocessed, the printed output from this reprocessing must be destroyed to avoid sending two identical invoices to the same customer for a single order.

Fallback procedures cover the steps to be taken if the system is anticipated to be unavailable for a long while. Fallback processing can be provided by manual procedures or by transporting the processing to a fallback site (another computer in a different location, ready to take over). One of the oft-cited advantages of distributed systems is that one site may be out of service without affecting the others. Moreover, the surviving locations may be able to absorb the workload of the failing site.

Backup procedures concern the routine copying and storage of files, program libraries, supplies, and documentation so that they will be available if needed, in particular for fallback purposes.

User Training Planning

Planning for training is primarily driven by three considerations: who is to be trained, what training they need (learning objectives), and what resources will be required.

The role and level of the personnel to be trained determines the general scope of the training. Training for management can often be reduced to an informal presentation of an hour or two. Clerical personnel may need formal training in the new system, a period of practice, and possibly an introduction to new workstations and new control techniques.

In some cases, the initial training is not dispensed to users, but to other trainers, who will then deliver their knowledge to the users. This approach, known as training the trainers, can be very effective when large numbers of people are to be trained. Moreover, trainers from either the corporation's training department or the user's own department are likely to be more effective, do a more professional job, and be better accepted by the trainees than a training team of IS professionals.

The resources required depend on the number and types of people to be trained, as well as the information content of the training. Usually, when classes are conducted, a maximum instructor-to-student ratio of 1:7 to 1:20 is aimed for, depending on the difficulty of the subject matter.

Self-study training can sometimes be used when the classroom approach is not appropriate. This technique is especially valuable when the ultimate user is a customer or when large populations of casual users have to be trained. Both printed programmed instruction manuals and computer-based training are possible tools.

The best option may be to incorporate into the system itself a training mode that gives the user access to the system and to a controlled set of transactions or other activities and that lets the user interface with the system. The only difference between training and real modes is that operational files are not updated and output documents are marked as being facsimiles. This approach is expensive, however, and it must be designed into the system. The great advantage is that it can be used long after conversion to train new operators, for whom it may be difficult to schedule classroom teaching.

Training Development and Conduct

In many large corporations, an internal training department can help develop training materials. In other cases, the project team may have to do without assistance. If so, the developers of the training materials should be aware of some general guidelines for effective training, such as the theory/examples/practice approach.

Suppose that the system is for rental agents for a large housing authority. One of the training objectives is to learn to use a waiting list form. The agents will first be told what data is on the form and how to process it (theory). Then they will be shown how several sample situations are treated on the form (examples). Finally, they will be paired off, with one agent playing the role of an applicant and the other filling in the form (practice).

The rental agents example concentrates on the acquisition of a skill. In modern systems development, the additional need for attitude formation is increasingly recognized. The best approach to teaching attitude is probably to keep in mind how the system is likely to benefit its users. An acronym to help training developers focus on this need is WIIFM, which stands for

"What's In It For Me?"—a question that is subconsciously asked by all users during training. Providing answers to WIIFM can be done by stressing throughout the training how the training and, by association, the system will help the trainee do a better job with less effort, improving the company or the user's department at the same time.

Those who conduct training sessions should be aware of the following major considerations:

- The trainees are adults, often older, more experienced, and more mature than the instructors. An effort must therefore be made not to appear patronizing or overbearing. It is perfectly normal for an instructor to know less than the audience in the domain of expertise of the audience. In fact, better results will be achieved if the instructor can draw on the participants' expertise and experience to make the training more relevant.

- The role of the trainer should not be that of a lecturer. Much more will be learned in a friendly, informal atmosphere, where everybody participates in the discussion. The trainer should act somewhat like the impartial leader described in Chapter 7, encouraging all to participate while preventing the most vocal participants from monopolizing the discussion. In addition, the trainer must keep the group on track and provide continuity.

- The trainees also have a role to play. They can contribute their own experiences and discuss different points of view in a constructive manner, helping the group stay on track and encouraging others to participate.

- Successful presentations are those where the presenter has physical presence and the material is well structured. Some presenters have the required physical presence almost naturally. Others must work hard to achieve it by paying attention to those factors that communicate the presenter's interest in the subject and the audience: eye contact, spontaneous gestures, varied movements, and proper use of the voice.

  The structure of the presentation refers to the way the introduction sets the tone and the expectations, the pacing of the delivery, good transitions between major subjects with summarizing and questions, and an appropriate ending that relates the topic to its objectives or to other parts of the course.

- During the presentation (or sometimes after a formal presentation), there will be discussions. These can be initiated by the trainer asking the audience a general question or directing a specific question to an individual. The audience will also ask questions, especially once they feel at ease with the instructor. The most difficult part is to get the discussion started; the next most difficult thing may be to stop it.

  During the discussion, the trainer should be careful to respond positively to audience statements by reinforcing good responses ("That's a good point") and by avoiding flat disagreement, keeping the discussion open even if the participant's response was inappropriate.

OPERATIONS PROCEDURES DEVELOPMENT

DP operations procedures have already been mentioned as part of the overall documentation to be developed during implementation. Specifically, the computer operations procedure manual is written exclusively for DP operations. Most of the others—security, control, performance, recovery/restart, fallback and backup procedures—have aspects that apply to DP operations.

Writing procedures for DP operations and training the operators to run the computer part of the application are not very different from user procedure writing and user training. The main difference is that DP operations handles applications from many different functional areas and cannot be expected to have a very deep understanding of the purpose and the functional architecture of each application. In addition, internal control principles should preclude DP operations from making business decisions normally made by the users.

As a result, the flow of an application should be as uniform from day to day and as automated as possible. Uniformity and automation are easily achieved with on-line applications, where the main role of DP operations is to start up the system in the morning and take it down at night. In addition, DP operations is responsible for recovery and restart, but if the recovery/restart procedures have been designed in accordance with the precepts in Chapter 16, this responsibility becomes largely routine.

Batch processing is more difficult. Part of the task of simplifying the running of the application is achieved by good design. For instance, no program should be allowed to request a response from the system operator. Any options, parameters, and dates that vary with each execution of the program should be entered by a user in a parameter file at the start of the run. If the operator's attention has to be drawn to some exceptional condition, such as an input file being out of balance, the program should be interrupted and the rest of the job abandoned, either by causing a program error (not a halt) or by returning an abnormal return code to the operating system. In the latter case, this return code may signal to the operating system that some other program, required for recovery, is to be run, simplifying the operator's task even more.

Some actions can be taken to automate operations once the programs have been designed, coded, and tested. Properly used, the operating systems job control facilities may chain programs and jobs together so that they can run to their normal end without the operator's intervention. In addition, restart points and procedures must be identified. For instance, one tactic may be to keep all the work files intact until the end of the batch process. Thus, the process can be restarted at any point in a series of programs and only the work that failed is redone. If a file is updated randomly, it may be necessary to back out the updates before restarting or restart the process against a backup copy, as in an on-line environment. In other cases, a program may be so long that there would not be time to reexecute it in its entirety, should it fail towards the end. For instance, an overnight program that takes 10 hours under normal circumstances might fail because of a program error, a hardware problem, or an operator mistake after 9 hours. To run the program over again would bring the total time required to 19 hours (plus the time required to fix the cause of the failure) on that night: it would probably not be done on time. In such extreme cases, the programmer, in cooperation with DP operations, must introduce checkpoints into the program. A checkpoint is a pause in a program where its state (working storage, file buffers, etc.) is recorded on an external medium. An associated restart facility enables the operating system to load the checkpoint from the external medium, position all the files at the point where they were at the checkpoint, and restart the program. If a checkpoint is taken every one or two hours, the time required to recover from failures is decreased correspondingly.

DP operations must also make sure that output gets directed to the appropriate medium. This concerns tape files and files on other removable magnetic media, whether sequential master files, backup copies of data bases, or interface files sent to customers, suppliers, or other locations. Clear operator instructions and proper use of the operating systems file and library control facilities help distribute output correctly. Printed output must be sent to the proper printer and instructions for mounting the proper continuous form, if required, must be developed. Each DP operations department tends to have its own techniques and standards for printing and processing reports.

Finally, as explained in Chapter 17, the control and security procedures must be developed. An example will illustrate what requires to be documented. For any sequential master file, a minimum of three generations should always be kept to ensure that the current version can be re-created if it is lost. Thus, for a daily application, a master file created on Monday must be kept through the end of processing on Thursday, three days later. A file created on Thursday must be kept until the end of processing on Tuesday, or even Wednesday if the Monday should happen to be a holiday—up to six days. The most widely used technique is to have the operating system create an expiration date for the file a given number of days after the date on which it is created. The number of days between creation and expiration is called the retention period of the file. A proper retention period ensures that no error of manipulation will accidentally destroy the file while it might still be needed. In the example, the daily file would require the retention period to be six days. For a monthly application, a retention period of 100 days would probably be prudent, given the variability of the number of days per month and the fact that the scheduling of monthly applications often varies by a few days.

FILE CONVERSION

In many cases, the application requires a new data base, new master files, new records in existing files or data bases, or new fields in existing master records. When most applications were conversions from manual systems, the strategy was to start a file creation process several months before the sched-

Figure 21–3 **Typical File Creation Application**

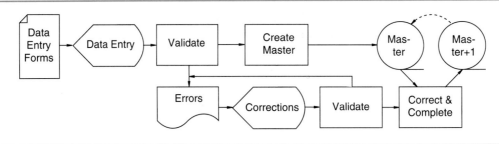

uled application cutover date. Thus, the master file would be loaded and ready when required. During those months, user personnel would prepare data entry forms for each record to be created—customer, product, supplier, personnel—in addition to their normal duties. Data entry personnel, often the future data entry clerks of the application being developed, would enter the data on computer-readable media. To populate the master file, operations would run a mini-application (see Figure 21–3), which would have to be ready, programmed, and debugged at a fairly early stage.

This strategy created a heavy transient workload on users, data entry, and DP operations alike. Some of the workload could be reduced by using temporary personnel and resorting to outside service bureau processing; the cost was still substantial.

Nowadays, this way of converting files is still encountered on occasion. Much more frequently, most of the information required to create the new master file or data base already exists on some electronic medium. For instance, a new utility billing system created today will usually replace an existing one that has a fairly complete customer file. The conversion from one to the other may be a simple restructuring exercise. In this case, all the data for the new data base exists on old master files, but the new data base has a different structure (for instance, because it is a data base rather than a sequential tape file). The problem is then easy to resolve: a program is developed to read the old files and create the new. This program can be run the day before cutting over to the new system (see Figure 21–4).

Even in this simple case, it is prudent to have a dry run some weeks before cutover. In general, the integrity requirements for a data base will be much higher than for a sequential file, and the conversion program should identify any related problems. For instance, in converting a customer file, some customer records might contain sales representative numbers of salespersons who have left. An obsolete sales representative number might not be of any functional consequence if the customer is inactive, but the data should be cleaned up before the new data base is created. All these problems should be identified and corrected on the old files before the final conversion run is made (see Figure 21–5).

Figure 21–4 **One-Time Conversion of Files from Existing Files**

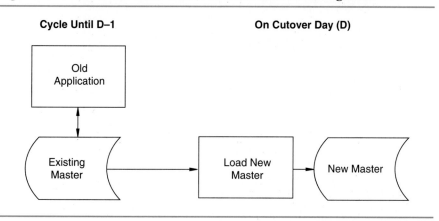

Sometimes, however, the file conversion cannot take place overnight, on the day before cutover. With large files, the process might be too long. More probably, the existing files do not have all the data required. There are three approaches to solving this problem. The first and most common is to convert the existing files a few weeks before cutover and have users complete the new file during the transition period. The problem with this approach is

Figure 21–5 **Conversion of Files from Existing Files after Cleanup**

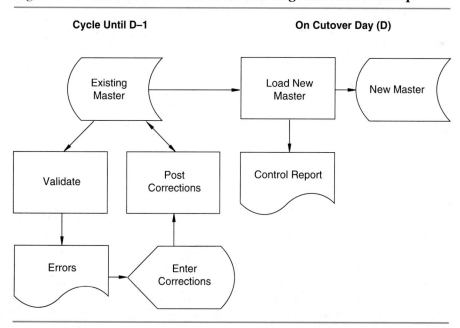

Figure 21–6 **Gradual Conversion of Files from Existing Files**

that the old file continues to live and be updated during the time that the new file is being completed. Stringent controls must be put in place to ensure that all the updates to the old master are reflected in the new one as well, so that the two are synchronized on cutover day. The shorter the period between the initial file conversion and cutover, the easier it is to ensure synchronization (see Figure 21–6).

The second approach is to modify the existing system to accommodate the supplementary information without necessarily processing it. The data is simply stored on the master file records. This approach eliminates the prob-

Figure 21–7 **Modifying Existing File Design before Conversion**

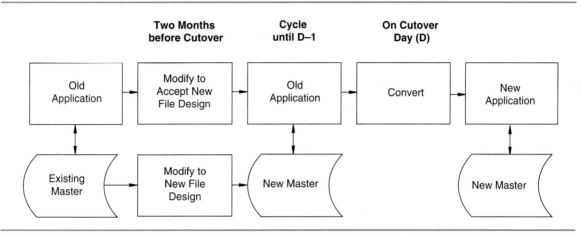

lem of maintaining two versions of the same file for several weeks or months. Naturally, the cost of modifying the old application may be prohibitive, as one of the main reasons for replacing applications is that they have become hard to modify (see Figure 21–7).

The third approach can be taken when the new data is not required on cutover day but can be completed as new transactions come in. For instance, if the new customer address file should have a nine-digit zip code instead of the five-digit zip code that existed on the old file, this change can probably be implemented gradually.

CUTOVER AND FOLLOW-UP

On cutover day, the new system is brought up instead of the old one. If it has been possible to test the system on one or two pilot sites, the risks are not too great. Most of the practical difficulties have probably already been shaken out, and the remaining problems are not likely to be catastrophic. The installation team already has experience in answering user questions and allaying their concerns.

If the system is started without the benefit of a pilot test, the situation is likely to be different. All the resources and fortitude of the team will be required to solve the problems, answer the unexpected questions, and make last-minute changes. If system testing has been properly performed, most of the really serious problems have been resolved already, and temporary solutions can be found for the remaining ones; but it will be hard work, and the pressure is high. This pressure is likely to continue for several months; in most cases, about half the total installation team should be available for three to six months after cutover.

During this time, it is critical to display discipline in change management. Each problem must be documented and each change request from users acknowledged. For each problem, it is best to find a temporary solution so that as few changes as possible are made to the computer system under pressure, when maintenance analysis is likely to be too quick and testing is likely to be superficial. The ideal way to handle such changes is to group them into a controlled release, due some months after the initial installation. Chapter 22 describes how the process of change can be controlled.

Summary

User procedures document the manual aspects of a system, including human-computer interfaces. Such documentation may be either manual or paper-based, but on-line documentation is easier for users to access from their workstations. It also eases the burden of preparing and distributing updates.

Of the three types of user documentation, task guides are most common today. They are less complete than reference manuals and are also organized differently. Reference manuals are complete descriptions of systems components (e.g., forms, reports, procedures) presented in sequence. Task guides, on the other hand, list the tasks most likely to be encountered by an employee and explain how each is handled. Rather than prepare complete reference manuals, some IS departments save the training materials for the new system's operations and use them in place of a formal reference manual. Training manuals do not replace a formal reference manual satisfactorily. Task guides available to all employees coupled with reference manuals available to a few of the most experienced employees provide a good balance for most situations.

Other types of procedures that require formal documentation include computer operations, security procedures, performance procedures, controls, recovery/restart, and fallback and backup procedures.

A successful implementation requires that users be well trained in the new systems operations. Considerations in developing a plan for training users include: (1) who is to be trained, (2) what training they need, and (3) what resources will be required. Management users of the system require less training than personnel who will be working more closely with the system. When large numbers of users must be trained, training the trainers is effective and does not unduly burden the project team. Building a training component into the system itself is often the most effective strategy in the long run. If the organization has a training department, the project team should use it to help develop training materials and conduct training sessions.

Some of the major considerations for the conduct of training sessions are (1) to treat the trainees as adults, (2) to avoid the role of a lecturer, (3) to encourage participation by the trainees, (4) to aim for structured presentations delivered by trainers with an appropriate physical presence, and (5) to manage discussions during the training sessions.

Developing procedures for DP operations is facilitated if guidelines are followed during design that lead to streamlined operations in the first place.

Most systems today involve the creation of new system files or data bases from existing electronic media rather than from manual records. Even though today's systems simplify the effort, file conversion still requires careful planning to ensure that the new system begins with correct data in its master files.

Following cutover to the new system, the project team must be available to deal with inevitable problems. Such problems can be minimized with well-planned and executed testing and training. In most cases, however, about one-half the installation team will need to be available for a period of three to six months for post-cutover problem resolution.

Review Questions

1. What are some of the advantages of on-line documentation?

2. Distinguish between the three types of user documentation manuals.

3. What functional tasks might you expect to find covered in a well-designed set of user procedures?

4. To what technique does the phrase "training the trainers" refer?

5. What is the advantage of incorporating training into the system itself?

6. What is a program checkpoint?

7. What are the three primary approaches to file conversion?

8. What are some of the techniques used to minimize post-cutover changes to the new system?

Discussion Questions

1. Under what circumstances might it be more appropriate to distribute reference manuals rather than task guides to users?

2. Why do users often prefer to be trained by other users or professional trainers rather than by IS personnel? When might users prefer to be trained by IS personnel?

3. Cite as many situations as you can where a self-study approach to training might be the most appropriate option.

Mini-Case

Northwest Distributors. Northwest Distributors operates a mail-order business in tools, hardware, and home supplies from its offices in Seattle. Two years ago, it engaged the firm of Harwood and Hancock (H&H) to assist with the design and installation of a new customer information system. Northwest's existing system had been in operation for over ten years and was becoming increasingly difficult to maintain properly. In addition, the mail-order business was getting much more competitive each year, and Northwest's marketing manager, Ron Zayots, was dissatisfied with the demographic data in the present system's files.

The new system's design expanded the customer data base by adding several new fields, and the system itself contained several new functions and reports that Ron wanted.

The development project had been a difficult one. H&H had agreed to do the work for a fixed fee, and the project had taken more time than Dick Zimmer, the H&H project manager, had estimated. Dick was concerned that unless shortcuts could be found in the project's remaining tasks, he would come in well over budget and might find his job on the line.

Two of the major tasks remaining are training user personnel and developing a strategy for building the new data base. Dick has decided to recommend the following approaches for these two tasks at the upcoming meeting of the project steering committee:

- Northwest is to take responsibility for training users on the new system and for developing all training materials and procedure manuals. Dick is going to argue that this strategy will be better accepted by the users and will assure all concerned that Northwest employees understand the new system.

- Required new fields will be added to the file by Northwest personnel following conversion.

Dick has discussed these ideas with Ron Zayots. Ron told Dick to expect some resistance at the steering committee meeting from Ron himself as well as from Janis McDonald, the supervisor of customer service operations. Ron wants the new file to contain the new data fields right from the start. He said the new system would not be considered complete or H&H's work complete until the new fields are in the customer master file. Janis McDonald was not pleased with Dick's approach, because she maintains that her personnel deserve to be trained by professionals, not by amateurs, and that her people are so busy already that they want to minimize the time for training on the new system. She is familiar with on-line documentation from her previous employer and wants to know why such a technique could not be implemented with Northwest's system.

Question for Discussion

1. What suggestions do you have for Dick as he prepares for the steering committee meeting?

Maintenance

After an introduction to the maintenance problem, Chapter 22 explains the various possible causes for maintenance. It describes an approach to the organization of maintenance by grouping modifications into versions, releases, and temporary fixes to the system. Next, it describes the actual process of maintaining a system: filling out a change request, organizing the maintenance team, and performing the modifications. Last, the chapter refers to how existing systems that are being maintained are integrated into the systems plan, thus closing the cycle of systems development.

Learning Objectives

- Understand the importance and the difficulty of solving maintenance problems.
- Describe the six major causes of maintenance and their frequency in different stages of the life of a system.
- Describe the differences between system versions, system releases, and temporary fixes to systems.
- Describe how maintenance requests are initiated through a change request form.
- Be aware of the possible ways to organize the maintenance team to support version and release control.
- Understand how the maintenance work is actually performed.

THE MAINTENANCE PROBLEM

Most mature installations devote approximately three-quarters of their analyst and programmer resources to maintaining existing applications. For an application lasting 20 years, not an unusual figure, maintenance can cost from two to five or more times the original amount spent on development (see Figure 22–1). Maintenance is considered an unglamorous job, and maintenance workers are easily discouraged. Often, too, management compounds the problem by assigning the best workers to development and average or mediocre ones to maintenance, where, in fact, greater intelligence and technical know-how is required.

Figure 22–1 **Cost of Maintenance**

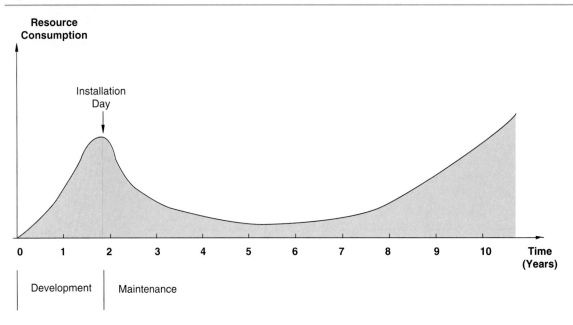

The cost of development and maintenance is the area under the curve

Yet little attention has been paid to maintenance in the literature and in available products. This situation is starting to change. A number of books have been written, research on maintenance problems has been initiated in many universities, and several tools have emerged since about 1985 that can help maintenance programmers produce better quality work.

Perhaps one reason maintenance has so long been neglected is that the latest development techniques have always promised that they would all but eliminate the maintenance problem. When structured programming emerged in the 1970s, its promoters argued that the elimination of GOTO statements would make all programs understandable and therefore maintainable. Today, the supporters of object-oriented programming and design claim that one of the main benefits of their approach will be to reduce maintenance efforts.

The claims made on behalf of these methods have merit. Some of the design techniques described in this book are also justified mainly by their effect on maintenance. However, few if any serious studies have actually quantified the maintenance benefits of new methods of design and programming. Because systems last for up to 20 years, by the time such a study was completed, the technique that it applies to would be out of date.

Most maintenance problems are not related to design and programming style but rather to management difficulties and poor testing practices. Cer-

Figure 22–2 **Generic Causes of Maintenance**

Changing reporting needs
New hardware and software
Changing business operations
Changing business environment (customers, suppliers, regulatory agencies)
Cumulative effect of maintenance

---

tainly, all software houses that distribute systems or application software to a large number of customers have found that it is more cost effective to maintain systems in versions and releases than to implement changes day by day, as they are requested. These software houses also have advanced testing practices; they use independent testing teams and regression testing techniques for system modifications. They are also more willing than most corporate IS departments to assign high-quality people to the maintenance and support jobs.

TYPES OF MAINTENANCE

Figure 22–2 lists some of the most frequent causes of maintenance. Maintenance and enhancements are treated together, although some authorities distinguish between them. These causes can be plotted against the curve of the cost of maintenance (see Figure 22–3). As can be seen, in the early days of operation of the system, bugs and minor functional enhancements dominate.

Figure 22–3 **Causes of Maintenance over Time**

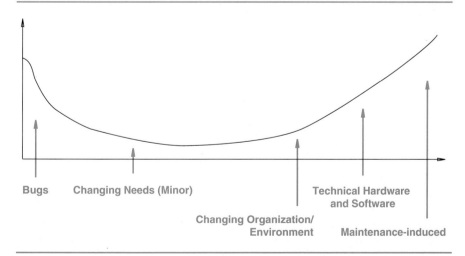

Bugs   Changing Needs (Minor)

Changing Organization/
Environment

Technical Hardware
and Software

Maintenance-induced

The minor functional enhancements continue to be a factor throughout the life of the application. Solving a problem usually creates (or reveals) a new problem. If a management report on causes of personnel turnover helps reduce turnover, the report is no longer required in its present form. It must be modified or replaced by another report that helps solve some other current problem, such as lack of training effectiveness, recruiting difficulties, or absenteeism.

Then, after a few years, additional causes for maintenance appear: major functional enhancements that are the result of gradual external changes. These new needs do not appear immediately for two reasons: first, some of them have been anticipated at the design stage and can easily be implemented (they become minor instead of major). Second, some problems accumulate gradually, with the users working around the system to meet new requirements, for instance, by supplementing computer-prepared reports with manually prepared graphs or PC-based spreadsheets. At some point, the work-around becomes too cumbersome for the users, who then request a major enhancement to streamline these nondesigned, nonarchitected, spontaneously generated layers of minor modifications.

Technical causes of maintenance follow a similar pattern. The evolution of the technical architecture of the installation for the first few years can be anticipated and built into the application. Later, more substantial changes are necessary to keep the application up to date. For instance, migrating to a new operating system or a new data base management system may require substantial rewriting of the application. New design and programming methods may also justify technical rewriting of parts of an application. For example, an application written 15 years ago in assembler may have to be rewritten in COBOL, just because the IS department no longer has enough personnel with assembler language competence. (A drawback of changing development methods to make applications more maintainable is that numerous changes in style make it more and more difficult for maintenance programmers to understand the programs they are to maintain, which have all been created with different standards, styles, and tools.)

Towards the end of the life of a system, previous maintenance becomes a major cause of new maintenance. Keeping a program or an application well structured is extremely difficult when it is modified several times in succession. Too many patches on a garment may make the original fabric and style all but invisible. The resulting degradation of the program structure does not increase the number of maintenance requests, but it does increase the unit cost per request. It can also result in fewer maintenance requests actually being accepted. Many requests get turned down with the following justification: "The program is too old; it works fine now, but we don't dare touch it any more." When this justification is invoked frequently, there is good evidence that the entire application ought to be redeveloped.

VERSIONS, RELEASES, AND FIXES

Software houses, and now more and more in-house IS departments, organize the maintenance efforts so that changes are implemented in successive versions of the system, successive releases of each version, and, if required, fixes distributed between releases.

In general, new **versions** of a system are created for major changes, either functional or technical. What distinguishes a version is that it must be tested as thoroughly as the initial implementation: integration test, system test, and acceptance test. Generally, the test data must be redesigned or substantially overhauled. Substantial user documentation revisions are required, and users may have to be partially retrained. A new version is therefore a large effort and should not be undertaken more than once every two to five years.

New **releases** of a system incorporate minor modifications at periodic intervals, usually about every six months. This period is a compromise between the cost of a new release and the frustration of users who might have to wait a year or more for relatively minor requests to be honored. Testing is also thorough, but generally, the existing test data can be used with only minor modifications. Thus, the test results can largely be checked automatically by comparing test results to those saved from the previous release. Testing using the existing test data to verify that unchanged parts of the system continue to function as before is called regression testing; it is a fundamental requirement of proper maintenance and one of the main arguments for implementing maintenance in releases rather than continuously. Documentation changes must also be made; however, they are usually minor and can be distributed as addenda or as loose-leaf replacements. Retraining is the exception rather than the rule.

Finally, some modifications cannot wait for the next release. They may be required to correct bugs discovered during operations, or they may be due to sudden changes in the environment, for instance, the critical need to match some competitor's offering immediately (as one suspects happened in 1988, when one frequent-flier program's offering of triple miles was matched within a few weeks by two of its competitors). In these cases, **temporary fixes** are applied to the system immediately. Often, no documentation change is required: if the fix was for a bug, chances are that the documentation described the way the system was supposed to operate rather than the incorrect way in which it actually worked. Testing is necessarily summary; it would be too expensive to conduct an entire regression test cycle every time a fix is posted.

This kind of fix must be strictly temporary; it has to be put in as a separate request to be addressed in the next release as well, so that it can then be properly analyzed, designed, programmed, tested, and documented.

The lack of rigorous testing of temporary fixes implies a high risk of errors caused by the fix, just as the use of untried drugs to treat a medical condition often induces unanticipated side effects, some of which can be

Box
22–1

Configuration Control

The distribution of systems over multiple locations has created the need for a new discipline, called configuration control. Maintenance requires changing the system, so that each component—program, data base design, hardware, documentation—may exist in different versions in different locations. Configuration control consists in keeping track of these different versions and planning for their implementation at each site, while avoiding incompatibility problems.

Examples of problems that may arise are the following:

- A bug is discovered in a program. The correction of this bug is different in version 1 than in version 2. To distribute the correction to all the users of the program, it is necessary to know which users have version 1 and which ones have version 2.

- A data interface between a distributed site and a central site is changed. Therefore, a program change is necessary at every site. However, there is no way to guarantee that all the changes will take place at the same time. During the period where both interfaces must exist, some solution must be devised for their coexistence. The central site must accept both interfaces and know which distributed site uses which.

- A new site is created. If the software has hardware dependencies (for instance, if version 1 does not support laser printers but version 2 does), the right components for the new hardware configuration must be assembled, tested for compatibility, and shipped.

- An existing site wishes to change hardware. It must first upgrade its software environment to a baseline that supports both the current and the planned hardware, regardless of functionality changes. (This upgrade is called *positioning*.)

These types of problems have long been known to computer manufacturers who distribute systems software in the current version to their customers and then ship updates to fix bugs or to migrate to new releases.

The same problems also exist in nondistributed systems, in cases where there is a high degree of integration between subsystems on the same site. A case in point is with subject data bases. As the design of a subject data base changes, the systems that share the data base must evolve in concert.

Finally, configuration control problems may arise when changes to the design of a system are requested and authorized during development. If the design of an interface changes after one of the programs using it has been developed, that program must be modified. The problem is to make sure that all the programs or modules affected by a change are synchronized when integration testing starts. If they are not, integration testing will probably discover the discrepancies, but at a much greater cost.

Very few configuration control tools exist in today's commercial environment. The use of data dictionaries with proper version control can help; but for the actual source and object code of programs, most installations have a manually controlled series of separate programming libraries for different versions of the programs and the data structures. The proper libraries are selected at compile time, with the objective of creating object code libraries that contain compatible versions of each module. If there is no compilation phase, as in many fourth-generation languages, a step replacing the compilation must be performed to make sure that the proper versions of source programs are made available in production.

more serious than the condition that the drug was supposed to cure. The following precautions should be taken:

- No temporary fix should be made to the automated part of the system if there is a manual bypass available.

- An honest effort should be made to test the effects of the fix on those parts of the system that are the most likely to be adversely affected. The practice of using live data to test the fix (in particular the practice consisting of rerunning the same data that caused the bug to appear) is not to be condoned. Properly designed test data, including the case that made the bug appear, should be used; test results should be precalculated; all test output should be checked. Ideally, at least the entire unit test cycle for each module that is modified should be updated to incorporate the new test case and rerun. If there are too many cycles, this requirement may be somewhat relaxed, but the lack of complete testing should at least be documented.

- Because the risk of errors is so high, a fallback procedure must be planned, so that the temporary fix can easily be reversed if necessary.

- Temporary fixes should be withdrawn and reimplemented for the next new release as a permanent modification.

PROCESSING CHANGE REQUESTS

At the heart of the maintenance process is the change request. This form is filled in by the user liaison person, an IS professional with the responsibility for maintaining contact with the various users. (The help desk is part of the user liaison's responsibilities, although it is usually manned by junior personnel on a rotating basis.) The change request form should accommodate both enhancements and reports of problems and errors (see Figure 22–4). The change request may be initiated by a user or potential user, by DP operations, or by the user liaison.

Each change request is assessed as to its completeness, urgency, and probable cost. A form is not complete unless its explanation of what is requested or why it is requested allows the maintenance group to evaluate its importance and its cost; incomplete forms are sent back to the initiator. If the form is complete, the request is classified as a candidate for a bypass solution, a temporary fix, an enhancement in the next release, an enhancement in a future version, or it is refused. In some cases, the request may be refused because the change has already been made, unbeknownst to the originator of the request. In other cases, it is refused because it is not deemed to be cost-effective or because it is in contradiction with some other, accepted change.

This initial classification is based on a very high-level evaluation of the request. In many cases, this evaluation is performed in a committee of IS department management and lead analysts so that each member can con-

Figure 22–4 **Change Request**

```
                    INSTALLATION   TOOL                              A825
               CONDOR TELEPHONE COMPANY                             CHREQ
                    CHANGE   REQUEST

PREPARED BY: Alan Forlink        DATE: 4 June 1994     VERSION:          PAGE 1
LOCATION:    Marketing Springfield Area               STATUS:  Submitted

PRIORITY (CHECK ONE):

  __  HIGH   xx  MED    __  LOW        DATE REQUIRED:    End 1994

   SHORT DESCRIPTION:  Separate Billing address for residential customers


DETAILED DESCRIPTION:  Some residential customers have a need to have their monthly

telephone bills sent to a different location than where the equipment is installed.

Since we already do this for corporate customers, it should be easy to provide for

residential customers as well. _____

_____

_____

_____


   REASON REQUIRED:  Customer requests (privacy, convenience) in increasing numbers

over the past five years. _____

_____

_____


TO BE FILLED IN BY ANALYST:

PROGRAM/PROCEDURE AFFECTED      EST EFFORT     VERSION      ASSIGNED      DEADLINE
--------------------------      ----------     -------      --------      --------

Order Entry Procedure           25 days        _____      _____      _____

POE735                          5 days         3.5          _____      _____

Convert Existing Customers?     60 days        _____      _____      _____
```

tribute detailed knowledge of some aspect to the discussion, and so that priorities and resources can be distributed evenly over applications. Typically, such a committee meets once a week. A weekly schedule does cause a problem for emergency requests, which must be fixed without delay. An exception procedure is then required which, however, does not preclude the requested change or problem report from being reviewed at the next maintenance committee meeting.

Because the initial classification is made without much analysis, it is subject to later change. In particular, if a problem is classified as urgent and subject to a temporary fix, a bypass solution may be devised to avoid a modification to the automated part of the system. In other cases, a seemingly minor modification may turn out to have major ramifications once it is studied in detail, and the corresponding request may be changed from a "next release" to a "next version" or "refused" classification.

Once the request has been classified, its originator is notified of the disposition and the request is turned over to the maintenance team for action at the appropriate time.

ORGANIZATION OF THE MAINTENANCE TEAM

The maintenance team is now responsible for analyzing each change in detail. The team's responsibilities include the following:

- Identifying all programs, files, procedures, and documentation requiring to be changed.
- Documenting how the change is to be implemented.
- Estimating the time required to implement the change.
- Performing an economic analysis of the change: implementation costs, operation costs, savings.
- Coding the change.
- Testing the change.
- Modifying the procedures and the documentation.
- Training users and DP operations, if required.
- Converting files that need to change.
- Coordinating the actual implementation of the change with other changes.

These responsibilities constitute a miniature of the entire life cycle of a project. Quite some time will elapse between the analysis and design of a change and its actual availability; therefore, a version and release approach to maintenance will require freezing the change requests some time prior to the planned availability of the release. Any new request arriving after the freeze date will be scheduled for the following release.

Figure 22–5 **Synchronizing Releases**

A technique that has been used successfully to deal with this timing issue is to divide the maintenance team into two subteams, which work on alternative releases. For instance, the first team will be implementing changes while the second team accepts and analyzes change requests. When the first team has implemented its release, the change requests for the second team are frozen, and it starts implementing those requests that have already been received, while the first team starts receiving fresh requests. The synchronization of the two teams is depicted in Figure 22–5.

In this scheme, the requests for change that arrive during the initial implementation cycle can already be assigned to a maintenance cycle before release 0 of the system has even been implemented, so as to ensure that release 1 is ready no more than three to six months after release 0 (see Figure 22–6).

Fred Brooks, in *The Mythical Man-Month*, recommends that the second version of any system should be a complete technical rewrite of the first version, without any functional enhancements at all.[1] His reasoning is that lack of experience and design compromises in the initial version combine in practically every case to make the first version a poor-quality product. By concentrating exclusively on correcting implementation errors in version 2, a high-quality basis for further evolutions can be obtained. Brooks also adduces the reason that most people tend to go overboard in version 2 and produce a system that incorporates every idea that was even considered in the initial implementation, but rejected because of time pressures. His reasoning is that if the idea or function did not deserve implementation then, it probably does not now. The only way to prevent overdesigning version 2 is to impose the strict discipline of avoiding innovation altogether.

Figure 22–6 **Overlapping Development and First Releases**

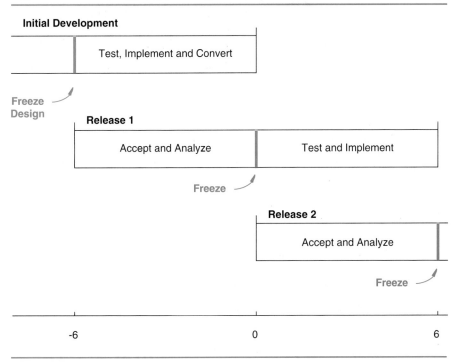

Brooks was writing from the perspective of a software vendor; the strategy that he recommends is probably most relevant for systems that are distributed to many sites.

PERFORMING THE WORK

Because the substance of the work associated with a new release starts when the change requests are frozen, all the existing requests can be reviewed together. Those that affect similar areas can be grouped and assigned to a single person, thus minimizing the chances of two analysts simultaneously trying to change the same program. Normally, consolidation will somewhat reduce the total estimate of the work to be done. This reduction can serve as a security margin for making sure that the next release is delivered on time.

Next, an economic analysis is made for each change request (see Figure 22–7). The economic analysis may result in some changes being rejected or delayed, if they turn out to be less profitable than others. This could free up some resources, which could in turn be used to unfreeze a few selected changes that may have come in after the initial deadline. These changes should be selected not so much on their absolute merit as on the synergy that they may have with other, scheduled changes.

Figure 22–7 **Economic Analysis of Maintenance**

```
MARKETING                        DESIGN TOOL                          CD-20
ORDER ENTRY                      SUBURBAN  PUMPS                       ECONS
             COST/BENEFIT OF SUMMARY SALES REPORTING MODIFICATION

PREPARED BY:   MARYANN UNGER     DATE: 08JUN94      VERSION: 1         PAGE 1
APPROVED BY:   HANS ABKORP       DATE: 22JUN94      STATUS:

                                                          Amount
                                                          ------
1.    One-time Change Costs
------------------------------------------------------------

         Personnel expense -
            50 workdays analyst                            6,000
            100 workdays programmer                        8,000
            30 workdays clerical                             960

         Machine hours cost -
            20 CPU hours                                  12,250

         Equipment and supplies -
               Paper and office supplies                    100
            25 reels magnetic tape                          625
                                                       ----------
                        Subtotal                          27,935
                                                       ----------

2.    Recurring Costs and Savings
------------------------------------------------------------

         Clerical costs - Annual -
            5 workdays/month                               1,920

3.    Intangible Costs and Benefits
------------------------------------------------------------

         Customer satisfaction - translating possibly to
            100 fewer local calls per month:  yearly      (4,000)
                                                       ----------
                        Subtotal                          (2,080)
                                                       ----------

4.    Payback Period
------------------------------------------------------------

         27,935/2,080 = more than 13 years
```

The work is then assigned to analysts and, later, to programmers; it proceeds much as in the regular life cycle.

In some cases, a detailed analysis will reveal that the modification is much more complex than initially thought. A change in classification or resources allocated may then be necessary. If, as a result of the detailed analysis, the cost of a modification increases substantially beyond what was initially evaluated, a fresh economic evaluation may be justified.

In truth, few installations actually perform cost/benefit analyses for maintenance work. In most cases, maintenance is performed on the basis of qualitative judgment ("sounds like a good idea"). One of the merits of the release and version approaches is that cost/benefit analyses are consolidated and can therefore be made more significant. Ordinarily, it is also much easier to perform an accurate analysis of the economic impact of a change than of an entirely new system because there are not nearly as many factors of uncertainty.

RELATIONSHIP WITH SYSTEMS PLANNING

The maintenance process feeds information to the systems planning process. Systems planning usually takes place at an initial point, with updates being made to the systems plan at more or less regular intervals—ideally once a year, in conjunction with the business planning cycle of the organization.

Some information about maintenance costs is useful for systems planning. The amount of resources allocated to each existing system for new releases and especially for new versions and the cost/benefit history of the application will help indicate to the systems planners when the economic life of an application is approaching its end. Thus, the effort to redevelop the application from scratch can be planned well in advance.

Summary

Maintaining installed systems is a major cost of operating a mature IS department. It is not unusual to find three-quarters of the programmer and analyst resources devoted to maintaining installed systems rather than to developing new applications.

Of the various types of maintenance, minor functional enhancements are to be expected throughout the life of the system. Major functional enhancements tend to appear after the system has been in operation for a few years, as do maintenance requirements caused by technical reasons. As a system ages, previous maintenance performed becomes a major reason for new maintenance, as the system becomes so "patched" that maintenance is increasingly difficult for anyone to perform.

Some in-house IS departments are adopting the policy of versions and fixes used by software houses. Fixes are installed as problems are corrected, and new versions are released when major modifications are made. Each new version incorporates all fixes installed since the last version was released. Careful attention must be given to procedures for testing fixes and new versions.

The change request form and accompanying procedures provide a systematic way of recording user requests for changes and for classifying them, assigning priorities to them, and managing their execution.

Maintenance teams install changes in a process that is similar to the development life cycle in miniature. Some IS departments will have two maintenance teams working on the same system at one time. When one team is implementing changes on a given release of the system, the other team is analyzing change requests and planning for their implementation in a subsequent release.

Although many departments do not attempt formal cost/benefit analyses on each maintenance request, the adoption of the release and version technique permits change requests to be grouped, thus reducing overhead costs.

Finally, the maintenance process should be structured so that it provides a continuous feedback to the systems planning process. Thus, systems planners are made aware of when an installed system is approaching the end of its useful life and is becoming a candidate for replacement.

Selected Readings

Martin, J., and McClure, C. *Software Maintenance: The Problem & Its Solutions*. Englewood Cliffs, New Jersey: Prentice-Hall, 1983.
This book is James Martin's view of maintenance. Although it has been less influential than many of James Martin's other books, it is still worthwhile reading.

Parikh, G. *Handbook of Software Maintenance*. New York: John Wiley & Sons, 1986.
Girish Parikh is the best-known author today specializing in maintenance. This book is one of the most representative of his views, but there are several others that are also valuable.

Review Questions

1. What are some of the most frequent causes of maintenance?

2. What are some of the indications that a system is becoming too difficult to maintain and should be replaced?

3. What is the distinction between a program fix and a new version?

4. What are some of the precautions that should be taken if temporary fixes are made to a system in actual operation?

5. What are some of the benefits of using formal change requests for maintenance?

6. Why does Fred Brooks, in his book *The Mythical Man-Month*, recommend that the second version of a system be a complete technical rewrite?

7. What information should be communicated from the systems maintainers to the systems planners?

Discussion Questions

1. What techniques can be employed in the systems design and programming phases to make the resultant system more easily maintainable?

2. Give several examples of the phenomenon that "solving a problem creates (or reveals) a new problem."

3. What are the pros and cons of organizing maintenance efforts into two teams as suggested in the chapter?

Mini-Case

CJ Automotive Supply Corporation. CJ Automotive Supply Corporation is a large automotive parts supplier and distributor located in Detroit, Michigan. Its IS department has been an integral part of the company's operations since 1962 when a computer was installed to perform various accounting-related applications. The IS operation has grown to the point where it now includes applications in all functional areas of the business including an up-to-date computer-integrated manufacturing application and an electronic data interchange (EDI) application between CJ Automotive and its major customers. The company has two large mainframe computers, several minicomputers, and hundreds of PCs. Most of this hardware is tied together on a sophisticated computer network.

Like most companies that have been running computer applications for a considerable number of years, CJ Automotive finds that it must devote a substantial portion of its programmer and analyst resources to maintaining existing computer resources. Dave Lambert, the director of MIS at CJ, is concerned about the ever-rising cost of maintenance. He is concerned about not only the percentage of resources he must devote to the area, but also the difficulty of keeping maintenance personnel motivated. Turnover of maintenance personnel is twice that of personnel working on new development. Exit interviews show that most maintenance personnel who leave consider their work to be tedious and removed from the leading edge of technology.

You are an independent consultant in the information systems field. Dave has called you and asked you to come to his office so that he could determine whether you would be able to help him devise a plan to reduce his costs of maintaining the existing applications.

Questions for Discussion

1. What questions would you want to ask Dave about the environment surrounding the maintenance function at CJ Automotive?

2. What suggestions could you put together for ways to make the maintenance assignment more interesting and challenging?

Note

1. Brooks, F. *The Mythical Man-Month*. Reading, Massachusetts: Addison-Wesley, 1975.

Technique

Implementation Data Dictionary

INTRODUCTION

A major part of the program specification package described in Chapter 20 is the description of the program's data. The data is also described to the data base management system (as explained in Section V) and to any test data generators used during testing (see Chapter 20). In addition, data dictionaries produce cross-references that help maintenance analysts assess the impact of proposed changes.

Data dictionaries were initially created in the early 1970s to centralize and coordinate all these descriptions of data. They were thus the ancestor of CASE tools, and they are still at the core of the installation functionality (program generation, coding, testing) of most serious CASE tools today. Indeed, the emerging notion of *repository*, the facility that stores and retrieves descriptions of all aspects of a system, design as well as code, data as well as procedures, is directly based on the concept of data dictionary.

DEFINITION

A data dictionary system is a computer-based application to maintain descriptions of data used in an installation, on a project, or for a given data base.

The data dictionary produces machine-readable data descriptions for programs that manipulate the data described. Examples are COBOL Data Division statements and DDL (Data Description Language) statements for the data base management system.

The dictionary also produces printed or displayed output to help analysts and programmers in the following:

- Locating in which files and programs data are used.
- Specifying the meaning of data to avoid duplication and misunderstandings.
- Describing processing rules and in particular validation rules for input data.
- Depicting relationships that reflect the data model established during design.

Most data dictionaries in use today are implementation-oriented. In other words, they have facilities for describing actual files, records, and data elements as they will be represented on the physical files and in memory. The data model (the conceptual or logical levels) may be represented as well, but only by assimilating the model to a file or set of files. The activities of data modeling are usually not well supported.

Repository-based CASE tools, which maintain distinct descriptions of data structures at the requirements analysis and implementation levels (with a generalized audit trail facility to track how one is transformed into the other) are not yet prevalent. Some of these have adequate data modeling facilities but are weaker on the implementation side.

Manual, paper-based data dictionaries have been attempted, but they have not been successful.

A SAMPLE DATA DICTIONARY SYSTEM

The system flow of a sample data dictionary system is shown in Figure 1. It includes the following:

- Interactive input of data descriptions that update the data dictionary.
- Batch input of data descriptions from other sources (useful for converting existing data definitions from a DBMS, for example).
- Control reports on the update activity.
- A query and reporting facility.
- A facility for generating data definitions for the DBMS, the programming language in use, and various productivity aids.
- A generator of recompilation requests in answer to the question: "Given that such-and-such a record or element has been changed, which programs need to be changed and/or recompiled?"
- A test/production version control facility.

Figure 2 is the data model that underlies the data dictionary. The model covers not only the data definitions, but also the process definitions (programs, conversations, batch jobs) that use the data definitions. Figures 3 through 6 show sample outputs from the data dictionary.

CHARACTERISTICS OF DATA DICTIONARIES

Data dictionaries can be characterized by the type of information they contain (data elements, records, or other); how they interface to other facilities; whether they are active or passive; and how they assist in version control.

Information Content

A minimal data dictionary has facilities for describing data **elements and groups** of data elements. A data element is one that cannot be further subdivided, such as an account number, an amount, a job title, a department name, an estimated delivery date. Each data element is described only once in the data dictionary.

Figure 1 **Sample Data Dictionary System Flow**

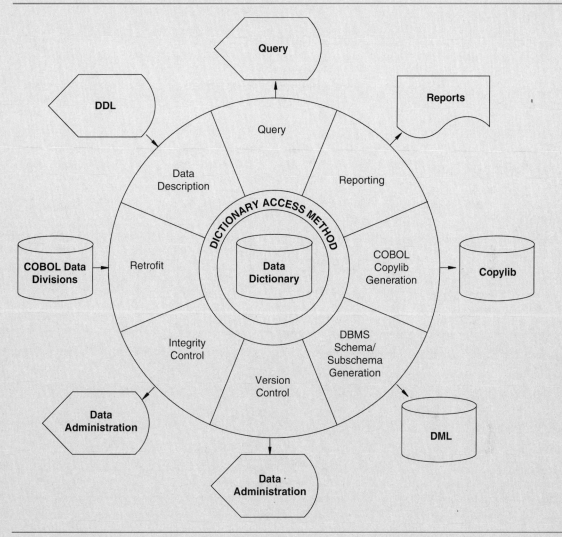

A data group is a record, a segment, or a row of a table made up of several data elements. It can also, in most systems, be a partial record made up of several elements that belong together. An address, for example, is a group made up of a number, a street, a city, a state or country, and a ZIP or other postal code. A higher-level group such as a record can be made up of a mixture of data elements and other groups.

Even if a data element or a data group is used in many different records, each of them is described only once in the dictionary. Each data element has

Figure 2 **Data Model for a Data Dictionary**

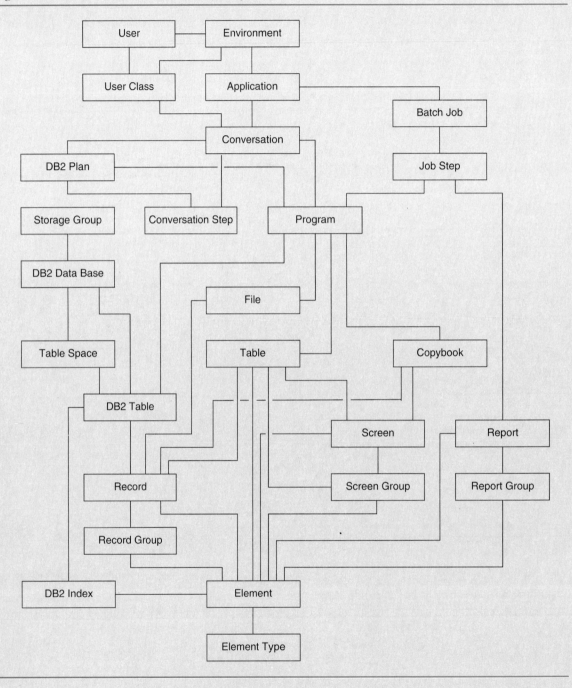

Figure 3 **Sample Element Description**

This example is taken from a data dictionary that does not support data type analysis as described in Chapter 14.

```
PERSONNEL                      INSTALLATION  TOOL                    D710
PAYROLL                         SUBURBAN PUMPS                    WMES0041
                    DATA  ELEMENT - SCREEN-ERR-MSG-NUM

PREPARED BY:  R. WESTERGREN      DATE: 27APR89         VERSION: 1.1      PAGE 1
APPROVED BY:  JIMMY WEBER        DATE: 05MAY89          STATUS:  D
DESCRIPTION: MES error message number.  This field will appear in MES symbolic
             maps and will be decoded by MES into the corresponding error message
             field on the screen.


TYPE:           MSG-NUM (Message Number -- see D711)


            Length     Format       Precision   Structure
            ------     ------       ---------   ---------
SCREEN-        5       ALPHA                       09
REPORT-        5       ALPHA                       09
INTERNAL-      4       NUM                                   Usage: C


DB2 COLUMN NAME:
COBOL NAME:                SCREEN-ERR-MSG-NUM
ASM NAME:
PL/1 NAME:


HORIZONTAL LITERAL:               Error Message Number
SHORT LITERAL:                    Err Num
FIRST VERTICAL COLUMN HEADING:    Err
SECOND VERTICAL COLUMN HEADING:   Num
THIRD VERTICAL COLUMN HEADING:


SCREEN INITIAL VALUE:             Spaces
INTERNAL INITIAL VALUE:           0 (Zero)


VALIDATION RULES
----------------


TEST TYPE:      Range
FROM:           -9999      TO:      +9999


DECODE TABLE NAME:  Table name provided in the screen definition defaulted by SM with
                    a name for the application.

                    System-level message table (for sign-on, sign-off and security
                    checking) will be WMESTMSG.
```

Figure 4 **Sample Segment Description**

```
REPORT NO. : RPT0760                                          PAGE 001
SEGMENT    : D610.UERRMSGS
IMAGE      : INTERNAL                                         12DEC93
                        SEGMENT REPORTING (COBOL)


                   SEGMENT CHARACTERISTICS
- - - - - - - - - - - - - - - - - - - - - - - - - - - - - - - - - - - - -
  DATA LAYOUT: MES-ERROR-MSG-RECORD
  DESCRIPTION: ERROR MESSAGE RECORD LAYOUT FOR CODES TABLE.  USED BY MES TO
               DECODE ERROR MESSAGES.
               (SAME COPYBOOK AS WERMT010)
         TYPE: R
  COBOL NAME: UERRMSGS
 COBOL PREFIX: MEMR
     ASM NAME:
   ASM PREFIX:
    PL/I NAME:
  PL/I PREFIX:
       KEY ID: {D610.WERMG002}
     ASC/DESC: A
 TOTAL LENGTH: 85



                   MEMBERS
- - - - - - - - - - - - - - - - - - - - - - - - - - - - - - - - - - - - -
  DOCUMENT ID            ITEM TYPE   ITEM NAME              FMT LEN PRC USG BYT
  - - - - - - - - - - -  - - - - -   - - - - - - -          --- --- --- --- ---
  D610.WERMG002          GROUP       WERMG002
    D710.WMES0041        ELEMENT     PWBSP-SCR-ERR-MSG-NUM   N   4       C    2
    D710.DAUSR004        ELEMENT     USER-LANGUAGE           A   1            1
    D710.WMES0033        ELEMENT     MES-MSG-SEQ-NUM         N   3       D    3
    D710.WMES0057        ELEMENT     MES-ERR-MSG-DATA        A  79           79
```

a single name by which it is known to every designer and programmer. The data element description corresponds.to the characteristics of the data type described in Chapter 14. Unfortunately, many records contain two or more data elements that are of the same type. For instance, a bank transfer contains two account numbers, the "from" account and the "to" account. These two account numbers need different names and are usually considered to be two distinct data elements by the data dictionary. Very few data dictionaries existing today recognize the notion of type.

Some facilities (usually in connection with productivity aids such as report writers, program generators, fourth-generation languages, and application generators) style themselves data dictionaries, but can describe data

Figure 5 **COBOL DATA DIVISION Input
Generated from Segment Description**

```
RPT0210                                    12DEC93  17:20:01  PAGE 001
                         INSTALLATION TOOL
                          CODE GENERATION
                          COBOL COPYBOOK


***   COPYBOOK D615.UERRMSGS        IS BEING PROCESSED
***   WARNING...TOTAL LENGTH IS IGNORED ON D610.UERRMSGS
***   COBOL COPYBOOK FOR D615.UERRMSGS   HAS BEEN GENERATED WITH WARNINGS ***


COPYBOOK GENERATION PROCESSING TOTALS
            NUMBER OF COPYBOOKS REQUESTED            :  1
            NUMBER OF COPYBOOKS GENERATED SUCCESSFULLY :  0
            NUMBER OF COPYBOOKS GENERATED WITH WARNINGS:  1
            NUMBER OF COPYBOOKS GENERATED WITH ERRORS  :  0




  01  WSER-UERRMSGS
  *****************************************************************************
  *   RECORD UERRMSGS                              GENERATION DATE  12DEC93  *
  *                                                                         *
  *   ERROR MESSAGE RECORD LAYOUT FOR CODES TABLE FILE.   USED BY MES TO    *
  *   DECODE ERROR MESSAGES.                                                *
  *   SAME COPYBOOK AS WERMT010                                             *
  *                                                                         *
  *****************************************************************************
      05  WSER-WERMG002.
          10  WSER-PWBSP-SCR-ERR-MSG-NUM
                                   PIC S9(4)   COMP
                                               VALUE ZEROES.
          10  WSER-USER-LANGUAGE   PIC X       VALUE SPACES.
          10  WSER-MES-MSG-SEQ-NUM PIC 9(3)    VALUE ZEROES.
      05  WSER-MES-ERR-MSG-DATA    PIC X(79)   VALUE SPACES.
```

elements only within records. If both the customer master record and the order header contain the customer number, these facilities require that the length and type of the customer number be fully described in both places. Each customer number could be named something different, such as CUS-TOMER_NUMBER and CUST_NO, thus causing undocumented synonyms. Conversely, two different elements could be called by the same name in two different records without the so-called data dictionary objecting. In reality, such a facility is not a data dictionary but rather a facility to store record descriptions, on a par with COBOL copy libraries.

Figure 6 **Sample Cross-Reference of Where-Used Report**

```
                        SUBURBAN PUMPS
                   DATA DICTIONARY REPORTING
                   CROSS-REFERENCE WHERE-USED

 12DEC91              FOR ITEM S0000015 element              PAGE 001


 S0000015  element  ITEM-NUM
        AIN11001  group  *** DESCRIPTION REQUIRED
            AINIM10  screen  INVENTORY INQUIRY ITEM LIST
                AINILIST  step  ITEM LIST
                    AINI  conversation  INVENTORY INQUIRY
            AIN2P20  screen  ITEM INVENTORY SELECT
                AIN2LIST  step  AIN2 LIST
                    AIN2  conversation  ITEM INVENTORY MAINTENANCE
        AIN1M20  screen  INVENTORY INQUIRY MULTI-WAREHOUSE
            AINIWLIST  step  MULTI-WAREHOUSE ITEM LIST
                AINI  conversation  INVENTORY INQUIRY
        AINOD010  record  INVENTORY-ITEM-TABLE
            AINOD010  db2 table  INVENTORY ITEM TABLE
            AINOD010  copybook  INVENTORY-ITEM-TABLE
            TINOD010  db2 table  INVENTORY ITEM TABLE
            TINOD01  db2 table  INVENTORY ITEM TABLE
            TEMMTEMP  db2 table  INVENTORY ITEM TABLE
        AINOG001  group  ITEM-WHSE-AVAIL-KEY
            AINOR010  record  INVENTORY-ITEM-WHSE-AVAIL
                AINOR010  copybook  INVENTORY-ITEM-WHSE-AVAIL
                    AIOMOD  program  DB2 TABLE I/O MODULE
            SCE10001  copybook  WAREHOUSE-ITEM-RECORD
                SCE1C060  program  WAREHOUSE INVENTORY LIST
                AIN2C010  program  ITEM INVENTORY PROMPT
                    AIN2PRPT  step  AIN2 PROMPT
                        AIN2  conversation  AIN2
                WCG5I051  program  WCG5
                ATESTC01  program  TEST CONVERSATION
                ATESTC02  program  TEST DESCRIPTION
                TEMMTEMM  program  TEST TEMM PROGRAM
        SCEOD011  record  ORDER-ENTRY-LINE-TABLE
            SCEOD011  db2 table  ORDER ENTRY LINE TABLE
            SCEOD011  copybook  ORDER-ENTRY-LINE-TABLE
        SCE1M40 screen ORDER ENTRY LINE ITEM
            SCEMLINE step LINE ITEM
                SCEM conversation ORDER ENTRY MAINTENANCE
```

Minimal data dictionary facilities are present in practically all data base management systems. In addition to element and record descriptions, these dictionaries also describe other DBMS entities: file structures (the hierarchy of records going into a physical data base such as IBM's IMS); views (the results of join and project operations performed on a relational data base and presented for manipulation to a user); and so on. Because these facilities usually cannot extend their reach beyond the data base that they document, they have difficulty meeting some of the main objectives of data dictionaries.

In addition to field and record descriptions, a useful data dictionary should contain descriptions of **files, data bases, and programs** that use those files and data bases. (For this discussion, reports and screens are assimilated to files.) Thus, the data dictionary can be queried about where an element or a group is used so that the impact of a change can be analyzed. This characteristic is especially useful during the design and implementation stage of development, when data descriptions are not yet complete and definitive. On a large system, a data dictionary helps ensure that all the team members are kept up to date on seemingly minor design decisions.

In addition, those dictionaries that contain file and screen descriptions can support the generation of programming language statements required to use the screens in on-line conversations and the files in batch programs. This simplifies the task of the programmers by eliminating a tedious, uninteresting, and error-prone job of copying paper descriptions and translating them to the appropriate syntax.

Interfaces

All productivity aids such as fourth-generation languages and application generators require data descriptions, just as COBOL requires a Data Division in every program. Ideally, each data dictionary should generate the data descriptions required by each productivity aid. However, each productivity aid uses its own conventions and formats. Therefore, most data dictionaries simply provide access to the data dictionary structure, so that each installation can create programs that will format the data definitions to be accepted by those productivity aids in use at that installation. Many data dictionaries have active user groups, a good source for such programs.

Programs to format data descriptions for a productivity aid can be created only if the productivity aid in question accepts data description input in batch mode from files. If data descriptions can be entered only interactively, via a screen, then it is not very useful to have the data dictionary generate this input.

Active versus Passive Dictionaries

Dictionaries have the most merit if they are the only possible source for data descriptions. If COBOL programmers are free to choose between dictionary-generated Data Division statements and hand-coded ones, a programmer will sometimes resort to coding by hand because it is quicker, because the data dictionary has not been updated, or because the programmer has not learned about the benefits of a data dictionary. The hand-coded version may then differ from the data dictionary version of the data, negating the main benefit of the dictionary——to be an exhaustive description of all the data in an installation or on a project.

So-called passive *dictionaries* do not address this problem. *Active dictionaries* address it by forcing the programs to refer to the data dictionary whenever a data description (length, format, precision) is required. (A good example of an active dictionary is Cullinet's IDD, the data dictionary used by the IDMS data base management system.) Even for active dictionaries, the solution is only partial; it only applies to DBMS operations and not to classical files.

Another approach would be to have the data dictionary integrated with the program development system, particularly the compiler. This approach would cause a recompilation when the data dictionary is changed and force the compiler to use only the data dictionary as a source for describing data. This approach has not yet been implemented on large-scale, commercially available systems. In most cases, the only way of forcing the programmers to use the data dictionary is through procedural means.

Version Control

The last main feature of a data dictionary is the support of several versions of the same data. This feature is required because changes cannot be made instantaneously. When a record description changes, a team is set up to modify all the programs that use the record. Some programs will be changed today, others tomorrow, and some at the end of next month. The change cannot be implemented in production until all the programs are changed and the files that contain the modified record are converted to the new format. In the meanwhile, one of the programs affected by the change may need some urgent modification——perhaps because of a bug. That program will therefore need to be recompiled with the old version of the record description. Similar considerations apply during the design of a large system. Changes may be proposed by one group, evaluated by another, and finally accepted or rejected by whoever has that authority. In the meanwhile, those not immediately touched by the evaluation of the modification must continue to work with the old version of the data.

A good data dictionary therefore needs a version control facility with two or more versions of the data descriptions for test and production, together with a convenient means of transforming test data descriptions to production and vice versa.

WHERE USED IN THE LIFE CYCLE

Most data dictionaries are designed to be used during the implementation and maintenance phases of the life cycle. In these phases, programmers incorporate data definitions into programs and productivity aids, data base administrators maintain the data base descriptions, and maintenance analysts query the data dictionary as one step in evaluating where a proposed change would have an impact.

Attempts have been made to use the same dictionaries in the design phase of a project to record data design decisions both for user approval at the end of design and to carry over to the implementation phase. Attempts have also been made to use data dictionaries to support entity-relationship modeling. In both cases, problems have arisen. The main difficulty is that during data modeling and data design some of the characteristics of data captured by a good implementation-level data dictionary are not known. Physical representation format is one of these characteristics.

The current trend is for CASE tools to provide their own data dictionary or data description facilities and for the contents of the design-level dictionary to be transportable to an implementation-level dictionary. The ability to transport data from the design level to the implementation level also implies that existing data descriptions can be transported from the implementation-level dictionary for reuse by design teams who are creating systems that use, at least in part, existing data. This feature, however, is not widely available in CASE tools.

EXISTING TOOLS

Since the advent of CASE tools, independent data dictionary software products have decreased in importance, although they may still exist in installations that acquired them in the late 1970s or early 1980s.

All data base management systems have some type of data dictionary function, as do fourth-generation languages. Some of these facilities fall short, however, because elementary data descriptions must be repeated for each record in which the element appears. Thus, unless good naming conventions are strongly enforced, these facilities do not provide reliable where-used cross-reference listings.

All CASE tools have some dictionary functionality. How installation-oriented it is (and how useful it will be for producing COBOL and DBMS data descriptions as well as in maintenance) often depends on the origin of the CASE tool. If the tool originated as a program generator, dictionary functions are likely to be strong; if it came from an analysis/modeling tool, those functions are likely to be weaker.

CRITERIA FOR USE

The implementation and enforcement of a single data dictionary by the entire IS department is a major undertaking. It implies reorganizing part of the department to create a data administration function with new job descriptions, possibly hiring experienced data administrators, and training all the analysts and programmers in the use of the data dictionary. Such a step should not be undertaken without top IS management commitment.

If a data administration function as such does not exist for the IS department, each major development project must provide its own data administration function by acquiring the data dictionary software and designating project team members to keep the data dictionary up to date and enforce its use. Even if no data dictionary software is available in the department, a minimal system providing most of the functions required during development of a single project can easily be developed. The project team can use whatever data description facilities are available in a CASE tool. Alternatively, the team can use a fourth-generation language to create a data dictionary that will accept data element, record, screen and report descriptions; print them out; and generate DBMS, COBOL, and other tool output.

Selected Readings

Ross, Ronald G. *Data Dictionaries & Data Administration*. New York: AMA-
    COM, 1981.
    This book is the most useful reference on data dictionaries.

EXERCISES

1. Review and critique the data dictionary functions of tools that you have available:
   a. CASE tool
   b. Micro-based DBMS (dBase III, Rbase)
   c. Fourth-generation language (Focus, Oracle)

2. Design a minimal-function data dictionary to cover the entity-relationship and data element design components of this book. Evaluate the effort to program and test such a system on a micro-based DBMS such as dBase III.

3. Use a CASE-based data dictionary function to document one of the data structures established when you studied entity-relationship modeling (described in Section V). Create a complete set of paper reports from the dictionary. Contrast the use of paper output and on-line query. Contrast the features of the CASE tool with those you would expect to find in an installation-oriented data dictionary.

Value Chain Analysis

THE VALUE CHAIN

All organizations consist of a collection of value activities that are performed to design, produce, market, deliver, and support their products or services. Value activities can be viewed as building blocks by which an organization creates products or provides services valuable to its customers. An organization's value activities can be listed systematically using the value chain framework. Developing the value chain and analyzing value activities in detail provides the analyst with an understanding of how an organization performs its activities, how activities interact, and what the relative importance of each activity is.

VALUE CHAIN COMPONENTS

The value chain consists of primary and support activities and added value, as illustrated in Figure A1–1. Primary activities are activities involved in the physical creation of the product or service, its sale and delivery to the buyer, and the support after the sale. Support activities complement the primary activities by providing such functions as human resources, procurement, technology development, and administrative support. Added value, sometimes called margin, is the difference between the collective cost of the value activities and the amount customers are willing to pay for the organization's product or service. In a profit-making organization, added value is the equivalent of pretax profit. In a not-for-profit organization, added value represents the benefits achieved less the total cost of creating such benefits.

Primary Activities

There are five generic categories of primary activities involved in any industry:

- Inbound logistics includes activities associated with receiving, storing, and disseminating materials and other inputs necessary to create the product or service. Examples are warehousing and inventory control.

- Operations activities are associated with transforming inputs into the final product form. Examples are such activities as machining, assembly, and packaging.

Figure A1–1 **Value Chain**

- Outbound logistics activities are associated with collecting, storing, and distributing the product to customers. Examples are activities such as finished goods warehousing, order processing, and delivery.

- Marketing and sales activities are associated with methods of persuading buyers to purchase a product or service and providing them with the means to do so. Examples are activities such as advertising, sales efforts, and retailing.

- Service activities are associated with providing after-sales services such as installation, repair, or follow-up services, which enhance or maintain the value of the product or service delivered.

Each cell can be broken down into distinct activities. Figure A1–2 illustrates how operations activities might be listed for a manufacturer of chocolate bars.

Support Activities

Support activities can be divided into four generic categories:

- Procurement activities are associated with the acquisition of all inputs necessary to produce the product or provide the service. Examples include activities such as purchasing raw materials, searching for new supplier sources, and monitoring supplier performance.

- Technology development activities are associated with the design and creation of the product or service. Examples are activities such as product design, technology selection, or development of a new service line.

- Human resource management activities are associated with all aspects of hiring, training, evaluating, and rewarding personnel. Examples are activities such as hiring, administering benefit programs, or conducting training programs.

Figure A1–2 **Value Chain of Chocolate Manufacturer**

- Firm infrastructure activities are those activities that collectively support all elements in the value chain. Examples are activities such as general management, planning, finance, and legal.

The dotted lines for the support activities in Figure A1–2 reflect the fact that procurement, technology development, and human resource management are often associated with specific primary activities as well as supportive of the entire value chain. Firm infrastructure is not associated with specific primary activities but supports the entire value chain.

APPLYING VALUE CHAIN ANALYSIS

Figure A1–3 is a completed value chain for a commercial airline company, ASAP. The information necessary to prepare such a value chain is usually gathered through interviews with user personnel. Analysts familiar with a particular industry are able to determine quickly whether the lists of activities in each category of the value chain are complete, since similar activity lists will be found in the value chains of companies in the same business.

Although the identification of value chain activities is sometimes difficult, the basic principle is to look for the following types of activities:

- Activities that have a high potential for increasing the added value of an organization's product or service.

Figure A1–3 **Completed Value Chain for Airline Company**

	Inbound Logistics	Operations	Outbound Logistics	Sales and Marketing	Service
Firm Infrastructure		• Assess Government Regulation • Analyze Route Structure • Develop Market Forecasting Model			
Human Resources Management	• Hire and Train Personnel • Set Wages and Work Rules	• Schedule and Supervise Crews - Flight - Ground		• Recruit, Hire and Train Marketing/ Sales Force	
Technology Development	• Research Ticketing and Resevations • Research Meal Preparation		• Reassess Information Needs - Reservations - Operations - Accounting/ Billing	• Develop Feedback for Marketing • Develop Media Coverage	
Procurement	• Obtain Aircraft Spare Parts and Ground Equipment • Obtain Airport Terminal Locations • Purchase Insurance	• Purchase Meals • Purchase Fuel • Purchase Baggage Handling Equipment • Purchase Automated Reservation Systems		• Buy Media	
	• Manage Spare Parts Inventory • Manage Meal Logistics	• Handle Baggage • Maintain Equipment • Operate Ticket Counter • Operate Gates • Operate On-Board Systems • Schedule Maint'ce	• Schedule Routes • Manage Reservations • Manage Downtime Operations	• Determine Pricing Strategy • Determine Commissions • Ensure Travel Agent Relationship • Monitor Contribution of Scheduling	• Ensure On-Time Strategy • Continue Interlining Service • Offer Other Customer Services

- Activities that represent a significant or growing portion of cost within the organization.

Functions such as operations or marketing contain broad activities that must be further subdivided into several levels of narrowing activities in order to assist an analyst's understanding. The level to which activities should be subdivided depends on the purpose for which the value chain is being created. For example, high-level value chains are often used to compare and contrast firms in the same industry. A more detailed value chain could point analysts to areas in which opportunities to reduce costs or increase added value exist.

In any situation, value chains help analysts identify areas for further study and possible improvement. For example, ASAP's value chain may suggest questions such as the following:

- How is baggage handled? Can the activity be automated?
- Are self-ticketing machines used?

- What benefits might be derived from a higher investment in personnel training?
- How is scheduling performed?

In the ASAP example, if scheduling were selected as an activity that would benefit from further study, it would be analyzed using either a hierarchical technique (see the Technique to Section I) or data flow diagram (see the Technique to Section III). For example, a data flow diagram for the scheduling activity is illustrated in Figure A1–4. The data flow diagram has broken down the scheduling activity, identified all inputs and outputs, and identified interfaces with other activities. Interfaces can be within or outside the organization.

- Internal interfaces such as sales and load data come from ASAP's sales function. Passenger service provides information concerning customer service and requests for new service. Maintenance provides the aircraft maintenance schedule. Human resources provides training and monitors governmental or union rules.

  The completed schedule contains information required by other functions. Marketing needs the schedule to develop sales strategies, maintenance needs the schedule to plan maintenance schedules, human resources needs the schedule to schedule flight crews and ground personnel, and information services must update its files for the on-line reservation system.

- In this example, there is only one external interface. ASAP's selection of routes and departure times depends in part on the actions of its competitors. Thus, information on competitors' routes and schedules is used in the determination of ASAP's route frequency and times.

Analysis of activities, their inputs and outputs, and their interfaces can help uncover operational inefficiencies. Changing how an activity is performed or deleting unnecessary steps can enhance efficiency and reduce cost. Sources of customer dissatisfaction can also be identified. For example, if customer requests were missing from ASAP's scheduling activity, an analyst would probably recommend that it be used as an input to the process of selecting routes and flight times.

Review of the data flow diagram for ASAP's scheduling activity might prompt questions such as the following:

- Is the sales data captured by marketing adequate for analyzing routes?
- Is ASAP receiving a large number of customer complaints?
- How effectively does ASAP monitor the scheduling and pricing actions of its competitors?
- Are ASAP's maintenance costs in line with industry standards?
- Which scheduling activities can be improved by automation?

Figure A1–4 **Data Flow Diagram of ASAP Scheduling Activity**

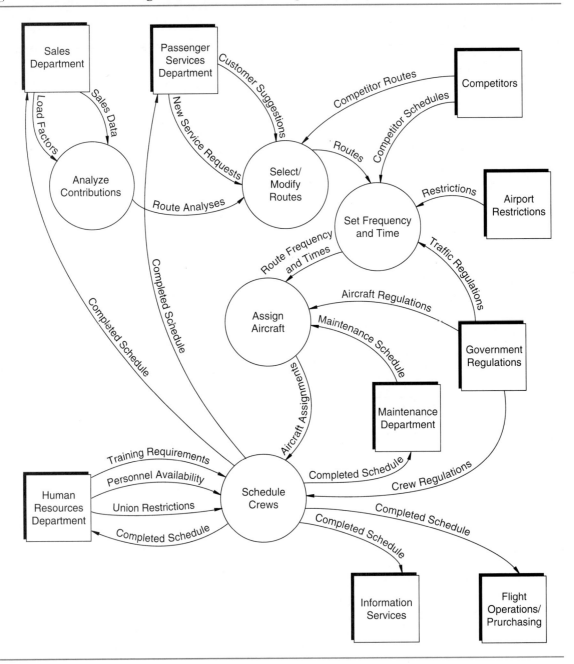

Figure A1–5 **ASAP Cost Map**

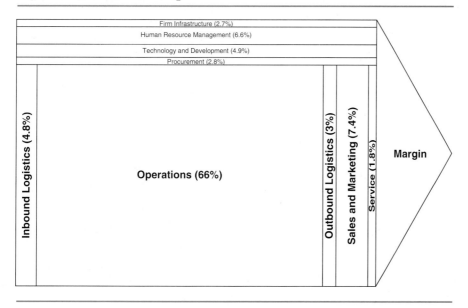

Answers to these and other questions would help analysts generate recommendations to improve ASAP's business. Recommendations for change would then become a part of ASAP's business plans.

COST ANALYSIS TOOLS

Three cost analysis tools form a systematic framework for cost analysis:

- Cost maps
- Cost drivers
- Asset maps

All three draw information from the value chain. Cost maps associate cost with the value activities, and asset maps associate assets with the value activities. Cost drivers are factors that influence the cost of an activity, causing it to increase or decrease.

Cost Maps

Cost maps express the cost of each activity in terms of percentages of the total cost. The cost map for ASAP is illustrated in Figure A1–5. Preparing a cost map requires that costs be distributed to specific value activities. In practice, this often requires a redistribution of costs from the way they are kept in the accounting records because, in many cases, costs are not classified pre-

Figure A1–6 **ASAP Cost Map with Breakdown of Operations Activity**

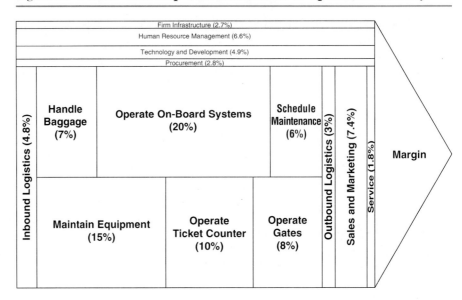

cisely according to activities. For example, the salary of an aircraft maintenance manager may be classified as "management salaries" when in reality 85 percent of the salary should be associated with the maintenance activity.

Activities on the cost map may be further aggregated or disaggregated in accordance with the following guidelines:

- Disaggregate, or separate, activities that represent significant or rapidly growing percentages of cost

- Aggregate, or group, activities that represent small, stagnant, or decreasing percentages of cost

Applying these guidelines to ASAP, the operations activity, which represents 66 percent of the costs, would be separated into its six components, as illustrated in Figure A1–6.

Cost maps are useful for identifying high-cost activities as targets for cost reduction efforts. For example, 20 percent of ASAP's operations costs are spent in the operation of on-board systems. Significant savings could result if this activity could be performed more efficiently.

Cost maps are also useful for making comparisons between competitors in a particular industry. Although the information to make precise comparisons is not always readily obtainable, much of it is public information. What is not available publicly can be obtained or imputed through observation or other means. For example, the number of maintenance employees and their average wage may have been disclosed in a newspaper article concerning a competitor's labor contract negotiations. This information, combined with knowledge of the

Figure A1–7 **Generic Cost Drivers**

Generic Cost Driver	Description	Examples
Scale	Cost of activities are often subject to different efficiencies at different volumes.	Longer production runs, buying in bulk.
Learning	Cost of an activity can decline over time due to learning that increases efficiency.	Work is better scheduled and organized once worker is familiar with job details.
Capacity Utilization	Fixed costs can create a penalty for underutilization.	Selling excess facilities and skills.
Linkages	The cost of an activity is frequently affected by how other activities are performed.	Inspection and after-sale service linkages with suppliers.
Interrelationships	Cost can be affected by interrelationships with other SBUs within a firm.	Sharing an activity such as order processing between two SBUs.
Integration	The level of vertical integration in an activity may influence its cost.	Owing a service instead of contracting out, e.g., payroll.
Timing	When an activity is performed can affect its costs.	Raw materials may be cheaper at certain times of the year. Being the first in the market helps establish a brand name.
Discretionary Policies	Policy choices that a firm makes will affect activities' costs.	Service policies, wages paid, quality policies.
Location	The geographical location of an activity can affect its cost.	Differing cost of labor, raw materials, energy, and transportation.
Institutional Factors	Usually outside firm's control. This cost driver can influence the cost of an activity very heavily.	Government regulations, unionization.

number of airplanes in the competitor's fleet by type and age may be enough to estimate their maintenance costs with a sufficient degree of accuracy.

An organization derives important information about itself by classifying its costs according to activities. Very often, organizations may find that certain activities cost them much more than was thought. Usually, there is a tendency to focus cost improvement efforts on primary activities. A cost map, however, may indicate that support activities represent a larger portion of total costs than was thought and are thus a more logical target for cost reduction efforts.

Cost Drivers

Cost drivers are factors that influence the cost of an activity. One way to reduce costs is to work on changing cost drivers. Cost drivers affect the unit cost, not the total cost, of an activity. Cost drivers can cause unit costs to increase or decrease. Categories of generic cost drivers, together with examples of each, are illustrated in Figure A1–7. The generic categories are useful as a starting point for identifying cost drivers for an activity.

Scale. The cost of value activities often exhibits different levels of efficiency at different volume levels. For example, if the same item is requested by several different departments, purchasing them together in one order from a single vendor could result in lower unit cost because of price concessions from the vendor and a reduction of effort within the purchasing department.

Learning. The cost of an activity can decrease over time as a result of organizational learning that increases efficiency. For example, when a new product is manufactured, production rates are lower and scrap rates higher at first because employees are not familiar with the processing steps and make more mistakes. As they become more familiar with the process, they produce items faster and better, thus reducing the item's unit cost.

Capacity Utilization. When a value activity has a substantial fixed cost, a penalty is paid for underutilized capacity. Resources not utilized represent the loss of potential revenues. For example, every empty seat on an ASAP flight represents revenue lost forever. Controlling underutilization requires studying patterns of usage and taking steps to minimize fixed costs. In the ASAP example, it may be possible to increase utilization by either filling empty seats with passengers flying on incentive fares or by using smaller planes on routes on which current capacity is chronically underutilized.

Linkages. The cost of an activity is frequently affected by the way another activity is performed. Such connections between activities are called linkages. Two broad types of linkages exist: internal (within the organization's value chain) and external (within the value chains of other organizations, for example, buyers or suppliers). Linkages create the opportunity to lower the combined cost of linked activities. ASAP's inventory management system is an example of an external linkage acting as a cost driver. ASAP's suppliers keep an inventory of spare parts in anticipation of orders from ASAP, parts that would otherwise need to be held in ASAP's inventory. ASAP also keeps an inventory of the same parts in case the suppliers are out of stock when maintenance needs to be performed. The inventory levels for both ASAP and its suppliers could be reduced if the suppliers were aware of ASAP's demand patterns. Because spare parts for aircraft can be expensive, exploiting the linkage between ASAP and its suppliers could produce substantial savings.

Interrelationships. Any form of sharing among strategic business units (SBUs) represents an interrelationship. The most significant form of interrelationship is when a value activity can be shared with other SBUs. In ASAP, there are two SBUs: cargo and passenger service. Maintenance for the planes used by both SBUs are performed by the same maintenance unit. Sharing resources is a potential means of achieving economies of scale, decreasing the learning curve, and increasing capacity utilization.

Integration. Activities can be performed by an organization's own employees or by external vendors. Integration (performing an activity in-house) may be more cost-effective for some activities and deintegration (engaging external vendors to perform all or part of an activity) may be the better choice for other activities. This choice is commonly called the "make or buy" decision. For example, meals aboard ASAP's flights are prepared by an external caterer. ASAP could operate a catering service of its own and integrate the preparation of meals into its operations if it would be beneficial to do so.

Timing. The cost of a value activity is often affected by the timing of its acquisition or performance. For example, ASAP's fuel may be purchased at a lower cost during certain times of the year, or at times when the price is at a low point because of excess supplies. Many companies will purchase computer time from third parties during nighttime hours, when it is offered at the lowest price.

Discretionary Policies. Discretionary policies are those that management can set and change almost at will. Employee benefits, high quality, and liberal merchandise return policies are examples of how discretionary policies can affect costs.

Location. The location of a value activity can affect its cost in several ways. The prevailing cost of employees, office space, raw materials, and energy can vary widely by country or by region within a country.

Institutional Factors. Institutional factors (e.g., governmental regulations, taxes, labor laws) are the final major cost driver. They can be significant factors for some industries. Favorable institutional factors such as tax incentives can lower costs. Unfavorable factors such as tariffs can increase costs. For example, strict government regulations for the maintenance of aircraft have a heavy cost impact on ASAP.

Identifying cost drivers and their effect is not always an easy task. Three methods are usually employed in practice:

* Quantitative Measures.

    One method often used is to measure the efficiency of an activity using quantitative nonmonetary measures such as yield, scrap rates, and labor hours to probe the sources of cost changes in a value activity. For example, if it were determined that the average time to take a customer's reservation by telephone was too high, steps could be taken to reduce it, possibly by investing in additional employee training.

* Internal Experience.

    Another method is to examine an organization's internal experience. Analyzing cost levels at different levels of activity may help to clarify scale economies.

Figure A1–8 **Cost Drivers**

	Inbound Logistics	Operations	Outbound Logistics	Sales and Marketing	Service
Firm Infrastructure			• Institutional Factors (Government Regulations, etc.)		

Human Resources Management			• Human Resource Policies
			  - Unions
			  - Hiring Policies		

Technology Development			• Global Scale		
Procurement			• Procurement Policies • Linkages with Suppliers • Global Purchasing Scale		

	• Location
	• Linkage with Suppliers
	• Timing
		• Learning
		• Policy Choices
		• Timing of
		  - Asset
		  - Purchases
		• Economies of Scale
			• Order Size
			• Interrelationships
			• Global Scale
				• National Scale (Advertising)
				• Buyer Concentration
					• Local Scale (Interlining Services)
					• Interrelationships with Other Lines of Business

- Interviews with Experts.

     Individuals who have extensive knowledge of a value activity can answer "what if" questions about the effects of changing various cost parameters. For example, the head of ASAP's marketing and sales department could answer such questions as:

     What if we exclude travel agents and sell tickets directly to passengers?

     What if we increase or reduce the permanent sales force?

     What if we establish a marketing link with a national carrier?

     Answers to such questions can help an analyst determine if there are integration, capacity utilization, or linkage cost drivers for the marketing and sales activities. Decision support systems are often very helpful in analyzing such questions as these.

Figure A1–8 shows the cost drivers for some of ASAP's major activities. By knowing what drives the cost of an activity, ASAP's staff can take steps to reduce the cost. For example, if learning is a cost driver in some of the operations activities, then hiring more experienced personnel or starting a more

Figure A1–9 **ASAP Asset Map**

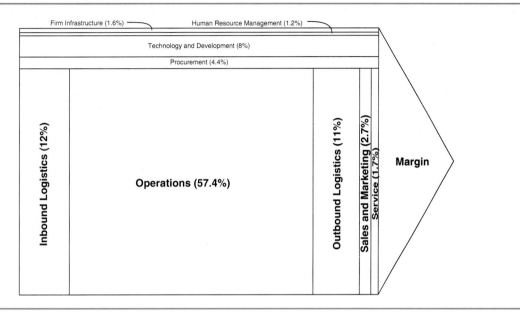

comprehensive training program should be considered. Locating its reservations clerks and supporting computers in a low-cost region of the country may drive down the costs of the reservations activity.

Cost drivers are key in helping an organization analyze its costs. Cost maps associate costs with value activities and highlight high-cost activities. Cost drivers help the analyst understand factors affecting costs so that steps can be taken to control them.

Asset Maps

Asset maps are similar to cost maps. However, instead of assigning costs to value activities, assets are assigned. On the asset map, assets for each value activity are assigned as a percentage of total assets, both fixed and current. Figure A1–9 is the asset map for ASAP.

Assets should be assigned to the activities that employ, control, or greatly affect their use. Like costs, information on the value of assets can be extracted from the accounting records. Asset accounts must usually be regrouped to correspond to activities. For example, ASAP's motor vehicle asset account would be assigned to several activities. Luggage trucks would be assigned to baggage handling, fuel trucks to equipment maintenance, and food trucks to managing meal logistics.

Like cost maps, asset maps are most commonly used for comparison with competitors. The main objective in comparing asset maps is to highlight any unusual allocation of assets in competitor organizations. This could provide some insight into the competitors' strategies. If ASAP discovers that a competitor who normally purchases its airplanes suddenly leases several new ones instead, it may mean that the competitor is planning to replace the new planes in a short period of time or that it is trying to conserve its capital for some reason.

Summary

The objective of value chain analysis is to help an organization better understand its activities and costs and search for ways to enhance its position in the competitive arena. The value chain and analysis of value activities are the base on which the other tools are built. In building value chains, primary and support value activities are identified, categorized, and analyzed. Costs and assets are assigned to value activities in building cost and asset maps. The costs of each activity are expressed as a percentage of total costs and total assets, respectively. To reduce costs, the behavior of costs must first be understood. Identification of cost drivers for each value activity assists in the process of understanding cost behavior. Taken collectively, the tools discussed in this appendix can be of great help to analysts searching for opportunities to apply information technology.

State Transition Diagrams

State transition diagrams are used to represent the behavior of so-called *finite-state machines*. Finite-state machines are data entities, business transactions, or system components (such as conversations) that can take on any one of a finite number of states. These states have specific transactions that cause the entity to make a transition from one state to another. State transition diagrams are widely used in systems software; they are applicable to many other fields but are generally not understood by many analysts.

An example of a state transition diagram is given in Figure A2–1. The schematic represents the state of a person relative to a corporate retirement plan and the various transactions that can affect that state. The possible states are represented by circles labeled with the designation of the state, and the transitions by the labeled arcs between states. The figure shows that a person who is fully vested and 65 years old or more can apply for benefits and become retired. A person who is not fully vested and leaves the company is eliminated from the plan.

Another example of the use of a state diagram is given in Figure A2–2. This graph represents part of a parser of a COBOL compiler. (A parser is the part of a compiler that recognizes elements of the language in the source code and validates that these elements obey the language's syntax.) Most of the circles are not labeled; this is because the intermediate states are only useful as partial steps towards verifying that an entire COBOL statement is correct. Errors (unauthorized transitions) are assumed to be processed by a subroutine, which is not represented on this diagram.

Figure A2–3 represents a lower level of parsing for the COBOL compiler, that which isolates a word and determines whether it is a reserved COBOL word, a valid data name, or a numeric or text literal. The state machine represented by this diagram can thus be used by the one represented in Figure A2–2.

An alternative format for state transition diagrams is the fence diagram, illustrated in Figure A2–4. This figure reproduces the retirement plan example, but with states being represented by vertical lines and transitions by arrows drawn between lines.

Figure A2–1 **State Transition Diagram for Retirement System**

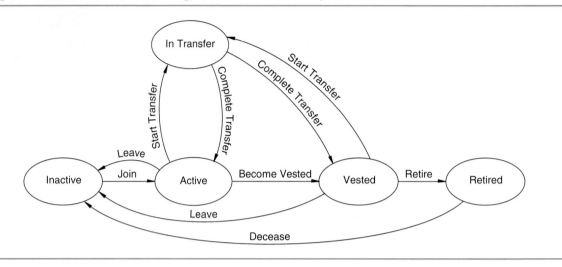

Figure A2–2 **State Transition Diagram for COBOL Parser (Partial), Version 1**

Figure A2–3 **State Transition Diagram for COBOL Parser (Partial), Version 2**

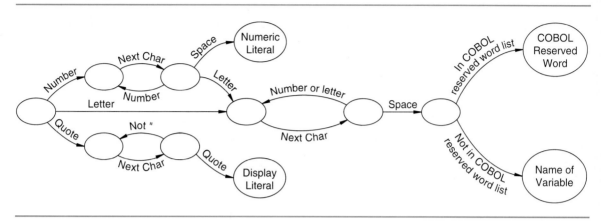

Figure A2–4 **Fence Diagram for Retirement System**

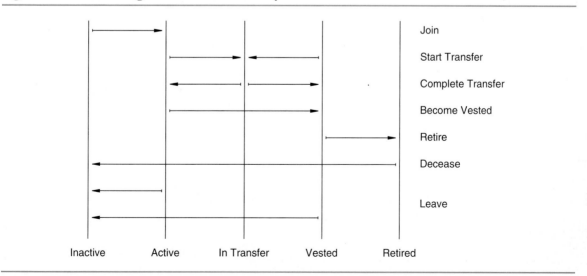

Figure A2–5 **State Transition Matrix**

State	0	1	2	3	4	5	6	7	8	9	10	11
Transition:												
Number	1		1									
Letter	7		7						7			
Quote	4					6			7			
Not Quote					4							
Next Character		2			5			8				
Space			3							9		
In Table										10		
Not in Table										11		
Final				F			F				F	F

Both types of diagrams are excellent communications tools. For rigorous analysis, another form of representation, the state transition matrix (see Figure A2–5), may be useful. This matrix represents states along one dimension and inputs (or attempted transitions) along the other. In this matrix, each cell must be filled in with the next state reached (or an error indication) and the other actions to be taken, such as the creation of an output message.

State transition diagrams are useful whenever the entity to be analyzed can take on five or more states and when the logic for accepting and processing transactions is complex and depends heavily on the state variable. For instance, whereas yesterday's transaction systems guided the operator heavily through a menu-driven, form-filling dialog, today's transaction systems tend to give much more freedom to the user in selecting the next course of action. Consequently, many more unpredictable sequences of events may arise; finite-state machines are excellent for analyzing how these events should be processed.

A limitation of state transition diagrams is that they appear to be able to represent only one variable. When the entity being processed has two independent variables, either two independent state transition diagrams (with two separate sets of transitions) are required or the state variable must be transformed into a single two-dimensional variable. This was implicitly done for the retirement illustration, where the states of vestedness and the age were combined (e.g., "fully vested" and "over sixty-five").

One of the advantages of finite-state machines is that they are quite easy to program in a generalized way, so modifying the state transition logic only requires updating a table in memory, representing the state transition matrix.

3

Computer Graphics

INTRODUCTION

In his landmark book, *The Visual Display of Quantitative Information,* Edward R. Tufte gives the following reasons why a graphical display of quantitative results is often much more effective than a numerical display:

> Modern data graphics can do much more than simply substitute for small statistical tables. At their best, graphics are instruments for reasoning about quantitative information. Often the most effective way to describe, explore, and summarize a set of numbers—even a very large set—is to look at pictures of those numbers. Furthermore, of all methods for analyzing and communicating statistical information, well-designed data graphics are usually the simplest and at the same time the most powerful.[1]

Information from today's computer systems is often presented in the form of graphs. Current display technology and software tools have made it relatively easy to accommodate a user's preference for a graphical display of output in place of or in addition to numerical displays. Graphical presentation of computer output is most often found in decision support systems (DSS) and executive information systems (EIS).

Writing of the importance of graphical presentations for EIS, John F. Rockart and David W. De Long said:

> The availability of new presentation formats—particularly graphics—has an important impact on the way executives think about information. But graphics is not the only formatting advantage provided by the computer. The CEO at one major food distributor took advantage of the computer's ability to combine tabular, text, and graphic data on the same page to satisfy his idiosyncratic way of looking at data.
>
> Most commonly, graphics are used for standard performance reports or to present the results of ad-hoc queries. The president of Banco Internacional found that a graphic display of profits versus goals and forecasts provided a picture over time and revealed dynamics of the business he had not previously recognized. Derwyn Phillips, Gillette's executive vice president, implemented his EIS largely to review performance reports graphically. Phillips believes that executives can get too caught up in minor variances when looking only at numbers. The key is in seeing trends, he says, not minor blips, and graphs help management do that.[2]

In a DSS or EIS environment, it is frequently a single user who decides on output format designs, depending on his or her individual preferences. In some cases, the IS analyst may not be involved in the process at all. There will, however, be many opportunities for the IS analyst to assist users in selecting a graphical presentation format. Thus, it is important for IS analysts to be aware of good design principles for the presentation of quantitative information in a graphical format.

TYPES OF GRAPHS

There are several types of graphs encountered in practice. Each is discussed briefly and illustrated in Figures A3–1 through A3–9.

- Pie charts are used to show the proportions of components to the whole. The graphic can give a much better sense of the relative importance of a given component than if one merely views a table of numbers. This is illustrated in Figure A3–1. Figure A3–2 is an "exploded" pie chart, used to draw the attention of the viewer to one of the components.

- Line graphs are used to plot the interaction of two variables on x and y coordinates as illustrated in Figure A3–3. It is customary to plot the independent variable along the x-axis and the dependent variable on the y-axis. Figure A3–4 overlays another line graph on the first so that the user can easily compare two different years.

- Time series graphs are commonly used to show how a parameter varies over time. Time is the independent variable and is thus shown along the x-axis. Figure A3–5 is an example.

- Bar graphs are often used in place of line graphs, for example, highlighting changes in magnitude (see Figure A3–6). Bar graphs can also be in stacked format, as shown in Figure A3–7.

- A specialized form of bar graph is the histogram (see Figure A3–8). This type of graphic shows a frequency distribution of the dependent variable. (Ordinary bar graphs are often also incorrectly called histograms.)

- Scatter diagrams are used to plot x-y coordinates of two variables that are believed to correlate statistically with each other. Once the scatter diagram is prepared, the viewer can choose between various standard statistical techniques to determine the degree of correlation (see Figure A3–9).

GRAPHICAL EXCELLENCE

The design of a graph is an important factor in whether it will communicate effectively. Edward Tufte lists five general principles of graphical excellence that apply equally well in the more specific case of computer graphics design:

> Graphical excellence is the well-designed presentation of interesting data—a matter of *substance*, of *statistics*, and of *design.*

Figure A3–1 **Simple Pie Chart**

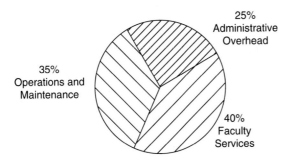

**Ivy University
1990 Operating Budget**

25%
Administrative
Overhead

35%
Operations and
Maintenance

40%
Faculty
Services

Figure A3–2 **Exploded Pie Chart**

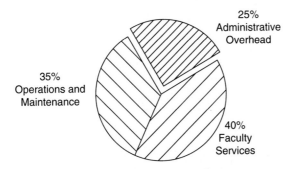

**Ivy University
1990 Operating Budget**

25%
Administrative
Overhead

35%
Operations and
Maintenance

40%
Faculty
Services

Figure A3–3 **Line Graph**

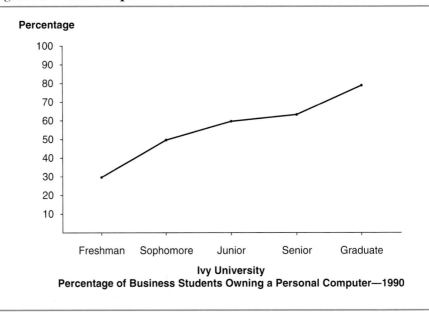

Percentage

Ivy University
Percentage of Business Students Owning a Personal Computer—1990

Figure A3–4 **Line Graph with Two Variables**

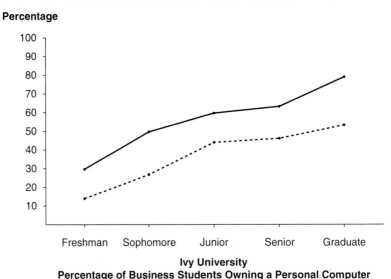

Percentage

Ivy University
Percentage of Business Students Owning a Personal Computer
1988 Compared with 1990

Figure A3–5 **Time Series Graph**

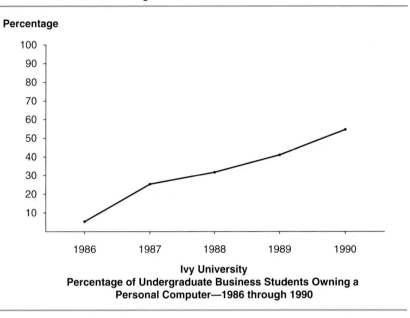

Ivy University
Percentage of Undergraduate Business Students Owning a
Personal Computer—1986 through 1990

Figure A3–6 **Bar Graph**

Two-Dimensional Standard Bar

Three-Dimensional Standard Bar

Figure A3–7 **Stacked Bar Graph**

Two-Dimensional Stacked Bar

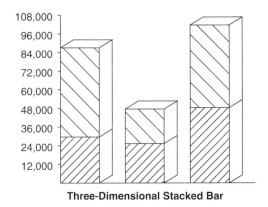

Three-Dimensional Stacked Bar

Figure A3–8 **Histogram**

Figure A3–9 **Scatter Diagram**

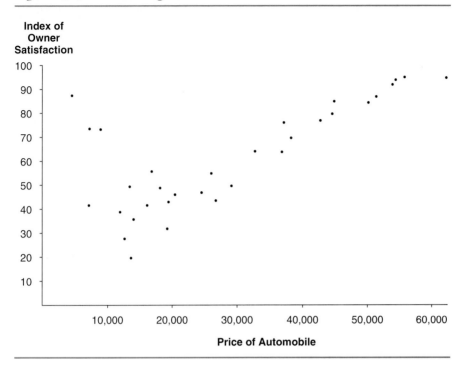

Graphical excellence consists of complex ideas communicated with clarity, precision, and efficiency.

Graphical excellence is that which gives to the viewer the greatest number of ideas in the shortest time with the least ink in the smallest space.

Graphical excellence is nearly always multivariate.

And graphical excellence requires telling the truth about the data.[3]

The last point bears some elaboration. A graphics designer can either deliberately or inadvertently miscommunicate the meaning of data behind a graph by the way the graph is designed. Designing a graph that is an accurate representation of the underlying data is called graphical integrity.

GRAPHICAL INTEGRITY

Tufte identified six principles of design that will help ensure graphical integrity:

The representation of numbers, as physically measured on the surface of the graphic itself, should be directly proportional to the numerical quantities represented.

Clear, detailed and thorough labeling should be used to defeat graphical distortion and ambiguity. Write out explanations of the data on the graphic itself. Label important events in the data.

Show data variation, not design variation.

In time-series displays of money, deflated and standardized units of monetary measurement are nearly always better than nominal units.

The number of information-carrying (variable) dimensions depicted should not exceed the number of dimensions in the data.

Graphics must not quote data out of context.[4]

Figure A3–10 is an illustration of a graph that violates some of these principles. Figure A3–11 is an example of a graph that presents the same underlying data with integrity. Tufte's book contains many wonderful illustrations and should be read by anyone with an interest in the subject of graphical displays.

Notes

1. Tufte, Edward R. *The Visual Display of Quantitative Information.* Cheshire, Connecticut: Graphics Press, 1983, p. i.

2. Rockart, John F., and De Long, David W. *Executive Support Systems—The Emergence of Top Management Computer Use.* Homewood, Illinois: Dow Jones-Irwin, 1988, p. 141.

3. Tufte, *Visual Display,* p. 51.

4. Tufte, *Visual Display,* p. 77.

Figure A3–10 **Graphic Lacking Integrity**

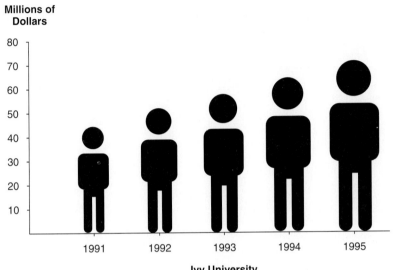

Ivy University
Increase in Administrative Overhead Expense
1991–1995

Figure A3–11 **Graphic with Integrity**

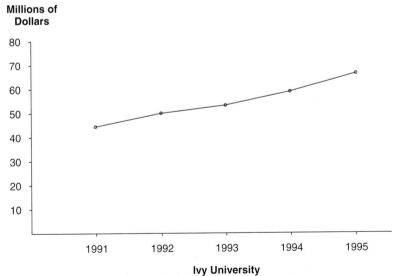

Ivy University
Increase in Administrative Overhead Expense
1991–1995, in Constant 1991 Dollars

Index

Abbreviation, data name, 422–423
Acceptance testing, 614, **641**
Access, 536
Accurate (output), **257**
Adams, D., 549
Ad hoc reporting architecture, 508
AECLAIMS system, 23
Aetna Life & Casualty, 23
Affinity analysis, 189
    matrix, 183–190
After-image logging, 498–499
AI. *See* Artificial intelligence
Airlines
    flight scheduling for, 115
    and information systems, 36
Alerts and warnings, 361–363
Alphanumeric codes, 441
Alter, Allan E., 58n
American Express, 23
American Hospital Supply, ASAP
    system, 22
Analysis
    definition of, 194
    top-down vs. bottom-up, 232
Analyst, program, 621
Analytical approach, the, 564
Analytical business process
    techniques, 43, 44
Analytical Hierarchical Process (AHP), 261
Anderson, Howard J., 12n
Animation and full-motion video, 358
Application architecture, 474
Application controls, 533–539
    specifications of, 534–535
Application development
    backlog, 106–107
    evaluation criteria for, 131
Application focus, 14
Application generators, 71
Applications prototypes, 369
Application software packages, 154
Architecture. *See also* Program design;
    type of architecture
    ad hoc reporting, 508
    application, 474
    batch, 476, 502
    for on-line updates, 494–497
    patterns of technical, 68, 69
Artificial intelligence (AI), 142–143

ASAP system, 22
Asset maps, 711–712
Assignment, 424
Associations (relationships), 466
Asynchronous (postconversation) posting,
    494–496
Atkins, William, 120, 123n
ATMs, 22
Attributes, 379, **383**
    assigning to entities, 398–403
    nonkey, 436
    as noun, not adjective, 402–403
    selecting, 397–398
Attribute types, 383
Audiovisual aids, for JAD, **214**
Audit trail, 293
August, J., 221
Authorization, 535
Automatic teller machines (ATMs), 22
Automation
    early, 38
    office, 60, 62–63
    office systems, 141–142
Automational business process
    techniques, 43, 44
Automobile manufacturers, change and, 36
Availability, 559–560
    problems of, 563–564
Available (system), **257**

Backup copy, 498
Backup procedures, 659
Bar chart, summary of, 590
Bar codes, 332
Bargaining power
    of buyers, 19
    of suppliers, 19
Bar graphs, 718, 721
    histogram, 721
    stacked, 722
Basic approach to conversion, 585
Batch, turnaround time, 556
Batch architectures, 476
Batch control, 540
Batch design document flow, 289
Batch processing, 502–514
    and procedures development, 622
    reporting, 511–514

resource consumption in, 573–574
    trends in, 521
    update and, 503–511
    validation for, 502–503
Batch program design, 502–514
    and on-line design, 579–580
Batch system, validation program,
    542–543
Batch terminal simulator, 639
Batch turnaround time, calculation of, 575
Battle order chart, 93
Before-image logging, 500
Behavior, system, 236–237
    stimuli/response context diagram, 236
Behavior model, 231
Benchmarking, 564–565
Benefits, and quality, 256
Best, Laurence J., 522
Biggs, Charles L., 120, 123n
Billing and collection system, 192–193
Birks, Evan G., 120, 123n
Blackman, Maurice, 523
Blumenthal, Michael, 15, 31n
Boehm, Barry, 9n, 10, 12n
Bottom-up analysis, 232, 379, 404–406
Boyce/Codd normal form, 408
Bricklin, Dan, 354
Brooks, Fred, 580, 619, 648, 651n, 681,
    685n
BSP. *See* Business Systems Planning
Budget and schedule, and quality,
    256–257
Buffered terminals, 314
Bug-free, 257
Bugs, 482. *See also* Debugging
Business area analysis, 227, 231–233
Business event, 300, 301
Business function/data matrix, 184
Business function data models,
    405–406
    and user views, 405–406
Business entities, identifying, 144
Business integration, achieving, 243–244
Business lines, improving position in, 21
Business organization environment, 34
Business problem understanding, 198
Business process
    composition of, 33–34
    freezing of, 39

information technology impact on, 42–47
integration of, 38–39
overall, 244
prototype development, 44–47
Business process change, 33–57.
    See also Change
Business process/entity matrix, 187
Business process reengineering (redesign), 37–38, 40–48
five steps in, 40–47
at Ford Motor Company, 38, 39
information technology levers, 42–44
principles of, 40–47
process identification, 41–42
and prototypes, 42–44, 44–47
vision and objectives, 41
Business systems
decision support, 141
departmental, 142
executive information, 143
expert, 142
management information, 140
office automation, 141
pyramid of strategic, tactical, and operational, 138, 140–143
transaction processing, 140
Business Systems Planning (BSP), 128, 156
operational process identification, 138
schematic representation of, 130
Business transaction, 301
Buyers, bargaining power of, 18, 19

Candidate keys, 434
Capacity, 170–171, **556**
and end-user computing, 170–171
production, 170
Capacity utilization, 707, 708
Capital investment analysis, 591–595
Cardinality, 462
Care Monitoring System, 114–115
Carter, Allen, 241n
CASE (computer-aided software engineering), 168, **302**
data flow diagram editor of, 267
and hierarchical programming, 94–95
and matrix affinity analysis, 183
CASE tools, 78–79
Casework, 301, **453–454**
Cash, James I., 24, 29, 70, 129
Cash Management Accounts (CMA), in securities industry, 22
Centralized and decentralized information systems departments, 66–67, 68–70
Chandy, K. Mani, 576
Change. *See also* Business process change
implementing organizational, 51–53
nature of, 48
resistance to, 48–51
social, 48
Change in the business environment, 15
Change in the nature of applications, 15
Changemasters, The, 52
Change requests, 677–679

Chen, Peter, 466, 469
Chief information officer (CIO), 64–65
Child entity, 393, 431
Cho, Chin-Kuei, 648
Clarity, and dialog design, 318
Classification, 233, 535
Clean-room methods, for testing, 645
Cleland, D., 80
Clerical work, historical, 37
CMA, 22
Coad, P., 245, 247n
COBOL, program structure, 90
COBOL DATA DIVISION input, and data dictionary, 693
Codd, E. F., 431
Codes, 437–442
documentation requirements for, 441–442
Combination of key of both parents, 433
Command, 354
Command language, 306, 312–313
sample dialog with, 312
Communications software, 171–172
Competition
historical perspective on, 14–15
and information systems change, 36
Competitive advantage, information technology and, 13–31
Competitors, rivalry among existing, 18, 19–20
Composite key, 433–434
Computer-aided design (CAD), 358
Computer-aided design and manufacturing (CAD/CAM), 15
Computer-aided engineering (CAE), 358
Computer-aided software engineering (CASE) tools, 71
Computer-based applications, data designs for, 373
Computer graphics, 717–725.
    See also Graphics
Computer operations procedures, 659
Computer personnel, resistance to, 49–51
Computers
centralization vs. decentralization and, 68–69
uses of, 14
Computer-to-computer facsimile, 357
Computing, business, 34
Concatenated keys, 432, 435
of parents, 432
Condition, 604
Configuration control, 676
Consistency, and dialog design, 318–319
Consistency of redundant information, 451–452
Constantine, Larry, 226, 267, 278, 526n
Constraints, and matrices, 188–189
Constraints on derived data, 452
Construction of Object-Oriented Programs, The, **510**
Context–sensitive help, 315
Control flow, 72, 273
Control procedures, 659
Controls
application, 528–529, 533–539

data base, 547
data entry, 540–543
direct file, 546
error sources, 529–531
general, 528
general systems, 531–533
objectives of, 535
privacy issues and individual rights, 547–549
processing, 543–546
and reporting, 546–547
and security, 527–552
sequential processing, 544–546
systems interface, 547
and transaction origination, 540
transaction processing control techniques, 539–547
Conversational mode, 485, 488
inquiry with terminal paging, 490
Conversation design, for on-line program design, 485–497
Conversation flow document, 320–322
sample, 321
Cooperative processing, 520
Corporate data model sample, 150–151
Correspondence management, 357
Cost analysis tools, 705–712
asset maps, 711–712
Cost/benefit analysis, 588–591
components of, 588–591
in feasibility studies, 116–119
worksheet, 117
Cost drivers, 707–711
generic, 707
identifying, 709–711
Cost maps, 705–707
Costs, reducing, 126
Cotterman, W. W., 158
Couger, J. D., 158
CPM (Critical Path Method), 75
Creeping commitment approach, 106
Creeping maintenance, 176
CRUD matrix, 185
Current logical system, omits the analysis of, 230
Custodial activities, 230
Cut-off processing, 518–521
Cutover, 667–668

Data
loss of, 302
Data administration, 423
Data analysis, alternative tasks and deliverables for, 377
Data base balancing, 546
Data base controls, 547
Data base design, 375
Data base integrity, 445–447
constraints, 450–453
referential integrity problem, 447–450
Data base management system (DBMS), 167, 375
Data bases, 140–141, **695**
errors in, 445–447
file conversion, 663–667
and information modeling, 380

integrating with text, voice, and graphics, 403
intertwined with world, 381
overlap with world, 381
as world model, 381
Data communications, 171–172
Data dependencies, 233
Data-dependent help, 315
Data design, 371–377, **374, 375**
goals of, 373–374
key tasks and deliverables, 374–377
management information systems (MIS) and decision support systems (DSS), 375–377
transaction processing systems, 374–375, 376
Data dictionary, 237, 238, 622
active vs. passive, 695–696
characteristics of, 688–696
COBOL DATA DIVISION input and, 693
cross-reference of where-used report, 694
data model for, 689
implementation, 687–698
in life cycle, 696–697
sample element description, 691
sample segment description, 691
sample system flow, 689
tools for, 697
use criteria, 697–698
version control of, 696
Data-driven design, 506
structure chart for, 507
Data element design, 421–444
naming elements, 421–423
Data entry
controls over, 540–543
form for, 336
types of, 541
Data entry application flow, 493
Data flow, 271, 272, 273
from external entity, 289–290
to external entity, 290–295
without external entity, 295–297
turnaround document and, 297
Data flow diagrams (DFDs), 87, 237–240, 267–278, 297, 386
constraints, 273–274
definition of, 267
equivalent techniques, 275
leveling, 97, 274
in life cycle, 269–271
marked with batch, on-line, and manual domains, 298
samples, 239, 268, 704
symbols, 271–273
use criteria, 276–278
Data generators, for testing, 633–635
Data hiding, 423–424
Data model
for bill of materials, 397
initial project, 385–388
Data modeling
at Bailis, Kronberg, Kendall & Son, 372–373
business function, 405–406

Data processing, 60
traditional placement of, 61
Data redundancy, 398–403
Data requirements
analyzing, 144–149
data classes, 145
data wage, 144
and process/data matrix, 145, 146–148
Data retrieval, 430
Data sharing, 126
Data storage, ad hoc inquiries and, 296
Data store, 228, 272
replicated, 273
symbols, 273
Data synthesis, 232
Data traffic matrix, 185
Data type analysis, 423–429
date as data types, 425–426, 427
defining operations, 426–428
definition of types, 424–425
documentation requirement for, 428–429
examples of types, 425–426
frequently used types, 426
Date, Chris, 409, 413, 415n, 443, 523
Davenport, Thomas H., 37, 40, 41n, 42, 44n, 54, 58n
Davis, A. M., 65, 82n
Davis, Gordon B., 49n, 80, 109, 120, 123n, 158, 549
Dayton-Hudson Department Stores, 23
DBMS. *See* Data base management system
Debugging, 629, 638, 644–645
Decision support systems (DSS), 141, 300–301, 375–377
computer graphics and, 717
Deere & Company, 23
Degree of relationships, 411
De Long, David W., 717, 724n
De Marco, Tom, 226, 267, 274, 275, 278
Deming, W. Edwards, 251
Departmental systems, 142
Deregulation, 14
Derived data, 410
Design, 4, 5
completion of, 582–583
of document flow, 297–298
of forms, screens, and reports, 329–348
guidelines for, 358–364
of input forms, 334–335
for performance, 553–579
process, 471–477
program, 479–526
report, 335–342
Design decision, 259
Design drivers, quality characteristics as, 259–261
Design phase, of user interface design, **284,** 285
Design process, 76–79
as modeling, 77–78
from models, 78
as problem solving, 77
as transformation, 78–79

Desktop metaphor, **354**
Macintosh desktop, 355
Development environment, 166–169, 473
Development procedures (DP) operations, 662–663
Development resources, lack of, 164–165
DFDs. *See* Data flow diagrams
Diagnostic assessment, and organization change, 52
Diagramming, hierarchical, 83–98
Dialog boxes, 363–364
Dialog design, 299–318
choosing dialog types, 304–318
and conversation flow documentation, 320–322
designing, 287
dialog type characteristics, 325
elements of good, 318–320
and logical unit of work, 300–301
styles of, by terminal type, 314–317
Dialog structure, 474
Direct file controls, 546
Direct manipulation, 306
Discretionary policies, 707, 709
Disintermediation, as business process technique, 44
Disk access time, 569–571
calculation of estimated disk I/O times, 571
Distributed data processing (DDP), 172, 174–175, 492
Documentation
of conversation flow, 320–322
for integrity constraints, 454–455
on-line vs. paper, 655
Documentation requirements
for codes, 441–442
for implementing relationships, 437
Documentation techniques, hierarchy chart, 83–98
Document flows, designing, 289, 297–299
Documenting keys and relationship implementations, 438
Documenting strategies, for functional requirements, 235–240
Documents, specifications of, 225
Domain checking, 450–451, 542
Domain variables, 259
Double-clicking, 354–355
Dow Jones News/Retrieval, 25
Doyle, M., 221
Dragging, 355
Drucker, Peter F., 50, 58n
Dunn, Robert, 648
Duration, 427

Ease of learning, 258
Ease of use, 258, 303
of forms, reports, and screens, 333
Economic analysis
of maintenance, 681–683
presentation to management, 596
Economic feasibility, 110
Economic summary
for information systems, 591–595
sample, 592

Economies of scale, 19
EDI. *See* Electronic data interchange
Efficient and effective utilization, 536–537
Eiffel, 510
Either-or-relationship, 464
Electronic data interchange (EDI), 290
    application examples, 290
    systems, 19, 48
Elements and groups, 688
    data, 688–695
Eloquent Systems Corporation, 115
Emergent properties, 79
Employees, terminated, 531
End-of-conversation posting, 494, 495, 597
End-user computing, 154
    capacity and, 170–171
    specialists, 71
Enger, N. L., 158
Enterprise modeling, 128
    methods, analysis framework and, 131, 137, 138
Entities, 379, **382,** 388–397
    attribute assignment to, 398–403
    in bill of materials, 396
Entity life-cycle diagram, 236–237
Entity-relationship-attribute model, 384
Entity-relationship diagram (ERD), **231,** 237, 459–469
    benefits of, 379–382
    criteria for use of, 467
    entity-relationship model, 379–491
    equivalent techniques for, 465–467
    for lending library, 460
    in life cycle, 461–462
    for manufacturing company, 461
    mechanized tools for, 464–465
    rules for, 462–463
    for university, 460
    probable changes analysis, 410–412
Entity types, 383
Entry barriers, 17, 18–19
Environment
    of business organization, 34
    development, 166–169, 473
    operating, 199
    production, 169–172, 473
Equipment, and software disparity, 165–166
Equipment inventory check function, description of, 419
Ergonomics, 343–344
Errors
    data base, 445–447
    generic causes, 530
Error sources, 529–531
    human, 529
    natural forces, 530–531
    technical failures, 529–530
Essential systems analysis, 226, 229–231
Estimating, 75
Evaluation methods, 260–261
Event-driven process, 480
Excessive abbreviation, 422–423
Executive information systems (EIS), 143
    computer graphics and, 717

Executive sponsor, in JAD, **213**
Expert systems, 142
External entities, 271, 272. *See also* Data flow
    data flows and, 289–297
Extract program, structure of, 513

Facsimile, 15
Factory quadrant, 25
Fallback procedures, 659
Family tree, 83, 84
Feasibility studies, 105–123
    cost/benefit analysis in, 116–119
    determining project feasibility, 110–115
    examples of use of, 106–108
    feasibility types, 109–110
    objectives and organization of, 105–106
    for selecting and assigning project priorities, 107–108
Federal Express, Package Locator System, 44
Felt need, lack of, 50
Fence diagram, 713
    for retirement system, 715
Fields, 404
File and data base records, 404
File balancing controls, 544–545
File conversion, 663–667
    approaches to, 665–667
    creation application, 664
    from existing, 665, 666
    system modification, 666–667
File-driven process, 480
Files, 695
    Interface, 516
    shared master, 515
Finite-state machines, 713, 716
Finkelstein, Clive, 128, 158, 231, 232, 414
First-mover disadvantages, 26–27
Five forces
    interaction of, 20
    model, 13, 17–20
Five normal forms, 408–409
Fixed-function terminals, 314–315
Fixed help text, 315
Flavin, Matta, 469
Flexibility, and quality, 258–259
Flores, F., 251, 265n, 325, 328n
Flow of data, 228
Ford, business process reengineering at, 38, 39, 47
Foreign key, 429, 430, **435,** 449
Form design, 329–331
    preprinted forms, 332
    principles of, 333–334
Form-filling, 305, 307–309, **353**–354
Forms and reports, 404
Fourth-generation languages, 168, 169, 519
Free-form dialog, 313
Freezing, of business process, 39
Functional analysis
    business area analysis, 231–233
    essential systems analysis, 229–231
    object-oriented analysis, 233–235
    structured systems analysis, 227–229

Functional organization, of IO department, 65–66
Functional prototyping, 368–369
Functional requirements, 225–247
    analysis strategies for, 226–235
    definition of, 225–226
    and quality requirements, 249–250
    strategies for documenting, 235–240
Functional specifications report, 582
Function charts, 86, 96

Gane, Chris, 220, 226, 267, 274, 275, 278, 413, 444n, 465
Garlitz, Wilbert 0., 345
Gate Assignment Display System (GADS), 115
General Electric, Appliance Park facility, 14
General systems controls.
    See Systems controls
Generation data sets, 545–546
Generic life cycle, 4, 5. *See also* Life cycle
    feasibility study and, 106, 107
Generic quality attributes, 255–256
Generic strategies, and strategic business planning, 13, 20
Geographical business process techniques, 42, 44
Gibson, Richard, 31n
Gilb, T., 264, 265n
Gilbreath, R., 80
Gildersleeve, Thomas R., 55, 106, 120, 123n, 198, 220, 223n, 598
Glaser, Ted, 529
Gonzalez, Richard, 100–101
Goodhue, Kirsch, 158
Goody, Sam, 44
Graphical user interfaces (GUI), 306, 313, 349–366
    elements of, 359–364
Graphics, 141
    computer, 717–725
    excellence of, 718–723
    graphical integrity of, 723–724, 725
    processable graphics, 358
    types of, 718
Group technology, for JAD, **214**

Halpin, T. A., 467
Hammer, Michael, 37, 55, 58n
Hare, W. H., 552n
Harold, F., 158
Henderson, John, 129, 161n
Hevner, A., 247n
Hierarchical chart, for menu structure, 324
Hierarchical diagramming, 83–98
    battle order, 93
    book structure, 87
    COBOL program structure, 90
    and data flow diagrams leveling, 97
    essay structure, 86
    family tree, 83
    formal rules for, 87–94
    function chart, 96
    Jackson program structure diagram, 95
    line of succession, 85

mechanized tools for, 94–98
organization chart, 94
program structure chart, 88
pseudo-code, 89
table of contents, 86
U. S. Army ranks, 92
Warner program structure diagram, 95
Hierarchies
biology taxonomy as, 393
depiction of, 87–94
enterprise organization chart, 394
program structure chart, 88
types of, 88
High I/O times, 562
HIPO diagrams, 276, 277
Histogram, 721
Homonyms, 422
Hospitals
billing system, 111
information system in, 2–3
Hotel reservations, new system for, 115
Hudson, Michael, 22
Human error, 529
Human factors, systems with poor, 51
Human resource management, 700

IBM. *See also* JAD
Business Systems Planning (BSP), 100, 128
Information center IBM Canada, 71
Multiples Marketing Program, 612–613
Icons, 355
Illegal transactions, and illegal state, 453–454
Image processing, 356–358
at Northwest Airlines, 351
Immediate posting, 494, 496–497
Implementation, 4, 5, 611–616. *See also* Implementation phase
key tasks and deliverables, 613–616
Implementation data dictionary, 687–698. *See also* Data dictionary
Implementation of relationships, 429
Implementation phase, of user interface design, **286**
Inbound logistics, 699
Increasing the MTBF, 563–564
Individual rights, privacy issues and, 547–549
Industrial engineering, 37–40
and clerical work, 37
Industry structure alteration, 20
system examples, 22
Information Center, 71
Information Engineering, 128, 226
Information gathering. *See also* Interview; JAD
observation and, 218–219
questionnaires and, 218
sampling, 219
Information modeling, 380
Information needs, matrix of, 130, 132–133
Information resource management, 16
Information security, 533
Information set, 508

for complex, fanned-out hierarchy, 512
with detail records in storage, 509
for simple hierarchy, 508
Information systems. *See also* Systems planning
changing, 35–37
deducing processing and information requirements, 240–243
economic summary for, 591–595
executive, 143
freezing specifications of, 597
and hospital success, 2–3
infrastructure planning, 163–182
layers of, 35
management control over, 528–529
supportive role of, 16
technical architecture of, 473–475
Information systems analyst, In JAD, **211–212**
Information systems departments, 192
centralized vs. decentralized, 68–70
decentralized, 66–67, 68–70
functional organization of, 65–66
matrix organization of, 67
organizational place of, 60
organization of, 65–72
policies and procedures of, 531–533
product line organization of, 66–67
reporting level of, 64
supportive role of, 63–65
trends in, 71–72
Information systems development. *See also* Life cycle; Systems development life cycle
design process in, 76–79
feasibility studies, 105–123
hierarchical charts in, 86–87
implementation of, 611–616
life cycle, 3–12, 72–76
and personnel organization, 69, 70
and requirements analysis, 191–196
transformations in process, 261
Information systems specialists, and technician-user gap, 14–15
Information technology (IT), 14
and business computing, 34
capabilities and organizational impacts, 44
and competitive advantage, 13–31
competitive use of, 15
for developers, 166
and first-mover disadvantages, 26–27
in hospitals, 2–3
identifying levers, 42–47
management understanding of, 16
and not-for-profit sector, 27–29
role of, 16
strategic grid, 24–26
usage challenges, 34
Infrastructure activities, 701
Infrastructure planning, 163–182
Infrastructure specialists, 71–72
Inheritance, 233
of modifiable attribute, 398–401
Inherited attributes, 407–409
In-house custom development, 155

Inmon, W. H., 414
Input forms, design of, 334–335
Input/output design, sample, 333
Input/output media, choice of, 331–332
Installation. *See* Installation phase; Installation planning; Systems installation
Installation phase
standard activities of, 589
of user interface design, 286
Installation planning, 583–588
conversion plan, 584–586
detailed, 586–588
test plan, 583
user training plan, 584
Institutional factors, as cost drivers, 707
Integrated systems, 38–39, 101
Integration, 707, 709
Integration testing, 614, **641**
Integrity, in graphs, 723–724, 725
Integrity constraints
documentation requirements for, 454–455
sample of rules, 456
sample state transition network diagram for rules, 457
specifications of, 445–458
Intelligent workstations, 314, 315
Interface design. *See also* Interfaces; User interface design
batch interface, 289
factors in, 288
on-line data flows, 289
on-line dialogs, 287
Interface files, 516
Interface messages, 516
Interface requirements. *See also* Graphical User Interfaces
direct manipulation metaphor, 353–356
image processing, 356–358
self-learning systems, 350–353
Interfaces, 695
easy to use, 303–304
requirements for knowledge workers, 349–358
to other systems, 514–518
user, 279–286
Internal experience, and cost driver identification, 709
International competition, 36
Interorganizational system (IOS), 48
and process integration, 47–48
Interviewing, 201–210
acceptance cues in, 207
conducting, 205–210
and cost driver identification, 710
data-gathering note headings, 206
and JAD, 197–223
opening and closing techniques, 204–205
planning and scheduling, 202–204
preparing for, 202
process of, 202
restating responses during, 208–210
silence during, 210
Intrapreneurs, 36

Invisible backlog, 106–107
IOS. *See* Interorganizational system
IS. *See* Information systems
Islands of technology, 60–63
IT. *See* Information technology
Iteration program structure, 89, 604
Iterative development, 4, 8–9
    and life cycle, 9

Jackson, Michael, 506, 523
    diagram, 47
    program structure chart, 86, 89, 95,
        608, 609
JAD. *See* Joint Application Design
JAD session, 386
Japan
    quality in, 251
    U.S. competition with, 36
Johnson, Deborah G., 548, 550, 552n
Johnson, E., 365
Joint Application Design (JAD), 210–219
    alternatives to, 217–218
    approach, 192, 193
    conducting session for, 216–217
    costs and benefits of, 218
    DFDs and, 269
    documenting, 217
    interviewing and, 197–223
    room layout for, 215
    types of participants in, 211–213
    uses of, 210–211
    workshop preparation, 213–215
Juran, J. M., 251
Just-in-time inventory systems, 19

Kanter, Rosabeth Moss, 29, 52
Keen, Peter G. W., 49, 58n
Kent, W., 415n
Key analysis , 429–437
    and identifying key, 431–435
    implementing relationships and, 435–437
King, W., 80
Knowledge management, business
    process techniques, 43, 44
Knowledge workers, 40
    interface requirements for, 349–358
Konsynski, B., 22n, 55

Languages
    and methods and tools, 168–169
    natural, 316–317
    and system design, 78–79
Learning, as cost driver, 707, 708
Leveling, 270, 274
Lewin, Kurt, 48, 49, 58n
Life cycle. *See also* Generic life cycle and
        systems development life cycle
    approach selection, 74
    data dictionary in, 696–697
    DFDs in, 269–271
    entity-relationship diagrams and, 461–462
    generic, 4, 106–107
    hierarchical charts in, 86–87
    implementation and, 611
    of information systems development,
        72–76

interative development and, 9
    matrix in, 188–189
    phases, objectives, deliverables, 6
    program structure charting in, 603
    prototyping impact on, 11
    of system development, 3–12
    waterfall, 4–8
Line graphs, 718, 720
Line of succession, 83, 85
Linger, R., 247n
Linkages, 707, 708
Location, as cost driver, 707, 709
Logical unit of work, 300–301
    case as, 302
    determining, 301–302
Logistics, 699, 700
Long-range planning, 16
Loops, 604–605
Lotus Development Corporation, and
    barriers to entry, 19

Macintosh computer
    desktop, 355
    pull-down menu, 353
Magnetic ink character recognition (MICR),
    294, 332, 390
Maintenance, 4, 5, 671–685
    causes of, 673–674
    cost of, 672
    creeping, 176
    and data dictionary, 696–697
    economic analysis of, 681–683
    generic causes of, 673
    processing change requests, 677–679
    and systems planning, 683
    team organization, 679–681
    types of, 673–674
    version and release approach to,
        679–681
    and work performance, 681–683
Management, 292. *See also* Project
        management and chief information
        officer (CIO), 64–65
    as external entity, 292–293
    support of, 155–156
Management cycle, traditional, 73
Management information systems (MIS),
    140, 375–377
    data design flow for, 377
Management report, 596
Management review meeting, 596–597
Management values, 259
Manuals
    procedure, 657–659
    types of, 655–657
Manual systems, feasibility study for
    mechanizing, 113–114
Many-to-many relationship, 463
Marketing plan, for system, 653
Marketing/sales activities, 700
Mark sensing, 292, 332
Martin, James, 77, 79, 80, 82n, 123n, 128,
    158, 190, 226–227, 231, 306, 328n,
    345, 413, 443, 465, 523, 684
Matrices, 233
Matrix affinity analysis, 183–190

Matrix organization, of IS department, 67
McClure, C., 684
McCubbrey, D. J., 123n
McFarlan, F. Warren, 24, 29, 55, 60, 70,
    82n, 118, 119n,120, 123n, 129
McKeen, James, 582, 601n
McKenney, James L., 24, 29, 60, 70, 82n,
    129
McMenamin, Stephan, 226, 229, 245
Mead, Kirtland C., 27, 31n
Mechanizations, feasibility study for,
    113–114
Mechanized tools
    and data flow diagrams, 274–275
    and entity-relationship diagrams,
        464–465
    and hierarchical diagramming, 94–98
    and implementation data dictionary, 697
    and matrix affinity analysis, 189–190
    and tools for prototyping, 369–370
Mellor, Stephen J., 414
Memory requirements, calculation of, 574
Menu choices, 305, 307–309
Menus, pull-down, 363
Menu selection, 352–353, **354**
Merrill-Lynch, CMA of, 22
Messages, 233
Message transmission times, 561–562
Method, the, 217, 218
Methods and tools, 168
Metrics, selecting, 261–262
Meyer, Bertrand, 510
Microfilm, 332
Microsoft Word Ruler, 353
Miller, G. A., 98n
Mills, H., 247n
Modeling, 141
    in object-oriented analysis, 233–235
Model only the essentials, 230
Morison, Robert F., 27, 31n
Moss, Stephen, 219
Motivational feasibility, 110
MTBF (mean time between failures), 563
MTTR (mean time to recover), 563, 564
Multi-exchange inquiry application flow, 487
    pseudo-codes, 488, 489
Multiples Marketing Program, 612–613
    master schedule, 614
Mumford, Enid, 55
Mythical Man-Month, The, 680

Natural language, 79, 316–317
Net present value, 591
    sample overall economic summary
        using, 594
Network design, 171–172
New entrants, threat of, 17, 18–19
New product development, 21
New products/services, companies
    creating, 25
New York State Retirement System, 472
Nijssen, G. M., 467
Nolan, Richard L., 130, 161n
Nonconversational mode, 487, 489
Nonintegrated systems, 101
Nonkey attributes, 436

Nonkey dependency, 451, 452, 454–455
Nonumeric data, 427
Normal forms, 408
Normalization, 406–412
Northwest Airlines, image processing
  system at, 351
Not-for-profit organizations
  and competitive advantage, 13
  information technology for, 27–29
Null values, 427
Nulty, Peter, 223n
Numeric, 424–425

Object-oriented analysis, 227, 233–235
Object-oriented design, 510
Object-oriented interface, **355**
Objects, 233
Observation, for information gathering,
  218–219
Observers, in JAD, **212**
OCR. *See* Optical character recognition
Office automation, 60, 62–63, 141–142
Olle, T. W., 245, 247n
Olson, Margrethe H., 49n, 65, 80, 109,
  120, 123n
One-to-many relationships, 448–450, 463
One-to-one relationships, 450, 463
On-line applications, and procedures
  development, 662
On-line data entry, 490–494
On-line help, and interfaces, 352
On-line program design, 480–501
  backup, recovery, and restart in, 497–501
  and batch design, 479–480
  conversation design, 485–497
  functional hierarchy of, 481
  session sign-up and, 481–484
On-line resource consumption, 573
On-line response time, 555
On-line transaction output, 294
On-line tutorials, 350
On-line update, 494–497
On-line vs. paper documentation, 655
OPEC, and supplier bargaining power, 19
Open-ended questions, in interview,
  205–207
Open Systems Interconnect (OSI) model,
  171
Operating costs, 588
  and cost/benefit analysis, 588–591
Operating environment, 199
Operational feasibility, 109
Operational problem, and feasibility
  studies, 111–112
Operational processes
  grouping/splitting, 138
  identifying, 138, 139
Operations activities, 699
Operations procedures development,
  662–663
Operator-directed dialogs, 304, 306
Optical character recognition (OCR), 290,
  332, 358
  handwritten form, 291
  printed form, 293
Optical technology, 290

Order entry function description, 417
Organizational change, 201
  four-phase program for, 52–53
  implementing, 51–53
Organization chart, 38, 94
Organization/function matrix, 137
Organization/goal matrix, 186
Organization redesign, 52–53
Organization transformation, 53
Orientation meeting, for JAD, **215**
Outbound logistics, 700
Output report design, 329–331

Packaged application software, 154
Paging, 344–345
Palmer, John, 226, 229, 245
Parallel operations, 585
Parent entity, 393
**Parent key with a sequence number,
  431,** 432
Parikh, Girish, 684
Parker, M., 158
Parnas, David L., 482, 483, 526n
Participative development
  iterative, 4, 8–9
  prototyping, 4, 9–12
Passive dictionaries, 696
Payroll systems, 61–62, 63
Performance
  definition of, 553–554
  and dialog design, 319–320
  measures of, 554–560
  and quality, 257
Performance design, steps for, 560–564
Performance measures, availability as,
  559–560
Performance modeling, 368
Performance procedures, 659
Personnel, systems development and,
  69, 70
Personnel requirements planning,
  172–176
PERT (Project Evaluation and Review
  Technique), 75
Phased approach, 106
Phased conversion, 585–586
Phillips, Derwyn, 717
Physical security procedures, 533
Pie charts, 718
  exploded, 719
  simple, 719
Pilot testing, 583
Plan for implementing, 169
Planning, strategic business, 16
Plant tour, 199
Porter, Michael, 1, 13, 17, 20, 29, 129, 149
Positioning, 676
Power users, 305
Practice mode, and user interfaces, 351
Prestel, 280, 281
Pretty-printing, 644
Privacy issues, and individual rights,
  547–549
Problem statement, 198
Procedure manuals, 657–659

Process, 228
Process box, 271
  alternative, 275
  expansion of, 270
Process/data matrix, 145, 146–148
Process design, 471–477. *See also*
    Program design
  key tasks and deliverables, 476–477
Process-driven design, 504
  structure chart for, 504, 505
Processing change requests, 677–679
Processing controls, 543–546
  transaction, 536
Processing rules, 436–437
  relationship implemented by, 431
Process model, 231–232
Processor time, 568–569
  MIPS ratings, 569
  number of machine instructions per
    function, 568
Procurement activities, 700
Product delivery process, 34
Production environment, 169–172, 473
Product line organization, of IO
    department, 66–67
Products, new, 21
Product/service improvement, companies
    involved in, 23
Products/services, new, 25
Profit-making organizations, and
    competitive advantage, 13
Program design, 479–526
  batch, 479–480, 502–514
  on-line, 479–501
  strategies for, 482–483
Program-directed dialogs, 304–305
Programming, 617, 618–622. *See also*
    Testing
  organizing and managing, 618–619
  planning, 619–620
  program specifications, 620
  supervisor's role in, 625–628
  unit testing and, 630–640
Programming languages, 168
Programming structures, 89
Programs, 695
Program simulator, 368
Program structure charting, 86, 88,
    603–610
  constructs for, 605–607
  equivalent techniques, 607–608
  formal rules of, 604
  illustration of chart, 604
Project data model, 406
Project feasibility, determining, 110–115
Project management
  control, 75–76
  execution, 75
  organization, 72–74
  planning, 74–75
  and systems development life cycle,
    72–76
Project risk, 118–119
Project-specific variables, 259
Prompting, 305, 306
  example of, 310–311

Prototypes, development, 44–47
Prototyping, 4, 9–12, 71
    of conversation flow, 320
    domains for, 368–369
    impact of, 519
    life cycle impact of, 11, 519
    mechanized tools for, 369–370
    tools for, 367–370
    in user design phase, 654
Pseudo-code, 89, 610
Pseudo-conversational mode, 487, 488
Pull-down menu, 354, 363
Purchasing system, description of, 387

Quality
    as absence of defects, 252–253
    definition of, 250–252
    generic feedback loop, 253, 254
    measurement of, 261–262
    systems development feedback loop, 255
    and user expectations, 254–255
Quality attributes, 250
Quality circles, 251
Quality control, testing and, 614–616
Quality requirements, 249–265
    functional requirements and, 249–250
Quantitative measures, to identify cost
    drivers, 709
Questionnaire, 218
    preinterview, 202, 203
Queuing, 557
Quillard, J., 158

Rapid analysis, 217, 218
Ratio numbers, 427
Recovery, from errors, 257
Recovery/restart procedures, 659
Redesign. See Business process
    reengineering
Reducing the MTTR, 564
Reduction of data redundancy, 382
Redundancy
    of attributes, 409
    consistency of information, 451–452
Reengineering, 37–38. See also Business
    process reengineering
    business process, 40–48
Reference manual, 655–656
Referential integrity, 447–450, 542
    one-to-many relationships, 448–450
    one-to-one relationships, 450
Reichard, K., 365
Relational database technology, 167, 473,
    509
Relationships, 379, 383
    analyzing, 388–397
    in bill of materials, 396
    documentation requirements for, 437
    either-or, 464
    with entities and subentities, 465
    entity to itself, 463
    implementation of, 429, 448
    with keys, 435–437
    many-to-many, 463
    nongraphic representation of entities
        and, 468

one-to-many, 463
one-to-one, 392–393
point and two-dimensional surface, 437
transforming into entities, 388
Relationship types, 383
Releases, 675
Reliability, and quality, 257
Report design, 329–331, 335–342
    definition form, 347–348
    of detailed (control) report, 341
    exception reporting, 339
    for management reporting, 340
    principles of, 333–334
    report frequency, 339–340
Reporting, and batch processing, 511–514
Reporting controls, 546–547
Report printing program, 514
Reports
    complex structure, 515
    printed, 331
    purposes of, 336
    trend analysis in, 337, 338
Repository, and data dictionary, 687
Requirements analysis, 4, 5, 191–196,
    374, 375, 386
    functional requirements, 225–247
    interviewing, 197–210
    JAD, 210–223
    and quality, 249–265
Resource loading, 172
Resource requirements, estimating,
    564–574
Resources, development, 164–165
Response times, 257
    and performance, 554–557
    problems, 561–562
Responsibility reporting, 513
    hierarchical, 517
Restart/recovery procedures, 497–501
Return on investment (ROI), 591
    sample overall economic summary, 593
Reverse engineering, 231
Rinaldo, J. A., Jr., 123n
Risk, project, 118–119
Rockart, John F., 130, 149, 158, 161n,
    220, 717, 724n
Rock-Evans, Rosemary, 413
Ross, Ronald G., 414, 458, 698
Royce, W. W., 4, 5n, 6, 10, 12n
Rueb, Richard, 532
Rule-based expert system, 368
Ruler, 352–353
Rumbaugh, James, 414
Run-to-run controls, 544

Saaty, Thomas, 261, 265n
SADT, 275
Sampling, 219
Sarson, T., 226, 267, 275, 278
Sauer, Charles H., 576
SBU. See Strategic business unit
Scale, 707, 708
Scanned images, 356
Scatter diagrams, 718–723
Schaller, C., 549
Schedule, and quality, 256–257

Schedule feasibility, 110
Scheduling, 75
Schema, 375
Scope, 231
Screen design, 331, 342–345
    highlighting, aesthetics, ergonomics,
        and, 343–344
    operator guidance, 342–343
    output from, 332
    paging and scrolling, 344–345
    principles of, 333–334
    style of, 475
Scribes, in JAD, 212
Scrolling, 344–345
Sears, and credit market, 18
Securities industry, CMA in, 22
Security, controls and, 527–552
Security procedures, 659
Sequence, 604
Sequence programming structure, 89
Sequential business process techniques,
    43, 44
Sequential processing controls, 544–546
Serial number, 431
Service activities, 700
Service order system, 416
Services, new, 25. See also
    Products/services
Session leader, in JAD, 212
Session sign-on, 481–484
Shared master files, 575
Shlaer, Sally, 414
Shneiderman, Ben, 306, 328n, 345
Short, James E., 37, 40, 41n, 42, 44n, 54,
    58n
Shryock, J. R., 123n
Silver, D., 221
SIMULA, 234, 510
Single-exchange inquiry
    application flow, 486
    conversations, 485
Smalltalk, 510
Social change, 48
Social model of change, 48, 49
Social Security Administration, data
    restructuring by, 100–101
Social uncertainty, fear of, 50–51
Software
    and equipment disparity, 165–166
    for work plans, 587
Source code, 79
Specification document, 225
Spiral model, of systems development life
    cycle, 10
Spreadsheet, 172, 173–175, 354
Spreadsheet package interface, 288
SQL, 167
Stable foundation, 382
State diagram, 713
State transition diagram, 237, 323,
    713–716
    for COBOL parser, 714, 715
    matrix, 716
    for retirement system, 714
Static program analysis, 644
Statistical testing, 644–645

Sticky cursor, 315
Storage dump, 638
Strategic business plan, 129–130
  and systems plan, 125
Strategic business planning, 16
  in competitive environment, 13
  five forces model, 17–20
  framework for, 17–24
  generic strategies for, 20–21
Strategic business unit (SBU), 20, 155
  interrelationships among, 708
  value chain for, 23–24
Strategic grid, 24–26
Strategic quadrant, 24–25
Strategies
  for analyzing functional requirements,
    226–235
  for documenting functional
    requirements, 235–240
  sharing, 126
Straus, D., 221
Structure chart, 476
Structured systems analysis, 226,
  227–229
  data dictionary, 238
  logical system, 228, 229
  physical system, 228, 229
Structured walk-throughs
  control sheet, 624
  participants in, 622–623
  point sheet, 626, 627
  of program, 622–625
Stub testing, 636, 637
Subject data base approach, 144, 152
Subschemas, 375
Substantiation and evidence, 535–536
Substitute products or services, threat of,
  17, 19
Subsystems, 33–34
Subtypes
  and relationships, 389–390, 391
  representation of multiple, 390, 391
Superentities, 389–390, 391
Suppliers, bargaining power of, 18, 19
Support activities, 700–701
Supportive role of information systems, 16
Support of top management, 155–156
Support quadrant, 25–26
Surrogates, 431
Suspend-and-resume technique, 315
S.W.I.F.T., 172, 294
Synonyms, 422
System implementation, and data
  dictionary, 696–697
System log, 546
System master files, 584
System requirements, 225
System response time, 555
System review, 197–200
  checklist for, 199, 200
  interviewing and, 201–210
Systems. *See also* Information systems
  definition of, 33
  design and installation of new, 60–82
  feasability study for creating new,
    114–115

quality attributes of, 255–259
  sources of, 154–155
Systems architects, 72
Systems controls, general, 531–533
Systems development
  implementation of, 611–616
  quality feedback loop in, 255
Systems development life cycle, 3–12
  approach selection, 74
  data dictionary in, 696–697
  spiral model of, 10
Systems installation, 653–670. *See also*
    Maintenance
  and configuration control, 676
  cutover, 667–668
  file conversion and, 663–667
  and maintenance, 671–685
  operations procedures development,
    662–663
  user procedure development and
    training, 655–661
Systems integration, 62–63
Systems interface controls, 547
Systems life cycle, system projects and,
  59–82
Systems plan, 385
  and cost reduction, 126
  data sharing, 126
  establishment of, 125–161
  organizational issues and, 176
  and strategic business plan, 125
  strategy sharing, 126
Systems planning, 4, 5, 374
  approaches to, 99, 127–129
  benefits of, 125–127
  identifying projects, 149–152
  and maintenance, 683
  organizing, 155–157
  project evaluation, 131, 134, 135
  purpose of, 102
  and strategic business plan, 129–130
Systems projects
  evaluating, 153–155
  grouping of, 136
  identifying, 149–152
  product/service/resource identification,
    136
  strategic planning/management control
    processes, 136–138
  and systems life cycle, 59–82
Systems with poor human factors, 51
System testing, 614, 641

Table of contents, as hierarchy, 86
Tables, codes and, 437–442
Task guide, 657
Taylor, Frederick, 37, 40, 251
Technical failures, 529
Technical feasibility, 109
Technical specifications report, 583
Technician-user gap, 14
Technology
  for developers, 166
  and dialog/help styles, 314
  feasibility study for replacing, 112, 113
  merging "islands" of, 60–63

special-purpose, 92
  Videotex and, 280–282
Technology-development activities, 700
Technology infrastructure planning,
  128–129
Telecommunications, 60, 62–63
  and hospital success, 2–3
Télétel, 280–282
Temporary fixes, 675
Terminal paging, 490, 491
Terminals
  block-mode (buffered), 319
  buffered and unbuffered, 314
  coexistence of multiple types, 317–318
  Testing, 614–616, 617
  acceptance, 641
  clean-room techniques for, 645
  data preparation, 642
  debugging, 644–645
  execution of, 643
  integration, 641
  log, 640
  phases and objectives of, 616
  planning of, 642
  of program, 628–629
  and quality control, 615
  results evaluation, 643
  static program analysis, 644
  statistical, 644–645
  system, 641
  unit, 630–640
  walk-throughs, 639
Test plan, 583
Test run, of program, 637
Third-generation language, 168
Throughput, 557
  as performance measure, 554
  problems, 562–563
Throughput requirements, 257
Time series graphs, 718, 721
Timing, 707, 709
Tools, methods and, 168
Top-down analysis, 232, 379, 384–403
Top-down approach, in waterfall life cycle
  model, 6
Total quality management, in design
  process, 263
Total response time, calculation of,
  572–573
Trace option, 638
Tracking business process techniques, 44
Training
  development and conduct, 660–661
  user, 659–660
Training documentation, 657
Transaction, 301
  illegal, 453–454
Transactional business process
  techniques, 42, 44
Transaction analysis, 482
Transaction constraint approach, 453
Transaction documentation, 290–292
Transaction-driven process, 480, 481
Transaction origination, controls of, 540
Transaction processing, 131–136
Transaction processing control

objectives of, 536, 537–539
techniques of, 539–547
Transaction processing monitor,
    167–168
Transaction processing systems, 374–375,
    380
    data design flow for, 376
    flow of, 537
    tastes and deliverables of, 376
Transaction restart, 501
Transcription errors, 540
Transform analysis, 482
Transformation rules, 388–396
Transmission time, 565–567
    calculation of, 567
    and multimode network, 567
Treacy, Michael, 39
Tree diagram, 393
Trend analysis report, 337
    bar graph format, 338
TRW, 25
Tufte, Edward R., 717, 718, 724n
Turnaround document, 297
Turnaround times, 257
Turnkey systems, 155
Two-phased commit, 492

Unbuffered terminals, 314
Understanding Computers and Cognition,
    288
Understand the data model, 382
Uniqueness, 429
United States Army ranks chart, 92
Unit price, 399, 400
Unit testing, 614, 630–640
    annotated program specifications, 632
    control sheet, 631
    executing, 637
    loading test data, 635, 636
    preparing data, 633–636
    result evaluation, 638–640
    test cycle control sheet, 634
Universal Produce Code (UPC), 295
UNIX, 510
Update, and batch processing, 503–511

Usability, and quality, 258
Usability lab, 612
User acceptance, Videotex system and,
    280–282
User acceptance test, 196
User dialog, and natural language,
    316–317
User friendly, 303
User interface, 368
    graphical, 349–366
    on-line help, 352
    Self-learning systems, 350–353
User interface design, 279–286, 288.
    See also Interface design
    definition of, 283
    in installation phase, 286
    key tasks and deliverables, 283–286
User participation, in development cycle,
    654–655
User procedure development and training,
    655–661
User procedures, 657
User relationships, and system review, 200
User representative ideal, 156
Users
    classification of, 305
    in JAD, **211**
    perspective of, 241
User training
    planning for, 659–660
    program, 584
User views, 405–**406**

Validation, 75, **542**–543
    batch transaction, 502–503
Value chain, 21–24
    generic, 21–23
    for strategic business unit, 23–24
Value chain analysis, 13, 699–712
    applying, 701–705
    components, 699–701
    cost analysis tools, 705–712
Venkatraman, N., 129, 161n
Venue, for JAD, **214**
Verification, 75

Versions, 675
Very large scale integrated (VLSI) circuit
    design, 358
Videotex, 280
Visual Display of Quantitative Information,
    The, 717
Vitale, M., 22n, 26, 31n
Voice output, 332
Volume, 556
VTOC (Visual Table of Contents), 86

Warnier, Jean-Dominique, 506
Warnier chart, 86, 89, 95, 393, 476
Warnings, 361–363
    box, 363
Waterfall life cycle, 4–8
    costs of, 6, 7
Weinberg, G ., 648
Weinberg, V., 247n
Weir, Mary, 55
Wetherbe, James C., 220
White, George, 532n
Windowing, 344–345
Windows, 359–361
    auxiliary, 362
    main vs. child, 360
    one per zone, 362
    overlapping, 361
Winograd, Terry, 251, 265n, 325, 328
WISDM, 217, 218
Wiseman, Charles, 29
Wood, J., 221
Word processing packages, 367–368
Work plans, software for, 587
Workstations, 314
WYSIWYG, formatting control and, 357
WYSIWYG editing, 356

Yourdon, Ed, 226, 237, 245, 247n, 267,
    275, 278, 481, 482, 526n, 648

Zachman, John, 152, 157
Zero defects, 251
Zuboff, Shoshana, 40